#77295-1

SINS OF THE FATHERS

Moral Economies in Early Modern Spain

HILAIRE KALLENDORF

Sins of the Fathers

Moral Economies in Early Modern Spain

UNIVERSITY OF TORONTO PRESS
Toronto Buffalo London

© University of Toronto Press 2013
Toronto Buffalo London
www.utppublishing.com
Printed in Canada

ISBN 978-1-4426-4458-8

Printed on acid-free, 100% post-consumer recycled paper with vegetable-based inks.

Library and Archives Canada Cataloguing in Publication

Kallendorf, Hilaire
Sins of the fathers : moral economies in early modern Spain / Hilaire Kallendorf.

Includes bibliographical references and index.
ISBN 978-1-4426-4458-8

1. Spanish drama – Classical period, 1500–1700 – History and criticism. 2. Spanish drama (Comedy) – History and criticism. 3. Deadly sins in literature. 4. Ethics in literature. I. Title.

PQ6105.K34 2013 862'.309353 C2012-908470-0

University of Toronto Press acknowledges the financial assistance to its publishing program of the Canada Council for the Arts and the Ontario Arts Council.

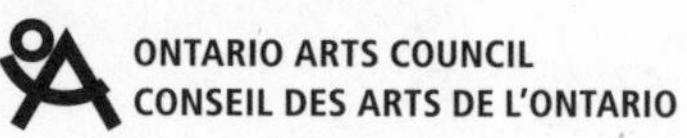

University of Toronto Press acknowledges the financial support of the Government of Canada through the Canada Book Fund for its publishing activities.

For my son Barrett,
child of grace,
which covers
a multitude of sins.

Contents

Foreword: A Note on Method ix

Acknowledgments xiii

Introduction 3

Part One: Residue

1 Pride & Co. 15
2 Greed Breaks the Bag 45
3 Lusty Lads and Luscious Ladies 74

Part Two: Transformation

4 Loath to Call It Sloth: The Plus Side of *Pereza* 97
5 That Gnawing Hunger: The Plus Size of Gluttony 112
6 Angry Young Murderers 133

Part Three: Emergence

7 Disappearing Deadlies: The End of Envy 155
8 Parents and Lies: The Decalogue on the Rise 174
Conclusion: The Self Discovered by Sin 202

Epilogue: To Avoid Reductionism 209

Notes 213

Bibliography 367

Index of Comedias 387

Index 401

Photo section follows page 178

Foreword: A Note on Method

Fuente clara la Comedia, de preciosas perlas rica.

– Lope de Vega[1]

With all humility, and never forgetting that Pride is the chief Deadly Vice, I would like to suggest that this book appears on the cutting edge of a new kind of research. It sees the early modern Spanish dramatic text corpus as a vast archive of moral knowledge, a valuable repository of collective cultural memory. The irony, of course, is that these plays were meant to be performed, and as such, the *comedias* and *autos sacramentales* as genres occupy a unique liminal space between the archive and the repertoire. The interplay between the archive and the repertoire as modes of cultural knowledge has been commented upon recently by performance studies scholar Diana Taylor:

> "Archival" memory exists as documents, maps, literary texts, letters, archaeological remains, bones, videos, films, CDs, all those items supposedly resistant to change. Archive, from the Greek, etymologically refers to "a public building," "a place where records are kept" … [T]he archival, from the beginning, sustains power. Archival memory works across distance, over time and space; investigators can go back to reexamine an ancient manuscript, letters find their addresses through time and place, and computer discs at times cough up lost files with the right software. The fact that archival memory succeeds in separating the source of "knowledge" from the knower – in time and/or space – leads to comments … that it is "expansionist" or "immunized against alterity." What changes over time is the value, relevance, or meaning of the archive, how the items it contains get interpreted, even embodied … There are several myths attending the archive. One is that it is unmediated, that objects located there might mean something outside the framing of the archival impetus itself. What

> makes an object archival is the process whereby it is selected, classified, and presented for analysis …
>
> The repertoire, on the other hand, enacts embodied memory: performances, gestures, orality, movement, dance, singing – in short, all those acts usually thought of as ephemeral, nonreproducible knowledge. Repertoire, etymologically "a treasury, an inventory," also allows for individual agency … The repertoire requires presence: people participate in the production and reproduction of knowledge by "being there," being a part of the transmission … The repertoire both keeps and transforms choreographies of meaning …
>
> Certainly it is true that individual instances of performance disappear from the repertoire. This happens to a lesser degree in the archive. The question of disappearance in relation to the archive and the repertoire differs in kind as well as degree. The live performance can never be captured or transmitted through the archive … Embodied memory, because it is live, exceeds the archive's ability to capture it. But that does not mean that performance – as ritualized, formalized, or reiterative behavior – disappears. Performances also replicate themselves through their own structures and codes. This means that the repertoire, like the archive, is mediated. The process of selection, memorization or internalization, and transmission takes place within (and in turn helps constitute) specific systems of re-presentation. Multiple forms of *embodied acts* are always present, though in a constant state of againness. They reconstitute themselves, transmitting communal memories, histories, and values from one group/generation to the next.[2]

According to this definition, sin, too, is a performance, a reiterated behaviour, an embodied act, and discourses about it transmit values from one generation to the next.

So in a very real way, cruelly, we find ourselves doubly removed from our object of study. In looking at what the *comedias* and *autos sacramentales* have to say about sin, we are watching a performance of a performance – except that we are not even that close, really, since by and large we can only read these plays instead of experiencing them in the theatre. Thus, by the very nature of this project, its referential surfaces will inevitably be mixed. This phrase refers in parallel to both the referential surfaces of actual artistic performance, i.e., the theatrical space of the stage, and the rough edges of textual surfaces perpetually bumping up against one another as they come into contact: stage plays versus treatises by *moralistas*, etc. Yet another set of rough edges may be detected if we begin to break each genre down into its respective subgenres; and this simple reality has required me to make some difficult decisions, just as an artistic director might have to make some tough calls in the process of directing a play. For example,

I have chosen to include the *autos sacramentales* as part of this same cultural milieu, forming a continuous (or at least coterminous) dramatic tradition with the *comedias* and involving nearly all of the same players: they were performed by the same actors, written by the same playwrights, for the same audience. This choice is probably debatable, in much the same way that a stage director's decision to incorporate certain props or combine different styles of costume might generate controversy.

But such artistic and philological decisions do not change the fact that this book makes creative use of newly available technologies, and as such it participates in the growing wave of digital humanities scholarship.[3] Without the 800 *comedias* digitized by ProQuest in the Teatro Español del Siglo de Oro database, a project this ambitious could not have been attempted. I am satisfied by the rigorous scholarly standards of the TESO editorial team but have opted to modernize spelling and punctuation in order to facilitate online searches of the digital version of this book. I have retained authorial attributions as they appear in the database, although at times noting where authorship is contested or doubtful. I have chosen to eliminate dates of publication since they often do not reflect even the same decade of the first performance of a play and only distract from a consideration of the entire *comedia* corpus qua corpus. This decision was a careful one, requiring much deliberation. The reader should note that each playwright's dates of birth and death are listed next to his name in the primary source bibliography at the end of the book. The focus here is not on change over time, for example from one decade to the next or between generations of playwrights, but instead on the whole seventeenth century and its enormous output of *comedias* and *autos sacramentales*. As such, it promises to enhance and complement existing scholarship but does not claim to replace it. This study would have been impossible without the 800 *comedia* plot summaries offered by David Castillejo, the categorization of the *comedia* corpus in terms of subgenres by Ignacio Arellano, and so forth.[4] We stand on the shoulders of giants. As one of my senior colleagues commented to me recently, this all-encompassing, large-scale kind of research was not possible even a short time ago. It remains to be seen whether it will give birth to a new trend of broadly comparative, cultural studies–based criticism which revolves around more than a handful of canonical plays.

Finally, sin may seem a little outmoded these days,[5] but it was not so for early modern playwrights and their audiences. Cultural studies as a methodology opens up new vistas. In the new freedom of our postmodernity, we need no longer rely on any one shared foundation of religious beliefs and assumptions. Even atheistic scholars or readers can benefit from considering sins as nodes of cultural anxiety.

What does or does not constitute a sin, and how it is performed, can tell us much about the culture surrounding a specific religious belief. Like us, early moderns were grappling with inherited forms – both archives and repertoires – and struggling to figure out which sins were still relevant and why. The messiness of their search can give us hope as we, too, strive to adapt traditional notions of spirituality to meet the exigencies of postmodern life.

Acknowledgments

My most significant intellectual debt incurred in relation to this project is to Richard Newhauser, who directed a five-week National Endowment for the Humanities seminar on the topic of the Seven Deadly Sins at Cambridge University which I attended during the summer of 2004. I have benefited enormously from his expertise. This project was funded by a Mid-Career Fellowship from the Howard Foundation at Brown University. I gratefully acknowledge this assistance. In the course of researching and writing this book, I have also received financial support from the Glasscock Center for Humanities Research, the College of Liberal Arts, the Department of Hispanic Studies, the Program in Religious Studies, and the Program in Comparative Literature at Texas A&M University. On the personal level, I wish to thank my friend and colleague Donnalee Dox for providing valuable insights. For one happy semester we met weekly to discuss our respective projects. Thanks to Laci Templeton for daily notes of encouragement while I wrote the bulk of the manuscript, as well as for delicious dinners she cooked (providentially!) while I was writing the chapter on Gluttony. My mother, Mickie Richey, was the first pair of eyes to read each chapter as it rolled off the printer. Her unfailing enthusiasm in discussing the book's themes on the phone was an invaluable source of inspiration and support. Finally, I would like to thank my sister, Sarah Johnson, for volunteering to serve as my older son's nanny in Cambridge during that summer of 2004. I could not have attended that fateful seminar otherwise.

SINS OF THE FATHERS

The urge to classify is a fundamental human instinct; like the predisposition to sin, it accompanies us into the world at birth and stays with us to the end.

– A. Tindell Hopwood

If the work of comedy is to correct the vices of men, I do not see by what reason some vices would be privileged.

– Molière

We spend our time breaking the ten commandments, and that is why society is possible.

– Jacques Lacan

Introduction

Aun las malas intenciones se heredan en las familias.

– Juan Pérez de Montalbán[1]

This book begins with a curse. In the second instalment of the Hebrew Pentateuch, which later became the second book of the Christian Old Testament, the great saga of Exodus is played out as a real-life drama in the desert. Near its point of culmination, at the exact moment when he brings down from the mountain the Ten Commandments (later to be inscribed on stone tablets, written by the finger of God), Moses prophesies that Yahweh will visit the sins of the fathers upon their children. The voice of the prophet relays God's somber warning: "I am the Lord thy God, mighty, jealous, visiting the iniquity of the fathers upon the children, unto the third and fourth generation."[2] This message took on a deeply personal resonance for me recently as I completed the process of writing a memoir with my own father. The understanding of generational cycles is crucial, I came to realize, for any attempt to comprehend one's own life.

And so it is also as we make the cognitive leap from microcosm to macrocosm, in our new age of concern over fiscal instability, global warming, and a host of other problems we are passing on to our heirs. As a mother of two, I am acutely aware of the potential impact of my words and actions on the impressionable consciousness of my young sons. But in order to break the cycle, we must first try to analyse it – to exorcize these demons of the past and break their hold on our collective future.

These comments, of course, presuppose a recognition of the very category of sin, not necessarily a given in our postmodern age. It goes without saying that sin was one of the major organizational concepts of early modern thought, notwithstanding recent attempts to trace heretofore-suppressed histories of atheism in the early modern world.[3] But whether or not we accept notions of good and evil, right and wrong – and even regardless of whether our ancestors did – it is nonetheless undeniable that sin has proven to be one of the most important loci of artistic and creative energy in the history of the Western world. It has inspired countless treatises, proverbs, confessors' manuals, and stage plays. Psychologists point to it as a primary source of much of the baggage we carry around, both individually and collectively. As I have examined elsewhere, in the Romance languages the word *conscience* is linguistically indistiguishable from *consciousness*, a telling indicator of the inescapable shadow cast by this concept upon the most minute intricacies of everyday life.[4]

Why are notions of sin so important? It may be argued that fundamentally, notions of sin shape our notions of self:

> The self, says a modern philosopher, has been discovered by sin. The merely logical self-consciousness does not have such a power. Without practical knowledge about oneself, produced by the experience of law and guilt, no practical self-consciousness … could have developed.[5]

As Paul Tillich further concludes in his powerful *Morality and Beyond*, "the self discovers itself in the experience of a split between what it is and what it ought to be." Before they sinned, Adam and Eve never looked down to realize they were naked. It is almost as if, in a radical rewriting of Descartes's famous dictum *I think, therefore I am* ("cogito ergo sum"), the new mantra for the early modern and subsequent periods became instead *I sin, therefore I am*. Thus we see that in a very real way, in the history of ideas as well as the history of each individual, the self is somehow discovered by sin.

In my first book, *Exorcism and Its Texts*, I explored the topos of exorcism in literature as a way of examining larger issues of subjectivity. Then, in a study titled *Conscience on Stage*, I looked at representations of conscience in early modern Spanish stage plays as evocations of playwrights' intimate knowledge of the science of casuistry, or case morality. Now I would like to continue this meditation on early modern religious thought with an in-depth study of various early modern sins. Some of the best sources for details about Renaissance sins to be found in the archives are Renaissance confessors' manuals, dusty tomes filled with examinations of conscience, suitable penances to be assigned, specific moral advice, as well as questions interrogating thought, word, and deed to register even the most minor infractions. But by their very nature, these fascinating sources raise the somewhat complicated question of taxonomies.

Taxonomies are considered odd and old-fashioned today. Technically the word refers to laundry lists or catalogues of words, abstract concepts, or concrete things organized under headings and subheadings into elaborate hierarchies of genres and subgenres, species and subspecies. The most common current example might be found in botanical or zoological field manuals, where we look up specific plants or animals for the purpose of verifying to which branch of which family they might belong. The same thing might be done for chemical compounds or viruses in medical encyclopedias or textbooks. The assumption behind these types of routine inquiries is one of consummate order: that the universe is a neat and tidy place where everything fits into its own particular slot.

This fundamentally optimistic, positivistic world view traces its roots to the European Enlightenment, when a new spirit of scientific inquiry offered hope that the world was imminently manageable.[6] But the exertion of this type of encyclopedic control over vast amounts of information also has an earlier, more hidden history. The taxonomic impulse goes back at least as far as the scholastics, those medieval giants who pored over every available manuscript in order to incorporate all opinions on a given topic, whether ancient or modern.[7] Furthermore, medieval taxonomies were not limited to bestiaries, alchemy, astrology, and primitive medical texts. Instead, this irrepressible classificatory urge extended itself also into the realm of moral thought. There it found fertile ground to multiply and fill the earth, as sins were dissected with an ever-finer scalpel. Original broad categories such as *mortal* and *venial* gave way to ever-more-subtle distinctions. This endlessly expanding web of moral knowledge came to be known as *casuistry*, or the science of case morality.

The best and, to my knowledge, only survey of early modern Spanish casuistry is Elena del Río Parra's *Cartografías de la conciencia española en la Edad de Oro*.[8] There she rightly describes confessors' manuals and *summas* for confessors as tools for effectively mapping the moral landscape. The critical value of this work cannot be overstated. But as I mentioned in my review of her book, a crucial blindspot is its failure to address the competing classificatory systems by which these volumes themselves were organized.[9] Despite a chapter titled "Taxonomías del pecado" – a label which can only be considered, in this context, a misnomer – Del Río Parra does not address the tension between those manuals which derive their chapter structure from the Seven Deadly Sins and those which instead base their layout on the Ten Commandments. (Many guides for confessors bear witness to an uneasy combination of both – see figure 1.) Instead, her chapter focuses on certain extreme penances such as excommunication without interrogating the competing conceptual frameworks which produced them.

Why does it matter? Who cares whether early modern confessors viewed sin more in terms of the Decalogue or the Capital Vices? Abstruse as this question may seem, this topic has generated heated debate among scholars. As we shall see, taxonomies – which in this case I prefer to think of as complex moral economies – are important because of their ramifications for individual agency and subjectivity. By the phrase *moral economies*, I do not mean to invoke seminal anthropological studies by Sidney Mintz and James C. Scott which helped to redefine the field of political economics in the second half of the twentieth century.[10] In other words, this book is not primarily about economics in a literal sense, although the chapter on Greed does contain multiple instances of actual economic transactions. Instead, I mean rather to indicate that competing moral taxonomies such as the Ten Commandments and the Seven Deadly Sins contain elements that were traded, substituted, reversed, and exchanged in a complex ethical calculus which acted figuratively as an economy of sins and souls during the time we now call the early modern period.[11] Beliefs and attitudes became, in some sense, commodified, just as surely as did works of literary art. The paradoxes inherent in this system – or rather, this set of competing systems – have been noted by previous scholars.

In his now-classic essay "Moral Arithmetic: Seven Sins into Ten Commandments," John Bossy first argued that the Ten Commandments, as the foundational document of first Jewish and then Christian monotheism, inspired an individualistic approach to sin, and that this approach was something new, or at least newly rediscovered, in the late Renaissance:

> After the sixteenth century, a different moral system was universally taught in the West: the scriptural (though not New Testament) catalogue of the Ten Commandments. It may seem odd to suggest that, for the average person, the Decalogue was in 1600 a relative novelty, but so it was. In the early church it seems to have been treated as part of the old law from which Christians were anxious to distance themselves. St Augustine … had asserted its fundamental validity for Christians, and sought to make it the base of Christian moral teaching; but until the thirteenth century he had not been widely followed. From that point … the Commandments began to make headway, but it was not until the universal diffusion of the Catechism in the sixteenth century and after that their dominance of the moral scene was established.[12]

The Catechism he referenced here was the *Catechism of the Council of Trent* (1566), a crucial text that endorsed the Decalogue as the definitive moral code by which all Catholics should live.[13]

Now, the Commandments which fit Bossy's model best are undoubtedly the first three, all having to do with the direct relationship between God and an individual. After elaborating this hypothesis, Bossy went on to contrast this allegedly individualistic or private stance with the more communal one he saw as embodied in the medieval construct of the Capital Vices.[14] Although, paradoxically, the Seven Big Ones (which at certain times have been eight)[15] postdated Exodus by many centuries – and putting aside for a moment the fact that they are not even biblical – Bossy nonetheless saw them as representing a medieval, and thus communal, and thus more primitive approach to sin than the one fostered by the Ten Commandments. The Renaissance, he argued, as an age of heightened individuality, witnessed a return to the more private, direct approach exemplified by Moses on the mountain speaking face to face with God. While this argument has since been partially discredited, it remains an important critical juncture in the historiography of early modern morality.[16]

In *Religious Authority in the Spanish Renaissance*, Lu Ann Homza uses Bossy's argument as a point of departure but then proceeds to demonstrate how Spain is different from the rest of Europe. Judging from the tables of contents as well as the indices of Spanish confessors' manuals, she notices a prevalence of the Seven Deadly Sins model in Spain long after it had been jettisoned in similar books being published elsewhere. (There is some artistic evidence for this also; see for example Hieronymus Bosch's mammoth cycle of *The Seven Deadly Sins*, still on display at the Prado Museum in Madrid [figure 2].)[17] Homza offers a syncretistic explanation for this persistence: "Spaniards' works make it impossible to dismiss the importance of the communal milieu ... they continued to employ the Seven Deadly Sins as a taxonomy... . Spaniards read the Decalogue as the Seven Sins."[18] Regardless of the cause, the result of this perceived anomaly – aside from demonstrating yet again a phenomenon known to European intellectual historians as Spanish exceptionalism[19] – is to provide a unique laboratory for postmodern cultural critics to dissect an early modern clash of world views.

In my book *Conscience on Stage* I was able to document the indebtedness of early modern Spanish playwrights to Jesuit casuistry. The current study takes that research several steps further by looking not just at conscience in general but instead at playwrights' treatments of specific sins. This study operates on the assumption that taxonomies are important, not because they are necessarily credible or in vogue today, but because early modern people themselves considered them useful as lenses through which to view their world. By looking at the ways in which Spanish playwrights dealt with specific sins, we can hope to learn something about early modern conceptions of both self and society. If it turns out that a disproportionate number of dramatists conceptualize sin within the framework of the Ten Commandments, then perhaps the subtle result is an individualizing tendency which has been intuited by some scholars but, at least until now, not fully substantiated within *comedia* studies. On the other hand, if the stage plays contain references to the Vices in overwhelming numbers, then perhaps the effect of the theatrical experience is to reinforce hegemonic ideals of community.

To my knowledge, no one has studied before either the Seven Deadly Sins in the *comedias* or dramatic references to all ten of the Ten Commandments.[20] In proposing a new strategy for confronting the longstanding problem of coming to terms with the massive *comedia* corpus, this study does both. Its chapter structure mirrors the organization of many confessors' manuals in the archives: eight chapters, roughly focused on each of the Seven Deadly Sins, at the same time discuss specific Commandments which are relevant for each particular Vice.[21] Even for early modern moral arithmetic, to borrow Bossy's phrase, they are not an exact fit. I will argue that three out of seven Sins (Pride, Avarice, and Lust) persist as relevant categories, finding easy equivalents in the list of Ten Commandments. These are the moral residue, in theoretical terms posed by Marxist critic Raymond Williams, which remains as a curious holdover from the medieval period.[22] Three further Vices, Sloth, Gluttony, and Anger, are liminal cases, transmuted or redefined within the culture in order to fit the new dominant paradigm. The remaining Capital Vice, Envy, simply finds no neat equivalent among the Ten Commandments. The end of Envy, I shall argue, marks the end of an era when received values seemed no longer relevant for early modern life.

To fill the moral vacuum these largely discarded cultural preoccupations created, two items from the Decalogue rose to take their place. Once again, these are Commandments (to honour parents, as well as the injunction against lying) which find no easy equivalent in the list of Capital Vices. In the eighth chapter, I will argue that these two Commandments were uniquely suited to address new moral challenges arising within the context of Spanish Renaissance court culture. Finally, the last section attempts to draw some tentative conclusions about which taxonomy or organizational system, or some combination thereof, might have been favoured by Golden Age dramatists.

The ramifications of this study are wide and far-reaching. In what has become one of the mainstays of *comedia* criticism, José Antonio Maravall argued in the 1970s that the Spanish Golden Age *comedia* was evidence of a directed culture which he took to be symptomatic of the Baroque. In a startlingly crisp pronouncement, he dismissed notions of individual agency as irrelevant when it came to interpreting the period's drama: "el 'soy quien soy' … [n]o se trata de afirmar un ser íntimo, ni una esencia individual, ni un yo interior."[23] Here Maravall makes reference to a key phrase, *soy quien soy*, which has been debated by *comedia* scholars – as well as Hispanists more generally – ad nauseum, most notably in a classic article by Leo Spitzer.[24] The accepted view has been that, to use Althusser's term, the ideological apparatus of the state precluded even the slightest hint of individual agency.[25] This position would later be echoed by the so-called New Historicists, who by and large limited their assessments of English Renaissance drama, particularly Shakespeare, to seeing plays as cultural byproducts of social energies circulating aimlessly without guidance by the master hands of individual geniuses.[26]

The most sustained critique of Maravall was published a decade ago by Melveena McKendrick in the introduction to her magisterial monograph *Playing the King*. In this book, she argued that "close reading of the Spanish plays themselves suggests not an ideologically monolithic and complacent drama, but one which is multivalent and which potentiates ambiguities and subversive readings." She went on to insist that

> the view that the Spanish establishment, let alone the whole of Spanish society, thought with one mind and spoke with one voice is patently absurd ... On the contrary, debate of a wide range of social, political, economic and literary concerns ... was extremely lively, often heated, in this so-called monolithic society ... [T]he concept of state propaganda as elaborated by twentieth-century repressive régimes is simply not applicable to any seventeenth-century society.[27]

Her mantra of "propagation, not propaganda" is a salutary corrective to the excesses of Maravall and the New Historicists.

Convincing as it is, McKendrick's argument appeared in a book-length study devoted to one particular playwright. This is unfortunately all too typical of much work published in this field, which tends to sidestep broader questions about the history of ideas by focusing instead on single authors, plays, or genres. More general and all-encompassing recent correctives to Maravall's approach – focusing on presence or subjectivity, and with particular relevance for Spanish Golden Age studies – have been offered by William Egginton and George Mariscal, but these brilliant studies rarely touch upon the subject of sin, and never upon its taxonomies.[28] Thus the critical need for the present work.

This book harnesses the formidable capacities of digital search engines to tackle the intimidating challenge of grappling with a vast corpus of surviving *comedias*. Early modern Spanish sources often speak about the new genre of the *comedia nueva* in global terms, but this is a liberty of which our hyper-specialization as scholars has deprived us. This book takes a global perspective, organized around notions of sin, to adhere more faithfully to Lope de Vega's original dictum that *comedias* could in fact be a *speculum vitae*, a mirror of life and morality. In doing so, this book brings us closer to these works of art as they were originally conceived.

However, this book was not written exclusively for Hispanists. As a scholar also of Shakespeare and the English Renaissance and Baroque periods, I have tried to offer whenever possible and relevant a comparative perspective to illuminate these plays. In a recent article I wrote comparing Shakespeare and Lope de Vega, I was amazed to find out how many works of scholarship have been published allegedly comparing these two dramatic giants, a disproportionately small number of which succeed in going beyond a few airy generalities to get down to substantive, specific points of contact.[29] In these pages, wherever a particularly apt parallel case has proven appropriate – *The Merchant of Venice*, for instance, makes an appearance in the chapter on Greed – I have not hesitated to use my comparative training to offer a broader European context for phenomena happening in Spain. In my opinion, too frequently Hispanists live on their own proverbial island. It is high time we get in touch with scholars and ideas from other disciplines.

My hope is that professional Hispanists, but also that ever-elusive general reader, particularly of Hispanic heritage, might find in this book the equivalent of one gigantic therapy session. That has certainly been my experience while writing it. These dramas play out timeless tales of love, honour, integrity – and treachery. They give voice to our highest ideals of what constitutes friendship, or patriotism, or self-sacrifice. They also reveal a seamy underside of crass violence and selfish motivation.

Setting aside for a moment Lope de Vega's protestations to the contrary, the anti-Aristotelian *comedia* form as a genre is a highly stylized, totally unrealistic ritual of innuendo and metaphor which could hardly seem further removed from the harsh realities we face today.[30] Moreover, its frequently moralizing tone, sometimes finely calibrated to suit the often-whimsical taste of Inquisitorial censors, would seem, at first glance, to offer little in terms of insight into actual human behaviour.[31] But while this dramatic genre may prove alienating to many contemporary readers and viewers, I would argue that – upon closer reflection – it offers unparalleled glimpses of early modern struggles with sin, temptation, and consequences.

This mode of scholarship approaches the *comedias* as performances of specific sins but also as repositories or archives of moral wisdom. These are not to be confused with archives of historical facts. The latter may be found in Inquisitorial *procesos*, notarial documents, and library inventories, not to mention baptism records, last wills and testaments, dowry lists, and shipping manifests. In general we cannot expect to find this level of historical accuracy or specificity in the *comedias*.

What we can find, however, is the Derridian *trace* of moral attitudes and perspectives on ethical dilemmas ranging from piracy to Adultery to Murder.[32] The nuggets or morsels of wisdom contained in these plays appear not in the canned dialogue or far-fetched and preposterous plots, but rather in the pithy moral sayings uttered off the cuff in asides or dramatic soliloquies which stand out in stark contrast to the main story line. Richard D. Woods has amassed a collection of 3,500 Spanish proverbs; this number offers us a mere glimpse of the vast living repertoire of moral knowledge that was being enacted both on and off the *comedia* stage.[33] This book – in humanistic fashion, as opposed to the more quantitative social science tradition – is an effort to retrace a geneaology of those myriad performances.[34] These dramas constitute only one archive among many and thus do not claim to afford a panoramic view of Spanish culture. It is likewise important to allow for different linguistic registers, rhetoric, satire, allegory, and any number of other deliberate or unintentional literary distortions. But keeping in mind Lope de Vega's dictum in the *Arte nuevo de hacer comedias en este tiempo* about drama being the mirror of life, if we are looking for traces of early modern Spanish moral attitudes, the comedia *corpus* at very least offers us a good place to start.[35]

This way of reading the *comedias* is consonant with what we know in other contexts about Renaissance reading practices. In Craig Kallendorf's recent study of commonplace books, he shows how the goals of early modern readers whenever they approached canonical classical texts were often not the same ones we bring to those same texts today.[36] Their primary purpose in reading Virgil, for example, was not to find out about ancient cultures, nor to admire Golden Age Latin stylistics or turns of phrase, but instead to rack up a new batch of pithy aphorisms they could salt into their own essays or speeches. The survival of Renaissance commonplace books in manuscript – essentially home-made scrapbooks from which authors shamelessly concocted their own plagiarized brew – along with marginal annotations in the original fifteenth- and sixteenth-century printed editions from which they were pirated, demonstrates the pervasiveness of this (by now, foreign to us) reading practice. Lope de Vega himself mentions both memory books (*libros de memoria*) and the printed commonplace books or miscellanies used to produce them (*libros de lugares comunes*) in his 1632 closet drama *La Dorotea*.[37] Furthermore, from surviving copies we can see that overwhelmingly high percentages of these harvested *dicta*, it turns out, had to do with pious behaviour and morality.[38]

More than one disaffected critic has failed to find a human side to the *comedia*.[39] But I would note that it is precisely the critical inattention to sin which could account for this absence. The *comedias* are not, nor were they ever meant to be, autobiographies; they do not offer the sort of self-revelatory passages characteristic of, say, lyric poetry or that "new" genre emerging in the Renaissance, the novel. But it makes no sense to me that plays written during the same period in which novels first became popular would prove utterly devoid of that elusive quotient we have come to call subjectivity.

This book is a journey through time, wading with the reader through miasmas of guilt, struggling through a slimy, icky morass of specific sins, in search of a *trace* of something we might recognize as individual consciousness. The process of writing it has been like pawing through a box of old photographs in the attic in search of some vague family resemblance. The ink might be faded, the image distorted, but often the search will, in the end, be rewarded in the arch of a grandmother's eyebrow or the angle of a cousin's chin.

If the sins of the fathers will be visited upon the third and fourth generations, then it's high time we started dealing with our moral inheritance. Who knows? We might even find clues to behaviour patterns of today.

PART ONE

Residue

1
Pride & Co.

TULIO: Ved la arrogancia que toma.
CAYO: De tales padres la hereda.

– Lope de Vega, *El honrado hermano*[1]

First among the Vices, Pride sails onto the early modern Spanish stage at the prow of the ship.[2] The first head of the hydra representing the Deadly Sins, she is constantly being lopped off, only to grow back again with renewed ferocity.[3] Pride is described alternately in the *comedias* as a poison and a vampire, drinking the blood of its victims amid horrific screams.[4] But this is only the beginning. Root of all evil, Pride engenders even more terrible progeny.[5]

Why would Pride necessarily be seen as the worst Vice? Why not Anger, Avarice, or any other of the prime candidates? Indeed, at later times and in different places, alternative sins have been raised to the status of ultimate Ur-Sin or fallacy: witness the current expression favouring Avarice, "love of money is the root of all evil." But in the early modern period this was definitely not the case, nor was there much argument over which Sin was considered deadliest.[6] This apparently puzzling fact may be explained in a single word: Lucifer. Pride was the worst Sin because it was the one committed by the devil himself: "Luzbel cayó del cielo, por soberbia, y arrogancia."[7] It becomes, then, the most likely Sin of his imitators: "imito a Luzbel, en el caer de la altivez de mí mismo" and "no es bien que así, imite al Querub soberbio, cayendo tal Serafín."[8] Pride is consistently referred to as infernal or hellish, as in the phrase "mi infernal altivez."[9] The devil himself – "aquel monstruo tan rebelde, que a Dios mismo se atrevió soberbio y loco, aquél que tantos delitos cometió" – appears in appropriate costume to lament his eternal loss: "soy … aquel Espíritu Noble, que perdió por su soberbia Gracia, Patria, y Hermosura."[10]

It is perhaps indicative of Pride's prevalence in early modern Spanish society that there are more synonyms for it than for any other Vice. If psycholinguists are right, and the number of words we have to describe a certain experience serves as an index for the degree of complexity used to think about that phenomenon,[11] then the mere fact that there are so many synonyms for Pride in the early modern Spanish lexicon should give us pause. The most frequently encountered synonyms for the noun form include *altivez*, *soberbia*, *vanidad*, and *arrogancia*.[12] Strings of adjectives for "proud" also proliferate.[13]

One of the most fascinating things about the way Pride was understood during the early modern period is that it was considered to be a natural condition. This seems counter-intuitive, since we postmoderns have been conditioned and socialized to think of sin as a choice. But the evidence is clear: *comedia* characters consistently refer to it as natural or even, in some sense, originary. One quickly becomes accustomed to such utterances as "Esta natural soberbia, desde que nació, la tuvo" and "la natural, altiva, soberbia condición fuerte."[14] *Comedia* characters, particularly women who don't seem to fit the dominant gender paradigm, are particularly insistent on this point: "por mi natural condición, tan arrogante, tan altiva, tan soberbia soy."[15] These references to nature also often allude to birth, as in "El haber así nacido soberbia, y desvanecida," or to childhood: "indicio, sobre muchos, que desde su tierna infancia, de su soberbia tenemos, y de sus fieras entrañas."[16] But Pride is not seen as an infantile developmental phase which adults necessarily have the good fortune to grow out of; adults, too, are routinely described as proud in terms which would seem to indicate a constant or unchanging condition.[17] We can reconcile the theological dilemma which would appear to follow from this deterministic world view with reference to Original Sin and its explicit connection to Pride: "comiendo el hombre soberbio la fruta del Paraíso."[18] It makes sense that the devil, taking the body of a serpent, first infected the earthly paradise with the Sin of Pride when he tempted Eve to make herself like God by gaining access to the knowledge of good and evil.[19]

Perhaps stemming from this primordial incident, Pride is seen to have infected the natural world. It pervades the four elements: earth, wind, water, and fire.[20] Now this again might seem curious to the postmodern reader. Have we somehow stumbled into a pantheistic realm where even the natural world rises up in rebellion against God? While some version of this scenario may be possible, considering Neoplatonic interest during the Renaissance in natural objects and their allegedly magical properties, it is more likely that from nature, playwrights were merely harvesting a treasure trove of striking visual images they could use to illustrate various aspects of this root of all Vices.[21] They could use mountains to warn about falling from Pride's height; they could use wind to warn about torrents of prideful words; they could use swiftly flowing rivers to warn of proud impatience; and they could use fire to describe Pride's angry rages as well as the unquenchable thirst for power which Pride engenders.[22] All of these images appear repeatedly in the *comedias* as unforgettable visual aids to understanding this Sin.

As part of Pride's contagion of all things natural, it is also seen to pervade the animal kingdom. This happens both more generally and with regard to specific animals. The butterfly and the eagle are both chastised for daring to soar too high, with the former being singled out for critique as an ambitious creature who forgets its lowly, worm-like beginnings.[23] Dogs may be man's best friends, but they also share in his foibles; they are the object of particular scorn for the foolish arrogance they show when barking at the moon.[24] More ferocious creatures are characterized by arrogance, albeit not so foolish: the lion and the wild boar are both seen as logical vehicles for Pride.[25] The peacock is prideful because he is vain.[26] But unsurprisingly, given his antics in the Garden of Eden, the animal most often associated with Pride is the serpent.[27] This bloody predator is seen menacing the heels of his innocent victims, until his neck is forever crushed, his power symbolically broken, by the sinless Virgin Mary and her saintly imitators who step on his head.[28]

Once the spiritual serpent of Pride bites, its human victim is infected. As we have seen, this primordial act occurred first in the Garden; but since then, this scene has been re-enacted every time a person has succumbed to Pride and then blamed the devil. This perverse form of the phenomenon later theorists have labelled scapegoating can happen repeatedly within the same lifetime.[29] Indeed, one playwright is of the opinion that "crece con los años la arrogancia."[30] But this is the exception that proves the rule; by and large, Pride seems to be mainly the province of youth, with young men being the category of persons most susceptible to its influence.[31] Young men are seen as capricious and imprudent, loving liberty and resisting discipline.[32] They are seen for a time as riding on the shoulders of good luck, like Alexander the Great.[33] But the Baroque *desengaño* of memento mori reminds us and *comedia* audiences that sooner or later, all will end up in the grave: "ese orgulloso mozuelo que te amenaza con guerra, medirá presto la tierra."[34] Until then, we are left with the prototypical scenario etched in our minds starkly, as if in daguerreotype, of the naked, rebellious youth who shakes his fist at God: "Desnudo el rebelde Joven, de su pérfida arrogancia movido."[35] This is an indelible image of treacherous and voracious arrogance.[36]

Where precisely is Pride located in the body of this arrogant youth? Here there seems to be some transference from the animal world, since like the serpent whose neck is crushed by the Virgin, most adherents of this Vice end up suffering from sore necks. Sometimes necks are trounced upon, as was the case with the snake; at other times they are voluntarily lowered, as when love conquers Pride of birth.[37] The solution to an unruly neck which keeps rising up is a bridle. The *comedias* speak recurrently of reins or bridles – like those used for a horse – as concerted efforts to control the Sin of Pride. One character remarks that the proud man needs a bridle, like a coward needs a shield: "Freno al soberbio, y al cobarde escudo."[38] Sometimes Pride is explicitly referred to as an unbridled horse, as in "desbocado

Caballo de mi altivo pensamiento, que por el Aire corría desvanecido, y soberbio."[39] The person riding such a runaway transport will inevitably fall: "del desbocado caballo de mi arrogancia, en el suelo caigo ... postrado."[40] Often it is a king or other ruler who must bring his *subjects* into *subjection* by imposing needed control and guidance: "quiero que a tan necio orgullo pongan obediente freno vuestros Reyes."[41] Without this restraint, the proud person is said to run wild: "el soberbio, osado, atrevido, y cruel, con rienda suelta corre el campo."[42] Even the ocean is pictured as needing the bridle of the beach to rein in its fury: "esta desierta playa, que del mar la soberbia tiene a raya."[43]

Another place where Pride is located on the body is inside a puffed-up chest. The prideful person is described as having "lleno de arrogancia el pecho," with other plays confirming that "el pecho ... ha sido el centro de altivez, y de soberbia."[44] The arms and hands extend out from the chest, and these body parts are described as proud based upon their role in doing battle: "y pues para que conozcas nuestro valor sólo espera la arrogancia de mi brazo."[45] Another possible explanation for Pride's placement in this part of the body is that the chest is where the heart is located, and hearts are also often described as arrogant.[46] In fact, punishment for Pride sometimes involves ripping the proud person's heart right out of his chest: "que del pecho mismo de Gonzalillo le saque aquel corazón altivo."[47] But the heart is not the only thing residing in the proud person's breast, which also becomes the seat of eternal torment if this Sin goes uncorrected: "tormento eterno tiene en el pecho bárbaro vestido de soberbia, arrogancia, crueldad e ira, venganza, enemistad, odio y mentira."[48] Here we see that the inevitable result of uncontrolled Pride is eternal torment.

Another crucial part of the body for locating Pride is in the eyes – not so much because they flash with prideful arrogance (although this too occurs in these plays), but because they go blind, at least metaphorically, as a result of white-hot ambition.[49] In the *comedias*, Pride is the downfall of many a valiant warrior who becomes so blinded by arrogance that he can no longer fight effectively: "A muchos valientes ciega la arrogancia, y los humildes humillaron su soberbia."[50] This proud person must be convinced or persuaded to renounce Pride, thereby opening his eyes:

PECADO: Persuadid su vanagloria.
MUERTE: Convenzed su ceguedad.[51]

Blind Pride inevitably leads to bloodshed, as with the knight who is "tan ciegamente atrevido, tan sangrientamente osado."[52]

But although blind, she is also beautiful; for Pride is not exclusively the province of men.[53] In fact, at least as frequently Pride is described in feminine terms, usually in relation to physical beauty. The *comedias* speak eloquently of "la arrogancia que engendra la hermosura" and lament, "O cómo corren parejas la arrogancia, y la hermosura."[54] In typical Baroque fashion, this is not so much natural as affected or artificial beauty: "La mentira, y la abundancia acompañan la arrogancia con la afectada belleza."[55] The prototype for this Sin of beautiful Pride is Mary Magdalene: "De una vana presunción, Soberbia de la hermosura, Magdalena pide Cura."[56] But arguably, at least in the eyes of the *moralistas*, as well as some playwrights, beauty was a problem for sinners long before Mary Magdalene's time.[57] In a theatrical exploitation of the ambivalence of this conceit, now a thousand beautiful suitors multiply this originary arrogance in an impressive visual array: "mil hermosas pretendientes, que con arrogancia vienen, porque … es la hermosura de sí misma gloriosa."[58]

Once again – and perhaps we hear echoes of Eve – woman's Pride is described as natural by both moralists and certain playwrights: "Yo, que por mi natural condición, tan arrogante, tan altiva, tan soberbia soy."[59] These "naturally" proud women are described in both feminine conduct manuals and certain plays which followed their logic as impertinent and unwilling to listen, as in "no me escuchó Beatriz, porque ha estado impertinente con más soberbia que nunca."[60] These women are alternately ungrateful, fierce, and merciless ("altiva, ingrata, y fiera"), as when Semíramis coldly declares: "Poco mi soberbia altiva se enternece de tu llanto."[61] Their rage can at times be placated, as with the "Mujer, que altiva, y soberbia, en algún tiempo se ve desairada."[62] But Pride resurges in these women in response to drastic life events, such as being married off by one's brother or being held prisoner.[63] Sometimes female Pride is expressed collectively or with consciousness of a group identity, as when Calderón's Doña Clara calls herself the avenger of women: "yo, que tan altiva, y soberbia, me llamé la vengadora de las mujeres."[64]

This line of reasoning naturally leads us to a consideration of that cross-dressing, gender-bending star of early modern Spanish theatre, the *mujer varonil*. Full of swaggering braggadocio, she struts across the stage looking great in her tight pants. This pretty homicide is "tan soberbia, altiva, y fuerte en la guerra" that she is diabolically identified with the "scandal of Men," as when Soberbia (appearing as a *mujer varonil*) talks directly to Lucifer: "en mí, Luzbel, una Dama ves tan vana, y tan altiva, que escándalo de los Hombres la llaman por lo homicida."[65] Indeed, Pride is explicitly associated in the *comedias* with this stock character:

> VELA: ¿Tan altiva es Doña Elvira?
> RAMIRO: Es muy varonil mujer.[66]

The Amazon woman is particularly known for her Pride, as is the Tartar Celaura in Rojas Zorrilla's *Los celos de Rodamonte*. Examples abound.[67] But perhaps for our purposes, the more interesting example of the proud woman is not so extreme.

Rather than looking for her out on the battlefield, we should start right in the home.

A prototypical example of a "normal" – that is, conforming to the norm in the sense of not cross-dressing – woman who is prone to the Sin of Pride is the titular character Jezabel in Tirso de Molina's *La mujer que manda en casa*. Based on the biblical Queen Jezabel from the book of First Kings, the literary version indulges in sexual orgies and is an avid idolatress of the pagan god Baal.[68] As in the Old Testament account, she orders the slaughter of the Hebrew prophets and persecutes Elijah, God's mouthpiece. The most spectacular scene of this play would have undoubtedly been Elijah's miraculous escape from her by being raised to heaven. (The machinery used in these stage productions was often quite sophisticated.) At other points in the play she attempts Adultery by trying to seduce the Jew Naboth, although in reality her primary motivation is to gain control of his vineyard. Another spectacular scene would have been her famous end, as she is seized forcefully and thrown to her death from a balcony.

Thus we see that even a wife can be prideful. Although she does not literally wear the pants, this proud woman's subversion of male patriarchy is perhaps even more insidious. Instead of escaping to the battlefield, she instead stays inside the home – the *casa* of the play's title, even if her house is a palace – to subvert male patriarchal dominance from within. Her complete subjugation of her husband Ahab consistently makes him look rather pathetic. The play's title contains an obvious admonition to wives not to overpower their husbands.

The domineering wife is not the only example of the ways in which Pride bends gender. In the same manner that the *mujer varonil* and the controlling wife take on traditionally male characteristics, so the implicitly homosexual dandy takes on traits normally associated with females. Let us not forget that Lucifer himself, known as the most beautiful angel, "por lo hermoso era soberbio."[69] As I have studied elsewhere, the physically attractive, seductive Counter-Reformation devil was a commonplace of the Baroque period.[70]

Perhaps the most famous pagan equivalent for the Christian devil's vanity is Narcissus, who falls in love with his own image while gazing into a pool of water.[71] His early modern heir is the titular character in Guillén de Castro's *El Narciso en su opinión*, a play which was later imitated by Agustín Moreto in his more famous *El lindo don Diego*. In the original version, Don Gutierre is mocked behind his back by all the other characters, including his servant Tadeo, for being so enamored of himself that he has eyes for no one else:

GUTIERRE: Otra vez mirarme quiero.
TADEO: Gustarás mucho de verte.
GUTIERRE: ¿No ves que cuando me veo
a medida del deseo,
me contento con mi suerte? …

TADEO: Recelo algún mal suceso,
si es verdad lo que se dice
de aquél, [¿]como se decía?
quien dio a la muerte más fría
la vida más infeliz.
Pues que se mató bebiendo,
y no menos que agua pura,
perdido por su hermosura
en la fuente.

In fact, Gutierre is so in love with himself that he announces he is looking for a woman who resembles him physically. (His servant asks jokingly in response, "even if she were as bearded as you?")[72] He takes forever to get dressed. His servant even claims to have caught him embracing his own shadow.[73] Throughout the play he assumes that every female he encounters has fallen for him already; at one point, he announces "Imán soy de las mujeres" – the Golden Age equivalent of "I'm a chick magnet." The other characters, especially his servant Tadeo, take advantage of this weakness to deceive him into wooing a servant girl and thinking she is a high-born lady. When all the pairs of lovers break off into couples at the end, he is left alone – with good reason, since the only person he has ever really loved is himself:

Don Gutierre, pues tan ciego,
tan desvanecido, y fácil,
de sí mismo se enamora,
con su parecer se case.[74]

Here the father figure in the play, Don Pedro, remarks flippantly, "let him marry his own image in the mirror." But Gutierre, ever deluded, is just as happy with this. He sees ladies only as accessories he can put on or take off at will. And this leads us to our next point of discussion about Pride.

* * * * *

Traditional or avant-garde, male or female, proud characters in the *comedias* – starting with Pride herself in the *autos sacramentales* – are almost universally associated with high fashion. This trend once again goes all the way back to the Garden of Eden, where God Himself played tailor to Adam and Eve by fashioning for them garments made out of animal skins to cover their nakedness. For this reason we find the line in Tirso de Molina's aptly named *Santo, y sastre*, "la culpa fue la inventora de gala, y soberbia tanta: cortó ropas el delito."[75] As I have explained elsewhere in an article devoted to costumes worn by the Deadly Vices, Pride is typically pictured in the *autos sacramentales* as wearing fancy clothing, particularly a plumed hat.[76] A representative set of stage directions written by Calderón himself reads: "sale la Soberbia con un Sombrero de Plumas en la Mano."[77] She also wears a lavish cape or mantle of brilliant colour made of silk spun by the insidious worm of ambition: "Real Púrpura le adorne, que tejió de mis tareas la altiva ambición, gusano, que artificioso desea las entrañas que le hila."[78] Pride and the Mal Genio it infects are to be recognized by their lavish costume: "Por estas Plumas, y Telas doy, vano, altivo, y soberbio, conocer de mí, que sólo ponérmelas yo merezco."[79] Various *comedia* characters are likewise instantly recognizable as prideful when they stride onto the stage dressed in elegant attire; for example, "Llevaba Octavio altivo, y arrogante el guante, como pluma en el sombrero."[80] The dandy Don Gutierre in Guillén de Castro's *El Narciso en su opinión* is said by his servant Tadeo to own one outfit adorned with 6,500 buttons.[81] The practice of wearing au courant clothing, such as the newly fashionable shorter sleeve, could potentially lead to vainglory, in what is an unmistakable reference to sumptuary laws: "manga corta al uso, mas no de suerte que parezca vanagloria."[82] In Philip II's austere court – as well as, to some extent, that of his son Philip III – nearly everyone was concerned with avoiding conspicuous consumption.[83]

The plumed hat worn by Pride carries with it still further connotations.[84] It calls attention to the raised forehead, another body part frequently associated with Pride: "Ya veo, que la frente es la Región de la Soberbia."[85] The punishment for a proud soldier is often to crush his forehead: "en la arena sus carros estampastes: Quebrad la altiva frente de Federico airado."[86] But the feathers themselves are also seen to carry special significance. Because they are made from birds' wings, they recall the high flights of the proud creatures they once adorned: "alas son, que la Soberbia de tu propio ser nacido, a grandes cosas te eleve." The repentant sinner gives back this plumed headgear in Calderón's auto *El año santo en Madrid*, saying: "Toma, Soberbia, esas Plumas, que ya tus Alas no quiero."[87]

Although it may seem small to the point of insignificance, this detail leads us to the strange synthesis which was Christian humanism during the early modern period. The identification of plumed hats with birds' wings reveals an imaginative Baroque dexterity unfamiliar to our sensibilities.[88] I would postulate that furthermore, these are not the wings of just any bird. Instead they form an oblique reference to Icarus, who flew too close to the sun, and, by extension, to Phaethon, who could not control the immortal horses pulling the sun's chariot. Many other mythological figures are mentioned in connection with Pride in the *comedias*, including the one-eyed giant Polyphemus; Tesiphonte, murderer of Adonis; Perseus; and Atlantis, who was metamorphosed into – no surprise here, considering the proud mountains we have seen above – a mountain as a punishment for Pride.[89] Even Jupiter is referred to repeatedly as proud.[90] But it is Icarus and Phaethon who seem to be most inextricably connected to Pride within the early modern Spanish paradigm.

"Ícaro altivo," as he was known to early modern audiences, reached the sun on wings of wax, only to fall when they melted.[91] Phaethon likewise, being the son of the god Helios or Apollo, bore a natural affinity to the sun. Upon meeting his father, and being granted a boon of his choice, he requested permission to drive the sun's chariot for a day. His wish was granted, but unable to control the sun's horses – here we remember the unbridled horse metaphors already noted for Pride – he fell to the earth. Calderón de la Barca thematizes Pride's fall in his mythological play *El faetonte*, which according to some scholars may have been written on the occasion of the painting of the mythical figure of Phaethon on a ceiling of the Royal Palace in Madrid.[92] In this play, Thetis unknowingly addresses Phaethon as "Ignorado hijo del viento, que sólo a tanta soberbia él pudiera dar las alas."[93] The irony, of course, is that he is the son of the sun, not the wind. Other characters, likewise, notice his proud disposition even before his true identity is revealed. For example, Epafo (whom Phaethon believes to be his brother) rails at him as they engage in a fist fight: "no sufriré desde aquí de tu siempre altivo, fiero espíritu otro desaire." Amaltea addresses him as "villano, al fin, mal nacido, que esa soberbia altivez de tu presunción, castigue su mismo espíritu."[94] Her words turn out to be prophetic, as his Pride will soon receive its punishment. Phaethon is not the only proud character in this play; his beloved Thetis also speaks self-consciously of her own Pride, presumption, and arrogance.[95] In what must have been a spectacularly staged scene, Phaethon rises to the heavens with his mother, Climene, to meet his father Apollo and request the chance to drive the sun's chariot. In the dramatic version, he becomes distracted while driving when he notices Epafo trying to abduct Thetis on the earth below. The out-of-control chariot veers too close to the earth, scorching the Ethiopians' skin. Phaethon falls from the chariot and Eridano drowns. A more literal visual depiction of Pride's fall could hardly be imagined.

While Spanish Golden Age interest in classical mythology may be typical of the Renaissance, once again we see here a synthesis of pagan and Christian sources. For every reference to Icarus or Phaethon in the Spanish *comedias*,[96] we find several corresponding ones to Biblical figures. Judás Macabeo of the apocryphal Book of Maccabees, a Scriptural text accepted by Catholics as canonical, is said to be proud, as is Haman of the Esther story.[97] But of all the Old Testament figures, it is Goliath who comes to symbolize the epitome of arrogance. The Philistine giant felled by a shepherd boy's slingshot became the archetypical scenario for Pride going before a fall. In Calderón's auto sacramental *El Arca de Dios cautiva*, we see the Philistines boasting of Goliath's strength to the Israelites: "Para cada uno de vuestros Soldados, trae su arrogancia ciento, y más." In what modern psychologists would call a supreme act of transference, Goliath himself refers to his young opponents here as proud: "Locos Jóvenes, cuya arrogancia, si yo hubiera de temer, temiera … en premio de su arrogancia, lleven el honor de ser Goliath el que los mata."[98] But at the end of this dramatic spectacle, as well as others by the same author, the audience could indulge in some edifying Schadenfreude as it saw "postrada de Goliath la Soberbia."[99]

Imagining historical wars such as the one between the Israelites and the Philistines gave early modern Spanish playwrights the opportunity to meditate about the pridefulness of war in general. They refer to war as "O guerra soberbia, altiva, sangrienta, homicida y fea" and to an army as "armado con lucida infantería, y vana soberbia armado."[100] This characterization of war goes all the way back to the Roman god of war, Mars, who is consistently referred to as proud.[101] During the early modern period, new technologies of warfare were causing what had before amounted to mere skirmishes to wreak more widespread devastation.[102] In this new technological era, even military innovations such as landmines are described as being, by extension, full of arrogance.[103] But even more traditional warfare could partake of this representation, if by sheer force of numbers one side could intimidate another:

> CONDE: ¿Que en fin ha desembarcado?
> PALADIO: Con arrogancia espantosa. Dos mil hombres tiene en tierra.[104]

Playwrights had to resort to dialogue to convey such images because, unlike with Hollywood cinema, they could not fit 2,000 warriors on stage.

These, of course, were not just any wars that contemporaneous Spaniards were fighting. The so-called Golden Age witnessed the peak period of Spain's world dominance. Much blood and ink were spilt defending Spain's alleged right to invade and conquer, and these tensions also played out in the nation's theatre. Playwrights recalled other great conquerors of world history, such as Alexander the Great, whose invasions they justified by allusion to his "civilizing" mission of giving laws.[105] The Spanish conquistadores could also seek justification for their actions in their own history by recalling the Carthaginians who, in centuries past, had invaded the Iberian Peninsula, driving the Goths into the mountains, from which they eventually launched the Reconquest.[106] Similarly, the Spaniards themselves had invaded the native tribes living on the Canary Islands in 1494, a historical episode which later inspired Lope de Vega's play *Los guanches de Tenerife, y conquista de Canaria*.[107] Traditionally, early modern Spaniards' favourite role models for conquest were the Romans, to whom they were able to trace their lineage back in a direct line to Julius Caesar.[108]

But curiously, though early modern Spanish playwrights at times seem gratified to recall their Roman heritage, at other times they almost seem to blame the Romans for a legacy of Pride, which went on to become Spain's perceived national Vice. It is common to find general references to "la arrogancia Romana" or more specifically to the "vile" Roman senate: "ese vil senado Romano, arrogante, altivo."[109] In fact, throughout the *comedias* the word Roman becomes virtually synonymous with "arrogant":

> CURIACIO: Extraña arrogancia muestra.
> HORACIO: Muestro que Romano soy.[110]

The moral and pragmatic judgment made upon Roman arrogance is unequivocal: "Roma con su triunfo y arrogancia jamás estuvo en paz."[111] It is one lesson from history which early modern Spaniards notoriously neglected to take to heart.

Just as early modern Spanish conquerors self-consciously imitated their Roman precursors, they retained the language of Pride to talk about their own conquests. Calderón refers to that "Comunero del Imperio, mi soberbia," and in another play he has his character Cintia declare, "no sólo de mi altivo valor el Imperio es."[112] In Lope de Vega's *El valiente Céspedes*, a warrior play contemporaneous with the semi-autobiographical picaresque soldier's tale *Varia fortuna del soldado Píndaro* (1626) by Gonzalo de Céspedes y Meneses, the titular character, Céspedes, describes a vast empire reaching from "la Scitia helada hasta las Indias de Ofir." Trillo replies: "Brava arrogancia … muy bien me advertís de ciudades conquistadas."[113] It is well known that the *comedias* are rife with references to "New" World riches, but what has perhaps not been recognized before is that these often occur in the context of Pride: "podía enriquecer su soberbia con el oro de otras Indias, más ricas."[114]

Paradoxically – and here we might remember the Spaniards' complicated historical memory with reference to the Romans – we note that Pride suddenly gets transferred from the conquistadores to the native peoples they conquer. This is true especially in the "New" World context. Caupolicán in Lope de Vega's *Arauco domado por el excelentísimo señor don García Hurtado de Mendoza* says to the indigenous chieftain Tucapel: "Huélgome que tendrás justo castigo, Soberbio Tucapel, de tu arrogancia." In the same play, a character on the other side of this epochal battle, Filipe de Mendoza, makes reference to "la arrogancia de Galvarino, Indio fuerte, aunque de malas entrañas."[115] The mestizos, who were the product of miscegenation between Spaniards and conquered native peoples, are singled out in the *comedias* as being especially prone to the Vice of Pride, perhaps because their claim to Spanish heritage gave them occasion to lord it over their less fortunate indigenous relatives: "la ambición, y la soberbia de un mestizo, de un bastardo."[116] But ironically, the very humility of "vile" Assyrian slaves is said to reflect the arrogance of their Roman (read: avatars for early modern Spanish) conquerors: "viles esclavos, que muestran en su humildad mi arrogancia."[117]

This complex interplay of racial projection and transference was not limited to the people groups Spain set out to conquer.[118] Anyone they fought against or with whom they had even passing unpleasant contact could be vilified later in their literature as proud. References to other "prideful" nationalities in the *comedias* are too numerous to count, starting in fact with entire continents, such as Asia.[119] Greeks, Italians, English, and even Albanians are mentioned in the context of Pride, as is the Duchy of Saxony.[120] It should come as no surprise, given the vexed relationships within the Iberian Peninsula, that the Portuguese are often criticized as proud by early modern Spaniards.[121] And given Spain's long-standing rivalry with France, as well as territorial disputes over the region of Navarre, it is logical to find more references to Frenchmen as proud than to the inhabitants of any other country within Europe.[122]

But a special place in the early modern Spaniard's moral universe was reserved for Muslims. As Barbara Fuchs has shown in her provocative book *Exotic Nation*, all things Islamic were viewed within Spain at this time as paradoxically both alien and quotidian. Thus any criticisms of Muslims became at the same time criticisms of Spain's own heritage, considering the 700+-year history they shared. The Arabic peoples with whom Spaniards had the most contact after the Reconquista came from either North Africa or Turkey. The Turks certainly receive their share of derogatory comments, such as "la arrogancia del Turco" and "el Turco viene orgulloso, porque cuatro pueblos quema."[123] But it is the North African Muslims, particularly the corsairs or pirates known to seize Christian prisoners, whom early modern Spaniards came to see as the greatest threat.

In what Eric Griffin would term a deliberately Otherizing gesture of ethnopoetics, the *comedias* associate African Pride with barbarity: "de aquel bárbaro furor, y del Africano orgullo."[124] The Spanish Christians of the Reconquest propose, "Que lancemos del Reino Castellano los moros, que con Bárbara arrogancia lo inquietan."[125] In Calderón's allegorical *autos sacramentales*, the figure of Pride is identified with "the African sect": "la Secta Africana, que hoy es la Soberbia ufana."[126] The Spanish Catholic king is lauded as the scourge of the "Moors": "un Rey de oro, gloria del honor Christiano, temor del orgullo Moro."[127] But not all encounters with Arabs turn out successfully:

> ZERBÍN: ¿Que va furioso el Capitán Cristiano?
> ISABELA: La arrogancia del Moro le desvela.[128]

On the *comedia* stage, the proud shouts of Muslim warriors can still be heard echoing down through the centuries: "Oyó entre otros la arrogancia que el Moro a voces repite."[129] There are also Arabic characters in these dramas who refer to themselves in terms of Pride, as when a Muslim woman says to her brother, "no permita Alá que del Cristiano … triunfe tu orgullo, pues dolor tan fiero, será insufrible para la ansia mía."[130] Some plays thematize Muslim/Christian interaction to the point of giving us a blow-by-blow of specific battles of the Reconquest: "ya está el Reino sujeto a pesar del Moro altivo, porque Zaro se rindió" and "Cuando partí de Cartama topé a Reduán soberbio con una escuadra de Moros."[131] Theatregoers would have been delighted to hear about the fall of proud Muslim warriors at the hands of their own "saintly" heroes: "Castigada la soberbia de Aveniucef, en sus Muros tan derrotado se encierra."[132] Early modern Spaniards appear to keep fighting the Reconquista over and over again obsessively in their minds and on stage, until "de los moros cesa la arrogancia injusta y loca."[133] The fight against the "Moors" continues to exert appeal as a voyage of fantasy in early modern Spanish texts, such as the one in which a character declares: "si tuviera en África esa espada, yo venciera la Morisca arrogancia bizarra."[134]

The Pride of the Muslims is seen in these texts to be derived from the founder of their religion, Muhammad. As a Christian warrior says, "espada en mano, hemos de salir a triunfar de la arrogancia de Mahomet."[135] But the Pride of this sect is traced in the *comedias* even further back, all the way to Abraham's son Ishmael, born to the maidservant Hagar: "Línea de Ismaél, y Agár, de quien descendí, de tanta soberbia lleno, que con Nombre de Agareno, Dios ninguno conocí."[136] The discourse of Pride is placed directly into the prophet's own mouth by the playwright Francisco de Rojas Zorrilla, who thematizes the downfall of the "false" religion of Islam in *El profeta falso Mahoma*. In the third act of this play, Muhammad himself declares, "pues ya por mi soberbia me he querido condenar." His statement refers to the lasting effects of Pride, namely eternal condemnation. By identifying Muhammad so explicitly with the Sin of Pride, early modern Spanish playwrights have effectively managed to demonize him through connection to Lucifer, whose hallmark was Pride. This impression is solidified by Muhammad's own account of his fall: "Válgame el infierno, sean mi iras quien me castigue, quien me arroje mi soberbia ... Caí de la nube densa a ser escándalo al mundo."[137]

Early modern Spaniards were nothing if not zealous in defending their faith. References abound not just to Muslims as proud, but to heretics in general as arrogant. Unsurprisingly, we find references to "Lutero lleno de torpe arrogancia" which cast Martin Luther in roughly the same light as Muhammad.[138] Calderón's *El sitio de Breda*, recalling a Spanish battle in the Netherlands, and Lope de Vega's *Angélica en el Catay*, set in China, both cast the Catholic conquests in those territories as the defeat of arrogant barbarians: "Hoy el Cristiano derriba, del Bárbaro la arrogancia, rompe, atropella, y cautiva" and "hoy espero que el cuello dome a esta herética arrogancia, Religión dañada y torpe."[139] But religious zeal was also working here in combination with more pragmatic concerns. In the same breath, we see Calderón's characters referring to Muslim religion and to the Arabs' predilection for piracy: "aquesa Religión, que siempre altiva infesta nuestros mares."[140] In fact, in one of his *autos sacramentales* Calderón even dresses up Pride in the costume of an infidel pirate: "tú, Soberbia, en infiel Pirata de sus Mares te transforma."[141]

Now, with all this finger pointing and name calling taking place on the early modern Spanish stage when it comes to other races and religions, one might expect Spaniards themselves to come out smelling like the proverbial rose. But this could not be further from the truth. By some strange act of simultaneous rejection and appropriation of the cultural capital embodied by sin and its manifestations through different character traits, Spanish Renaissance playwrights also accuse themselves and their countrymen of being arrogant. In fact, as we saw earlier with the sheer number of synonyms for Pride, references by Spaniards to themselves as proud far outweigh their criticisms of anyone else. The term Spanish becomes synonymous with proud, as in "la soberbia y Española gente" and "Brava arrogancia Española."[142] At the same time, various characters refer to a peculiarly Spanish brand of Pride, such as "¡O qué Española arrogancia!" and "Ya no se puede sufrir esta Española arrogancia."[143] Spanish Pride is undoubtedly mixed with valour, as in "después de haber vencido la Española arrogancia cuanto topa." It has the advantage of making Spanish soldiers more formidable in warfare; thus we see Spain's Flemish enemies plotting, "humillemos esta Española arrogancia."[144]

Miguel de Cervantes describes the proud, prototypical Spaniard in *El gallardo español*: "parece que en él sólo hizo asiento la arrogancia."[145] In what Barbara Fuchs has described as a Janus-like ambivalence, Spain here gazes inward at itself at the same time as it gazes outward to observe others' impressions:

> CELIO: Tengo cara de Francés.
> MARCELIO: Mas de Español la arrogancia.[146]

An aptly titled play about mutual deception, Guillén de Castro's *El engañarse engañado*, presents the arrogant Polish view of Spaniards as displaying more bravado than true bravery: "de Polonia arrogante, diciendo, que el Español funda en la arrogancia el trato, y no en la espada el valor."[147] Lope de Vega's *Del mal lo menos* goes even further, declaring that Spanish arrogance is all empty wind: "Todo es viento la arrogancia Española: ¿quién osara mostrar a un Rey tan arrogante cara?"[148] Spanish playwrights themselves seem to be aware of the apparent contradiction here, using alternative words for Pride to describe Spanish soldiers, French soldiers, and Turks. We see this complicated dynamic in action when a French soldier – symbolically represented in the figure of the city of Paris – exclaims, "de mis Lises experimentaron fieros los Turcos con *mi arrogancia* todo el desvanecimiento de *su soberbia*, manchando con su Sangre mis aceros."[149] But early modern Spaniards, considering themselves naturally proud, would not seem to want it any other way: "no quisiera que la bizarría Española, naturalmente soberbia, a otro afecto se persuada."[150]

Any student of Spanish geography and demography understands the importance of regional distinctions. So the question might well be asked: are Spaniards of different regions referred to with the same frequency as being proud in the *comedias*? Basically all of Spain's regions and their inhabitants are mentioned at some point in connection to Pride, such as "arrogancia Leonés" or "dándole los Catalanes favor con mucha arrogancia."[151] Galician Pride is seen to be a blend of the Spanish with the Portuguese varieties: "si arrogancia no es de Español y Portugués, verá mi patrón Gallego, con esta espada de fuego, toda el África a sus pies."[152] Granada and Andalusia are both seen as having lost their Pride through the humiliation of being occupied by Muslim invaders: "Granada perdió su orgullo y brío" and "vea la Andaluz soberbia, su orgullo desvanecido … hasta las torres mismas de Córdoba."[153] Even subjection by fellow Spaniards is unwelcome and evidently results in a certain loss of face, as when Castile refuses to roll out the red carpet for its new Aragonese king: "Alborótase Castilla con tener Rey de Aragón; que su altiva condición piensa que afrenta, y humilla." In the same play, the Castilians protest, "no es razón que con arrogancia tanta venga a poner Aragón sobre Castilla la planta."[154] Indeed, Castilian Pride, or "Castellana arrogancia," becomes almost legendary, with fables of Salamancan bravery adorning the ancient wall of this Castilian city: "historias, ò las fabulas, once Salamanca tiene, que con mayor arrogancia su muro antiguo ennoblecen."[155] In Tirso de Molina's *Adversa fortuna de don Álvaro de Luna*, the titular character vows: "he de domar, vive Dios, el orgullo Castellano."[156] But Spanish playwrights, at heart, were poets; and they could not resist the Baroque seduction of witty plays on words. Whether or not the Aragonese were in fact particularly arrogant, a favourite pun from this period seems to have been the alliteratively splendid "de Aragón la arrogancia."[157]

* * * * *

Perhaps it is time to step back for a moment and ask: why should Spaniards have considered themselves to be particularly proud? How does this fit in with the rest of what we know about early modern Spanish culture – and more specifically, what we know about the genre of the *comedias*? It has long been recognized that one of the major thematic preoccupations in the *comedias* is honour.[158] If we can tie Pride to this theme with textual evidence, then we shall add one further layer to our understanding of this complex moral economy.

Pride is connected to honour very explicitly in the *comedias*. In fact, the two words often appear as synonyms for each other.[159] It is common to find characters making such declarations as "yo con toda la arrogancia mía profeso honor con alta valentía."[160] Honour is routinely referred to as high or proud, such as in "como a tu honor altivo faltas, y a tu decoro te niegas" or "¡que una razón, o que una sinrazón pueda manchar el altivo honor, tantos años adquirido!"[161] Proud honour is to be tested, "hacer prueba de mi honor altivo," but it can also make one miserable: "tú con altiva arrogancia, o recelos de mi honor, vida miserable pasas."[162] Finally, proud honour fights against offence until it is avenged properly: "Válgome de mi honor, que altivo intenta pelear con mi agravio hasta vengarle."[163]

The popular and at times prohibited practice of duelling was the preferred way to avenge wounded honour.[164] Duels, likewise, often appear in the *comedias* in the context of Pride. Sometimes swordplay is the object of burlesque comedy in these theatrical works, as with the swaggering braggart without much substance behind his style: "La espada con arrogancia sacó, entre otros camafeos, con muchísimos meneos, y poquísima sustancia."[165] But more often in the *comedias*, duelling is portrayed as deadly serious, for these playwrights knew better than to miss such a prime opportunity for showmanship. The very act of challenging someone to a duel is portrayed as proud and therefore worthy of punishment: "he de empezar castigando el altivo atrevimiento de llamarme a desafío."[166] Duelling is seen as the right of a gentleman; but even within those rights, it can still be viewed as a cruel practice designed to humiliate one's opponent publicly: "usando de todo el fuero, concedido a Caballero, le llama altivo, y cruel a público desafío."[167] There were pamphlets and treatises published at this time arguing both for and against this dubious practice, and the Count-Duke of Olivares wrote a memorandum in 1638 pondering the question of what would be the most effective means to stop duels among the noblemen at court.[168] Calderón thematizes this contemporary controversy in his *El postrer duelo de España*. It was considered particularly unseemly to challenge someone of lower rank: "y más si contra un villano sacarla, obligado, debe, porque altivo se le atreve cuerpo a cuerpo, y mano a mano."[169] The women whose tokens the knights wore, or whose standards they bore, were also guilty of vainglory: "es necia la que por su vanagloria con el galán a quien ama de ser querida blasona."[170]

As we may assume from the cultural relic of duelling which survived as a holdover from the medieval period, Pride is seen here as the province of the more elevated social classes. Many of the specific characters described as proud are noble men and women, or at least those with significant social-climbing ambitions: "cuán altiva es la Condesa" and "vaya de aquel pensamiento altivo con que a ser Conde aspirabas."[171] Noblemen are alternatively described as confident and presumptuous: "¡Qué altivo y presuntuoso, qué confiado y lozano os mostráis, Marqués!"[172] Their Pride causes them to do things – such as entering someone's home without permission – which are considered unacceptable within the normal social order: "¿tanta es, Don Pedro, la osadía de tu briosa arrogancia, que así en mi casa te entras?"[173] Often servants or friends of noblemen are found trying to persuade them to temper their Pride: "Sosiega el fiero y orgulloso pecho Noble, Suero Velázquez, no te alteres."[174] Kinship or some other special relationship to the king often gives them the courage to act outrageously, as does the young Aurelio in Lope de Vega's *El amigo por fuerza*: "un pariente del Rey, hombre orgulloso y mancebo, de costumbres atrevidas y de propio nombre Aurelio."[175] In fact, sometimes Pride even impels these nobles to sedition: "Para cualquier traición tiene el Conde inclinación, arrogancia y rebeldía."[176] This is because Pride bears with it a certain impatience with the ebb and flow of the normal course of events; as the king says in Guillén de Castro's *Las mocedades del Cid*, "Tiene del Conde Lozano la arrogancia, y la impaciencia."[177]

Drawn to its healthy population of proud noblemen, Pride thus becomes a more or less permanent resident of the court. We see courtiers striding across the stage dressed with arrogance, as in "Caballero de la Corte que vestido de arrogancia venís a quitarme el bien que solicitan mis ansias."[178] Pride is consistently referred to as a characteristic of the court, along with its bedfellows, flattery and ambition: "Mírale haciendo trofeos de las galas que ostentó la soberbia Cortesana, la lisonja y la ambición."[179] In Biblical and historical fiction plays such as Tirso de Molina's *Tanto es lo demás como lo de menos*, based on the parable of the talents as well as the story of the Prodigal Son, Spanish playwrights often looked for parallels to their own situation. One can only assume that Tirso saw a mirror of Spanish court culture when he had one of his characters make the observation, "Corte soberbia es Egipto."[180] In fact, the Deadly Sins as a group came to be uniquely identified with courtly Vice: "a seguir hoy Cortesano los rumbos de mi Apetito: Soberbia, Avaricia, Envidia, Pereza, Ira, Gula, Amigos, a vosotros vengo."[181]

The Pride of courtiers leads them to indulge in self-seeking preoccupations, such as the concern over lineage (*limpieza de sangre*) and coats of arms.[182] Golden Age Spaniards came under intense scrutiny as to their lineage, with some wealthy *conversos* buying the equivalent of a fake family tree.[183] The reason for this was that anyone with a known Jewish background was in grave danger of persecution by the Inquisition, which was ever on the lookout for signs of judaizing activities.[184] These notarial documents are scoffingly called charters of vainglory in a play by Lope de Vega, *La pobreza estimada*, where he praises the moral benefits of poverty: "hojas de que fundó la más noble ejecutoria, cédulas de vanagloria que da firmadas el mundo."[185] Other *comedia* characters come across as proud due to their heritage, such as the young man who goes around proclaiming loudly that he is the son of the town's chief shepherd – as if that were some mark of great distinction: "Ese Joven, que diciendo viene altivo, y arrogante, que es Hijo del Mayoral."[186] The flip side of this equation is of course not wanting to be of lowly origin, such as the son of an ironworker: "su orgullo no consiente ser hijo de un vil herrero."[187] The multiple identity swappings and resulting confusion characteristic of so many *comedias* mean that some characters believe themselves to be noble when in fact they are not: "hoy presunción enemiga … Mi soberbia burladora, hijo noble de Ricardo me llamó."[188]

Once a nobleman's lineage is proven, then he may display his family's coat of arms. These insignia too are explicitly framed in terms of Pride: "bruñe de oro sobre negro, unas letras esculpidas, de su arrogancia concepto."[189] In what can only be seen as a slap to the monarchy, Calderón goes so far as to let Pride march across the stage, bearing a standard emblazoned with the royal coat of arms: "con un Estandarte … y la Soberbia en el suyo las Armas Reales."[190] The trappings of Pride furthermore most often include immense wealth, such as golden chariots and shining crowns said to be enamelled with arrogance: "llévame a Roma a prisa, y en carro de oro mi arrogancia pisa" and "ahora enlaza sus sienes de piezas de oro esmaltadas de arrogancia."[191]

We might anticipate that the inverse of this logic would also hold true – that the poor would be valorized as humble in the *comedias*. This certainly does happen sometimes, as when Tirso moralizes in *La Dama del Olivar*: "Dios desprecia tal vez de los hombres la altivez, y antepone la pobreza."[192] Lope de Vega, likewise, would seem to associate riches with Pride, and poverty with humility, as in *La pobreza estimada*. In his *La fe rompida*, he has one of his characters introduce his *villano* father in positive terms: "Éste en efecto es mi padre, no por la riqueza altivo, sino humilde labrador en traje compuesto, y limpio."[193]

But on closer inspection, the *comedias* offer a more complicated picture, one in which Pride is not necessarily synonymous with wealth, any more than poverty translates easily into humility. Poor people can also be guilty of Pride, largely in their efforts to imitate the upper class: "Hasta el villano criado su loca arrogancia imita."[194] In the *comedias* we find repeated injunctions by noblemen designed to keep the *labradores* in their place, as in "que se recoja la desmandada y orgullosa gente."[195] Often we find a character expressing amazement at the incongruity of finding such Pride in so lowly a subject: "¡Notable altivez de pobre!" and "¿escucháis la arrogancia del villano?"[196] Juan Ruiz de Alarcón would seem to advise that Pride be suppressed until there is wealth to validate it: "Y así mientras pobre fueres, el ardiente orgullo doma."[197] But once again, we see poor labourers expressing an innate Pride which they claim is natural or inborn: "pobre estoy, así nací, ved mi arrogancia, y mi talle."[198] This Pride of the lower classes undoubtedly posed a threat to early modern Spanish social order. An upstart such as the lady-in-waiting Anne Boleyn, who rose in English society to become queen to King Henry VIII, thus becomes emblematic in the Spanish imagination of the social dangers to which Pride can lead if left unchecked: "es Ana mujer altiva, su vanidad, su ambición, su arrogancia, y presunción la hacen a veces esquiva, arrogante, loca."[199]

One exception to this apparently inviolable social hierarchy would be those who answered the military vocation. As we have seen earlier in our discussion of warfare, soldiers are consistently described as proud, but not necessarily in pejorative terms, as for example when Calderón's character Joab refers to "el orgullo del ejército, que osado la batalla nos dispuso."[200] Likewise in Antonio de Zamora's *El custodio de la Hungría, San Juan Capistrano*, Cardenio asks: "¿no veis dos Soldados, cuya altiva arrogancia, al Río corta las cóleras fugitivas?"[201] Pride is particularly evident in military leaders such as generals or captains, as in "aunque de arrogancia llena a tan fuerte Capitán."[202] In Calderón's auto sacramental *El socorro general*, the traitorous nation of Israel acts as a female general who "soberbia, y arrogante tocó Cajas, armó Gentes, y arboló sus Estandartes."[203] Nevertheless, there seems to be some ambivalence regarding the excusability of this Vice in this context, as when Calderón's Prince Fernando reminds his soldiers: "no se emplean nuestras armas aquí por vanagloria."[204]

Another exception to the normal social hierarchy occurs for poets. This is a favourite topos for playwrights, since here they get to criticize fellow practitioners of their very own profession: "así verás mil personas, Poetas de pintar monas, llenos de arrogancia en vano."[205] Censors often take the opportunity in the preliminary prose added to printed editions of plays to comment on the Pride of literary authors, as when Joseph de Valdivielso, in his *aprobación* for a volume of works by Lope de Vega, alludes to "las plumas que más remontadas con ilustre vanagloria vuelan por nuestra España."[206] Sometimes Pride is translocated in early modern historical memory as having belonged more to the country's remote literary past, as with "Cierto Poeta temprano, que escribe por vanagloria."[207] But repeated statements within the *comedias* cast aspersions more generally upon Spain's contemporaneous intellectual elite: "Da el saber sin fundamento arrogancia y presunción."[208] In fact, in some passages Pride is seen to be inseparable from knowledge: "es tan inseparable la altivez presumida de los que saben algo."[209] Science – in the more general sense of any sort of knowledge, from the Latin verb *scire*, meaning to know – is seen as forming a canopy of Pride over its devotees: "mis Ciencias, Trono de mi Majestad, y Dosel de mi soberbia."[210] However, intellectual charlatans can also hide their lack of knowledge under this same tent: "los que ahora tratan de estos estudios, con más arrogancia que ciencia."[211] This is especially true of magicians, such as Calderón's *mágico prodigioso*, who admits: "sin estudios tuve tan grande arrogancia, que a la Cátedra de Prima me opuse."[212] Here he makes reference to an academic chair which is still the mark of distinction in Spanish universities today. *Comedia* characters even potentially make specific reference to the moral instruction of confessors and preachers in identifying Pride with academic letters: "Las letras, según el Cura, causan al sabio soberbia."[213] In Calderón's great market of the world, intelligence or genius is sold in the shop or boutique of Pride: "el Buen Genio está en la Tienda de la Soberbia."[214] Pride is even conscripted to serve in the literary battle between *conceptistas* and *culteranos*, as when Lope de Vega criticizes the *culteranos*, such as Luis de Góngora, who want to "Por vanagloria adulterar la lengua."[215]

In the midst of all these myriad uses we have found for the Deadly Vices framed as cultural capital, we might well ask whether Pride is seen to enter the realm of the political. Not surprisingly, it does. Of all the figures associated in the *comedias* with prideful behaviour, one of the most frequently encountered is the king or emperor himself. The king is viewed as someone who arrogantly offers his hand to be kissed, as in Lope de Vega's *El piadoso aragonés*: "a besar les dio la mano con arrogancia."[216] We can imagine how it pains the pious Calderón de la Barca to "ver las Majestades con soberbia servidas siempre desvanecidas con locas vanidades."[217] The most powerful emblem of the ruler's Pride is his crown: "coronóse al fin venciendo, y … en su frente altiva las hojas de oro y laurel del sagrado Imperio insignias."[218] Here we see the golden laurel wreath invoked as one of the specific trappings of sacred Empire, a reference to the Holy Roman Empire of the Spanish ruler Charles V but also an allusion more generally to Spain's belief in its divine right to rule.[219] The neck of the potential ruler who wishes to wear this wreath – particularly if he does not deserve it – is described as proud: "ese altivo cuello que pensaba coronarse."[220] Thus the old man Emanuel warns Lisarco, king of the Philistines, that his attempts to "conservar tu Monarquía, y Emperador del Orbe Coronarte" are nothing more than vain arrogance: "porque si altivo tu rigor porfía."[221] The sorceress Cenobia similarly boasts that she would trick the proud Emperor into bowing at her feet: "había de ver a mis plantas el poder de un soberbio Emperador."[222]

The *comedias* are rife with references to tangible symbols of kingly or imperial power, which we might properly call the architecture of empire. These symbols include castles, which are often described as high and arrogant, as well as thrones, which embody the power of the ruler who sits on them. The palaces of the wealthy are characterized as arrogant both in terms of their height and in terms of their size: "ese gigante de piedra, ese Palacio del Duque, esa fábrica soberbia (cuyos altos chapiteles compiten con las Estrellas)."[223] Palaces are consistently seen as perched up high, out of reach for normal folk who marvel at their splendour: "¿No ves aquese palacio, por cuya altura soberbia, sólo el Sol señalar puede la distancia de su alteza?"[224] Baroque playwrights relish the possibilities for wordplay inherent in the synonym for Pride, *altivez*, as when one character warns, "tu arrogancia castigaré en un Castillo" and another replies, "Notable *altivez*."[225] Indeed, proud castles often serve as places of prison or punishment, as in Calderón's *La vida es sueño* or in Antonio de Solís's aptly titled play *El alcázar del secreto*: "Y ordenaba, por Diana, en ese Alcázar soberbio, presa estuviese."[226] Some of these high castles, such as Calderón's *El castillo de Lindabridis*, bear the further mystique of being enchanted: "este encantado Castillo, a cuya frente soberbia se abolla el Viril del Cielo."[227] The most diabolical resonances of all come from the high walls of the devil's own court: "hay murallas, donde tiene su Corte, y altivo Alcázar el Demonio."[228]

Likewise, monarchs' thrones are seen to represent their most probable Vice, as in "de su fiereza ha de estrenar el Trono de su orgullo."[229] The throne room in all its glittering splendour is criticized for being ostentatious: "doradas salas, donde tiene la grandeza la silla de su arrogancia, digo, de su ostentación."[230] We must remember that in this period, and also still today, thrones could symbolize religious as well as secular authority, the most important investment of which – for Catholic Spaniards – was placed in the pope.[231] Thus it is with particular horror that Calderón imagines the audacity of Cardinal Volsius, who sought to usurp the pope's rightful authority by sitting on his throne. As he schemes in *La cisma de Inglaterra*, "si por vosotras medro a tan excelso lugar, me pienso altivo sentar en la Silla de San Pedro."[232]

This architecture and furniture of empire extends out from the enclosed space of the throne room into the public courtyard and beyond. Thus we see rulers erecting statues to themselves in public places where more people will see them: "en la plaza, esa que el aire embaraza, de su soberbia testigo."[233] In fact, statuary and art more generally are seen to be tainted by Pride's contagion because of the frequently self-serving uses to which they are placed; thus we see Lascivia in Calderón's *A tu próximo como a ti* saying that Christ "ha de derribar de mi soberbia la Estatua."[234] Art is seen as potentially Pride-inducing, going at least as far back as ancient Egypt, a magnificent ark from which is still displayed as a landmark to impress the ladies in Spanish Naples: "cuya pintura fue excelente, copioso de figuras, e inscripciones, ocupaba soberbio aquel distrito, opuesto a las pirámides de Egipto."[235] Triumphal arches served a similarly decorative as well as symbolic function: "Pudieron arcos triunfales, dar soberbia a la ventura" (see figure 3).[236]

Even more practical architectural creations such as bridges (see figure 4) and towers could be seen as prideful, as in Calderón's *La Puente de Mantible* about the gigantic bridge constructed for the purpose of separating the territory of Charlemagne from the feared Africans. In this play, Guido and some Frenchmen are captured by Africans and imprisoned in a tower which is described as proud: "Ves esa fábrica altiva, cuyo soberbio homenaje con la frente abolla el cielo."[237] Similarly, in Antonio de Zamora's *Amar, es saber vencer, y el arte contra el poder*, another high, proud tower is also used as a prison: "tenía preso Lidoro en la mansión umbría de ese Torreón soberbio."[238] Of course, the most famous tower associated with Pride in early modern Spaniards' collective cultural memory is the biblical Tower of Babel, thematized in Calderón's *La torre de Babilonia*.[239] This *auto sacramental*, which was probably performed in the Plaza Mayor of Yepes for the Feast of Corpus Christi in the year 1637, and presumably included props such as an actual tower, centres around the legendary Pride of the Old Testament figure Nimrod (Nembrot), who, according to medieval tradition, built the Tower of Babel.[240] He was a great hunter, praised in the book of Genesis, and he loomed even larger in Golden Age imagination as an anachronistic conflation with one of the race of giants born from fallen angels who had copulated with humans before Noah's flood: "Hombres nacen Gigantes, a ser aborrecidos del Cielo por su soberbia cruel. Chus, de Cam hijo, ha engendrado a Nembrot, cuya altivez de todo el Género Humano piensa apellidarse." Here we see Nimrod's lineage recited faithfully: he was the son of

Chus, who was the son of Cham, who was the son of the great Noah himself. Nembrot is harangued in the play by an Angel who chastises him for presuming to pry into heavenly secrets reserved for the knowledge of God alone:

¿Cómo lo puedes negar
disforme Monstruo feroz,
si este Prodigio del Mundo,
del Cielo esta Permisión,
en tantas lenguas publica
el castigo de tu error?
Siendo figura esa Torre,
que el viento desvaneció,
de todos cuantos soberbios
con osada presunción
pretenden examinar
Secretos que guarda Dios …
Llegar a tocar el Cielo
tu soberbia presumió, y pisar la azul Campaña
de la Esfera superior …
Pues aquel que lo intentare,
como tú intentastes hoy,
ver los Cielos, ése hará
Torres contra el mismo Dios,
y merecerá el castigo,
que tu culpa mereció.

His downfall came to be emblematic as a negative exemplum or warning to anyone who might presume to seek knowledge which was beyond human capacity to grasp: "para escarmiento, de cualquier presunción … la soberbia de Nembrot."[241] In a stunning visual display, we can imagine the theatrical tower which must have been used as part of the scenery being knocked down right in the middle of the Plaza Mayor.

* * * * *

In the cursed cacophony to which proud humanity is condemned in the generations after Babel, are all attempts to organize around a common cause doomed to failure?[242] The verdict of the *comedias* on this question is not reassuring. In *El alcalde mayor*, one of Lope de Vega's many meditations on governing authority, we find the blanket statement: "La sombra de los gobiernos es la arrogancia."[243] In another one of his plays about kingship, *Dios hace reyes*, we find a reference to the desirability of finding "tal embajada, que la soberbia del Estado enfrene."[244]

As we have seen above, Pride needs a bridle even on the personal level; how much more so when the Pride involved is viewed as the collective Sin of the state. For persons familiar with Spain's history, it should come as no great revelation that the very embodiment of the state's Pride at this time appears in the person of the king's favourite, or *privado*. Thus we find the virtuous Queen Isabel of Portugal complaining in Rojas Zorrilla's *Santa Isabel reina de Portugal* about "Carlos, Privado del Rey, este vasallo, que altivo, tirano de aqueste Imperio, hasta la cumbre ha subido."[245] Given the author's life dates (1607–48), we can guess that this character is really a veiled reference to the notoriously corrupt Conde-Duque de Olivares (1587–1645), the *privado* or royal favourite of King Philip IV of Spain.[246] Years later, Calderón would recall this same figure in *El mágico prodigioso*, a play in which the devil recounts his rise to *privado* or *valido* status at God's court in heaven: "[me] llamó Valido suyo, cuyo aplauso generoso me dio tan grande soberbia, que competí al Regio Solio, queriendo poner las plantas sobre sus dorados Tronos."[247] Even the *privado*'s family could be elevated to high social status under this system, as when Lope de Vega's character Bato refers to the arrogance of the king's *privado*'s daughter: "¡O qué graciosa arrogancia! ¿Siendo hija de un Privado del Rey?"[248]

As John Elliott explains in *The Count-Duke of Olivares: The Statesman in an Age of Decline*, the foremost critique of this *privado* and others like him was that despite the appearance of fairness, he was tyrannical:

> Throughout his career Olivares stoutly upheld the standard Castilian ideal of government by counsel … but he was quite determined that the chosen policy should be his own. To ensure this happy outcome, he had to make certain that his views were well supported, and for this he needed friends and adherents well distributed through the court and the government … There were few among the grandee houses of Castile who could resist the offer of a lucrative viceroyalty or a major court post, and by dangling high offices and honours before them Olivares could hope to secure supporters in strategic positions, and neutralize his enemies.[249]

The *comedias*, likewise, repeat this charge of heavy-handedness: "mucho más que todos es dañoso un tirano de un Rey favorecido."[250] Such tyranny in the *comedias* is almost uniformly associated with Pride: "aquel tirano altivo mata a quien lo dice airado."[251] Pride, along with Envy, is seen as a natural effect of having the power to command.[252] A tyrannical king is seen as making foolish decisions through arrogance, even if that means giving away his entire kingdom.[253] The Pride of a tyrant is viewed as merciless, as in "Mira, que de su arrogancia e ira ninguna piedad se espera."[254] It defeats maturity and oppresses the soul.[255]

This extreme version of Pride is thematized in Juan de la Cueva's *Comedia del príncipe tirano*, the titular character of which refers to a pseudo-historical figure,

Prince Licimaco, who followed ancient precursors as a poster boy for bad behaviour: "el poderoso era intolerable, el noble altivo, el fuerte soberbio, el rico vanaglorioso, el juez sin clemencia, y el sabio maldiciente."[256] Actions such as his are further described in the *preliminares* to the work as a plague on the country, "Esta plaga."[257] As Alban Forcione notes, early modern Spain had more than its fair share of tyrannical rulers, many of whose avatars found their way onto the stage, and their Pride is criticized in these plays with suitable vehemence.[258]

Could a ruler's Pride become so flagrant, within early modern paradigms, as to justify revolution? Surprisingly, evidence from the cultural archive of the *comedias* suggests that it could. One of Lope de Vega's characters says openly to the king, "el Reino descontento de esa tu arrogancia está."[259] In what could just as easily have been a cryptic reference to the Comuneros' Revolt (1520–1), another one of Lope's characters makes reference to the fact that "los Grandes con orgullo y brío querrán alzar la frente a la corona."[260] Juan de Matos Fragoso, in *El traidor contra su sangre*, thematizes treason as proud, when the king describes the treasonous rebellion of his subject Mudarra: "Mudarra, atrevido, sin esperar mis decretos, contra mis leyes altivo … sin mi licencia, a mis preceptos remiso."[261] But just as often, treason would appear to be justified within early modern moral imaginations, as with the *pueblo*'s revolt against civil authority in Lope de Vega's *Fuente Ovejuna*.[262]

The only unified image produced by these apparently contradictory passages is an eminently Baroque one, namely, the fleeting nature of all earthly power. It is fair to say that the textual tombs[263] of especially the later *comedias* are marked with skulls placed next to crowns and sceptres, just as we see in Hendrik Andrieszen's still life of *Vanitas* (1635) (see figure 5), where these memento mori symbols serve as a sober warning to the viewer.[264] The literary equivalent of this painting is Calderón de la Barca's *La vida es sueño*, in which all power to rule is implicitly criticized as a fantasy and a delusion.[265] In this play, Prince Segismundo, the rightful heir to the realm, is locked up in a tower by his father the king in response to a terrible prophecy spoken near the time of his birth. Given a chance suddenly to come out of the tower and appear in the royal court, Segismundo lashes out at those around him, acting like the brute he has been conditioned to become. Imprisoned in the tower once more, he wonders in the context of Pride whether his chance to rule was merely a dream. As his allegorical avatar, Hombre, in Calderón's *auto* version of this same subject matter, exclaims: "Pero (¡Cielos!) el orgullo reprimamos, por si ahora también soñamos."[266] In the *comedia* version, Segismundo's sympathetic jailer, Clotaldo, laments as he watches the young prince's confusion: "Ay de ti, que soberbia vas mostrando, sin saber que estás soñando." Whenever he talks about ruling, he seems to ramble delusionally, his royal blood becoming hot and agitated as he rebels against his imprisonment: "tocando esta materia de la Majestad, discurre con ambición y soberbia, porque en efecto la sangre le incita, mueve, y alienta."[267]

Based on evidence we find in the *comedias*, it would not be too great a stretch to conclude that all Pride is a fleeting fantasy. It is described repeatedly in those terms, as in "una altivez engañosa, y una necia fantasía de pensar con vanagloria."[268] As we have seen, the King of Babylon is emblematic of this arrogant fantasy: "les dejó su fantasía, y el Rey de Babilonia su arrogancia."[269] Arrogance offers the delusion that a vanquished man has instead won his battle: "¡A, qué extraña arrogancia de hombre bravo que ya vencido, vencedor se juzga!"[270] Like Freud's repressed libido, Pride keeps returning: "La hierba que con los pies desvía, oprime, y quebranta, parece que se levanta con más orgullo después."[271] In this moral economy, as Slavoj Žižek has theorized, fantasy can effectively become more real than reality: "la vida se vuelve nauseabunda cuando la fantasía que media nuestro acceso a ella se desintegra."[272]

Eventually, the delusions of Pride lead to insanity. Once again, the *comedias* are unequivocal on this point. As Lope de Vega's Fineo says of the prince Ciro in *villano* garb: "de Ciro la arrogancia ya debe de ser locura."[273] Tirso's self-deprecating titular character in *La santa Juana* asks herself, "¿Qué arrogancia es ésta vuestra? ¿Qué altivez, y frenesí?"[274] In Pérez de Montalbán's *Amor, privanza, y castigo*, Tiberio complains about Seyano as "un hombre que desprecia lo mismo que yo respeto. [L]oco, altivo, y sin prudencia, estima la vida en poco."[275] Judas Iscariot is likewise described as both proud and insane.[276] Pride causes sinners to ramble on without ceasing: "Dice con vana arrogancia dos mil locuras, señor."[277] The ultimate revenge for this sort of prideful behaviour is to see crazy Pride put back in its place, prostrated before a higher authority: "que para venganza sobra ver de esta suerte postrada su altiva soberbia loca."[278]

But just exactly how realistic is this scenario? Can Pride ever really be tamed? Some passages seem to characterize it as difficult to root out, inflexible but paradoxically resilient enough to reappear like the heads of the hydra: "inflexible mi soberbia, aun cuando más castigada, menos reducida."[279] Indeed, several characters speak of their own or others' Pride as never humbled: "el nunca humillado orgullo mío" or "el nunca domado orgullo, la juvenil arrogancia."[280] Others flatly declare Pride to be invincible.[281]

So morally speaking, is there a glimmer of hope in this bleak picture? Luckily, still operating here, even within the constraints of Counter-Reformation severity, we find the workings of grace and humility to be sufficiently powerful to counteract Pride and its misery. Along with towers, thrones, and high palaces; along with tyrannical villains; the *comedias* are also filled with prostration scenes which literally emblematize reconciliation with God and the Church and the concomitant restoration of the rightful hierarchy of the social order.[282] Indeed, the very poetics of the *comedia* as a genre seems to require a comic reversal, one or more marriages, or the restoration of peace to the kingdom at the end of the play. These prostration scenes could of course be spectacularly effective in performance. We see in the *comedia* corpus multiple examples of this trend, beginning once more with nature and the animal kingdom and continuing all the way up to the emperor. We see fierce, thundering storms on the proud sea which all of a sudden mysteriously cease.[283] We imagine the *locus amoenus* of Paradise, where animals who are natural enemies of each other will lie down together: "en el sacro Paraíso, se postraban obedientes, ya el Rinoceronte altivo, ya el jabalí ensortijado, ya el tigre a manchas vestido."[284] This miraculous end to all the conflict caused by Pride extends itself to the human realm as well: love conquers Pride in human relationships, both in the private sphere and on the world stage of wars between nations.[285]

But is this idyllic picture always necessarily the outcome? Unfortunately, no. In fact, these amicable resolutions prove all too often to be the exception to the rule. What is much more common is to see spectacular falls from grace, where prideful people come down from their delusional flight only through a crash landing in which there are no survivors. "¿[Q]uién subió soberbio, que no cayó?" asks Calderón in *El purgatorio de San Patricio*.[286] "[M]ísero trofeo de la soberbia serás," he predicts in *La gran Cenobia*.[287] Even Lope de Vega, whose personal pecadillos were too numerous to count, knew in his heart of hearts that "no hay soberbia humana, sin contradicción divina."[288]

The *comedias* are full of warnings against Pride, and in this they do fulfil a certain pedagogical mission. A typical *comedia* audience might be intrigued by such thought-provoking questions as, "¿para qué te precias de libre, con pecho altivo? [M]ira que es en el soberbio siempre mayor el castigo."[289] Not to mention the blood-curdling punishments for Pride they might witness on stage, such as when Lope's character menaces another with cutting out his tongue: "conviene … cortarle aquella lengua que habló con arrogancia en nuestra mengua."[290] The *autos sacramentales* provide allegorical tableaux with figures representing each of the Vices as well as their adherents, and also their punishments. In these works we see even more starkly the final dramatic conversion or scene of repentance, as when Cuerpo (the Human Body) announces, "Ya no hay vanidad en mí, ni soberbia, ni altivez; conozco la desnudez con que a este Mundo nací."[291] Biblical plays, likewise, such as Lope de Vega's *La hermosa Ester* offer remarkably vivid word pictures of proud sinners figuratively drowning if they refuse to repent: "De su caballo cayó en el mar de su arrogancia."[292] This strange mixing of metaphors – how does one ride a horse in the ocean? – does not detract from the basic point of the moral lesson. Even if there is no evident punishment – even if they appear to have escaped wrath – those who are prideful already bear within themselves their own torment: "éstos ya traen consigo la pena de su arrogancia, porque hay muy poca distancia de la soberbia al castigo."[293]

The most raw historical memory in the minds of *comedia* audiences at this time would have been the defeat of the Armada in 1588. Without question, this was a national disgrace. The multiple references to it in the *comedias* indicate that this was a wound which Spain kept on licking well into the second half of the seventeenth century. It was a blow to the national psyche which priestly playwrights exploited in order to warn of the dangers of Pride: "Rota, y deshecha la armada, que fue con vana soberbia pesadumbre de las ondas."[294] But covert references to the Armada's defeat in the *comedias* are not limited to only the most blatant allusions to Spain's ignominious defeat by the English. In a literary technique recognizable as *in typo* or the invocation of historical type,[295] playwrights also obsessed over other great naval battles which could be seen as in some sense mirroring their own situation. Thus an armada was sent out against Alexander the Great to divert him from arrogance, much as the Spanish must have seen their mission against Sir Francis Drake.[296]

These dramatists also resurrect as a counterpoint to the defeat of the Armada their own most glorious naval victory of the period, the battle against the Turks at Lepanto (1571), in which Miguel de Cervantes famously lost the use of his arm – thus the nickname of which he professed to be proud, *el manco de Lepanto.*[297] Not surprisingly, these playwrights also cast this naval battle in terms of Pride. The Turkish fleet "[con] pompa venía aprestando cuerdas para maniatar Cristianos; ¡qué locura! ¡qué soberbia! Pero viendo nuestra Armada, con voz turbada, y suspensa, dijo Alí: Habéisme engañado."[298] This battle, commemorated at length in Agustín Moreto's *La traición vengada*, must have served as a comfort for proud Spaniards who were still lamenting the Armada's loss.

Perhaps it is easier to moralize philosophically about Pride's defeat once you have already been the one to suffer humiliation. Thus we see in Lope de Vega's *El triunfo de la humildad, y soberbia abatida*, published a mere thirty years after Spain's debacle at the hands of the English, the most extended meditation on Pride and its consequences to be preserved from this period. In this play, two brothers represent Pride and Humility in their actions until an accident of fate reverses their roles. The once-proud Prince Trebacio suddenly finds himself working as a coal bearer and a stable hand. Their ironic role reversal is complete at the moment when he throws himself at his brother's feet so that he can literally step on his body in the process of ascending to the throne. (No one ever accused this play of subtlety.) Some of his former dignity is restored when his brother then recognizes him and makes him a count as a consolation prize. Suffice it to say that he has learned his lesson. In all likelihood, he will never engage in such prideful behaviour again.

* * * * *

And so it goes – through all its vicissitudes, Pride remained very much relevant as an organizing category for moral life in early modern Spain. Is this perhaps because Pride, considered to be the root of all other Vices, was thought to be of such overwhelming importance that it was the last to get thrown out in the transition from medieval to Renaissance world views? Is it because Pride bore affinities to other preoccupations, such as the honour code, which have long been considered permanent features of Spain's cultural landscape?[299] Or is there some other reason?

In what little remains of this chapter, I would like to propose that one possible explanation for Pride's continued relevance is its potential assimilation of two out of the Ten Commandments. If Bossy is right, and the history of ideas in the West chronicles a gradual displacement of one moral system, the Seven Deadlies, by another, the Decalogue,[300] then surely the Capital Vices – such as Pride – that survived the longest would have been those which accommodated themselves most comfortably to the new system. The fact that Pride bears close connections to two of the Ten Commandments – namely, the injunctions against Idolatry and taking God's name in vain – would seem to indicate that as a cultural construct, this entity had an excellent insurance policy. If people still chose to see sin through the lens of the Seven Deadlies, all the better; but if they consciously or unconsciously began to participate in this intellectual and moral transition, Pride could still hop onto that bandwagon through its association with Idolatry and swearing. Let's take a look at how this works.

Pride in the *comedias* is specifically linked to Idolatry. In the *autos sacramentales*, she is often clothed in the garb of pagan religion: "la Soberbia, vestida de infiel sacrílego afecto, de réproba secta."[301] In fact, Pride is characterized repeatedly as sacrilegious.[302] In some plays, there are explicit scenes of idol worship or pagan practices, such as in Calderón's *El amor, honor y poder*, when Enrique offers his soul to the sun with vain arrogance: "Al Sol, con vanos antojos, y con arrogancia loca, ofrecí el alma en despojos."[303] The same author's *Judás Macabeo* invokes the memory of Nebuchadnezzar, the proud, idolatrous pagan king who threw Daniel the prophet into the lions' den: "aquel soberbio Nabuco, que por ser Dios, sus estatuas sobre los Altares puso."[304] In this play the sin of Idolatry is vividly literal. Another great villain of the Spanish theatre, King Peter the Cruel, was known for Pride to the point of presumption against the Deity: "Tú que altivo, y loco, ser deidad presumes, atrevido a Dios."[305] But even less legendary figures could be guilty of idolatrous Pride: "qué vanaglorioso está, que soberbio se antepone a las deidades celestes."[306] The devil himself declares that his Pride impelled him to declare war on God: "moví guerra al mismo Dios … inflexible mi soberbia."[307] Prideful putting of oneself on the same level with God is idolatrous because it is tantamount to usurping divine authority: "poderoso eres, mas no es razón que exageres con tal soberbia tu estado. Arrogante, a Dios te igualas."[308]

Similar connections may be made between Pride and Blasphemy, or taking the Lord's name in vain.[309] A "barbarous" king is described as both blasphemous and proud: "Blasfemo, bárbaro Rey, soberbio, y desvanecido, no prosigas, no prosigas."[310] A less lofty character is threatened with having his tongue cut out for the boldness of his Blasphemy: "te saque también la lengua, por blasfemo, y atrevido."[311] Yet another character reports (how, we are not sure) that he has inflicted the same punishment on himself: "me corté toda la lengua con que atrevido y blasfemo ofendí de Dios el nombre."[312] Nimrod of Babylon – whom we remember from Calderón's auto *La torre de Babilonia* – appears as the epitome of Blasphemy, Idolatry, and Pride, illustrating well the confluence of these sins in the minds of early modern Spaniards: "comenzó Nembrot su Reyno. Fabricó muchas ciudades, pero soberbio y blasfemo persuadía a sus vasallos negasen su Dios eterno."[313] As we have seen already with Pride, Blasphemy is considered likewise by Spaniards to be a specifically Spanish problem related to arrogance:

> CONDE DE FUENTES: ... Voto a Cristo.
> MARISCAL: Si bien por la arrogancia que en ti veo pareces Español.[314]

Interestingly, we find in the *comedias* evidence not just of a connection between Blasphemy and Pride, but of a growing awareness among Spaniards at this time of where the injunction against Blasphemy comes from. In other words, we see references not just to the prohibition, but also to its source.[315] Thus we find questions like "Vive Dios, ¿ha de jurar un Cristiano? ¿Y el mandamiento segundo quebrantar?" and warnings such as "quiero os, señora, avisar, que nunca habéis de jurar, porque es contra el Mandamiento segundo."[316] The act of breaking the Second Commandment is recognized as a grave sin ("aunque yo soy pecadora, nadie ha de tener licencia de jurar en mi presencia, que es gran pecado") which merits eternal punishment: "Ay blasfemo, en la experiencia cuando padezcas abismos de penas, siempre inmortales."[317]

Even in comic contexts, this prohibition is seen as deadly serious; in one humorous exchange, a *labrador* is enjoined to swear an oath with the incentive that if he does, he will receive some bread. The *villano* declares, "Que no me cumpre jurar, había yo de infernar mi alima por tantico pan [*sic*]."[318] The temporal punishment for Blasphemy was bad enough, as we find in the archives: according to the *Siete partidas*, a Spanish code of law dating from the thirteenth century, a person's lips were to be branded with the letter "B" if he or she was found to be even a second-time offender in this area.[319] Ultimately Blasphemy is seen in the *comedia* repertoire as a cancer burning up the best of Europe, which is, of course, the Catholic kingdom: "ver que tanto cáncer pase tan adelante, y su infernal blasfemia, que lo mejor de vuestra Europa abrase, el Católico Reino."[320]

Transplanted back four centuries and across an ocean, Octavio Paz might have concurred. In his now-classic study of Latin American, particularly Mexican, psyches, *El laberinto de la soledad*, he lamented the persistent addiction of Hispanics to using swear words: "los españoles se complacen en la blasfemia y la escatología."[321] What Paz may not have realized is that the roots of this vice go back at least as far as the early modern period in Spain.[322]

* * * * *

Many more examples could be proffered of all three sins examined in this chapter: Pride, Idolatry, and Blasphemy. But true to form, Pride has already expanded to fill the space available. Since Pride is the root of all Vices, its chapter is necessarily longer than many of the others in this book. But by considering the biggest residual Sin first – along with two of the Commandments it assimilates – we have also set up a paradigm to use for examining the other Vices and Commandments.

In a chapter titled "Dominant, Residual, and Emergent," Raymond Williams offers a theoretical formulation which seems uniquely applicable here:

> By "residual" I mean something different from the "archaic," though in practice these are often very difficult to distinguish. Any culture includes available elements of its past, but their place in the contemporary cultural process is profoundly variable. I would call "archaic" that which is wholly recognized as an element of the past, to be observed, to be examined, or even on occasion to be consciously "revived," in a deliberately specializing way. What I mean by the "residual" is very different. The residual, by definition, has been effectively formed in the past, but it is still active in the cultural process, not only and often not at all as an element of the past, but as an effective element of the present. Thus certain experiences, meanings, and values which cannot be expressed or substantially verified in terms of the dominant culture, are nevertheless lived and practised on the basis of the residue – cultural as well as social – of some previous social and cultural institution or formation.[323]

This formation, in the case at hand, is the list of Seven Deadly Sins, which up until the Renaissance had been *the* dominant organizing principle for moral thought.

Now, with this paradigm in place, let us move on to Avarice and Lust, two of the other residual Deadly Vices which, along with Pride, remain equally resonant in Spain during the early modern period.

2
Greed Breaks the Bag

[L]a codicia cruel abrió camino en el mar, otro mundo supo hallar.

– Lope de Vega, *El piadoso veneciano*[1]

Busque entre los Indios oro la fiera codicia humana que mar, y montes allana.

– Lope de Vega, *La prisión sin culpa*[2]

As Raymond Williams reminds us, "against the pressures of incorporation, actively residual meanings and values are sustained."[3] Just as we saw Pride rear its ugly head in so many plays in the last chapter, now we can watch the broad brush strokes of a collective portrait of Greed begin to emerge. Like the cartoon character Speedy Gonzalez, popular on US television in the 1950s, the residual figure of Avarice may at times seem elusive. But after combing through hundreds of *comedias* looking for references to Greed, we begin to see certain patterns or recurrent themes appearing in relation to this Vice. Let us pause to examine these so that we will recognize Avaricia/Codicia furtively guarding its stolen treasure.

At first, Greed would seem to be glittering and golden, arrayed in costly finery and dripping with jewels.[4] He reclines on soft cushions of rich beds and has the leisure, like the legendary King Midas, to count his gold obsessively, over and over again.[5] But no sooner does this impostor take the stage, than he is unmasked. His bag of money breaks, and his desk begins to sink into a chasm from the weight of all the gold on top of it.[6] Fleeing through the forest, the greedy man reaches into a bird's nest, hungry for an egg, only to be bitten instead by a venomous snake.[7] He is perpetually thirsty, but his drink turns out to be a strange concoction of opium and arsenic – a beverage as hallucinatory as it is deadly.[8] Formerly mimicking the ant, scurrying around and saving, he grows wings only to become food for a bird of prey.[9] Tricked by the Renaissance alchemist's sleight of hand, he discovers that the gold he was chasing did not even turn out to be real.[10] A grave robber himself, he suddenly looks down to find the worm of Avarice gnawing on his own entrails.[11]

Avarice, otherwise known as Greed: this Vice, perhaps more than any other, taps into the familiar Baroque topos of *desengaño*. Described as a sudden moment of recognition or disillusionment, *desengaño* has long been recognized as a hallmark of the Baroque age.[12] As Spain's imperial power starts to wane, increasingly its Greed appears as a phantom, a fleeting fantasy of "New" World cities paved with gold which never quite materialized.[13] By its very nature, Greed can never be satisfied; but due to overly inflated expectations during the Age of Discovery, the period immediately following it must have been a time of anticlimactic letdown. Not fed by tangible riches longed for by conquistadores, Avarice instead entered the realm of fantastic imagination, becoming illusorily "la codicia de un soñado Tesoro."[14] Another passage by the same playwright further locates the place of Greed within the realm of imagination and desire: "podrá ver las joyas más excelentes, que la codicia imagina, el arte pule, y guarnece el deseo."[15] But as we saw in the last chapter on Pride, sometimes fantasy is more potent than reality.[16] Let us trace the broad outlines of this shadow.

* * * * *

There are at least two kinds of Greed in the *comedias*, both equally dangerous. The first is the kind where the rich man, like the one in the New Testament parable, turns a deaf ear to the poor. When he asks the poor man, Lazarus, for a drink in the afterlife, he finds him reclining peacefully on Abraham's bosom.[17] In deference to the parable, greedy *comedia* characters are almost invariably depicted as insatiably thirsty.[18] Like a vampire, Avarice convinces its victims to bleed themselves dry.[19]

But the other kind of rich man not only fails to spend money on other people; he does not spend it to feed himself either.[20] Thus we see this character as the ultimate hoarder who denies himself even basic sustenance in order to amass more wealth.[21] Both kinds of Greed lead to misery: the avaricious person is perpetually weighed down by anxiety and care, burdened by the vigilance of watching over his treasure.[22] A perpetual insomniac, he can find no rest.[23] He is consumed by Greed to the point of being suffocated by his own riches.[24] At the point of death – he perishes, appropriately, of apoplexy – he is aptly and unattractively compared in the *comedias* to a pig.[25]

But lest we feel too sorry for this figure, these plays make it clear that Greed is a choice. Countless avaricious persons are seen to give entry to Greed or somehow spiritually to open the door to this affliction.[26] However, there are certain classes and ages of people who, in the dramatic repertoire, seem more naturally prone to contamination by this Vice.[27] Let us pause to view the panorama of this moral landscape in greater detail.

First of all, as with Pride, Avarice is not limited to men. References to greedy women abound in the *comedias* also, as in "de la mujer el vicio de la codicia avarienta" and "Es la moza algo avarienta."[28] In fact, some (but not all) blanket statements made on stage by *comedia* characters might at first seem to indicate that Greed is perceived to be *more* common in women.[29] Addicted as they are to fine furnishings and fancy dresses, women in early modern Spain were known for their Greed.[30] Avarice was often depicted allegorically dressed as a woman, and greedy women were said to be willing to go all the way to hell in order to get money out of their greedy male counterparts.[31] How many of these references in the plays may be dismissed as stemming from misogyny on the part of male playwrights would be difficult, if not impossible, to determine.

Be that as it may, on certain points these dramatists seem unanimously to agree. For example, Avarice is more frequently associated with certain age groups. On the *comedia* stage, Greed seems to be distinctly the province of the old: "la codicia civil, (que a toda vejez infama)."[32] Young people are seen as profligate,[33] while the old tend to be misers. This trend once again can be true of either man or woman; for example, "¡O cuánto puede en una vieja avara la codicia del oro[!]"[34] But more often, the miser in the *comedias* is a greedy old guy, as in "de un avaro viejo la codicia" – a line occurring in Lope de Vega's appropriately named *La niña de plata*, in which Enrique de Trastámara tries to seduce a young woman and her aunt with his wealth.[35] In fact, the predominant stereotype of the avaricious character in the *comedias* is a stingy older gentleman as viewed by younger characters; for example, a father, father-in-law, or even an uncle.[36]

Spanning the gamut of ages as well as both genders, and touching upon issues like contemporaneous economic conditions, this Vice offers a unique vantage point from which to view early modern cultural trends and social problems. But a funny thing about sin in the early modern period – or, for that matter, any era – is that it is remarkably democratic. Perhaps this levelling effect seems more jarring to us when we are presented with evidence from the Renaissance because of the profoundly undemocratic nature of early modern Spain's hereditary monarchy. All classes in early modern Spanish society were prone to Avarice, it is true; but in this period as in so many others, Greed manifests itself in different ways for different strata of society.

For nobles, Greed was seen as a natural liability accompanying their foreordained state in life. As one *comedia* character asks another, "¿No os agrada esta grandeza? ¿El oro no os da codicia? ¿El oro, que honra el valor y la nobleza acredita?"[37] Greed could also be seen in the nobility's preoccupation with issues of inheritance, with the totality of a person's net worth or estate being summed up in that magical word *hacienda*. His *hacienda* or estate may be seen to fit a rich person's Greed, or it may be seen to produce Greed in an individual who, prior to receiving this inheritance, may not necessarily have been prone to this particular Vice.[38] Heirs are seen vying over their inheritance in the *comedias*, in much the same way as a last will and testament might be contested during probate today.[39] The practice in Spain of primogeniture, or the custom of leaving the bulk of the family's wealth to the first-born, meant that younger siblings even found motivation to kill their older brothers and sisters in order to rise to the top of the pecking order.[40] A chilling illustration of Greed offering incentive for Murder appears in the lines of a wealthy female character from Cervantes's *El gallardo español*, whose greedy brother wanted to bury her alive: "Vi que mi hermano aspiraba, codicioso de mi hacienda, a dejarme entre paredes, medio viva."[41] A similar fate is suffered by Inés in María de Zayas's *La inocencia castigada*, in which her husband, her brother, and her sister-in-law cemented her into a chimney.[42]

The famous *enredos* or entanglements of the *comedias* arguably become even more complex once Avarice is thrown into the equation. Greed is nearly always assumed to be a motive, even when it is not.[43] In a plot that is somewhat parallel to that of a contemporaneous English Renaissance drama, *The Phoenix* by Thomas Middleton (probably performed before King James of England on 20 February 1604), Tirso de Molina's *Del enemigo el primer consejo* presents a character who pretends to be dead in order to allow the woman he loves to keep his inheritance.[44] He is then interested to see what happens to his estate: "así en Milán publicóse mi muerte por la codicia de intereses sucesores."[45] Even where foul play or treachery is not involved, the younger generation in these plays is seen to be waiting around for the older one to die so that the family riches may be inherited.[46] They are perpetually worried about the older generation's impressions of them and whether their progenitors might be persuaded to change their financial bequests accordingly.[47]

These concerns over inheritance were particularly complicated by marriage arrangements which transferred wealth via a woman's dowry into a different family:

> [hay] una relación significativa entre el matrimonio y una actividad comercial de compra-venta en la que el sujeto se cosifica al trasladarse al terreno sémico de los productos adquiribles mediante una transacción monetaria … [D]os campos semánticos … convierten al matrimonio en un buen negocio para los jefes de familia impulsados por una mentalidad calculadora característica del mercader.[48]

This degeneration of a sacrament into a financial or economic transaction is symptomatic of a larger, more gradual process of secularization which Max Weber has dubbed significantly the "disenchantment of the world."[49] This chapter is where the moral economies of this book's title become most literalized. The *comedias* are clear on this point: a nobleman was expected to marry according to factors other than love ("que el honor a un Caballero / le ha de casar, y no el gusto").[50] The concern over arranged marriages as an incentive to Greed was so great that they were actually prohibited by the Council of Trent:

> Earthly affections and desires do for the most part so blind the eyes of the understanding of temporal lords and magistrates, as that, by threats and ill-usage, they compel both men and women, who live under their jurisdiction, – especially such as are rich, or who have expectations of a great inheritance, – to contract marriage against their inclination with those whom the said lords or magistrates may prescribe unto them. Wherefore, seeing that it is a thing especially execrable to violate the liberty of matrimony, and that wrong comes from those from whom right is looked for, the holy Synod enjoins on all, of whatsoever grade, dignity, and condition they may be, under pain of anathema to be *ipso facto* incurred, that they put no constraint, in any way whatever, either directly or indirectly, on those subject to them, or any others whomsoever, so as to hinder them from freely contracting marriage.[51]

Nonetheless we find references to specific sums of money meant to serve as incentive dowries in the *comedias*, such as "Mal hacéis en no aceptar casamientos tan honrados, que con treinta mil ducados ninguno puede rabiar."[52] The most elaborate item-by-item recital of the contents of a woman's dowry – which reads like the early modern equivalent of a contemporary bridal registry – appears in Lope de Vega's *San Isidro labrador de Madrid*. In this play, the bride's father rattles off for her intended husband all the gifts he so generously offers in exchange for taking her off his hands:

> Yo quiero,
> decirte el dote primero . . . .
> Yo te doy primeramente,
> mil maravedís en plata,
> y en oro. . . .
> Entre ellos hay un escudo,
> que treinta años he guardado,
> tan bueno, limpio, y dorado,
> como cuando hacerse pudo.
> Porque desde que cayó
> en mis manos, le guardé
> para esta ocasión, no sé
> si le gastarás, o no.
> Pero si aquella sin ley,
> a gastarle te obligare,
> haz por tu vida, que pare

en comprar un gentil buey.
Sin esto te pienso dar
dos colchones, y un jergón,
y advierte, que nuevos son,
que no te quiero engañar.
No ha diez años que se hicieron,
ni seis veces se han lavado,
seis sábanas de delgado
lienzo, que en dote me dieron.
Cuatro almohadas, y un banco,
una silla de costillas,
trébedes, sartén, parrillas,
y un paño de manos blanco.
No ha un año, que estaba entero,
y en toda su perfección,
mal le dé Dios al ratón,
que le hizo un agujero.
Dos sargas de linda mano,
la una tiene a David,
y el Gigante, que en la lid,
tendió en el verde llano.
Ella está a medio traer,
porque era el lienzo algo flojo,
fáltale al Gigante un ojo,
pero no se echa de ver.
La otra tiene pintado
el Pródigo, que dirás,
que viendo en la artesa estás,
los lechones, y el salvado.
Están con ojos extraños,
mirando el Pródigo esquivo,
y tan gordos, que ha de estar vivos,
tuvieras para dos años.
Sin otras cosas así,
que por menudencias dejo,
te daré peine, y espejo,
y por no cansarte aquí,
no te digo los vestidos,
y camisas de tu esposa,
tus camisones es cosa,
que revientan de pulidos.

Ella lleva allá también
su arca grande, donde puso,
aspa, lino, rueca, y huso,
que sabe gastar muy bien.
Para después de mis días,
una viña, un pegujar,
y algo más hay que te dar,
sin tres cabras con sus crías.[53]

Given such a lengthy laundry list, literally, it should come as no surprise that sometimes young couples themselves, uncoerced by parents or lords and magistrates, chose to marry advantageously of their own volition, basing their choice of spouse not on love, but on economic considerations which came perilously close to out and out Greed. Thus we see *comedia* characters reportedly deciding to marry someone else – even someone considerably older – because an older woman was probably already widowed and thus possessed a higher dowry:

DON FRANCISCO: Su intento es casarse con mi tía, por codicia del dinero.
MARGARITA: ¿Pues tú no tienes buen dote?[54]

The reverse of this scenario occurs in Lope de Vega's *La pobreza estimada*, a play in which Dorotea is faced with a choice between a rich lover or a poor one. Writing to her father for advice (he is a captive in Algiers), she asks him which she should choose. He wisely counsels her to marry the poor man. She takes his recommendation, but within a year the couple's poverty has ruined their marriage. Her husband journeys to Morocco and manages to ransom his father-in-law, who goes back with him to Valencia just in time to keep Dorotea from falling for her rich former suitor. This didactic play on the virtues of poverty nonetheless succeeds in foregrounding – almost in spite of itself – the deleterious effects of economic necessity upon high-minded ideals such as love.

We also see in the *comedias* instances of dowries being stolen outright, as in "también la robó todo su dote."[55] Dowries could take the form of money, land holdings, livestock, linens, jewellery, or even the sumptuous clothing a bride was given to wear. In fact, the lavish clothing so popular in the Renaissance was more than just fashion; it effectively became an alternative system of portable wealth.[56] It was common for young courtiers to own a different three-piece suit for every day of the week, and monarchs or heirs of great estates had to undergo a formal ceremony of *investiture* – involving the public donning of ornate garments – in order to receive their inheritance.[57] Thus we find lines specifically relating Greed to fashion or clothing, such as "la codicia del vestido," "Codicioso de las telas," and "Ya tras mis vestidos anda, qué codicioso."[58] There are similar lines relating diamonds, gold chains, and lavish clothing to Avarice.[59] Ladies' dresses are seen to be stolen or surreptitiously interchanged, both on and off stage, in an effort to reapportion assets or otherwise shake up both moral and financial economies.[60] Not surprisingly, perhaps, given what we have already seen of early modern Spanish misogyny, a woman's petticoat where she can hide stolen objects is seen as particularly emblematic of Avarice.[61]

Given the very real economic issues involved – and noting again the aforementioned misogyny – it is no wonder that we find fathers in the *comedias* effectively marrying off their daughters to the highest bidder: "el padre avariento venda al oro la libertad de sus hijas" and "me mandó mi avaro padre intentar este triste casamiento."[62] As one sad *comedia* character commiserates with another, "yo sé que vuestro padre codicioso de hacienda, os ha casado."[63] A certain old and tyrannical character by the suspiciously Arabic-sounding name of Alí is said to sell his daughter's beauty to a wealthy son-in-law: "tu viejo tirano Alí, que yo sé que es codicioso, y que ya vender procura, tu inestimable hermosura a yerno más poderoso."[64] Even in situations where the quid pro quo is not stated in such bald terms, Greed and the potential for gain are said to be factors.[65] And once again, male characters are not the only ones to blame; it is not uncommon, though certainly less so, to find mothers who are similarly blinded by Greed. As one daughter vents, "Mi primero casamiento mi madre, a quien tanto ofusca la codicia del dinero, hizo con violencia injusta."[66]

But the older generation does not bear exclusively the weight of this Vice in the context of marriage. Prospective sons-in-law are seen as equally opportunistic, to the point that they are essentially equated with thieves.[67] Even widowed females could play the field, safe in the knowledge that their fortunes would attract numerous suitors: "bien moza has enviudado, y con hacienda, que ha dado codicia, si tu quisieras, [a] más de seis pretendientes."[68] Sometimes Greed could be combined with Lust – in traditional symbology of the Seven Deadly Sins, a likely pairing – to produce dual motivations for getting married, as in "ya veréis los casamientos, que unidos me ofrecerían la codicia, y el deseo."[69] Some lower-class women were undoubtedly also looking to marry up, as in the situation of the foolish young lady who is looking for a suitably wealthy marquis: "de algún Marquesote, codicia del dinero, pretende la bobería de esta dama."[70]

In fact, financial gain seems to have been such a common motive for tying the knot that some lovers in the *comedias* feel the need to protest that this is not in fact their intention: "¿echando a mi noble amor sanbenitos de codicia? Tan lejos de apetecer tu estado, estoy por quererte."[71] This striking image of Greed as an Inquisitorial *sambenito*, or garment of shame worn by heretics and then hung in the parish church even after they were burned at the stake, to remind their children in the most literal way of their fathers' sins (see figure 6), gives us a vivid picture of the stigma still carried by Avarice at this time within early modern Spanish culture.[72]

Unfortunately marriage was not the only context where men made a profit off of women. Prostitution, or "buying love," was also becoming an increasing problem in Renaissance Spanish society.[73] As Mary Elizabeth Perry has demonstrated in the case of Seville,

> [a]rchival evidence from early modern Spain suggests that legalized prostitution developed not only in response to socioeconomic problems, but also as an expression of a larger consciousness about women and sexuality ... Female sexuality threatened not only the public order ... but also male independence ... The legal brothel served to control this sexuality, both inside and outside the brothel. Although there was active opposition in the early seventeenth century, legalized prostitution persisted in Seville.[74]

But this social problem was not limited to Seville. In fact, wagons carried prostitutes in travelling brothels from village to village at certain designated times every year.[75] In April 1574, Alain Saint-Saëns notes that it cost 16 *maravedíes* to have sexual intercourse with a prostitute at a brothel in Córdoba, only 4 *maravedíes* less than a theatre ticket in Madrid a few years later in 1606.[76]

These archivally documented cultural preoccupations with controlling sexuality and the profitable industry it generated likewise are played out in the *comedia* repertoire, where pimps and procurers are universally portrayed as avaricious ("¿Seré alcahuete? No inquiete mi codicia") and as thieves ("Déjame, hermana, con este ladrón de procurador, que yo le arañaré toda la cara").[77] They negotiate specific forms of payment, such as diamonds:

> LEONOR: ¿Quieres pago?
> MILLÁN: ... ¿No es justo? ¿Quieres que sea alcahuete del campillo?
> LEONOR: Toma este diamante.[78]

These figures pertain to the marginal fringes of society, where servants venture out at night to procure sexual services for their masters: "es alcahuete el criado, aquí, y allí codicioso. Éstos se llaman ventores."[79] This tradition in Spanish literature goes all the way back to Fernando de Rojas's late medieval closet drama *Celestina*, in which the titular character from the lower class serves as a go-between for the nobleman Calisto and his lady, Melibea. Like with this classic *tragicomedia*, almost universally recognized as being more tragic than comic, such plots and subplots often end very sadly.[80]

Still lower on the moral ladder, even below pimps, would have to be those trafficking in human slaves. According to Robert Davis, the early modern period saw an increase in slaving activity throughout the Mediterranean.[81] In Spain, specifically, there were at least four kinds of slaves, to be determined according to how and when a person entered a life of servitude. As Ruth Pike explains in *Penal Servitude in Early Modern Spain*,

> There were several kinds of slaves, their classifications reflecting their mode of acquisition, that is, by capture, purchase, private donation, or judicial sentence … The enslavement of prisoners of war was a well-established custom in the Mediterranean world. Christians enslaved Moslems and Moslems retaliated in kind. The majority of the Moslem prisoners of war were North Africans (Moroccans, Algerians, and Tunisians), but there also were Moriscos (converted Spanish Moslems) and renegades … Once captured they became *esclavos del rey* (royal slaves), and were sent to serve on the galleys. When military forays and expeditions failed to provide sufficient numbers of prisoners, royal officials purchased slaves, but they had to be Moslems because legally only infidels could be enslaved on the Christian galleys. The standard price for these slaves remained at 100 ducats apiece in the sixteenth and seventeenth centuries, but in the eighteenth century it was somewhat higher, usually around 130 ducats. Most often the money utilized in these purchases came from the sale of old and unserviceable galley slaves who customarily were auctioned off to the highest bidder.[82]

Some statistics of early modern persons who were thus sold as merchandise may be estimated based on the number of galley slaves required to row a single ship: 180 to 200 per boat. In the Battle of Lepanto (1571) alone, some 80,000 slaves participated by way of manning the oars. In an urban setting, a typical large city like Seville would have contained about 6,000 slaves throughout most of the sixteenth century. Atlantic ports such as Lisbon, Seville, and Salé (Morocco) all boasted booming slave markets.[83] Some scholars estimate that in 1600 there may have been as many as 100,000 slaves in Spain.[84]

Multiple references to human trafficking in the *comedia* repertoire point to the pervasiveness of this problem. In Calderón's *La niña de Gómez Arias*, the titular character elopes with a young woman but then grows tired of her, so he decides to sell her to the "Moors." Ironically, her Arabic buyer Cañeri's behaviour towards her appears more civilized than her Christian seller's. As he negotiates his purchase of her, his words signal attachment beyond a mere token esteem: "¿Pues cómo dudas si quiero comprarla, que un mundo entero daré, Cristiano, por ella? Pídeme por su hermosura cuánto avariento tesoro trajo a retraer el Moro a esta bárbara espesura."[85] As this and other passages suggest, female slaves were often chosen for their beauty.[86] In the case above, the pretty girl is being traded for "greedy treasure"; but more often, slaves were simply stolen and then hidden away, presumably so that their greedy masters could profit from their uncompensated labour: "un esclavo que le hurtó allí le trajo a esconderlo."[87] The most common references to human trafficking and Greed occur in the context of the so-called Moors:

CELIO: Guarda, Marcelio, del moro que de vidas y tesoro anda codicioso.
MARCELIO: Tente, que no busca Castellanos.[88]

But if not Castilians, then whom might the "Moorish" slave traders be seeking? A clue to this mystery may be found in such polyvalent phrases as "robo de mulato," which could mean either that a mulatto of mixed race was stolen or that he stole something.[89] On the other side of this racial equation, Christian traffic in African and Morisco slaves was, at this point in Spanish history, still a booming business.[90] Early on in the "New" World conquest, captured indigenous natives were also brought to Spain as slaves.[91]

An unusually complicated scenario – one destined for tragic repetition in subsequent centuries in Latin America under military dictatorships – arose whenever Morisco children were snatched from their families at birth or shortly thereafter and adopted by Christian families to raise as their own.[92] The *comedias* allude to similar kidnappings by Christians of Jewish children:

JUDÍO: Este Cristiano me acaba de robar a este mi hijo.
CADÍ: ¿Para qué quiere el niño?
SACRISTÁN: ¿No está bueno?
Para que le rescaten, si no quieren
que le críe, y enseñe el Padre Nuestro.[93]

Infant snatching was unfortunately practised on both (or rather, several) sides of the confessional divide, as children were kidnapped when they were as little as two months old: "vive Dios, que os tengo de hurtar un niño antes de los meses dos."[94] These ominous lines are spoken on stage by a Christian sacristan to a Jew. Muslim pirates sailing in frigates may have begun snatching Christian infants in retaliation for the Morisco children who had been relocated during the expulsion.[95] For example, a Christian character laments in Lope de Vega's *Los esclavos libres* that "Moorish" pirates have stolen his children: "en Perpiñán Moros cosarios me robaron mis hijos, de que tengo papeles."[96] Although this was occasionally done for religious rather than financial motives, most of the time Greed also entered the picture:

> In Tangier and Hone, in Orán, Algiers, Bougie, Bizerta, and Tunis … Muslim corsairs armed galleys and light vessels that they launched against Christian ships … [T]hey assaulted the Spanish coasts, plundered towns and churches, and captured hostages, who were made slaves … After a few days or weeks on the sea, the "fortunate and happy" corsairs returned to Algiers, *"cargados de infinitas riquezas y cautivos"* [loaded with infinite riches and captives], spoils that were easily multiplied because they sailed three and four times a year – or more – in search of human bounty.[97]

Besides the possibility of selling captives into slavery, an additional way in which Greed became relevant to kidnapping was when the kidnappers demanded a ransom, or *rescate*.[98] This ransom could be any sum up to and including the entire value of a person's estate, as in "¿Rescatarle no es mejor? Cien barras vale mi hacienda."[99] Sometimes wealthy prisoners even changed their names in an attempt to avoid paying a higher ransom: "mudéme el nombre, y fue cautela mía, por no hacer mi rescate más preciado."[100] As early as the twelfth and thirteenth centuries in Spain, kidnapping and the subsequent ransom of prisoners had become a very profitable and highly organized business:

> Spanish towns developed a system of licensing professional ransomers … These individuals, who were named by the crown or councils, were privileged persons, traveling under safe-conduct across the military frontier between Christian and Islamic Spain. They were usually merchants who maintained regular traffic with the Moors and who were charged with ransoming captives as well. For their services, [they] … were paid 10 percent of the ransom price.[101]

We witness actual scenes of ransom prices being negotiated in the *comedias*, as for example in Lope de Vega's *La pobreza estimada* – although in this case, no money changes hands, since one prisoner is traded for another:

> LEONIDO: En trueco sólo pido
> Mi viejo suegro.
> AUDALLA: El viejo, y tu rescate.[102]

We also see Arabs buying or trading Christian prisoners on the speculation of how much ransom money they will fetch, with obvious appeals to Greed on both sides: for example, the sum of 100 gold doubloons was tossed around in the case of only two captives.[103] As we have seen, the ransom money was typically raised by family and friends, to whom captives wrote letters from their dungeons, begging for help; references to these letters likewise abound in the *comedia* repertoire:

> FELISARDO: La cólera ciega mucho,
> que templéis la vuestra os ruego
> señora con este pliego.
> DOROTEA: ¿Es de Argel?
> FELISARDO: De Argel.
> DOROTEA: ¿Qué escucho?
> FELISARDO: A Denia llegó un navío,
> con viento airado, y contrario
> de un Redentor Trinitario,

y diola a un pariente mío,
que aquí me la despachó.
DOROTEA: ¡O letras de mi cautivo!
A buen tiempo la recibo.[104]

In this particular case it is a daughter who receives a long-awaited letter from her imprisoned father, to whom she has written asking advice about which suitor to marry. Eventually it is the son-in-law who journeys to Algiers to rescue him. But this is an unusual scenario. More frequently, as we have learned, the negotiations were performed by Trinitarian or Mercedarian friars, familiar figures who also are called in the *comedias* by name:

Vino a Valencia
un Redentor Trinitario,
éste conoció en Argel
los afligidos esclavos,
que fueron de aquesta tierra
cautivos, y aprisionados.[105]

The whole industry of captive redemption is allegorized in Calderón's auto sacramental *La redención de cautivos*, a drama emphasizing Christ's salvific work on behalf of humanity held captive by sin. In this play, the galley ship of the human species carries its chained captives across the sea. Their identity is unmistakable, as they come out on stage wearing *alquiceles*, which were "Moorish" garments resembling cloaks. According to Luis Vázquez Fernández, this *auto* may have been written on the occasion of an actual redemption of a North African captive by the Trinitarian or Mercedarian orders during the playwright's youth:

> Las redenciones se anunciaban, públicamente, en la Villa y Corte, señalando el día que los redentores salían de su convento madrileño, las "provisiones" que llevaban para la redención, qué familias tenían gente suya cautiva, e iba a ser redimida. Todo el pueblo participaba. Y en la fiesta y procesión del *Corpus Christi* se pedía por el feliz éxito de la redención proclamada. Hasta fines del siglo XVI no solía permitirse sacar dinero de España, y se redimía con "mercancías" diversas.[106]

Specific reference is made on stage in the play to Argel – in this case, a double entendre, since the word is also an abbreviation of *Arcángel*, that is to say, Gabriel, who announced the redemption of humanity while Jesus was still in Mary's womb – as well as to Pedro Nolasco, founder of the church of La Merced in Madrid, and Juan de Mata, founder of the Trinitarian Order.[107] The dates 25 March and 25 December are mentioned, in order to coincide with the Feast of the

Immaculate Conception and Christmas, respectively, but also to the amount of time the voyage normally took from Spain to North Africa.[108] Emmanuel the Redeemer even negotiates on stage with Furor over the price of the captives, just as the Spaniards had to do with the Muslims.[109]

The ransom intended to redeem captives effectively assigned a price to human life – a harsh reality which played to the Greed of their captors, who found themselves tempted to demand the highest possible ransom amount or sum earned through a sale transaction. The Christians did this as well, as we see from the titular character of Lope de Vega's *Pedro Carbonero*, who makes his living by selling or trading "Moors": "Pedro vive de robar Moros, que en este lugar vende, trueca, y acomoda."[110] But more frequently, it was the Muslims who were selling their Christian captives, a scenario so frequent that some pious Spaniards even left provisions for *la redención de cautivos* to be done as a charitable work after their death in their wills.[111] One poor *comedia* character recounts his adventure of first being attacked by a band of Saracens, then being taken to Algiers, and finally being sold as a slave: "aquel bando Sarracino que me robó en el camino, dentro de Argel me vendió."[112] Miguel de Cervantes, the renowned author of *Don Quijote* and also a playwright, had suffered a period of captivity in Algiers which inspired the plots of several of his dramas.[113] He was only one of many early modern Spaniards to suffer this fate. Oded Löwenheim explains the direct causal relationship of the Morisco expulsion in 1609 to the increase in piracy:

> The result of the expulsion of the Moriscos was the opposite of what its planners had hoped: the corsair attacks on Spain and its Mediterranean shipping actually increased after the expulsion of the Moriscos. Thus, many authors dub the early seventeenth century the golden age of Barbary sea predation ... The expulsion of so many Spanish-speaking people who knew the Spanish coast intimately, together with their desire for revenge and the need to prove loyalty to their coreligionists in the Barbary Coast, made the Moriscos a much greater threat than they were in Spain.[114]

The Morisco expulsion effectively created a different kind of Golden Age, one for piracy – which by definition was a profession whose greedy practitioners lived off of stolen plunder.[115] Of course piracy had existed before the expulsion, but the seventeenth century saw a drastic change in the corsairs' operational patterns. Suddenly, there was more than a 20 per cent increase in the number of captives snatched not from the seas, but from Spain's own shores.[116]

We see literary evidence of this historical shift towards raiding the coasts in *comedias* such as Agustín Moreto's *El esclavo de su hijo*, in which the Christian Roberto is captured as a young boy by eighty corsairs, who perform a successful raid on Valencia.[117] He later returns as a corsair himself, now using the

"Moorish" name Abdenaga, to kidnap other Christians by snatching them right out of Spain:

SIDÁN: Notable, Abdenaga, es tu heróico pensamiento,
pues pones tan continua diligencia,
en robarle sus hijos a Valencia.
¿No es ésta la Ciudad donde naciste,
y donde de seis años cautivaste?
ABDENAGA: De mí pienso, Sidán, que lo supiste,
de algunas veces que conmigo entraste
en esta tierra.

An old hermit heralds his arrival, warning the villagers to flee from what was evidently a common occurrence, a Muslim pirate raid:

Váyanse a la Hermita, hermanos,
huyan de dar en las manos,
de los cosarios del mar.
Que un renegado de Argel,
con diez bajeles de guerra,
asombra toda esta tierra,
hecho apóstata cruel.[118]

We shall return to this play in a moment, but this last phrase brings us to a related topic, that of apostasy. One frequent scenario which might not be considered often enough by early modern historiographers in the context of Greed is the syndrome known as turning renegade, from the Spanish verb *renegar* (to deny vehemently), otherwise known as renouncing one's faith. According to contemporaneous observer Antonio de Sosa, over half of the inhabitants of Algiers in the 1570s were so-called Turks by profession – that is, renegades.[119] As María Antonia Garcés explains,

> most of the "renegade" Christians who had abandoned the true path of God had become Muslims either because they rejected the work of slavery or because they favored a life of freedom, marked by the pleasures of the flesh. Evidently, the captives, soldiers, or mercenaries who converted to Islam were thorns in the sides of the Christians, particularly the Spaniards, who saw them as the most blatant representatives of accommodating and pliable morals. These men or women broke not only with their religious creed but also with most of the mental and cultural categories of their society.[120]

But although the religious aspect of conversion is the one most often emphasized, the material benefits of turning renegade were nothing to scoff at either:

> When these men adopted the Muslim religion, their owners generally offered them letters of credit and gave them slaves and money. And later, *"muriendo [los turcos] sin herederos reparten con ellos sus bienes y hacienda como sus hijos y generalmente a todos los que aún no eran libres los dejan libres antes que mueran"* [if the Turks die without heirs, they divide amongst the renegades their possessions and estate as if they were their children, and generally they free all of those who had not been freed before they die].[121]

As we hear from the mouth of this contemporaneous observer, one thing which is possibly not well enough understood about early modern Spanish morality is that Greed could also serve as a motive to turn renegade and forsake the Christian faith.

Once again, we find specific evidence for this in the *comedias*, as in "aqueste Cristiano quien le trajese a ser Moro, por codicia del tesoro que ha prometido su hermano."[122] The dilemma of the renegade is thematized most extensively in Agustín Moreto's *El esclavo de su hijo*, in which – as we have seen – the renegade Roberto (now known by his Arabic name, Abdenaga) later laments the choice he made to turn his back on his religion and his homeland:

> Pues que la flaqueza en mí
> me pidió, que el alma trueque:
> por el disfrazado gusto
> de un mal logrado deleite.
> Negué mi Ley, y fue causa
> de que por ello valiese;
> fueron de Ícaro las alas
> los favores de los Reyes.
> Anduve en corso diez años
> con mil cosarios valientes,
> haciendo cosas notables,
> y todo en favor de Infieles.
> Murió el cosario Audenau,
> y por razón de su muerte
> me vi cosario, y señor
> de diez armados bajeles.[123]

Here he freely admits that a prime motivation for denying his faith was Greed. His options were to languish as a Christian in a Muslim prison or turn renegade and rise through the ranks of the corsairs, eventually commanding ten armed pirate ships. What a powerful testimony to the hold this Deadly Sin still had upon the early modern Spanish imagination.

* * * * *

Thus we see that early modern Spanish playgoers faced the Deadly Sin of Avarice both at home and abroad, as they navigated threats of Murder by greedy relatives as well as worrying over treachery they might encounter on the high seas. But once again, before we start to feel too sorry for early modern Spaniards being snatched by pirates, the *comedias* remind us in no uncertain terms that the dangers they faced while sailing on the ocean were sometimes viewed as divine punishment for their imperial ambitions. Once again – while references to Jews, gypsies, Venetians, and other people groups abound – it is for themselves that early modern Spaniards reserve the most potent criticism with respect to Avarice. In Lope de Vega's *El Nuevo Mundo, descubierto por Cristóbal Colón*, a demon delivers lines which can hardly be read as anything other than a devastating critique of Spain's imperial project. Speaking of the conquistadores, he says: "No los lleva Cristiandad, sino el oro y la codicia. España no ha menester oro, que oro tiene en sí."[124] Later on in the same play, Dulcan accuses the Spanish explorers: "Con falsa relación y falsos dioses … nos venís a robar oro y mujeres."[125] In the same author's *Arauco domado*, Tucapel delivers a similarly passionate invective against the Spaniards: "Ladrones, que a hurtar venís el oro de nuestra tierra, y disfrazando la guerra dezís que a Carlos servís, que sujeción nos pedís?"[126] In Agustín Moreto's *El Cristo de los milagros*, a character is caught in the very act of conquest, as he is said to be carrying off "en talego de avariento la Indiana moneda rubia."[127] Gold was not the only object of Greed to be found in Spain's "New" World colonies, which also boasted natural resources such as pearls: "oro, y más perlas hay en ella, y mayor codicia arguyen Indias del sol y de estrellas."[128]

One of Spain's wealthiest colonies, the former home of the vast Inca empire, was the Viceroyalty of Peru. Its capital, Lima, was described by contemporaneous eyewitnesses as the City of Kings.[129] The Spanish-born soldier Don Josephe de Mugaburu offers a shimmering account of Lima's glittering jewels, which he witnessed in a procession honouring the Virgin Mary as part of a novena in April 1644:

> [H]er statue was removed from its niche and taken in procession to the cathedral. Accompanying it were [images of] a great number of saints of the same [Dominican] order, including Saint Dominic, and an angel with the words of the Hail Mary made out of many pearls and diamonds. The statue of Our Lady had more than two million jewels and pearls; such was the sight to be seen in this City of Kings.[130]

This image of Lima as the epitome of colonial wealth is carried over into the *comedias*, as in the case of a character named Don Pedro de Medina, who journeyed to the "New" World, like so many of his Spanish contemporaries, with the goal of seeking his fortune: "don Pedro de Medina, que a las Indias después pasó mancebo a la codicia del dorado cebo. Casóse en Lima."[131] It is no accident that he ended up marrying there. In fact, the very mention of the city of Lima conjured up for many early modern theatregoers an instant picture of immense wealth: "en Lima tenía un millón de hacienda con más codicia que Midas, gradóles el tesoro."[132] By extension, the town of Cuzco was also seen as wealthy enough to attract the Greed of imperial overlords, as in "la inobediencia de quien con ciega codicia al Cuzco tiranizaba."[133] Once again we see an unflattering picture of colonizing Spaniards motivated not by evangelism so much as by blind Greed.

Whether specific places in the "New" World are mentioned in these plays or not, the evocative word Empire became virtually synonymous with Avarice. The Greed of empire was responsible for causing war among neighbours: "guerra entre dos vecinos, y parientes, debe de ser codicia del Imperio."[134] It also caused *comedia* characters to leave their spouses and children: "¿Cómo, o dónde dejas hijos, y marido, por codicia de un Imperio, y el nombre real altivo?"[135] Greed is ultimately seen as homicidal in the misery it has caused since at least the time of the legendary King Midas: "Ha hecho tantos fuertes de homicidas la mísera codicia del Imperio, y el oro matador de Craso, y Midas."[136] In what Craig Kallendorf has described as an unexpected act of self-criticism, writers such as Alonso de Ercilla (1533–94) – author of *La Araucana* and a contemporary of Lope de Vega – were turning the very discourse of empire against itself as they focused on the downtrodden, the conquered, and the marginal figures in their literary recastings of imperial Rome's greatest epic poem.[137]

A veritable pamphlet war was waged as early modern thinkers traded thoughts on possible justifications for empire,[138] and a frequent argument marshalled to support the exploitation of "New" World resources was the long tradition within moral philosophy of justification for taking spoils during warfare.[139] Imperial Spaniards could point to well-established precedents for seizing the spoils of war, a custom also criticized by priestly playwrights in the *comedias* as being avaricious: "Satisfizo su hambre el fuego, como su sed la codicia con los robados despojos."[140] Untold wealth was reallocated during the Renaissance as armies sacked conquered cities in search of valuable plunder.[141] We find such contemporaneous historical echoes disguised only thinly by Golden Age playwrights like Lope, who chose more remote chronological settings for historical dramas, namely the period when the Romans had conquered Spain: "Saqueóse la ciudad la codicia y apetito, hallaron riquezas, ropas, perlas y rostros divinos."[142] The occupied Netherlands likewise became happy hunting grounds for greedy Spanish mercenaries, those soldiers of fortune immortalized in Lope de Vega's *Los españoles en Flandes*. One of these is depicted in the *comedias* as making his living exclusively off the spoils of war, to the point that Greed became metaphorically the sheath for his sword: "vivió primero en Flandes de robar ricos despojos; en la codicia envaina el blanco acero."[143] In a similar scenario, Spanish soldiers sacked the Dutch city of Maastricht in Lope's *El asalto de Mastrique, por el Príncipe de Parma*. Sometimes these mercenary soldiers were motivated less by personal Greed than by religion or the desire to offer lavish gifts to their ladies: "viene al ejército ahora este bellaco, por codicia que tiene de hacerte rica en el primero saco."[144] In this age of artistic connoisseurship, not only was Greed seen as feeding the hunger for riches, but pillaged art could also promise a feast for the eyes.[145] More commonly, Greed was denied even the potential excuse of becoming aestheticized. The real goal of taking spoils, both from the "New" World colonies and from other European nations with which the Spanish were at war, was that elusive metal which remained, then as well as now, the main object of Avarice or Greed.[146]

This insatiable thirst for metal was fed by the discovery, over the course of the sixteenth and seventeenth centuries, of a wealth of mineral deposits within Spain's "New" World territories. The mining industry was developed by the Spanish government incrementally during the first few decades after the establishment of permanent settlements in its colonies.[147] Thus early modern Spanish playwrights could lament, "Cuánto metal (que se encierra, por huir *nuestra avaricia*, para ser del mundo guerra) supo sacar la codicia, despedazando la tierra."[148] Avarice was seen alternatively as lurking in the earth itself ("cuánto avara en sus minas la tierra oculta") or in human nature; in this view – which may sound eerily familiar to postmodern environmentalists – man is seen to be, through Greed, engaged in a tragic war with his own environment: "el oro, la plata, el cobre, y el hierro, vive en las minas profundas, y no se libra por eso de la avaricia del hombre, aunque le escondan sus cerros."[149] The specific metals mentioned in connection with mining include both silver ("plata en Potosí nacida") and copper: "la cobre creciendo la maldad, y la codicia en la de yerro, con que vio la tierra hurto."[150] The violence done to "New" World territories in pursuit of these precious metals is graphically described as carving out holes in Mother Earth's breasts.[151] In this cataclysmic upheaval, the centre of the earth opens her gaping mouth to swallow up those who would steal her riches, thus demonstrating "el avaro anhelo del centro de la tierra."[152] One could speculate that archivally documented earthquakes, such as the one experienced in Guatemala in 1651 or the one which devastated Lima in 1655,[153] might have been viewed by early modern Spaniards as punishment for violating the earth's sanctity. In what can only be seen as a subversive critique of official government policy, Spanish playwrights use these images in their repertoire to warn of the dangers of Greed and repeat a Baroque memento mori to encourage a return to greater simplicity. Such was the only possible antidote to this spiritual disease.

* * * * *

But Greed followed the Spaniards across the ocean – or perhaps more accurately, it flowed with the Atlantic Ocean's waves in both directions. On their way back to the Iberian Peninsula in the years following its "New" World encounters, Spain's heavily laden ships were prone to more peril than just pirates.[154] They were also frequently dashed by shipwrecks, which could be considered another form of divine punishment.[155] At the very least, the ocean was viewed as a place of danger to which seafarers exposed themselves by their Greed.[156] Characters speak of the ocean taking revenge upon those guilty of Avarice, as in "hoy el mar se venga de mi codicia, sin ser de oro, de plata, ni perlas."[157] By extension, the sea itself is even seen as avaricious because it sucks up treasure from the ships it sinks: "las riquezas arrojadas al mar, siempre codicioso."[158]

Even if they did make it back intact, Spanish galleons often fell prey to the Greed of merchants and moneylenders who had financed their voyages in the first place: "El mercader marinero con la codicia avarienta cada viaje que intenta, dice, que será el postrero."[159] Merchants were notorious for adjusting their ledgers to the detriment of those who bought their goods or borrowed money from them: "el mercader vaya a ajustar libros, y cuentas, que es codicia demasiada."[160] In Tirso de Molina's *El mayor desengaño*, Viso exclaims, "¡O avariento mercader, que el interés ha podido tu valor poner en venta!"[161] In fact, the very word *mercader* became synonymous with Greed: "Gran codicia en vos se encierra, muy mercaderes quedasteis."[162] The newly discovered trade routes opened up by the voyages of exploration led to a bonanza for the early modern entrepreneur, who "codicioso esquilma las Orientales riquezas, sus drogas, y especierías."[163] The riches of Africa suddenly became more available, as did gold and silver from as far away as the previously ignored continent of Antarctica.[164]

The seafaring merchant of this time period is perhaps best portrayed in Calderón de la Barca's auto sacramental, *La nave del mercader*. In this play, the Merchant describes the bargain he has struck with the ship's owner:

> Viendo, pues, digo, esa Nave,
> pedí al Autor que la hizo,
> su gobernarle; él piadoso,
> o liberal, o benigno,
> de mí quiso fiarla, en fe
> de que a granjearle me obligo
> las soberanas riquezas
> de un Nuevo Mundo, en que he oído,
> que entre otros muchos haberes,

hay un tesoro escondido.
Preciosa una Margarita,
y unos frutos de Infinito
precio, que a ciento por uno
rendirán, a fuer de trigo,
en cuyo empleo podremos
quedar honrados, y ricos.[165]

The owner authorizes the use of his ship, as long as the Merchant brings it back full of "New" World riches, the profits from which they plan to share. The Merchant claims to carry such marvellous cargo to trade in the "New" World territories that he expects to turn a 100 per cent profit on his investment. Such a high rate of return is almost certainly literary hyperbole; even the shrewdest investments were not likely to pan out so well. But the fact that the Merchant seeks such a profit is all that concerns us here.[166] The figure of the wealthy, seafaring merchant in his multiple avatars was an established stereotype during the early modern period.

These rich merchants were most frequently assumed to be either Jewish or Venetian, with Christopher Columbus's native Genoa being another Italian city often mentioned in connection with moneylending.[167] Almost from time immemorial, Jews had been seen as "naturally" avaricious: "viendo la paga cuantiosa, y siendo ella tan naturalmente avara, como todo su Hebraísmo, atento al logro, y ganancia."[168] Thus the Hebrew in Calderón's loa *El veneno, y la triaca* speaks of "lo avaro de mi esquivez."[169] The allegorical figure of Avarice in another of Calderón's *autos sacramentales* makes his entrance on stage wearing a beard, which at this time could have been recognizable as Jewish (see figure 7).[170] Sometimes in the *comedias* we find Jews lumped together with atheists and other heretics, but the unifying thread is usually either their supposed propensity for theft or, more generally, their alleged Greed.[171]

One thing that might not be immediately obvious to postmodern readers is that Jews and Venetians may have been at least partially synonymous in the minds of some early modern audiences.[172] In fact, Venice was the site of the original *ghetto*. One only need think of Shakespeare's *The Merchant of Venice* to conjure an image of the grasping Shylock greedily exacting his pound of flesh from the Christian Antonio:

SALERIO: Why, I am sure if he forfeit thou wilt not take his flesh. What's that good for?
SHYLOCK: To bait fish withal – if it will feed nothing else, it will feed my revenge. He hath disgrac'd me, and hind'red me half a million, laugh'd at my losses, thwarted my bargains, cool'd my friends, heated mine enemies; and what's his reason? I am a Jew.[173]

As Robert Davis and Benjamin Ravid have shown in their recent edited collection *The Jews of Early Modern Venice*, a sizeable Jewish community lived there during the Renaissance. Some estimates place their number at 2,500 by the year 1600.[174] As I myself have demonstrated in a different context for the field of printing history, there is tangible evidence that some of these Venetian Jews were refugees from Spain.[175]

Jewish Venetians, or their Renaissance avatar which may more properly be termed a cultural amalgamation, were defamed above all for their practice of usury. Usury was controversial because a verse in the Old Testament specifically prohibited it between brothers, that is, co-religionists ("Thou shalt not lend to thy brother money to usury" [Deuteronomy 23:19]). Yet the Jews were the most notorious practitioners of usury, at least in the popular imagination. Brian Pullan explains how both Jews and Christians rationalized the situation to get around this prohibition:

> lending by Jews had been justified on the grounds that ... they could lawfully apply a double standard to co-religionists and to aliens: to lend at interest to fellow Jews was prohibited, but to charge interest to Christians was legitimate. It could even be argued that lending at interest was neither a service nor a means of making a living but a chastisement inflicted on idolaters to divert them from idolatry.[176]

This debatable practice of charging interest as a condition for lending money – now accepted as standard procedure – was still, at the time when these playwrights were writing, condemned in some circles as greedy, as in the reference to "el avaro que encierra usuras."[177] But this was a vice seen as necessary and one which was effectively condoned by the state. As Pullan affirms,

> Jewish bankers could be openly taxed – the rates they charged being geared to the taxes they were expected to pay – or, like other pawnbrokers, they could be formally fined for their usurious activities even when these had been officially condoned by authority, the fine becoming in effect a licensing fee.[178]

The tradition that usury had originated with Jewish merchants only reinforced the stereotype of them as avaricious, a myth which traced its origins at least to Judas Iscariot and the evil King Herod.[179]

Both of these Jewish villains are resurrected on the *comedia* stage. Judas Iscariot is vilified as "el Apóstol que a Dios dejó vendido ... avariento sea," while the allegorical figure of Avarice is pictured as carrying a white flag bearing the five wounds of Christ, which Judas caused.[180] Avarice becomes the overriding theme of Antonio Zamora's *Judás Iscariote*, in which the ex-apostle betrays Jesus for a mere thirty pieces of silver. In Zamora's version, Judas explicitly apotheosizes Greed: "Avara complexión mía, en tus manos pongo toda mi esperanza."[181] In this play, Avarice is seen as an unfaithful, internal burning of the soul.[182] In terms reminiscent of images we saw in the last chapter for Pride, Avarice is portrayed here as an unbridled beast who blinds its victims as they charge ahead madly in pursuit of worldly gain: "demos rienda, demos rienda al desenfrenado bruto de mi avaricia." Judas implicitly asks who permitted Avarice to blind him so and blames the powers of darkness for desiring his eternal loss.[183]

Judas is not the only Biblical/historical figure reviled for his Avarice. Lope de Vega cites the ancient historian Josephus as a credible authority who had testified to King Herod's Greed.[184] Tirso de Molina thematizes the Greediness of this wicked king in his comedia *La vida de Herodes*. In this play, Herod stops at nothing, stealing even the intended wife of his older brother Faselo. Instead of receiving the just punishment for his actions – indeed, he is condemned to be executed – he is saved when Caesar Augustus marches in and rescues him due to his own long-standing feud with Marcus Aurelius, Faselo's protector. Caesar then proceeds to make Herod king of Jerusalem. This is the same king who, later in the play, receives word from the Wise Men that the Baby Jesus has been born and orders the Slaughter of the Innocents in order to preserve his kingdom. This rather lengthy biblical episode is recounted most succinctly in Guillén de Castro's *El mejor esposo*, part of the second act of which is devoted to Mary and Joseph's flight into Egypt to flee King Herod:

> por milagro le buscaron,
> y le adoraron tres Reyes.
> Por lo cual celoso Herodes,
> un demonio se le mete
> en el ambicioso pecho:
> y viendo que no le pueden
> traer el divino infante,
> ha mandado que degüellen
> los niños, siendo deudor
> de tanta sangre inocente.[185]

Thus Greed is linked to Murder in this literary-historical figure who will stop at nothing to consolidate his hold on a position of political power which, like his brother's intended wife, was not even rightfully his in the first place.

But to return to Spain – in Spanish drama the Jews had to be located in ancient Israel, or the Roman empire, or else in some place like Venice, in early modern imaginary geography,[186] because they had officially been expelled from Spain by the Catholic Monarchs in 1492:

> The blood-libel accusation at La Guardia in 1490–91 brought anti-Jewish feeling to a fever pitch. While many attempts were made to annul the Decree of Expulsion, they were all to no avail. By the end of July 1492, the last openly practicing Jews had left Spain … [A] reasonable guess … could put the number who left Spain in 1492 at between 100,000 and 150,000.[187]

This was out of an estimated 300,000 openly professing Jews, who had previously comprised the backbone of the mercantile class. In the fourteenth century, Jews had accounted for 5 per cent of the total population of Spain and Portugal.[188] The result, of course – with ramifications extending down to the present day – was the great Sephardic diaspora.[189]

This mass exodus of Jewish people left Spain divested of much of its material and cultural wealth:

> Apart from the importance of the Jews as administrators and financiers, the place of their community in the finances of the treasuries is well illustrated by the fact that in 1294 the Jews paid 22 percent of all direct taxes in Aragon and in 1323 paid 35 percent of all Catalonian taxes.[190]

Golden Age lexicographer Sebastián de Covarrubias, in his entry for the word *judío*, lamented that in retrospect, the Catholic Monarchs had shown precious little foresight regarding the economic ramifications of their decision: "En España han habitado judíos de muchos siglos atrás, hasta que en tiempo de nuestros abuelos, los Reyes Católicos, sin reparar en lo que perdían de sus rentas, los echaron de España."[191] In addition to their personal assets, the Jews were valuable to the Spanish crown because of their traditional role as tax collectors.[192] One of the prime motivations for "New" World conquest may have been, at least in part, an effort to replace some of the gold and silver carted off by Jews during their forced exile.[193]

The wealth they did take with them, as well as efforts to divest them of it, quickly became the stuff of legend: "Jews arriving in Oran, Algiers, and Fez were slaughtered by Berbers who believed they were hiding gold in their stomachs."[194] Other European rulers, quick to take advantage of Spain's poor judgment, saw the potential for financial gain and offered wealthy Jews a safe haven.[195] In the decades following Queen Isabel the Catholic's expulsion of the Hebrews – and certainly within a century after this event – the Spanish economy was plunged into crisis due to the sudden absence of Jewish capital, in addition to failed economic policies.[196]

This economic strain is reflected in the *comedia* corpus by the presence of *pícaros*, gypsies, petty criminals, and every sort of down-and-out trickster imaginable. As evidenced in the archives, beggars became a real problem as events conspired to produce a higher number of vagabonds in Spain than in any other country in Europe:

> [T]he failure of the urban *comunero* revolts was symptomatic of the opposition that, as early as 1521, arose between a stymied nationalist capitalism based on local industry and the international capitalism successfully supported by the Emperor. Already by the latter half of the sixteenth century, these events had led to such interrelated factors as the chronic lack of employment in both agriculture and industry, heavy taxation, and the general rise in prices, all of which contributed to make the number of vagabonds in Spain the highest in Europe. The various Poor Laws decreed in Valladolid in 1523, Toledo in 1525, Madrid in 1528 and 1534, and in Zamora, Salamanca, and Valladolid in 1540, had failed to stem the flow of paupers circulating from one urban centre to another.[197]

The contemporaneous pen and ink sketches of beggars and cripples by Hieronymus Bosch (1450–1516) (see figure 8) give us some idea of what these swarms of vagrants must have looked like.[198] In *Discourses of Poverty: Social Reform and the Picaresque Novel in Early Modern Spain*, Anne Cruz employs Foucauldian terminology to describe a discourse which arose in Spain as duelling *tratadistas* vied with each other to have the last word on what should be done with the poor and similarly marginalized Others:

> The interrelated problems of vagrancy and lack of employment first arose in the sixteenth century under Charles V's monarchy; they worsened substantially during Philip II's reign, and were further complicated by the religious dissensions that sprang up throughout the Spanish Empire and which gave rise to other marginalized groups … Perceived by most Spaniards as a threatening alien force unrestrained by national boundaries and unchecked by Old Christian morality, these displaced and marginalized "others" were soon blamed for the disorder and chaos enveloping the country. Together with the poor, such heterodox elements as Protestants, conversos, moriscos, and gypsies were judged deleterious to the social well-being and therefore requiring of increased distribution and control by the state.[199]

Once again, if we turn to Spain's dramatic repertoire, we see how the Deadly Vices become a lens through which playwrights choose to view social problems, as when Calderón de la Barca writes of "la discordia, que hay entre Avaro, y Mendigo."[200] This *mendigo* or beggar was not a mere metaphor. In the *comedias*, we find out that prime locations for beggars to accost the more affluent in search of timely donations were everyday places such as public markets: "los Mercados, es también donde acude la codicia de los Pobres, que el manejo del dinero facilita tal vez la Limosna más al que importuno mendiga."[201] Other places considered prime for begging were the ports where ships docked, laden with foreign wealth from abroad.[202]

But even those who were not actually beggars still could be living on the fringes of society; these social misfits are almost universally described as avaricious. In some *autos sacramentales*, Avarice is dressed as a *villano*,[203] while in the *comedias* a simple villager falls into the trap of gold: "el villano cayó en la red del oro codicioso, como en la liga el pajarillo simple."[204] Paradoxically, the ambitious *labrador* is seen as greedy for carrying his tools, in what may be read as a concerted effort to keep unruly commoners in their place.[205] In an age where social unrest could quickly degenerate into outright rebellion, the *comedias* record an uneasy tension between social groups.[206] Dramatists with noble pretensions – let us not forget that several of them had courtly ambitions – perhaps left traces of this prejudice in lines such as "ser el hurto el villano de los Vicios."[207] On the other hand, these playwrights' attempts to placate the greedy mob – we find such telling lines as "que sosiegue el codicioso pueblo dividido en bandas" – reveal a nagging uncertainty or even concern for personal safety which must have been attendant upon everyday life.[208]

While the villages were the province of *villanos*, their counterparts in more urban areas would have been household servants.[209] Once again, here we see portraits of Greed breaking down more or less predictably along class lines. Domestic servants are referred to on stage in the *comedias* as greedy or as thieves, just like such lower-class figures as tavern- and innkeepers.[210] In lines reminiscent of Don Quijote's misadventures in the inn, Tirso de Molina's play *Antona García* refers to "mesones y posadas donde vive la codicia. Todo en la venta se vende."[211] These haunting words refer not just to merchandise, but to prostitutes like Cervantes's Maritornes who sold their bodies to any traveller by the wayside; we might recall here Hieronymus Bosch's painting *The Pedlar* which includes in the background an inn with a prostitute in the doorway (see figure 9).[212] The atmosphere of a typical inn is admirably recreated in Tirso de Molina's comic interlude *La venta*. In this short *entremés*, characters hurl insults at each other in a heady stream of vituperation centring around accusations of thievery and Greed: "Ladrón potro, ladrón archiladrillo, y tátara Pilatos, casamentero infame de estómagos, y gatos."[213] Generally speaking, inns were seen as likely places to get robbed: "un ladrón en una venta cual veis aquí me ha robado."[214]

Travellers in Cervantes's and Tirso de Molina's Spain were not just in danger of being ripped off by innkeepers; they were also threatened by professional robbers and bandits lying in wait for them around the next bend in the road:

> In 1643, the Council of Castile noted of two bandit gangs operating in La Rioja and led by the gypsies Matías and Chaparro, respectively, that they were particularly dangerous "because they offer refuge and asylum to fugitive soldiers from the Aragonese army" … Francisco de la Puente Montecillo Miranda, a deserter who had escaped … "had gone around with gypsies and other undesirables, carrying pistols and other arms, and robbing and mistreating the travellers they encountered" … As far as *moriscos* were concerned, while they had long been involved in banditry in

> the south and south-east, there were now reports that both they and gypsies were active as bandits in central and western Castile, too … Banditry was an endemic problem in the south, in the kingdom of Valencia, and, to a slightly lesser degree … in Catalonia.[215]

The *comedia* repertoire of course also records traces of this scurrilous cast of characters: "este Capitán de una cuadrilla de Bandidos, desde el Monte va, y viene, con la codicia de robar al Publicano, a la Ciudad."[216] Bandits were thought particularly to lurk in the mountains: "un Ladrón … Bandolero de estos Montes."[217] We watch as they assault passers-by, or at very least demand that they surrender their possessions: "Primero que el paso adelantes, rindo las joyas, y los Talentos que contigo llevas."[218] Sometimes we see robber bandits fighting over their booty.[219] In particular danger were the many pilgrims who ventured out each year to visit Santiago de Compostela, Rome, or one of Catholicism's many other sacred shrines.[220] References to these pilgrims often invoke the parable of the Good Samaritan in the New Testament, who assists the poor man beaten by robbers and left for dead.[221] In an alternative twist, *comedia* characters may even be heard advising each other to pretend to have been wounded by robbers in order to gain sympathy – a plausible excuse, since this was evidently a common occurrence.[222]

But perhaps even more terrifying, due to the perpetual proximity of their menace, were the gypsies who populated not just the roadways, but Spain's very cities and towns:

> In 1674, writing from Andalusia, Manuel Montillo complained that marauding bands of gypsies had plagued the region for 40 years and that neither on the open road nor in populated areas were people safe from them … [I]n 1639, Pedro Marcos, *alcalde mayor* of Palenzuela, was instructed to pursue and apprehend "troops of gypsies" who had used two nearby villages as bases from which to carry out robberies in the surrounding areas. In particular, it noted, they had ransacked a coach on the road from Burgos to Valladolid, stripped and robbed the *alcalde mayor* of Noreña (Asturias), waylaid many students on their way to Salamanca, and raped "many women," before making good their escape by crossing into a neighboring jurisdiction.[223]

In 1631 Juan de Quiñones published a *Discurso contra los gitanos* in which he bragged about how he – in his legal capacity as *alcalde* in Madrid – had hanged five gypsies he had arrested for the crime of robbing the mail from the Netherlands. He left their quartered bodies by the side of the road to discourage other gypsies from committing similar thefts.[224] Since they made their living by stealing, these nomads were portrayed as notoriously avaricious, to the point that Avarice itself is compared to a gypsy: "Y también es gitana la avaricia, vive Dios, que de engaños, y dobleces no he de creer la hipócrita noticia, que le apoya."[225] The Greed of gypsies is thematized in act 3 of Antonio de Solís's *La gitanilla de Madrid*, in which a gypsy claims the right to steal as part of his time-honoured way of life:

> Sabe el Cielo como parto
> con el pobre el caudalejo
> de lo quinto, y de lo hurtado,
> que me toca de derecho:
> el hurtar en las Iglesias
> es pecado, y muy mal hecho,
> que no tiene otro peor modo
> de quebrarse el Mandamiento.
> Nadie me trabe en alhajas
> la ejecución, si hay dineros,
> que el trato es como perrillo
> que siempre busca a su dueño,
> y el dinero no conoce
> al dueño de ayer.[226]

In one scene of this play, two gypsy thieves are captured and brought out onto the stage. They give Don Pedro a box which contains family jewels as well as a portrait of Isabel's mother, along with a book which tells the story of Isabel's long-lost sister's disappearance years ago. Like Muslim pirates, gypsies were also known to steal Christian children; and this is in fact what happens in the play by Solís. The gypsy Preciosa turns out to be a Christian child, the sister of Isabel, who had been stolen by a gypsy band as a little girl.[227] Gypsies considered it their right to steal and to live off of what they had stolen. However, the gypsies' internal code of honour required them to refrain from stealing in holy places such as churches. As the saying goes, there is honour even among thieves.

Undoubtedly, early modern Spanish playwrights could have encountered some figures from this cast of real-life characters while on their way walking home from the theatre. But true to form, these dramatists also bring their subject matter into even more personal perspective as they write about the greedy people with whom they personally had the most contact: printers and booksellers. Thus Juan Pérez de Montalbán complains of "la codicia de los Libreros, y la facilidad de los Impresores," while a volume of Calderón's collected works begins with a preliminary "Advertencias a los que leyeren" warning of "La Codicia de algunos Libreros, y la ignorancia de muchos Trasladantes."[228] In the front matter printed to accompany his *A María el corazón*, in a Prologue reprinted from the first edition of the first volume of his *autos sacramentales*, Calderón likewise excoriates the printers of pirated editions of his works: "pues no contenta la codicia con haber impreso tantos hurtados escritos míos."[229] As always, meditations on sin are the most potent when they are brought into the realm of our own personal experience. This is just one of the many ways in which early modern playwrights made their subject matter come alive for their audiences.

* * * * *

So we see that Avarice, like its first cousin Pride, was still very much relevant as an organizing category for understanding sin in the early modern period. Once again, I would postulate that one possible explanation for this was the extremely close connection of Greed to two of the Ten Commandments. The Seventh Commandment, "Thou shalt not steal," and the Tenth, "Thou shalt not covet thy neighbor's goods," both form a neat segue from medieval into early modern world views. Easily assimilable into existing discourses of Avarice, this particular pair of Commandments, at least, reinforced the Capital Vices' injunctions against damaging the whole community by the individual instance of harming one's neighbour. Pre-eminently social evils, these Sins continued to be recognized as such in an effort to promote community cohesiveness and civic order.

As we saw earlier with Pride, references to Greed in the *comedias* specifically invoke these two Commandments in a uniquely early modern synthesis of competing moral systems. References to the Seventh Commandment against stealing are relatively straightforward and usually also include one of the synonyms for Greed or Avarice; for example, "O cuando en el silencio el *hurto* atento con la dormida noche se conforma, *Codicioso* villano atrevimiento."[230] Some of these assign a biblical motive – coveting – to Theft, as in "No había de codiciarle el ladrón."[231] Allusions to the Tenth Commandment are even easier to spot since they usually include the infrequent phrase "others' goods," or *bienes ajenos*, which *comedia* characters are enjoined repeatedly not to covet: "Desear bienes ajenos, es pecado" and "Con el debido decoro Mentís, que en bienes ajenos, no hay posesión."[232] Sometimes these references conflate coveting with the related Vice of Envy, as in "el ajeno bien no envidies; ni quieras de otro la hacienda."[233]

Thus we see that Greed remains relevant in the early modern period (in intellectual history terms, we might call this another residue) and even receives reinforcement from the once again popular set of moral instructions which was the Decalogue. This was, after all, the "new" set of precepts which came to prevail during this time period in the rest of Europe. Now let us move on to the next Deadly Sin, Lust, to see whether it, too, remains residually relevant – and if so, how – to early modern Spanish moral economies.

3
Lusty Lads and Luscious Ladies

Y vosotros, descendientes … quedaréis escarmentados.

– Lope de Vega

[T]he social location of the residual is always easier to understand, since a large part of it (though not all) relates to earlier social formations and phases of the cultural process, in which certain real meanings and values were generated. In the subsequent default of a particular phase of a dominant culture there is then a reaching back to those meanings and values which were created in actual societies and actual situations in the past, and which still seem to have significance because they represent areas of human experience … which the dominant culture neglects, undervalues, opposes, represses, or even cannot recognize.

– Raymond Williams[1]

Lust makes her entrance on stage as a lady lounging on top of the seven-headed hydra representing the Seven Deadly Sins: "Juan, que le vio de más cerca allá en Patmos, dice, que es Hidra de siete Cabezas, en cuya escamada espalda, lasciva Mujer se asienta."[2] She beckons alluringly from a golden tower, holding a golden cup in her hand.[3] A cousin to Pride and his variations, such as Narcissus, she also appears with a mirror for admiring her own beauty.[4]

By extension, Lust appears in the *comedias* in so many sensual details. The trappings of Lust are silks, beds, and plunging necklines.[5] Lustful women wear silks ("toda vestida de seda, y por ventura dejada por adúltera"), but then so do men ("vístase amoroso amante el hombre torpe, y lascivo sedas, que el gusano teja").[6] This is, after all, the age where gentlemen still wore tights. Lust could be illustrated provocatively on stage through immodest dress:

CELINDA: Más hermosa estás así.
BLANCA: Es el traje más lascivo.[7]

Lust was also associated with baths, cosmetics, and curled hair.[8] Perfume and sweet-smelling substances such as amber were believed to provoke one to Lust: "ámbar pondré en tu boca, si es que a lujuria el buen olor provoca."[9] As described by Leah Middlebrook in *Imperial Lyric*, all of these characteristics may be seen as pertaining to highly advanced civilizations which – though previously warlike – had succumbed to pleasure and thus begun a slow process of decline.[10] The Romans, otherwise emulated by the Spaniards, were seen as pathetically hanging on to an empire which had started to crumble once it became more effete: "qué graciosos son los Romanillos llenos de afeite, baños y lascivia."[11] The diminutive ending on the word *Romanillos* makes this comment particularly condescending. It must be remembered that at this time, "New" World natives were also thought by Spaniards to be more lustful because they bathed so frequently.[12] The contrast between the austere warrior ethic and undisciplined hedonism may perhaps best be seen in Tirso de Molina's play *El Aquiles*, which dramatizes the Homeric scene of the warrior refusing to fight the Trojans. Instead he is accused of lounging in his luxurious tent: "¿Por los muros los tapices? ¿Qué delicados matices, seda que lascivo tocas? Todo el mundo se hace bocas contra ti."[13] But as Middlebrook has argued so convincingly with regard to lyric poetry, and Sidney Donnell, Sherry Velasco, and Julio González-Ruiz have done in reference to the theatre, this feminized figure of Achilles is possibly emblematic of many, if not the majority, of Spanish courtiers at this time.[14] As their warrior culture started to evaporate, and the age of epic passed, Spanish noblemen had leisure time available for pleasurable dalliance. Let us look at some of the metaphors in the plays for these amorous pursuits.

Metaphors for Lust in the *comedias* include magnets, magic, clinging vines, proliferating weeds, beggars who leave their own country, and deserters who board a renegade ship. Lust is viewed as the magnet which draws the senses inexorably towards Vice: "es preciso el ser la Lascivia imán del Sentido." It casts spells like the Sirens, who lured Odysseus's men to take their own lives by diving into the sea: "la Lascivia usa de la Sirena el hechizo que le descamine."[15] The figure of Lust is associated with proliferating nature, as she appears bearing a profusion of roses and other flowers: "la Lascivia en una Fuente [trae] todo género de Rosas, y demás Flores."[16] By extension, she is herself a clinging vine which wraps itself around her victims until they are hopelessly entangled: "esta yedra lasciva, y esta vid trepadora fresnos, y olmos enlazan."[17] She is as promiscuous as a rapidly spreading plant or weed: "La Clicie que amar aspira, gigante de amor, descuella su púrpura y su jazmín tan lasciva, e inmodesta, que trocados los efectos surten colores diversos."[18] As Calderón de la Barca allegorizes in *La viña del Señor*, these weeds may look beautiful, but actually they prove deadly.[19] When she takes human form, Lust appears disguised as a slutty villager or even a beggar: "el Lascivo, en el Mendigo, que pródigo abandonó su patrimonio, y labró de su culpa su castigo."[20] Forsaking her own ship (i.e., her husband), she boards a renegade, adulterous frigate which bears her towards exotic lands. But instead of arriving safely, this ship's passengers never reach port; instead, they shipwreck and drown in a sea of lascivious, profane love.[21]

This shipwreck reminds us that once again Lust, along with all the rest of the Vices, participates in the Baroque topos of *desengaño*, or the disillusionment which follows seduction by deceptive appearances. Appearing to be fire, Lust only leaves one covered with soot: "disfrazado en llama tibia, cubre en muchas cenizas la Lascivia."[22] At first Lust seems to have a good smell, but then it turns out instead to have a pungent, unpleasant odour.[23] Lust steals the heart ("robando el corazón la Lascivia al Hombre") and possesses it ("todo afecto lascivo es dueño del corazón").[24] It digs a mine in a person's psyche, "adonde abrió su brecha la mina de la Lascivia." Along with the Devil and the World, Lust forms an unholy Trinity of the three foremost enemies of the soul: "Ya sé, que son el Demonio, el Mundo, y la Lascivia los tres más enemigos del Alma."[25]

But Lust in the *comedias* is not confined to the realm of allegory. Even the most casual reader or viewer of this dramatic art form is aware that Lust provides much of the titillating, sensationalistic material for these stories. In the *comedia* corpus we in fact find every sort of sexual perversity: rape,[26] sodomy,[27] incest,[28] bestiality. In a calculated throwback to classical mythology, we literally find references to women having sex with bulls and horses: "qué escogió (en historias hallo) Semíramis a un caballo, Pasifae lasciva a un toro."[29] In a slightly more palatable euphemism, bestiality became known simply as *el pecado nefando*, the nefarious sin, as in one *comedia* character's injunction to another: "es pecado nefando casarte con un Jumento."[30]

In the case of incest, we should keep in mind that standards for this sin were much higher than today's, with sex being prohibited within three to four degrees of even spiritual kinship, defined as the relationship stemming from a godparent's responsibility to a godchild and extending even to later generations of these two biologically unrelated families.[31] Certainly sex with a sister-in-law – although again, the two people involved were not biologically related – would count as incest: "y demás de esto, con su cuñada cometió un incesto."[32] But the *comedias* are also filled with activities which would fit the definition of incest by any standard. Such are sons having sex with their mothers ("corras a los delitos más atroces, y en torpe incesto de tu madre goces") and bragging about it later ("te quise hacer del todo abominable, cometiendo contigo torpe incesto");[33] sisters accused of loving their brothers inappropriately, as occurs with Leonor and Diego in Antonio de Solís's *El doctor Carlino*;[34] and go-betweens who facilitate, albeit silently, sexual relationships within families, as in "ha sido de aqueste incesto tercera muda."[35] Occasionally in the *comedias* we find all of these sexual vices lumped together in a single character: "miraba en un sujeto escalamiento, violencia, incesto, estupro, adulterio."[36] This unfortunate creature – normally the Antichrist or some other suitable villain – is caught "cometiendo en un acto deshonesto, fuerza, adulterio, estupro, y torpe incesto."[37]

Given this extensive panorama of sexual vice, it is no wonder that we find abundant evidence of concerns over the morality of this theatre. The notoriously austere King Philip II was so hung up on the potentially negative impact of the *comedias* on his subjects that he shut down the theatres at least twice, using as an excuse the deaths of royal family members and the requisite period of mourning which followed.[38] In Manuel de Guerra y Ribera's official *aprobación* (a document granting an official stamp of ecclesiastical approval) for the published edition of Calderón de la Barca's *Agradecer, y no amar*, this rather severe doctor of theology and professor of philosophy at the University of Salamanca complains about the immorality of even classical theatre, specifically Jupiter's Adultery as celebrated in the plays of the Roman dramatist Terence:

> Mira celebrado el joven el adulterio de Júpiter ... en la Comedia de vuestro Terencio se excusa el perdido joven del adulterio, mirando la tabla de Júpiter ... ¿Se deleita un perdido con el adulterio? Pues mira a Júpiter, y de su vista saca materia.

He continues to vilify the god Jupiter by further accusing him of incest with his own daughter: "y para llenar enteramente la grande hazaña de incestuoso, intentó contra su hija abominables, y torpes licencias." He rants on in the same passage: "¿Qué paciencia podía tolerar invocaciones a un Marte adúltero, y a Venus incontinente?"[39] In another one of his plays, Calderón himself protests that the goddess Venus behaves no better than a public prostitute: "Venus, pública ramera, delitos hizo de amor."[40]

Given these potent critiques, how did Lust win the battle for the hearts and minds of Spanish playgoers? Although most of these playwrights were also ordained priests, some of them – most notably Lope de Vega, without contest the most prolific and promiscuous dramatist of the period – were also notorious womanizers.[41] But whatever salacious details might have circulated about their private lives (the question might well be asked: was there even any such thing as privacy in the early modern period?),[42] that did not mean they were granted licence to celebrate Lust openly on stage. Instead, in what can only be viewed as a supreme act of repression, they explore this Deadly Sin in tantalizing detail, all the while distancing themselves from any clear, direct connection to the historical and dramatic contexts in which it appears. Lust is almost ubiquitous in these plays, but more often than not it is assigned a context that is at once both long ago and far away: i.e., everywhere but Spain.

Lust is seen as suffusing the humanistic realm of the pagan gods: "Plutón, y Apolo lascivo" and "Venus lasciva ... Marte adúltero."[43] The ever-randy Lope de Vega, in lines spoken on stage by one of his characters, seems to relish imagining the hot sex being had by the gods: "cuando Venus lasciva, y tierno Marte, en Chipre estaban una ardiente siesta."[44] Lope's classicizing play *El laberinto de Creta* offers him further opportunity to explore the Lust of the pagan deities, even if he has to admit that their behaviour is scandalously scurrilous. Perhaps making his comments more palatable to Inquisitorial censors, he refers in this play to "lascivo Jupiter, Deidad indigna de tan alto nombre." Jupiter is later characterized in the same play by his sexual victim as "Dios lascivo que en Toro trasformado me ha quitado la honrosa vida."[45] In addition to the gods, Lust in the *comedias* is also exhibited by mythological creatures such as the satyrs and fantastic animals stemming from Greek and Hebrew religious traditions.[46]

But moving away from the realm of fantasy into historical episodes of lustful human interaction, early modern Spanish playwrights found ample material in their history books. The ancient Greeks, Romans, and Egyptians were all reputed to be lascivious, and these stereotypes were exploited by dramatists to the hilt. Beginning with classical Greece ("Egisto es este, que en lascivo juego con Clytemnestra alegre había vivido"),[47] they could then move on to Troy ("como el Troyano huésped olvidado del hospedaje con lascivo intento su hija le robaste"),[48] and from there to Rome via the dalliances with Dido by the otherwise pious Aeneas, Rome's founder.[49] We have already witnessed, above, the stereotype of late-empire Romans debilitated by luxury; these references are only multiplied as the Christianized Romans' lasciviousness comes to be seen as more culpable, since they ought to know better.[50] Even the more warlike Romans of the pre-Republican era are not spared contumely on the grounds of Lust; thus we find Sexto Tarquinio, the infamous rapist of Lucretia, immortalized in the historical drama *La libertad de Roma*, by Juan de la Cueva, as "Sexto Tarquinio, aquel cruel incesto."[51] Most classicists would consider the high point of Roman civilization to be the time of Julius Caesar; his close associate Mark Antony is vilified in the *comedias* for succumbing to the wiles of Cleopatra as "aquel Marco Antonio que tan lascivo murió." Perhaps due at least in part to association with her, all of Egypt came to be associated with Lust, as in "la tierra del lascivo Egipto."[52]

Egypt bore lustful connotations not only as a result of its most famously lascivious queen; according to the Old Testament, as repeated in the *comedias*, it was also in Egypt that the patriarch Joseph had to resist Potiphar's wife's adulterous advances: "vino a esta extranjera Patria de Egipto, donde lascivia, viciosa hermosura incasta, le redujo a vil prisión."[53] Other biblical figures, usually villains, were also dominated by Lust. Thus in the Hebrew Scriptures we find the adulterous Queen Jezabel ("Adúltera Jezabel, que al demonio sacrificios ofreces")[54] as well as that brother/sister couple, Amon and Tamar, who were guilty of incest. As another *comedia* character predicts to Tamar, her situation is most convenient, for "en el incestuoso Amon tendrás hermano, y marido."[55]

In the New Testament, King Herod's brother's wife Herodias, with whom he had an incestuous relationship, asks for John the Baptist's head on a platter because he, as God's prophet, has condemned her illicit affair.[56] It turns out that this is a classic case of the sins of the fathers being revisted on their children: this Herod's father, of the same name – the King Herod who ordered the infants slain near the time of Jesus's birth[57] – had likewise been involved according to legend with a woman named Mariadnes, whom he suspected of Adultery. We witness this scenario in Tirso's *La vida de Herodes*, in which King Herod – in a Baroque apostrophe – realizes belatedly how evil her influence has been: "Aparta, adúltera cruel, que ya engaños llegan tarde."[58] Alternative sexual lifestyles are likewise readily apparent in a well-known character from the Gospels, the Samaritan woman who has had five husbands and to whom Jesus delivers the living water discourse at Jacob's well. This figure proves so compelling that Calderón chooses her to represent the Vice of Lust in one of his *autos sacramentales*: "hace una Samaritana el Papel de la Lascivia."[59]

In addition to chronological distance as a strategy for removing Lust to the realm of the long ago and far away, early modern Spanish playwrights had at their disposal the ploy of transposing their scenes to increasingly remote geographical locations. We have already witnessed the use of Greece, Troy, Rome, Egypt, and even Judea as sites of Spanish anxiety about sex. But as we saw in earlier chapters with other Vices such as Pride and Avarice, the Spaniards' favourite punching bags likewise when it came to Lust were, more often than not, their Arabic enemies known simply as the "Moors." Perhaps as a justification for Reconquest, or perhaps revealing anxiety over the persistent Morisco presence in Spain, or maybe even as a fantasy they allowed themselves to indulge in about a people group that was at once both alien and familiar,[60] Spanish playwrights spun out imaginary tableau scenes of Moorish harems engaging in all sorts of lascivious behaviour: "Ya con el amor lascivo sobre alcatifas de seda requiebran noches, y días las Moras."[61] In addition to this Paradisiacal vision of an Islamic harem of virgins – which might have captured the imagination of early modern theatregoers in much the same way as it captures the imaginations of would-be fundamentalist martyrs today – there was another stereotype generally accepted about Muslims, even though it was probably similarly inaccurate. This was the assumption that Islamic people groups, including Turkish Arabs as well as Muslims from so great a distance as Ethiopia, were more prone to commit incest with their mothers: "esto mismo usáis los Turcos, y Moros, los Etiopes, que incesto, se casaban con sus madres."[62] This imputation of sexual sin by the Spaniards – and its removal to ever-more-remote realms, such as Ethiopia – became at once a strategy for distancing themselves from their centuries-old political and military rivals, and an outlet for anxiety over "Moorish" corruption of their own sexual mores. Let us not forget that the Hapsburg line became debilitated through decades of inbreeding, as when Philip IV married his niece Mariana in 1648. The specific charge of incest against the Muslims betrays a growing discomfort with the proximity of their cohabitors throughout the Iberian Peninsula. In lashing out against Muslims, they are again attributing sexual sin to *somebody else*; but given the degree of intermingling evidenced by Mudéjar art, architecture, and literature of this time period, Spaniards were also engaging in navel-gazing about their close relatives – and, ultimately, about themselves and their families.

This stereotype of the "Moors" as lustful can also explain a telling exception we find to the rule of long ago and far away which is adhered to by so many Golden Age playwrights when it comes to the open or even celebratory depiction of Lust on the stage. Through the legend of La Cava, in which Count Julian persuaded the Muslim Musa to invade Spain in retaliation for King Rodrigo's seduction of his daughter Florinda (a story retold in countless ballads and epic poems), Spaniards reminded their children and their grandchildren that ultimately Spain had been lost through Lust: "España ... por un Rey que fue lascivo se perdió la vez primera."[63] The Sin of King Rodrigo was neurotically obsessed over in the retelling, in a syndrome which still speaks to Spain's national psyche:

> [T]he storied Islamic invasion of the eighth century had come as a result of Visigothic sexual inconstancy ... [I]t had been the "original sin" of the Goths themselves that brought on seven hundred years of Moorish rule and the resultant potential for miscegenation ... [T]he Spanish chroniclers themselves were quite aware of the negative implications of a genealogy derived from "Rodericke king of the Gothes" ... [T]he appeal to a Gothic past did raise the specter of a primordial Christian purity. But this lineage also destabilized the very "whiteness" it sought to recover, opening the door to all manner of genealogical manipulation and falsification as Spaniards sought to establish lineal "cleanliness" – a notion that Black Legend polemicists were all too eager to exploit as laughable.[64]

By way of precedent for this episode in Spain, the Lust of Paris for Helen was remembered as having been the doom of Troy: "Troya se abrasó por aquel Griego adulterio."[65] In a logical extension of this scenario, other kings and princes in the *comedias* became types of Prince Paris and King Rodrigo, as early modern Spaniards re-enacted on stage the primordial drama of their national tragedy. This is the case in Lope de Vega's aptly titled *La fe rompida*, where the young, lustful King Felisardo is described by another character as "Mal considerado Rey, mozo mal aconsejado de amor lascivo engañado."[66] A similarly lascivious king appears in Tirso de Molina's *La mujer que manda en casa*, in which the character Elias exclaims: "No blasones impiedades, lascivo y bárbaro Rey, hijo del esclavo Amri, consorte de Jezabel." We have already seen the biblical episode on which this play is based.[67] Another character refers later in the same drama to "ese Rey torpe y lascivo" and "esa Reina hambrienta de honras." He sums up the cultural-moral status of the royal couple, "con ellos no hay honor."[68]

But to step back for a moment – how exactly can this royal husband and wife be described together as lustful? We shall see later in this chapter how Lust is often conflated with Adultery.[69] Perhaps it speaks once again to the Spanish psyche (these are, after all, the same people who would later become, under Franco's regime, devotees of a veritable cult surrounding the memory of a chaste Queen Isabel la Católica) to discover that early modern Spaniards were so uptight as to even consider Lust sinful within marriage.[70] Contemporaneous confessors confirm the existence of this so-called Sin: "El acceso conyugal después del parto, durante los días de la purgación … es pecado venial … Ni tampoco es pecado alguno el negar el débito, cuando se pide con exceso, y nimia repetición."[71] Here we see that sex after childbirth between spouses is considered sinful, and married couples are encouraged not to have intercourse excessively or with prolix repetition. It was also considered sinful to ejaculate prematurely on purpose in order to avoid pregnancy; in this case sex between married people was labelled just as malicious as Adultery.

Lust within marriage is thematized in Lope de Vega's *La Historia de Tobías*, a story from the Catholic Apocrypha which Rojas Zorrilla also adapted in a different play.[72] In Lope de Vega's version, a couple is told they should not marry because the foolish prospective husband is too lustful: "que mal os podréis juntar, si trae este necio esposo lascivo amor enojoso." The poor husband-to-be protests that his love for his wife is pure: "no he mirado mi esposa con voluntad lasciva y codiciosa."[73] But to no avail. In a supernatural turn which might not play well on a modern stage, a voice from heaven gives a demon permission to kill Sara's lascivious husband:

> VOZ: Licencia te doy que mates de Sara el lascivo esposo.
> DEMONIO: O precepto venturoso, de esto me huelgo … .

The demon hastens to take advantage of this unprecedented opportunity: "Allá voy; mano, apretad el cuello al lascivo esposo, que le es a Dios enojoso no ver limpieza y verdad. *Han de tratar los casados limpiamente el matrimonio*."[74] This scene of the demon sneaking into the couple's bedroom with God's permission, so that the Archangel Raphael can bind him and hold him over the fire, is illustrated in a sensational contemporaneous painting, *The Marriage Bed of Tobias and Sarah* (ca 1660), created by Jan Steen in what was formerly the Spanish Netherlands (see figure 10).[75]

In the same way that we find married couples worrying over whether their sexual contact might be lustfully sinful or not, we also find grown children in the *comedias* worrying over their parents' chastity or lack thereof. Thus we find the god Cupid in Lope de Vega's *Adonis, y Venus* declaring, "Tengo tan aborrecida la [condición] de mi lasciva madre, y el ver que al cielo mi padre ofenda."[76] He obsesses over what we might call, in the most literal sense possible, the sins of the fathers. These lines recall a contemporaneous classic of world literature, Shakespeare's *Hamlet*, in which the eponymous young prince worries about the (un-) chastity of his mother Gertrude. In this play we find the lines:

> Mother, you have my father much offended …
> Such an act
> That blurs the grace and blush of modesty,
> Calls virtue hypocrite, takes off the rose
> From the fair forehead of an innocent love
> And sets a blister there, makes marriage vows
> As false as dicers' oaths, O, such a deed
> As from the body of contraction plucks
> The very soul, and sweet religion makes
> A rhapsody of words. Heaven's face does glow
> O'er this solidity and compound mass
> With heated visage, as against the doom;
> Is thought-sick at the act.[77]

So we see that concerns of this nature were endemic to the early modern period, and not necessarily confined to Spain or even to what is often caricatured as its especially uptight form of Catholicism.[78] We shall see later in this chapter how the ultimate unknowability of a woman's sexual purity could lead her offspring to practical concerns over inheritance as well as Hamlet's existential angst.

Throughout this book we have been looking at sins as nodes of cultural anxiety, and it is perhaps indicative of the degree of anxiety which Lust attracted that the punishments for this Sin, as documented in both the archive and the repertoire, were more severe than for any other. These might include harsh prison, as in the case of a chaste queen accused of Adultery unjustly: "¡[que] la Reina en duras prisiones viva de esta suerte baldonada de adúltera, y fementida, cuando es de virtud ejemplo!"[79] Or they might involve exile, as when the Queen of France in Lope de Vega's *Ursón y Valentín, hijos del rey de Francia* "fue hallada en adulterio y por el Rey desterrada."[80] Most often the fair punishment for Adultery was determined to be death: "Di, ¿cuando hace un adulterio una mujer no merece la muerte?"[81] Here a *comedia* character seeks affirmation from an interlocutor to support the existing social and moral order. Still, a wedge of doubt is driven into spectators' minds by a character who dares to question the justice of this sentence.

The male party caught in Adultery, if he was a commoner, was destined to suffer the same punishment as the female. As the king reports in Lope de Vega's *La inocente Laura*, "Ya Ricardo el adúltero villano va por los pasos de su justa muerte."[82] Contrary to other, more hypothetical, punishments, this one was really enforced on the stage, even for noble women: "hoy morirá la adúltera Duquesa, hoy morirá."[83] But in particularly heinous cases, mere death was deemed insufficient. Instead, some further indication of her crime's extremity was required: "que quien supo cometer adulterio, es menester que muera desesperada, de todos desamparada."[84] This requirement that the adulterous woman die in despair could be interpreted to mean that she be burned alive: "que la que adúltera sea, la saquen a quemar viva."[85] The male adulterer was to be punished by ripping out his eyes: "la ley compuso, que al adúltero sacasen los ojos."[86] This punishment for Adultery is thematized in Agustín Moreto's *La fuerza de la ley*, in which the king Seleuco institutes this law for the realm but then finds himself obliged to inflict it on his own son Demetrio, whom he has forced to wed a woman he does not love. Recognizing his own responsibility for his son's downfall, he decides to share the punishment with him and thus orders that one eye be removed from each.

But as we see from these examples, the terms of this discussion have shifted ever so subtly; for it is actually Adultery that is being punished in these passages – not Lust. This could simply be due to the fact that Adultery was easier to prove; after all, who could imagine a courtroom where the prosecuting attorney attempted to prove lustful intentions?[87] But it could also indicate a larger shift in cultural mores and expectations such as the one we have been chronicling in this study. Adultery is prohibited in the Sixth Commandment, while Lust is a Deadly Vice; therefore, if we see a transition away from talking about Lust and a move to reframe the discussion in terms of Adultery, the consequences might be interesting for religious and intellectual history. Let's take a look at some of the literary evidence.

In quite a few of the *comedias*, Lust and Adultery appear side by side as nearly equivalent terms: "Descrimen a Venus lasciva, a Marte adúltero."[88] Lust is used interchangeably with Adultery, as in this catalogue of the Ten Commandments: "no tendrás ajeno Dios; ni el nombre jurarás de él; santifícale sus fiestas; honra a quien te ha dado el ser; ni homicida, *ni lascivo seas*; el ajeno bien no envidies; ni quieras de otro la hacienda; ni la mujer."[89] Calderón's auto sacramental *El año santo de Roma* conflates the Seven Deadly Sins and Ten Commandments to the point of invoking a specific Commandment, number Six ("thou shalt not commit Adultery"), but instead referring to it as the precept against Lascivious Love:

> CASTIDAD: [M]i Precepto es contra el Amor Lascivo.
> ALBEDRÍO: Siendo su Precepto el Sexto …[90]

This literary passage, at least, would seem to reflect the kind of historical conflation of the Seven Deadlies with the Decalogue which Homza describes.[91]

Any ultimate verdict on this question would have to be as mixed as the evidence. Even so, there would seem to be a slight shift towards the Commandments and away from the Seven Deadly Sins in the area of sexual morality.[92] We start to see some *comedias* where Adultery is thematized to the near-complete exclusion of Lust. A case in point is Lope de Vega's *La buena guarda*, in which a repentant adulteress laments her past offence. She confesses to the Virgin Mary, the Catholic paragon of chastity, that she is lost: "Con lágrimas lo digo, Virgen bella; adúltera soy ya, yo voy perdida." This already-bad situation is made worse by the fact that she is a nun who used to be the abbess of her monastery. She no longer feels herself worthy to call Christ her Spouse: "sé, Esposo, que me aguardas; Esposo dije; ay de mí, adúltera soy, desata corazón estas dos fuentes." She mourns her betrayal of Christ, her mystical Husband: "La que siempre os ofendió, la adúltera del esposo más honrado, y más hermoso, que el cielo a la tierra dio."[93] Given that this was an age when women were often forced into the convent less out of vocation than out of social or economic necessity, one can only wonder what this same play might have looked like if it had been written from a woman's perspective.

In fact, there are multiple red flags alerting us to the bias of misogyny in these plays about Lust. The same adulterous woman from Lope de Vega's *La buena guarda*, discussed above, actually ends up begging to be punished: "vos me habéis de dar como a adúltera castigo." Another female character in Lope de Vega's *Los Porceles de Murcia* pronounces her own punishment to be just: "mi marido justamente, como a adúltera, e infame, darme la muerte pudiese."[94] Have Spanish women of the theatre internalized this shame, this stigma to the extent that they acknowledge their own culpability? Or are we simply witnessing here, once again, the prevalence of male voices to the detriment and even exclusion of their female counterparts?

A particularly egregious example of misogyny in connection with Adultery which appears in both the archive and the repertoire was the barbarous custom of allowing men to decide a woman's guilt or innocence in a joust. Duelling, sometimes in the form of mounted combat between knights, had been used in the Middle Ages to let God decide who was in the right when it came to Adultery as well as other kinds of disputes.[95] Not surprisingly, vestiges of this medieval world view still linger in the *comedias*, especially those set in a feudalistic context. In Lope de Vega's *El testimonio vengado*, the queen's two sons and their supporters accuse her of Adultery: "os acusan de adulterio."[96] Later these traitors are called upon to sustain their charge in mortal combat: "los reto de traidores, diciendo que te levantan el adulterio que afirman con Sesse, cosa que espanta; aplazóse el desafío."[97] In another play by the same author, Princess Isabela is likewise charged with Adultery. Her accusers are also challenged to prove their claims by placing them before divine arbitration in the form of a joust: "conforme al fuero de Alemania, la mandase prender, y los testigos sustentasen en campo su adulterio." One of the witnesses against her, Rodrigo, insists: “Yo digo que sustento el adulterio.” His interlocutor, Enrique, seems to object to this by-then-rather-quaint idea of proving her guilt or innocence by such an antiquated method. Instead, he appeals to reason: “Si sabes que es verdad, la razón basta.” Nevertheless, her beloved is urged to sally forth to prove her innocence: “el que dice que tu amada Isabela ha sido adúltera, susténtelo en campaña, y no permitas que muera una mujer con inocencia.”[98]

As this old-fashioned means of deciding who was in the right receded into the mists of cultural memory, there arose to take its place in the prevailing discourse a nascent obsession with proof, witnesses, and newfound legalism.[99] With this newly legalistic approach to sin came higher standards regarding the burden of proof, including the call for witnesses, signed documents testifying to what was seen, physical evidence left at the scene of the crime, and so forth.[100] In this new approach to domesticating sin in the early modern period, first came the accusation, accompanied by oaths that the accuser was telling the truth: “la llamó infame, y ramera, y adúltera a su marido, y jurando en mi presencia.”[101] This accusation was often sustained by testimony, as in Lope de Vega’s appropriately named *El testimonio vengado*, where one of the king’s loyal subjects declares openly the queen’s infidelity: “de todos sustento y del Rey … que es adúltera la Reina y la afrento de mil modos.”[102] This testimony often became very public, extending even to the whole empire: “se puso contra mí, contándome el adulterio, que de él se dijo al Imperio.”[103] But the transition to a newly legalized system of dealing with sin was incomplete; at least in some dramatic texts, punishment was meted out merely on the basis of one such witness: “una Reina honrada testigo de este misterio que fue hallada en adulterio y por el Rey desterrada.”[104]

It is of course characteristic of any such transition in intellectual history to find, as we have been noticing, vestiges or residues of the old belief system coexisting side-by-side with the new. The new system, in this case, demanded proof. Increasingly in the *comedias* we find women asserting their right to have the charges brought against them proven or at least corroborated before they are punished. Thus in Lope de Vega’s *Los Porceles de Murcia*, we find the alleged adulteress Lucrecia exclaiming: “Digo que sin más probanza por adúltera me mates.”[105] The assumption of Adultery, in this case, stems from a woman’s bearing twins, or – in this case – septuplets, which were considered divine punishment for fornication. In this play, it turns out that Lucrecia is punished by God for insulting Ángela as an adulteress after Ángela has merely borne twins. In this divine arithmetic, she is made to pay seven times over, and have her own reputation stained, for making unfair assumptions about the other woman’s chastity. This is complex moral arithmetic indeed.

Examples abound of similar instances where characters accuse each other of assuming Adultery without proof. María Mercedes Carrión calls this type of scene "an evidentiary maze that drove spouses to distrust, hypocrisy, suspicion."[106] In Lope de Vega's *El ejemplo de casadas* – a play whose title indicates that it was meant to serve as a mirror of wives, in line with the long-established *mirror of princes* tradition – Enrico says to Fabia: "Quieres tu adulterio ver si no probado, entendido."[107] The play's complete title, *El ejemplo de casadas y prueba de paciencia*, affirms a concern over proof. This proof in the case of Adultery could take many forms, including "cuchillo, cordel, o toca."[108] One very tangible way of proving a woman's involvement with a man other than her husband was thought to be the discovery of letters, tokens, miniature portraits, or other objects exchanged between lovers in the course of their affair. This of course is what happens with Desdemona's handkerchief, embroidered with a distinctive strawberry design, in Shakespeare's *Othello*.[109] In this play, Desdemona loses the handkerchief – which had actually been a gift from her husband, the Moor – only to have it used by Iago to wreak havoc with her marriage. Once the handkerchief is in his possession, he shows it to her jealous spouse in alleged proof of her unfaithfulness. To her peril, this tangible sign proves utterly devastating. To avoid having a similar situation arise, a female character in Juan Pérez de Montalbán's *Teágenes, y Clariquea* seeks a *prenda*, or token, to prove her innocence. As a third party explains to her husband, the wife "temió ser de adulterio convencida, y así por no tenerte sospechoso, otra prenda buscó." In this case the tangible proofs of the truth of the matter include a ring and a handwritten letter.[110] A ring given by King Felisardo to Lucinda similarly proves his seduction and abandonment of her in Lope de Vega's *La fe rompida*. These *prendas* or tokens provided opportunities for effective manipulation of tangible props or visual markers in performance.

Also pertaining to the rhetoric of legalistic proof for criminal behaviour was the word *indicio*, defined by Sebastián de Covarrubias, Spain's foremost Golden Age lexicographer, as "[s]ospecha, la señal, el barrunto, la huella de alguna cosa oculta que se desea saber."[111] Of course, *indicios* could be misleading; and the gulf of ambiguity opened up by this possibility forms the basis for the play *Los indicios sin culpa*, by Juan de Matos Fragoso. In this drama, the indicators are of two kinds: one written in ink, the other written in blood.[112] When Carlos intercepts a letter which persuades him of his sister Porcia's dalliance with Octavio, he comes to her house at night to slaughter both of them. He only succeeds in killing Octavio; but the bloody scene he leaves behind, along with the wounds on her breast inflicted by his sword, form the *indicios* which are later interpreted and misinterpreted by other characters in what could only be described as a Golden Age version of the hit TV series *Crime Scene Investigation*:

AGUADO: Y pues la sangre ves, y no conoces
de qué causa procede, no des voces,
sino Médico experto,
la causa busca, pues el mal es cierto.

ENRIQUE: ¿Cómo?
AGUADO: Por las señales
de aquesta sangre, encontrarás tus males.
ENRIQUE: Toma, Aguado, una vela.[113]

The only substantive difference here between this scene and *CSI* is the use of a candle instead of a flashlight. Later in the same play, when Enrique finds Porcia alive, he interrogates her about his friend Octavio's death in a speech which provides the perfect occasion for one Golden Age playwright's meditation on the inherent ambiguity of *indicios*:

Escucha, Porcia, que soy
como un juez, y de mi agravio,
y de la muerte de Octavio
haciendo la causa estoy;
y es fuerza en estos enojos,
bien que los indicios mientan,
bien que lo contrario sientan,
creer lo que ven los ojos;
que no sirve de consuelo
en las dudas que me abrasan,
saber que en este mundo pasan
por la permisión del Cielo,
que ni culpa, ni disculpa,
ni severo, ni propicio,
muchas culpas sin indicio,
muchos indicios sin culpa,
y aunque tu estés inocente,
y sin culpa en el delito,
hallo contra ti en lo escrito,
información evidente.[114]

This last phrase highlights both the new emphasis on legal evidence and its only evident or apparent nature in the absence of scientific scrutiny. But despite their notorious unreliability, these indicators were nonetheless used routinely to decide matters of grave import, concerning the life or death of the accused parties. In an age without DNA, people had to go with their hunches, or at least with their best efforts to interpret whatever information might be available.

One especially persuasive indicator of a wife's involvement with another man was any plot that might be uncovered to do away with her spouse. This scenario unfolds in Francisco de Rojas Zorrilla's *El profeta falso Mahoma*, in which an adulterous wife poisons her husband: "de aqueste adulterio estaba claro el indicio, le dio veneno a su esposo."[115] Of course, in certain rare cases the offending couple might literally be caught in the act – *in flagrante delicto* being the technical term. This would seem to have happened so infrequently that *comedia* characters are overheard taunting each other with the very absence of this infallible proof:

RUPERTO: ¿Hasme hallado en adulterio?
FLORIS: Basta, tú lo has de pagar.[116]

A husband might even disguise himself with the goal of catching his wife in bed with another man, at times journeying as far away as a different country to do so. As one aggrieved husband confides, "en ir a Francia estoy determinado, que sabré del adúltero sospecho, en otro traje, y con fingido pecho."[117] In some extreme cases the stated goal is to get there in time to kill the offending parties before the act can occur. Apparently successful in this dubious endeavour, Belardo apostrophizes to his sword: "o espada, que al fin deshaces un adúltero concierto."[118]

Failing that, the ultimate proof was judged to be a pregnancy resulting from the alleged Adultery. This scenario takes on particular resonance when the pregnant woman is the Virgin Mary, impregnated by God before the birth of Christ. It will be remembered that even she was accused of Adultery, a highly awkward situation dramatized in Juan Bautista Diamante's *El nacimiento de Cristo*, where an ignorant character says maliciously of her: "estando preñada, probado está el adulterio."[119] As her husband Joseph asks in a different play written about the same subject matter, "¿Mas puede haber engaño en lo visible?" This was evidently spoken at a point when she was already visibly pregnant. A few lines further on, he becomes agitated at the prospect of prosecuting his beloved before the Divine Judge:

mas de haber concebido
la acusan las señales evidentes,
y con grande violencia
vence la confianza la evidencia.
¿Qué haré? ¿Daré piadoso
crédito a lo que vi, o a lo que creo? ...
¿Daré razón del caso
al tribunal supremo, y eminente?
Mas ay, qué penas paso,
¿qué será si castigo una inocente?[120]

Here poor Joseph finds himself in the classic double bind: if he divorces her, then he risks punishing an innocent woman; but if he stays married to her, then his honour will be jeopardized. Other women in Mary's situation, of course, did not have the convenient excuse of an Immaculate Conception to use to cover their tracks.

Ultimately, all of this evidence went before a judge. The *comedias* chronicle the transition from an all-knowing Divine Judge to His very human and fallible counterparts, as we see in an indignant exclamation by a pope accused of Adultery: "a mí me acusaron al Imperio, como si fuera mi Juez humano, no menos que de infamia de adulterio. ¡A qué no llega el pensamiento humano!"[121] The secular judges presiding over these cases were in fact all too human; and in the absence of modern science, one wonders how many of the verdicts they handed down must have been inaccurate. But the transition from Divine Judge to human judges also bespeaks a concomitant shift in underlying world view. Namely, the issue in question is: at what point does a *sin* become a *crime*?[122]

This tension reverberates throughout Agustín Moreto's *La fuerza de la ley*, one of the first instances I have found in the *comedias* in which Adultery is referred to as a crime instead of a sin. The words "crime of Adultery" are presented in an explicitly legal context: "preso por haber incurrido en el crimen de adulterio, está sentenciado en vista en la pena de la Ley."[123] It is also worth noting that the accused here is a man. Perhaps with a more rigidly secular, legal approach to human misconduct there was an auxiliary shift away from the double standard as far as gender.[124] We shall look at this in greater detail below.

This of course does not mean that – in the same theoretical terms we have invoked repeatedly throughout this study – the residue of consciousness of sin does not endure well into the early modern period. Indeed, the same era which produced Banquo's nightmare of the bloody dagger, the sure sign of a guilty conscience in Shakespeare's *Macbeth*,[125] also produced such telling lines as these, from Lope de Vega's *La buena guarda*: "dormí mal aquella noche, imaginando la espada del cielo sobre mi cuello del adulterio en venganza." At this point an extraordinary thing happens – the guilty sinner enters a church and imagines that the crucifix turns its back on him:

Fuime a la Iglesia otro día,
que aún no era bien de mañana,
y quitándole el sombrero
a un Crucifijo que estaba
sobre los arcos del claustro,
le vi volver las espaldas …
Erízaseme el cabello
de imaginar tales ansias
como entonces recibí …
No me atreví a hablar Carrizo,
ni a oír Misa.[126]

This ghoulish nightmare of a knife hanging over one's head or a crucifix miraculously turning its back affords powerful testimony to the psychological sensation of guilt perpetuated by the sins of the fathers.

We also see a tension between divine and secular authority in the reasoning of some characters who see a rift between the two. Thus we hear a character philosophizing, in Tirso de Molina's *Escarmientos para el cuerdo*, that God is the founder of the true law: "Dios fundó el derecho verdadero." This character uses this first principle as the basis upon which to build a case accusing another character, Manuel, of Adultery. He speaks to Manuel's first wife: "y así infiero, que es adúltero Manuel para con él, casado con vos primero."[127]

But if there is a tension between secular and divine authority, it would almost seem that worldly powers win out upon the *comedia* stage. Besides obsessing over Lust as a Sin, early modern Spanish theatrical characters seem far more worried about potential stains on their honour. In fact, given a choice between criminality and loss of social standing, early modern Spaniards seem to choose the latter as the greater evil: "ilícito amor, adulterando la Ley, adultera también de esperado Esposo el Honor."[128] In cases of Adultery, both guilty parties' honour was said to be affected: "me va el honor tuyo, siendo mi honor mismo, con adulterio y agravio incurro en el mismo duelo."[129] As we have seen earlier from evidence in the archives, the likely punishment for dishonour was death, often burning at the stake; and this historical reality likewise makes its appearance in the theatrical repertoire. For example, we read the lines "muera la que mi honra deshace y vitupera. ¡Ah, Casandra lasciva, cruel Casandra, digna siempre de arder en mayor fuego!"[130] But the significant thing about Spanish notions of honour as reflected in the theatre is that even if you kill the guilty party, the dishonour to one's name still lives: "Si yo a mi hija mataba, como adúltera y lasciva, dejaba deshonra viva, que para siempre duraba."[131]

To reflect this excruciatingly harsh moral and social reality, a stronger word was needed even than *dishonour*. That word was *infamy*. In an essay for the collection *Sexo barroco*, Francisco Tomás y Valiente offers a useful definition of this term which highlights its special relevance for the current study: "infamia propiamente dicha … es decir, que la pena del delito … se traslade hereditariamente a los descendientes del delincuente."[132] In confirmed cases of Adultery in the drama, a common word used to describe its deleterious effects on the family in question is *infamy* or one of its derivatives, as in "Mi casa habéis infamado con vuestro lascivo amor" or "una hija de vuestro Conde se infama de adúltera."[133] The steps of the adulterer are seen by one king as tracing a path to his infamy: "Parece que las pisadas del adúltero me avisan, que sus plantas viles pisan de mi infamia las moradas."[134] Often the words *infamy* and *honour* are uttered together, as if with one breath: "Suelta, adúltera, resuelta en la infamia de mi honor."[135] This newly emphasized concept of infamy is explicitly thematized in Juan de la Cueva's

El Infamador. In this play, which in some ways anticipates Tirso's Don Juan character in *El burlador de Sevilla*, Leucino attempts to ruin the reputation of Eliodora, a woman who has resisted his amorous advances.[136] He realizes that her infamy will be the best retaliation for his own humiliation. Her family is in fact so devastated by his accusations against her that her father attempts to poison his own daughter in order to repair his tattered honour.[137] Of course, such infamous affronts to one's reputation must be suitably avenged. As another of Tirso's aggrieved characters warns, "Si saliere de noche Ludovico, el adúltero infame que me afrenta, verás de mis agravios la venganza."[138]

Now, we should be clear on this point: what is at stake here is the public reputation of a person or a family, not that person's internal integrity. The classic though loose distinction of *honor* vs *honra* – with *honor* referring to a person's internal, personal morality, versus the social category of *honra*, the fate of which lies in the hands and mouths of others – goes back at least as far as the ancient Greeks, who distinguished between *aretē*, or personal honour, and *timē*, or social reputation.[139] The *comedias* show nefarious instances of adulterers sneaking around, often trusting erroneously that they will not be found out: "[persiste] el adúltero en fiarse, que podrá del secreto socorrerse."[140] There is even the intimation in the *comedias* that the sin itself is not so bad, as long as it remains a secret: "cuando es secreto el adulterio, no viene a ser con tanto vituperio."[141] Even the accusation of Adultery – regardless of whether it was justified – could result in a permanent loss of honour to the accused, as we see in Juan Ruiz de Alarcón's appropriately named drama *La crueldad por el honor*: "pues aunque allí no cometiese Bermudo adulterio, la opinión es del honor el verdugo."[142] But as we see in this passage, in the theatrical repertoire at least, opinion is ultimately what matters, a tendency which may in fact have kept Spaniards locked in to a medieval, communal world view. If the Ten Commandments were seen as placing a greater emphasis on the individual, that shift in emphasis could only be embraced by hypothetical Spaniards who were not too busy worrying about the opinions of others. It would take many more generations before this residue of medieval mentality disappeared.

But aside from questions of religious or theological emphasis, Lust also raised pre-eminently practical concerns. These were such pressing issues as legitimacy of children and the bequeathing of inheritance. In the early modern period more than now, bastardy was dangerous because it threatened to overturn the natural order. We see this clearly in Tirso de Molina's nightmarish *La república al revés*. In this dramatic enactment of a familiar Baroque trope, the upside-down world,[143] an aggrieved father bemoans his daughter's pregnancy with a bastard child: "¡Adúltera Carola, cielo injusto! ¡Carola de un adúltero preñada!"[144] An adulterous woman, through her illegitimate progeny, was seen to leave a stain on the family's bloodline. Where royal families were concerned, and sons stood to inherit entire kingdoms, blood purity became even more of an issue. As the King of France says to the queen in Lope de Vega's *Ursón y Valentín, hijos del rey de Francia*, "Agradece, infame mala, que aquesa adúltera planta en tu sangre no resbala."[145] In the same dramatist's *La campana de Aragón*, a queen stands to lose the entire realm of Aragon after being accused of Adultery: "estando el Rey en la guerra, de adulterio la acusaron; tuvo a Aragón por herencia."[146]

In pragmatic terms, a bastard son, particularly the product of incest, was not legally allowed to receive an inheritance: "no legitima la ley al que de incesto ha nacido."[147] The one exception to this was if the father took legal action to legitimize his bastard son, as Christopher Columbus did – acting through the Spanish legal system, since the woman involved was Spanish – with his illegitimate son Hernando Colón.[148] This is what happens in Juan de Matos Fragoso's *Los indicios sin culpa*, where the aging Don Diego acknowledges his illegitimate son Enrique and promises finally to wed the boy's mother, Madama Clori, so that he will have the legal right to inherit his father's estate.[149] In the *comedias*, we also see a mother worrying to her bastard son over the fate of his inheritance if her Adultery comes to light through the indiscretion of a dying grandfather: "abuelo tan necio, que en la muerte me declara por adúltera, y a ti del justo derecho aparta de legítimo heredero."[150] Perhaps an even worse ignominy fell upon the child whose paternity remained unknown: "O tú, adúltero aborto, de quien el nacimiento no se sabe."[151]

This paranoid fear of disorder is voiced in the *comedias* in a couple of extreme cases where playwrights were granted cultural licence to compile aggregate portraits of ultimate villains. Among their other perceived failings, both Muhammad and the Antichrist were viewed originally as bastard children. There is a long tradition of bastardy among villains, the logic of which dictates that the natural product of a morally depraved act will exhibit similar depravity.[152] In this way, pagan idols were seen as the mere bastards of their gods: "Adúltero hijo de Bael, que en uno, y otro Metal forma."[153] While children conceived out of wedlock might not always show evidence of physical deformity – of which contemporaneous *relaciones de sucesos* loved to publish pictures circulating in all their tabloidesque detail (see figure 11)[154] – they were thought to be trapped in an inescapable cycle of moral monstrosity.[155]

Spain's confessional prejudices at this time dictated, of course, that one of these bastard-villains be Muhammad. In Rojas Zorrilla's *El profeta falso Mahoma*, the prophet himself details his monstrous lineage: "Emina forzó mi madre, estando su esposo vivo; de aquesta adúltera junta, de este incestuoso delirio, se halló mi madre preñada." He later concludes that his own sin of Adultery repeats that of his mother: "he sido adúltero hijo de aquella homicida."[156] In Juan Ruiz de Alarcón's *El Anticristo*, another arch-villain is seen to be the dastardly product of an incestuous union. Another character asks him in exasperation, "¿no te bastó ser parto incestuoso de el que, siendo tu abuelo, fue tu padre?" Just in case we missed it the first time, this complicated relationship is reiterated in the same play: "Tú, fuiste de tu abuelo padre y tío, abominable incestuoso efecto." The Antichrist's own mother speaks unlovingly of this bastard within her womb: "en mi vientre creció el agravio mío a publicar por fuerza mi secreto." The man with whom she committed this incest, a character named Manzer, ends up being stoned in punishment: "Pues este (no os engañe) incestuoso hijo fue de Manzer, que fue apedreado en castigo."[157]

But this case is unusual in more ways than one. For starters, women seem to have been punished for Adultery far more often than men. As mentioned earlier, whether this tendency is attributable to misogyny on the part of male playwrights or to women's internalization of cultural scripts passed down to them by their mothers and grandmothers, Lust does appear to take on disproportionately feminine characteristics in the theatrical repertoire. Part of this undoubtedly has to do with dictates of subgenre within the playwrights' source material; for example, when Lope de Vega adapted Bandello's novella about the Duchess of Amalfi and shaped it into a tragedy, or when Andrés Antonio Sánchez de Villamayor wrote *La mujer fuerte, asombro de los desiertos, penitente y admirable Santa María Egipciaca*, drawing upon medieval hagiography.[158] It would be logical to assume that earlier attitudes towards Lust may have been incorporated by dramatists along with borrowed source material. For instance, one parent in the *comedias* echoes the warnings of Proverbs, where a young man is advised to avoid the evil temptress: "deja esa vana mujer, y su lascivo comercio. Deja, hijo de mi vida, el vano amor."[159] Another, echoing the moralists, refers to a lascivious woman's amorous fire, so powerful that it prostrates and captivates its unwitting male victim.[160]

Now, in all fairness, this pattern may also be partially attributable to demographic trends. It is a fact that during this period, Spanish men were often absent from their homes for extended periods of time. Whether exploring or settling "New" World territories, fighting as mercenaries in European wars, or governing Spain's provinces in the Netherlands, Portugal, or southern Italy, Spain's menfolk were often the proverbial absentee landlords. Their absence logically led to concern over their wives' faithfulness back at home. In one play, Albano asks Flora: "¿luego tú adúltera has sido, ausente de tu marido?"[161] This potential danger could extend to queens as well as their female subjects, as with one queen who "estando el Rey en la guerra, de adulterio la acusaron."[162] In fact, the phrase *adúltera en ausencia* became synonymous with women who took advantage of their husbands' absence to make the proverbial hay: "lágrima no llora, es falsa, es fiera, es traidora, es adúltera en ausencia."[163] It is perhaps no accident that in contemporaneous emblem books, Occasio appears as a female (see figure 12). This figure is typically recognized by her exaggerated forelock, which a knowing man will seize in the spirit of carpe diem.[164]

In a deliberate move of *captatio benevolentiae* aimed at male theatregoers, some playwrights even offered juicy tips for how to tell if one's wife has been unfaithful;

for example, "que la adúltera casada de su dueño está quejosa."[165] On the flip side, wives with absent husbands in the *comedias* worry that they will be accused unjustly: "no diga mi esposo ausente, que fui adúltera, y me maten."[166] One can only wonder whether audience members, both male and female, might have picked up from these plays certain strategies they found useful for solving their own moral dilemmas. In this way the *comedias* truly would have functioned, as Lope de Vega prescribed that they should, as a *speculum vitae*.[167]

* * * * *

In conclusion, we might say that Lust remained relevant as a cultural category, but also became more secularized as sin became redefined or domesticated as a crime. As such, it pertains to the residue of the medieval mindset which saw sin as more social or communal in nature. This is particularly true in the case of Adultery, with which Lust was often conflated, because it produced a stain of dishonour upon one's family in the eyes of the community. Ironically, the nascent secularization of the legal system did not necessarily result in a rejection of medieval paradigms.

However, this chapter chronicles several important steps of the inexorable march towards modernity. It could even be said that the transition towards the Decalogue – evidenced by the privileging of the concrete act of Adultery over some amorphous notion of Lust – resulted in a greater interiority available to Spanish subjects. This enhanced opportunity for subjectivity might result from a tacit acknowledgment that feelings without actions were difficult to legislate or prosecute, and private emotion should not be intruded upon. In this sense, the account here presented offers a concrete example of a Deadly Sin which potentially defies strict classification as a more communal Vice.

In fact, we might well begin to question at this point whether Bossy's whole scheme is too simplistic. Are all of the Ten Commandments really geared towards individuals? Or perhaps only the first three? Are the Seven Deadly Sins really so communal after all? This one scholar's totalizing, reductionist argument – accepted unquestioningly by many scholars of religion – begs for further nuance. We shall return to some of these questions in this book's conclusion and epilogue. For now, let it suffice to say that Lust is the last of the Seven Deadly Sins to remain relevant to early modern Spain in its (un)adulterated form. We shall see in the next section how three of its counterparts underwent a radical cultural transformation or metamorphosis.

PART TWO

Transformation

4
Loath to Call It Sloth: The Plus Side of *Pereza*

No es el ocio delito donde el descanso es primor.

– Juan Bautista Diamante, loa for *Alfeo, y Aretusa*

El descanso de hoy, quizás será pereza mañana.

– Pedro Calderón de la Barca, *El gran príncipe de Fez*[1]

With this chapter we inaugurate the second section of this book, "Transformation," which will look at three more of the Seven Deadly Sins in various phases of cultural evolution. In the first section, "Residue," we examined Pride, Greed, and Lust as holdovers from a more medieval and hence possibly more communal way of viewing vice. Now we shall turn to Sloth, Gluttony, and Anger as symptomatic of still-largely-intact capital offences, but with some surprising and often fascinating variations. As we recall from previous discussions of concepts such as *dominant*, *residual*, and *emergent*, medieval organizational categories for moral thought did not disappear in the early modern period; instead, they came to be dealt with in increasingly ingenious ways. Raymond Williams calls the next phase of this process of cultural change *incorporation*:

> A residual cultural element is usually at some distance from the effective dominant culture, but some part of it, some version of it – and especially if the residue is from some major area of the past – will in most cases have had to be incorporated if the effective dominant culture is to make sense in these areas. Moreover, at certain points the dominant culture cannot allow too much residual experience and practice outside itself, at least without risk. It is in the incorporation of the actively residual – by reinterpretation, dilution, projection, discriminating inclusion and exclusion – that the work of the selective tradition is especially evident.[2]

The processes he describes – "reinterpretation, dilution, projection, discriminating inclusion and exclusion" – seem to me equally well served by the term *transformation.* In this eminently messy narrative, some of the Vices persisted while others drifted out of the picture. Still others suffered change to the point of being altered until they were almost unrecognizable. It is to this phenomenon that we shall turn now as we begin our exploration of the next three of the Seven Deadly Sins.

* * * * * * *

The Latin term for Sloth, *acedia*, becomes alternatively *ocio* or *pereza* in the Spanish, two terms which are explicitly connected in the *comedias*.[3] While laziness is considered natural to man, it is nevertheless a foolish, vile, infamous, and barbaric enemy which flees from work and must be fought: "es en nuestra naturaleza el ocio de la pereza gran contrario."[4] It is a base weakness or brutish negligence which must be overcome or left behind.[5] It is a waste of time, a frivolous distraction which is in fact doubly culpable.[6] It makes one's life useless and worthless.[7] Allegorical images used to convey the negative valences of Sloth include a millstone of lead around one's neck ("el plomo de la pereza").[8] Sloth inspires its victims to procrastinate and causes great inconvenience.[9] It delivers one into the hands of deception.[10] It delays both departures and arrivals and generally detains progress.[11] It produces sins of omission rather than commission.[12]

Sloth causes one to fall slack with his walking pace, as when the allegorical figure of Pereza declares in an *auto sacramental*, "Pues yo del paso me quito," or when a *comedia* character notices of two others, "¡Jesús, y con la pereza que entrambos mueven las plantas!"[13] It inspires digressions from one's proposed route and unplanned stops along the way.[14] It destroys people's good intentions and reinforces their bad habits.[15] The allegorical figure of Pereza appears in one of the *autos* dressed as a leper covered with sores, a graphic image explained later in the same dramatic work as representing the person who is paralysed by sin.[16] Alternatively it is pictured as a set of hydra's heads which grow back as soon as they are cut off.[17] Its progeny is a poison[18] which produces lethargy in both lips and legs.[19] As sluggish as the donkey, it causes fatigue.[20] It sinks one into profound sleep for exaggerated time spans lasting as long as thirty weeks.[21] The vile sleep of Sloth causes one not to want to get out of bed.[22] It makes people stay the same for fifty years: "con vida torpe y ociosa … estén así cincuenta años."[23] Associated with Lethe and oblivion, Sloth is an infamous tomb: "hoy yacen en el infame sepulcro de la pereza."[24] It is thus suitably depicted using images of stagnation and decay. Sloth changes a person into a mass of worms: "que corrompido, y deshecho te le convierta en Gusanos la pereza de tu afecto."[25]

The medieval system of feudalism exhorted workers to be industrious. "Don't be lazy!' – thus went the familiar moralistic harangue. The *comedias* certainly contain such warnings as, "El que vive libremente vida estragada, y ociosa … muere como ha vivido."[26] The title of this play is derived from a familiar proverb meaning "good riddance," *Con su pan se lo coma*. In some of these dramas, Sloth appears as the direct enemy or opponent of virtue: "en fin el ocio la virtud destierra."[27] The pedagogical *autos sacramentales* in particular were in the business of exhorting Christians to fight the urge to stay in bed ("has de llevar oponiendo a Pereza Diligencia"), using as a weapon against it qualities considered to be its mirror opposites, namely vigilance and care.[28] They of course offered the appropriate carrot along with this stick – that is, the promise that those who succeeded in conquering Sloth would thereby achieve happiness: "no es más lograr la dicha que vencer a la Pereza."[29] These allegorical, deliberately dogmatic works by and large insist that God is offended by Sloth: "Dios, ofendido de la dormida pereza en que vivimos, piadoso con sus ruidos nos despierta."[30] At times these injunctions take on overtly misogynistic tones, as for example with the male playwright's assertion that "pues en algo esta mujer, si está ociosa, ha de ocuparse."[31] On this point, the moralists and some male playwrights seem to have agreed: women were expected to keep their hands busy with sewing or embroidery – anything to avoid being idle.[32]

But Sloth was not exclusively a feminine Vice; the charge of laziness was also a familiar complaint by female characters against their husbands.[33] Nor was it, evidently, limited to secular life. Monks and nuns were expected not to sit still for a moment ("Que … este Fraile no sepa estar ocioso un instante, que la túnica remienda"), and especially not to delay in fulfilling their vows.[34] The result for the early modern Spanish psyche, at least as reflected in the theatre, was a self-imposed diligence – one might even say surveillance – immediately recognizable to readers of Michel Foucault's *Discipline and Punish*.[35] Counter-Reformation injunctions against Sloth had been internalized to the extent that the character Belisa could say in Lope de Vega's play about her, "Tráeme luego labor, no me vean tan ociosa."[36] Work was endowed with moral qualities almost (though anachronistically) anticipatory of Max Weber's Protestant work ethic.[37]

But in typical Renaissance fashion, Sloth's antagonists combined moralistic attacks with arguments which appealed to reason and pragmatism. Renaissance medicine condoned an active life, that is, physical exercise, as part of the regimen for maintaining good health. Thus physical activity was prescribed in Tirso de Molina's *El amor médico* as a remedy for lovesickness: "Guardarse de estar ociosa, hacer mediano ejercicio, y echar a parte congojas."[38] Conversely, laziness prevented one from becoming physically and spiritually robust: "poco robusto para el mismo gusto está flaco, y perezoso."[39]

Viewed as both a personal and a social disease, *Pereza* targeted primarily two age groups: youths and old men. Youths were considered to be particularly prone to Sloth's seduction, which could cause young men to shipwreck if they were not careful.[40] Then as now, it was a perpetual challenge to keep young people occupied ("dar qué hacer al ocio de la juventud lozana"), it being almost impossible to "entretener sin ocio la juventud."[41] This difficulty applied especially to students who did not attend to their studies or went on vacation, with their resulting ignorance also being referred to as lazy: "cuán perezosa tu ignorancia reposa en su bárbaro olvido."[42] At the opposite end of the age spectrum, Sloth was depicted allegorically as an old man with a cane. He was so tired that he did not even walk towards that which was good.[43] The *comedias* pass scathing judgment on old men such as this, asserting that it would be better for them to die than to become old and lazy.[44]

A further negative valence of Sloth in the *comedias* may not be immediately obvious to the non-Renaissance specialist. Beginning at least in medieval times, the Deadly Sin of Sloth was also associated with a humoural imbalance known as melancholy. As described in *The Noonday Demon*, this malady was understood as roughly the equivalent of what we might refer to as clinical depression.[45] This is an association carried over into the *comedias*. In these plays, Sloth is connected in a general way to sadness (as in "es ocioso el dolor, y el sentimiento es ocioso"), which is said to be a monster that devours human lives.[46] But it is also connected specifically to melancholy by name, as in "el ocio suele causar melancolía y tormento."[47]

Melancholy was thought to be caused, among other contributing factors, by too much empty time; it was problematic to "entretener la pena, y melancolía, que el temor, y el ocio cría."[48] This melancholy produced by Sloth is described in the *comedias* as a mortal illness: "es una melancolía, y una enfermedad mortal. Es el ocio suspensión, en que está el mismo sentido sin moverse detenido."[49] As explained by scholars of humoural medicine, melancholy was considered to be a particular danger for monks and nuns because their solitary way of life was conducive to loneliness and depression. This association, too, is carried over into these plays, especially in the numerous hagiographical *comedias de santos*. The titular saint of Juan Bautista Diamante's *Santa María Magdalena de Pazzi* declares that Sloth has turned her into an inert lump: "me tiene como una masa." She reiterates in what modern-day psychologists would recognize as the catatonic (as opposed to the agitated) form of the illness, "con qué pereza … voy a lo que antes deseaba tanto."[50]

But melancholy is not limited in the *comedias* to saintly figures. At one point, a *comedia* character refers to another as "en tu tristeza ocupada, y en tu ocupación ociosa."[51] Of course, melancholy also appears with special relevance in the pastoral landscape, such as Agustín Moreto's *La fingida Arcadia*, one of whose characters declares, "Aprovecharme procuro de aquel ocioso desvelo, en que las tristezas mías … me pusieron."[52] Sad lingering over the memory of past loves, as well as pining away for the absent beloved, were considered the sine qua non of pastoral as a genre. If

Sloth still bore some negative moral valences in early modern Spain, it also served as a necessary precondition for the creation of much of its best literature.[53]

* * * * * *

The apparent sublimation of Sloth via absorption into the pastoral world now offers us an appropriate segue towards thinking about some of its more positive valences.[54] In its positive construction, Sloth may appear at first as a guilty pleasure, as in "que la felicidad nos tuviese en ocio envueltos, y el ocio en vicios."[55] Here we note that Sloth is still mentioned in the context of Vice. But soon we begin to notice references to Sloth as something rather to be enjoyed: "De este, pues, ocio apacible gozaba yo, ya lo sabes."[56] Sloth is depicted as a solace for life's disappointments: "el sosiego blando del ocio dormido" and "gozando el solaz de mi poltrona pereza."[57] In fact, Sloth is portrayed as a continual solace: "Pereza … en continuo solaz de Juegos, Bailes, y Amores."[58] In its less hedonistic form, Sloth can be used simply as a synonym for rest, although this characterization may sound as spurious as the character's name which appears next to it: "Espurio, que el descanso, y ocio ama."[59] But as we read further, we cannot help but notice the *comedias* insisting that Sloth is sometimes acceptable: "¡Qué quietud tan misteriosa! ¡Toda la humana tarea es primoroso descanso!"[60]

Particularly after harsh labour, the entire planet rests: "el Planeta hermoso ausente, a los trabajos da reposo, con lasciva licencia se mezcle el apetito y la insolencia."[61] After a hard day's work, men all over the world give themselves over to delicious leisure: "Los diurnos trabajos reparando, los hombres al sabroso ocio entregándose."[62] When a worker is tired, he treats himself to an appropriate amount of rest: "Si cansado me siento, feliz a la fatiga el ocio iguala, pues un templado viento me consuela, me alivia."[63] One can almost picture the speaker of these lines swinging contentedly in his hammock.

In this iteration, Sloth offers repose for the body and rest for the feet:

> PIMIENTA: Y pues ya al cansancio pide que déis al cuerpo reposo, aquí puede a los cuidados hurtar instantes el ocio.
>
> MULEY: Bien dice, Daraja mía, descansen tus pies.[64]

Sloth is the place where not just the body, but also the soul's ambition, rests: "con tanto empeño descansar la ambición en ocio, y sueño."[65] We find lines invoking the peaceful tranquillity of candlelight meditation, which of course must be enjoyed alone in sweet silence: "en el dulce silencio, sin ocupación se mira, de *un ocio, que no es defecto*."[66] We should note that here an early modern Spanish playwright chooses to cast Sloth defensively in terms of a positive moral judgment.

Sloth indulges an appetite for sweet delights: "delicias, que patria son del descanso, y el ocio."[67] It invites one to deep sleep upon soft beds of embroidered sheets and downy pillows:

LAURINO: Aquí tu almohadilla tienes.
MATILDE: ¿Que ociosa, Rosela, vienes?[68]

Here *lazy* seems more the equivalent of *tired*. The slothful person is portrayed as free of cares ("ocioso, libre, y sin ningún cuidado"), for all his powers are delivered into the hands of rest.[69] The lazy individual is free even of all thought: "no es mal don el ocio a quien no piensa."[70]

Once again, it will come as no surprise to Renaissance specialists to find connections between and among Sloth, melancholy, and romantic love.[71] We find in the *comedias* numerous references to Sloth in an amorous context, such as "me agrada, señora, la paz del ocio amoroso."[72] Love is said to thrive where there is leisure to pursue it; and in this way, Sloth acts as an incubator for sweet fantasy.[73] Even where it is not directly responsible for igniting the flames of amorous passion, leisure time nonetheless opens the door to such activities: "Entra por el ocio amor tirano de las potencias."[74]

This association goes back at least as far as classical antiquity, to characterizations of the god Cupid as a plump cherub who loafed around shooting arrows at the hearts of unsuspecting humans. Cupid, too, makes a cameo appearance in numerous *comedias*, where he is invoked as "amor, ociosa deidad" and "mi amor … ese dios ocioso."[75] Antonio de Solís's *El amor al uso* refers to the experience of being in love as "esta ociosa prisión de ese Dios rapaz." In the same play, a character resolves not to succumb once more to love's lazy captivity: "de no enamorarme … pienso redimir mi libertad de este ocioso cautiverio."[76] In a similar vein, in Lope de Vega's *El Amor enamorado*, a character addresses Cupid directly, accusing him of deliberately targeting those who are lazy: "Los que te acogen son hombres desocupados, que viven en ocio torpe."[77] The Golden Age was prime time for courtiers, the epitome of these *hombres desocupados*.

It stands to reason that scenarios of courtly love are most often spun out in the context of the royal court. The *comedias* make frequent reference to "el afecto amoroso de algún Caballero ocioso."[78] They even allude specifically to the seat of the Hapsburg empire in Madrid: "ya en Madrid cortesano su amor mano sobre mano, gastase ocioso los días."[79] At the royal palace as well as in private houses at the capital, courtiers sat upon chairs and entertained one another discreetly, whiling away the lazy hours: "silla tienes en esta sala sin falta para cuando estés ocioso, y yo a manera de dama, que te entretenga discreta."[80] As tokens of their affection, they exchanged portraits, which incidentally also had to be painted while the subject was sitting still.[81] Paradoxically, popular songs exhorted lovers – in the spirit of carpe diem – *not* to be idle, but instead to seize the day to enjoy their love while they could.[82] This conflicting advice must have left more than one early modern lover confused.

* * * * * *

In the 1960s, the hippies used to say, "make love, not war." Early modern Spaniards seem to have anticipated this injunction. In the *comedias*, repeatedly, we find the "ocio de la paz" contrasted with the "furor de la milicia."[83] In fact, leisure is equated with peacetime: "Quien dice paz, dice ocio."[84] In Calderón's *El lirio y la azucena*, we find this illuminating exchange between Paz and Ocio:

> PAZ: ¿Quién tengo yo que me haga compañía?
> OCIO: Quien irá a la Paz siguiendo, para vivir descansado.

In this same work, Spain's happy peace is contrasted with another unnamed country's state of turmoil: "Ocio, y Paz juntos salieron de otra Patria."[85] As an added affirmation, Ocio confirms to Paz as they walk along together, "juntos hemos de ir, puesto que no hay Ocio, donde hay Guerra." The current, albeit temporary, peace of the realm means that warships can be disarmed: "Bien podéis desarmar vuestras galeras, que en ocio, amor, y sueño sepultado, su vida pasa."[86] The prophet Isaiah's comforting words predicting a future era when swords would be transformed into ploughshares seem to have found curious resonance for playwrights in Golden Age Spain.[87]

In historical plays such as Lope de Vega's *El último godo*, alternatively titled *El postrer godo de España*, Spain looked back in its history to a mythical, idyllic time of peace before the Muslim conquest – itself a memory now receding into the mist: "en la paz hermosa, estaba la gente ociosa." In this same play, a character remarks nostalgically: "esta tierra ha mucho que está sin guerra perezosa paz gozando."[88] At various points during the period in which these plays were being written, Spain was once again peaceful: "Y así mientras ocio, y paz tenga España."[89] But Spain was at peace not necessarily for all the right reasons, in the judgment of some of her playwrights, who lamented that she could not afford to fight wars when she was busy fighting plagues and other domestic crises at home: "alma quieta, y vida ociosa piden tiempos apestados."[90] This tension is thematized in Juan Bautista Diamante's appropriately titled *Triunfo de la paz, y el tiempo*, one of whose characters invokes Morpheus as the god of rest: "Morfeo, que custodia de la paz lisonjera en su ocioso descanso tienes la preeminencia."[91] But of course Morpheus morphs, the sleeping tiger wakes up, and Spain must return to war once again. As the king says to one of his warriors in Lope de Vega's *El mayorazgo dudoso*, "apenas gozas la paz de aquesta tu amada tierra, ocio, descanso, y solaz, cuando en volver a la guerra estás."[92]

When Spanish soldiers became impatient with peace, they made war ("¿Qué aguardas? Pues la gente ya de ociosa [vida] impaciente, con ánimo Cristiano vencer espera"), brandishing their swords and lances in bloodthirsty anticipation of the battle ahead.[93] As we might expect, the discourse of honour quickly became a part of this discussion. One character expresses his impatience to fight, precisely in terms of rejecting Sloth: "No puedo tener la espada en ocio, porque envainada no da honor, antes afrenta."[94] In the old warrior ethos, nobility precluded idleness: "que no sufre la [espada] que es noble estar ociosa en la vaina."[95] The epic warrior of classical antiquity was exhorted to leave the comforts of home for the battlefield: "Dejad, dejad la pereza, las armas toma en las manos, acórdaos que sois Romanos."[96] During the Golden Age period of Conquest and Reconquest, the early modern Spanish soldier was similarly urged to take up his sword once again: "levantar, señor y saca luego la espada, que tenían envainada ocio, descanso, y amor."[97] War games were specifically prescribed as an antidote to courtly boredom: "Ninguna cosa destierra tanto el ocio, ni parece al trabajo de la guerra."[98]

But despite all this hawkish chest beating, we are left in the *comedias* with the inescapable impression that many early modern courtiers simply refused to fight. On the most literal level, they commanded each other to abandon their swords: witness Angélica's "ten la espada ociosa" or Don Quijote's "Básteos el ocio, armas mías."[99] Despite the fact that Sloth was frequently equated with cowardice ("pereza, y cobardía" and "tu ocio cobarde"),[100] we witness a deliberate recasting of the decision not to go to war as merely the suspension of valour. As we see in Lope de Vega's appropriately named *Contra valor no hay desdicha*, "ociosa la Majestad tendrá suspenso el valor."[101] Valour could similarly be said to be sleeping ("estoy en las caricias del ocio, adormecido el valor").[102] While valour slept, the use of arms was suspended, or – as Derrida would have it – deferred, in an infinite postponement of the business of warfare.[103] It was replaced instead with the leisure of joyous feasting: "nos tiene el uso suspenso de las Armas, dispensando el ocio de los festejos."[104]

In its more chaste, less hedonistic version, this rejection of the old warrior ethos could also find expression in the mystical *vida retirada*. This trope appears often in hagiographical dramas. For example, in Tirso de Molina's comedia de santos *Los lagos de san Vicente*, Don Tello seeks "la soledad ociosa, y la tierra de suyo tan fragosa."[105] The seeming paradox of saintly Sloth is thematized most saliently in Lope de Vega's *San Isidro labrador de Madrid*. The stage version follows traditional hagiography in dramatizing the life of Isidro, a lowly field hand whose extraordinary devotion is rewarded by divine assistance with his labours. His boss Juan de Vargas becomes outraged at rumours that Isidro is neglecting his fields due to the fact that he spends all his time in church: "va al campo a mediodía, que pasa una vida ociosa … [a] sombra de hacerse santo." As the plot unfolds, the boss interrogates two other labourers, Lorenzo and Esteban, to try to figure out what is going on:

JUAN: ¿Eso pasa de mi hacienda?
ESTEBAN: Esto es lo menos que pasa.
JUAN: Buen labrador tengo en casa,
  a buen dueño se encomienda.
LORENZO: ¿A las diez a trabajar?
[ESTEBAN]: A las diez, y a mediodía.
JUAN: ¿Medrará la hacienda mía?
ESTEBAN: Ha dado Isidro en holgar.
  Y no ha sido mala traza,
  la que rezar ha tenido,
  pues con ser Santo fingido,
  andarse holgando disfraza.
  ¿Quién le mete a un labrador,
  más que en servir?
JUAN: Y dices bien.
LORENZO: Todos murmuran también,
  que se pierde tu labor.
  Los mozos, que arando están,
  de esa parte del molino,
  como es el campo vecino,
  y antes que amanezca van.
  Espántanse de mirar,
  con la pereza que baja,
  pues cuando Isidro trabaja,
  ya vuelven de trabajar.
  Échale de tu servicio.

The irony, of course, is that Juan's fields look better than ever because angels have been sent to plough them in Isidro's absence. Once he realizes what has been happening, far from firing Isidro, the boss instead rewards him with – you guessed it – a day off.[106]

But aspiring saints were not the only ones to seek out-of-the-way places where they could rest. In fact, in the *comedias* an ideal restful place – the classical *locus amoenus*[107] – became as important as the leisurely activities which could be enjoyed there. We find references to the search for this sort of idyllic spot, because "para estar ocioso le falte lugar al gusto."[108] It could be up on a mountain or on a nobleman's country estates.[109] In one of Antonio Zamora's plays, a character describes Ariobates, a monarch who actually gives up his throne to enjoy the quiet pleasures of country life: "trueca a delicias del campo los cuidados de la Corte."[110] Sometimes the desirability of this tranquil space is highlighted by a nostalgic memory of it or a complaint regarding its absence. As Carlos says regretfully in Agustín

Moreto's *El desdén, con el desdén*: "Ya sabes, que a Barcelona, *del ocio de mis estados* me trajeron los cuidados de la fama."[111] Similarly, an older character in Juan Ruiz de Alarcón's *La prueba de las promesas* speaks remorsefully of the decision to leave the quiet city of Toledo for life at the court in Madrid: "troqué el ocio de Toledo a la inquietud Cortesana."[112] This attitude echoes the Horatian *beatus ille* theme of praise for the country life so famously expounded in Antonio de Guevara's *Menosprecio de corte y alabanza de aldea*.[113]

Another important aspect of rest or leisure time which must be relevant for any discussion of literature from this time period was the role *ocio* played in the creation of literature itself.[114] Leisure offered the time to cultivate the life of the mind, a familiar half of the dichotomy in the arms vs letters debate. We find frequent references in the *comedias* to peace time or leisure offering the speaker an opportunity to study and learn: "el blando ocio de la paz me dé a las letras."[115] The *locus amoenus* topos is also relevant here, for characters often speak about the pursuit of letters occurring in a remote, tranquil place: "En mi retirado albergue, entregado al blando ocio de mis estudios estaba."[116] Solitude is crucial for furthering the life of the mind: "me pongo discursos, que siempre vagos dictaron soledad, y ocio."[117] In fact, intellectual curiosity, along with the leisure to pursue it, is spoken of as an obligation incumbent upon discreet individuals: "La curiosidad es ocio de obligación en discretos."[118]

For better or worse, leisure time is necessary for books to be written.[119] Early modern writers were urged to invoke the Muses in moments of leisure.[120] As Leah Middlebrook has shown persuasively, new genres of lyric poetry were being cultivated during this period for the very specific purpose of entertaining nobles at the court. We find reference to this type of courtly poetry also in the *comedias*: "la Poesía Castellana … para entretener un mes la ociosidad de la Corte."[121] In what can only be termed a metaliterary moment, the *comedias* themselves, in the context of *ocio*, are called licit diversions for their audiences: "Estas … Comedias … lícitos divertimientos del ocio."[122]

This new devotion to leisure we have been describing – in which warriors laid down their swords to take up their pens or else take up residence in a monastery – was part and parcel of the new culture deliberately fostered at the court. A courtier, "un Cortesano ocioso,"[123] was supposed to be leisurely to the point of being caricatured as lazy; conversely, we find explicit rejections (which nevertheless also serve as fairly accurate depictions) of the unproductive courtly lifestyle, such as, "no me quedo en la Corte, dando al ocio lascivos daños."[124] At court, one was expected to have time to engage in such frivolous pastimes as jousting contests, those "concursos nobles de gente ociosa."[125] The feminized, enervated courtiers described by Sidney Donnell in *Feminizing the Enemy* still grasped at vestiges of manliness; for example, they clung to the fiction that these knightly competitions were really designed to showcase their bravery: "os puso en ese ocioso certamen vuestra osadía."[126] Certainly the older, wiser heads at court saw through this charade; thus we find occasionally a voice of prudence who objected to these dangerous and extravagant displays. Of course, such a party pooper was quickly overruled. Later we overhear him throwing up his hands in exasperation: "es vano mi cuidado; porque ¿quién puede estorbarle a la ociosa juventud de la Corte este ejercicio?"[127]

Another courtly pastime which at least retained the semblance of manliness was hunting. Once again, *la caza* is framed explicitly within the discourse of leisure: "La caza que del ocio nos defiende, nos convida a buscar las soledades" and "siendo el alivio del ocio la agreste marcial palestra, cazando en estos contornos."[128] But not even hunting was possible by courtiers who had become so effete that they no longer wanted to ride a horse. We find complaints in the *comedias* about the new vogue for horse-drawn carriages, which had earlier been reserved for ladies or perhaps monarchs riding in processions.[129] Now not even horseback riding was maintained as a manly tradition by courtiers, who instead preferred to slouch behind a coach's curtains. Further proof of this decline in knightly abilities is evidenced by the fact that applicants for the honour of being dubbed a *Caballero de Santiago* (Knight of the Order of Santiago) had to own a horse and demonstrate their ability to ride it.[130] Knights were reduced to proving they had skills which previous generations would have taken for granted.

For the most part, the other leisure activities in which an effeminate courtier indulged ("un afeminado Caballero, que en las delicias de la Corte duerme") were not even covered over with a veneer of masculinity.[131] Instead, the leisurely, bordering on lazy, courtier engaged in a host of more typically feminine activities, foremost among them being idle chatter or gossip.[132] Indeed, gossip is referred to in the *comedias* as the food which sustains leisure: "tratamos de murmurar, que éste es el manjar del ocio."[133] Free time gave people the opportunity to invent fabulous stories which did not always redound to the good credit of their friends and neighbours: "Ellas son fábulas viles, que el ocio infame inventó."[134] Such rumours were as damaging as they were unnecessary: "Tendría de nuevas tan excusadas la culpa algún Cortesano ocioso."[135]

The same idle tongues which propagated rumours also played elaborate practical jokes: "unos y otros son enredos, que eslabona por burlarnos algún ocioso discreto."[136] The resulting confusions and misunderstandings were of course the stuff of which standard *comedia* intrigue was concocted. Saintly characters occasionally objected to the frivolity of this type of humour, as when Tirso's Saint Juana objects to her *padrino* in *La santa Juana*: "Padre, dejémonos de eso, que es ocioso disparate."[137] But they were the only ones objecting, as the rest of the theatre erupted in laughter. Not just jokes, but also songs could fill the vacuum produced by courtly leisure; we find characters alluding to music as an acceptable way to pass the time.[138] Games were also a popular leisure activity, whether or not they involved gambling: "Jugar tasadamente lo que puede, un hombre que procura, estando ocioso, un rato entretenerse se concede."[139] Or courtiers might alternate playing games with reading a book: "entretener la pena … que … el ocio cría, ya en jugar, y ya en leer."[140] Or else they might take a stroll through the garden, a space which had become increasingly feminized, as when a formerly manly male character asks rather pitifully, "¿Yo en el ocio, en el halago, de un jardín de femeniles adornos acompañado?"[141]

Is this the pathetic state to which the formerly brave Spanish epic warrior had been reduced? In her important book *Imperial Lyric*, Leah Middlebrook describes the newly fashionable non-warrior courtiers thus:

> In contrast to the *diestro braço*, "now the sword, now the pen" is an early modern aesthetic topos conditioned by the political and social strictures that were being levied on where, when, and how far the courtierized aristocrat could raise his arm … [T]o identify with the formula implied a primary subordination to power … [T]he new courtly fashions and codes of behavior … had been formed in response to the consolidation of crown control over its formerly spirited and unruly noble subjects… [T]he Spanish courtier … was a figure for the subjection of the aristocrat … [S]ixteenth-century articulation of arms and letters would become a site for the emergence of symptoms of anxiety and ambivalence about the repositioning of the nobility within Spanish culture.[142]

Although her book covers primarily lyric poetry, some of her conclusions about Golden Age culture in general are relevant here. In the *comedias* we find certain residues of the old warrior mentality definitely present, as with the assertion that "No se adquiere el nombre honroso con el ocio, el juego, el vicio, sino con el ejercicio del acero."[143] But early modern Spanish stage characters almost seem torn between divided loyalties as they strive to juggle the competing demands placed upon them: "partí en acciones diversas, entre el ocio, y la fatiga, con las armas, y las letras."[144] They want to have their cake and eat it too.

It is a testament to Sloth's complexity during the early modern period that we find so many traces of this delicate balancing act between the inherited Horatian ideals of moderate *otium* and *negotium*.[145] For, ultimately, early modern Spanish courtiers had to concern themselves with both: "Los mozos, los Cortesanos a veces hablan de *ocio*, mas remiten su *negocio* a la práctica de manos."[146] Indeed, Erasmian moderation dictates that leisure be seen as the parenthesis of work: "ser el ocio paréntesis del trabajo."[147] Without work, leisure could not be properly enjoyed, and vice versa; the plight of the new landowning class, the *hidalgos*, who thought it beneath them to till their own soil, was perhaps nowhere better dramatized than in this period's greatest novel, *Don Quijote*. Arguably, this self-styled knight errant would not have had the leisure to pursue his fantasy without the socially induced burden of a petty nobleman's *ocio*.

If we look carefully, we start to see here an incipient destabilization of formerly fixed categories such as leisure and work. In Juan Bautista Diamante's *El nacimiento de Cristo*, Joseph the carpenter, who is also Christ's stepfather, says, "El trabajo que se toma porque se destierre el ocio, no fatiga."[148] Evidently, whether leisure was pleasurable or not depended on whether it was freely chosen or enforced: "Que en el ocio hay diferencia, si es buscado, o si es preciso."[149] Ultimately these categories were turned inside out, to the point where we find a bored character exclaiming, "el ocio es grandísimo trabajo."[150] In light of such comments, we might well ask: what counted as Sloth? What counted as leisure? How can we tell the difference between the two?

At this point in Spanish history, as we have seen, traditional moral categories were in flux. Previously accepted distinctions begged for greater nuance. As we try to unravel some of Sloth's complexity during the early modern period, we must keep certain questions in mind: namely, who was accused of being lazy? Who was doing the accusing? What was the social class of each party, respectively? How might the author's position in society have impacted his attitude towards these subjects?

Of the many angles we could take as we approach these knotty difficulties, two seem to emerge naturally from the dramatic material. These in turn could be extended to a larger discussion of the residual/transformative role of the Seven Deadly Sins in Spanish Golden Age society. The first of these two approaches views Deadly Vices such as Sloth as lenses through which to examine social problems. The second views the Deadly Sins as potential instruments for class oppression. Let us pause to examine each of these in turn.

It is notable that in the *comedias*, much of the time when Sloth is treated as a Vice it is in the context of persistent social problems such as vagrancy, theft, and criminality. In these instances, the groups being targeted for their laziness are usually gypsies, robbers, or marginalized *pícaros*.[151] The city planners and magistrates responsible for maintaining social order were adamant – even through their mouthpieces speaking on stage – that Sloth contributed to crime. Thus Juan cautions the king in Lope de Vega's *El villano en su rincón* against theft of goods by vagrants: "No se lleve alguna cosa, que anda mucha gente ociosa, y que vive de hacer mal."[152] Conversely, a city was considered free of such petty criminals as long as it did not harbour a large population of loiterers who might, at any moment, decide to make mischief: "Estar limpia una Ciudad de gente ociosa es la causa, de no haber hurtos, y muertes."[153] Noble characters on stage repeatedly warned their peers to avoid "[el] ocioso … vulgo siempre desbocado."[154]

The other persistent residue of this medieval category for Vice occurs when it is used as a convenient instrument for class oppression. Evidently it was morally acceptable for noblemen themselves to be lazy: "con peones mal regidos, damas, y Reyes fingidos busca[n] en ocio vil regalo."[155] In the *comedias*, Sloth is associated repeatedly with wealth, as in "os tienen en blanda paz ricos, y alegres, el ocio."[156] It is also tied to extravagant generosity, as when the Count in Lope de Vega's

El soldado amante declares, "Ojalá viniese a ser, libre, regalón, y ocioso."[157] This was the type of profligate gift giving expected in exchange for courtly favours. Rich women in particular were actually *supposed* to be idle ("mujer sola siempre ociosa, y rica, y loca, que basta"), although they sometimes complained of being bored if there were no men around to entertain them.[158] Some noblewomen may in fact have been waited upon by a hundred servants, if the exaggerated figures thrown about in the course of *comedia* dialogue are to be taken at face value. As the maid Lucía says to the lady Blanca, "preciosa te miro acompañar de la cuadrilla noble sirviendo, y trabajando ociosa de cien gentiles hombres."[159] However, this is more likely a case of literary distortion falling under the rubric of hyperbole; and as such, it should probably not be taken too seriously.

Noblemen in the *comedias* also often come across as bored or at least restless, as in "inquieto yo del ocio con que siempre mi madre me crió."[160] Their leisure time extended indefinitely, to the point that it became burdensome ("el ocio fue nuestra mayor fatiga").[161] But there would appear to be no help for it; courtly protocol dictated that they leave their work to someone else: "Hombre al ocio atento, el trabajo a otro dejas."[162] Noblemen in the *comedias* exhort their servants to work hard so they won't have to: "Que deseches de ti toda pereza, y a lo que pido vayas sin reposo."[163] In Antonio de Solís's *El alcázar del secreto*, Laura asks the gardener contemptuously, "jardinero … ¿cómo tan ocioso estás?"[164] Even a priest in a monastery (which – we must remember – was often a refuge for second sons of noblemen under the system of primogeniture) barks orders to the cook: "Vaya luego, ponga la comida al fuego, ¿no advierte que ocioso anda? Vaya, guise de comer para aquestos padres hoy." The poor chef, Junipero, replies in pitiful tones, internalizing the accusation of laziness: "Siempre, padre, ocioso estoy, soy malo, ¿qué puedo hacer?"[165]

In the context of master/servant relationships, the *comedias* recall the parable of the talents from the Gospels, in which various servants are judged according to how well they managed their master's money.[166] Popular wisdom held that in any contest, the lazy person would never win the prize.[167] Thus lower-class characters themselves speak ambitiously of earning a living by avoiding laziness: "Por no estar ocioso en casa a buscar la vida vengo."[168]

One avenue for social mobility, then as now, was the army. With the new use of lower-class foot soldiers or *tercios* came the possibility that even a *labrador* could seek professional opportunity in the military:

> [T]he Spanish *tercios* and the Swiss pikemen … [were] blocs of soldiers drawn from the general ranks of the populace. As the success of various imperial wars was credited to the increased use of these kinds of troops … a discourse of generalized male Spanish prowess displaced references to the *diestro braço* in Spanish poetry and prose.[169]

This discourse also appears in the *comedias*: "no dan honra a su linaje rendidos al ocio vil, sino terciando la pica."[170] These new Renaissance men – of whatever background – realized that Sloth would only prevent them from bettering their lives ("Yo pongo mi piedra, que quien tiene pereza no medra").[171]

A popular refrain predicted that the lazy person would soon be forgotten, a sad fate not to be desired by Spaniards obsessed with *fama*.[172] Occasionally servants in the *comedias* even hoped their inherent laziness would not contaminate their masters: "aunque mi amo es noble, temo no le avillane mi pereza."[173] Their masters seemed to realize what was happening when this process started to occur, but declined to blame laziness for their decrease in productivity: "los sentidos nobles voy entorpeciendo, sin temer que la pereza pueda culpar el efecto."[174] Instead, they seemed to sink willingly into the seduction of Sloth: "así es hoy perezoso el sueño de nobles sentidos dueño."[175] The poorer classes, needless to say, did not enjoy this same luxury.

Thus we see that while Sloth remains an important cultural category during this period, in the *comedia* at least it appears as a highly unstable one. Moses himself – the giver of the Ten Commandments – rails against this Deadly Sin, along with Gluttony, in Calderón's auto *La serpiente de metal*: "¡O Villanas Pasiones, o Afectos viles, de Gula, y Pereza!"[176] We note, of course, the adjective *villanas*, which effectively attributes these Vices to the villagers. But just as often, we find references which endow this Sin with positive valences. Taking a cue from Moses, let us turn now to Gluttony, the other Deadly Vice he mentions in the same breath with Sloth. We shall witness this Deadly Sin, too, in a moment of cultural transformation which resists the tidy organization of grand, sweeping narrative.

5
That Gnawing Hunger: The Plus Size of Gluttony

En mí son Católica la razón, y Epicúreo el apetito.

– Juan Ruiz de Alarcón, *Todo es ventura*

¿Un cilicio, o unas martas? ¿Un ayuno, o un almuerzo?

– Pedro Calderón de la Barca, *El gran mercado del mundo*

Fue el arrepentimiento fin del apetito mío.

– Lope de Vega, *El postrer godo de España*[1]

Gluttony still appears as a medieval Vice to be avoided in the *autos sacramentales.* In fact, Gluttony was considered the first Vice to occur in the world, when Eve and then Adam took a bite of the forbidden apple: "ofendido Dios de ver la golosa inobediencia, que fue sugestión de Adán."[2] In the *autos,* Mundo or World is told to prepare an inn full of delicious food to waylay the human pilgrim: "prevénle tú una Posada llena de Aparatos ricos, Delicias, Comida, y Juego."[3] In this rather shady roadside establishment, Gluttony cooks dinner for the other Vices: "no sólo come, y bebe; mas hace, y guisa Viandas para cuantos Vicios se albergan en su Hostería."[4] The figure of Gluttony herself accepts the responsibility of providing the food for this party: "me ha tocado a mí, (que en efecto soy la Gula) preveniros las Viandas, en cuya alegre dulzura, cuanto corre, nada, y vuela registro."[5] She prepares fish, fowl, beef, and every kind of game at her table. This same type of lavish feast is thematized in Calderón's *La cena de Baltasar*: "Una opulenta Cena, de las delicias, y regalos llena."[6] It is a banquet that offers an endless parade of exquisite delights.[7] This trope reappears in countless *autos,* where the Vices beckon Man to partake of their bounty: "Ven, Hombre, donde te esperan, entre amorosas delicias de Peregrinas Bellezas, Perfumes, Galas, y Joyas, las golosas opulencias."[8] The Pilgrim or, alternatively, the passengers of life are invited to enter Gluttony's inn to share in this magnificent repast: "A la Casa de la Gula, Pasajeros de la vida, que aquí está el Placer."[9] In a type of Baroque kaleidoscopic refraction, the topos of the singular banquet multiplies into various parties, even spilling out into the gardens.[10] The pilgrim becomes "consumido en Delicias, y Placeres, Juegos, Galas, y Mujeres,"[11] to the point that his senses are possessed or intoxicated by them.[12] Passing most of his life devoted to the proverbial secular trinity of wine, women, and song, he at first gives little thought to the consequences of his actions.[13]

Gluttony – along with its first cousin, Lust – perverts one's course and impedes devotion.[14] These two Vices are connected through the problematic word *Apetito*, which intentionally mixes love and eating metaphors.[15] Basically Gluttony is understood to mean indulgence in food past the point of being hungry ("Bien ser la Gula en comer sin Apetito se indicia"), or the Vice of one who uses resources to buy food to the exclusion of all other necessities.[16] A glutton overeats to the point of vomiting.[17] There is, however, a fine line between eating until one is satisfied and eating past the point of feeling full. Finding the balance between *satisfecho* and *harto* could be a matter of spiritual as well as physical discernment.[18]

As an umbrella Vice, Gluttony also included drunkenness. The figure of Gula sometimes shows up with a basket of fruit but also appears in many of the *autos* with a cup or *copa* used to imbibe alcohol.[19] Furthermore, we find specific references to wines or "preciosos Vinos" in the context of Gluttony.[20] As with food or sex, it was the over-indulgence in alcoholic beverages which was thought to constitute sin.[21] But one's measurement of alcohol intake could be deceptive, particularly with favourite Spanish drinks such as *sangría*, where the flavour of fresh fruit appeared to dilute the wine.[22]

Representations of Gluttony on stage were not limited to the *autos sacramentales*. Gula appeared in the *comedias* in the context of hospitality (as in "aquesas delicias del hospedaje"), with special feasts prepared to honour the arrival of an illustrious personage ("allí banquetes prevengo, de tales personas dignos honre nuestros vellocinos Vuestra presencia").[23]

Even country people could extend the customary hospitality by offering fresh game or fish they had caught.[24] *Romerías* were often made in the guise of pilgrimages to country shrines, involving day trips during which much mischief was made, including Gluttony: "Romerías de no decentes cantares, de no templadas Bebidas, y Viandas."[25] Thus it would seem that at least in some sense, Gula was both a common and a culturally sanctioned Vice.

However, if we look more carefully, we find that Gluttony was primarily a Sin among the wealthy, beginning with the king and queen themselves. In the *comedias* we find descriptions of bad kings who are wholly delivered over to sensual pleasure ("vos todo entregado al ocio, al apetito y torpeza, mal podréis vivir buen Rey"), as well as evil queens like Cleopatra of Egypt who host lavish banquets to consolidate their power.[26] Even inoffensive monarchs were customarily fed exotic or delicate foods which were considered too expensive or simply unsuitable for the common palate ("los Reyes … en sus mesas curiosas los delicados manjares.")[27] Wealthy households could boast big houses as full of servants as they were of desserts: "casa con tal Fausto de criados, con tal Filis de viandas, dulces, y bebidas."[28] One witness to such a scene reports: "entré a verlos comiendo. ¡Tanta plata, tantos platos, de tantos manjares llenos! Tanto servicio y criados, éste entrando, aquél saliendo."[29] These bustling banquet scenes, replete with squires and pages tasting hors d'oeuvres on the sly, must have been commonplaces on stage as well as at court.[30] It will be remembered here that Gluttony appears in the catalogue of Vices to which courtiers specifically are said to be prone.[31]

Courtiers were not the only ones reputed to be notoriously gluttonous. This Vice provided a convenient opportunity for playwrights – even though many of them were themselves priests – to voice a strain of anti-clericalism we might find surprising if we were not already familiar with similarly damning evidence against priests appearing in the picaresque genre.[32] In various *comedias*, too, priests are satirized for being gluttonous, as when one character says to another bitterly, comparing him to a cleric: "tú te huelgas como un padre de comerlos, y yo ayuno como un puto, pues ni los toco, ni veo."[33] Just in case this was not explicit enough, we find references made to specific theatrical priests by name: "Bueno está ahora, fray Francisco, que engorda con ayuno y penitencia, como otros enflaquecen."[34] In defence of the church, there was a certain belief that priests, like monarchs, should eat food dignified enough to be suitable for those who served God's altar.[35] But in one particularly scandalous *auto sacramental*, Gula appears bearing a flag with a picture of a cardinal's hat on it.[36] This could hardly be interpreted as anything other than a not-so-subtle jab at the fat cats who were living in high style off their ecclesiastical benefices.

* * * * *

In sum, then, the Epicurean theme of carpe diem resonates powerfully through both the *comedias* and the *autos*. It appears most frequently in the context of memento mori, as in "Comamos hoy, y bebamos; Humana Naturaleza, que mañana moriremos."[37] In one of Calderón's *autos sacramentales*, the figure of Gluttony appears as a mouthpiece for the Epicure's creed: "Si mañana a la muerte todos caminan, vívase oy."[38] The ancient Epicureans themselves are mentioned as the inspiration for this philosophy ("mi Mesa, Altar de los Epicuros, la Gula, y Lascivia tengan a mi Vientre por mi Dios"), in particular their leader, Epicurus himself.[39] The idolatrously pagan aspect of this Vice is repeated in other *autos*, where not only does one's stomach become one's god, but Gluttony actually renders rites of worship to the palate: "O tú, Gula, que insaciable, de Manjares avarienta, al Paladar rindes cultos."[40] Also mentioned in this context we find the legendary ambrosia, a sweet nectar imbibed by the pagan gods.[41]

But even the most riotous partying brought a bitter aftertaste in this Baroque age of *desengaño*. Exquisite food such as stuffed pheasant was suddenly replaced by rotten bread and raw onions.[42] What used to be a bewildering variety of delicacies was now reduced to a steady diet of the same old thing.[43] By a clever theatrical sleight of hand, a table full of food was made to appear on stage and then just as quickly to vanish, leaving nothing other than smoke and dust – and most probably, the lingering smell of food – in its wake.[44] One is reminded here of the dinner party hosted by a ghost in Tirso de Molina's *El burlador de Sevilla*, in which the appetizers and entrées range from scorpions to snakes to fingernails.[45] This was a Counter-Reformation theatrical experience incorporating all the senses, drawing as it did upon Jesuit meditation techniques in which the penitent was instructed to taste, smell, hear, touch, and visualize the object of that particular meditation.[46] We find a similar strategy being used in Calderón's extended theatrical meditation on food, *Los alimentos del hombre*, in which Appetite is particularly interested to check out the food situation.[47] In one of his other works, this playwright asks a poignant question: "¿cómo quieres, cuando va hambriento un Vulgo, que ya sepa el Apetito de él?"[48] In other words, the sad truth is that the common man or *vulgo* is not so much concerned about Gluttony as he is about meeting the basic requirements of daily sustenance.[49] Gluttony suddenly ceases to be relevant when all the food has disappeared.

By the time we reach the Baroque period, the medieval Vice of Gluttony itself has decayed like a hunk of mouldy cheese.[50] As the Baroque age progresses, images of Gluttony become increasingly deformed and grotesque.[51] We find a proliferation of love and eating metaphors, both of which consume one as a termite consumes wood.[52] What appear to be delicious seeds are in fact corrupt wickedness: "Semillas, siendo en el efecto estragos, lo que al parecer delicias."[53] One *gracioso* appearing as a mouthpiece for Gula, appropriately named Gulín, rides onto the stage seated on a donkey because he is too fat to walk. He announces his entrance proudly, as with a trumpet: "el primero que anda a mula, trompetero de la gula, que por eso soy Gulín." Another character calls him deformed: "Disforme estás para amante, que la gula corpulenta, en fe … en ti se aposenta."[54] He calls himself happily enough the slave of Gluttony ("De la gula esclavo soy"), but ultimately in the same play we see how a self-described Idolatry of food leads quite literally to getting burned. In the last act, a character named Nineucio is sitting at a table when he actually catches on fire from plates of food which begin to ignite.[55] He screams in agony: "llamas de inmortalidad, castigos de Dios eterno. La gula en que idolatré manjares me da de fuego, hidrópica sed me abrasa, ten piedad."[56] His insatiable thirst is that of the weary traveller following a mirage, that glittering water that appears always just out of grasp upon the horizon.

Even in the *autos sacramentales* – that last bastion of medievalizing morality plays – food begins to appear more as a tantalizing chimera: "¡la idea me representa *a lo lejos*, de Banquetes, y Delicias, de Holguras, y Pasatiempos!"[57] Characters accuse each other of fantasizing about food, as in "Tú te entretienes con tan sutiles sueños y manjares, que deben de ser estas fantasías."[58] Perhaps in a half-hearted attempt at rationalization, banquets are now seen to be artificial anyway, lacking substance: "ya en banquetes donde pudo igualar la ostentación, la riqueza al artificio."[59] They impoverish those who indulge in them, reducing even the richest to beggarly stature: "la Gula, pues rica empobrece a limosnas."[60] During this period, presumably the rising costs of lavish banquets started causing some noblemen to go bankrupt, as with one gentleman who finds it necessary to dismiss his servants in order to pay for other excesses: "despide hasta sus criados, por mujeres y por juego, por banquetes, y por bravos, que le ha puesto en más extremos."[61] According to picaresque tales from the period, one way for impoverished nobles to give the false impression they had plenty of food was to use toothpicks obtrusively so everyone would think they had just enjoyed a good meal.[62]

In the *comedias*, increasingly, we find plaintive notes which may be interpreted as signs of real-life economic distress. One knight was reported to have spent 3,000 *maravedíes* on parties, banquets, weapons, and armour: "Caballero, tres mil maravedíes, por Dios bendito, en galas, en banquetes, y en acero."[63] Courtiers increasingly found that the lavish courtly lifestyle consumed all their resources. As they spent beyond their means, it was of course their servants who first started to feel the squeeze: "Hace más que un Alejandro, fiestas, juegos, y banquetes, consume el dinero todo, sus criados le aborrecen."[64] Hosts started making excuses to their guests that if they had just come a day earlier, they might have found more to eat.[65] Alternatively, party planners began to limit the guest list out of worry that the food and wine would run out.[66]

When there was no food left, the call to meal time, even in the convent or monastery, became instead a call to fasting:

> PEDRO: Mande tocar a comer.
> ESPESO: Será tocar a ayunar.[67]

This scenario proved particularly cruel when the person left with no food was the cook, who by virtue of his office had to stand over the stove and smell what all the other people were eating.[68] One character even asks why he must dwell on torments instead of delicacies, when normally – then as now – food was considered one way to escape momentarily from life's troubles.[69] But this solace was not available for all. We find intriguing clues to the situation of noblemen who hid themselves to avoid the obligation of hosting banquets: "oculto, don Juan, para no obligarme a ostentación, ni a banquetes, *cosas que ya no se hacen*."[70] This last line is indicative of a faint memory still lingering of a former time when Spaniards had enjoyed greater prosperity.

There is evidence of an actual food shortage in Spain during this period:

> Malnutrition was widespread, both through sheer ignorance about diet, and through shortages of famine proportions, as in the 1590s and around 1650: two of Calderón's *autos sacramentales*, *La semilla y la cizaña* and *El cubo de la Almudena*, both performed in 1651, were written against a background of grain shortage and bread riots. The Spanish language is full of proverbs about bread, and bread still plays an important part in Spanish meals. In the seventeenth century, in a society which was still largely agricultural, the role of bread was fundamental. We cannot know how often grain was affected by ergot, the then uncomprehended fungus which made bread poisonous, but the title of a lost *auto* attributed to Calderón, *La peste del pan dañado*, suggests that outbreaks were frequent enough to be significant.[71]

As Meg Greer explains, the most acute suffering from hunger was experienced within Spain in the years between 1645 and 1652, when a series of bad harvests compounded by flooding produced the serious possibility that part of the population might starve to death. She notes that during this period, hunger-related uprisings occurred in Granada, Córdoba, and Seville. She also cites a report from the President of the Council of Castile to Felipe IV denying requests for grain to be sent from Madrid to other regions such as Andalucía, with the reason being given that such a decision would provoke the *madrileños* to riot.[72]

We find traces of anxiety regarding lack of food likewise in the *comedias*.[73] A character refers to a meal portion as "tan triste porción, que no puede ser ración de un avariento, o de un niño."[74] Before, Spain had been blessed with plentiful agricultural produce, when feudal farms had functioned and crops had flourished: "que no hay regalo, que a la mesa de la Gula sirva platos de deleite, que el campo no lo produzca."[75] But now no one envies Spain's food: "No envidia esta pobre vida, nuestra rústica comida."[76] Early modern Spaniards voiced hunger pangs on stage in tones so loud we cannot avoid hearing them moaning, "yo muero aquí de hambre."[77] They lay awake at night, unable to sleep for being hungry: "la noche es toda tristeza, hambre, cansancio."[78] Their relentless poverty gave cause for untold misery: "en tan infeliz miseria … ¡da lástima mi pobreza!"[79] The bottom line is, Gluttony was not a problem for *pícaros* who could not afford food.[80]

* * * * *

In fact, in the *comedias* as well as the *autos sacramentales*, we find multiple direct echoes of the picaresque.[81] In one *auto*, Culpa walks onto the stage wearing the garb of a *pícaro*, following Appetite the way a young servant would follow his blind master.[82] In the *comedias*, lower-class characters frequently complain that other *villanos* steal food from them.[83] Bodigo asks the Demon in a play by Agustín Moreto, "Si de las alcorzas mías quedo en ayunas, ¿por qué tú me mueles la comida?"[84] The situation was acutely desperate if even the demons were hungry. One picaresque character named Juanete satirizes the catechism by claiming that as a child, instead of studying church doctrine, he learned to steal food: "a ser rapaz, fui niño de la Doctrina. Para ser goloso igual, en acto más importante, fui paje, luego estudiante."[85] Another is caught in the act of stealing food when he is hungry: "Anda, bellaco goloso, que te han cogido por hambre."[86] As with the picaresque genre per se, servants in the *comedias* complain to their masters that they often go hungry: "Como asisto a un desvalido, pienso que ayuno."[87] One exclaims that even dogs are given food to eat by their masters, as he requests permission to take some food for himself: "pues no hay perro que con amo ayune, dejàrme llevar de aquéste quiero."[88] We find servants and masters arguing about skimpy rations:

JULIO: Ni os entiendo, pues de vos siempre me quedo en ayunas.
DUQUE: ¿Pues te falta qué comer?[89]

We also find hypocritical masters who claim to be solicitous for the state of their servants' souls, when in fact all they really care about is saving a few pennies by not feeding them properly: "hombre en fin, que nos mandaba a pan, y agua ayunar los Viernes, por ahorrar la pitanza que nos daba."[90] Remember that this was an age when kings did not always feed their subjects well either: "Rey mío, ¿da usted de almorzar conejo? Porque estamos en ayunas, y el cómo se da comiendo."[91] Here we see a king feasting on rabbit for lunch while his underlings starve.

Alongside this picaresque motif there coexisted other, potentially contradictory, stereotypes. One of these was certainly the stock character of the *villano* or *gracioso* who – akin to his famous contemporary, Sancho Panza – lived to eat. The scruffy innkeepers who ran a humble restaurant or *mesón* by the side of the road were often pictured as either gluttonous themselves or as tempting potential customers – especially foreigners looking to enjoy Spanish cuisine – to indulge in this Vice.[92] As we saw earlier, the allegorical figure of Gula appears dressed as an innkeeper in at least two of the *autos sacramentales*.[93] Cooks or chefs, above all, were lower-class characters frequently described as gluttonous: "la ensalada llevo. ¿Qué mandas? Que a buscar voy un goloso cocinero, para cuatro platos dulces."[94] Waitresses also were thought to indulge in this Sin, perhaps on the sly.[95] Even a male carriage driver is described as "gran bebedor, mal contento cochero, libre y sin alma y goloso cocinero," along with a male opera singer who is a "tiple goloso, contralto loco, tenor siempre necio, contrabajo bebedor."[96] Hungry gypsies complete the picture of those gluttonous – that is, hungry – individuals, existing on the mere fringes of society, who are always living from one meal to the next.[97]

"Donde no hay muchos manjares, es amor mal comedor" – in other words, nothing is pleasurable when one is hungry.[98] Sometimes hunger is experienced as a punishment, or while one is in prison; but many times characters in the *comedias* specifically attribute their lack of food to poverty: "Viéndote en pobrezas tantas, que en tu ayuno a firme apuestas."[99] Witness this exchange between Innocence and Gluttony in one of Calderón's *autos sacramentales*:

GULA: ¿Pues cuándo faltó a ningún Caminante en la Casa de la Gula?
INOCENCIA: Cuando sin dinero.

In the same play, Gluttony announces her transformation into the figure of Appetite: "yo, que la Gula fui, el Apetito seré, que es el disfraz de la Gula."[100]

As we have mentioned before, these two terms, Apetito and Gula, are complicated and in some ways problematic; but over and over again, we see that the problem is not so much Gluttony as it is Appetite – in this case, signifying simply base hunger. A child first experiences Appetite when it cries for its mother's milk: "mas niño asiste al Hombre, pues no hay infancia sin apetito."[101] These stage characters long for Appetite, with the goal of merely ending their hunger: "Quién al Apetito viera, que matara la hambre."[102]

Does Gluttony morph into Appetite when she's out of money? We find references indicating that what had once been a pleasurable indulgence is now a burden.[103] In Calderón's auto *El nuevo hospicio de pobres*, Appetite appears as a blind beggar loitering on the steps of the building.[104] Appetite begins to be mentioned more in the context of hunger than of satiety, as in the lines of one character who vows that he's so hungry, he'll eat anything: "Como quien tiene apetito de comer, que le da gana cualquier rústico sustento."[105]

By and large, what we find here is a discourse of paucity, a conversation about lack. We are reminded incessantly of deprivation, as in "la privación es causa del apetito."[106] These characters bleat plaintively about their lack of money: "no hay ayuno peor, que el ayuno del dinero."[107] In Anne Cruz's *Discourses of Poverty: Social Reform and the Picaresque Novel in Early Modern Spain*, we find a context for this dialogue about need:

> The complex dislocations, both symbolic and social, that propelled Spain into the early modern period generated divergent discourses in response to the increasing numbers of marginalized poor that emerged in the early sixteenth century. [T]his study … focuses on the articulations of poverty and its relief through charity and social reform in both the picaresque and non-fictional texts … [T]his new kind of fiction … discloses the authors' preoccupations with the increasing disenfranchisement of the poor. From Lazarillo de Tormes, who arrives in Toledo when the Poor Laws are enforced, to Estebanillo González, whose hunger compels him to join the Hapsburg armies, the *pícaros* contend daily with both social disenfranchisement and physical deprivation.[108]

Cruz's book offers a starkly different picture of early modern Spain, one in which beggars wandered the streets. In the *comedias*, too, we see characters reduced to begging for breakfast, comparing themselves explicitly to the *mendigos*, who must have been a familiar sight.[109] We see hungry figures who consume every last morsel, not leaving behind a single crumb.[110] We hear rumours of feigned maimings as cripples hobble onto the stage, begging for a meal, while onlookers whisper about whether their injuries are real or pretended, since the handicapped stood to profit from increased sympathy.[111] Even higher-class characters who have not had to beg before will soon be reduced to begging in order to buy food: "Ya esto acabó, no hay que hacer enredos ya, ni mentir; mañana habrá de pedir limosna para comer."[112]

There was a belief that rich people had the obligation to feed the hungry, based not only on Saint Paul's injunction to do so but also on the assumption that God had made the basic food humans needed for survival, and therefore it was – to some extent at least – to be considered common property.[113] Yet the Sin of Gluttony is directly connected in the *autos sacramentales* to a scorn for the poor, as the gluttonous man eats all he wants without a thought for the scrawny beggar child who goes hungry.[114] Even the famous still-life paintings of this era – often showing dead fowl and foodstuffs strewn across the table, half-consumed – while representative of the delicacies enjoyed by some, also must have mocked those who could not afford such a sumptuous repast (see figure 13).[115] The allegorical figure of Gula alludes to these types of paintings in one of the *autos sacramentales*: "En Imágenes Pintadas los deleites represento."[116] She may or may not have carried one of these paintings onto the stage.[117] In a similar example, an abhorrently wasteful *comedia* character offers a word picture of one of these half-eaten feasts in the lines, "Pues servidme los manjares más costosos, y porque envidien más, se derrame todo." This evil character taunts the hungry with his waste, reminding them sarcastically that he has extra food to throw to his dogs: "¿no habréis sentido que os falten estas viandas, que yo estoy echando a mis canes?"[118] Another malevolently sadistic character says it feeds his Appetite to see others go hungry: "Pues tráiganme de comer, que no hay para mi apetito, como ver a otros hambrientos, y sírvame de principios."[119] This mess of overturned tables, with food scattered all over the floor, must have been a standard tableau scene, for it is repeated in various *comedias*.[120]

An interesting side note to the portrayal of hungry early modern Spanish subjects on the *comedia* stage was the similar depiction of starving, heroic "New" World explorers in the same venue. It was the greedy Spaniards' Appetite for wealth, it will be remembered – from our extensive coverage of this theme in our Greed chapter – which sent the explorers out to discover new lands in the first place: "A del Humano Apetito, Mercader a quien fió sus Indias el Mar, sus Aromas."[121] The impact of "New" World exploration on Old World cuisine has been studied extensively.[122] On the one hand, "New" World delicacies such as turkey meat became all the rage in Spain, and we find explicit references to such newly popular delicacies in the theatre.[123] The explorers did in fact encounter many of the exotic spices prized so highly in Europe: "un árbol solo pudiera sazonar cuantas cocinas tiene la gula en España, y estarále agradecida a don Gonzalo Pizarro."[124] The notion of well-seasoned food also appears repeatedly. It must be remembered that spices were doubly sought after because of their preservative function.[125] It was believed that seasoned food could be preserved longer – and potentially, thus feed more people – than food which had not been so preserved.

But one of the great ironies of "New" World exploration was that the explorers themselves often went hungry. Even when they found new sources for exotic spices, they sometimes went without basic foodstuffs to keep them alive.[126] Explorer figures in the *comedias,* the protagonists of a subgenre I like to call dramas of discovery, complain that one can live on papayas, coconuts, and pineapples for only so long. One of them recounts a weary trek through virgin territory: "caminamos, a vista del Briáreo Marañón, no hallamos otras delicias que ñames, ajíes, papayas, guayabos, cocos, y piñas, porque iguanas, y alcatrazes fuera pedir gollorías." Evidently even the iguanas were in short supply.[127] When early modern Spanish soldiers – in the "New" World and elsewhere – wanted to celebrate a victory, often they did not have adequate culinary means to do so: "[con] muestras de alegría, la artillería dispara, mas no nos hizo banquetes, ni brindó más que con agua."[128] Here the sad soldiers offer a half-hearted toast using only water, since they have no wine. Similarly, when Spanish citizens returned to their country, they often lacked the proper means to celebrate:

CASTRO: Si de aquesta batalla sale mi honor como debe, y a España me vuelve
Dios, a este ayuno haremos fiesta.
MUDARRA: Desdichada tierra es ésta.[129]

One of the few creatures left who could indulge a passion for Gluttony in early modern Spain was the lowly ant, an insect who could still afford to follow its Appetite.[130] And then there was the mouse, that sturdy rodent still able to forage for food.[131] Times were so desperate that *villanos* even stole, or at least were stingy about giving, food for the horses. For this act of desperation, one simpleton is chastised:

LEONARDO: A don traidor, que ahora pagaréis lo que al cuartaguillo
hicistes estar ayuno, ¿acordastes? [*sic*]
MELCHIOR: Pues pecador fui yo a Dios.[132]

When early modern Spaniards had not a speck of flour left in the house, they had no choice but to go hungry ("no haber polvo de harina en casa, nos dábamos al ayuno") or, as a last resort – metaphorically, at least – to feed on their social inferiors, as we see in the following exchange about a foolish nobleman who has squandered his estate:

MARQUÉS: ¿Es rico?
TADEO: Pudiera serlo,
que es varón calificado;
señor es de seis aldeas,
pero con empeños tantos,
que los vasallos se come
crudos, cocidos, y asados.[133]

Here a feudal lord is reduced to "eating" his vassals. Only a few generations later, the Spanish artist Francisco de Goya would paint a horrific image of Saturn devouring his children (see figure 14) – a fitting image for Spain at this time of crisis, as it turned inward upon itself and devoured its young.[134]

* * * * *

At this time of intense cultural transition, we find Gluttony juxtaposed with its antidote: abstinence. Abstaining from all or some types of food for a specified period of time was a practice known as *ayuno*, or fasting, which was usually connected to some kind of religious devotion. The allegorical figure of Gula refers to these devotional practices as a foil or antidote for Gluttony. This figure of Gluttony says in one of Calderón's *autos*, "Sin mí, a Ayunos, y Cilicios"; and later in the same play, one of the other characters says to Gula, "toma, Gula, los Ayunos, que desde este instante ofrezco."[135] In another *auto*, self-flagellation and fasting, both typically penitential practices, are served as the first courses of a perverse banquet.[136] In the same drama, devout beggars are contrasted with gluttonous spendthrifts:

HOMBRE: Míseros Mendigos son, devotamente compuestos.
GULA: Si los que padecen Hambre, y sed, hoy viven contentos, *¿qué acción le queda a la Gula?*[137]

Arguably the hungry were not actually content, as in these lines from the play, but instead were being encouraged by the authorities, including playwrights, to try to be content with their lot in life. In any case, the conclusion remains the same: there was essentially no place left for Gluttony in this culture.

The relationship of religious fasting to Gluttony was not always so simple. Some characters are told to indulge in Gluttony now, since they will undoubtedly have to fast later: "hinche el Jergón, que para eso de padecer, y ayunar, harto tiempo hay en la Vida."[138] Other allegorical pilgrim figures in the *autos* are seen avoiding Gluttony specifically through the strategy of fasting:

DEMONIO: ¿Por la Gula también pasas?
PEREGRINO: Ayuno estoy de cuarenta días.[139]

Here the Pilgrim imitates the technique used to resist temptation by Jesus in the desert, where Satan also tried to tempt a hungry Christ to turn stones into bread. This New Testament episode is dramatized in Calderón's autos *La cura, y la enfermedad* and *El valle de la zarzuela*.[140] The specific tool used by Gluttony to tempt its would-be victims was the sense of smell; this detail is conveyed rather indecorously in the phrase "sin duda es ésta la gula, que tienta por los hocicos."[141] Christ was preceded by several Old Testament figures who likewise resisted the Sin of Gluttony through a period of fasting in the wilderness. These included Elijah and Moses, both of whom were commanded by God to fast for a symbolic number of days or years, usually when a punishment from the vengeful deity was expected.[142] Both of these figures are referenced explicitly in the *autos sacramentales* as well as various *comedias* where characters decide self-consciously to imitate them.[143]

Several allegorical figures in the *autos* are shown resisting the temptation to Gluttony, as when Gentilismo says in Calderón's *El tesoro escondido*, "yo de la Gula me abstendré."[144] In the *comedias*, too, fasting is specifically juxtaposed to overindulgent eating as its mirror opposite.[145] A spiritual justification is offered for this practice, namely that while the soul was being sustained by sufficient spiritual food, then it was reasonable for the body to fast from physical nourishment: "donde el alma come, el cuerpo es razón que ayune."[146] Saintly characters languishing in captivity in Algiers speak of suffering hunger, here portrayed as a sort of involuntary fasting, but being sustained instead by their faith:

FLORENCIO: Hambre, castigo, y prisión
me dan por pena, mi Dios,
mas padeciendo por vos,
dulces las cadenas son …
Regalo al desabrimiento,
de la perdida porción,
que es gusto del corazón
ver el apetito hambriento …
JACINTA: Y si carecéis de Pan,
alzad de la tierra el vuelo,
y comed del Pan del Cielo
que en el Padre Nuestro os dan.[147]

Here a hungry Appetite is said to bring joy to the heart. Only a mystic or a masochist could find pleasure this way. But even non-martyr characters are exhorted to practise this type of pious devotion, as in "ayune a santa lealtad, que es muy buena devoción."[148] Fasting was included in instructions to nuns, along with self-flagellation.[149] Saintly characters in hagiographical dramas defend their choice to fast as obeying a command by God. For example, the titular character in Juan Bautista Diamante's *Santa María Magdalena de Pazzi* retorts: "Tú quieres que de regalos a la gula satisfaga, cuando Dios manda, que sólos me alimentan pan, y [agua]."[150] Later in this same play, Gluttony and fasting are once again explicitly juxtaposed: "entre abrojos de la gula, entre sedientos ayunos." *Abrojos* were thorns placed on the end of a whip used for self-flagellation. Here divergent options are displayed cruelly as the saint gluts her senses not with food, but with violent self-punishment.

Obviously there were dangers involved with fasting too much. Excessive fasting was known to result in physical weakness: "Cuerpo ayuno, y desvelado fácilmente se empereza."[151] It could cause one to become too thin: "viendo mi flaco sujeto, me dijo, no ayune tanto."[152] After a prolonged fast, some characters feel sorry to see each other looking so skinny.[153] Even those who are fat, if they are fasting, protest that they are still hungry, as in "Yo, señor, tengo gran cuerpo y cuando manda la Iglesia, ayuno como los otros; mas es mi hambre tan fiera."[154] Some characters rebel against fasting, as in the following exchange:

BUEN GENIO: Hoy es día de ayunar.
INOCENCIA: Hagámosle de comer.[155]

Others protest that they were made to fast on the wrong day of the week, as in "me hizo ayunar el lunes sin ser ayuno."[156] One character even curses the day he was ordered to stop eating lunch as well as afternoon snacks: "fue de mi edad el tener obligación, y en mandándome ayunar, maldito el día he dejado de almorzar, y merendar."[157] Here he blames his adult age for imposing an obligation he might otherwise have managed to escape, presumably if he had still been young enough to remain exempt.

Some characters request permission from their superiors to cease fasting, as in "que me dé licencia, de que deje de ayunar."[158] The people who were in charge of commanding someone to fast or stop fasting were normally either their doctors or confessors.[159] These superiors could absolve their charges from a vow to fast if they saw that it was starting to cause real suffering – such as severe migraine headaches – or to be prejudicial to their health.[160] Monks and nuns were expected to fast as part of the vows taken at their ordination.[161] But even some non-priestly characters made the decision to fast of their own volition, deciding for whatever reason that it was better for their physical or spiritual health.[162] There are numerous instances of characters who – without being under any obligation at all – just decide to fast or keep fasting.[163] One character who has already been fasting for nine days on the occasion of a nine-day *novena* is advised to extend it to ten, with *salud* or health cited as the rationale.[164] Perhaps this person needed to diet.

Fasting was expected of all Catholics on certain specified occasions, and it is to this more routine fasting to which we shall turn our attention now. Here we encounter an unanticipated intersection with the Third Commandment to keep the Sabbath, and not just in offhand jokes about eating too many sweets or in the familiar popular refrain *por oír misa, y dar cebada, nunca se perdió jornada*, which eventually became the title of a *comedia* by Antonio Żamora.[165] In the next section, I hope to argue that in Catholic Spain, for all practical purposes, the observance of the Sabbath was redirected towards Fridays, when the devout were instructed to refrain from eating meat. The injunction to keep the Sabbath lost its punch in a culture where hearing mass every day was expected. To prove this point, it will be necessary for me to take the reader on a short excursus regarding early modern church attendance. Eventually the relevance of all this to Gluttony will be made clear.

* * * * *

Early modern Spaniards did not attend church just at Christmas and Easter, although those feast days were a certain minimal bar for how often they were expected to receive communion.[166] As with believers today, they went to church on the occasions of weddings and funerals, but they also went to mass on special feast days or saints' holy days, especially for their patron saints.[167] There is also evidence in the *comedias* of a certain expectation that they attend mass every day, as with the advice: "mi voz te aconseja … la Misa cada día, cuidando de la limpieza del alma."[168] In fact, the key difference between types of church services was that a sermon was preached on feast days, while on normal days the mass was limited to the liturgy of the Eucharist by itself.[169] Daily mass might be said for the souls in Purgatory; for a special request, such as finding a lost object; or a special intention, such as good health or the safety of a loved one.[170] Masses were even said for the purpose of dubbing someone a knight.[171] These masses were paid for by donations, often at the bequest of someone who had died and arranged in his will for masses to be said for his soul.[172]

This all goes to show that going to mass was serious business, at least for those sectors of the population who were particularly devout. We find pious references in the *comedias*, but especially in the *autos*, to "el Excelso Misterio de la Misa," "el grande Sacrificio de la Misa, que Oblación logra el Fiel," and to the mass as being a North Star to guide both body and soul ("la Misa norte del cuerpo, y del alma").[173]

In Calderón's auto *La devoción de la Misa*, he explains "cuánto el Misterio de la Misa incluye, y cierra, desde la primera Edad del Mundo":

> conteniendo la Misa la ley, que culpas confiesa, la que Preceptos escribe, la que Misterios aumenta, siendo el nombre de la Misa, traducido de la Hebrea frase, Hacimiento de gracias: y de la latina lengua Missa, enviada Oblación del Hijo al Padre en Ofrenda.[174]

The censors for these plays were also serious about attending mass. Fray Manuel de Guerra y Ribera relates, in his *aprobación* for a volume of collected works by Calderón, how he prayed to God every day at mass for inspiration: "todos estos días he pedido a Dios en la Misa, me alumbre, e inspire."[175] The austere Hapsburg monarchs were known, at least publicly, to be similarly devout. Calderón describes Maximilian of Austria in *El segundo blasón del Austria*: "cada mañana en la MISSA, en ... Devoción tanto se arrebata, y fervoriza."[176] It was believed that God blessed the Catholic faithful through divine beneficence: "el que la Misa oye, Dios con él benigno se muestra."[177] The mass was seen to work like a sort of vaccine or amulet against evil.[178] In sum, then, this was an investment of time and energy which would reap eternal interest: "el Cielo galardona la devoción de la Misa."[179]

In the *autos sacramentales* in particular, the playwright's pedagogical mission was to educate the average person as to what the mass was all about. In Calderón's *Los misterios de la Misa*, the figure of Ignorance admits, "Todo el Año voy a Misa, y yendo, y viniendo a ella, al cabo del Año no sé de la MISSA la media."[180] Part of the problem here was illiteracy: "mal cantará misa aquél que el A,B,C ignora."[181] Some unlettered fools who even served as altar boys did not know how to respond *amen*, but still they came to mass so they could gobble up the extra communion wafers afterward.[182]

Pious playwrights such as Calderón used a good part of their time spent writing about daily church attendance to chastise those who did not live up to this obligation: "En no oírla cada día, no solamente es tibieza del perezoso, sino descortesía grosera, que se hace a Dios." They even worried that once Catholics started to slip in this area, they might soon begin to slide in all the others: "si yo ahora, negligente, o perezoso faltara a aqueste precepto, ¿en mí peligraran todos?"[183] In some ways, Sunday was still considered a day of rest, particularly for labourers who could stay in bed on that day of the week.[184] But increasingly it came to be identified instead with more practical concerns, such as clean clothes; for example, every Sunday, one was supposed to change shirts (thus we find references to "mudar cada Domingo camisa").[185]

In this moment of cultural transition, Sunday eventually became more of a party day than an occasion for religious devotion: "cuantos en San Sebastián son de fiesta, y de Domingo."[186] Symptomatic of this anxiety are Juan de Zabaleta's moralistic exhortations in his treatises *Día de fiesta por la mañana* (1654) and *Día de fiesta por la tarde* (1660) to make use of leisure time to further the soul's profit:

> día de fiesta … es día de hacer mucho, aunque a ti te parece que no es día de hacer nada … El ocio no es no hacer nada, porque éste es ocio de muertos, sino hacer algo que deleite o que no fatigue. En el ocio en no haciendo algo bueno es preciso caer en hacer algo malo.[187]

This passage forms an interesting echo of our previous discussion about Sloth. However, judging from the titles of such works as Francisco de Luque Fajardo's *Fiel desengaño contra la ociosidad y el juego* (1603),[188] these moralists' admonitions often went unheeded.

The reality of this situation led some characters to question why they should have to get out of bed so early to go to mass on Sunday: "¿De qué sirve madrugar el Domingo a Misa tanto?"[189] Some even questioned why it was important to go at all:

> DON ALONSO: ¿Han de quedarse sin Misa?
> DON TORIBIO: ¿Qué dificultad es ésa?[190]

Masses were typically short, so many characters began to question what, if anything, they were really missing.[191] The religious quality of the ceremony was notoriously bad, as we see from the following exchange:

> AGUADO: Iba a rezar a la Iglesia,
> porque tengo devoción
> de oír maitines.
> SARGENTO: Buena es ésa.
> AGUADO: Era muy mala, Sargento.[192]

Monarchs or the wealthy didn't have to go out to attend mass at all; they could just hear the liturgy performed in their own private chapels.[193] Some particularly spoiled individuals were willing to sally forth only if the weather was mild.[194] The especially privileged could even choose to hear mass while staying in bed, although this was looked down upon unless there was illness involved.[195] Soldiers and hunters were allowed to celebrate mass outdoors, while sailors had little choice but to celebrate it onboard the ship.[196] If some early modern Spaniards went to church at all, it was more as a social event: "La que ir a Misa desea el Domingo de mañana, no lo hace por Cristiana."[197] They did it out of habit ("hacer decir a la siguiente Aurora una Misa, la cual oigo devoto, por costumbre, o piedad") or the desire to see friends.[198]

Most often in the *comedias*, mass appears as a furtive chance for lovers to see each other. Many a Celestinesque love story begins with the words: "Oyendo en San Jorge Misa el pasado día de fiesta, vi una mujer."[199] The lovers would gaze at each other in church instead of paying attention to the service: "En san Juan el Domingo en el sermón, siendo de mi corazón vuestros ojos piedra."[200] One woman admits that she got all dressed up to go to church, but not out of any sort of religious devotion.[201] Men were often even more distracted: "Oyó Misa, que en mi vida me vi más inquietamente divertido."[202] The challenge, of course, was to remain quiet in church: "Adusto viene, ¿cómo en Misa he de callar?"[203] The lovers might exchange tokens surreptitiously, as this gallant reports: "estimada prenda la di, con què en un instante despejo misa, e Iglesia. Cesó el no oído Oficio, que me holgara."[204] Salacious *comedias* even include cases of outright solicitation during mass. As one woman recounts, "he resistido vergonzosa, y hoy me ha solicitado estando en Misa, y sabe Dios si yo lo he echado en risa."[205] She does not seem to have taken this overture too seriously. In one rather blasphemous line, the church itself is called a pimp or go-between: "juntos oído Misa habemos, dándonos san Antonio el templo suyo, por medianero."[206] Alternatively, a man might follow a woman home from church with the intention of sending love letters later. As one woman reports, "Siguióme después en Misa, hubo terceros, y cartas."[207]

Even if these characters did not misbehave in church, many things could happen along the way. One female character is described as always choosing a faraway church, presumably with the goal of being seen by men en route.[208] It is no surprise that these shenanigans generated palpable cynicism. Some characters reached the point where they were willing to hear anything *except* mass: "Cualquier cosa oirá, no siendo Misa."[209] Of course, an avowedly irreligious character such as Enrico in Tirso's *El condenado por desconfiado* refuses to go to mass under any circumstances, even if he is about to die: "En mi vida Misa oí, ni estando en peligros ciertos de morir."[210] By the time the Baroque age drew to a close, Sunday had literally become a day just like any other, as we see in the flippant "San Domingo, san Miércoles."[211] It is safe to say that the Third Commandment was honoured more in the breach.

I would like to propose the rather novel argument that early modern Spaniards showed their piety in other ways – namely, through punishing their bodies by fasting. In this moment of transition we have been describing – a precarious moment of tension between competing moral systems, the Decalogue vs the Seven Deadly Sins, neither of which survived entirely intact – old forms were being discarded or transformed in response to new pressures. I shall argue that the Sabbath per se ceased to be relevant in a culture which promoted daily church attendance, and some of whose members in any case did not seem to take mass very seriously. Instead, the practice of fasting – involving, as it did, a real sacrifice in the form of abstaining from food – became an outlet for early modern piety which may best be understood as the rough equivalent, at least in spirit, of Sabbath-keeping. The result was a drift away from the Deadly Vices towards the Ten Commandments as the dominant moral paradigm, but with important changes even to the Decalogue in its interpretation. Let us see how this works.

* * * * *

Certainly in the *comedias* there are some joking references to fasting, as when a man loses his Appetite due to lovesickness and pretends to hold a vigil of abstinence for his beloved as if she were a saint.[212] Another character in a play by a different author accuses a woman of pretending to fast for material gain.[213] We find select instances of picaresque profiting from others' genuine piety with regard to fasting; for example, "que podamos de consuno yo, y nuestro hermano, de ayuno hacer mucha colación."[214] But mostly we find serious references to fasting in the context of pious devotion, as in "ayunar con tal fervor … en la oración ocupado" and "discreción tan religiosa, tome ayuno, y oración."[215] As one character predicts of pious women, they are likely to be found either whipping themselves, fasting, or praying.[216] In Cervantes's hagiographical drama *El rufián dichoso*, about the conversion of a picaresque ruffian into the saintly Cristóbal de la Cruz, his new devotion is described as including fasting as part of a complete religious regimen: "su oración es continua, y fervorosa, *su ayuno inimitable*, y su obediencia presta, sencilla, humilde, y hacendosa."[217]

Truly devout fasting was frequently combined with self-flagellation. These two practices went hand in hand in countless passages, such as "el ayuno, y diciplina, en que siempre es vigilante," and the rather graphic description which begins, "pues sobre las penitencias que vos sabéis, tan extrañas, tanto ayuno, y disciplinas que se da, casi inhumana, con las cadenas."[218] It is no accident that both of these references occur in hagiographical dramas. Fasting was sometimes practised in solitary confinement or as a form of intercessory prayer.[219] It was also often mentioned in the same breath with giving alms, as in "Más vale la oración santa, ayuno, y limosna rica, que los tesoros guardados."[220]

But fasting was not only a signifier for extraordinary religious devotion. Then as now, ordinary Catholics were expected to refrain from eating meat on Fridays during Lent.[221] The same was true of feast days which happened to fall on a Friday. Occasionally the fasting for these feast days might be extended for up to a year.[222] Widows were expected to engage in fasting while in mourning.[223] As her uncle Lucencio says to the young widow Leonarda in Lope de Vega's *La viuda valenciana*, "Y Dios te lleve adelante ese cilicio, y ayuno."[224] Fasting was sometimes undertaken by single women in conjunction with a vow of chastity.[225] They might abstain from all food starting at dawn: "a mi Elvirilla su esclava traer algo que comer, que ayuno desde hoy al alba."[226] We see an all-day fast being used as an excuse for not accepting a dinner invitation in this dialogue with Saint Julian in Lope de Vega's *comedia de santos* about him:

CONTADOR: Coma conmigo.
JULIÁN: Hoy ayuno, otro día podrá ser.[227]

This form of diurnal fasting could be practised as often as three times a week.[228] Some religious orders took vows of perpetual abstention from meat (they did eat fish).[229] A variant of this perpetual vow might be an every-Friday abstinence from meat, even when it was not during Lent.[230] Fasting could be used as a punishment or a test of one's virtue.[231] Breaking a vow of fasting was considered to be a serious sin: "qué importuno, pues no se quiebra un ayuno, y es mucho mayor pecado."[232] But successful fasting was seen as providing the devotee with a foretaste of paradise: "Basilio al ayuno llama, imagen del vivir quieto del paraíso."[233]

* * * * *

So did Gluttony remain relevant at all in a culture where large segments of the population were starving? Where even the noblemen who did have enough to eat were likely to choose to show piety through the very practice of abstaining from food? In the last section of this chapter, I shall argue that it did – but not necessarily in the ways one might have reason to expect. In early modern Spain, Gluttony becomes transmuted and transformed. The trope of the heavenly feast appears in countless *autos sacramentales* and is too prevalent an image to be ignored. Let us explore this final phase of Gluttony's metamorphosis as we finish up what has, admittedly, been a wild roller coaster ride through various early modern conceptions of sin and devotional practices.

It is worth remembering that the *autos sacramentales* as a genre were performed every year during the *Feast* of Corpus Christi.[234] What even some scholars of early modern drama have perhaps failed to realize is that often this celebration was literalized to incorporate actual food.[235] In Corpus Christi cycle plays during this same time period in England, the bakers' guild, for example, would bake loaves of bread to use as theatrical props. Then they themselves would act in the play and when it was over, they would toss the loaves of bread out into the audience.[236] Similarly, in Madrid a drawing of plans for the Corpus Christi dramas of 1644 shows a temporary stage in the Plaza Mayor to be erected just to the left of the Panadería, or bakery, which was the main building on the town square at that time.[237] The symbolism of physical bread pointing to Christ the Bread of Life would not have been lost on the plays' audience. In 1651, likewise, Calderón wrote a pair of autos, *El cubo de la Almudena* and *La semilla y la cizaña*, against the background of the bread riots mentioned earlier.[238] As Meg Greer explains, "[t]he word 'almudena' derives from the Arabic word 'almud,' a measure of grain, and the 'almudaina' or 'almudena' was the place in which seed grain was measured, bought and sold." She further notes that in the same play, the figure of Apostasía clarifies on stage that the Almuden is supposed to be understood as the Panadería or Casa de Pan:

> When in the auto's miracle, the Virgin de la Almudena knocks down the walls to save Madrid, she reveals hidden within them a great supply of wheat, miraculously fresh, whether new-sprung from stone or conserved thus for centuries ... Calderón's explanation of "Almuden" as "Casa de Pan" also functioned as a subtle underlining of the importance of municipal structures in the supply of bread, and of their intertwining with the monarchical presence in the city.[239]

This is clearly a case where a return to the physical circumstances of these plays' original performances can illuminate certain otherwise mysterious aspects of their meanings.

In a gesture which is perhaps best interpreted within the context of Counter-Reformation spirituality, along with aforementioned Ignatian meditation techniques of imagining with all the senses, deeply theological playwrights such as Calderón de la Barca offered their viewers a heavenly feast as an alternative to compete with the increasingly scarce earthly one: "Mesa a que yo fui convidada, ofreciéndoles en ella Divinos Manjares."[240] According to this vision, God in His divine Providence provides spiritual food which is unapologetically attractive: "su Providencia Sabia previno con una Cena, de tan sabrosas Viandas, que han de alimentar, no sólo las Vidas." This heavenly feast feeds the soul, not just the body: "Mesa franca, siendo del Alma, y del Cuerpo Alimento las Viandas."[241]

What we have here is Gluttony transposed to a heavenly key. It is transvalorized in the process to become a Virtue instead of a Vice. The Eucharistic truth that God is the Bread of Life is literalized by such titles as Calderón's *El verdadero Dios Pan*. This bread imagery goes all the way back to the Old Testament, when heavenly manna fell from the sky ("aquel llovido Maná, que unión de manjares fue").[242] This manna was imagined by Golden Age Spaniards to include every possible flavour in one food, and to taste as sweet as honey:

> tendrás para Vianda un Pan, y Vino, en quien mil distintos Manjares cifrados verás; pues el Maná del Desierto, que neutral sabor fue, hallarás en la Mesa, más dulce que la Miel, del Panal de la Boca del León.[243]

The all-sufficiency of manna was due to its encompassing power: "que en una Vianda sola os dé todas las Viandas."[244] This trope is repeated in multiple instances, as in "serán las demás Viandas del blanco Maná compuestas, que dieron las Nubes."[245]

Manna was also prefigured in the sheaves of wheat gathered by Jesus's ancestor Ruth, as we see in Calderón's auto *Las espigas de Ruth*.[246] In fact, her humble gleanings are transformed in the *autos* into the most precious delicacies imaginable: "tan preciosos manjares, que lleguen a incluir en la Espiga de Ruth."[247] The Baby Jesus, her descendant, is born in Bethlehem, a Hebrew name which means House of Bread, a fact which likewise does not go unnoticed by Calderón.[248] We find allusions to New Testament feasts as well, such as the banquet prepared to welcome home the Prodigal Son.[249] The theatrical theophany of Christ as Lamb of God is here presented visually in the most literal terms: "en medio una Mesa grande adornada de Viandas, y en ella un Cordero, y dos luces."[250] We know from extant stage directions that in performance, this table bearing the Passover lamb was wheeled out on a cart, with the character of Moses standing beside it in the wagon. The stage directions read, "En el segundo Carro una Mesa, con Viandas, y en un plato un Cordero, y Moisés en pie."[251] Thus the Old Testament was visually linked to the New in one theatrically seamless transition.[252] The literalized doctrine of transubstantiation was revealed in the true composition of the Eucharistic bread as actually being meat – that is, Christ's flesh: "llegando a saber, que sus delicias paran en ser sus Viandas tan raras, tan exquisitas, como que Carne el Pan sea." The intellectual project of the *autos* is thus unmasked as that of "examinar de Viandas tan Divinas la razón."[253]

The notion that words, also, could serve as spiritual food was self-consciously developed by these playwrights as a deliberate rhetorical project, or what Calderón calls "este raro Argumento de que son Palabra, y Trigo Viandas del Alma, y del Cuerpo."[254] To illustrate visually the spiritual truth behind this heavenly feast, one of the movable carts used to perform the *autos sacramentales* was divested of the lavish food which had formerly been displayed upon it. The earthly feast was then replaced with a heavenly one, symbolized by a simple chalice and the Eucharistic host: "el cuarto Carro la Fe en la Mesa, quitados los Manjares, y puesto en ella un Cáliz con Hostia."[255] Instead of the adulterous woman who had previously represented the figure of Gula, instead we now see a female type of the Virgin Mary offering spiritual sustenance to believers: "Tomad, tomad las Viandas, que nos ofrece Benigna la Piedad de una Mujer."[256]

In a supremely metaliterary moment, the theatrical experience itself is offered up as a visual, auditory, and intellectual feast for its viewers:

> A vuestros gustos ofrezco,
> Madrid, este nuevo plato,
> si os sabe bien le tendréis,
> siempre a punto, y sazonado.

Unlike with physical food, with this literary food they should never become too full: "Y de estos varios manjares, que en la mesa del teatro, os sirve la voluntad, nunca lleguéis a estar hartos."[257] The *comedia* as well as its characters are said to be seasoned with witty dialogue and comic humour.[258] But these metatheatrical moments never overshadow the central theological message. Corpus Christi is a mere earthly precursor to the future heavenly feast in which the audience is invited to participate: "os espera la ventura de veros Viandas Eternas."[259] Only at such a moment of extreme cultural transition could a Vice like Gluttony undergo such a profound metamorphosis.

6
Angry Young Murderers

Por las iras heredadas.

– Juan Bautista Diamante[1]

Anger is unquestionably one of the most powerful of the Vices, consuming mountains and laying high outcroppings of rock to waste: "la ira ásperos montes consume, altos Mármoles derriba."[2] The histrionics associated with Anger made it exceptionally theatrical and thus peculiarly susceptible to adaptation for the *comedia* stage. This very subject matter calls attention to itself as theatre, as when one angry character threatens, "ha de ser Parma un teatro de la venganza, y la ira con el fuego de mi agravio. Toca alarma."[3] Time and again playwrights manage to sound the alarm to alert their audiences to the presence of Anger in their works, be it through representations on stage or on the printed page. Unlike the other Deadly Sins, Anger bears a particular form of typography which came to be associated with it. These typographical conventions served to announce its presence visually on the page in the same way that an actor's gestures might announce Anger's entry on the stage. By printing parenthetical asides, playwrights in conjunction with typographers collaborated to signify Anger visually as outside and apart from normal experience (see figure 15). These parenthetical interpolations typically appear strung together in a series, the cumulative effect of which manages to convey successfully the extent of a character's rage: "con mayor desaire vencido (de pena muero) de mayor (rabio de ira) poder (de cólera tiemblo)" or "Elena (¡muero al pensarlo!) Cristiana (¡rabio al decirlo!) en busca (¡qué sentimiento!) del Madero, (¡qué delirio!)."[4] Alternatively, Anger is conveyed on the printed page of the *comedias sueltas* through a series of first-person, present-tense verbs set apart by commas, as in the following examples:

> "Rabio, lloro, peno, y gimo."
> "Muérome, rabio, suspiro, abrásome."
> "Ya rabio, desconfío, muero, y ardo; ya mi castigo siento."[5]

A more extreme example occurs in Pérez de Montalbán's *Cumplir con su obligación*, where no fewer than sixteen staccato first-person verbs are shot out in rapid succession: "Velo, duermo, sufro, callo, amo, olvido, rabio, peno, huyo, sigo, siento, lloro, ardo, hielo, vivo, muero."[6] It seems safe to say that this technique proved more effective in print than in performance.

However, playwrights succeeded in communicating the experience of their characters' Anger performatively in other ways. The visible and audible components of Anger enacted on stage include yelling, argumentation and insults, weeping and concomitant blindness, impatience or rushing around, and physical violence. All of these techniques would have made for spectacular theatre. Let us explore each of them in turn.

In the *comedias* we find characters bursting onto the stage, yelling and screaming in order to express their rage. Witness this fearsome description of Bernardo del Carpio in Juan de la Cueva's *La libertad de España*: "Y así lleno de Saña furiosa la voz terrible levantando al cielo, convocó aquella esquadra valerosa."[7] These actors were not necessarily screaming *at* anyone, just screaming.[8] We hear characters describe themselves as rending the air with their cries: "Yo furiosa, y ofendida, hendiendo a voces los aires."[9] Half the time they are yelling insults.[10] We get to eavesdrop on what some of these insults were: "Ya no lo pude sufrir, y de ira, y coraje lleno, le dije, bárbaro, bruto, de seso, y razón ajeno."[11] We overhear the warrior Achilles reaming out his enemies.[12] Many characters, when they become incensed, turn increasingly argumentative, like a lawyer: "En las cosas de la ira está retórico el pecho."[13] But others are actually less prone to argue, because they become confused.[14] In this case, they are actually angry that anyone else can think clearly enough to form rational arguments.[15] In the heat of the moment, they utter thoughtless words which cannot be retracted.[16]

Another visible sign of Anger enacted on stage is weeping: "hay lágrimas también que el coraje las arroja, dando suspiros al aire."[17] Tears come rushing out as Anger manifests itself through the eyes.[18] It might be thought that this form of Anger would only be found in female characters, but the *comedias* state explicitly that this is not the case; indeed, tears cried from rage were imagined to be consummately compatible with masculine honour: "Las lágrimas de coraje no hacen al honor ultraje, antes su fuerza acompañan."[19] This is the Golden Age version of today's pop psychology maxim, "Real men do cry."[20]

One thing is also certain: tears cried from Anger are beyond consolation, as in "Si llorara la terneza, me pudieras consolar, mas cuando llora la ira, está de más el consuelo."[21] Another result of this weeping is that it makes the angry person blind.[22] It makes one so blind that he forgets his obligation even to blood relatives: "¡Ha bárbara pasión ciega de la ira, que irritada, ni aun de su sangre se acuerda!"[23] As one character states baldly, Anger has no eyes.[24] Other physical symptoms include losing the colour from one's face, turning white or red,[25] trembling ("De ira tiemblo" and "de coraje estoy temblando"),[26] and sweating profusely.[27] The senses become confused, while patience is exhausted.[28] The angry person is specifically described as impatient, as in "yo cruel, colérica, e impaciente." In fact, impatience leads to more Anger.[29] Soon it is no longer possible to dissuade the angry person with rational arguments.[30] The angry person will not wait: "¿Qué colérico habrá, que quieto aguarde?"[31] Instead, she goes rushing around, fleeing the provocative incident or person.[32] In one particularly comical example, the allegorical figure of Anger is said to leave in a huff from the very performance of the *auto sacramental*: "Que se ha soltado la ira del Auto del Corpus hoy."[33] We can only imagine the impact of this visual representation of Anger and its propensity to run away pouting.

The ultimate manifestation of Anger on stage is physical violence. Again, the voyeuristic aspect of this sort of slapstick comedy routine, which nonetheless could turn deadly, made for great theatre.[34] In the *comedias* we find references to angry characters hitting each other, ripping each other's clothes off, and just generally trampling everything in sight: "por lograr mi bárbaro coraje, cuanto encuentro atropello."[35] The tendency here is to tear enemies apart, as when one angry character boasts: "bien pudiera, como herido can rabioso, a cuantos vienen contigo despedazar."[36] There are scenes of actual or reported stabbing, whipping, or beating with a board.[37]

These are all fairly standard theatrical fare and as such would not by themselves be worthy of comment. But then things start to get more creative, as when characters threaten to cut each other's tongues out ("Ella me ha muerto, ¿no ves que rabio? De celos muero; la lengua cortarte quiero") or command their subordinates to hang women by their hair from trees ("las mujeres colgad de los cabellos por los árboles; muero, rabio, deshágome; ¿qué es esto?").[38] In one particularly smelly example, a character reports having been threatened not just with a good whipping, but with being covered in bacon grease: "Este bárbaro feroz, ayer colérico dijo, que nos había de azotar, y pringarnos con tocino." As Scott Taylor explains, this was not a figment of Tirso's imagination, but instead an actual punishment: "'pringar' … referring to a punishment given to slaves involving hot grease applied to the wounds sustained from a whipping."[39] One can only hope, for the actors' sake – and given the presence of stray dogs roaming the streets near outdoor theatres – that the performance practice for this scene was not overly realistic.

Sometimes the physical violence of Anger was not directed outward at enemies or adversaries, but instead turned inward by an angry person upon him- or herself. The psychology of this phenomenon would be the assumption that depression is Anger turned inward.[40] We see here nervous nail-biters ("las manos me muerdo, y rabio de ver que en tu casa estoy") as well as furious women who rend their own garments ("Furiosa el pecho se rasga").[41] Characters threaten hyperbolically to rip their own hearts out.[42] They end up a bloody mess as Anger turns quickly into savage cruelty: "cuanto enojo dio la ira al ejercicio sangriento fue uso de su crueldad."[43]

As we might expect from other literary treatments of the Vices we have encountered, Golden Age playwrights employ metaphors from nature to achieve maximum visual impact in the minds of their audience as they describe Anger and its effects. Anger is likened to the sea or to its miniature, a swiftly flowing fountain.[44] In a further extension of this water imagery, Anger is compared to a thunderstorm, which at that time was believed quite literally to be a manifestation of God's displeasure: "Alguna gente ha entrado a rogar su Dios temple la ira de los truenos, y rayos, que ya cesan."[45] This imagery could also appear figuratively, with lightning in particular being used to describe the effect of words spoken in Anger upon a wounded heart: "Loco estoy, de celos rabio, rayos mis palabras sean."[46]

The static electricity of lightning could of course produce fire where it struck, and it is to this family of symbolism that we shall turn next. The discourse of Anger is filled with words for burning, such as *arder* and *abrasar*: "Rabioso furor me abrasa"; "en ira, y en coraje ardo"; and "lleno de ira, y de coraje ardiente."[47] An angry woman is said to be on fire: "colérica, será incendio, ira, estrago, y rabia."[48] In fact, Anger is said to *be* fire.[49] In one humorous line, a character asks whether given that Anger is fire, it could ever produce actions that were cold as ice: "siendo fuego la ira, ¿quiere que la acción sea hielo?"[50] Anger's fire is inextinguishable, to the point of comparison with a continually erupting volcano.[51] Rage erupts from an angry person like the flames from Mount Etna.[52]

Angry people, not surprisingly, are compared to animals in these dramas, in a further effort to situate their extraordinary behaviour within the natural world. We find epic catalogues of angry beasts, such as "lebrel rabioso, tigre fiero, áspid pisado, león pardo, bravo toro," along with evocations of animals who were not normally violent but had turned so after having been stricken with the plague (thus we find "la ira de apestadas Aves").[53] Some of these creatures were mythical, such as the hydra – a being, as we have seen, often associated iconographically with the Seven Deadly Sins – or the basilisk, a hybrid of a rooster's head combined with a serpent's tail.[54] One particularly striking image of Anger comes by association with the biblical lobsters of the Apocalypse.[55] A more mundane characterization occurs when Anger is likened to a rabid dog, as in "Como perro herido rabio, de rabia mortal herido."[56] Another frequent comparison is made to a venomous snake.[57] Angry characters first present themselves as tied, bound, or bitten by the asp of wrath.[58] In an especially vivid image, snakes feed on their bosom: "ceben las Víboras, que en mi Pecho se alimentan de la ira."[59] They are filled with venom to the point of bursting ("Reventar de mi veneno" and "reviento, rabio de la ponzoña que cría el dolor").[60] The venom threatens to rush out as from a snake which has been stepped on.[61] Sometimes the venom might stay hidden, but always it seeks to be released: "Una, y mil veces rabiosa solicita con cautelas verter su infame veneno."[62] This occurs most often through poisonous words, as in "suele ofender con veneno de la lengua y de la ira."[63] It could also simply be exhaled: "veneno exhalo desde el pie al cabello."[64] Occasionally the venom is specified, as when Calderón refers to it as hemlock, the same deadly poison drunk by Socrates when he was ordered to commit suicide.[65] This poisonous spiritual substance results in animal-like behaviour by humans, for "No es en las fieras, y animales sólos a quien la ira del vengarse alcanza."[66] We see angry men bleating and kicking like goats as well as angry women who seem to morph into snakes.[67] We even find disturbing language describing brutal acts normally associated with self-cannibalism ("su Verdugo, y su homicida: como el que rabioso y loco se ceba en su carne misma") and – though this metaphor belongs more properly to a later time period – self-vampirism: "Y quien sale de una batalla infernal, con hidrópico coraje de beber mi sangre propia."[68] Even when Anger once again turns outward, repeatedly we note a bloodthirstiness which we would associate with vampires, though Golden Age playwrights probably would not have.[69] *Ira* is commonly associated with thirst that can only be sated by drinking the blood of one's victims.[70] This pattern places us squarely in the realm of madness, towards which Anger has been leading us inexorably all along.

The discourse of madness is employed routinely in the *comedias* to convey the experience of Anger. Angry figures in these plays are characterized alternately as frenzied, senseless, or crazed.[71] In one particularly telling example, a technical term from casuistry, *synderesis*, is harnessed to bear a new type of cultural freight: "Di que estoy ciego, estoy loco. Di que tengo, porque rabio, el sinderesis perdido."[72] *Synderesis* was a term coined by Saint Jerome to mean "the immediate apprehension of the first practical moral principles of the natural law."[73] Given the centrality of casuistry to the *comedia*'s poetics – as I have established at length in my book *Conscience on Stage* – this image of a conscience lost through rage may strike us as uniquely poignant.

In another twist that is of special interest to me personally, given the topics of my previous research, characters often explicitly connect demonic possession to Anger.[74] This should come as no great surprise, considering Anger's privileged relationship to Hell: "la ira del Reino horrible, del eterno olvido."[75] Prototypes for Anger in the *comedias* often include supernatural entities such as Satan. One representative passage describes the devil as angry: "pues hay pluma, que compara al demonio, a un can rabioso."[76] We must not forget that in the *autos sacramentales* and even the secular drama, an actor dressed as Lucifer would appear on stage as one of the characters. When this happened, he was given the lines we would expect to convey his raving.[77] At least he is in good company: a whole pantheon of pagan gods and figures from Greek and Roman mythology join the chorus to intone the discourse of Anger.

Mythological figures appearing in connection with Anger in the *comedias* include Jupiter, Saturn, Jove, Hercules, Diana, and Pallas or Athena.[78] We also find reference to the Fates, as in "Ceda el valor a la ira de los hados."[79] We find further allusions to the Furies, who in some instances are called by their individual names: "empiece de mi furor también la ira: o Sumejera, que de las tres furias eres la que más a Marte asiste, en aquel bruto reviste toda la saña que adquieres."[80] But Renaissance playwrights also drew profitably upon the Christian tradition. Biblical figures invoked as emblematic of Anger include the Egyptian Pharaoh ("ve que habla el Psalmista de los tormentos, que dio rabioso a los Israelitas Faraón, cuando en tirano Imperio los oprimía") as well as the King of Persia, who sacked Jerusalem: "Empiezo: Cosdroes Rey Persiano, ministro de la ira el más tirano, saqueó a Jerusalén cuando reinaba."[81] Tracing the phenomenological history of Anger through the ancients into early modern times, we might well ask ourselves who, among these dramatists' contemporaries, they considered to be especially prone to Anger at the time when they wrote. It turns out that the Portuguese in particular are vilified in the *comedias* as being terribly susceptible to falling under Anger's sway: "igualmente la ira Portuguesa añadió a Troya, si no lástimas, cenizas." In a similar example from the same play, one character offers to avenge another, claiming as his special qualification the fact that he is Portuguese: "permite, señor, vengarte la ira de un Portugués, que tu honor va a restaurar."[82]

It will come as no surprise to experienced readers of early modern texts that another group targeted for criticism regarding Anger would be women. We find such prejudicial stereotypes as "temo que es mujer, y en ellas arde la ira" and "más rigurosa, más fiera traición, que en humano Pecho la ira de Mujer engendra."[83] An effort is made to claim that women, in general, are more prone to Anger than men.[84] Women even say this of themselves: "el verme alterar te admira, no sabes ya que es la ira mayorazgo en las mujeres."[85] The shrewish, angry women we encounter in the *comedias* specifically include stepmothers, like the one who appears in fairy tales such as *Cinderella*: "Casóse luego y temiendo de la madrastra la ira."[86] However, some say women only act angry because it is fashionable: "pues no es la ira, entre las mujeres, más que gala."[87] Ultimately this misogyny remains unconvincing, due to a simple fact: Anger is associated predominantly with warlike behaviour, and most (though not all) women in the *comedias* are not warlike. There are some key exceptions, such as the *mujer varonil*. As one of these gutsy girls declares defiantly, "soy mujer, y en mi pecho está en su punto la ira. Dame esa espada."[88] We can easily picture her brandishing a sword. But in general, Anger is associated more with men because early modern men tended to be more militantly violent.[89]

In this vein, Anger is often mentioned in the *comedias* in the context of specific weapons. Figuratively speaking, Anger is said to be a knife.[90] On a more literal level of interpretation, concrete stage props would have been used to bolster the mention of specific weaponry in these texts. Most common among these is the sword: "la ira dispense de su acero siempre airado."[91] The sword wielded by one of these belligerent men could unleash his Anger and send it flying into orbit: "mi acero rayo será, que desata la esfera de mi coraje."[92] We see angry warriors bearing swords, menacing their enemies face to face or waving them in their eyes, calling them by name with fearsome cries: "con su acero, a voces te va llamando y con coraje diciendo, que te ha de dar el castigo."[93] Other weapons mentioned in the context of Anger are pistols, bullets, and rapiers.[94] Alternative options might be a dagger or a knife, or perhaps even arrows, with which Andalusians were thought to be particularly adept.[95] We see the image of an angry soldier on the battlefield sharpening a pike with flint: "O cómo el pico arrogante, colérico, y presuroso amuela en los pedernales."[96] Anger is associated closely with weapons, to the point that the allegorical figure of Ira appears carrying a sword, selling swords, or dressed as a bandit firing pistols in the *autos sacramentales*.[97]

Another close association of Anger which is not unrelated to warlike behaviour is that of youth. As was the case with the later British literary and cinematic movement from the 1950s and 60s known as the Angry Young Men, back in the Renaissance, Anger was already considered the near-exclusive province of youth.[98] We find characters attributing episodes of Anger to youthful lapses, such as "tu edad deja vencerse de la ira."[99] This dangerous time of youth is inevitably contrasted with old age, in which the fire of Anger has already been spent: "yo soy viejo, y tengo ya la ira y valor templados."[100] As we shall see below, young men were thought to suffer from an inflammation of the blood which coursed burning through their veins as long as they were still in their tender years; in comparison, old men's blood was as thick as phlegm.[101] In fact, old men's grey hairs are likened to the spent ashes left over from the fires of their manhood.[102] However, not all old guys are so tame: "en su edad … las cenizas guardan de la ira algún calor."[103] Even still, angry behaviour is not recommended for older people because it detracts from their *gravitas* ("Mucho desdice la ira de la anciana gravedad").[104]

Occasions for youthful Anger might include jealousy or reaction to an affront. Anger appears in the *comedias* often in the context of romantic jealousy, as when the king in Alarcón's *Los pechos privilegiados* declares, "Ya el rabioso desatino de los celos me enloquece."[105] Jealousy is said to rule with a crown and sceptre over Anger, which means it must do its bidding the way a subject obeys a monarch or a god: "viven mis ardientes celos, dioses que hoy en mi coraje, tienen la corona, y cetro."[106] Anger may be aroused by a lover's disloyalty in a jealous partner who looks for answers but then does not believe what she hears: "pues la que más celosa se muestra, más colérica y furiosa, más entonces desea satisfacciones, aunque no las crea."[107] This is especially true when a man finds a love letter written by his lady to another, where every word becomes a wound and every letter becomes a sharp dagger.[108] No one will be able to restrain this jealous passion: "¿quién a enfrenar será bastante la cólera furiosa de una pasión celosa?"[109] We shall look later in this chapter at the ramifications of this discourse of the passions. One particularly astute playwright sums it all up in the maxim, "love is an angry accident": "amor es un colérico accidente."[110]

Anger could also be aroused in response to a perceived affront, such as an insult or a social slight to a sensitive recipient.[111] This incident could be as simple as a breach of decorum or even what might be interpreted as an insulting tone of voice ("Responde tan altiva, que mi coraje aviva").[112] Sometimes it could be a literal slap in the face, but more often the culprit was a licentious tongue, as in "la ira que alborota tu lengua licenciosa."[113] Anger would obviously be provoked by a lie, a logical enough association without the elaborate etymology typically applied to it of the Latin *mens* + *ira*, an allusion to which we find in the phrase "me suspendió la ira de su enojosa mentira."[114] Anger could even arise in the face of an unspecified offence.[115]

Basically any new cause of annoyance could give occasion for wrath.[116] But the most extreme provocation to Anger in Spanish Golden Age society was usually the desire for revenge. Anger is intimately intertwined with revenge tragedies in these dramas, as we see from lines such as "me enciende la ira, a tomar venganza."[117] Characters become angry at the slightest hint of betrayal, as for example by two erstwhile friends: "no es posible, que haya consejo, que no atropelle la ira; en vengarme me resuelvo de dos traidores Amigos."[118] The most frequent scenario, however, is for revenge to be enacted in the wake of a death, especially a close relative, such as a father ("Mas mi Padre es éste, rabio ya por hacer su venganza").[119] Among the Deadly Sins, Anger might be said to predominate in cases of honour. As one character states succinctly, "es colérico el honor."[120]

In the most extreme cases – and let us not forget that the *comedias*, by and large, present exactly that: extreme cases[121] – the end result of Anger can be the taking of a human life. What we have here is yet another liminal instance in which a Deadly Sin came to be viewed in terms of the Ten Commandments. The Fifth Commandment's injunction against Murder was well known, and yet the *comedia* stage is filled with spectacular scenes of homicide.[122] How are these Murders presented on stage, or narrated later if they occur off the set? In what terms are they posed, and how does this terminology situate these actions within competing moral economies? It turns out that the facile segue from Anger to Murder is illustrative of larger trends within early modern Spanish society.

Angry characters on stage frequently talk about wanting to kill someone, as with the lines, "Muero, rabio en pensarlo, ¿que me detengo pues? Quiero matarlo."[123] But there is a big difference between just talking about it and actually doing it or having it done.[124] Anger is repeatedly offered as an explanation for why someone could have killed someone else, as when Leonor describes a potential killer as "Tan rabioso, que no dudo que allí la diera la muerte."[125] Other characters simply assume that this is what happened.[126] Some of these massacres are recounted later in particularly gruesome terms, as with "Sin duda viene de coraje ciego, él lo ha muerto, no deja de él pedazo."[127] At other times the threat of future murderous action is spoken in the third person, as when an angry warrior pledges to avenge a wrong done to a lady, even if it means killing the emperor in the process.[128] Or – in what must have made for a particularly suspenseful scene – the threat is made directly to the offending party: "sabré estimarte, dueño, como amante. Pero si no, enojada, rigurosa, colérica, briosa, impaciente, severa, y ofendida, te enseñaré, quitándote la vida."[129] We must note that this warning is issued peremptorily by an Amazon queen, one of the aforementioned stock characters known as the *mujer varonil*.

Sometimes, when threatened in this way, the intended victim begs for mercy, once again situating his or her plea within the context of Anger: "no me mates, Alejandro; ten la ira, Federico."[130] Even when avoided, the danger is still acknowledged, as when Lirio warns, "Vete, antes que mi inhumana rabiosa furia te mate."[131] Anger has left many a young girl orphaned when the men in her life have fought duels to protect her honour. As Calderón reminds us in *Duelos de amor, y lealtad*: "cuantas desamparadas Bellezas huérfanas dejó la ira."[132] The *comedias* leave little room for doubt: death is the true daughter of Anger ("la muerte … que hija sea de la ira").[133] Eventually this moral and philosophical position leads to a transfer of emphasis from a Deadly Sin to one of the Ten Commandments.

* * * * *

As we have seen in previous chapters, such as the one devoted to Lust, the Golden Age was a period of incipient criminalization in which, for the first time, certain sins came to be viewed as crimes. The shift in emphasis from Anger to Murder was no exception. In plays which participate in this transition to a legal framework, if Anger is mentioned at all, it applies more to the temperament of the judge: "confesar el delito, con claro arrepentimiento, mitiga en parte la ira del juez que es sabio y recto."[134] It is fascinating to watch the terminology of repentance and confession being tranferred from a sacramental/penitential context to a secular, legal one. We might have expected to see the phrase *confesar el pecado*, to confess the sin, but instead we find *confesar el delito* – to confess the crime, in a clear reference to a courtroom setting. In an even more elaborate reversal of received categories, now all of a sudden the criminal is not the one being found guilty, but instead it is the judge: "¿Qué cosa en el sentenciar, la ira puede templar, como hallarse el juez culpado?"[135] In fact, nothing mitigates a judge's Anger like his own acknowledgment of guilt.

What we find here is a messy mixture of two or even three competing frameworks: three, if you consider two competing moral economies – one based on the Ten Commandments versus one based on the Seven Deadly Sins – plus a third, secular variety which employs instead the terminology of lawsuits and courtrooms to replace what used to be references to casuistry and confessional booths. This is truly a complicated picture. In the *comedias* we do still find some attempts to use Deadly Vices to excuse crimes, or vice versa, as in "Hace justa la ira que consigo, el detestable crimen."[136] But it is hard to ignore the fact that increasingly, these actions were referred to as crimes – that is, *crímenes* or *delitos* – as opposed to sins, whether mortal or venial. In a few particularly fraught cases, there could even be a direct conflict between the visions of ecclesiastical and secular authorities regarding a specific wrong action and how it would be defined. The special case of uxoricide in the wake of Adultery provides one illustrative example.

Studies have been done of an entire subgenre within the *comedias* known as the wife-murder plays. These spectacular dramas of uxoricide served as the perfect arena for contending factions in what was increasingly a battle to domesticate, contain, and define sin:

> One cannot dispute that there were laws permitting wife murder and documented cases of such actions in the sixteenth and seventeenth centuries, and that seventeenth-century Spain was concerned with both lascivious behavior and honor. Husbands such as one finds in the wife-murder plays did exist, and, in large part, they were the products of social tensions that forced them to eliminate their wives in order to fulfill what they considered to be more important personal considerations … The laws were not unified in granting to the husband the power of life and death over their wives in matters of honor, and both the laws and their enforcement changed considerably over time.[137]

The most nuanced treatment of these laws and their changing interpretations by both moralists and jurists appears in Daniel Heiple's essay "The Theological Context of Wife Murder in Seventeenth-Century Spain." In this study, Heiple traces the wife-murder laws all the way back to the Roman *Lex Julia*, through the medieval *Fuero real*, to the *Recopilación de leyes*. His verdict is unequivocal: if two lovers were caught in Adultery, "the law specifically allowed the husband to kill with impunity the wife and her lover on his own authority."[138] The confessors' manuals, however, did not concur with the law of the land. Following Saint Augustine and Saint Thomas Aquinas, they condemned Murder in any form and refused to sanction these honour killings as an ethical course of action. But as Heiple points out, the fact that confessors were addressing these issues at all, by definition, left open a moral loophole:

> While no Spanish theologians actually argued in print that a husband could kill with moral impunity his adulterous wife and her lover on his own authority, the fact that each takes up the question suggests that it functioned as a disputed question which allowed the probabilists to accept the less probable solution.[139]

As Jenaro Artiles explains, these husbands – and the confessors who advised them – managed to convince themselves that they were not in fact taking revenge so much as channelling the wrath of God to perform the role of divinely sanctioned executioners. In fact, in some cases they even believed they were saving their wives' souls:

> En el castigo del causante de la deshonra en el drama del siglo de oro, como en la vida real, no hay la menor idea de venganza, sino una convicción profunda de ser, el marido en el caso del honor conyugal, el padre en el de la hija, la mano ejecutora de la justicia de Dios, necesaria a veces para restablecer la balanza y hasta, como se nos ofrecen ejemplos repetidos y se expresa en alguna comedia, para la salvación eterna del alma del merecedor del castigo.[140]

Postmodern readers, especially students, tend to find this sort of casuistical contortion remarkable.

Probably the best-known drama from this group of plays is Calderón's classic *El médico de su honra*.[141] In this play, Mencía is a faithful wife to Don Gutierre, who nonetheless becomes suspicious of her fidelity when her old lover Prince Enrique shows up in town. Gutierre surprises her in the act of writing a note to Enrique, which he believes to be a love letter (but which is really a Dear John). Gutierre calls a Jewish doctor and orders him to bleed his wife to death. When the doctor is led blindfolded to and from Mencía's room, he leaves bloodstains on the walls with his hands as evidence to help him find the place again later.[142] Don Gutierre confesses to the king that he has murdered his wife; but the king, finding his suspicions of Adultery plausible enough, does not punish him. Instead, he marries him off immediately to one of his previous girlfriends.

The crux of the dilemma explored in this drama revolves around the fact that at this time, secular law permitted husbands to slay their adulterous wives, though canon law did not.[143] These plays' insistence on exploring this subject matter, with all of its complex ramifications, demonstrates how effective these playwrights were at pointing out inconsistencies between the secular and religious frameworks in which they lived. The tension between these competing moral economies goes beyond even the one we have been describing throughout this study, the struggle between a more communal world view as exemplified by the Seven Deadlies and a more individualistic one as represented, albeit somewhat problematically, by the Decalogue. But the deeper tension is related to the superficial one in the sense that increased legalization of society meant, at least potentially, greater protection of individual rights. The messy mixture of terminology in these quotations reveals that these competing frameworks were not necessarily judged to be incompatible, but instead jostled each other side by side in an increasingly uncomfortable coexistence.

Part of this growing discomfort with overt reliance on the Seven Deadly Sins as a moral framework may stem from a certain uneasiness with legislating intangibles. After all, a narrowly defined crime such as wife-killing was easier to prosecute than an intention or an emotion such as Anger.[144] It still remained relevant in the sense of being a readily identifiable motivating factor, but increasingly the emphasis fell less on Anger than on the concrete actions it inspired.

Besides, how could Anger be wrong if even God felt it sometimes? In their more didactic iteration, the *comedias* are filled with general references to divine wrath, such as the ire of Heaven ("la Ira del Cielo")[145] or of the supreme gods, whose disdains were deemed unknowable by man: "de divinos desdenes no entienden humanos pechos."[146] Renaissance dramatists drew upon a long classical tradition of humans fleeing the pagan gods' wrath, as when Calcas pleads in Juan de la Cueva's classicizing *La muerte de Ajax Telamón*, "Fuerte Agamenon, la ira de los Dioses aplaquemos, y nuestros yerros purguemos."[147] In a further messy mixing of terminology, this language of purging errors almost sounds like a pagan version of the Catholic sacrament of confession. More often, in the *comedias* we find deliberate allusions to the Christian God's wrath, as in "la ira de Dios fuerte y divina."[148] God is said to be outraged by such sins as Adultery ("rebelde y adulterina, pues no merecéis piedad, sentiréis de Dios la ira"), but obviously not as much as the husband, who is the one chasing her – often literally – with a dagger on stage.[149] All sin is loathsome to God,[150] but we cannot resist the feeling at times that instead of the open-air *corral* theatre we have somehow strayed into a revival tent of the American Great Awakening, where Jonathan Edwards preached his famous sermon, *Sinners in the Hands of an Angry God*.[151] These priestly playwrights' rather frantic calls to repentance ("mira que irritas de Dios la ira, y tarde has de arrepentirte") suggest that God's Anger can only be placated by religious fervor: "se puede aplacar de Dios la ira el continuo fervor."[152]

If God's Anger was not culpable, then surely a righteous form of Anger for human beings was also possible, however rarely it was meant to be invoked. But certain truly subversive references to righteous Anger from the Bible, such as Samson slaying the Philistines ("valor Cristiano, como las de Sansón, juntas un día, quiere la ira derribar por tierra"),[153] reverse moral categories to the point where we are left feeling unsure whether Anger is necessarily a bad thing. In traditional biblical hermeneutics, Samson was seen as a prototype of Christ,[154] Who would later also engage in righteous Anger when He cleaned out the moneylenders' tables from the temple.[155] But in a further layer of texture for this already dense passage, Anger becomes not the source of Samson's strength, but instead a metaphor for the Philistine banqueting hall whose columns he breaks to collapse the building, killing all who were inside – himself included. This literally colossal act of multiple Murder is sanctioned in the Bible because it was directed against God's enemies. And as we might have expected, early modern Spaniards grant themselves a similar licence to commit Murder whenever they are fighting against infidels and heretics: "encontrando unos Herejes perjuros, colérico me obligaron a sacar la espada."[156] There is no escaping the historical fact of the Murders committed as part of the Crusades or the Reconquest. When it comes to exterminating heresy, Anger is redefined to the point of extinction, suddenly ceasing to be a Sin itself and instead bringing an end to the sins committed by Others: "para que se borre … la iniquidad, y … de sus abominaciones destruyendo la ira fiera, y dando fin al pecado."[157] These problematic passages offer us a complex picture of what can only be termed one of the messiest transitions ever to occur in Western moral and intellectual history.

So what happened to Anger as its star started to wane on the horizon of early modern Spanish drama? Did it disappear? Did it cease to be relevant altogether as a defining moral category? Was it replaced by something else? If so, by what? Did it continue to coexist with its replacement? Or did it morph into something new completely, some other entity no longer recognizable as one of the Capital Vices? In this case, it is this last option which seems to have prevailed. If not entirely unrecognizable, at least Anger became so secularized that it could hardly be classified as a Sin any longer. Let us explore this thorny knot of historiography further.

When the Seven Deadly Sins had by and large finished their performance on the early modern stage, they did not simply grab their props and exit stage right. They hung around for a while. To obtain permission from the director to do this – in our hypothetical, metaphorical scenario – they had to blend into the scenery. The way they did this, in terms of *mentalités*, was to metamorphose into passions, affects, or humours.[158] It has long been noted that the Renaissance witnessed a revival of, as well as Paracelsian challenges to, Galenic medicine.[159] But here, finally, we have proof both that Spain participated in this trend and that the preoccupations of erudite humanists found their way onto the popular stage. Let's see how this works.

Increasingly in the *comedias* Anger is redefined as a passion, as in "La ira detén, porque es pasión desigual."[160] It is something to which someone gives way: "dio lugar en todo el pecho a la cólera, y la ira. Ya de esta pasión soy todo."[161] As such, it is something that one can put on like a garment.[162] It alters the blood ("dando a un hombre ocasión, la ira, como pasión natural, su sangre altera").[163] Alternatively, at other times Anger evolves in the *comedias* into what was known as an affect, a concept not fully understood by some readers today.[164] According to the Golden Age lexicographer Sebastián de Covarrubias, *afecto* may be defined as "pasión del ánima, que redundando en la voz, la altera y causa en el cuerpo un particular movimiento, con que movemos a compasión y misericordia, a ira y a venganza, a tristeza y alegría; cosa importante y necesaria en el orador."[165] In these plays, Anger or rage is said to fight or struggle against or in an affect, such as with the line, "La rabia emboce, que en mi afecto lidia." At other times, Anger appears to morph into an affect, as with the question "¿por qué mudaste aquella ira en este afecto?"[166] But also, at one point Calderón de la Barca offers a specific definition of Anger *as* an affect based upon physical symptoms: "el Afecto de la Ira ... es Sangre inflamada, que al corazón se retira."[167] Blood is also said to be burning as Anger reaches a feverish pitch: "la ira se cría de espíritu, y sangre ardiente." This talk of blood rising, retracting, or burning should immediately make us suspect that we are in the realm of humoural psychology.[168]

Unruly as they sound, the affects were thought to be something that could be controlled or deliberately transferred or channelled into a different course of action, as in "cuando vos os entregáis al despecho, desde el amor a la ira trasladáis vuestros afectos."[169] An affect could pass via the voice from, say, dismay to Anger.[170] Anger was not the only Deadly Vice to metamorphose into an affect, which then could be said to rule over a person and his actions.[171] Indeed, affects could be said to conquer the passions, as in Juan Bautista Diamante's significantly titled *Pasión vencida de afecto*.

In this play, the King of Albania has two daughters. The law stipulates that the oldest daughter must inherit the crown, or else it will pass to the enemy prince of a neighbouring kingdom. A further legal requirement is that she must marry in order to be eligible to govern. Deeply resenting this imposition, the daughter, Fénix, resists marrying because she does not wish to be made subject to a man. Ultimately she is wooed by a junior prince of Thebes, who sings to her instead of trying to cajole her into marrying him. By keeping a respectful distance, he gains both a bride and a kingdom. As Jodi Campbell notes, this gentle approach to taming the passions is reflected well in the play's title, which announces the moral of the story:

> Federico wins her love by singing to her, trying to charm her rather than emphasizing her obligations to marry. This approach is echoed by the servants, who comment that "tyranny should know that the attractive accomplishes more than the unpleasant." It is also underlined by the title, in which Fénix's passion (not to be dominated) is overcome by her affection for Federico. In other words, a ruler, or anyone else, who wishes to impose his will would do best to appeal to the interests of those on whom he wishes to impose it.[172]

Here we see that within Golden Age *mentalités*, an affect could indeed prove more powerful than a passion.

It is a very short step indeed from the discourse of passions and affects to the formal language of the humours. Anger here shifts terminology slightly, becoming instead a choleric humour: "Que ha gran tiempo que padece de humor colérico, y triste."[173] In fact, all lovers are said to suffer from this malady: "Señor, todos los amantes tienen colérico humor."[174] As we saw previously, romantic

Anger affects primarily those who are jealous: "como el humor colérico predomina, en el celoso … yo estaba febricitante de envidia."[175] It is typical of this new medicalization of sin – comparable to the nascent secularization we saw earlier in a legal context – that there is a renewed emphasis on actual physical symptoms. This last passage mentions a physical symptom, a fever, but we should also note the cameo appearance of another one of the Seven Deadlies, Envy. This last of the Capital Vices will be the subject of our next chapter. In the meantime, for the person who suffers from a choleric humour, an excess of blood incites him to strange dreams while he sleeps: "como al humor, ẏ condición aplace la cólera al colérico, a su dueño la sangre incita a semejante sueño."[176] This psychological – as opposed to physical – symptom nonetheless corresponds to a nascent medicalizing mentality which strove to document the minutiae of diseases and the concrete ways in which they were made manifest.

Humoural medicine, in turn, also influenced a newly rational discourse of cure. Rationality had temporarily been made subject to or even been displaced by Anger, but now we find explicit appeals to rationality as a way to counteract its pernicious effects:

> PRÍNCIPE: Rabio de enojo, Belardo.
> BELARDO: Con razón, témplate en él.[177]

There are certainly still some vestiges of religious arguments against Anger, but increasingly we see these supplanted by appeals instead to clear understanding and prudence, as in "¡Con qué cordura reporta su colérico despecho!"[178] We find characters being told to calm down, as when Agamemnon commands in Juan de la Cueva's *La muerte de Ajax Telamón*, "Vuestra encendida pasión sosegad."[179] Anger-prone hotheads are encouraged not to get mad until they know the full story: "Reporta, señor, la ira, hasta que la culpa sepas."[180] The pen is mightier than the sword, as words are seen to win out over war games: "¿qué fuerza oculta tienen tus palabras, puesto, que de mi ardiente coraje has aplacado el incendio?"[181] The best approach to take in response to an angry individual is a humble, honest answer, which frequently will cause the person's Anger to dissipate:

> El enojo me ha quitado
> la risa, y respuesta honesta,
> porque una humilde respuesta,
> templa el corazón airado.[182]

The right word spoken at the right time, particularly if it produces laughter, can act as a ray of sunshine, dispelling the cloud of someone's rage: "¿fue rayo, que despedía la nube de su coraje?"[183] Ultimately the discourse of fury is replaced by the language of sacramental confession, which – in a paradoxically secularizing turn – in this case seems to be more about repeating the reassuring words of ritual, "yo confieso," than about receiving absolution from the priest.[184] In a prescient precursor to pop psychology, we find hints about breaking the cycle of Anger: "del Duque la ira quiebra, y llegue el desenojo."[185]

Increasingly we encounter arguments against Anger not because it is wrong or sinful but simply because it's undignified, particularly for what was at that time the world's foremost superpower: "La vil venganza, y la ira son indignas del imperio."[186] Anger is deemed unworthy of Spanish nobility: "mira, que no es nobleza la ira, y el perdonar es valor."[187] It is beneath Spanish poise, inducing behaviour relegated to the barbarians ("No queráis seguir el bárbaro impulso de la ira") or to lower-class *pícaros*, akin to beggars ("Mira que dar lugar a la ira, es de hombres de baja suerte").[188] Anger places a fool's cap upon its victim's head.[189] It no longer works as a good excuse for bad behaviour.[190] In contrast, Anger that cedes to wise counsel is elevated as the consummate example of reason of state: "razón … de estado, hacer que la ira al consejo ceda."[191] Such is the burden and responsibility of noblesse oblige.

In line with this new rationality, we find cameo appearances of angry people calming down ("perdiendo voy la ira") or describing others who are recovering from their rage ("Clara, no te turbes, mira que de tu esposo la ira se viene templando ya").[192] We witness characters repenting of their Anger or pronouncing maxims about how quickly the angry person will regret his actions.[193] He soon decides it's not worth it – "Ya os habrán dicho, que yo, Príncipes, la ira templada, quiero más daros honores, que tomar una venganza" – as Anger turns instead to Pity.[194] The formerly angry person is here encouraged to make amends, often via the symbolic gesture of proffering peace ("En paces quiero resolver la ira").[195]

Anger's recovery is often achieved by putting some time and distance between one's self and the provocative incident: "que al fin se entibia la ira cuando el tiempo se interpone."[196] Eventually we find recovering rage-aholics looking back and even laughing about it later: "de cuando en cuando me hacen rabiar; y después me río de ver, que rabio."[197] A telling sign of this new discourse of rationality applied to Anger occurs in the multiple references we find to what was known as the mirror cure: "el espejo, de él se dice, que templa la ira, en poniendo al colérico su imagen delante."[198] The idea here was that the ridiculous image of a person's own angry, red face would immediately cause him to calm down once he saw it: "para templar la ira, es bueno mirar su rostro un hombre al espejo."[199] This scenario must have proven particularly entertaining in performance.

The classic case in the Old Testament of an angry person recovering from his rage occurs in the episode of David and Saul, where the young shepherd boy plays on his harp to soothe the troubled spirit of the Jewish king.[200] This early example of the use of music therapy to treat psychological disturbance was called, by

Renaissance critics, an exorcism.[201] But while it may involve supernatural elements, this interpretation ignores the discourse of Virtues and Vices as the lens through which Golden Age dramatists viewed this scene. In Calderón's *La primer flor de el Carmelo*, the young David, future king of Israel, says, "venza mi humildad de Saúl la ira."[202] In another auto, *El indulto general*, Calderón once again makes reference to "Las Armas sí, que la ira de Saúl a David entrega."[203] The fact that King Saul was sleeping as David played him a lullaby has also been overlooked in some interpretations. It is significant that sites of Anger were specifically pinpointed on the body and that Anger was said to be sleeping inside a person's chest.[204] The allegorical figure of Ira appears bearing a breastplate to call attention to the part of the body where Anger was traditionally located.[205] There Anger was thought to lie sleeping until aroused: "si en ti duerme la ira, en mí la hallarás despierta."[206] Then, in soldier's or cattleman's terms, Anger applied a sharp spur to the heart: "la ira pone al corazón espuela."[207] In the *comedias* we find medical procedures such as bleeding, often with leeches, to remove rage ("Sangrarme quiero, porque traigo la sangre requemada, corrompida, colérica, dañada, adusta, hecha materia, y repodrida")[208] or counteracting one humour with another: "lo colérico aplacara con ponerle lo sanguino."[209] But we also find such common-sense remedies for Anger as simply going to sleep, as in "el tiempo que el venenoso coraje de mis nunca muertas iras, rendido al sueño, descanse."[210] We are certainly far removed from the discourse of sin and punishment if all it takes to fix the problem is a nice little nap.

One of the most characteristic elements of the discourse of Anger had been reports of the experience of being carried away, out of control, or suspended, a sensation brilliantly described for the mystical context in Elena del Río Parra's essay on *suspensio animi*.[211] Interestingly, the language often used to describe Anger ("la ira te arrebata" and "la ira arrebata a la suspensión")[212] is the same language used to describe pious mystical ecstasy. Of characters who give way to its influence, it is said that Anger controls them in the same way that the Holy Spirit guided the actions of saints and *beatas*.[213] This is very complex moral territory indeed. But increasingly, we find that the discourse of being out of control or suspended gives way to a counter-discourse of reins and restraint, as in "refrena de sus iras el coraje" or "Detén un poco tu furiosa ira."[214] In a humorous example of reason reining in Anger, one character tells another to just shut up and leave: "mas será bien que la razón recoja las riendas a la ira, calla, y vete."[215]

If that's what it takes for them to regain control of themselves, then so be it; we should note that it also provides a clever way for a dramatist to end a scene. But even in the most serious moral context of Murder described earlier, increasingly *comedia* characters warn each other not to give way to Anger in the first place:

SEMÍRAMIS: No le mates, señor, tente.
MENÓN: Suspende la ira.[216]

Noblemen in particular are encouraged to make an exception to the dictates of honour and show themselves instead to be more benign.[217] Getting rid of Anger will allow them to see more clearly a situation's causes and effects.[218] This wisdom is most often proffered in the tone of fatherly advice ("Refrena o hijo el alterado pecho, no te entregue la ira al enemigo") or sage counsel spoken by a trusted counsellor to a king.[219] Much like the modern popular psychology book *Love Is a Choice*, about the dangers of co-dependency, Anger is seen here to be a decision.[220] Those who give in to it often regret it later.[221] We see here a remarkable degree of self-awareness and interiority for what have traditionally been dismissed as flat characters (witness the reflection, "Tentando me está la ira").[222] This self-awareness, at least potentially, offers literary characters greater autonomy by putting them in control.

Here we might think of Joseph Gillet's classic essay on novelistic autonomy, which he claims was more or less invented during the early modern period.[223] Why should the same period that produced *Don Quijote* not afford some autonomy to its dramatic personae? In the *comedias* in the context of Anger we find such declarations of autonomy as "Mucho me aprieta la ira, y la refreno" and the flat statement, "la ira templo" (the modern equivalent would be, "I've got it under control").[224] We find characters who choose to mitigate wrath, even in the face of obstinence, or at least adjust it to fit the offence.[225] We also hear apostrophes to Prudence, a Virtue thought to mitigate this Deadly Vice, as in "Gobernadme vos, prudencia, no deis lugar a la ira, que cuando con pasión mira, hace al engaño evidencia."[226] One telling speech specifically invokes the discourse of free will to put Anger in line with a person's deliberate choice: "sea ésta la vez primera que la ira, y la voluntad caminen por una senda."[227] As Melveena McKendrick has effectively established, this was not a stage where characters were mere puppets of the hegemonic church/state monolith.[228] This is not the Golden Age theatre you thought you knew.

Ironically, what we see here is that in the end, individualism wins out, but not only because of a shift towards the Ten Commandments. Perhaps more than any other of the Seven Deadlies, Anger is defined increasingly in terms of the concrete actions it inspires. The foremost of these relates directly to the Fifth Commandment, which prohibits Murder. The *comedias* engage with this Commandment extensively, especially in the recognized subgenre of wife-murder plays. But this is not the only metamorphosis this Capital Vice undergoes. In a peculiarly messy mixing of linguistic registers – we might even call this the code switching of morality – Murder evolves into a crime, not a sin; and Anger suddenly becomes a passion, affect, or humour instead of a Vice.

Are we confused yet? Well, we should be. Transitions are never tidy. But Anger is the last of the Seven Deadly Sins, I shall argue, that even persists in recognizable enough *form* to be *(trans)formed* miraculously in the theatre into the stuff of performance magic. The final Capital Vice, Envy, will lose its identity altogether – always a danger on the stage, where identities are perpetually tried on, changed, or discarded.[229] The next chapter, on Envy, marks the end of an era. It sounds the death knell for the Deadly Vices as the primary organizational categories for moral life in early modern Spain. At the pinnacle of world power, Spaniards had no one left to envy but themselves. Thus Envy ceased to resonate, as it experienced a profound metamorphosis on the way to becoming a Virtue. It is to this type of radical remapping of the moral landscape that we shall turn in this book's third section, "Emergence."

PART THREE

Emergence

7
Disappearing Deadlies: The End of Envy

Darás … envidia a los otros Reinos.

– Francisco de Rojas Zorrilla, *Persiles, y Sigismunda*

Todos miran, al Español, porque admiran la envidia de su poder.

– Lope de Vega, *El blasón de los Chaves de Villalba*

Pues a no haber qué envidiar dejara de ser envidia.

– Juan Bautista Diamante, *El nacimiento de Cristo*[1]

In this book's first section, "Residue," we saw how the Deadly Vices of Pride, Avarice, and Lust persisted as primary organizational categories for moral thought in Golden Age Spain. In Part II, "Transformation," we saw how Sloth, Gluttony, and Anger underwent drastic facelifts to stay au courant. Now, in this book's final division, "Emergence," we shall see how Envy died and two Commandments arose to fill the cultural vacuum left by its absence. However, we must be careful that in the process of deconstructing one grand narrative, we do not merely create another: in the language of Raymond Williams,

> [b]y "emergent" I mean, first, that new meanings and values, new practices, new relationships and kinds of relationship are continually being created. But it is exceptionally difficult to distinguish between those which are really elements of some new phase of the dominant culture (and in this sense "species-specific") and those which are substantially alternative or oppositional to it: emergent in the strict sense, rather than merely novel. Since we are always considering relations within a cultural

process, definitions of the emergent, as of the residual, can be made only in relation to a full sense of the dominant.[2]

Envy is the perfect vehicle for giving us this full sense of the dominant, since its rejection occurred in response to Spain's dominance over half the world during this period. We shall soon see how this works.

Envy is certainly still present in the *comedias*. It is defined quite simply as the shadow of fame.[3] Appearing as the snake that bites the heart – or sometimes alternatively as the scorpion's tongue – it manufactures venom using as ingredients the pleasures of others.[4] It is lightning which strikes one down from on high.[5] In its more pedestrian form it appears as a weevil nibbling in the pantry, thereby ruining the foodstuffs one has worked so hard to save up.[6] It is an incurable itch that never goes away, no matter how hard one scratches.[7] It is never absent from human activity, even if one tries to escape from it by flying to the moon.[8] It is the distorted lenses of eyeglasses which, instead of helping a person to see better, instead make him even more blind.[9] It is the moth who gets burned up from hovering too close to the flame.[10] It is the process by means of which honey attracts flies.[11] It is the single blow which shatters glass.[12] It is the spear which goads the bull in a bullfight.[13]

In its simplest form, Envy is seen as a Vice for villagers, "la envidia villana."[14] It appears dressed as a country person in the *autos sacramentales*.[15] A rustic's passion is Envy's child.[16] Envy spoils the drinking water by mischievously putting her hand into the fountain.[17] Country people are seen as weighed down by Envy, much like the beasts of burden with whom they work daily, tilling their fields. They are acutely aware of their own predicament: "hecho una portátil tienda soy, como bestia cargado, envidioso a quien ha dado pesadumbre ajena hacienda."[18] This beastly imagery is carried over into even more literal descriptions of Envy as asinine, such as "al cochino regalaba tanto, que al jumento mismo, daba envidia, que esta falta, es muy de asnos."[19] In a clever theatrical sleight of hand, Envy is attributed by playwrights likewise to their own audiences, but only to the riffraff who attended their plays in the open-air *corrales*. The comment is actually an agile play on the word *corral*: "el coral está en los labios, y la envidia en los corrales."[20] This works because of the word's similarity to *coral*, or coral, which is also the colour of a woman's painted red lips. Here the dramatists got by with a blatant insult which they probably would not have attempted against the upper class.

For these common folk, Envy is mentioned in the same breath with Greed: "pasó la envidia a deseo, si ya no a codicia necia."[21] It is also collapsed together with the last half of two different Commandments, namely numbers Nine and Ten, both having to do with coveting something, either a wife or material possessions, that belongs to one's neighbours – a concept simplified in the *comedias* until it boils down to a single word: *ajenos*. Thus we find such expressions as "Envidia de los ajenos me mata,"[22] in what is clearly a conflation of this Deadly Sin with these two Commandments. In fact, Envy is collapsed into the two Coveting Commandments to the point that Moses himself, in Calderón's auto *La serpiente de metal* – which takes as its subject matter the episode in the desert where a bronze serpent lifted up on a staff becomes a prototype for Christ by curing the Israelites of their illness – apostrophizes Envy in terminology reminiscent of the Decalogue: "¡O! Afecto de Envidia, a cuánto del *bien ajeno* te agravias!"[23] *Bien ajeno* seems to be the catch-all phrase for anything good that can happen to someone else which would, in turn, make that person enviable.

In general, noblemen are not immune to Envy; they are just envious of non-material quotients: friendship, love, talent, and so forth – all things which money cannot buy. If money is an issue for them, it becomes sublimated.[24] Instead, in what may be seen as a feat of Baroque dexterity in the form of a cognitive leap, the Ninth and Tenth Commandments are transposed here to the realm of non-material assets. Instead of *bienes ajenos*, or others' goods, we now see characters who covet others' skills or virtues, their cultured learning, their refined good taste, their pleasure, their good luck or fortune, or their happiness or joy.[25] This Envy of course extends to physical attractiveness or beauty, especially for women.[26] Normally in the *comedias* Envy of this kind is limited to leading comments about a pretty face, although occasionally a playwright takes us up and down a woman's body with his voyeuristic gaze.[27] This sort of Envy was more brazenly expressed regarding the gorgeous bodies of naked indigenous women, which were said to be so softly luminous that even the moon envied them.[28] As we saw earlier in our Lust chapter, "barbaric" peoples were thought to be more lustful; perhaps it was also somehow permissible to gaze at exotic foreign women lustfully.

As one might expect – and this was true then as it is now – youth was frequently envied by old age.[29] Intelligence or ingenuity was envied in an era which still valued scholastic disputes.[30] Another often-envied quality was skill at sword fighting, or – in this increasingly superficial Baroque era – merely the outward trappings of a soldier.[31] In fact, Envy appears in one of Calderón's *autos sacramentales* bearing the standard, or flag, of Spain's military orders.[32] Envy could also be provoked by someone's musical ability, artistic talent, or social fame.[33] It is possible to be envious of such intangible quotients as friendship, as thematized in Lope de Vega's aptly titled comedia *El amigo hasta la muerte*, which serves as a sort of extended meditation on what it means to be a friend. One character is described by another character in this play as being "envidioso del amistad que entre los dos ha visto."[34]

Needless to say, romantic love became a frequent context for Envy. It has often been noted that in the *comedia*, love triangles abound.[35] It might be thought that Envy would occur more often in the context of illicit love, and at first this seems to be the case.[36] But then we begin to realize that it doesn't matter – married or single, the grass always looks greener on the other side of the fence: "El casado al libre envidia, y el libre envidia al casado."[37] Every woman is said to envy a good marriage, along with pretty clothes.[38] Even at the wedding, there will be guests who cast an envious eye on the happy couple: "Que burlada, y que envidiosa en mis bodas te has de ver."[39] The legendary *celos*, or jealousy, of the *comedias* can ultimately be traced back to Envy: "lo mismo es celoso, que envidioso."[40] In fact, arguably Envy is the sine qua non for romantic attachment.

Proof of this intrinisic conceptual relationship may be found in Antonio de Zamora's *Siempre hay que envidiar, amando*. In this elegantly insubstantial pastoral drama, the title becomes the repeated refrain to a song performed intermittently by musicians and singers on stage:

> Si el ajeno mal pretendo,
> el proprio bien despreciando,
> es, porque, para el que ardiendo
> empieza a envidiar queriendo,
> siempre hay que envidiar, amando.

Other verses of the song continue to play with the same concept:

> CANTA MIRTILA: No hay en amor venturoso,
> que no tenga un envidiado.
> CANTA ERITEA: No hay en amor desdichado,
> que no tenga un envidioso.[41]

As the shepherd Alcino remarks concerning the scorn of his beloved, in romantic love there is a fine line between hope and Envy.[42] Later in the play he asserts that the human experiences of love and jealousy are so closely identified with one another that no one will blame a lover for exacting revenge.[43] Of course, the pastoral ambience is so tranquil that the only revenge he has in mind is erasing the offending lover's name with the point of his dagger. At another point he declares that his soul is burning with Envy, when the more common expression would be to say that it is burning with love.[44]

All of this could of course happen again the second time around, especially to women, after their first husbands died. We witness this phenomenon in Tirso de Molina's interlude *Las viudas*, in which one widow says to another: "a decir verdad, Leonor hermosa, más que triste me tienes envidiosa, qué ventura tan grande que has tenido."[45] One common motivation for remarriage was to produce an heir so that one's family line would continue.[46] Like the two anonymous women who appeared before King Solomon, ladies could be envious of one another's good fortune in childbirth: "Envidiosa Gila ... del hijo, que sin sazón, parió Marina."[47] This was particularly important at a time when infant mortality rates were many times greater than what they are today.[48]

Once their children had grown up, women could be jealous of one another over the accomplishments of their offspring: "Doña Sancha está envidiosa, viendo en estos regocijos sin fama sus siete hijos."[49] More often than not, Envy occurred in the context of social position, as in "¿No os causa ... envidia ver que es Duque de Ferrara Alejandro?"[50] It is perhaps worth remembering that in Spain's church/state, as throughout much of the Catholic world, this stratification could be religious as well as secular:

FRAILE 2: O envidia necia.
PAPA PÍO: Inquisidor le nombro de Venecia.[51]

Indeed, Envy was said to have permeated even the religious orders, as for example over the sale of benefices or plum political appointments by the pope.[52]

We see, therefore, that Envy was ubiquitous, and that it had become accepted as part of court culture. Envy is called courtly on numerous occasions and even dubbed a daughter of the court.[53] Spanish knights were said to be full of Envy: "los Caballeros están llenos de envidia."[54] In fact, Envy is described using the language of jousts.[55] The horses, spears, and gay costumes of jousting tournaments are said to kill men with Envy.[56] Envy appears as a mother who gives birth to the monster of palaces ("al monstruo de los Palacios, del odio, y la envidia hijo"), or alternatively as the basilisk (a fabulous serpent) of the palace who is comfortable in its natural habitat, having been raised at the court.[57] Envy hides herself in courtly courtesies like a snake lurking in a flower bed: "la envidia, monstruo infame, disimulado en lisonjas, como entre flores el áspid."[58] These *lisonjas* include both flattery and applause.[59] The court was forever chasing after its latest minor celebrity, infatuated with the charms of whichever lucky man or woman was fashionable until another darling rose to take his or her place.[60] One of the most common symptoms of Envy is murmuring, a vice which we still see practised against celebrities today (witness the golfer Tiger Woods).[61] These murmurs can be so soft and insidious as to resemble the wind: "que de envidioso el viento fingió el susurro."[62] Courtly flattery carries Envy just as sound carries an echo: "cortesanas galas, los ecos de la envidia lisonjera."[63] Murmuring can cover everything from favours shown, to properties inherited, to fortuitous events which have occurred, to courtly offices appointed.[64] It chips away at loyalties little by little, using flattery to insinuate itself with the powerful.[65] Envy deceives through disguise,[66] donning in particular the winning garments of love ("en traje de amor la envidia cubierta anda") or friendship ("amigos fingidos, que el bien ajeno les mata, de su envidia persuadidos").[67] The disguise theme is repeated in the context of espionage, a favourite theme of *comedias* due to its inherent intrigue.[68] In fact, Envy is often pictured as the spy who never sleeps: "¿pero cuándo Envidia, y Mentira duermen?"[69] The all-seeing eyes of Envy are most commonly imagined as the hide of a tiger or the tail of a peacock, both animals covered with markings which resemble eyes.[70] In Calderón's auto sacramental *Los encantos de la Culpa*, Culpa or Fault addresses Vista or Sight with the words, "Vista, que manchado Tigre has pacido este Desierto, pues envidioso eres, ojos que sientes bienes ajenos."[71] Note here once again the language of the Commandments being conflated with the Seven Deadly Sins. In the same play, this imagery is further explained as, "La Vista, en Tigre cruel fue de la Envidia despojos, que este Animal todo es Ojos."[72]

In this courtly landscape of spying eyes and ever-shifting alliances, ties binding courtiers to the monarch and to each other were ever tenuous and liable to fray. They could be solidified by letters, tokens, portraits, and so forth, almost like the *prendas* exchanged between lovers.[73] Motivated by Envy, disloyal courtiers – described as vicious wolves in sheep's clothing – surreptitiously broke the wax seals on documents so they could spy on official correspondence.[74] Even monarchs could be the targets of Envy, when they were not engaged in it themselves.[75] This was, however, somewhat unusual, since kings were considered in some sense untouchable or at least above the angst provoked by common human passions. Normally kings or princes in the *comedias* are seen to be above Envy, as when the princess in Calderón's *La cisma de Inglaterra* says: "Envidiosa de sus brazos estuviera, si en la Majestad cupiera envidia."[76] More frequently, it is the courtiers' relationships with the king that are prejudicially affected by Envy.[77]

Envy had appeared in the context of relationships at least since the Old Testament stories of brothers vying with each other for their father's, or even God's, affection.[78] The fraternal pairs Cain and Abel as well as Jacob and Esau were both remembered as having let their familial relationships degenerate due to Envy.[79] It will be recalled that Joseph, the favourite son of Israel's patriarch Jacob, was thrown into a well and left for dead by his older brothers, who were envious of their father's favour as displayed in the coat of many colours he gave Joseph to wear.[80] Joseph in turn became a sort of prototype for the Spanish *privado*, since he was the favourite of Pharaoh and effectively ruled his kingdom for him.[81] Any special relationship to the ruling monarch could be enough to provoke Envy, as happens for example with the post of king's chief accountant.[82] This is because a person's office, or *oficio*, was thought to bear with it a certain degree of honour.[83] Thus even the palace servants experienced Envy when they saw one of their peers apparently favoured ever so slightly over the others.[84] This was especially true of the *camareros*, men-in-waiting or chamber men, who dressed the king and waited on him in his private chambers.[85] But the most common context for Envy was the post of *privado*, or king's favourite, who frequently became the object of intense speculation at court.

Privanza was the high wall which Envy tried to scale.[86] At best, any person in power must have sensed that Envy lurked right behind him.[87] Theoretically considered a blessing, this post instead became a sort of black bean drawn by someone destined to become the target of concerted attacks.[88] The *privanza*, as it was called, or "king's favourite" slot, was explicitly referred to in this new age of military technology as the target at which Envy took aim.[89] These shots did not always hit their mark; as one frustrated *letrado* complains, "Mi envidia en vano porfía a este idiota derribar."[90] Instead, Envy often had to resort to digging potholes in the hope that the favourite might trip and then be left crying in the mud.[91]

From the king's perspective, he often found occasion to raise a courtier up to fill this favoured position. As King Meleandro of Sicily says to Arcombroto, "me ha dado ocasión para que pueda sin envidia levantarte a mi privanza, y grandeza. Pídeme mercedes, pide cuanto imaginas, y piensas."[92] These *mercedes*, or special boons granted, frequently became the cause for Envy.[93] Kings were not unaware of this; in fact, for political reasons, sometimes this was even their goal. As one king says in a play by Tirso de Molina, "premiaréle tanto, que envidia le tengan."[94] Kings who did not stand behind their *privados* – monsters who were, after all, of their own creation – were said to be failing to provide them with cover[95] (our equivalent expression would be "hanging them out to dry") or – in a move reminiscent of King David when he was trying to do away with Bathsheba's husband – shoving them towards the front lines of battle.[96] This could occur once the king grew tired of one *privado* and decided to shift his favour to another.[97] At this point, the old favourite might be exiled to make room for the new one.[98] This is what ultimately happened to the Count-Duke of Olivares, that famous *privado* of Philip IV whom we have already mentioned in the context of Pride.[99]

In this courtly game of cat and mouse, Envy became a cloak behind which covert critics of the *privado* could hide.[100] A specific *privado* named Beltrán Ramírez is held out in one historical drama, Alarcón's *El tejedor de Segovia*, as an example of a king's favourite who was trapped in a sort of morbid theatre by Envy: "¿no vistes vos a Beltrán Ramírez mandar el Reino, y de la envidia después en un teatro funesto los rayos de su privanza en humo leve resueltos?"[101] In this play, the *privado* finds letters incriminating two noblemen, Suero Peláez and his son Don Juan, of plotting with the *moros* against the king, Alfonso VI. But instead of succeeding in turning the king against them, he suddenly finds that they have instead turned the king against him, and he is executed by royal mandate. This scenario of the *privado*'s fall from grace is repeated in several plays.

The most famous example of a *privado* eclipsed by Envy in the *comedias* undoubtedly appears in *Adversa fortuna de don Álvaro de Luna, segunda parte*, based on the life of a real historical figure.[102] In this play, which forms part of a pair (it is the second, companion piece to the first instalment, titled *Próspera fortuna de don Álvaro de Luna, primera parte*), the story is told of the famous *privado* of King

Juan II of Castile, whose spectacular fall from grace ended in his being hanged in the plaza of Valladolid on 2 June 1453 by express order of the same king who had formerly held him in such high regard.[103] The play ends, fittingly, with the words "Y con este triste ejemplo, de la envidia, y la privanza, acabe aquí el gran eclipse del resplandor de los Lunas."[104]

Envy's ubiquity at court meant that everyone felt the double-edged sword of either envying or being envied: "no hay hombre tan desdichado que no tenga un envidioso, ni hay hombre tan venturoso que no tenga un envidiado."[105] In fact, most courtiers were seen as simultaneously envying and being envious: "siempre ha sido envidioso, y envidiado."[106] Poets at court – and here we catch an inside glimpse of the playwrights' own profession – were described as alternately envious, if they wrote bad poetry, or envied, if their work was good: "aprendes con ser Poeta una ciencia trabajosa, si es imperfecta, envidiosa, y envidiada si es perfecta."[107]

But for many early modern Spaniards, the balance definitely tilted in the direction of being envied: "de todas por mi buen gusto [más] envidiada, que envidiosa."[108] As one admirer says to a character named (in a not-so-subtle reminiscence of Petrarch) Laura, "la hermosura divinamente adornada … más de ser envidiada, que envidiosa os asegura."[109] In fact, in many instances we find early modern Spanish stage characters professing not to feel Envy at all, as with a nobleman who hypothesizes that "tan contento me viera, que poca envidia al Príncipe tuviera."[110]

There is something very strange going on here. As we read these references, we slowly begin to realize that as successful empire builders, early modern Spaniards felt themselves more objects of Envy than subjects who experienced it: "¿No soy yo la que provoco a envidia, y temor el suelo?"[111] At the top of their game, there was nothing left for them to experience Envy towards. As Calderón predicts through the voice of Envy in an *auto sacramental*, "retiraráse la Envidia, que sobre Nobles, atentos, *no les queda qué envidiar*."[112]

Spaniards at this time fancied themselves the Envy of "barbaric" nations, "tanta envidia en bárbaras naciones."[113] Imperialistic plays written in praise of the conquistadores and their conquests predict that there will never be a province discovered, however remote, which does not feel Envy towards Spain.[114] But Spaniards are also envied by their contemporaries of other European nationalities, such as the Italians and Germans (as one Spanish soldier brags, "a mi valor se inclinan, di a Italia envidia, y Alemania celos") or the French, who are considered to be particularly prone to Envy: "Ésta es traición de algún envidioso fiero, de mil que en París lo son."[115] Women of other nationalities are seen to be envious of Spanish women; as the *mora* Daraja says, "Confieso que me da envidia una mujer Española."[116] The official fiction, of course, was that within Spain's own empire, the nations it had conquered were bound to it by love, not Envy.[117] But despite such inconvenient facts as the defeat of the Armada, Spain's military might was still such that it bragged that its squadrons could conquer the whole world by force, if necessary.[118]

Its imperial flags were said to be the Envy of the sun, whose rays could not reach as far as their Spanish bearers had carried them.[119]

Spain's hubris extended to considering itself in favourable comparison through diachronic perspective to other great empires throughout world history, such as the ancient Greeks and Romans. Spaniards came to see themselves as occupying a truly unique place in history.[120] This was their stated ambition: to be envied by both ancients and moderns.[121] This happens when Lope de Vega addresses the Spanish monarch in his prefatory poem as "Príncipe generoso, de quien está envidioso El Griego, y el Romano."[122] The laurel wreaths to which Spain was entitled – or so the thinking goes – would provoke Envy even in Julius Caesar ("Fuera para mi laurel, el verde listón, que diera envidia a Césares") or Hector of Troy.[123] And Spain's Golden Age – self-consciously experienced as such while it was still unfolding – was seen as a couple of glorious centuries which Fame herself might covet.[124]

Literate early modern Spaniards invoked Pliny to show how the Envy of the world put them in a superior position: "Llamó Plinio menor al envidioso, y mayor con razón el envidiado."[125] With their portable empire, Spaniards could well claim world dominion.[126] Renaissance Spaniards saw themselves as the big fish in the pond, the gigantic ostrich who was envied so much by smaller birds that they wanted to pluck out his eyes.[127] Spain was the Sun envied by all the lesser stars.[128] In the realm of letters, too, Spaniards prided themselves on their place at the very pinnacle: "Ingenio Soberano … a quien las doctas frentes del Parnaso Español respetuosas rindieron sin lisonja, y sin envidia las inmortales Yedras de su Ingenio."[129] Characters in these stage plays are praised as being so smart that they surpass even ancient intellects like Plato and Marcus Aurelius.[130] When it was convenient, Golden Age Spanish men, normally not known for their departures from the era's misogyny, could even bring out examples of Spanish women who had distinguished themselves by their writing: "[en] Madrid hoy se ven mujeres, que hacen también versos, que envidia cualquiera."[131]

In the perennial debate over the efficacy of arms versus letters, early modern Spaniards arguably did not have to choose. They were good at both. In this epideictic vein, their courage was so great that a single Spanish soldier could claim to have killed 10,000 enemies: "Diez mil enemigos vuestros, aunque la envidia me oiga, he muerto con estas manos en asaltos."[132] These playwrights hearkened back to the Cid and his legacy for metaphors to use in describing their countrymen's military prowess: "¡sangre del Cid, cuyas hazañas gloriosas, son envidia a las ajenas, y ejemplo honroso a las propias!"[133]

As the above reference to the Cid demonstrates, it was particularly their blood lineage – and the mythical purity of their blood – which Spaniards felt gave them cause to provoke Envy even among the gods: "vuestros pechos nobles, han de ser de Marte envidia; muéstrese en vuestro valor hoy la sangre esclarecida."[134] Noble blood certainly provoked Envy on the part of those who could not count themselves among the well-born, as in "envidia de ver lucido nuestro linaje."[135] This was a trial that noble families were taught to anticipate, along with a concomitant desire to be esteemed, in a rather perverse iteration of the traditional noblesse oblige.[136] But in a face-off between two dynasties of equal rank – like the one which occurs in Lope de Vega's *La envidia de la nobleza* – Envy could cause noble families to clash: "¡o envidia entre dos linajes!"[137] It was due in part to this preoccupation over lineage that early modern Spaniards took such care not to let Envy stain their blood purity: "Noble, y limpio es mi linaje, si la envidia no le mancha."[138]

The trope of nationalistic Envy ("la envidia nacional") became a commonplace within the discourse of patriotism, as in "Daré a mi patria laureles, a quien la envidia despoja."[139] Envy might attempt to despoil Spain, but by and large, early modern Spaniards saw themselves as strong enough to resist Envy's attacks. They were able to deflect Envy's arrows and would not succumb to Envy's bites.[140] Time could not erase the grandeur of Spain's cities, nor could it disfigure the bronze and marble busts of her leaders.[141] Envy could not stain the Spanish woman's beauty.[142] Envy dissolved in tears at the sound of Spanish oratory.[143] Early modern Spanish characters gloat that Envy effectively falls at their feet: "Hoy he llegado a gozar puesta la envidia a mis pies."[144] With Envy beneath them, they hold Fortune in their hands: "[no] habrá pena ninguna que tema mi suerte, pues tendré la envidia a mis pies, y en mi mano la fortuna."[145] In the face of such power, the envious one becomes mute or, at very least, bites his lip.[146] Envy and ambition are enslaved by Spain just as surely as black Africans were bought and sold by their slave traders: "ambición … y envidia, yo esclavas traigo a mis plantas."[147] Ultimately, Spain shows Envy the finger.[148]

In this vein, early modern Spaniards or their literary prototypes are seen as so strong that they bring fearful horror to the planet.[149] Spaniards actually *wanted* to be envied because in this world view, not being envied translated into not being famous; for example, "un hombre como Álvar Fáñez quedó sin fama, y envidia."[150] In this moral economy, Envy somehow perversely became the source of all well-being: "donde no hay envidia, ni hay bien, ni hay fama, ni hay nombre."[151] These characters' (and their authors') worst fear was to be forgotten, a fate they believed could be avoided through extraordinary deeds.[152] Conversely, being envied brought fame to one's memory ("partí, dando gracias a Dios, despojos a tu armada, envidia al mundo, fama a tu memoria"), with the result that for every one Spaniard, a thousand rivals were said to envy him.[153]

In other words, Envy in the *comedias* is seen to follow in the footsteps of the powerful, but essentially it becomes more of an asset than a liability.[154] From the Spaniards' perspective, the only problem would be if the rest of the world were *not* envious of them. In a remarkable extension of this same idea, they see themselves to be the Envy even of pagan gods: "Ya galanes en el cerco, valientes en la

Palestra, fuimos envidia de Adonis, y fuimos de Marte afrenta."[155] Even the angels in heaven were said to be jealous of the Spaniards: "el Ángel envidioso, que ¡ay envidia soberana! viendo al hombre tan dichoso."[156] The devil himself was envious of Spaniards' sanctity. As one character boasts, "Como ve que soy tan santo, rabia de envidia el maldito."[157] Miracles in particular were said to generate Envy.[158] In the pagan realm, Love, the Fates, and the Furies were all envious of Spain.[159] Some of the most frequent references to Envy occur in the context of Fortune specifically. We see Fortune as envious of specific Spanish families, such as the Mazas of Aragon, immortalized in Antonio Zamora's *Cada uno es linaje aparte, y los Mazas de Aragón*: "no le quiso la fortuna esta vez, pues envidiosa, de que una sola familia se alzase con las Historias."[160] More generally speaking, Fortune is understood to be envious of valour: "fortuna y valor del uno el otro envidioso."[161]

Once we start digging further, we discover that Envy was always a part of Fortune's early modern iconographical reception. Envy is seen in the *comedias* as integral to Fortune's fierce condition.[162] Vile Fortune is called inimical to Spaniards' luck, erring in her solication of their ills: "la fortuna errante, envidiosa de mis bienes, y solícita en mis males."[163] These misogynistic playwrights go so far as to say that because of her Envy, Fortune is often pictured as a woman, an impression confirmed by even the most cursory glance through early modern emblems of Fortune.[164]

However, in this early modern equivalent of a catfight between competing grammatically female concepts, Fortune does not always win out. Envy is called more powerful; indeed, Envy inebriates Fortune to the point that she acts like she is drunk.[165] In fact, Envy herself is seen as a distinct entity – almost the equivalent to one of the pagan gods – opposed to the good of human beings: "la Envidia enemiga de cualquier humano bien."[166] But even in this iteration, Envy is ultimately said to be won over by the Spaniards' irresistible charm, as in "Príncipes tan bizarros, que aun los alaba la envidia."[167] One is reminded here of the line of Gucci perfume which includes the scents *Envy Me* and *Envy Me 2*.

Ultimately, moral categories become so reversed that Envy herself admires and celebrates the hero's deeds: "hizo cosas, que la envidia propia admiró por imposibles, y celebró por heroicas."[168] Envy herself is said to fear the Spanish Empire:

MARQUÉS: Dilate el cielo tu Imperio.
DON FERNANDO: Des a la envidia temor.
DON PEDRO: Celebre el tiempo tu nombre.[169]

At the height of world power, Spaniards have no one left to envy but themselves. They profess to have never even experienced Envy ("un hombre soy que en mi vida, ni tuve envidia, ni celos")[170] because Envy is only for their poor, hapless rivals who do not know how to acquire honour.[171]

A possible exception to this maxim comes in the form of a rhetorical flourish which is nevertheless indicative of early modern Spaniards' vexed relationship to Envy. If they are guilty of this Vice at all, then they will admit to having experienced it only in regard to themselves, as for example with the phrase "deciros puedo, que tuve envidia de mí"; "Es tan bella que tiene envidia de sí misma"; and "cuando yo misma de mí no vengo a estar envidiosa."[172] The person who is envious of him- or herself begins to feel suspicious of so much success.[173] Thus early modern Spaniards profess to be jealous of themselves to the point of admiring self-gazing.[174] Envy turned inward upon one's self also turns this moral category inside out; that is, communal Sin becomes an individual one, like music transposed to a different key. In Lope de Vega's *El desconfiado*, Don Fernando says, "Satisfecha dejo mi voluntad, de sí envidiosa."[175]

This self-reflexive cycle is traced in the *comedias* all the way back to the myth of Phaethon, who says in Calderón's *El faetonte*: "infiero, que soy el hombre primero que tuvo envidia de sí."[176] But someone somewhere introduced a mirror into Phaethon's myth, for Envy is also seen as a ray of light reflected by mirrors back onto its source, with the result being possible combustion.[177] In this strange play of reflections, Envy serves as a mirror in which one may view one's self: "la envidia … la sirvió de espejo."[178] In Juan de la Cueva's allegorical comedia *El viejo enamorado*, the figure of Envidia seems to apostrophize herself: "Triste envidia, que haces consumiendo en lágrimas tu vida congojosa."[179] Indeed, Envy is seen here as both self-reflective and self-consuming.

This condition is perhaps best thematized in Tirso de Molina's aptly titled *La celosa de sí misma*. In this play, Don Melchor comes to Madrid in order to wed Magdalena. But before he meets her, he catches a glimpse of her beautiful hand peeking out from beneath her veil. Not knowing she is in fact his betrothed, he falls in love with the mysterious woman of the hand who – in his imagination, as well as hers – begins to compete with the real Magdalena for his affections. Continuing to play the game, Magdalena alternates between veiling and unveiling herself in order to retain, in Melchor's mind, her feminine mystique. Thus she becomes, in effect, envious of herself in veiled form and the place she holds in her fiancé's heart. At one point, another character says to her: "Envidiosa de ti estás, y niegas lo mismo que eres."[180]

If we can succeed in analysing it correctly, this strange statement may help us pinpoint the moment where Envy turns to Pity. For one of the strangest permutations undergone by Envy in its bizarre journey across the early modern Spanish stage – and through early modern Spanish imaginations – is its metamorphosis into what would seem to be its own diametrical opposite. The cycle of Envy→Pity→Envy produces a peculiarly Baroque moment: you realize the person you envy should actually be pitied. The late Renaissance and Baroque age loved paradox.[181] Let us try to follow the logic by which this evolutionary process might unfold.

At first, Pity and Envy would seem to be mirror opposites, as in the lines "sin que sea mi amor lástima, ni envidia" or "mayor lástima te tengo que envidia."[182] Pity is required by the unfortunate, while being so successful as to provoke Envy becomes a sort of trophy: "Que dar lástima, es desdicha, y dar envidia trofeo."[183] These would seem to be distinct emotions one might feel towards two different people (as in "al uno para la envidia, al otro para el consuelo") or from two different people (as in "ocasionar pudiera en vuestra Alteza piedad, y envidia en mis enemigos").[184]

But then, all of a sudden, in the *comedias* we find them yoked together: "¡o cuánta pena, y envidia me das!"[185] This connection is repeated over and over, with the two emotions even being experienced similarly through tears.[186] At first it would seem that only a person who dies heroically could unite these two declared enemies: "Sólo un muerto heróicamente juntara la lástima con la envidia, enemigas declaradas."[187] But then we realize that even for average people, they are actually two sides of the same coin: "la lástima se hizo envidia."[188] There is not that much emotional distance between them: "la distancia ... de la lástima a la envidia."[189] This rhetorical strategy was called a zeugma, or the yoking together of apparently disjunctive elements.[190] In this game of perspectivism, what is to be envied by one person may be pitied by another: "viendo que en alguno sea lástima la que fue envidia."[191] Spaniards are exhorted to have compassion, not Envy, for the less fortunate: "tenles lástima y no envidia, muévete a la compasión."[192] This is portrayed as the more prudent choice, for Envy is fleeting and quickly turns to Pity once you see what another's life is really like.[193]

In Calderón's auto sacramental *Psiquis, y Cupido*, we witness this exchange between Free Will and Faith:

ALBEDRÍO: ¿No tenéis envidia de ellas?
FE: Lástima, no envidia, tengo.[194]

We watch, astonished, as Envy literally morphs into Pity: "si envidia causó tu bien pasado, mayor lástima de tu mal presente."[195] This change can occur suddenly from one day to the next: "ayer eran envidia del mundo, y hoy dan lástima."[196] The king's favourite can turn prisoner, while the most ardent patriot can find himself an exile from his country: "¿Ayer favorecido, hoy preso? ¿Hoy sin estado? ¿Ayer causando envidia, hoy escarmiento?"[197] Just as it was possible to envy one's self, now it is possible to feel sorry for one's own misfortune: "se prueba de esta suerte, con cierto silogismo, la lástima, y envidia de sí mismo."[198] Here we witness the same turn inward observed earlier, as *comedia* characters speak in the first person about their reversals of fate.[199]

In an unanticipated twist of historical linguistics, the two words Envy and Pity ultimately came to be used interchangeably during this period. We find references to *envidia* where the context clearly indicates that the concept intended is *lástima*. An example would be: "de envidia de las heridas lloraban sangre los ojos."[200] Phantasmagorical imagery aside – and this is meant in a very literal sense, since the quotation comes from a passage in Calderón's *El galán fantasma* – this is not the only way in which Envy would suffer a total transformation during the early modern period. Spain, at the pinnacle of world power, was the object of Envy and in turn pitied everyone else. Conveniently located at the point of maximum Virtue, at least in the Machiavellian sense of *virtù*, Spain lacked Envy because it had no need for it.[201] We shall soon see how Envy makes the journey from Vice, through nihilism, to ultimate revalorization as Virtue – a novel concept known as *envidia virtuosa*.[202]

What we have reached here is the End of Envy as we know it. In a supreme gesture of Baroque *desengaño* which approaches nihilism, the early modern Spanish subject seeks oblivion, a state of forgetting where one is neither envied nor envious: "durara en la calma de mi estado, ni envidioso, ni envidiado."[203] One character leaves a memorial to oblivion: "memorial al olvido: déjame en aqueste estado, ni envidiado, ni envidioso, donde, ni aflija al dichoso, ni consuele al desdichado."[204] If these rather zen *comedia* characters feel any passion at all, it is only for their honour.[205] Aside from that, they are ready to say goodbye to the world: "A Dios mundo, a Dios lisonjas, galas, necedad, soberbia, envidia, falsa amistad."[206] In a passage written in praise of the honest life, Lope de Vega's character Cardinal Gerónimo declares that Rome can have its pleasures – he prefers to eat and drink simply:

> Quédate invicta Roma
> con tu soberbio fausto,
> tu envidia, y ambición, que yo me vuelvo
> adonde beba, y coma,
> sin este censo infausto …
> Desde aquí me resuelvo
> a volverme al Egipto,
> a ver mis Monjes santos.[207]

At the very top of his profession during his life – and still the most prolific Spanish playwright of all time – Lope could clearly afford to judge other writers' work without Envy.[208] In what New Historicists would term a deliberate act of self-fashioning, Lope repeatedly presents himself as above Envy. He writes in his "Égloga a Claudio": "mi llaneza me retira de toda envidia."[209] This desired state of tranquillity and contentment finds its way into his dramatic works, where it is described in terms which echo both the relevant Vice and its corresponding Commandments: "pero si *bienes ajenos* no te han de hacer *envidiosa*, contenta estarás también."[210] This state of forgetting is described by Calderón de la Barca as a sweet abyss: "y así … tendré en tan dulce abismo, yo lástima, y envidia de mí mismo."[211]

This trope recalls both the *beatus ille* of Horace and the pastoral *locus amoenus* of classical antiquity. This idyllic, peaceful setting held a perpetual fascination for Lope de Vega, who returns to it in several of his plays.[212] In *La carbonera*, a rustic country home is described as a "casa donde pienso que su dueño no envidia al Rey en la suya." In the same play, it is observed that "en su rústico albergue no envidia un pobre villano los Palacios de los Reyes."[213] Lope de Vega returns here to the same subject matter which had occupied him earlier in *El villano en su rincón*, in which a rustic Everyman, Juan Labrador, delights in the country life and professes to be content with his lot, even if he never lays eyes on the king. It turns out that the king, who often hunts in Juan's neck of the woods, runs across the tombstone the *labrador* has prepared for his own future use, in the engraving upon which he waxes eloquent. There he praises the quietness of country life and insists that he has no use for the court. The king becomes determined to meet Juan and convince him that life at court is really superior to life in the sticks. Juan ends up receiving the king as a guest without knowing who he is. The king later reciprocates by receiving Juan Labrador at the palace. Juan eventually takes his children and goes with the king to Paris, where his daughter falls in love with the nobleman Otón. But despite the conventional happy ending – and the Cinderella story in miniature vis-à-vis Lisarda – there is an unmistakable nostalgia for the peace of the countryside and the simpler life they have had to leave behind.

This is all fine for the villager who already lives in the country, that is, he can be content with where God has placed him and not seek to change his fate. But what about the courtier who is used to the hustle and bustle of city life? Here is where a mystical strain runs through the Golden Age, for even courtiers in the *comedias* are seen to voluntarily give up their life at the palace – motivated in part by the virtuous Envy mentioned earlier – in order to forsake courtly intrigue and turn instead towards heavenly pursuits.[214] Even kings in the *comedias* are ready to trade places with lowly villagers if it means finding their true love.[215] This is perhaps the sort of earthly tranquillity that the Emperor Carlos V sought when he entered the monastery at Yuste after abdicating his throne. A similar situation is described concerning Juana la Beltraneja (1462–1530), another Castilian princess who may have wanted to "en un Monasterio ilustre, dar al mundo desengaños, envidia a sus enemigos, y a sus pesares descanso."[216] Lope de Vega himself describes, in a dedicatory letter appended to a published edition of one of his plays, his own search for a quieter life removed from the court: "que con dos flores de un jardín, seis cuadros de pintura, y algunos libros vivo sin envidia, sin deseo, sin temor, y sin esperanza."[217]

But these idyllic descriptions did not always match the reality. As Lope's last phrase indicates, the End of Envy could also mean the end of hope. After all, the person who cannot see his way towards brighter days ahead does not envy that which he does not know exists.[218] In a nutshell, what happens after the End of Envy? The answer is: Nothingness. This is why somehow, Envy must find an acceptable reincarnation. Under this ethos – the seemingly desirable state of oblivion – Spain would stay poor, a condition thematized by Calderón de la Barca in *El hombre pobre todo es trazas*. In this play, one character wisely remarks to the poor man of the title: "tú que en un estado estás permaneciente, jamás envidiado, ni envidioso; tu vivir sólo es vivir, no llegues a florecer."[219] Mere living is not flourishing.

The down side to this situation is obvious: the failure to thrive. It is now remembered that Envy could spur one to arms: "en valor también, hoy solicito, mostrar de mis hermanos envidioso, que si no los excedo, los imito."[220] This trope of admiration and imitation in the context of Envy becomes increasingly common as we see this Vice begin to morph on its way to becoming a Virtue.[221]

As it evolves rapidly during the early modern period, Envy is subtly transmuted into emulation, with these words often appearing yoked together, as in "la emulación envidiosa, y destemplada."[222] In fact, the very colour of Envy is seen to change in the process of this transmutation, as in "parda envidia, si no verde emulación."[223] Envy changes colours just as surely as it is transvalorized by means of a literary process through which, suddenly, traditional moral categories are now reversed. This colour change happens, as our chapter title indicates, when Envy ends: "Mudar de color pudiera, pues ya, señora, *mi envidia con tan buena suerte cesa*."[224] Envy is also equated with ambition and a positive example, as well as with motivation and competition: "se compitieron de suerte, que era gloriosa la envidia."[225] So how has Envy all of a sudden become glorious? Pretty soon Envy is out there in the open, making no apologies for its behaviour: "¡Qué clara muestra el Marqués su envidiosa emulación!"[226] If we read the *autos sacramentales* carefully, we find that Envy is actually the Pilot steering the ship.[227] This crazy tale forms an important chapter in the intellectual history of the Vices.

In what can only be termed a dramatic turn towards moral ambiguity, this former Deadly Sin actually ends up being valorized positively, as it spurs one on to greatness. Now we find characters who are said to be justly envious, as in "Envidiosa a lo menos justamente"and "mi justa envidia," with the most notable assertion of this concept occurring within the injunction, "vayas, y envidies (pues es la envidia justa,) varones tan felices."[228] Similarly, we find references to some form of Envy as being honourable ("honrada envidia") if it is felt in response to natural talent: "señales de naturaleza altiva, de caballeroso brío, que causara honrada envidia."[229] Envy is even termed generous and saintly under the right circumstances.[230] It is tied to noble desires.[231] By extension, Envy itself becomes noble as a new allegorical figure emerges: Noble Envy. Let us pause to witness the apotheosis of this hybrid creature.

The existence of Noble Envy explains such otherwise problematic references as "Envidia noble de tu Rey me abrasa" and "ardiendo en mi noble, envidioso frenesí está el alma."[232] This Noble Envy springs from epic valour: "Qué Noble envidia, nacida de generoso valor."[233] But at least within the pastoral fantasy, it can also arise from the observation of simple shepherds – that is, if they seem happy enough.[234] This noble form of Envy is tied specifically to Spain.[235] Sometimes it is contrasted with vile or village-like Envy, as in "con noble envidia ... y no con villana envidia."[236] But even this vile Envy can turn noble, as in "ha introducido esta prodigiosa nueva, que a la vil envidia ha hecho tan Noble, que yo la tenga."[237] Noble Envy is then transposed back from the moral into the material realm to the point that it is associated with the *hidalgos*, or landowning class: "no sé si acertare en llamarla envidia; sí, qué hidalga envidia."[238] The *comedias* even assure us that this redefined Noble Envy never goes beyond so-called decent sentiment: "¡que en los generosos pechos no pasa la envidia nunca de decentes sentimientos!"[239] It might be possible – difficult, but possible – to dismiss these passages as odd aberrations if it were not for the appearance of Noble Envy as an actual allegorical figure in one of Lope de Vega's *loas* written for the stage.

The apotheosis of Noble Envy occurs in Lope de Vega's loa *El vellocino de oro*. When she comes out on stage and announces her name, the other characters ask how she can truly be Envy if she is so beautiful.[240] They object that she was never depicted so in past ages.[241] Noble Envy explains: "El nombre, Fama, os engaña, que yo no soy esa Envidia, que las historias infaman. Soy aquella Envidia noble, que es virtud heroica y santa." She proceeds to give examples of great men throughout history who were spurred on by Envy: "Lloró Alejandro de envidia, que su padre no dejaba más tierra que conquistase ... Con envidia de Platón estudió cosas tan raras Aristóteles."[242] In sum, it becomes Envy that has spurred all human achievement.

We might pause, at this point, to reference our theoretical framework for the processes of cultural transformation we have just witnessed taking place:

> The case of the emergent is radically different. It is true that in the structure of any actual society, and especially in its class structure, there is always a social basis for elements of the cultural process that are alternative or oppositional to the dominant elements ... *A new class is always a source of emergent cultural practice*, but while it is still, as a class, relatively subordinate, this is always likely to be uneven and is certain to be incomplete. For new practice is not, of course, an isolated process. To the degree that it emerges, and especially to the degree that it is oppositional rather than alternative, the process of attempted incorporation significantly begins.[243]

This could not have been more true in Spain. As Stanley Payne explains, beginning in the sixteenth century in northern Castile, even petty noblemen who could not claim true aristocratic status were nevertheless entitled to an exemption from taxes due to a legal loophole: "The figures for the aristocracy do not include the tens of thousands of ordinary people in northern Castile able to claim petty *hidalgo* status and tax exemption from the sixteenth century onward because of local *fueros*."[244] Paul Hiltpold, in "Noble Status and Urban Privilege: Burgos, 1572," chronicles the controversy that ensued when these minor noblemen filed a petition with the city council in Burgos claiming entitlement to tax relief in an effort to consolidate their power:

> In 1572 the city council of the northern Castilian city of Burgos heard a petition seeking aid for a privilege of exemption from taxation for the noble-owned property in the *burgalés* hinterland. Most support for the petition came, quite naturally, from noble-status members of the council and their clients. But the petition was attacked as unjust by several members who feared lower-class resentment and who viewed the privilege as an attempt to strengthen the decaying economic and clientage power of an estate which no longer fulfilled its social functions. That such a vehement attack on the status of the nobility should come so soon in the early modern period suggests that the economic and social changes affecting all of western Europe in the sixteenth century had an impact on Castilian thought and governmental action as well.[245]

The nobility's status may have been assaulted – we have seen multiple examples in this chapter of noble status becoming a target for Envy – but ultimately, their rights were vindicated and their legal status remained intact. Thus they could pride themselves on being *hidalgos* (an abbreviation for *hijos de algo*, or sons of something); and by extension, they could continue to view themselves as objects of Envy.

The most familiar example of this new social class is without doubt Don Quijote, whose *hidalgo* status is heralded in the very title of Cervantes's famous work *El ingenioso hidalgo don Quijote de la Mancha*.[246] Edward Baker pens a eulogy for an entire generation of these idle, useless country gentlemen caught in the transition from medieval feudalism to nascent capitalistic practices now considered characteristic of the Renaissance. He calls them "a dying, although … still propertied, stratum of the lesser Castilian nobility in the historically ambiguous circumstance of slowly but very surely disappearing as a class fraction."[247] I prefer to see these lesser noblemen more as a new class emerging – asserting themselves, fighting for their rights before the city council in Burgos – than as an old social class dying out. Regardless, it should come as no surprise that, in Raymond Williams's terminology, this new social class would bring with it new cultural practices and structures of belief.

As Baker goes on to explain, Cervantes's masterpiece can in some senses be considered an allegory of these larger economic issues and social movements:

> Indeed, Cervantes' fable of madness can be read, at one level, as an allegory of that disappearance. Its protagonist lives in a very nearly self-sustaining, although only barely self-sustaining, agricultural economy, something very much like the so-called "natural" economies characteristic of European feudalism but common enough in a variety of pre-capitalist economic formations. "Natural" economies stood entirely or almost entirely outside the networks of even simple commodity production and exchange and, in the context of European feudalism, produced a surplus sufficient only for the reproduction, that is the physical survival, of the immediate household. This is the context of Don Quixote's poverty, which is of a kind not uncommon in both the Middle Ages and early modernity, where labor power is not yet fully commodified and money does not yet function as a generalized mediation of social relations. Consequently, rather than poor in an absolute sense – and in early modern Castile many *hidalgos* were literally destitute – Cervantes' character is relatively poor and in a very particular way: he is both moneyless and propertied.[248]

With the emergence of the new petty *hidalgo* and courtier classes, exemplified by Don Quijote and his literary contemporaries, came a new cultural practice: that of valorizing Envy in a positive way. This transition was still messy and incomplete – up to and including even linguistic confusion between Envy and Pity – but more pronounced than any other evolution of the Vices we have witnessed thus far.

* * * * *

With the near-total demise of what had once upon a time been a highly valued medieval moral construct, it is safe to say that Spain rooted itself firmly in the Renaissance era. Envy came to be redefined to suit political expediency. Now let us see how, in the face of the rapidly Disappearing Deadlies, a pair of "new" Commandments arose to take their place as a more or less stable feature of Spain's moral landscape. They turned out to be the equivalent of skyscrapers taking the place of squatty office buildings.

8
Parents and Lies: The Decalogue on the Rise

En fin, naces del pecado.

– Calderón de la Barca, *El gran teatro del mundo*[1]

As the old era waned and a new age dawned,[2] the Seven Deadlies became less prevalent as a paradigm for moral knowledge. Increasingly, the Ten Commandments arose (or rather, were resurrected) to take their place as the dominant locus of anxiety regarding sin and guilt. Or so the story goes. But as we have seen repeatedly throughout this study, things are seldom if ever that simple. In any period of transition, change happens in fits and starts – one step forward, two steps back – like a baby who is learning to walk. Not to mention that "progress" is one of those dubious essentializing terms which have been banished by postmoderns as pertaining to the old-style grand narratives (*grands récits*) we no longer find relevant. No, the picture we have been painting in these pages is more messy than that. At the very least, these two competing paradigms coexisted in Spain for an extremely long time; indeed, I am not convinced that either of them has been completely discarded to this day.

Nonetheless, it is possible to trace in the *comedias* certain emergent areas of cultural concern, specifically two items from the Decalogue, which rose to fill the moral vacuum left in the wake of the Seven Deadly Sins' demise. These two of the Ten Commandments are "Honour thy father and mother" and "Thou shalt not bear false witness." Neither one of these finds an easy equivalent in the list of Capital Vices. In this chapter, I will argue that these two emergent Commandments, in addition to their status as outliers which did not fit within the old paradigm, were uniquely suited to address new moral challenges arising within the context of the Spanish Renaissance court. As we shall see, these two injunctions bear special resonance for this patriarchal culture at this particular time.[3]

The first of these Commandments, the charge to honour one's parents, appears explicitly in the *comedias* both as a natural obligation and a divine mandate. We find references to obeying parents framed in general terms of what is socially acceptable; for example, one son declares, "es deuda al padre debida el serle el hijo obediente. En mi vida le ofendí, ni pesadumbre le di."[4]

But giving honour to parents is not only a debt or obligation, it is a Commandment; and *comedia* characters speak of it as such: "los hijos manda honrar los padres, ¿y el Conde su mandamiento quebranta?"[5] This holy Commandment commands the utmost respect: "Ay, ¿qué ha dicho contra el santo mandamiento de honrarás tu padre y madre?"[6] Like all the Ten Commandments, this one is understood to come directly from God: "mirad que Dios quiere se haga el mandamiento de los padres, y que os manda que le obedezcáis."[7] When it is not specifically referred to as a Commandment, it is often called a holy precept, as in "Mejor guardamos los preceptos santos de honrar los padres."[8]

These references show us how this Commandment was understood in theory; but what about how theory was translated into practice?[9] Here again we see characters adhering to both the spirit and the letter of the moral law as they honour their parents by asking permission before undertaking a major enterprise. For example, the titular character in Guillén de Castro's *El nacimiento de Montesinos* demurs, "Sin licencia de mis Padres no podré," and then asks his parents directly for their licence or permission to do as he wishes: "Licencia, padres, os pido."[10] *Comedia* characters are also seen fulfilling their parents' wishes. An example of this appears in the prologue to Lope de Vega's *El desposorio encubierto*, where the author writes to the young son of his patron: "Cumple Vuestra merced justamente los deseos a sus padres, en el cuidado que muestra en los estudios."[11] Then, as now, in addition to course of study or career, a common area of tension between parents and children involved the choice of a marriage partner. We shall have opportunity to examine this further below.

A willing obedience to parents is explicitly connected in the *comedias* to several larger themes or issues we have already encountered throughout this study. These include honour, nobility, wisdom, prudence, natural law, pragmatic concerns, and both earthly and heavenly rewards. Obedient children were thought to bring honour to their parents, as in the following wordplay on *ilustre*: "Ana ilustre, de tus padres honra y lustre."[12] An obedient son is likened to his father's coat of arms in the significantly titled *La obediencia laureada* by Lope de Vega, where we find the phrase "en un hijo obediente las armas de hidalgo son."[13] Spain prided itself on particularly well-behaved children, as we see from the following exchange between a Spanish nobleman and a foreign monarch:

DIANA: Brava nación la Española.
REY DE NÁPOLES: ¿Con qué estilos, y cuidados
  criáis los hijos queridos?
  Que en siendo tan bien nacidos
  os salen tan bien criados.

DON JAIME: Yo que en la pobreza mía
me vi tan sin esperanza,
procuré darle crianza
ya que hacienda no tenía.[14]

Here a good upbringing, thought to produce pious children, is seen to compensate even for lack of a monetary inheritance. The epitome of filial piety is to give one's own life for one's father, and we see an example of this too in these plays. One son declares his determination to free his father from captivity, even if it means risking his own life: "encamina a libertar a mi padre, por quien con noble codicia, deseo en cambio dichoso, dar por la suya mi vida."[15] The risk of one's life for one's parent – a literary trope extending all the way back at least to Virgil's *Aeneid*, where Aeneas flees Troy carrying his aged father on his back – is seen here as the highest form of nobility.[16]

It is worth pausing for a moment to remember here that this was the first Commandment to come with a promise. The Ten Commandments as delivered by Moses were thought to contain various prohibitions as well as positive exhortations, followed, in some cases, by promises of good to result if these rules were obeyed. An English translation from the Vulgate for this Commandment reads: "Honour thy father and thy mother, that thou mayest be long-lived upon the land which the Lord thy God will give thee."[17] This accompanying promise seems to have been familiar also to Spanish Golden Age playwrights. In the first act of Lope de Vega's *El piadoso aragonés*, the title of which is significant in the Virgilian context of filial piety mentioned above, we find this detailed piece of moral advice: "retirad la ambición, que quien desea corta vida a sus padres, nunca crea que se alargue la suya; sed discreto, que conforme tuviéredes respeto a vuestros padres, y obediente fuéredes, os le tendrán los hijos que tuviéredes."[18] The inter-generational wisdom of this message is particularly relevant for our study of generational cycles and the effects upon children of sins committed by their parents. This is a theme to which we shall return towards the end of our consideration of this particular Commandment.

Obedience to parents is called most just and saintly, and it is an obligation which weighs heavily on the conscience: "pesa en tu conciencia la justísima obediencia de tu padre, cosa es santa."[19] Not surprisingly, for the obedient child we find in the *comedias* a promise of heavenly rewards. This promise comes in the form of a divinely inspired increase in virtue:

HIPÓLITA: Tu hija obediente soy.
PEDRO: Tal virtud el Cielo aumente.[20]

Beyond religious didacticism, obedience to parents is justified further in the *comedias* by appeals to natural law and human nature, as in "el natural regalo, que por los hijos a los padres viene."[21] This filial attachment flows in both directions; as one character in Lope de Vega's *La serrana de Tormes* says to a parental figure, "De tu mano me viene el ser que tengo."[22] We find further examples from the natural world of animals that show filial piety, even certain species of birds that care for their aging parents: "dicen que a la vejez a sus padres estas aves piadosamente sustentan."[23]

But as Darwin would point out later, this solicitude is not entirely altruistic. There is a kind of egotism latent in any attachment of parents to their child, whom they see as an "Ángel, en quien como espejo lucidísimo justamente se miran sus padres."[24] This was of course the same argument invoked by William Shakespeare in the sonnets to a male lover whom he urged to procreate to ensure his immortality.[25] But self-interest is not limited to parents gazing for the first time upon their own reflection in their children's faces. The myth of Narcissus is a specific intertext invoked in the *comedias* to explain the bond of filial attachment: "Por el Amor de los Padres aqueste galán Narciso, que querer a quien da el ser, es quererse uno a sí mismo."[26] In this same prologue to *La Francesilla*, we find Lope de Vega quoting from Aristotle the three reasons why all children should be grateful to their parents: "Tres beneficios dijo Aristóteles, que debían los hijos a los padres. La causa del ser, engendrándolos: la del vivir, criándolos; y la del aprender, informándolos."[27] Here we see a typically Christian humanist synthesis of pagan along with spiritual wisdom.

Philosophical considerations apart, pragmatic concerns like the ones we saw for Lust of inheritance and succession appear in the *comedias* as still further guarantors of filial piety. In Guillén de Castro's *Cuánto se estima el honor*, a king names his son, the prince, to be his heir in the then-Spanish-dominated realm of Sicily. The prince replies, "Tu hijo obediente soy."[28] Likewise one of Lope de Vega's princes says, "soy del Rey don Juan hijo obediente."[29] Perhaps it is easier to be obedient with a kingdom hanging in the balance. Issues of succession and inheritance are mentioned in even more explicit terms in other plays, with specific monetary figures included; for example, "Para él tienen sus padres, porque es único heredero, diez mil ducados de renta."[30] This was a substantial enough sum to encourage even the most recalcitrant son to cooperate.

The general principle of obedience to parents is extended in the *comedias* to encompass the desired response to other authority figures: "tras el respeto debido a los Padres, has de Honrar tus Mayores, y Ministros."[31] Eerily, even Inquisitors were referred to as Father Inquisitors ("los padres Inquisidores, de nuestra Fe defensores"), as indeed were most priests.[32] In fact, by extension, obedience to fathers came to be viewed as a form of patriotism. This should come as no surprise, given the etymological derivation of *patria*, or country, from the same Latin root as for *padre*, or father (the Latin term in question being *pater*, the same term that gave birth to *patriarchy*). We find in the *comedias* repeated wordplays on these related terms, such as "¿Pues cómo, si te engañara, y fingido amor tuviera, padres, y patria perdiera, vida, y honra aventurara?" The woman to whom this warning was directed later repents of her actions, repeating this same *padres/patria* connection: "yo la que de Leonato fui engañada, y sin recato, padres, y patria dejé, y arrepentida lloré."[33]

This connection between father and fatherland is repeated in countless examples, such as "una hija inobediente, que contra su honor, y gusto de su patria, y casa ausente ocasiona su disgusto."[34] Conversely, disobedience to parents, in this moral economy, is equated to treason. In Lope de Vega's *El piadoso aragonés* – a play rife with references to fathers and children, some of which we have explored already in this chapter – one character exclaims: "¡Insolente un vulgo airado Majestades pisa! ¡Que tanto pueda un hijo inobediente!"[35] The rioting crowd is compared implicitly here to a disobedient son rising up against the father/state. The most extreme case of filial impiety would be patricide, a crime linked directly in the *comedias* to betrayal of one's country: "una infame patricida, que quiso anegar su patria."[36] Usually the motive for royal patricide is the desire to seize the kingdom for one's self: "La codicia del reinar tal vez los hijos ha hecho matar los padres."[37] Interestingly, in the *comedias* this crime is not exclusively the province of men, as we see in Lope de Vega's *El laberinto de Creta*, where a princess murders her father: "la traición … nos dio puerta y lugar. Mató Cila patricida al Rey su padre."[38] In the case of patricide the punishment must be immediate and is viewed as entirely justified within this moral system: "castigaron con la pena merecida, que el hijo que es patricida, y rebelde a su piedad, no espere, que es necedad."[39]

As Foucault has demonstrated convincingly in *Discipline and Punish*, the threat of punishment is a powerful force for regulating moral behaviour. The threat of punishment for disobedient children in the *comedias* is both temporal and eternal. Disobedient children cause worry for their parents (as one repentant daughter says, "cuánto verle desconsolado siento, pues llego a notar el cuidado que le doy, hija inobediente soy") and harm to themselves: "Hijas inobedientes, que al curso de los años anticipáis el gusto, destrúyaos Dios, los cielos os maldigan."[40] In fulfilment of the warning contained in the Commandment, they consequently lead shorter lives: "Ves cómo quien no obedece a los padres, Dios permite, que aquello el tiempo les quite."[41] They are disinherited by their parents, as with the character who "padres ha perdido: desheredóle en fin, forzoso efecto de un hijo inobediente y atrevido, contóme sus desgracias y pobreza."[42] Their worst punishment, of course, is eternal: "castigo en la otra vida y en ésta siempre al hijo inobediente."[43] One disobedient son laments his moral blindness in this area: "Fui hijo inobediente, estuve ciego, y el cielo me castiga."[44] God Himself is said to punish the disobedient child: "¿el Príncipe no siente, que castigos tiene Dios para un hijo inobediente?"[45] Such divine punishment comes like a lightning bolt from the sky, as when the king exclaims, "A, hijo inobediente, abrase un rayo tu enemiga mano."[46]

Figure 1. 7 Deadly Sins vs 10 Commandments

7 Deadly Sins	10 Commandments
1. Pride	1. No idolatry
2. Greed	2. No blasphemy
3. Lust	3. Keep the sabbath
4. Sloth	4. Honour parents
5. Gluttony	5. No murder
6. Anger	6. No adultery
7. Envy	7. No theft
	8. No lies
	9. No coveting wives
	10. No coveting goods

Note: This numbering of the Commandments follows a contemporaneous confessor's manual, Jayme de Corella's *Práctica de el confessionario* (Madrid: Antonio Gonçalez de Reyes, 1696), which uses this list to divide Tratados I–VIII. Each Tratado is devoted to one of the Commandments up until number 8. At the end of Tratado VIII, Corella appends a short chapter devoted to Commandments 9 and 10, which he considers merely a repetition of Commandments 6 and 7: "El Mandamiento nono, y dézimo, se reducen al sexto, y séptimo; y se pusieron estos dos últimos preceptos para enseñarnos, que no sólo se peca con la obra … sino tambien codiciando esas cosas" (144). This short passage provides a perfect example of the uniquely Spanish conflation of the Seven Sins and Ten Commandments as well as the greater "interiority" or "individuality" hailed by many scholars as being a hallmark of the Decalogue.

2. Hieronymus Bosch (1450–1516), *The Seven Deadly Sins*, Museo del Prado, Madrid. Photo courtesy of Art Resource.

3. Arch of Bera (Roman, 1st century BC, Via Augusta, near Tarragona, Spain). Photo courtesy of Art Resource.

4. Bridge at Alcántara. Photo courtesy of Art Resource.

5. Hendrik Andrieszen, still life of *Vanitas* (1635), last known to be held by Christie's of London.

6. Francisco de Goya, *Por haber nacido en otra parte* (*For Being Born Somewhere Else*) (ca 1808–14), brown wash drawing, Album C, number 85, Prado Museum, Madrid.

7. Rembrandt van Rijn (1606–69), *Bust of a Young Jew*, Kimbell Art Museum, Fort Worth, Texas.

8. Hieronymus Bosch (1450–1516), pen and ink sketch of beggars, Musées Royaux des Beaux-Arts de Belgique, Brussels. Photo courtesy of the Bridgeman Art Library International.

9. Hieronymus Bosch (1450–1516), *The Pedlar: The House of Ill Fame*, Museum Boijmans van Beuningen, Rotterdam.

10. Jan Steen, *The Marriage Bed of Tobias and Sarah* (ca 1660), Museum Bredius, The Hague. Photo courtesy of the Bridgeman Art Library International.

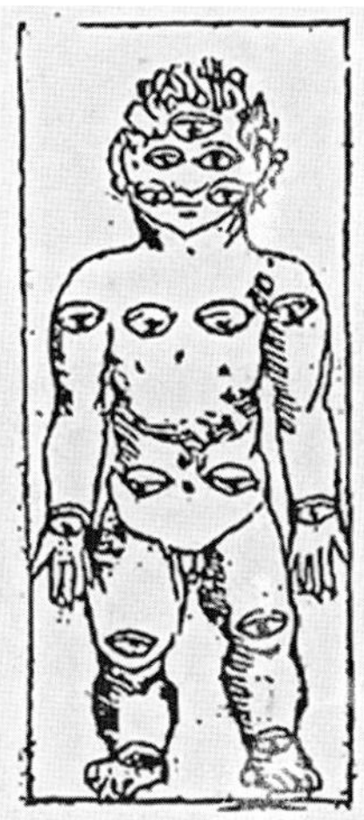

11. Baby born with 33 eyes, from *Admirables prodigios y portentos que se manifestaron en Bayona* (Barcelona: Lorenço Déu, 1613).

12. *Occasio* emblem from Andrea Alciato, *Los emblemas* (1584).

13. Pieter Claesz, *Still Life with Peacock Pie, Roasted Fowl, and Fruit* (1627), private collection / Johnny Van Haeften Ltd, London. Photo courtesy of the Bridgeman Art Library International.

14. Francisco de Goya, *Saturn Devouring His Son* (1819–23). Museo del Prado, Madrid. Photo courtesy of Art Resource.

lo indìcias?
Fè. Lo indicio,
de que yà Elèna ſu Madre
en Bretàña hà recibido
aquella Indeleble Marca
del Caracter del Bautiſmo;
y en fièl Peregrinacion
parte al Soberàno Olympo
de la Gran Jeruſalèn,
en buſca del Sacro Ligno,
que fuè Antidoto al Venèno
del Arbol del Paraíſo:
con cuyo exemplàr, no dudo,
que à ſus inſtancias movido
Conſtantino.
Gent. Calla, calla,
que al eſcucharlo, al oìrlo
tiembla el pecho, duda el labio,
falleze el aliento, el brio
ſe eſtremèze, el corazòn
flaquèa, delira el juizio,
y en las fieras confuſiones
con que vòy à hablàr, y gimo,
vna mordàza, en la lengua;
en la garganta, vn cuchillo;
en las entrañas, vn aſpid;
y en la viſta, vn baſiliſco:
Ethna ſoy, rayos arrojo;
bolcàn ſoy, llamas reſpiro:
Elèna (muero al penſarlo!)
Chriſtiana (rabio al dezirlo!)
en buſca (què ſentimiento!)
del Madèro, (què delirio!)
que ſepultado (què paſmo!)
yaze oculto, (què conflicto!)
Peregrina và (què aſſombro!)
à Jeruſalèn; (què abiſmo!)
pero què me deſaliento?
Què me ahogo? Què me aflijo
al veèr en mi Religion
ſoſpechoſo à Conſtantino?
Quando veèo, que ſu Campo,
deshecho, roto, y herido;
porque yà del Mar la Gente
toma tierra en ſus diſtritos,
ſe pone en fuga, diziendo
los eſtruendos mas diſtintos.
Suenan Caxas.
Dent. vn. El Grande Maxencio viva.
Otros. Viva; y muera Conſtantino.
Fè. Aunque de la lid le veèo
falìr, dexando perdido
el trançe de la Batàlla,
no por aqueſſo deſiſto
de mi Eſperança.
Gent. En qué puedes
fundarla?
Fè. En veér à dos viſos
hazerſe de lo Hiſtoriàl
Alegorico ſentido.
Gent. De qué ſuerte?
Fè. Oye: Oìd
quantos à mi vòz combido;
que à todos toca entendèrlo,
y à mì no mas que dezirlo.
En Conſtantino, que Ceſar
es de Roma, ſignifico
al Hombre en comun; pues tiene
del Orbe el mayòr Dominio:
que ſerà Hijo de la Igleſia,
fundo en ſer de Eléna Hijo;
pues la Igleſia es la que và
buſcando la Cruz de Chriſto:
Maxencio, en ſincopa, Magio;
ſu mas opueſto Enemigo,
es aquel Monſtruo, que vſando
de ſus Magicos echizos,
el Nombre acredita, pues
ſiempre es fantaſtico el vicio.
Eſſa Real Lid, en que aora
ſe ſignifica vencido,
es aquella primer Lid
del

15. Typography used to represent Anger on the printed page, from Calderón de la Barca, *La lepra de Constantino* (1717), in Calderón, *Autos sacramentales, alegóricos y historiales*, ed. Pedro de Pando y Mier (Madrid: Manuel Ruiz de Murga, 1717), 79.

As these violent meditations on filial interactions may reveal, honour or obedience to parents is not always cheerful. The trope of forced obedience to parental figures recurs frequently in the *comedias*, as when one daughter declares, "determinéme a ser hija obediente: verdad es que forzada obediencia."[47] It is possible to glimpse a complex network of power relations and mistrust in lines about overprotective parents who send spies out to watch their children's every move: "Son mis padres tan sutiles, que siempre traigo conmigo espías."[48] It is impossible not to think here of Michel Foucault's Panopticon, that masterpiece of nineteenth-century surveillance, where nobody was ever not being watched.[49] Although potentially anachronistic, as recent scholars have shown, this analogy is also not without potential relevance and resonance for Golden Age Spain.[50] Early modern Spanish parents were literally expected to keep their unwed daughters under lock and key: "pierdan se sabe los dineros sin la llave, sin los padres la mujer."[51] Here the parents are seen to act as a padlock on their daughter's virginal, corporeal treasure box. We seem to find a similar excuse made for parents' overzealous guarding of their children or keeping them under wraps in one *comedia* character's retrospective observation that "no me encerraron mis padres, sino para la crianza."[52] This child seems to understand that such quasi-captivity was intended for protection.

A particular case of forced obedience to parents was the practice of arranged marriages for daughters, a custom all too frequent in Spain during this time.[53] As one daughter laments, her marriage was not to her liking, nor to that of the husband forced upon her by her parents: "casáronme mis padres con Doristo, para mi muerte y a disgusto suyo."[54] It may be supposed that these contrived alliances could seldom end happily; instead, they brought much suffering under the guise of what Calderón calls a delirium of convenience. As one character describes the situation of a daughter forced to wed a man she did not love, "Casóse forzada en fin de sus padres: ay, delirio de la conveniencia, ¿qué te falta para homicidio?"[55] Here the foisting upon a daughter of an arranged marriage of convenience is likened to nothing less than murdering her. Even an obedience that would perhaps not qualify as forced tends to sound more abject when spoken by a daughter in these plays. Obedience to parents trumps free will for young girls, as we see clearly from the following exchange:

> SACERDOTE: A vuestros padres hablad.
> MARÍA: Sí haré, si me dais licencia, que hasta ahora la obediencia
> detuvo la voluntad.[56]

A synonym for *voluntad* or will is *libre albedrío*, that famous moral quotient which, according to Cervantes and other authors from the period, can never be forced.[57] Thus we find a disclaimer in Guillén de Castro's *El nacimiento de Montesinos* to the effect that parents are not always (although they are often) tyrants over their children's free will: "no del todo han de ser los padres al reprender, tiranos del albedrío."[58]

In Francisco de Rojas Zorrilla's *Los trabajos de Tobías*, the daughter Sarah says rather pitifully, "Tu hija obediente soy, haz de mí lo que quisieres."[59] Here she is saying, essentially, "do whatever you want with me." In a play which thematizes such reinforcements of the patriarchy, Calderón's *La niña de Gómez Arias*, the father threatens his daughter with being thrown into a convent if she refuses to comply with the arranged marriage he has planned for her: "Y si tu altiva soberbia intenta oponerse acaso a mi obediencia, un Convento te habrá de tener en tanto que te resuelvas; escoje, o el matrimonio, o el Claustro."[60] Here we may find post-modern theories of abjection, described by proponents of subaltern studies such as Julia Kristeva, to be particularly resonant.[61]

But most critics agree that the *comedia* as a genre supresses, or at least muffles, these faint, abject murmurings. It is a commonplace of *comedia* criticism that order must be restored at the end of the play – whether that order be social, economic, poetic, or moral. Thus we see that in the realm of obedience to parents, a repentant son promises to mend his ways: "Palabra os doy de enmendarme, y de ser hijo obediente, vuestra vida el cielo aumente."[62] This occurs in a play whose title, *El piadoso aragonés* (as we have mentioned), may echo the Virgilian epithet "pious Aeneas." The most obvious tying up of loose ends tends to occur at the end of these plays in the form of group weddings. Often not one, but several couples pair up at the end for a group ceremony that would make modern fathers envy the savings on wedding expenses.[63] My take on this – which is also not original – is that, as Jacques Lacan would have it, the reintegration of the social order mirrors a (re-)initiation into the symbolic order.[64] Incredibly, in one of his prologues Lope de Vega casts the entry into language in almost proto-Lacanian terms: "hablan la lengua Castellana, como nos la enseñaron nuestros padres."[65] According to the Law of the Father in the *comedias*, scandals always end in peace: "entre hijos, y padres estos escándalos siempre paran en paces."[66] This eery, forced imposition of order fails to contain the messy, slippery moral residue which, in Raymond Williams's terms, continues to ooze out around the edges of these plays.

* * * * *

Now, this is where things really get complicated. The discussion of early modern preoccupation with the Fourth Commandment, above, has assumed a fairly literal interpretation involving attitudes of biological children towards their biological parents. But the discourse of parenting was not limited during the early modern period in Spain to the purely biological. There were other, overlapping realms of discourse including authorship, self-fashioning, mysticism, and theology which employed this same terminology, but for very different purposes. Let us pause now to explore just a few of these.

It must be remembered that the language of parents and children always bears special resonance for authors. In the immortal words of Cervantes in his prologue to Part I of *Don Quijote*, authors normally consider their books to be their sons – although in this case, as Cervantes cannot resist pointing out with exquisite irony, he considers his work to be not his son, but rather his stepson.[67] The *comedias* echo and invert this recurring trope of parenting as authorship, like with the line "tus padres, autores de tu vida."[68] Similarly, when a character wants to enquire who a woman's father is, he asks instead who was her author.[69] There is necessarily a distinction made between divine and human fathers, with the honorific title of first Author always reserved for God (as one character poses the question rhetorically, "¿Dios no fue el Autor primero de cuanto vive?").[70] But even human fathers likewise are consistently called authors, as when Don Felis in Lope de Vega's significantly titled *Los enemigos en casa* hopes to act in such a way that "el autor de mi ser no se ofendiera."[71] There has been much interesting work done recently on authorship, printing, and parenting in early modern England,[72] and it would be fascinating to extend this scholarly trend into Golden Age Spain.

However, books are not the only alternative children of their authors. In the *comedias* we find the parent/child relationship being radically redefined in increasingly more complex ways. For men, we encounter echoes of the quixotic maxim, "cada uno es hijo de sus obras."[73] In this nascent Renaissance era of self-made men, lineage ceases to be so important, or at least takes a back seat to personal achievement. To illustrate this point, we must introduce a dialogue between two soldiers as recounted in a *comedia* by Calderón:

> [Un soldado] preguntó, ¿quién, después de haber nacido, había engendrado a sus padres? Y otro el soldado le dijo, que los padres del soldado sólo son sus hechos mismos.[74]

Here we find a radical redefinition of filial responsibility as early modern subjects declare their freedom to answer to no one but themselves.

Did this option exist for women? Undoubtedly not, at least not in the same way. But for women, there did exist the mystical option to marry God instead of a mortal man. This course of action is proposed by the Virgin Mary in Guillén de Castro's *El mejor esposo*, in the first scene where she professes a wish to consecrate herself to God's service in the Temple instead of performing every Jewish woman's duty to wed and procreate:

> Y así digo, pues nací
> en la obediencia inmortal,
> que … el derecho natural
> de mis padres para en mí

después de haberme ofrecido
al Templo.

She further defends her right to choose celibacy, even going so far as to argue before the high priest, "¿Quién puede negar, Señor, que el Virginio estado es al conyugal preferido?"[75] Now, it must be noted that in this play, Mary does not prevail in her desire: when God sends a dove from heaven to point out which man she is to marry (Joseph), she graciously accedes to His wishes. But it is fascinating to speculate about what might have inspired a Golden Age playwright to depart from the biblical account – in the New Testament, there is no indication that Mary wished to remain single – in order to justify a woman's right to choose an alternative lifestyle. This was potentially a choice which could be imitated by many a would-be nun or *beata*.

Early modern mysticism, in some sense, offered women a truly subversive option. They could resist the order from their parents to marry a man they didn't like, and the church essentially gave them carte blanche to do so as long as they entered a nunnery instead. If it is God's will, then it doesn't really count as disobedience, or so the thinking went. After all, God was their true Father, as evoked by the following lines: "más le cuadre, que decir que los padres … ha dejado, trueca por Dios, que es verdadero padre."[76] The church clearly had an investment in this position. Even as unassailable an authority as the Virgin Mary declares boldly that her natural duty to obey her parents effectively ends once she walks through the Temple door. This decision in favour of a religious life offers her a socially sanctioned manner to "resistir al debido casamiento."[77]

Thus we see that even in this seemingly uncontroversial area (who would not agree, at least in theory, that children are supposed to show respect for their parents?), the *comedia* resists containment or easy categorization and can't seem to stay on message. In an almost incredible example of the complex nuance with which some early modern playwrights approached moral problems, Calderón de la Barca – in *Las cadenas del demonio* – allows a character on stage to point out that even the Child Jesus disobeyed His earthly parents. After the observation made by another character that the Child Jesus is so special that three kings came to worship Him at His birth, the Demon replies, "Hombre es, pues sus padres le pierden del Templo a la puerta."[78] The reference, of course, is to the teenage Jesus's getting lost in the Temple, to the great distress of His mother Mary, who evidently travelled halfway home from Jerusalem before she even realized He was missing. She went back to find Him in the Temple conversing with the rabbis. This highly problematic scene is dramatized in the third act of Guillén de Castro's *El mejor esposo*, in which Joseph and Mary interrogate Jesus as to why He was disobedient. Mary laments,

Ay mi hijo, ¿qué te has hecho?
¿Cómo? ¿Dónde? Ay triste calma,
¿te perdí, fino del alma,
de los brazos, y del pecho?
¿Cómo no te lastimaste
de dejarme sola, y triste,
porque sin mí te perdiste?
¿Porque sin ti me dejaste?

She scolds Him for His lack of concern for herself and His earthly father, asking rather pitifully if it is their fault: "Hijo de mi corazón, ¿cómo nos tratáis así, a vuestro padre, y a mí? ¿Son culpas nuestras?"[79] These plaintive notes of discord would seem to indicate that this is not the traditional, idyllic view of the Holy Family.

In *Las cadenas del demonio*, the Demon claims that this disobedience of Christ towards His earthly parents in fact offers proof of His fallible or even fallen humanity. Now, we must hasten to point out that Calderón avoids any possible entanglement with Inquisitorial censors by placing these lines in the mouth of a demon. However, a knowledge of early modern demonology provides us with a needed context for understanding this cryptic ellipsis: demons were thought to be intimately familiar with the finer points of theology. As one demonologist puts it,

> Daemonum est & fuit magna potentia, astutia, & calliditas incredibilis, sapientia tanta, quanta in nullis alius creaturis praeter sanctos Angelos, perspicacitas acutissima.
>
> (Great is and was the power of demons, unbelievable their astuteness and cleverness, their wisdom was as great as any other creatures except the holy angels, their perspicuity most keen.)[80]

Thus the issue of Christ's possible disobedience of His earthly parents remains as a lingering question posed by the *comedias*. No fully satisfactory response is ever offered. Perhaps, as with the mystical marriages for women described above, the will of His Heavenly Father trumps whatever might have been said to Him by His mother about not running off. In these plays, it would seem that specific applications of the basic principle of obedience to parents remain as elusive as a teenage son with his own agenda.

The very title of this book, *Sins of the Fathers*, offers a chance to meditate on the many ways in which children are condemned to repeat the sins of their parents. After all, as these dramas remind us, "es la doctrina heredada en la natural escuela de nuestros padres."[81] We find some interesting twists on this scenario if we examine lines about parental sin and filial expiation from the plays themselves. Here we meet pious children who try to atone for their parents' sins, including Original Sin, as in "humilde os doy … ofrenda de la culpa de mis Padres."[82] But this recognition that parents have committed sins for which expiation is required is, by itself, subversive. In its acknowledgment that parental actions are bad, this piety cuts both ways. At the very least, it would appear to act as the proverbial double-edged sword.

We find in the *comedias* themselves some evidence of a counter-discourse to this effect, for example in lines reminding parents also of their obligations towards their children: "éste es amor paternal, no tratar los hijos mal."[83] Is this symptomatic of a grudging acknowledgment that some fathers do indeed treat children badly? Once again, there are Scriptural accounts such as Abraham's abortive sacrifice of his son Isaac upon the altar that would not earn their protagonists a spot on the cover of *Parenting* magazine.[84] A lesser-known, similar story appears in the Book of Judges, where a Hebrew warrior named Jephte makes a vow to the Lord that if He will deliver the Ammonites into his hands, then he will offer as a sacrifice upon the altar whomever comes to greet him first when he returns home from the battlefield. As fate would have it, the first person to run to greet him is his only daughter. This story is recalled in vivid detail in a speech made by the Virgin Mary, of all people, in Guillén de Castro's *El mejor esposo*:

> Y el gran Capitán Jepte
> nos da un memorable ejemplo,
> pues de la guerra al volver,
> honrando sus dignas sienes
> el victorioso laurel,
> y habiendo ofrecido entonces
> en cambio de tal merced,
> por víctima de las aras
> lo que la primera vez
> se le ofreciese a la vista
> poniendo en su casa el pie:
> acertando a ser su hija,
> tan piadoso, y tan cruel,
> consagrándola al Señor,
> satisfizo; y con tener
> sus inclinaciones ella,
> pagó la deuda por él.[85]

Here the father's actions towards his daughter are specifically labelled cruel, as she is made to suffer death unjustly in order for him to fulfil a rash promise which he arguably never should have made in the first place. There could not be a more literal example of the sins of the fathers being visited upon their children.

But in a strange inversion, some children in the *comedias* are seen to be the ones not just to suffer the punishment for their parents' sins, but actually to be the ones to punish their own parents ("a la horca van a dar los hijos, por estorbar, los castigos de los padres") in what amounts to an emotional – and sometimes quite literally physical – slap in the face.[86] These children end up cursing their parents in what can only be seen as an utter failure by the *comedias* to achieve their didactic mission. In Purgatory the condemned wail and gnash their teeth, cursing their progenitors: "En profundas cavernas se quejaban tristemente condenados, maldiciendo a sus padres, y parientes. ¡Tan desesperadas voces de blasfemias insolentes!"[87] It would be one thing if this were an isolated instance, but it is not. Again and again we find *comedia* characters cursing their parents in a nightmare of intergenerational strife: "Malditos mis padres sean mil veces, pues me engendraron."[88] In Guillén de Castro's *El Narciso en su opinión*, Brianda rails against the cruelty of her father's determination to marry her off against her wishes within the hour:

> Un padre riguroso,
> que pide, como injusto,
> fuerza a la voluntad, y ley al gusto.
> Sólo una hora le ha dado
> de término a mi muerte,
> o con rigor más fuerte
> resuelto, y arrojado
> por esposo importuno,
> de mis dos primos quiere darme uno.[89]

On top of parental cruelty, this father technically fosters incest by forcing his daughter to marry a close blood relative, for which a papal dispensation is required.[90] Similarly, in Lope de Vega's *El verdadero amante*, Belarda apostrophizes "O padre ingrato, avariento" while Danteo rails against "Padres fieros rigurosos." These are not groundless accusations; in this play, one cruel father is seen beating his son senseless ("Que a su cruel padre vi, que recios golpes le daba") and then throwing him out of his house ("Echóle de su cabaña, su padre fiero enemigo").[91] In some sense, this powerful counter-discourse subverts the entire system of the patriarchy: "los Reinos puede darlos la fortuna, y el poder; los padres sólo … el ser, luego ¿es justo el respetarlos?"[92] What started out an idyllic picture of parent and baby gazing at each other as in a mirror[93] has ended in a conflagration of curses.

Ultimately a surreal proliferation/multiplication of fathers leads to a veritably postmodern fragmentation: "hijos veréis, que como van creciendo, mil padres diferentes van teniendo."[94] The reduplication and refraction of these thousand fathers would be enough to confuse any child. Which one is real? Which one is false? Which one to obey? This shifting chaos of duplicity and confusion offers the perfect segue into our other resurrected Commandment for the early modern period, the injunction against bearing false witness. Implicitly and in subsequent reception of this Commandment, it became a prohibition against telling any sort of lie.[95] Just as the desperate – and only superficially successful – effort to preserve the patriarchy may have led to increased anxiety about fathers, the new court culture provided an ideal space for meditations on duplicity. It is to this final locus of preoccupation, or node of cultural anxiety, that we shall turn our attention now.

*****

> The process of emergence … is then a constantly repeated, an always renewable, move beyond a phase of practical incorporation: usually made much more difficult by the fact that much incorporation looks like recognition, acknowledgement, and thus a form of acceptance. In this complex process there is indeed regular confusion between the locally residual (as a form of resistance to incorporation) and the generally emergent. Cultural emergence in relation to the emergence and growing strength of a class is then always of major importance, always complex.[96]

At various points in this study we have looked at aspects of morality – such as the newly valued courtly leisure – as particularly relevant for a Golden Age Spain where the royal court exercised a centripetal pull on the rest of society. As Leah Middlebrook has shown convincingly in *Imperial Lyric*,[97] courtiers were that growing social class of which Raymond Williams speaks. Let us look now at one final aspect of Golden Age morality with special resonance for an increasingly courtierized culture.[98] This area has to do with deception and duplicity.

The Eighth Commandment, against bearing false testimony, was certainly familiar to Golden Age audiences. In the *comedias* we find explicit references to false witnesses of both genders, as in "Falsos testigos cohechó contra él el oro y la envidia, el poder y la soberbia" or "se quedan la Clavelita, y la Infanta, testigas falsas, y feas."[99] In Calderón's *El médico de su honra*, the *lacayo* Coquín protests jokingly, "Testigo falso me hacéis, y es ilícito contrato de enorme lesión."[100] His comment probably shows an awareness of this specific Commandment. During this period, false witnesses were available for sale and purchase at the right price: "como nos muestra el mundo el desengaño, compra testigos falsos el dinero."[101] In fact, the going rate appears to have been 100 *reales*: "¿Testigos falsos dudas? Por cien reales te vendrán a rogar."[102] The punishment for bearing false testimony was evidently having one's teeth pulled out, as we see from the king's continued banter with the *gracioso* above.[103] We see a reference to this customary punishment repeated in

Lope de Vega's *Servir a buenos*: "Una discreta llamaba, que era el agua su deleite, testigo falso el afeite, porque los dientes quitaba."[104] Even when the punishment was not carried out by earthly authorities, it was believed to be happening in the supernatural realm, as executed by a diabolical dentist who extracted one tooth for every lie uttered: "por cada mentira los está el diablo sacando una muela."[105] Finally, an explanation for those mysterious toothaches.

As we have been seeing throughout this book, while we have traced the complex and often incomplete transformations of moral concepts and their reception, here is another sin which gradually came to be redefined. Eventually an awareness of this specific Commandment morphs into a more general discourse about truth, falsehood, and lying, as in "la Verdad, con Testimonio fingido a nadie se ha de mentir."[106] Lying ultimately takes the place of bearing false witness in catalogues of sins. When characters demonstrate their knowledge of the catechism by rattling off the Ten Commandments, typically we find a general reference to lying instead of any mention of bearing false witness.[107] As with the false witness scenario, lies are said to be bought and sold for a price.[108] Sometimes instead of a monetary exchange, there is a different – but no less valuable – commodity which changes hands. In this moral economy, we find a lie being traded for revenge: "tú sólo te has de emplear en ayudarme a mentir, y ayudaréte a vengar."[109] In the sensationalistic *comedias*, often a lie is told when someone's life is at stake or the outcome of the dramatic work hangs in the balance.[110]

How are lies told? To illustrate falsehood visually, *comedias* turn to metaphors from the natural world. The moon was thought to lie since it only reflected the sun's light.[111] The wind lied through its whispered murmurs and soft, flattering caress.[112] Lies were compared to crystal because they appeared transparent.[113] They formed a web to trap the unwary, like a spider's net.[114] They could suck one in, like the sea swallowed a sailor in its vortex.[115] Night time was a liar because it covered up clandestine deeds.[116] Mirrors lied by reversing the image reflected in them.[117]

In contrast to the human world, the natural world and its inhabitants, namely animals, were typically portrayed as more inherently honest. A prime example – found in Antonio Zamora's *Judás Iscariote* – is the dog, not typically given to or capable of deceit: "un perro, que centinela de los silencios del sitio, jamás mintió a su sosiego el ladrón por el latido."[118] In this particular play, of course, the honest dog forms a marked contrast to lying Judas. But not all animals take on such honest connotations: the bird is implicitly likened to a lie because it flies in the same way that lies take flight.[119] Corporeal bodies in general, whether animal or human, are seen as a species of lie within a certain type of Renaissance world view rooted in Neoplatonism: "el alma es una verdad, y el cuerpo es una mentira."[120] All physical reality – particularly earthly beauty – becomes a lie when observed from an eternal perspective.[121]

Lies, since they are a pestilence coming from the mouth, are also likened to bad breath – the difference being that bad breath is accidental, while lying is a reckless choice.[122] The single body part most commonly encountered in the context of lying is the tongue: "la lengua, por callar su mengua, dijo que sí; pero mintió la lengua."[123] The tongue even lies to the voice: "Es posible que a su voz pasiones mintió su lengua."[124] Sometimes, to comic effect, the lips and the tongue are perceived as in some sense running away from the person who is talking: "¿Yo lo dije? No lo creas, debió de errarse la lengua."[125] The lips are the other part of the body most frequently associated with falsehood: "me harán creer tus ojos lo que mintieron tus labios."[126] Here the eyes are seen as complicit in deception, a trope repeated frequently ("Mintieron en Margarita ojos, donde se asomaron, lisonjas que me engañaron"), though sometimes it would seem that the eyes are privileged over the mouth because they lend themselves to truth verification: "mas ¿cuándo mintieron ojos que miran agravios?"[127] In a curious inversion of roles, eyes are said to be the only tongues that never lie.[128] This truism of eyes not lying is repeated in a play by Tirso de Molina, but with an interesting twist; this time the rhetorical question receives an answer involving the eyes' relationship to the soul:

ROGERIO: Los ojos, ¿cuándo mintieron?
LEONISA: Cuando no los rige el alma.[129]

One of the ways eyes *were* thought to lie was by crying when a person did not feel sorrow.[130] The heart, likewise, was thought not to lie, except when it did: "anuncia en esta ocasión mil cosas mi corazón, que nunca mintió en mi daño."[131] This last phrase, of course, implies that the heart could lie, just not to its owner's detriment.

In the same way that body parts were perceived to be capable of deception, so were such intangibles as thoughts, feelings, or suspicions, as in "mintieron mis pensamientos, y mintieron mis sospechas."[132] These feelings might even lie to or deceive the person who experienced them, as in "mi malicia me mintió."[133] Interest – normally shorthand for self-interest, but with economic overtones – was said *always* to lie ("siempre el interes mintió"), as was fame.[134] In fact, sometimes these non-concrete entities could lie even when the words accompanying them were not false: "No mintió el discurso mío, pero mintió mi deseo."[135] Desire in particular was notoriously unreliable.[136] But as the saying goes, actions speak louder than words; and even when words or feelings lied, actions were thought to tell the truth.[137]

Given this panorama of lies and their manifestations in humans, animals, and the natural world, what were the moral overtones of falsehood, and how did it fit into early modern Spain's larger moral economy? In what I call the straight or didactic reading, lying – at least in theory – was perceived as bad, even if theory did not always match practice. There are dramatic characters who state flatly, "es pecado el decir mentira."[138] We also find references to parents chastising their children with corporal punishment for lying, as in "Por mentir sólo, aunque niño, puse mi mano en su cara."[139] Adults are warned not to tell a lie on their deathbeds for fear that their dying words might condemn them to hell.[140]

Lying was thought to bear a special relationship to the Seven Deadly Sins, symbolically represented in the hydra with seven heads, through Lucifer, the Father of Lies.[141] More specifically, lies were imagined to go hand in hand with Envy, which frequently offered a concrete motivation for bending the truth.[142] We see here a synergy between two competing systems of moral thought – the Seven Deadlies versus the Ten Commandments – reminding us that transitions are always messy and the choice is seldom either/or, but instead (often resoundingly) both/and.

In line with this basic premise against lying, we find characters vowing not to do it for religious reasons, as in "yo no mentiré por cuanto Dios ha criado."[143] The moral standard of truthtelling, along with not stealing from others, was seen to define one's identity as a Christian: "Cristiano soy, aunque ignorante fiel, que nunca hurté, ni mentí."[144] To these religious reasons are frequently added philosophical ones, sometimes grounded in elaborate etymologies: "Ir contra mente es mentir; ¿qué hago en ir contra mi mente?"[145] This question highlights the basic irrationality of going against what one knows to be true. Some characters profess to be so unaccustomed to lying that they claim they don't know how ("yo en mi vida supe mentir, aunque sea en un pelo"), or that they hate both lies and those who tell them.[146]

However, increasingly we find these arguments grounded in more pragmatic than moral concerns. A lie cannot last ("aquella mentira, que de un peligro nos sacó, durar no puede");[147] the liar will get caught ("¿qué he de hacer, que estoy cogida en la mentira?"); and the only results of lying will be infamy and scorn ("mas de mentir, ¿qué se saca sino infamia y menosprecio?").[148] A lie risks the ultimate loss in Golden Age Spain, the loss of honour.[149] It weighs heavily on the conscience – so much so, in fact, that *comedia* characters jokingly warn each other that it might be hard to walk while staggering under such a weight.[150] Lying destroys trust and causes people forever afterward to view the liar with suspicion: "Necio, ¿cómo podré salir con esa invención? En sabiendo que mentí, y le engañé, no es forzoso tenerme por sospechoso [?]"[151] In Juan Ruiz de Alarcón's extended meditation on lying, *La verdad sospechosa*, the didactic moral of the story is announced resoundingly at the end: "que en la boca de él que mentir acostumbra, es la Verdad sospechosa."[152] But we should note that this message is posed more in practical than in ethical terms.

As we might have anticipated, given my earlier work establishing casuistry or case morality as the foundation for a poetics of the *comedia* as a genre,[153] lying is one of those sins which could be justified in some cases, such as when Isabel in Juan Pérez de Montalbán's *Los amantes de Teruel* admits, "mentí, erré; pero con mucha disculpa."[154] According to the Jesuitical doctrine of equivocation – which allowed Catholics to lie or at least withold information, especially when threatened by persecution for their beliefs – early modern Spaniards were left ample room to speak only partial truths.[155] In fact we encounter specific references to the doctrine of equivocation in the *comedias*, such as "que Amor me dé tan equívocas palabras, que sean mentira al oírlas, y verdad al apurarlas."[156] We also find allusions to special dispensations for lying, such as those afforded by manuals of casuistry: "señor, de este tu amigo no venga, que puede echar a mentir con un libro de dispensa."[157] This idea of receiving a special dispensation for lying appears repeatedly in the drama, as in "es también dispensado estilo, que las Infantas de Allende puedan mentir su poquito?"[158] This phrase is reminiscent of the familiar English expression *to tell a little white lie*.

In many of these plays, lies are considered not culpable if there is a good enough reason; as one character states baldly, "No es culpable una mentira, cuando excusa algún pesar."[159] Even more acceptable is lying just a little bit, or employing circumlocutions, as in "circunloquios … mentir por entresijos."[160] Most of the time this convoluted discourse is considered not exactly to be lying, just embellishing the truth or perhaps diluting it.[161] This could involve what we might recognize as softening the blow or sugar-coating the pill.[162] In certain situations, lying was even considered necessary, as in "Mentir ha de ser preciso" and "Aquí es menester mentir."[163] Characters describe themselves as being forced to lie, as in "Mas ¿qué he de hacer? Es forzoso, empiece a mentir el labio."[164] Here we get to witness a character's mouth starting to run away with him. Invoking the discourse of casuistry, characters could claim that a specific case might obligate someone to tell a lie ("El caso viene a obligarme, por deslumbrarla, a mentir"), with the ultimate justification offered being, of course, reason of state.[165] Finally, in the culmination of this process of what we have been calling a transformation of moral concepts, we see lying actually redefined as a pious act, under the right circumstances: "que decir por una amiga una mentira, obra es santa."[166] This sounds like it could have come straight out of a girlfriend advice column in *Cosmopolitan* magazine. Such radical rethinking of received moral categories is tantamount to nothing less than a redefinition of Vice and Virtue: "Que esta mentira virtud, y no culpa sea."[167] It is perhaps a measure of just how successful the Jesuits were in indoctrinating a whole generation of Spanish pupils.[168] At least during the Golden Age, their casuistical/equivocal ideology held sway.

Having acknowledged this basic fact, we can nonetheless differentiate to a certain extent among social groups to determine which ones were thought to be more prone to tell a lie. Far and away the biggest prejudice we see here is against women. It is not uncommon to find such vituperative outbursts as, "¡Ha fiera! ¡Ha ingrata! ¡Ha cruel! Qué pronto vive a mentir el ingenio en la mujer."[169] If women are seen here as lying, at least they are also viewed as smart or ingenious. The habit of "mentir mucho la mujer en cualquier tiempo" was so generally accepted by both moralists and some male playwrights that I have not been able to find much evidence in the drama of an accompanying counter-discourse.[170] In fact, women are said never to tell the truth, for their name is synonymous with lying: "que trate a una mujer verdad en nada, porque para mentir les basta el nombre."[171] Allegedly they don't know any better; as Roldán mouths off in Lope de Vega's *La mocedad de Roldán*: "Tras ser ruines las mujeres, ¿qué sabrán sino mentir?"[172] In more allegorical dramas of the period, Mentira is pictured as having the tongue of a woman.[173]

This depiction simply follows a long tradition of misogyny in which women were thought to be infused with lies from birth.[174] In Calderón's auto *La cura, y la enfermedad*, Inocencia declares, "mintió la Mujer antes que el Demonio mismo."[175] We find multiple oblique references to Eve leading Adam into temptation in the Garden of Eden.[176] Ever since this originary incident, women have been perceived not to fear lying.[177] Women – then as now – are seen to lie about such state secrets as their age: "Mintió, que yo sé que aquesta dama tiene más años que el Sol."[178] Some women try to defend themselves against the blanket accusation of lying, as in "saben los cielos que no he sabido mentir, aunque he nacido mujer, que no todas mienten."[179] They may not all do it, but at least they all know how.[180] In an ironic reversal, male characters even choose to dress or act like women in order to learn to lie better: "quiero aprender semblante de una mujer para acertar a mentir."[181] We shall explore the implications of transvestism – along with disguise more generally – for lying later on.

Whether as a result of contamination by women, or possibly more as a manifestation of the only chink in their armour, early modern Spanish men were allowed to lie when they were in love, although it was still considered ignominious: "mentir quien ama, es mengua."[182] In fact, the better a person knew how to lie, the better he would be (in practical terms) at wooing a potential mate: "negocios de amor, los que los dicen mejor, ésos suelen mentir más."[183] Falling in love was nothing but being lied to and lying in return: "el enamorar es mentir, y hacer extremos."[184] In fact, there is no truth in love, only lies.[185] We get the sense that all's fair in love and war, for "no afrenta una mentira, cuando engaña a una mujer."[186] Actually, a lover who does not lie is thought to be foolish, if lying could have advanced his cause: "Pues ¿qué amante, si no es necio, siendo parte apasionada, no mentirá en su provecho?"[187] Jealousy was one of those intangible entities which was thought almost never to tell the truth.[188] In fact, due to their propensity for bearing false witness concerning someone's fidelity, *los celos* are called sophistical enemies of domestic tranquillity.[189]

Romantic love would seem to be a fairly universal experience, and as such we might expect it to act as a great leveller when it comes to ethics and morality. However, in the *comedias* we find multiple statements to the effect that noblemen do not lie because it is beneath their dignity.[190] As one character asks another, "¿eres noble, si te defiendes, y amparas ya de vil mentira?"[191] Another example would be Don Gutierre's insistence in Calderón's *El médico de su honra* that "No os he de mentir en nada, que el hombre, señor de bien, no sabe mentir jamás, y más delante del Rey."[192] Another character states baldly that "nunca un Caballero puede mentir."[193]

Noble ladies, likewise, were to a certain extent considered immune from this vice: "La Marquesa Sirena lo confiesa, y no puede mentir una Marquesa."[194] It was generally agreed that the nobility were permitted to lie only in certain situations, such as when they were courting women ("un hombre principal puede mentir con las damas") or out of gratitude for a favour done to them.[195] There are definite overtones of social class accompanying many references to lying – who does it and how it is perceived – as when a lady says scornfully, "Siempre afrenta viene a ser el mentir, villano."[196] Lying is routinely associated with villagers:

> GENARO: ¿Puede mentir mi sospecha?
> JULIA: Sí, porque al fin es villana.[197]

The lower class, for their part, tend to pride themselves on lying better than noblemen; for example, in the case of gypsies, "veamos si saben los Caballeros mentir como los Gitanos."[198] There appears to be an invisible line drawn in the sand, placing an unspoken limit on socially acceptable lying.[199]

Very much a part of the hidden hierarchy for this moral economy seems to be the special case of kings. As a subject says to the king, "infamado en la lealtad, ninguno dice verdad. Sólo tú, señor, no mientes."[200] At first we might think that this is simply a case of an exceptionally honourable monarch, but then we realize there seems to be an exception made in the case of all, or at least most, kings: "Que no es de Reyes mentir, ni faltar a su palabra."[201] This truism is repeated in enough *comedias* that we may assume it was fairly widespread:

> DOÑA INÉS: ¿Crédito das a esas cosas? ¿No ves que son disparates?
> BEATRIZ: Pues ¿un Rey ha de mentir?[202]

Kings were believed to be God's representatives on earth and thus were felt to be above such banal immorality.[203]

When looking at how sins were perceived and by whom, it is fascinating to glimpse differentiations made between people on the basis of their standing in society. Noble masters would often forbid their servants to lie; we glimpse this dynamic when a lower-class servant exclaims, "el se[ñ]or Agricán mi amo no me dejará mentir."[204] Good servants are often described by their masters as honest, such as the squire who is "un buen escudero, que no sabe mentir."[205] As most famously exemplified in the *Celestina*, female servants often lied to protect their mistresses: "criadas, y amas tenéis pacto explícito a mentir."[206] In accordance with this breakdown along the lines of social class, lying is specifically referred to as a plebeian vice: "¡o vulgo, qué no sabrás encarecer, y mentir!"[207]

But in the *comedias* we also find curious traces of a real transition from the old moral order to the new. An example would be the lines,

> ¿Quién creerá, cielos, que sea el mentir un hombre honrado la cosa más torpe, y fea!
> ¡Y que haya trance en que agrade ver, que un hombre honrado mienta![208]

Here the clear implication is that people used to consider lying to be beneath an honourable man, but now it has become more generally accepted behaviour.[209] In fact, if we are to believe these play texts, everybody's doing it: "Eso que llamas mentir es, señor, tan ordinario."[210] From evidence found in the *comedia* repertoire, we cannot escape the impression that lying was both common and widespread (witness such blanket statements as, "todos suelen mentir").[211] In Quiñones de Benavente's significantly titled entremés *El murmurador*, we encounter the question, "Aqueso del mentir es pegajoso, mas ¿qué hombre hay, que no sea mentiroso?"[212] Trading accusations, characters claim to have learned from each other how to obfuscate.[213] Some of them express shame about lying, as when Nise declares, "¡Jesús, y qué desgraciada ando en mentir estos días!"[214] But others acknowledge the practical usefulness of lying with an eye towards social advancement.[215] In fact, it is often necessary to lie in order to uphold honour: "Caigo en lo que son honras de esta vida; todo es mentir."[216] This is a devastating portrayal of all-pervasive, generalized deceit.

The concomitant loss of innocence in turn makes the liar less gullible; a person who does not know how to lie assumes other people are just as ingenuous and, thus, tends to believe everything he or she hears.[217] Lying is fun: "Por Dios, don Diego, que el mentir es gusto."[218] It is fashionable: "Es muy al uso el mentir."[219] It makes one feel good: "quien bien miente, bien siente."[220] It can be profitable: "ya del mentir no dirá que es sin gusto y sin provecho."[221] In fact – particularly in the mouths of guys joking around with their pals – it is said to be the happiest thing: "Así lo siente un cofadre, que dice, que el mentir es la cosa más felize [*sic*]."[222] Besides, it has been around at least since the beginning of human history.[223] As with that first couple, Adam and Eve, married couples are particularly prone to lie to each other.[224]

Unfortunately one lie tends to generate another: "engaño a engaño añadiendo. A quien miente, he de mentir."[225] This character declares that a lie must be answered by another lie, until the situation becomes quite entangled.[226] Lying becomes a habit which is impossible to break.[227] One truth is followed by twenty lies, until veracity is mathematically outnumbered.[228] For those accustomed to lying, their interlocutors know they will lie even before they start talking.[229] For everything there is a season, but they lie throughout the year.[230] Soon there is a veritable Baroque proliferation of lies, as when the titular character in Antonio de Solís's *El doctor Carlino* declares, "Volveré a mentir de nuevo, y mentiré más, y más, y dure lo que durare, como mentira de pan."[231] Even an attempt to come clean after telling a lie can result instead in new fabrications.[232] A tongue that lies once will lie a thousand times.[233]

In a curious synecdoche by which the part came to represent symbolically the whole of Spanish society, lying was associated in particular with the court: "Bien digo yo, que en la Corte, pocos dejan de mentir."[234] Lying was synonymous with courtly flattery, adulation, and affectation.[235] At court, lying reached the altitude of social grace: "es en la Corte gracia, decir verdad por desgracia, y mentira por costumbre."[236] Character after character affirms that "todo es mentira en la Corte."[237] Soon after they arrived, courtiers learned how to lie: "Como vienes Cortesano, ¿ya te enseñas a mentir?"[238] Female courtiers and ladies-in-waiting had perfected lying to a fine art: "el uso de Señoras Cortesanas, que hacen gala del mentir."[239]

In this environment, it did not matter – great or small, old or young, man or woman – all became adept at the courtly lie.[240] This is a vice to which clerks and officials – those petty bureaucrats who were but cogs in the wheel of the new machinery of the imperial state – were thought to be peculiarly susceptible: "no he visto en mi vida tan excelente oficial, pensé yo, que mentiría, como lo suelen hacer."[241] Another character explains that it is natural for bureaucratic officials to lie because they are always having to invent excuses when something goes wrong: "que un oficial mienta, es cosa natural, porque con mentir se excusa."[242] Pretenders at the court were assumed to be lying whenever they spoke.[243] The climate had become such that in circles closest to the throne, lying was applauded and truth had been banished.[244] This was particularly true at the royal palace and, by extension, throughout the capital city of Madrid.[245]

One of the ways the court encouraged lying was by the emphasis placed there upon rhetoric and refined speech. We overhear characters applauding a lie as if it were a well-composed essay, as with the encomiastic "Qué bien compuesta mentira" ("what a well-composed lie").[246] Good lies are described as polished and well arranged or adorned, as in "ella hallará otra mentira tan aliñada, y compuesta, como la pasada."[247] Let us not forget that the Renaissance dramatist engages all the resources of classical persuasion, such as Aristotle's efforts to move the emotions: "mostrar que mentir sabe, mover afectos."[248] Humanist schoolmasters taught their pupils how to lie with wisdom, "mentir con lengua sabia," apparently without troubling themselves too much about the moral ramifications of this instruction.[249] We find the most accomplished practitioners of this art lying with dexterity and eloquence, to the point of convincing someone to believe 2,000 lies.[250] Playwrights even invoke the medieval troubadours to praise a lie which is particularly well crafted: "y si es mentira, está por Dios bien trovada."[251] This was especially true of the tall tales told by the *gracioso*, or fool, whose very job it was to lie.[252] These lies were often funny, as in "qué graciosa mentira."[253] Lying was thought to be indicative of intelligence because it required *ingenio*, or ingenuity.[254]

The recurrent trope of *mentir con arte* in the courtly context leads us naturally to consider lying as actual art, in the form of painting,[255] sculpture, embroidery, or even poetry. Within a Baroque aesthetic of artifice it was desirable and even necessary for painters to lie with their brushes; in fact – in an alarming reversal of moral categories – it was a sin for them to tell the truth: "dile al pintor que aprenda a mentir, porque es pecado decir verdad con pinceles."[256] Paintings are referred to as noble lies of nature.[257] Poets are thrown into the same lot with painters and other artists: "en materia de amores, los poetas, y pintores tienen de mentir licencia."[258] In a deliberate echo of Plato, we find frequent references to "Poética Mentira" and the implicit assumption that literary lies must have been composed by poetic liars.[259]

While paintings and other works of art were deemed meretricious, portraits achieved a special status in this hierarchy of artistic vice.[260] As Laura Bass elaborates convincingly in *The Drama of the Portrait: Theater and Visual Culture in Early Modern Spain*, this was a culture obsessed with simulacra as well as related literary motifs of doubling and disguise. Portraits of monarchs were especially prone to paint the ruler in a favourable light: "es mentira cuanto en cuadras de Príncipes se mira."[261] But as Bass proposes, this period's preoccupation with visual culture found a unique outlet on the stage, where dramatic foils, doubles, and cases of mistaken identity were already the norm:

> The risks inherent in the painted likeness of a person are what fuel the majority of the dramas of the portrait of the seventeenth-century Spanish stage, as portraits are misapprehended, surreptitiously painted, reduplicated, and often circulated without the sitters' knowing … This quintessentially baroque layering of levels of representation calls attention to theater and portraiture as homologous cultural and material practices with the power, at once seductive and perilous, to shape and unmake identities.[262]

Though Bass does not explicitly consider moral questions, her study might have benefited from an inclusion of the contemporaneous discourse about lies. Lies were specifically referred to as double dealings, or *tratos dobles*, and once again we see the Deadly Sins creeping into this moral equation.[263] We have already seen how Envy became an incentive to lie, but now we learn that the mechanism by which it did this was a double intention.[264]

Akin to the portrait, another form of theatrical lying and reduplication was related to the deceit of disguise. The concept of deception or disguise is mentioned many times in the context of lying, as in the phrase "mentiras disfrazadas."[265] This language works sometimes on a figurative (as in "el Príncipe Persiles mintió afectos disfrazados") but also on a literal level, as in "señor, hoy, que he reparado al mirarte disfrazado mentir patria, ser, y nombre."[266] Sometimes a disguise was donned with the goal of wooing a lover[267] or escaping detection; such was the case for many incidents of transvestism, as when Rosaura in *La vida es sueño* dressed as a man for the purpose of avenging herself upon Astolfo and eluding capture by her father, Clotaldo. A lie was also likened to cosmetics or makeup.[268] This was, after all, the theatre, where identities are fluid and can be manipulated with each change of costume.

In fact – and once again, here we see a complex theological transformation – by means of a gradual process of adding layers of resonance and association, lying came to be symbolized not just by disguise, but by clothing in general.[269] Lies are heavily adorned, while truth is naked.[270] Allegorically speaking, Mentira is known to be a notorious shape-shifter, appearing in a whole spectrum of disguises.[271] A scene from the auto *Llamados, y escogidos* demonstrates the emblematic relationship between the two, with Mentira stealing a cape from Truth with which she then slyly covers herself.[272] The inevitable conclusion to be drawn from this scene is that lies are preferred because they are well clothed, which makes them more socially acceptable: "No hay duda, que había de ser preferida Mentira que está vestida, a Verdad que está desnuda."[273] In a fascinating coda to this emblem, Golden Age playwrights go so far as to imagine Adam and Eve pursued by the Inquisition, who would have clothed them in *sambenitos* – the notorious Inquisitorial garments of shame – which are the Renaissance equivalents of humanity's first clothing, made from animal skins: "Adán, y Eva ensambenitan, la verdad anda desnuda, adornada la mentira."[274] (For a drawing of what a *sambenito* looked like, once again see figure 6.)

In lieu of a full costume change, sometimes playwrights opted to portray lies or their speakers with a more limited, but no less telling, change of masks. The danger is that a lie would be betrayed by the look on the liar's face: "que el mentir es calentura del alma, y sale a la cara."[275] It should be remembered that within Neoplatonic discourse, a person's facial features – particularly the eyes – were thought to be a window to the soul, making it impossible for the face to lie.[276] But what happened when the face was covered, as with a mask? As Diego says in Tirso de Molina's *Amazonas en las Indias*, "Quien el consejo y parecer que sigo contradijere (o envidioso, o loco) busca mi mal con máscara de amigo."[277] Even without such an obvious way to cover the face, lies generally relied on strategies of deception.[278]

* * * * *

In other chapters of this book, we have already explored a nascent obsession with proof and evidence that was characteristic of a move towards legality and secular authority. This was accompanied by a concomitant shift towards viewing a sin as a crime. This transition is nowhere more apparent than in discourse about truth and falsehood, where we find an increasing reliance on evidence to demonstrate guilt:

ELVIRA: Mira, que maltratas mi inocencia.
FERNANDO: ¿Mentir puede esta evidencia?[279]

The strongest secular argument against telling lies is in fact that the truth will be verified: "si alguna mentira finjo, será imposible que deje de averiguarse."[280] A lie will not be allowed to continue in circulation unless it receives accreditation from those who hear and repeat it.[281]

But whereas this is the discourse of proof we would expect to see – that is, disproving a lie by verifying the truth – in the *comedias*, surprisingly, we begin to see this discourse being reversed. Suddenly the discourse of proof is invoked to lend credit not to truth, but to lies, as in "qué mentira tan probada" and "Parece que se prueba esta mentira, y que tiene color de verdad."[282] Suddenly we find the rhetoric of validation being applied not to veracities, but to falsehoods, as in "hiciste tan válida la mentira."[283] This discourse of *validation*, in turn, takes on the resonance of the *validos* or *privados*, the king's favourites, a privileged position said to be occupied symbolically by Mentira:

SERAFINA: Mucho, pues, de ver me admira tan valida la mentira.
FEDERICO: Es huérfana la verdad.[284]

We see that Truth is orphaned here, in a society which prioritizes style over substance. In a particularly sinister iteration, just enough truth is mixed in to make lies seem more credible: "diréle la verdad antes, porque la mentira crea después, que así se acreditan comunmente mis cautelas."[285] In fact, a good or convincing lie is thought to be impossible unless it contains a germ of truth.[286] And in an alarming reversal, the evidence itself could be found to lie, as in "miente la evidencia misma."[287]

Whereas proof had previously been dependent on what was seen with the eyes or heard with the ears – or perhaps even what had been verified by a witness – now it could be demonstrated more fully through written accounts.[288] This transition to written culture, in theory, should have assured that truth would prevail. But lies could also be committed to paper, as for example with forged signatures: "recibí vuestras cartas, mas creí que hasta las firmas mintieron."[289] In a metaliterary tour de force which blatantly calls attention to the play's own status as fiction, characters brag about having written down enough deception to lend credence to their lies.[290] Written lies, in effect, provided a new form of counterfeit currency to circulate in this new moral economy.[291] Sometimes written lies could spur one to action, as in "con la espada firmáis lo que mintió el tal papel."[292] But other times a written lie could take on a life of its own.[293] A new awareness of this fact, so characteristic of the transition to print culture, results in multiple warnings not to commit lies to paper: "enmendaos en escribir, que no es seguro mentir."[294] This is particularly true once the manuscript page is printed, for now it becomes possible to find such telling lines as "el libro mintió."[295] Héctor Urzáiz Tortajada makes a comment in an article about the history of books in the Spanish Golden Age which seems strikingly appropriate in this context:

> Hay de fondo … una apelación al carácter mágico-religioso de la página escrita, a eso que se ha dado en llamar "taumaturgia bibliográfica," la atribución al libro de poderes que trascienden lo escrito, como una suerte de talismán.[296]

What we have here is a changing morality in response to print culture. Are written, especially printed, lies more permanent? We find some evidence of a growing mistrust of the senses as they are supplanted by the firmer, more solid medium of the printed page.[297] But an equally growing awareness that printed words, too, could lie soon led to a radical questioning of the very nature of truth and falsehood.[298]

Diego in Calderón's *El astrólogo fingido* points out the obvious: "la buena mentira está en parecer verdad."[299] But what happens when these categories are reversed to the extent that a lie actually *becomes* truth, and vice versa?[300] This is the situation described in the following dialogue between two characters in the same playwright's *No hay cosa como callar*:

> DON JUAN: Es cosa muy temeraria, que quieras hacer verdad tu mentira, a costa de mi paciencia.
> MARCELA: ¿Que es mi mentira verdad? Si es la que miente tu lengua.[301]

This process, which we might call ontological metamorphosis, begins when a lie is repeated often enough that it is actually granted the status of truth: "¡A quién esto no admira! Por verdad me contaron mi mentira."[302] If this happens frequently enough, even the originator of the lie starts to convince himself that it is true. Much confusion ensues.[303] The resulting discourse – "me llegué a persuadir a que en tal seguridad antes mintió mi verdad, que su error pudo mentir" – may best be described as elaborate, contorted paradox.[304] In Lope de Vega's significantly titled *El premio del bien hablar*, we find such inherently doubtful statements as "palabra os doy que mintió," akin to the so-called Liar Paradox, in which words are cheapened to the point that there is no good reason to believe this promise either.[305]

In what is perhaps the Golden Age's most extended meditation on lies and their consequences, Juan Ruiz de Alarcón's *La verdad sospechosa*, the inevitable but surprising conclusion, from a moral standpoint, is that "el mentir … puede decir verdad."[306] The atmosphere of the court, in particular, reverses moral categories, participating in the Baroque topos of the upside-down world: "Es ciencia la presunción, ingenio la obscuridad, el mentir sagacidad, y grandeza el ser ladrón."[307] We may detect here a critique of Góngora and the *culteranismo* movement in the allusion to ingenious obscurity, but the other critiques contained in this passage are levelled on the moral, not the aesthetic, plane. In fact, one character complains that the world has gone crazy, with everybody lying practically all the time: "Loco está el mundo, señor, porque si el mentir afrenta, ¿cómo tantos hombres mienten?" In the same play, this conversation continues as the other character notes that the world is painted with two faces, like Janus or a two-faced liar: "Píntanle al mundo dos caras: y si está tan recibido el mentir, como decís, ¿por qué es afrenta el *mentís*?"[308] Therein lies the paradox: on these shifting sands of morality, nothing is certain; lying seems universally accepted but continues to be (at least in a token sort of way) universally condemned.[309] In the epic battle between Truth and Falsehood, lies seem to win out; for when Elvira asks "¿Eso es mentira, o verdad?" Enrique answers, "Todo es mentira, señora."[310] This line from Calderón is actually echoed in the title of another play by him, *En esta vida todo es verdad, y todo es mentira*. In this play, the characters engage in extended dialogue in an effort to get at the crux of this ontological problem:

> LEONIDO: Cuando en tal confusion el sentido los admira, ¿mentira, o verdad?
> MÚSICOS: Mentira.
> ERACLIO: ¿Verdad, y mentira son? ¿Cómo puede ser?

Indeed: how can something be both true and false at the same time? Although it seems strange that a lie could tell the truth ("será la primera verdad, que la mentira haya dicho"), the play affirms that, conversely, truth can tell a lie: "mintiendo en la verdad, verdad la mentira dijo."[311] A Baroque love of paradox and riddles gives us such contorted phrases as "la verdadera mentira de aparentes realidades."[312] Ultimately this play would seem to conclude that it is beyond human capacity to decide, "que no hay humano sentido, que ser mentira, o verdad pueda afirmar," an argument which introduces once again the whole discourse of proof and affirmation we have been discussing.[313] This trope will already be familiar to readers of Calderón's most famous play, *La vida es sueño*, in which Prince Segismundo asks how it is possible to "saber si lo que se ve, y se goza es mentira, o es verdad: tan semejante es la copia al original."[314] Time and time again we run across the familiar Baroque lament of "siendo (como sabes) todo mentira, engaño, y quimera."[315] In a comic interlude meant to be sung, Luis Quiñones de Benavente offers a more humorous ontological meditation on the nature of truth in his entremés *La verdad*. In it we find lines characteristic of this same type of indeterminacy: "Jesús, quién le viera, por saber si es verdad, o mentira lo que de ordinario en el mundo se mira."[316]

One final case study from the *autos sacramentales* will serve to anchor this discussion firmly in the field of discourse studies. The play in question is *El laberinto del mundo*, by Calderón. In this drama, the figures of Truth and Lie take on classical overtones by their association with the Phaedra and Ariadne characters of Sophocles.[317] As they enact dialogue together, witness their fascinating exchange:

> MENTIRA: Somos las dos Hermanas, y ¿de una Naturaleza no son, Mentira y Verdad?
> VERDAD: Si son, o di, ¿quién engendra a la Mentira?
> MENTIRA: El Concepto que uno quiere formar de ella… .
> VERDAD: Luego es cierta cosa Mentira, y Verdad nacer de una Madre misma.[318]

Not only are they born of the same mother, but – in the sense that they both pertain to the *conceptista*'s realm of discourse – Truth and Falsehood turn out to be one and the same.[319] In fact, in this moral economy, lying becomes an acceptable way to arrive at truth: "o cuántas veces sacó verdad el que dijo mentira."[320] Lying can morph into truth in the space of time it takes to travel the distance between one person's mouth and another person's ear.[321] Along with this radical doubt, this crisis of rationality, in the purest of literary terms, what we are witnessing here is the triumph of fiction: "Ya no hay verdad, todo es mentira y ficción."[322]

* * * * *

This is a fitting end to the process we have painstakingly executed of placing each of the Deadly Sins and Ten Commandments under a microscope with a Golden Age lens. In a book about morality in drama, ultimately it is drama which prevails. But I find myself disagreeing with Lope on one important point: all discourse may be fiction in the sense of being shaped or made,[323] but it is not all necessarily a lie. I believe Golden Age dramatists left germs of truths about moral behaviour sprinkled throughout their plays, even if they tried to cover their tracks.

If we accept that the *comedias* – along with other preserved texts from the period – form an untapped archive of moral knowledge, then we may glean unexpected truths even from some throwaway lines which might previously have gone unnoticed. A stray line or two would not by itself be indicative of a pattern, but the sheer weight of evidence amassed by this study cannot be easily dismissed. These dramatists had a lot to say about ethical issues, and the often unresolved tensions in their works between competing moral systems do not belie that reality.

In the Conclusion that follows, we shall pause to ask the "so what?" question and try to make some sense of Spain's early modern moral heritage. In the case of the Mosaic injunction against lying, this Commandment was manifestly honoured more in the breach. But still the *comedias*' preoccupation with issues of veracity and mendacity demonstrates an awareness of – and a space of persistent relevance for – this moral concept. Without the original prohibition, its transgression would be meaningless. And so we close the curtain on this great collective psychodrama with a Decalogue that was emerging but still lacked hegemony. The transition from one moral system to another was far from complete. It was complicated, messy, and unfinished, as most such transitions tend to be. Let us now step away from the microscope to return to a more panoramic lens.

Conclusion: The Self Discovered by Sin

El Día que el Hombre peca, es morada del Demonio.

– Calderón de la Barca, *El diablo mudo*

Me han dado gusto los pecados cometidos.

– Calderón de la Barca, *La devoción de la Cruz*[1]

So after all this, we must ask: which moral system won out in the drama? And why? Among myriad possibilities, I see at least three options for ways we could have approached and interpreted this body of evidence. I shall summarize these three choices at the outset.

The first possible conclusion we could have reached is that a system of morality based upon the Ten Commandments won out. This reading might be supported by anecdotal archival evidence from the time period, such as bigamists being branded on the forehead with the number 10 to denote their flagrant violation of God's law.[2] As for why it triumphed, the answer would be that the Decalogue is at once both more biblical and more personal than competing taxonomies, foremost among them the one based upon the Seven Deadly Sins. One potential problem with this idea is that early modern Catholic Spain was not particularly known for its Bible reading. This outcome would have vindicated John Bossy without refuting Lu Ann Homza. In other words, it would have upheld the contention that there was a revolution in Europe right about this time in which sin increasingly came to be viewed through the lens of the Ten Commandments. In seeing sin this way, the faithful left behind the older, more communal perspective of the Capital Vices.

Homza points out that the latter taxonomy persisted in Spain long after it had been abandoned by the rest of Europe. This might still have been true, if we considered that the zenith of *comedia* production occurred during the sixteenth and seventeenth centuries, while Bossy's moral revolution is described as occurring earlier, in the fifteenth and sixteenth. Spain could still have been different, by virtue of being later to embrace this important change in the way morality was constructed. This argument buys into the theory known as Spanish exceptionalism.[3]

One crucial caveat to this reading would have underlined the differences in approach between dramatists and confessors – although, paradoxically, some of these were one and the same.[4] Even the most cursory glance at Spanish confessors' manuals from this time period indicates that Spanish confessors *were* slow to embrace this change and that even when they finally did, the Seven Deadlies still lingered: as Homza notes astutely, "Spaniards read the Decalogue as the Seven Sins."[5] But this strange persistence of the Capital Vices in the archives as organizing principles for confessors' manuals would not, in this reading, have necessarily spilled over into the repertoire or other areas of early modern life.

That is one possible interpretation, one direction in which the evidence might have led us. Another possible way to look at the evidence from the stage plays would have been to declare that the Seven Sins won out. This would have illustrated the Capital Vices' overall persistence in Spain as opposed to the rest of Europe – that is, Homza was right, and dramatists echo confessors. This view would have reinforced vigorously the critical doctrine of Spain as Other, studied recently by Barbara Fuchs in an interesting effort to trace Spain's rejection by the rest of Europe back to its maurophilia or "tainting" by Afro-Arabic culture.[6] However, in this reading I would have had to question Bossy's conclusions. Perhaps the Seven Sins system was not so communal after all. More than one scholar has criticized Bossy's overly simplistic reduction of competing moral economies into this bifurcation.[7] These critics see more personal or individualistic elements in the Seven Sins, while pointing to the communal nature of the last seven of the Ten Commandments (admittedly, the first three would be difficult to categorize as relating to anything other than the direct relationship between God and the individual). As medieval creations, the Capital Vices may have originated within a more communal milieu, but this does not mean that subsequent ages did not interpret them quite differently. Critics who embrace this perspective often couch their arguments in reception theory, on the grounds that in its *Nachleben*, a given text or idea may take on very different resonances from the ones originally associated with it.[8]

As is usually the case, as a literary critic trained in the rigours of Deconstruction, I prefer to seek a third term or *aporia*, refusing to accept the tyranny of Western logic and its tendency to think in terms of stark binaries. Instead of embracing either of these first two possible outcomes without reservation, I would opt instead for some combination or synthesis of both. Perhaps the moral system imagined in the *comedias* represents a unique blending of the more personal elements drawn from each moral code. This compromise approach recognizes that a play is not a confessor's manual. As the Structuralists and Formalists have taught us, careful attention to genre will reveal important similarities and differences between the two.

This reading specifically goes against the New Historicist treatment of all texts as somehow fundamentally the same. I refer here to their mantra about the "historicity of texts and the textuality of history."[9] Perhaps even in cases where dramatists and confessors *were* one and the same, they were able to make generic distinctions between plays they wrote in the evenings versus theological treatises they composed before noon. We do the same thing every day: when we are jotting down a grocery list, we are not composing a poem. When we are writing academic prose, it is not in the same mode as a letter to Grandma.

Ignoring Golden Age writers' ability to distinguish between one genre and another can only be done at our peril. These were smart people who were very prolific and immensely attuned to the contours of specific rhetorical situations.[10] If they had the ability to tell the difference, then so should we. It should not necessarily pose an insurmountable problem for us to find a somewhat different moral system played out on the stage versus in the confessional – or, in Diana Taylor's terms, the repertoire versus the archive.

But this more nuanced view, as usual, comes with its own complications. We might well ask: what were the selection criteria used by playwrights? How did they decide? How did they know when to invoke the Ten Commandments instead of the Seven Deadly Sins in order to support a given course of action? Or whether to reproach a given character for a moral failing according to one system or the other?

My gut instinct tells me that there is a tension here, betraying traces of an uneasy coexistence. While I would like in some ways to be able to argue the first outcome laid out in this section – it would certainly make the whole thing a lot simpler – I cannot wish away persistent evidence to the contrary. As is often the case with literary criticism, there is a sliding scale. Critics position themselves closer to one end of the spectrum or the other. The answers are seldom cut and dried, black or white. Moments of cultural transition are often messy and incomplete. This does not make the wave of change any less real, or any less worthy of our study.

If I had to choose which side of this sliding scale to lean towards – and this will come as no surprise to readers of my previous books – I would choose the side of subjectivity and individual agency. When I read these plays, I hear too many traces[11] of anguish, guilt, and remorse to say otherwise. These are early modern voices echoing through the centuries, clamouring to be heard. They deserve to be silenced no longer.

* * * * *

As we asked in our introduction, why does it even matter which moral taxonomy early modern Spanish dramatists favoured? Perhaps it is time to revisit the "so what?" question now, in light of all we have studied and analysed. We will see that the topic of sin and how it is conceptualized has wide ramifications for the classic self-vs-society dilemma.[12]

Consider this: the *comedia* has traditionally been considered the voice of a whole society, not of individuals. As Maravall so famously stated, "El teatro español es, ante todo, un instrumento político y social."[13] Here we see that up until recently, the *comedia* had been read as the mouthpiece of a fairly standardized social code.[14] Following the lead of scholars such as Melveena McKendrick,[15] my interpretation potentially changes that view. If instead we are able to discern individual voices of authors and characters – which before were perhaps barely even audible – then these oft-repeated critical assertions fall apart.

This critical hornet's nest in turn raises the spectre of the entire notion of the Spanish honour code. This concept has been debated ad nauseum, and it is highly unlikely that those arguments will end here. But I believe it is not too ambitious nor presumptuous to hope that this study might shed some light on this perennial problem – one which extends not just to the drama, but indeed to all of Spanish culture, even up to the present day.

In Spanish, there are at least two types of honour: *honra* versus *honor*, or social reputation as opposed to personal integrity or virtue. This dichotomy preserves distant echoes of the distinction in ancient Greek culture between *timē* (status or prestige) and *aretē*, or virtue.[16] The basic question is this: is the source of honour the self or other people? It would not be an exaggeration to say that how you approach this issue determines, in pragmatic terms, how you live your life.

The prevailing critical assumption with respect to early modern Spanish drama has been that *honra* is more important. Indeed, a database search on the two words reveals a high incidence of occurrences of *honra*: 2,866 instances in some 650 different plays. But these numbers, while to some degree indicative, fail to tell the full story. In comparison, *honor* occurs, in the same pool of roughly 800 *comedias*, some 9,410 times in 746 different plays. Attention to the context of individual occurrences – a thorough analysis of this will have to be saved for future research projects – would be useful here. But the simple statistics by themselves do tell us something about early modern moral and social preoccupations. *Honra* or social reputation remains a major concern in the *comedias*, but not to the complete exclusion of *honor* or personal integrity. In fact, the numbers would seem to indicate that *honor* is the overarching concern.

These comments lead us naturally to the thorny issue of *soy quien soy*. This legendarily problematic phrase is repeated at least 94 times in 81 *comedias*. It has been tackled in classic studies by such great critics as Leo Spitzer and Stephen Gilman.[17] Everyone seems to agree that based on sheer force of repetition, this must be a key phrase for understanding what the *comedia* as a genre is all about; as Spitzer postulates, "[e]l hecho es que en las obras del Siglo de Oro español nos hallamos a menudo con la frase *soy quien soy* (*por ser quien soy, siendo quien soy,* etc.) con que tal o cual personaje afirma su intención de no cometer una acción que contradiga a su verdadero ser."[18] A nobleman's appeal to his lineage, a lost prince's attempt to reclaim his identity, even a deliberate echo of the Jewish God Yahweh's mysterious pronouncement to Moses, "I am that I am"[19] (an interpretation which proves particularly problematic, given Isabel the Catholic's expulsion of the Jews from Spain in 1492) – these are only some of the many readings which have been imposed upon this problematic expression.

It is not necessarily my intention here to generate another one. But we cannot read many *comedias* for very long without asking seriously: what does that phrase really mean after all? If the self is in some way discovered by sin, then "I am who I am" becomes the product of all the sins I have ever committed.[20] In fact, it also becomes the product of all the sins my ancestors have ever committed, as the title of this book indicates. No one has ever studied this phrase in relation to moral taxonomies. I hope that by doing so in the light of new evidence established here, other researchers and I will be able to pour new wine into old wineskins. Of course they might burst … or get slashed by a crazy knight errant. But as the famous episode of *Don Quijote* demonstrates,[21] the result may be not a scholarly disaster, but instead a scene of enhanced complexity and artistic interest.

A frequent question I am asked when I give lectures on this material is: if this is all so obvious, then why has none of it been noticed before? I think any responsible answer to this question would necessarily be multifaceted.

The most simple answer is that the *comedias*' intricate polyrhythmic structure – so crucial to their success in the seventeenth century – poses immense challenges to readers and directors today. They are hard to read and hard to enjoy. They are an acquired taste which has been largely lost. Even native speaker scholars have confessed to me that they have no idea what some of the lines mean. Sometimes, in the process of dramatic creation, meaning was clearly sacrificed to considerations of rhyme. Succinctly stated, if we are not reading the *comedias* with gusto any more, then we cannot as readily be making new discoveries about their content.

There are of course thriving Golden Age programs in the US, not to mention Spain. In Madrid it is still possible to see *comedias* performed regularly on stage. There the *comedia* is actively preserved, a living repertoire, as an art form recognized to be a vital part of Spain's cultural heritage. But on the stage as well as in the classroom, one immediately stumbles across the problem of the canon. It almost seems as if there were some deliberate conspiracy to limit the number of acceptable *comedias* to, say, a dozen or fifteen. To judge from most graduate course syllabi or required reading lists, it looks like the number of *comedias* acknowledged to be great could not possibly exceed the number of works in the entire Shakespeare corpus. While this may even be true – as a comparatist, I have also concentrated seriously on his work – still it is no reason to ignore some of the many hundreds of other *comedias*. In my experience, even among those rare scholars who do read these archaic texts, most critics read only the same handful of plays.

One problem in this area is only just now beginning to resolve itself. This has to do with the availability of texts. In the digital age, hundreds of *comedias* have only just recently been made easily available to scholars for the first time. Digital search engines now allow for word searches of "Lust," "Avarice," "mandamiento," "pecado," and the like. This kind of research would not have been possible at the time when my own professors attended graduate school. Future graduate students will be able to launch brand new research programs, using texts and technology not available to previous generations.[22]

Another possible explanation for this apparent critical blind spot might be the nagging insistence on contrasting the *comedia* with other Golden Age genres such as lyric poetry, picaresque, and especially the novel which offer a wider range of expression for the individual subject. It is a critical commonplace that Cervantes's *Don Quijote* was the first real novel.[23] Studies abound about the emergence of autonomous characters, which define for many observers the true novelty of this new genre.[24]

These valid points merit careful consideration. My aim is not to detract one iota from the genius of Cervantes; complicating this matter even further is the fact that Cervantes himself was also a dramatist. But it makes no sense to me that the same country and the same time period that gave birth to the novel would produce theatre where that elusive and much-sought-after quotient we have come to call subjectivity was utterly lacking. Recent theoretical work in psychology may dismiss the very notion of subjectivity, insisting that it is socially constructed.[25] Perhaps all we ever have is endless posturing – an infinite series of masks to try on, the Hall of Mirrors at Versailles or, in serio-comical form, the stripper in David Lodge's academic satire *Small World* who keeps peeling off layer after layer without ever taking all of her clothes off.[26]

But I don't think so. Postmodern theoretical formulations are not always seamlessly applicable to Renaissance creations. If we hear a *comedia* character on stage confiding in a soliloquy about how guilty he feels for killing his father, I don't think we can discount the possibility that the priest/playwright who penned those lines was drawing upon sob stories he had heard from penitents in the confessional. Such is the living relationship between the repertoire and the archive. If that is not a trace of subjectivity, I'm not sure what is.

This, in turn, brings us to yet another nagging problem: many literary scholars are positively allergic to religion. As I argued in the introduction, inattention to sin has resulted in a critical muffling of any voices of agency or subjectivity struggling to break through the rigid constraints of this genre. I would say it is unusual – but not altogether impossible – to find novelistic, autonomous, or even subversive elements in the *comedias*. If we accept the premise that the self is discovered by sin,[27] then surely a genre this rich in depictions of sin onstage would have something to tell us about the people who were committing them.

Here it is necessary to recognize and acknowledge our own critical moment. The postmodern trend right now is to trace or uncover individual hidden histories of resistance to the prevailing grand narrative. An example would be Javier Espejo Surós's and Jesús Maestro's call for contributions to an anthology tracing the hidden history of atheism in Golden Age Spain.[28] In some ways the current study participates in that trend by unearthing certain subjective elements thought more properly to pertain to novels in the rather unlikely but fertile ground of three-act comic dramas. Well, what can I say? Cemeteries are unusually fertile.

It must be said here in the interest of nuance that this does not necessarily mean that previously accepted grand narratives about the *comedias* (read: Maravall and company)[29] have been entirely wrong. Usually there is more than a grain of truth to these accounts, or else they would not prevail for as long as they do. But they need to be at least updated, if not discarded altogether. Postmodern critics, those lovers of fragmentation, would say there is no such thing as a collective whole. All we ever have are heterogeneous collections of individual histories/experiences. So how could the Spanish drama serve as the voice of a nation if that homogeneous enterprise known as the church/state monolith was always already an illusion? Perhaps the previous critical unanimity has had more to do with critics' own historical moment than with the realities of a complex and not-so-golden Golden Age. Historiographically speaking, even that name betrays a totalizing view.

It is time to put the tarnish back on the golden aura by exploring the nasty, murky grime which is sin. Perhaps in doing so we will arrive at a closer approximation to the experience of theatregoers – and penitents – in early modern Spain.

Epilogue: To Avoid Reductionism

Hasta que arranque las raíces de la Culpa de la Heredad de mi Padre.

– Calderón de la Barca[1]

As demonstrated by a trendy pop culture book series published by Oxford University Press in conjunction with the New York Public Library, in addition to the January 2009 Seven Deadly Sins Week on the History Channel, as well as the Hollywood movie *Se7en* starring Brad Pitt, there has been a veritable explosion in recent years of renewed interest in the Capital Vices.[2] Conjuring images of the circles of hell in Dante's *Inferno*, perhaps the Seven Deadlies continue to seem more quaintly medieval – and certainly less controversial – than the Ten Commandments, those stern "Thou shalt's" and "Thou shalt not's" engraved on stone tablets and chiseled into children's memories as indelibly as they appear on the wall of the United States Supreme Court. Indeed, the continued depiction of the Decalogue in public spaces such as parks and government buildings has spawned a seemingly endless series of lawsuits demanding their removal on the grounds that they violate the basic American principle of separation between church and state.

Coming as I do out of this milieu, it is rather hard to imagine a Golden Age Spain in which church and state were not only not separate but instead formed one seamless whole. Indeed, the *comedia* art form – with its penchant for arranged marriages, restoration of order, and relentlessly happy endings – has been seen as the ultimate manifestation of Counter-Reformation dogmatism, particularly in the hands of a theologian such as Calderón. In this view, nothing is allowed to challenge or even question the pronouncements of the king, *comendador*, or other mouthpiece of the church/state monolith.

It is always important to recognize and if possible acknowledge one's own critical blind spots. I admit that my formation as a product of American democracy may at times colour my view of a culture and time period radically removed from my own. But the patterns I have noticed in the course of reading hundreds of Golden Age *comedias* simply do not fit the received critical narrative. Something else must be going on here. My suspicion is that generations of Spanish scholars such as José Antonio Maravall were perhaps unduly influenced by their own historical moment – namely, the critical consensus emerging out of the tragic shared experience of Franco's decades-long dictatorship in Spain. I suspect that, in part as a result of their own lived experiences, they saw in Golden Age Inquisitorial censorship a reflection of their own terror. Might this reactionary impulse, by which they showed themselves to be so much the products of their own historical moment, not have translated itself into disciplined fascism of the literary-critical variety? For in my experience, old-school, die-hard adherents of Maravall tend to be of a mindset that admits no dissent. Baroque Spain was "una cultura dirigida," period.

Or perhaps not. In their titillating, often scabrous, portrayals of sin on the stage, Golden Age dramatists' linkages to the picaresque are evident. But even in their less frequent scenes of tragic, as opposed to the much more usual comic, depictions of sin and its consequences,[3] Golden Age playwrights – those shrewd shades of Janus who have heretofore been viewed erroneously as simple mouthpieces of Counter-Reformation dogma[4] – often push the envelope to explore the conditions under which even the most outrageous sins might be permissible. The very titles of countless *comedias* confirm this: *El marido de su madre* (by Juan de Matos Fragoso), *El esclavo de su hijo* (Agustín Moreto), *La viuda casada y doncella* (Lope de Vega), to name just a few. These plays push past the limits of what could be considered, in any era, morally acceptable.

As Elena del Río Parra rightly notes, this affinity for the most extreme cases should be seen as a manifestation of Baroque aesthetics, the same passion for mannerism which inspired Bernini to sculpt figures who seem to leap out of the stone from which they were crafted.[5] But I would argue that this extreme-case mentality could also prove extremely subversive morally. Is it OK to murder one's parents? Under certain circumstances, says a play whose very title includes the phrase *dichoso parricida* (happy parricide).[6] What about the brother who almost commits incest unwittingly, not realizing that his beloved is in reality his long-lost sister? A similar scenario plays itself out in Lope's *El primero Benavides*, among others.[7] Should a woman caught in the very act of Adultery be murdered by her husband? Does a father owe greater allegiance to his treasonous daughter or his king?

Golden Age playwrights generate a proliferation of answers to these questions, but they may not always be the ones you might expect. What about situations in which one of the Commandments would seem to conflict with injunctions against the Seven Deadlies? Or vice versa? Which system takes precedence? In any given theatrical clash of world views, which system will ultimately take priority?

Renaissance dramatists not only reflect the tension between competing taxonomies; they actually play competing systems off one another and use the resulting tension to dramatic advantage. Is the person who rests on Sunday following the Ten Commandments by honouring the Sabbath, or might he instead be found guilty of one of the Capital Vices, the Sin of Sloth? Does the answer depend simply on one's moral vantage point? Should we even raise the issue of perspectivism here?

Concluding that early modern Spanish authors favour one taxonomy over the other would be too simplistic, just as previous generations of critics have oversimplified their attribution of Counter-Reformation dogmatism to these literary works. An alternatively postmodern, cultural studies approach – instead of imposing consensus – instead chooses to see productive tension.

Notes

Foreword

1 Lope de Vega (1562–1635), *Sobre una mesa de murtas*, loa.
2 Diana Taylor, *The Archive and the Repertoire: Performing Cultural Memory in the Americas* (Durham: Duke University Press, 2003), 19–21, emphasis mine. Taylor cites Michel de Certeau, *Heterologies: Discourse on the Other*, trans. Brian Massumi (Minneapolis: University of Minnesota Press, 1986), 216.
3 Recent years have witnessed a veritable explosion of digital search tools designed to approach the Golden Age theatrical corpus from new angles. Such projects include: Teresa Ferrer Valls, *Diccionario biográfico de actores del teatro clásico (DICAT)* (Kassel: Reichenberger, 2008); ARTELOPE, a database for the study and contextualization of works by Lope de Vega; Jonathan Thacker's Out of the Wings project at Oxford University, which focuses on English-language performance texts; and Meg Greer's Manos Teatrales project at Duke, a digital database of manuscripts. What are still lacking, in my view, are serious critical studies which will make use of these new research tools and go beyond the mere amassing of data to include actual analysis, synthesis, contextualization, and interpretation. It is this void in the critical landscape which this project desires to begin to fill.
4 For plot summaries of many of the plays mentioned in this book, see David Castillejo, *Guía de ochocientas comedias del Siglo de Oro* (Madrid: Ars Millenii, 2002). For a classificatory scheme organizing the *comedia* corpus by subgenre, see Ignacio Arellano, *Historia del teatro español del siglo XVII*, 4th ed. (Madrid: Cátedra, 2008), 129–39.
5 This phenomenon, by now widely commented upon, is the subject of Karl Menninger, *Whatever Became of Sin?* (New York: Hawthorn, 1973). See especially chapter 3, "The Disappearance of Sin: An Eyewitness Account," 13–37.

Introduction

1 Juan Pérez de Montalbán (1602–38), *Lo que son juicios del cielo*, Jornada 1.

2 Exodus 20:5b. The same curse is repeated after the Commandments have been inscribed by God's finger on the stone tablets, in Exodus 34:6–7. In this passage Moses addresses Yahweh as "the Lord God … Who renderest the iniquity of the fathers to the children, and to the grandchildren, unto the third and fourth generation." All biblical citations are to the Douay version: *The Holy Bible, Translated from the Latin Vulgate*, ed. Richard Challoner (New York: Douay Bible House, 1941).

3 A case in point is the forthcoming essay collection *Ateísmo, herejía y libertinaje en la España medieval y del Renacimiento*, ed. Jesús Maestro (Vigo: Academia del Hispanismo, in progress).

4 "In Romance languages such as Spanish, the word for 'conscience' (*conciencia*) is the same word used to refer to 'consciousness,' there being no way linguistically to distinguish between the two" (Hilaire Kallendorf, *Conscience on Stage: The* Comedia *as Casuistry in Early Modern Spain* [Toronto: University of Toronto Press, 2007], 198). Ned Lukacher also notes the "semantic and linguistic confusion between conscience and consciousness" (*Daemonic Figures: Shakespeare and the Question of Conscience* [Ithaca: Cornell University Press, 1994], 8).

5 Paul Tillich, *Morality and Beyond* (New York: Harper and Row, 1963), 67.

6 Illustrative of this impulse were scientists such as Carl Linnaeus (1707–78), a Swedish biologist who used taxonomies to classify plant and animal specimens.

7 Many scholars in fact trace taxonomies – including classificatory systems in more scientific fields such as biology – back to Aristotle. See Bennison Gray, "The Semiotics of Taxonomy," *Semiotica* 22.1–2 (1998): 127–50, at 14.

8 Elena del Río Parra, *Cartografías de la conciencia española en la Edad de Oro* (Mexico City: Fondo de Cultura Económica, 2008).

9 In *The Sixteenth Century Journal* 40.2 (2010): 560–2.

10 See, for example, James C. Scott, *The Moral Economy of the Peasant: Rebellion and Subsistence in Southeast Asia* (New Haven: Yale University Press, 1976); Sidney W. Mintz, *Sweetness and Power: The Place of Sugar in Modern History* (New York: Penguin, 1985); and B.S. Orlove, "Meat and Strength: The Moral Economy of a Food Riot," *Cultural Anthropology* 12.2 (1997): 234–68. Scott Guggenheim and Robert Weller offer a useful definition of moral economy in this context: "Moral economy concentrates on the system of rights and obligations that surround interpersonal and interclass relations in rural societies" (Robert P. Weller and Scott E. Guggenheim, "Moral Economy, Capitalism, and State Power in Rural Protest," in *Power and Protest in the Countryside: Studies of Rural Unrest in Asia, Europe, and Latin America* [Durham: Duke University Press, 1982], 3–12, at 3).

11 This perspective may, of course, be considered loosely Foucauldian. It was only after I finished writing this book that I discovered a passage from Foucault where he talks

about applying economic analysis to such seemingly non-economic phenomena as marriage, criminality, and the education of children. He ends up expanding the definition of economics to include most arenas of human conduct: "maybe the object of economic analysis should be identified with any purposeful conduct which involves, broadly speaking, a strategic choice of means, ways, and instruments ... deploying certain scarce resources – a symbolic system, a set of axioms, rules of construction ... to be used to optimal effect for a determinate and alternative end" (Michel Foucault, *The Birth of Biopolitics: Lectures at the Collège de France, 1978–1979*, ed. Michel Sennelart, trans. Graham Burchell [New York: Palgrave Macmillan, 2010], 268–9). In this paradigm the purposeful conduct would translate into moral conduct and the strategic choice would involve selecting from an array of such "symbolic systems, sets of axioms, and rules of construction" as the Ten Commandments and the Seven Deadly Sins.

12 John Bossy, "Moral Arithmetic: Seven Sins into Ten Commandments," in *Conscience and Casuistry in Early Modern Europe*, ed. Edmund Leites (Cambridge: Cambridge University Press, 1988), 214–34, at 215–16. See also Carla Casagrande and Silvana Vecchio, "La classificazione dei peccati tra settenario e decalogo (secoli XIII–XV)," *Documenti e studi sulla tradizione filosofica medievale* 5 (1994): 331–95.

13 *The Catechism of the Council of Trent*, trans. John A. McHugh and Charles J. Callan, http://www.catholicprimer.org/trent/catechism_of_trent.pdf.

14 For a history of the Seven Deadly Sins, beginning with their origins in a list made by the Roman poet Horace, progressing through their germination in the work of the early medieval monk Evagrius Ponticus (d. 399), and then their codification by Pope Gregory the Great (d. 604), as well as their popularization by Prudentius's *Psychomachia*, see Morton W. Bloomfield, *The Seven Deadly Sins: An Introduction to the History of a Religious Concept, with Special Reference to Medieval English Literature* (East Lansing: Michigan State University Press, 1952; reprint, 1967).

15 A list of eight *logismoi* or evil thoughts (Gluttony, Fornication, Avarice, Anger, Sadness, *Acedia*, Vainglory, and Pride) was first generated by Evagrius of Pontus in a treatise titled *On the Eight Thoughts*. For a recent English translation, see Evagrius of Pontus, *The Greek Ascetic Corpus*, trans. Robert E. Sinkewicz (Oxford: Oxford University Press, 2003), 73–90. This list was later condensed by Gregory the Great into the current set of Seven Deadly Sins.

16 A potent critique of Bossy and Bloomfield appears in Richard Newhauser, "'These Seaven Devils': The Capital Vices on the Way to Modernity," in *Sin in Medieval and Early Modern Culture: The Tradition of the Seven Deadly Sins*, ed. Richard Newhauser and Susan Ridyard (York: York Medieval Press, 2012), 157–88. Some muted criticism of this argument of Bossy's, amounting more to nuance than to opposition, appears in Simon Ditchfield, "Introduction" to *Christianity and Community in the West: Essays for John Bossy* (Aldershot: Ashgate, 2001), xv–xxix, at xxi–xxiv. However, many historians still repeat Bossy's argument uncritically; for example, Scott Taylor

remarks concerning the early modern Spanish man, "[h]is relationship with God was to supplant his relationship with his neighbors" (Scott K. Taylor, *Honor and Violence in Golden Age Spain* [New Haven: Yale University Press, 2008], 109).

17 Hieronymus Bosch (1450–1516) was a Dutch painter who lived in the Spanish Netherlands.

18 Lu Ann Homza, *Religious Authority in the Spanish Renaissance* (Baltimore: Johns Hopkins University Press, 2000), 166.

19 Dorothy Noyes offers a succinct summary of this historiographical trend:

> "SPAIN IS DIFFERENT." This notorious slogan of the Franco years, which invites foreign tourists to come and enjoy beaches, sangría, bullfights, flamenco music, and voluptuous women in black mantillas, both mirrors and emerges from the common eighteenth-century French assertion that "Africa begins at the Pyrenees." The idea of Spanish exceptionalism has been challenged by many recent historians (see Elliott 1989), and a few even deny Spanish "backwardness" in achieving modernity (Ringrose 1996). Catalans and Basques, among others, have long denounced Spanish exceptionalism as a myth that erases their own specificity and integration in Europe. The view from the Spanish interior, however, is and was more ambivalent. The notion of Spanish difference and the peculiar symmetry of Spanish and foreign accounts of it arise in a long history of mutual observation that became particularly acute in the period from the accession of Carlos III in 1759 to the Napoleonic Wars. (Dorothy Noyes, "La Maja Vestida: Dress as Resistance to Enlightenment in Late 18th-Century Madrid," *Journal of American Folklore* 111 [1998]: 197–217, at 197)

Noyes cites the work of John Elliott (*Spain and Its World, 1500–1700* [New Haven: Yale University Press, 1989]) and David Ringrose (*Spain, Europe, and the "Spanish Miracle," 1700–1900* [Cambridge: Cambridge University Press, 1996]).

20 The only scholar of whom I am aware to have made the connection between any Golden Age playwright and the curse from Exodus is Tom O'Connor, and that only with reference to Calderón: "A prominent theme in Calderonian theater addresses the biblical reality of how the sins of the parents are visited upon the children, involving them in guilt that requires of each some concrete expiation. Segismundo paid this debt in the tower… . Guilt is the human inheritance that cries out for relief" (Thomas A. O'Connor, "*La vida es sueño*, Reason and Renunciation, Versus *La estatua de Prometeo*, Love and Fulfillment," in *The Prince in the Tower: Perceptions of* La vida es sueño, ed. Frederick A. de Armas [Lewisburg: Bucknell University Press, 1993], 97–110, at 102–3). He does not develop these incidental comments any further. Nonetheless this study may be seen to fit broadly into a trend we have seen recently toward more analyses of early modern Spanish religion, several of them published by the University of Toronto Press, with topics ranging from the Inquisition, to legal discourses, to the

Catholic Universal Monarchy, to relations between church and state. See, for example, Ryan Giles, *The Laughter of the Saints: Parodies of Holiness in Late Medieval and Renaissance Spain* (Toronto: University of Toronto Press, 2009); Michael Armstrong-Roche, *Cervantes' Epic Novel: Empire, Religion, and the Dream Life of Heroes in* Persiles (Toronto: University of Toronto Press, 2009); Bradley J. Nelson, *The Persistence of Presence: Emblem and Ritual in Baroque Spain* (Toronto: University of Toronto Press, 2010); and María Mercedes Carrión, *Subject Stages: Marriage, Theatre and the Law in Early Modern Spain* (Toronto: University of Toronto Press, 2010).

21 In this book, the Capital Vices will be explored as they are acted out in actual scenarios by *comedia* characters on the stage. Elsewhere I have looked at emblematic costumes of allegorical figures of the Vices in Spanish Baroque *autos sacramentales* (Hilaire Kallendorf, "Dressed to the Sevens, or Sin in Style: Fashion Statements by the Deadly Vices in Spanish Baroque *Autos Sacramentales*," in *The Seven Deadly Sins: From Communities to Individuals*, ed. Richard Newhauser [Leiden: Brill, 2007], 145–82).

22 See Raymond Williams, "Dominant, Residual, and Emergent," in *Marxism and Literature* (Oxford: Oxford University Press, 1977), 121–7.

23 José Antonio Maravall, *Teatro y literatura en la sociedad barroca* (Madrid: Seminarios y Ediciones, 1972), 103. This quotation is taken from the chapter "La imposición del marco social sobre los impulsos individualistas" (The imposition of the social frame over individualist impulses).

24 Leo Spitzer, "Soy quien soy," *Nueva revista de filología hispánica* 1.2 (1947): 113–27.

25 See, however, an important critique of Maravall by Anthony Cascardi, "The Subject of Control," in *Culture and Control in Counter-Reformation Spain*, ed. Anne J. Cruz and Mary Elizabeth Perry (Minneapolis: University of Minnesota Press, 1992), 231–54, as well as the beginnings of one offered by George Mariscal in "History and the Subject of the Spanish Golden Age," *The Seventeenth Century* 4 (1989): 19–32, at 26–7. For Althusser's famous term, see Louis Althusser, "Ideología y aparatos ideológicos de estado" in *Ideología: un mapa de la cuestión*, ed. Slavoj Žižek (Mexico City: Fondo de Cultura Económica, 2004), 115–56. For an important new essay arguing for Althusserian modifications of theories first expounded by Américo Castro and Maravall, see Anthony Cascardi, "Beyond Castro and Maravall: Interpellation, Mimesis, and the Hegemony of Spanish Culture," in *Ideologies of Hispanism*, ed. Mabel Moraña (Nashville: Vanderbilt University Press, 2005), 138–59.

26 I refer here to the title of Stephen Greenblatt's *Shakespearean Negotiations: The Circulation of Social Energy in Renaissance England* (Berkeley: University of California Press, 1988). For an application of New Historicist approaches to *comedia* studies, see José Antonio Madrigal, ed., *New Historicism and the* Comedia (Boulder: Society of Spanish and Spanish-American Studies, 1995).

27 Melveena McKendrick, *Playing the King: Lope de Vega and the Limits of Conformity* (London: Tamesis, 2000), 1–14, at 4–7.

28 See William Egginton, *How the World Became a Stage: Presence, Theatricality, and the Question of Modernity* (Albany: State University of New York Press, 2003); and George Mariscal, *Contradictory Subjects: Quevedo, Cervantes, and Seventeenth-Century Spanish Culture* (Ithaca: Cornell University Press, 1991). Egginton prefers the notion of presence to Mariscal's subjectivity: "the sacrament of the Eucharist is the prototypical instance of that motion of mimesis as production of presence that characterizes both the magical worldview and the medieval experience of spectacle" (Egginton, *How the World Became a Stage*, 43). For a more recent further exploration of the notion of presence in the context of emblems which nonetheless unfortunately repeats many of Maravall's assumptions uncritically, see Bradley J. Nelson, *The Persistence of Presence: Emblem and Ritual in Baroque Spain* (Toronto: University of Toronto Press, 2010). For his part, despite the promising title of his study, Mariscal ends up denying unitary identity to early modern Spanish subjects to the point of obviating the very contradictions of which his title appears to deem them capable; instead they occupy "a series of subject positions lacking any permanent closure" (Mariscal, *Contradictory Subjects*, 6). He reiterates, "My argument … dissolves the notion of a unified individual" (5).

29 Hilaire Kallendorf, "Sex(y) Summer Solstice: Lope de Vega and Shakespeare Write Fantasies of Feminine Desire," *Comparative Literature Studies* (forthcoming).

30 Lope de Vega liked to emphasize his break with Aristotle's unities and the supposed realism generated thereby. See Lope de Vega Carpio, *El arte nuevo de hacer comedias en este tiempo* (1609), ed. Juana de José Prades (Madrid: Clásicos Hispánicos, 1971).

31 On Inquisitorial censorship of one of Calderón's plays, see Barbara Kurtz, "Illusions of Power: Calderón de la Barca, the Spanish Inquisition, and the Prohibition of *Las órdenes militares* (1662–1671)," *Revista canadiense de estudios hispánicos* 18.2 (1994): 189–217.

32 For an explication of the Derridian concept of *trace* with reference to casuistry, see Kallendorf, *Conscience on Stage*, 39.

33 Richard D. Woods, *Spanish Grammar and Culture through Proverbs* (Potomac: Scripta Humanistica, 1989).

34 I borrow the phrase *genealogies of performance* from Joseph Roach: "Genealogies of performance approach literature as a repository of the restored behaviors of the past. They excavate the lineage of restored behaviors still at least partially visible in contemporary culture, in effect 'writing the history of the present'" (Joseph Roach, "Culture and Performance in the Circum-Atlantic World," in *Performativity and Performance*, ed. Andrew Parker and Eve Kosofsky Sedgwick [New York: Routledge, 1995], 45–63, at 48). Roach cites Michel Foucault, *Discipline and Punish*.

35 "Humanae cur sit speculum comoedia vitae" ("Why comedy is the mirror of human life") (Lope de Vega, *El arte nuevo de hacer comedias en este tiempo*, line 377).

36 See Craig Kallendorf, "Commentaries, Commonplaces, and Neo-Latin Studies," in *Acta Conventus Neo-Latini Uppsalensis: Proceedings of the Fourteenth International Congress of Neo-Latin Studies*, ed. A. Steiner-Weber et al. (Leiden: Brill, 2012), 1:535–46.

37 The complete passages in context are as follows: "escribí un epigrama en un libro de memoria" and "Así son muchos, que cuanto hallan en Estobeo, la *Poliantea* y Conrado Gisnerio y otros librotes de lugares comunes, todo lo echan abajo, venga o no venga a propósito" (Lope de Vega, *La Dorotea*, ed. Edwin S. Morby [Madrid: Clásicos Castalia, 1987], 259, 343). Lope refers to the *Florilegio* of Estobeo from the fourteenth or fifteenth century as well as the *Poliantea* of Domenico Nani Mirabellio (1503).

38 To get some sense of the spectrum of content to be found in commonplace books, see Ann Blair, "Humanist Methods in Natural Philosophy: The Commonplace Book," *Journal of the History of Ideas* 53.4 (1992): 541–51; Ann Moss, "The *Politica* of Justus Lipsius and the Commonplace-Book," *Journal of the History of Ideas* 59.3 (1998): 421–36; and Lucia Dacome, "Noting the Mind: Commonplace Books and the Pursuit of the Self in Eighteenth-Century Britain," *Journal of the History of Ideas* 65.4 (2004): 603–25.

39 On this critical disaffection and a defence of the *comedia* as a genre offered in response, see John G. Weiger, "El juego de la originalidad: rasgo de la comedia frente a su carácter paradigmático," *Bulletin of the Comediantes* 35 (1983): 197–206. See also Arnold G. Reichenberger, "The Uniqueness of the Comedia," *Hispanic Review* 27 (1959): 303–16, as well as a rejoinder published by the same author under the same title in the same journal more than a decade later: Arnold G. Reichenberger, "The Uniqueness of the Comedia," *Hispanic Review* 38 (1970): 163–73.

1. Pride & Co.

1 Lope de Vega, *El honrado hermano*, Acto 1.

2 In response to the question "¿Quien eres tú, que vienes la primera?" Soberbia answers: "Soy la Soberbia, hermosa, y lisonjera Deidad de los Humanos" (Calderón de la Barca [1600–81], *El gran mercado del mundo*, auto sacramental). In another *auto* she appears at the prow of the ship: "da vuelta la Galera con la Soberbia en la Popa" (Calderón, *A María el corazón*, auto sacramental).

3 "y yo primer cerviz de la Hidra, como Hermosura, y Soberbia son casi una cosa misma" (Calderón, *El primer refugio del hombre, y probática piscina*, auto sacramental).

4 On Pride as poison, witness "el dañado tósigo de la Soberbia" (Calderón, *No hay instante sin milagro*, auto sacramental). For vampire imagery, in an exchange between figures representing the Vices of Anger and Pride, Anger says, "Ira soy, que vierte sangre." Pride replies: "Yo soberbia, que la bebe" (Calderón, *Los Lances de Amor, y Fortuna*, Acto 1). Another instance of Pride occurring in the context of blood is Calderón's *Afectos de odio, y amor*, where a character speaks of "mi orgullo ciego, talando a sangre, y fuego" (Jornada 2). The screams of Pride are "las horrorosas voces, idiomas de mi soberbia" (Calderón, *La devoción de la Misa*, auto sacramental).

5 "hijo de la soberbia engendró fetos mayores" (Calderón, *Judás Macabeo*, Acto 1).

6 For medieval debates over which Deadly Sin was worst, see Lester K. Little, "Pride Goes before Avarice: Social Change and the Vices in Latin Christendom," *The American Historical Review* 76 (1971): 16–49. As Little explains it, for a while Avarice took first prize as the deadliest Vice due to new economic developments in medieval Europe: "In the age of the Commercial Revolution some European thinkers ceased to regard pride as the worst of all vices and bestowed this signal dishonor instead upon avarice. Between the eleventh and fourteenth centuries … when European society experienced a profound structural transformation that brought a commercial economy, an urban culture, and a widespread use of money, European thought registered a corresponding shift in values within the traditional scheme of the cardinal vices" (16).

7 Lope de Vega, *La corona merecida*, Acto 3. Other plays similarly make reference to "la soberbia que al Cherub ha derribado" (Tirso de Molina [1584?–1648], *El mayor desengaño*, Acto 3). In a telling line from an *auto sacramental*, Culpa looks at Lucifer and says, "Texto hay, que fue soberbia tu delito" (Calderón, *El pintor de su deshonra*, auto sacramental). Still further works confirm Pride's status as the devil's predilect Sin: "ser de Luzbel el grande espíritu de Soberbia" (Calderón, *La primer flor de el Carmelo*, auto sacramental).

8 Tirso de Molina, *El castigo del penséque*, Acto 2; Tirso de Molina, *Don Gil de las calzas verdes*, Acto 1.

9 Juan Bautista Diamante (1625–87), *El jubileo de Porciúncula*, Jornada 3.

10 Calderón, *El purgatorio de S. Patricio*, Jornada 3; Calderón, *El cordero de Isaías*, auto sacramental.

11 For the most recent iteration of this controversial argument, which originated with the Sapir-Whorf hypothesis on linguistic relativity, see Leva Boroditsky, "How Language Shapes Thought," *Scientific American* 304.2 (2011): 62–5. Thanks to my linguistics colleague Veronica Loureiro-Rodríguez for bringing this article to my attention.

12 "la altivez, la soberbia, la vanidad, y arrogancia" (Calderón, *Mujer, llora, y vencerás*, Jornada 1). A similar litany occurs in the first person: "mi altivez, mi soberbia, mi ambición, y mi arrogancia" (Calderón, *La hija del aire, primera parte*, Jornada 2).

13 "bárbaro, arrogante, vano, soberbio, y desvanecido, altivo, loco, atrevido" (Calderón, *El alcalde de sí mismo*, Jornada 1).

14 Antonio Zamora (1662?–1728), *Amar, es saber vencer, y el arte contra el poder*, Jornada 2; Zamora, *El custodio de la Hungría, San Juan Capistrano*, Jornada 1.

15 Calderón, *Para vencer a Amor, querer vencerle*, Jornada 1.

16 Calderón, *El astrólogo fingido*, Acto 1; Diamante, *El cerco de Zamora*, Jornada 1.

17 "Hablando a Doña María, soberbia me respondió, como siempre" (Calderón, *El astrólogo fingido*, Jornada 2).

18 Tirso de Molina, *Santo, y sastre*, Acto 3. For a transatlantic perspective on the free will vs determinism debate during the early modern period, see Guillermo Lermeño, "Banned and Confiscated Books of the Jesuits," trans. Christopher Winks, in *Artes*

de México, Edición Especial: Biblioteca Palafoxiana (Mexico City: Transcontinental, 2003), 93–6.

19 Roger Shattuck also suggests that Eve, after eating the forbidden fruit, suddenly prides herself on being wiser than Adam: "With her new knowledge, Eve now fancies herself superior to Adam and freer than he. In the changed situation, she is tempted to lord it over him" (Roger Shattuck, *Forbidden Knowledge: From Prometheus to Pornography* [New York: St Martin's, 1996], 67).

20 Pride is seen upon earth primarily as frequenting high places such as mountains: "Monte soberbio, gigante que a los cielos te levantas, tu altivez soberbia abate sobre ese mísero vaso" (Francisco de Rojas Zorrilla [1607–48], *Los encantos de Medea*, Jornada 1). Air here is represented by its moving form, wind: "enojado el viento nos amenazó, cruel, y nos castigó soberbio, haciendo en mares y montes tal estrago, y tal esfuerzo" (Calderón, *El purgatorio de San Patricio*, Acto 1). The ocean is almost always characterized as proud: "O mar soberbia, y altiva" (Lope de Vega, *La firmeza en la desdicha*, Acto 2); and "la alta mar que soberbia no teme Sirenas ya" (Lope de Vega, *La Filisarda*, Acto 2). Rivers are also a perfect picture of this Vice because they sometimes flow with such force that they forget they are lesser bodies of water, not the sea: "río fugitivo, que hace golfo esa ribera, tan soberbio, tan altivo: que duda el río, si es mar" (Rojas Zorrilla, *Casarse por vengarse*, Jornada 1). Specific proud rivers found in the *comedias* are the Nile ("el Nilo con su soberbia te corta el paso" [Calderón, *El Joseph de las mujeres*, Jornada 2]) and the Danube ("Que suspendáis el orgullo impaciente con que el Danubio os peina" [Zamora, *El custodio de la Hungría, San Juan Capistrano*, Jornada 3]).

Fire imagery includes lines such as "ya la Soberbia que me inflama, me privó de pavesa de su llama" (Calderón, *El pintor de su deshonra*, auto sacramental); and "Soberbia Hermosura … nadie huyó de tu incendio" (Calderón, *No hay instante sin milagro*, auto sacramental).

21 On Neoplatonism and the supposedly magical properties of natural objects in a Golden Age Spanish context, see Hilaire Kallendorf, "Why the Inquisition Dismantles the *Cabeza Encantada*," *Anuario Cervantino* 1 (2004): 149–63.

22 Generic (for example, "vuelve a ese monte soberbio los ojos" [Calderón, *La vida es sueño*, Jornada 3]) as well as specific references to mountain peaks as proud may be found in the *comedias*. Specific mountains and mountain ranges mentioned include the Alps ("la fértil y clara orilla ni de los Alpes soberbio, las nevadas y altas cimas en efecto de la España" [Lope de Vega, *Bamba*, Jornada 2]), Mount Oeta ("Oeta, monte, que altivo, y soberbio, es empinando la frente verde columna del cielo" [Calderón, *Los tres mayores prodigios*, Jornada 3]), and the seven mountains of Jerusalem ("Invicta Jerusalén, cuya eminente soberbia, a coronarse de Nubes en siete Montes se asienta" [Calderón, *Llamados, y escogidos*, auto sacramental]). Prideful thirst is described as wanting to swallow mountains: "hidrópica su soberbia, se quiere beber los montes" (Calderón, *El Golfo de las sirenas*, Acto 1). Don Cruickshank traces a mythological

origin for this association: "Mountains symbolize pride, since they are associated with unlawful acts against authority, notably the attempt to conquer Olympus by piling Ossa on top of Pelion" (Don W. Cruickshank, "*El monstruo de los jardines* and the Segismundization of Clarín," in *The Prince in the Tower: Perceptions of* La vida es sueño, ed. Frederick A. de Armas [Lewisburg: Bucknell University Press, 1993], 65–78, at 66).

Wind imagery appears thus: "Paso, los humos exhala de tu arrogancia allá fuera" (Pérez de Montalbán, *El sufrimiento premiado*, Jornada 2); and "Toma, Soberbia, de tu vanagloria los Airones" (Calderón, *No hay instante sin milagro*, auto sacramental). When proud impatience appears as a river, it is impossible to "detener de un río la corriente, que corre al mar soberbio y despeñado" (Calderón, *La vida es sueño*, Jornada 3). There are numerous passages illustrating the intersection of Pride with Anger, for example "esa ira, con que tu orgullo alientas" (Calderón, *El lirio y la azucena*, auto sacramental).

23 On Pride's pervasiveness in the animal kingdom: "por causa de la indómita soberbia, de la fogosa arrogancia de los brutos" (Calderón, *Amigo amante, y leal*, Jornada 2). On Pride as an eagle: "Humillará su soberbia, caerá el Águila atrevida, siendo presa a los voraces lebreles" (Tirso de Molina, *La mujer que manda en casa*, Acto 3). Pride appears as a butterfly in the lines, "has visto una mariposa de un gusanillo nacer, y que altiva y ambiciosa más de lo que es quiere ser" (Pérez de Montalbán, *Amor, privanza, y castigo*, Acto 1).

24 "No es valor, ser temerario un hombre, es necia arrogancia, como los perros, que viendo la Luna creciente, ladran" (Lope de Vega, *El guante de doña Blanca*, Acto 2).

25 Pride is likened to a lion in the lines, "[¿]aunque fueras leona de estas montañas, humillara tu soberbia?" (Calderón, *Eco, y Narciso*, Jornada 1). The Indian lion in particular is singled out for comment, keeping company with such exotic creatures as the serpent and the harpy: "Indio león, sierpe, harpía, que Dios ha de castigar esa arrogancia" (Lope de Vega, *Adonis, y Venus*, Acto 3). Pride is also associated with the wild boar, as in "en un jabalí fiero envistas tu arrogancia" (Lope de Vega, *Adonis, y Venus*, Acto 3).

26 "pavón de la soberbia" (Zamora, *Judás Iscariote*, Jornada 3); "el pavón soberbio" (Lope de Vega, *El mayor imposible*, Jornada 1).

27 "el áspid de tu soberbia" (Zamora, *El lucero de Madrid, y divino Labrador, san Isidro*, Jornada 2); "la astucia Soberbia de incauta Serpiente" (Calderón, *A tu próximo como a ti*, loa for auto sacramental).

28 Serpent menacing the heels: "con mi rabia sangrienta morderé (Serpiente altiva) la Planta a esa Niña Bella" (Calderón, *La hidalga del valle*, auto sacramental); saintly women breaking its neck: "el astuto áspid, a quien la cerviz soberbia … pisáis limpia" (Diamante, *Santa Teresa de Jesús*, Jornada 2).

29 On the demon as scapegoat, see Hilaire Kallendorf, "The Demon as Scapegoat," in *Exorcism and Its Texts: Subjectivity in Early Modern Literature of England and Spain* (Toronto: University of Toronto Press, 2003), 140–8. For the critic who originated

this term, see René Girard, *The Scapegoat*, trans. Yvonne Freccero (Baltimore: Johns Hopkins University Press, 1986).

30 Lope de Vega, *El Genovés liberal*, Acto 3.

31 "O mozo intrépido, lleno de arrogancia, y ambición … armado de presunción" (Lope de Vega, *El piadoso aragonés*, Acto 1).

32 "más caprichos juveniles con arrogancia imprudente" (Juan Ruiz de Alarcón [1581–1639], *La verdad sospechosa*, Acto 2); "la libertad lozana, el nunca domado orgullo, la juvenil arrogancia" (Alarcón, *Mudarse por mejorarse*, Acto 2).

33 "advierte que este mancebo orgulloso viene en hombros de la suerte" (Lope de Vega, *Las grandezas de Alejandro*, Acto 2).

34 Lope de Vega, *El favor agradecido*, Acto 2.

35 Agustín Moreto (1618–69), *Los más dichosos hermanos*, Acto 2.

36 "un joven de altivez tanta, tan indómita soberbia, y tan voraz arrogancia" (Calderón, *Apolo, y Climene*, Jornada 2).

37 Necks are trounced upon ("tengo de poner las plantas sobre su cerviz altiva" [Calderón, *Luis Pérez el gallego*, Jornada 3]), versus voluntarily lowered: "sangre tan liviana, que a tan humilde Gitana incline el altivo cuello" (Cervantes, *Pedro de Urdemalas*, Jornada 3). One erstwhile lover reports that it has been "un año y más que se humilla a amor mi altiva cerviz" (Tirso de Molina, *Doña Beatriz de Silva*, Acto 2).

38 Lope de Vega, *Las cuentas del Gran Capitán*, Acto 1.

39 Calderón, *El orden de Melchisedech*, auto sacramental.

40 Calderón, *Los misterios de la Misa*, auto sacramental.

41 Moreto, *La fortuna merecida*, Jornada 1.

42 Calderón, *La vida es sueño*, Acto 1. A similar *topos* is invoked by the character who says to another, "tu soberbia no tiene quien le tire de la rienda" (Calderón, *El jardín de Falerina*, auto sacramental).

43 Calderón, *El monstruo de los jardines*, Acto 1. This image is repeated in other plays, which speak of "las Aguas; cuya soberbia, para que no se desboque, dorado freno de Arena tiene" (Calderón, *El diablo mudo*, auto sacramental).

44 Lope de Vega, *El triunfo de la humildad, y soberbia abatida*, Acto 3; Calderón, *Con quien vengo, vengo*, Jornada 2.

45 Zamora, *Cada uno es linaje aparte, y los Mazas de Aragón*, Jornada 3. A similar passage locates a person's compass, or sense of direction, in his feet and his arrogance in his hands: "llevar compás en los pies, y en las manos arrogancia" (Guillén de Castro [1569–1630], *El perfecto caballero*, Acto 1).

46 "que si alguna … me despreciase con altivo corazón" (Lope de Vega, *El perseguido*, Jornada 1).

47 Lope de Vega, *El bastardo Mudarra*, Acto 1.

48 Lope de Vega, *Roma abrasada*, Acto 3.

49 Eyes: "también tienen los ojos su modo de vanagloria" (Pérez de Montalbán, *Los templarios*, Jornada 1). Going blind: "una altiva ambición ciega" (Calderón, *Los tres*

afectos de amor, piedad, desmayo y valor, Jornada 2); "la ciega resolución de una altiva condición" (Calderón, *El astrólogo fingido*, Acto 1).

50 Lope de Vega, *El laberinto de Creta*; Acto 3.

51 Calderón, *El pleito matrimonial*, auto sacramental.

52 Calderón, *En esta vida todo es verdad, y todo mentira*, Jornada 3.

53 However, arguably Pride is made equivalent so frequently to male warlikeness that at least this militant type of arrogance is not often seen in women: "advierte que es arrogancia no vista en mujer" (Lope de Vega, *La doncella Teodor*, Acto 3).

54 Lope de Vega, *El Amor enamorado*, Preliminares de obra; Lope de Vega, *La Santa Liga*, Acto 2. Other plays reiterate that arrogance is the daughter of beauty: "Es hija de la hermosura, la arrogancia, y la locura" (Lope de Vega, *El favor agradecido*, Acto 2).

55 Tirso de Molina, *La mejor espigadera*, Jornada 2. On Baroque artificiality, see Duncan T. Kinkead, "Francisco de Herrera and the Development of the High Baroque Style in Seville," in *Painting in Spain 1650–1700: A Symposium*, special issue of the *Record of the Art Museum, Princeton University* 41.2 (1982): 12–23.

56 Calderón, *El primer refugio del hombre, y probática piscina*, auto sacramental.

57 "se arguya cuán antiguo es en el Mundo ser soberbia la Hermosura" (Calderón, *El pleito matrimonial*, auto sacramental).

58 Lope de Vega, *El premio de la hermosura*, Acto 1.

59 Calderón, *Para vencer a Amor, querer vencerle*, Jornada 1.

60 Calderón, *La crítica del amor*, Jornada 1. The most famous of these manuals from the period were Juan Luis Vives, *The Education of a Christian Woman* (1523), trans. Charles Fantazzi (Chicago: University of Chicago Press, 2000) and Fray Luis de León, *La perfecta casada* (1595) (Salamanca: Juan Fernández, 1595).

61 Calderón, *El astrólogo fingido*, Jornada 3; Calderón, *La hija del aire, segunda parte*, Acto 1.

62 Calderón, *Dicha, y desdicha del nombre*, Jornada 3.

63 In this situation, the brother asks, "y a mi hermana casé altamente, ¿es razón, que ahora soberbia, y vana, tenga esa vil pretensión?" (Lope de Vega, *Los pleitos de Inglaterra*, Acto 1). Cenobia is held prisoner in Calderón's eponymous *La gran Cenobia*: "mirad a Cenobia presa, veréis arrogancia, envidia, ambición, poder, y fuerza, puesto a mis plantas" (Calderón, *La gran Cenobia*, Jornada 3).

64 Calderón, *Mañanas de abril, y mayo*, Jornada 2. This line is reminiscent of an earlier *comedia* by Lope titled *La vengadora de las mujeres*.

65 Calderón, *La gran Cenobia*, Acto 1; Calderón, *El primer refugio del hombre, y probática piscina*, auto sacramental.

66 Calderón, *Cómo se comunican dos estrellas contrarias*, Jornada 1.

67 Amazon woman: "Es soberbia, impaciente, arrojada, imprudente" (Antonio de Solís [1610–86], *Las amazonas*, Jornada 1); Celaura: "oíd a Celaura, oíd, la Tártara más soberbia, que ha medido de la Francia las márgenes contrapuestas" (Rojas Zorrilla, *Los celos de Rodamonte*, Jornada 1). For a good overview of the *mujer varonil* figure, see

Melveena McKendrick, *Woman and Society in the Spanish Drama of the Golden Age: A Study of the* Mujer Varonil (Cambridge: Cambridge University Press, 2010). Another subtle discussion that focuses specifically on the cross-dressing aspect of this figure is María M. Carrión, "Woman in Breeches," chapter 6 of *Subject Stages: Marriage, Theatre, and the Law in Early Modern Spain* (Toronto: University of Toronto Press, 2010), 125–47.

68 The biblical version appears in 1 Kings 21 (3 Kings 21 in the Douay-Rheims version).

69 Calderón, *El Príncipe constante*, Acto 1.

70 See Hilaire Kallendorf, "Love Madness and Demonic Possession in Lope de Vega," *Romance Quarterly* 51.3 (2004): 162–82.

71 We hear echoes of this myth in several *comedias*, including Calderón de la Barca's *Eco y Narciso*. On the reception of the Narcissus myth in later literature, see Louise Vinge, *The Narcissus Theme in Western European Literature up to the Early 19th Century* (Lund [Sweden]: Gleerups, 1967).

72 Guillén de Castro, *El Narciso en su opinión*, Jornada 1; "al mirarme, me holgara / si una mujer alcanzara / que en todo me pareciera" (Guillén de Castro, *El Narciso en su opinión*, Jornada 1); "¿Aunque fuera tan barbada como tú?" (Guillén de Castro, *El Narciso en su opinión*, Jornada 1).

73 "Es tan tierno enamorado / de sí mismo, que a su sombra / suele alargarle los brazos" (Guillén de Castro, *El Narciso en su opinión*, Jornada 1).

74 Guillén de Castro, *El Narciso en su opinión*, Jornada 2; Guillén de Castro, *El Narciso en su opinión*, Jornada 3.

75 Tirso de Molina, *Santo, y sastre*, Acto 1.

76 See Hilaire Kallendorf, "Dressed to the Sevens, or Sin in Style: Fashion Statements by the Deadly Vices in Spanish Baroque *Autos Sacramentales*," in *The Seven Deadly Sins: From Communities to Individuals*, ed. Richard Newhauser (Leiden: Brill, 2007), 145–82.

77 Calderón, *El gran mercado del mundo*, auto sacramental. Alexander Parker confirms that Calderón wrote his own stage directions for his *autos sacramentales* (Alexander A. Parker, *The Allegorical Drama of Calderón: An Introduction to the* Autos Sacramentales [Oxford: Oxford University Press, 1968], 97).

78 "Pone el Afecto primero a la Soberbia un Manto rojo de Púrpura" (Calderón, *El indulto general*, loa for auto sacramental).

79 Calderón, *El gran mercado del mundo*, auto sacramental. These lines are spoken by Mal Genio.

80 Guillén de Castro, *La fuerza de la costumbre*, Jornada 3.

81 "Una vez le vi poner sobre un vestido de paño / más de seis mil y quinientos botones abellotados" (Guillén de Castro, *El Narciso en su opinión*, Jornada 1).

82 Lope de Vega, *Santiago el verde*, Acto 3. Some of the most theoretically stringent sumptuary laws were passed in Spain in 1623 by the Conde-Duque de Olivares (Don W. Cruickshank, *Don Pedro Calderón* [Cambridge: Cambridge University Press,

2009], 4). However, Cruickshank notes that since at least the 1570s the Cortes had been calling for legislation to control extravagant consumption (4). For a snapshot circa 1600 of which sumptuary laws were in place in Spain, see *Premática y nueva orden: de los vestidos y trajes, así de hombres como de mujeres* (Madrid: Pedro Madrigal, 1600), reprinted later as a curiosity in *Semanario pintoresco* 19 (1854): 242–3 (cited in Carrión, *Subject Stages*, 136, 217). For a history of Spanish sumptuary laws, see J. Sempere y Guarinos, *Historia del lujo y de las leyes suntuarias en España*, ed. Juan Rico Giménez (Valencia: Alfons El Magnànim, 2000), which offers in particular a useful summary of the *Decretos suntuarios* published during the reign of each monarch for the time period in question here: Carlos V, Felipe II, Felipe III, Felipe IV, and Carlos II (pp. 235–316 cover all of these).

83 King Philip II reigned from 1556 to 1598, nearly a half-century. Philip III reigned from 1598 to 1621. The austerity of Philip II's court was legendary. As Sir John Elliott laments, "these were the years in which Renaissance Spain, wide open to European humanist influences, was effectively transformed into the semi-closed Spain of the Counter-Reformation" (J.H. Elliott, *Imperial Spain: 1469–1716* [London: Penguin, 1990], 224). This was the time period in which the importation of foreign books was banned and Spaniards were discouraged from studying at foreign universities. All books printed in Spain had to be licensed, and the Inquisition moved quickly to stifle Protestantism with fiery displays of *autos-de-fe*. Michael Armstrong-Roche calls these suffocating restrictions "the quarantining of the country's intellectual life through ideologically sanitizing measures" (Michael Armstrong-Roche, *Cervantes' Epic Novel: Empire, Religion, and the Dream Life of Heroes in* Persiles [Toronto: University of Toronto Press, 2009], 163).

84 "sale la Soberbia con el Sombrero de Plumas" (Calderón, *El año santo en Madrid*, auto sacramental).

85 Calderón, *La serpiente de metal*, auto sacramental.

86 Lope de Vega, *La vida de San Pedro Nolasco*, Jornada 3.

87 Calderón, *El año santo en Madrid*, auto sacramental.

88 Similar examples of Baroque aesthetic sensibility in the realm of lyric poetry may be found in Hilaire Kallendorf and Craig Kallendorf, "Conversations with the Dead: Quevedo and Statius, Annotation and Imitation," *Journal of the Warburg and Courtauld Institutes* 63 (2000): 131–68. For instance, in one case the poet Francisco de Quevedo wrote a *silva* imitating Statius but took the imitation to an extreme typical of Baroque mannerism. In both poems, a tree branch bends all the way down to the ground; but in Quevedo's version, it goes even further – it breaks off: "his imitation of 'Arbor Atedii Melioris' reveals an impressive feat of Baroque virtuosity … [I]n typical Baroque fashion, he wrenched a striking image from its original context, invested it with philosophical significance and pushed the symbolic resonance to its logical conclusion" (Kallendorf and Kallendorf, "Conversations with the Dead," 155).

89 On Polyphemus: "Sola una luz en la frente tuvo Polifemo altivo, ésa Ulises le cegó con aquel tostado pino" (Lope de Vega, *La Filisarda*, Acto 1). Tesiphonte is urged to enter the body of a wild boar to infuse the animal symbolically with arrogance: "en un jabalí fiero envistas tu arrogancia, Éntrate Tesifonte en sus fieras entrañas para matar a Adonis" (Lope de Vega, *Adonis, y Venus*, Acto 3). About Perseus: "la arrogancia de Perseo va saliendo verdad" (Calderón, *Fortunas de Andrómeda, y Perseo*, Jornada 2). Atlantis's metamorphosis is described thus: "Que se convirtiese en Monte Atlante, por la soberbia con que intentó competir en las Judiciarias ciencias" (Calderón, *Fieras afemina amor*, Jornada 1). On the frequency of Pride's association with classical myths in the dramas of Calderón, see N. Erwin Haverbeck Ojeda, "La comedia mitológica calderoniana: soberbia y castigo," *Revista de filología española* 56 (1973): 67–93.

90 In the *comedias* Jupiter is often associated with Pride, while Saturn is associated with Anger: "Jupiter me dio soberbia de bizarros pensamientos, Saturno cólera y rabia, valor, y ánimo" (Calderón, *El purgatorio de San Patricio*, Acto 1). The legend of Jupiter and the crab is recounted in Lope de Vega's *Porfiar hasta morir*: "Jupiter, que en las arenas del mar su arrogancia vio" (Lope de Vega, *Porfiar hasta morir*, Acto 1).

91 Moreto, *El caballero del Sacramento*, Jornada 3.

92 David Castillejo, *Guía de ochocientas comedias del Siglo de Oro* (Madrid: Ars Millenii, 2002), 616. Castillejo cites David García Cueto on this point.

93 Calderón, *El faetonte*, Jornada 2.

94 Calderón, *El faetonte*, Jornada 1.

95 "a pesar de mi soberbia, mi presunción, mi arrogancia me obliga que a buscar venga ocasión" (Calderón, *El faetonte*, Jornada 2).

96 Icarus and Phaethon are frequent motifs even in non-mythological plays. For example, Envidia says to the Demon in Lope's *San Isidro labrador de Madrid*, "Ícaros fuimos los dos, que el rayo del Sol de Dios arrojó al mar del infierno" (Lope de Vega, *San Isidro labrador de Madrid*, Acto 2). Similarly, Abdenaga says in Moreto's *El esclavo de su hijo*, "soy Ícaro, que llegué al Cielo donde subí, y en su Esfera me abrasé" (Moreto, *El esclavo de su hijo*, Jornada 2). In a more extended comparison, Fortún in Lope de Vega's *La desdichada Estefanía* offers the following speech on a failed enterprise:

al cielo llegué y subí,
mas si he llegado, y caído,
yo he hecho lo que he podido,
fortuna lo que ha querido.
La conquista fue imposible
de quien fui Faetón altivo,
retrocedieron los astros,
y la elección se deshizo,

en lo más alto me vi,
del sol me llamaron hijo,
pero llegado, y caído,
yo he hecho lo que he podido,
fortuna lo que ha querido. (Lope de Vega, *La desdichada Estefanía*, Acto 2)

97 "a manos del soberbio Macabeo, que cruel tu poder destruye, ha muerto Gorgias soldado" (Calderón, *Judás Macabeo*, Jornada 3); "la soberbia de Amán" (Calderón, *El pleito matrimonial*, auto sacramental). A similar version of the same story may be found in Lope de Vega's *La hermosa Ester*.

98 Calderón, *El Arca de Dios cautiva*, auto sacramental.

99 Calderón, *La primer flor de el Carmelo*, auto sacramental.

100 Lope de Vega, *El asalto de Mastrique, por el Príncipe de Parma*, Acto 1; Lope de Vega, *Los pleitos de Inglaterra*, Acto 1.

101 "Marte altivo" (Calderón, *El amor, honor y poder*, Jornada 2); "sin ver del fiero Marte la intrépida arrogancia" (Lope de Vega, *La mayor victoria de Alemania de don Gonzalo de Córdoba*, Preliminares de obra).

102 On early modern military innovations in general, see Paul E.J. Hammer, ed., *Warfare in Early Modern Europe 1450–1660* (Aldershot: Ashgate, 2007). For a country-specific study of new military technologies in the Renaissance, see Rainer Leng, *Ars Belli: Deutsche taktische und kriegtechnische Bilderhandschriften und Traktate im 15. und 16. Jahrhundert*, 2 vols (Wiesbaden: Ludwig Reichert, 2002). See also Michael Murrin, *History and Warfare in Renaissance Epic* (Chicago: University of Chicago Press, 1994), for the impact of these new methods of warfare on a key literary genre.

103 "¿Qué minas brotan de arrogancia llenas?" (Calderón, *El sitio de Breda*, Jornada 3).

104 Lope de Vega, *El soldado amante*, Acto 1.

105 "Alejandro, que dio penetrando el mundo, leyes" (Matos Fragoso, *Amor, lealtad, y ventura*, Jornada 2).

106 "los Cartagineses, que de la primer Cartago de África su orgullo ardiente trajo a conquistar a España" (Calderón, *El segundo Scipión*, Jornada 1); "los últimos Godos, que sus montañas habitan por la arrogancia Africana, y la Española desdicha" (Lope de Vega, *Guardar, y guardarse*, Acto 1).

107 Siley says to the Spaniards in the play, "Vosotros que a Tenerife venís con tanta arrogancia" (Lope de Vega, *Los guanches de Tenerife, y conquista de Canaria*, Acto 2).

108 A good example of this cultural appropriation of Spain's Roman heritage is Lope de Vega's *Loa: Después, que el famoso César*, in which specific references are made to "bravos Españoles" whose charge it is to "vencer los Indios negros."

109 Lope de Vega, *El esclavo de Roma*, Acto 1; Lope de Vega, *El honrado hermano*, Acto 1.

110 Lope de Vega, *El honrado hermano*, Acto 2.

111 Lope de Vega, *El casamiento en la muerte*, Jornada 1.

112 Calderón, *La redención de cautivos*, auto sacramental; Calderón, *En esta vida todo es verdad, y todo mentira*, Jornada 3.

113 Lope de Vega, *El valiente Céspedes*, Acto 1. On this and other picaresque tales of soldiers' lives, see Anne J. Cruz, "From Pícaro to Soldier," in *Discourses of Poverty: Social Reform and the Picaresque Novel in Early Modern Spain* (Toronto: University of Toronto Press, 1999), 164–206.

114 Calderón, *Fortunas de Andrómeda, y Perseo*, Jornada 1. On the "New" World in the *comedias*, see R. Shannon, "The Staging of America in Golden Age Theater," in *Looking at the* Comedia *in the Year of the Quincentennial*, ed. Barbara Mujica and Sharon D. Voros (Lanham: University Press of America, 1993), 53–68, as well as Viviana Díaz Balsera, "Auracanian Alterity in Alonso de Ercilla and Lope de Vega," 23–36 of the same volume. See also James T. Abraham, "The Other Speaks: Tirso de Molina's *Amazonas en las Indias*," in *El arte nuevo de estudiar comedias: Literary Theory and Spanish Golden Age Drama*, ed. Barbara Simerka (Lewisburg: Bucknell University Press, 1996). For Spanish-language sources on the same topic, see three essays in particular on Spanish *comedias* set in, or written about, the "New" World: Fausta Antonucci, "El indio americano y la conquista de América en las comedias impresas de tema araucano (1616–1665)"; Teresa J. Kirschner, "Enmascaramiento y desenmascaramiento del discurso sobre el 'indio' en el teatro del 'Nuevo Mundo' de Lope de Vega"; and Luis Vázquez Fernández, "Impacto del 'Nuevo Mundo' en la obra de Tirso de Molina." All of these articles appear in *Relaciones literarias entre España y América en los siglos XVI y XVII*, ed. Ysla Campbell (Ciudad Juárez [Mexico]: Universidad Autónoma de Ciudad Juárez, 1992), 21–46, 47–64, and 89–124, respectively.

115 Lope de Vega, *Arauco domado por el excelentísimo señor don García Hurtado de Mendoza*, Acto 2.

116 Tirso de Molina, *La lealtad contra la envidia*, Acto 3.

117 Calderón, *La gran Cenobia*, Jornada 3.

118 For discussion of these key concepts, see Barbara Fuchs, *Exotic Nation: Maurophilia and the Construction of Early Modern Spain* (Philadelphia: University of Pennsylvania Press, 2009).

119 "sangrienta, y tan tirana la lid, que el Asia mueve soberbia" (Calderón, *¿Quién hallará mujer fuerte?*, auto sacramental).

120 The proud Greek is referred to as "Con su venida orgulloso está el Griego" (Tirso de Molina, *El Aquiles*, Acto 3). References to Italians tend to be focused on southern Italy, which was governed by Spain at this time; for example, "habrá quien castigue de Nápoles la arrogancia" (Lope de Vega, *Mirad a quién alabáis*, Acto 2). In reference to Englishmen: "No he menester más aprecio, cuando del Inglés orgullo voy a postrar el denuedo" (Zamora, *La poncella de Orleans*, Jornada 1). The reference to Albania appears in the lines, "sufrir la arrogancia, con que el de Albania te inquieta" (Lope de Vega, *El blasón de los Chaves de Villalba*, Acto 2). The Duchy of Saxony appears in two different plays in the context of Pride: "de ver corrido del Sajón la vanagloria"

(Pérez de Montalbán, *Los amantes de Teruel,* Jornada 2); and "rendir la soberbia de él de Sajonia" (Diamante, *El Hércules de Ocaña*, Jornada 2).

121 "Portuguesa vanagloria" (Calderón, *El Príncipe constante*, Acto 1). In the same act of the same play, the King orders: "Rinde la espada, altivo Portugués." In a different play by the same author, a character exclaims: "¡qué Portuguesa arrogancia!" (Calderón, *A secreto agravio, secreta venganza*, Jornada 2).

122 References abound to the "arrogancia Francesa" (Lope de Vega, *El casamiento en la muerte*, Jornada 1) and "la loca arrogancia del Francés" (Calderón, *El escondido, y la tapada*, Jornada 1), as well as to "la insolencia del Francés orgulloso, y desvarío" (Juan de la Cueva [1550–1609?], *La libertad de España por Bernardo del Carpio*, Acto 4). At one point a Spaniard reminds a Frenchman that he cannot act the same way abroad as he does at home: "Francés, que no es España Francia, donde puedan sufrirte esa arrogancia" (Cueva, *La libertad de España por Bernardo del Carpio*, Acto 4).

123 Cueva, *El saco de Roma, y muerte de Borbón, y Coronación de nuestro invicto Emperador Carlos Quinto*, Acto 1; Lope de Vega, *La Santa Liga*, Acto 3.

124 Lope de Vega, *La primera información*, Jornada 3. See Eric J. Griffin, *English Renaissance Drama and the Specter of Spain: Ethnopoetics and Empire* (Philadelphia: University of Pennsylvania Press, 2009).

125 Cueva, *La libertad de España por Bernardo del Carpio*, Acto 3.

126 Calderón, *A María el corazón*, auto sacramental.

127 Lope de Vega, *La ocasión perdida*, Jornada 3.

128 Lope de Vega, *Angélica en el Catay*, Acto 2.

129 Tirso de Molina, *Marta la piadosa*, Acto 2.

130 Zamora, *Cada uno es linaje aparte, y los Mazas de Aragón*, Jornada 2.

131 Lope de Vega, *El Sol parado*, Acto 2; Lope de Vega, *La envidia de la nobleza*, Acto 1.

132 Calderón, *El santo rey don Fernando, segunda parte*, auto sacramental.

133 Lope de Vega, *El Nuevo Mundo, descubierto por Cristóbal Colón*, Acto 1.

134 Calderón, *A secreto agravio, secreta venganza*, Jornada 3.

135 Zamora, *El custodio de la Hungría, San Juan Capistrano*, Jornada 3.

136 Calderón, *La semilla, y la cizaña*, auto sacramental.

137 Rojas Zorrilla, *El profeta falso Mahoma*, Jornada 3.

138 Tirso de Molina, *La lealtad contra la envidia*, Acto 1.

139 Lope de Vega, *Angélica en el Catay*, Acto 2; Calderón, *El sitio de Breda*, Jornada 3.

140 Calderón, *El gran príncipe de Fez*, Jornada 2.

141 Calderón, *A María el corazón*, auto sacramental.

142 Cueva, *El saco de Roma, y muerte de Borbón*, Acto 1; Lope de Vega, *El blasón de los Chaves de Villalba*, Acto 2.

143 Diamante, *El Hércules de Ocaña*, Jornada 2; Lope de Vega, *El caballero del Milagro*, Acto 2.

144 Calderón, *El sitio de Breda*, Acto 1.

145 Miguel de Cervantes (1547–1616), *El gallardo español*, Jornada 2.

146 Lope de Vega, *El casamiento en la muerte*, Jornada 3. Fuchs states her purpose "to complicate the story of an inherent, timeless Iberian opposition to the Moors by pointing out how Spain's very success in its consolidation as a nation was accompanied by a pronounced European denunciation of its Moorishness, particularly as northern Europeans came to rule and administer Spain" (*Exotic Nation*, 20).

147 Guillén de Castro, *El engañarse engañado*, Jornada 2.

148 Lope de Vega, *Del mal lo menos*, Acto 1.

149 Calderón, *Los encantos de la Culpa*, loa for auto sacramental, emphasis mine.

150 Calderón, *El encanto sin encanto*, Jornada 2.

151 Lope de Vega, *Quien más no puede*, Acto 3; Lope de Vega, *El piadoso aragonés*, Acto 2.

152 Lope de Vega, *El Sol parado*, Acto 1. Later in this passage reference is made to the brave sword of Galicia's patron saint, Santiago the Moor-Slayer.

153 Lope de Vega, *La Santa Liga*, Acto 1; Juan de Matos Fragoso (1608?–1689), *El traidor contra su sangre*, Jornada 2.

154 Lope de Vega, *La varona castellana*, Acto 1. The historical events represented in this play are the marriage of Urraca of Castile to King Alfonso of León, along with their union's eventual dissolution at the insistence of outraged noblemen of the realm.

155 Lope de Vega, *La mayor virtud de un rey*, Jornada 3; Lope de Vega, *El bobo del colegio*, Acto 2.

156 Tirso de Molina, *Adversa fortuna de don Álvaro de Luna*, Jornada 2. Some scholars attribute this play and its companion piece (*Próspera fortuna …*) to Antonio Mira de Amescua.

157 Lope de Vega, *El casamiento en la muerte*, Jornada 3.

158 See C.A. Jones, "Honor in Spanish Golden-Age Drama: Its Relation to Real Life and to Morals," *Bulletin of Hispanic Studies* 35 (1958): 199–210.

159 "mi altivez, mi honor, mi vanidad, mi soberbia, mi respeto, mi decoro" (Calderón, *El mayor encanto, amor*, Jornada 2).

160 Lope de Vega, *Quien todo lo quiere*, Jornada 3.

161 Calderón, *El alcalde de sí mismo*, Jornada 3; Calderón, *A secreto agravio, secreta venganza*, Acto 1.

162 Moreto, *El parecido*, Jornada 3; Lope de Vega, *Los Ponces de Barcelona*, Acto 2.

163 Pérez de Montalbán, *Cumplir con su obligación*, Jornada 2.

164 On duels in both literary and legal contexts during this time period, see José Luis Bermejo Cabrero, "Duelos y desafíos en el derecho y en la literatura," in *Sexo barroco y otras transgresiones premodernas*, ed. Francisco Tomás y Valiente et al. (Madrid: Alianza Universidad, 1990), 109–26. Bermejo Cabrero refers to treatises on duelling to make the distinction among three types of duels: "Los tratadistas del duelo llegan a distinguir tres modalidades: decretario (duelo a muerte), como fórmula más usual; propugnatorio (procurando no causar la muerte) y, finalmente, satisfactorio (a muerte, pero con posibilidad de aceptar antes un arreglo o composición" (114).

165 Moreto, *El lego del Carmen*, Jornada 1.

166 Calderón, *Los Lances de Amor, y Fortuna*, Jornada 3.

167 Calderón, *El postrer duelo de España*, Jornada 3.

168 Scott K. Taylor, *Honor and Violence in Golden Age Spain* (New Haven: Yale University Press, 2008), 5.

169 Guillén de Castro, *La fuerza de la costumbre*, Jornada 1.

170 Calderón, *El postrer duelo de España*, Jornada 1.

171 Lope de Vega, *El perro del hortelano*, Acto 2.

172 Alarcón, *Examen de maridos*, Acto 2.

173 Calderón, *La desdicha de la voz*, Jornada 3.

174 Cueva, *La libertad de España por Bernardo del Carpio*, Acto 3.

175 Lope de Vega, *El amigo por fuerza*, Acto 1.

176 Lope de Vega, *El rey sin reino*, Acto 1.

177 Guillén de Castro, *Las mocedades del Cid, Comedia primera*, Acto 3.

178 Lope de Vega, *Al pasar del arroyo*, Acto 2.

179 Tirso de Molina, *Doña Beatriz de Silva*, Acto 3.

180 Tirso de Molina, *Tanto es lo demás como lo de menos*, Acto 1.

181 Calderón, *El año santo en Madrid*, auto sacramental. This identification is enunciated more than once within the same play: "a ser Cortesano entre Envidia, y Pereza, Codicia, Ira, Gula, Soberbia, y Lascivia!"

182 On the concern about *limpieza de sangre*, see Linda Martz, "Implementation of Pure-Blood Statutes in Sixteenth-Century Toledo," in *In Iberia and Beyond: Hispanic Jews between Cultures (Proceedings of a Symposium to Mark the 500th Anniversary of the Expulsion of Spanish Jewry)*, ed. Bernard Dov Cooperman (Newark, DE: University of Delaware Press, 1998), 245–72.

183 Such was the case of Saint Teresa's family, which instigated a lawsuit in 1519 to claim *hidalguía*, thus effectively removing the traces of their Jewish lineage. See Tomás Álvarez, "Santa Teresa de Ávila en el drama de los judeo-conversos castellanos," in *Judíos, sefarditas, conversos: la expulsión de 1492 y sus consecuencias*, ed. Ángel Alcalá (Valladolid: Ámbito, 1995), 609–30, at 610. A study of the text of the lawsuit, located in the Archivo de la Real Chancillería de Valladolid, has been published in Teófanes Egido, *El linaje judeoconverso de Santa Teresa: pleito de hidalguía de los Cepeda* (Madrid: Editorial de Espiritualidad, 1986).

184 In Spain, the church demanded proof of blood purity dating back seven generations before permitting marriage to someone whose lineage had been called into question (Cecil Roth, *The Spanish Inquisition* [New York: Norton, 1964], 27). This was, however, an even more serious and ongoing problem in Portugal. On Inquisitorial persecution of judaizers and some differentiation as to its relative intensity by country, see Paolo Bernardini and Norman Fiering, eds, *The Jews and the Expansion of Europe to the West, 1400–1800* (Providence: The John Carter Brown Library, 2004), 245. Don Cruickshank comments on the irony of Jewish persecution by the

Spanish empire: "Christ may have been the Son of God, but having a Jewish mother would have excluded him from a range of posts in Habsburg Spain" (Cruickshank, *Don Pedro Calderón*, 319).

185 Lope de Vega, *La pobreza estimada*, Acto 2. This speech includes a lengthy vituperation against the *cartas de hidalguía*:

> Son las cartas de nobleza,
> de solar, y hechos notorios,
> libelos infamatorios
> contra la naturaleza.
> ¿Al que es vil recibe el cielo
> descargo de que es hidalgo?
> ¿Estima la muerte en algo
> al más hidalgo del suelo? (Lope de Vega, *La pobreza estimada*, Acto 2)

We might possibly glimpse here a personal complaint by Lope, who resented his own lack of noble status. On his vexed relationship to the court, see Melveena McKendrick, *Playing the King: Lope de Vega and the Limits of Conformity* (London: Tamesis, 2000), 211.

186 Calderón, *El día mayor de los días*, auto sacramental, Acto 1.

187 Calderón, *El sitio de Breda*, Jornada 2.

188 Tirso de Molina, *Amar por razón de estado*, Acto 1.

189 Lope de Vega, *El soldado amante*, Acto 1.

190 Calderón, *El año santo en Madrid*, auto sacramental.

191 Calderón, *La gran Cenobia*, Jornada 2; Lope de Vega, *El postrer godo de España*, Acto 2.

192 Tirso de Molina, *La Dama del Olivar*, Acto 3.

193 Lope de Vega, *La fe rompida*, Acto 1.

194 Lope de Vega, *La fortuna merecida*, Acto 3.

195 Cueva, *El saco de Roma, y muerte de Borbón*, Acto 1.

196 Calderón, *Auristela, y Lisidante*, Jornada 2; Tirso de Molina, *El árbol del mejor fruto*, Acto 2.

197 Alarcón, *La industria, y la suerte*, Acto 1.

198 Lope de Vega, *El caballero del Milagro*, Acto 3.

199 Calderón, *La cisma de Inglaterra*, Jornada 1.

200 Calderón, *La sibila del Oriente*, Jornada 2.

201 Zamora, *El custodio de la Hungría, San Juan Capistrano*, Jornada 3.

202 Lope de Vega, *El galán de la Membrilla*, Acto 2.

203 Calderón, *El socorro general*, auto sacramental.

204 Calderón, *El Príncipe constante*, Acto 1. The full context for this line is the speech:

no se emplean
nuestras armas aquí por vanagloria
de que en los libros inmortales lean,
ojos humanos esta gran victoria,
la Fe de Dios a engrandecer venimos,
suyo será el honor, suya la gloria. (Calderón, *El Príncipe constante*, Acto 1)

205 Lope de Vega, *La discreta venganza*, Acto 1.

206 Lope de Vega, *El Amor enamorado*, Preliminares de obra.

207 Lope de Vega, *El mayor imposible*, Jornada 2.

208 Lope de Vega, *El saber puede dañar*, Acto 3.

209 Tirso de Molina, *Adversa fortuna de don Álvaro de Luna*, Preliminares de obra.

210 Calderón, *El jardín de Falerina*, auto sacramental.

211 Lope de Vega, *La pobreza estimada*, Preliminares de obra.

212 Calderón, *El mágico prodigioso*, Jornada 1. Likewise, Joan of Arc, accused as a sorceress and thought to possess occult powers, says in Zamora's play about her: "que en mi ciencia se fía nuestra arrogancia" (Zamora, *La poncella de Orleans*, Jornada 3).

213 Tirso de Molina, *El melancólico*, Acto 1. On specific references to casuistry and confessors within Golden Age plays, see Hilaire Kallendorf, *Conscience on Stage: The* Comedia *as Casuistry in Early Modern Spain* (Toronto: University of Toronto Press, 2007). Burlesque treatment of the often obscure, always pedantic casuists was logically more frequent in Jesuit school drama. For illustrative examples of this parody of the *letrados*, see Kallendorf, *Conscience on Stage*, 30.

214 Calderón, *El gran mercado del mundo*, auto sacramental.

215 Lope de Vega, *Si no vieran las mujeres*, Preliminares de obra.

216 Lope de Vega, *El piadoso aragonés*, Acto 2.

217 Calderón, *El purgatorio de San Patricio*, Jornada 3.

218 Lope de Vega, *Si no vieran las mujeres*, Jornada 1.

219 On the divine right of kings, see Ernst Kantorowicz, *The King's Two Bodies: A Study in Medieval Political Theology* (Princeton: Princeton University Press, 1981), especially the section on "The Halo of Perpetuity," 78–86. As Kantorowicz explains it, this aura "indicated the bearer and executive of perpetual power derived from God and made the emperor the incarnation of some kind of 'prototype' which, being immortal, was *sanctus*" (80). For a recent application of Kantorowicz's interpretive model to Golden Age Spain, see Alban K. Forcione, *Majesty and Humanity: Kings and Their Doubles in the Political Drama of the Spanish Golden Age* (New Haven: Yale University Press, 2009).

220 Lope de Vega, *Las mudanzas de Fortuna, y sucesos de don Beltrán de Aragón*, Acto 3.

221 Pérez de Montalbán, *El valiente Nazareno*, Jornada 1.

222 Calderón, *La gran Cenobia*, Jornada 3. As she recounts, "pretendí vencer su arrogancia" (Calderón, *La gran Cenobia*, Jornada 3).

223 Moreto, *Hacer del contrario amigo*, Jornada 2.

224 Rojas Zorrilla, *Los encantos de Medea*, Jornada 1.

225 Guillén de Castro, *Las mocedades del Cid, Comedia primera*, Acto 3.

226 Solís, *El alcázar del secreto*, Jornada 1.

227 Calderón, *El castillo de Lindabridis*, Jornada 2.

228 Pérez de Montalbán, *El divino portugués, San Antonio de Padua*, Jornada 2.

229 Zamora, *Todo lo vence el Amor*, Jornada 2.

230 Lope de Vega, *Nadie se conoce*, Jornada 3. By extension, the furnishings of regular (i.e., non-royal) rooms can also be described as proud, as in the question "¿No es soberbia alfombra ésta?" (Rojas Zorrilla, *Lo que son mujeres*, Jornada 3).

231 For current theoretical discussion of the significance of the throne, especially an empty throne, see Giorgio Agamben, *Il Regno e la Gloria: Per una genealogia teologica dell'economia e del governo* (*Homo sacer*, II, 2) (Vicenza: Neri Pozza, 2007), 266–9.

232 Calderón, *La cisma de Inglaterra*, Jornada 1.

233 Tirso de Molina, *La celosa de sí misma*, Acto 1. In this speech, urban buildings are also viewed as arrogant and in fact compared explicitly to the grandeur of Babylon:

Usurpando a su elemento
el lugar con edificios,
de esta Babilonia indicios,
pues hurtan la esfera al viento. (Tirso de Molina, *La celosa de sí misma*, Acto 1)

234 Calderón, *A tu próximo como a ti*, auto sacramental.

235 Lope de Vega, *Las cuentas del Gran Capitán*, Acto 3.

236 Tirso de Molina, *La villana de Vallecas*, Acto 2.

237 Calderón, *La Puente de Mantible*, Jornada 2.

238 Zamora, *Amar, es saber vencer, y el arte contra el poder*, Jornada 3.

239 For expert commentary on this play, see the introduction to Valentina Nider's recent critical edition (Calderón, *La torre de Babilonia*, ed. Valentina Nider [Pamplona/ Kassel: Universidad de Navarra/Reichenberger, 2007]). Another Golden Age play written about this same subject matter is a relatively unknown *comedia* by Antonio Enríquez Gómez titled *Soberbia de Nembrot* (ca 1635).

240 Jacqueline de Weever, "Nembrot," in *Chaucer Name Dictionary* (New York: Garland, 1996), 252. Nimrod's legendary Pride appears frequently in other Golden Age dramas; for example, reference is made in Lope's *Virtud, pobreza y mujer* to "esta torre de casas, a donde mejor pudiera la arrogancia de Nembrot atreverse a las estrellas" (Lope de Vega, *Virtud, pobreza y mujer*, Acto 2). On possible props for this performance, see Françoise Gilbert, "Sobre 'La torre de Babilonia,' auto sacramental de Calderón de la Barca," *Criticón* 103–4 (2008): 331–41, at 332.

241 Calderón, *La torre de Babilonia*, auto sacramental. The Biblical account of the giants occurs in Genesis 6:2–4: "The sons of God seeing the daughters of men, that they were fair, took to themselves wives of all which they chose … Now giants were upon the earth in those days. For after the sons of God went in to the daughters of men, and they brought forth children, these are the mighty men of old, men of renown." On Nimrod, see Genesis 10:8–9, which reads "Now Chus begot Nemrod: he began to be mighty on the earth. And he was a stout hunter before the Lord."

242 See George Steiner, *After Babel: Aspects of Language and Translation*, 3rd ed. (Oxford: Oxford University Press, 1998).

243 Lope de Vega, *El alcalde mayor*, Acto 3. For more meditations by Lope about good government, see Alban Forcione, *Majesty and Humanity*, which focuses primarily on Lope's *El Rey Don Pedro en Madrid* and *El villano en su rincón*.

244 Lope de Vega, *Dios hace reyes*, Acto 3.

245 Rojas Zorrilla, *Santa Isabel reina de Portugal*, Jornada 3.

246 See J.H. Elliott, *The Count-Duke of Olivares: The Statesman in an Age of Decline* (New Haven and London: Yale University Press, 1988).

247 Calderón, *El mágico prodigioso*, Jornada 2. The Latin phrase *Regio Solio* refers to the royal throne. The phrase is found, for example, in early references to the kingdom of Asturias, the first Christian principality to be established after the reign of the Visigoths. See Claudio Sánchez-Albornoz, "*Sede Regia* y *Solio Real* en el reino asturleonés," *Asturiensia medievalia* 3 (1979): 61–86.

248 Lope de Vega, *Contra valor no hay desdicha*, Acto 1.

249 Elliott, *The Count-Duke of Olivares*, 134–5. It should not be forgotten that Olivares was so Machiavellian that he persuaded Francisco de Quevedo to write *Cómo ha de ser el privado* (1629) in which Olivares himself "appears, thinly disguised, as the anagrammatic Marquis of Valisero" (Cruickshank, *Don Pedro Calderón*, 74).

250 Moreto, *El esclavo de su hijo*, Jornada 3.

251 Lope de Vega, *El gran duque de Moscovia, y emperador perseguido*, Acto 2.

252 "envidia, y soberbia, que son del mandar efectos" (Rojas Zorrilla, *Los trabajos de Tobías*, Jornada 1).

253 "Esto quiere el Rey quitarte, y da por vana arrogancia todo su reinado a Francia, por sólo desheredarte" (Cueva, *La libertad de España por Bernardo del Carpio*, Acto 3).

254 Lope de Vega, *La carbonera*, Jornada 1.

255 "a su tirano quitara el orgullo, que vence la sazón, y el alma oprime" (Lope de Vega, *El mayorazgo dudoso*, Jornada 2).

256 Cueva, *Comedia del príncipe tirano*, Preliminares de obra. For more background on this pseudo-historical drama, see Ronald E. Surtz, *The Birth of a Theater: Dramatic Convention in the Spanish Theater from Juan del Encina to Lope de Vega* (Madrid: Castalia, 1979), 181.

257 Cueva, *Comedia del príncipe tirano*, Preliminares de obra. The full quotation reads: "Esta plaga ha redundado desde aquellos tiempos, hasta los nuestros, y de tal suerte

ha tendido sus contagiosos ramos, que todo es señoreado, y aun contaminado" (Cueva, *Comedia del príncipe tirano*, Preliminares de obra).

258 Forcione notes, "it is worth mentioning that there are certainly many more dramatic depictions of corrupt and sinful monarchs in the Spanish theater than both its celebrants and its critics have realized" (Forcione, *Majesty and Humanity*, 20).

259 Lope de Vega, *El mejor maestro, el tiempo*, Acto 1.

260 Lope de Vega, *La ventura sin buscarla*, Acto 3.

261 Matos Fragoso, *El traidor contra su sangre* (1658), Jornada 3.

262 Critics continue to debate this interpretation. Melveena McKendrick provides a particularly well-nuanced assessment: "the king, as God's vice regent, plays a crucial strategic role as a dispenser of justice, in … *Fuenteovejuna* ratifying without condoning the violent measures taken by the desperate peasants to protect their women … Critics never tire of pointing out that in spite of their superficially democratic, even revolutionary, spirit, the plays are, if anything, anti-feudalism but pro-monarchy … But this does not mean that they are a defence of absolutism" (McKendrick, *Playing the King*, 35).

263 I borrow this striking image from Leah Middlebrook, who applies it to lyric poetry (Leah Middlebrook, "Coda: The Tomb of Poetry," in *Imperial Lyric: New Poetry and New Subjects in Early Modern Spain* [University Park: Pennsylvania State University Press, 2009], 175–80).

264 Last known to be held by Christie's of London. For similar images which visually link earthly power to mortality, see Steven N. Orso, *Art and Death at the Spanish Habsburg Court: The Royal Exequies for Philip IV* (Columbia: University of Missouri Press, 1989).

265 See Anthony J. Cascardi, "Allegories of Power," in *The Prince in the Tower: Perceptions of* La vida es sueño, ed. Frederick A. de Armas (Lewisburg: Bucknell University Press, 1993), 15–26. Cascardi invokes Walter Benjamin to describe absolutist power as, at best, allegorical: "Absolutism thus becomes the ground of a power that is allegorical in the modern, Benjaminian sense: having first destroyed the authority of nature, absolutism goes on to reclaim nature's power as the legitimizing basis of its own. It supplants nature with what might be described as a series of secondary 'power effects,' whose artificial origins and historical contingency it attempts at the same time to conceal" (18).

266 Calderón, *La vida es sueño*, auto sacramental.

267 Calderón, *La vida es sueño*, Jornada 2.

268 Pérez de Montalbán, *El mariscal de Virón*, Jornada 3.

269 Lope de Vega, *Los hidalgos del aldea*, Acto 2.

270 Lope de Vega, *La amistad pagada*, Jornada 2.

271 Guillén de Castro, *El engañarse engañado*, Jornada 1.

272 Slavoj Žižek, "*Azul*, de Krzysztof Kieslowski, o la reconstitución de la fantasía," trans. Román Setton, in *Teoría de la cultura: un mapa de la cuestión*, ed. Gerhart

Schröder and Helga Breuninger (Buenos Aires: Fondo de Cultura Económica, 2005), 115–30, at 122.

273 Lope de Vega, *Contra valor no hay desdicha*, Acto 1.

274 Tirso de Molina, *La santa Juana*, Acto 3. This play is the first of three in a series. Tirso's trilogy of plays on this topic chronicles the life of Mother Juana de la Cruz, a Spanish mystic consulted by Emperor Charles V (not to be confused with the later eponymous Mexican nun).

275 Pérez de Montalbán, *Amor, privanza, y castigo*, Acto 1.

276 "para quien es altivo, injusto, atrevido, y loco, como tú, son las virtudes poco" (Zamora, *Judás Iscariote*, Acto 1).

277 Lope de Vega, *Contra valor no hay desdicha*, Acto 3.

278 Moreto, *Hasta el fin nadie es dichoso*, Jornada 2.

279 Calderón, *El jardín de Falerina*, auto sacramental.

280 Zamora, *Amar, es saber vencer, y el arte contra el poder*, Acto 1; Alarcón, *Mudarse por mejorarse*, Acto 2.

281 "es invencible su orgullo" (Matos Fragoso, *La devoción del Ángel de la Guarda*, Jornada 3).

282 On the direct connections between emblem books and *comedias*, see Manuel Ruiz Lagos, "Interrelación pintura/poesía en el drama alegórico calderoniano: El caso imitativo de la *Iconología* de C. Ripa," *Goya* 161–2 (1981): 282–9. Ruiz Lagos has identified the specific emblem book, Cesare Ripa's *Iconologia* (1618), upon which Calderón modelled the designs for costumes of at least three of the Deadly Vices: Pride, Anger, and Gluttony. I believe the case could be made for adding Avarice to this list. See Kallendorf, "Dressed to the Sevens," 163.

283 "El mar altivo su fiera frente humilló" (Lope de Vega, *El hombre por su palabra*, Acto 1).

284 Pérez de Montalbán, *El valiente Nazareno*, Jornada 3.

285 For the private sphere: "Ya sé que el más altivo, al más extraño le doma una mujer" (Lope de Vega, *El castigo sin venganza*, Acto 1). For the macrocosm we find such references as, "postren la arrogancia en concordia feliz, Savoya, y Francia" (Pérez de Montalbán, *El mariscal de Virón*, Jornada 1); and "a toda Francia, se deshizo su arrogancia, como las nubes al Sol" (Cervantes, *La casa de los celos y selvas de Ardenia*, Jornada 3).

286 Calderón, *El purgatorio de San Patricio*, Jornada 2.

287 Calderón, *La gran Cenobia*, Jornada 2.

288 Lope de Vega, *Las bizarrías de Belisa*, Jornada 3. For an account of Lope's numerous love affairs and how they later became material for his creative production, see Alan Trueblood, *Experience and Artistic Expression in Lope de Vega: The Making of* "La Dorotea" (Cambridge: Harvard University Press, 1974).

289 Calderón, *El amor, honor y poder*, Jornada 2.

290 Lope de Vega, *El hijo de Reduán*, Acto 2.

291 Calderón, *El pleito matrimonial*, auto sacramental.

292 Lope de Vega, *La hermosa Ester*, Acto 3.
293 Lope de Vega, *De cosario a cosario*, Acto 3.
294 Calderón, *El Príncipe constante*, Jornada 2.
295 Griffin, *English Renaissance Drama*, 109.
296 "a Macedonia una armada que divirtiera a Alejandro la temeraria arrogancia" (Lope de Vega, *Las grandezas de Alejandro*, Acto 2).
297 Cervantes, *El ingenioso hidalgo don Quijote de la Mancha*, ed. Luis Andrés Murillo, 2 vols (Madrid: Castalia, 1987), 2:33.
298 Moreto, *La traición vengada*, Jornada 1.
299 Fernando Díaz-Plaja relates Pride explicitly to honour in *El español y los siete pecados capitales* (Madrid: Alianza, 1980), trans. John Inderwick Palmer as *The Spaniard and the Seven Deadly Sins* (New York: Charles Scribner's Sons, 1967), 25–6.
300 See John Bossy, "Moral Arithmetic: Seven Sins into Ten Commandments," in *Conscience and Casuistry in Early Modern Europe*, ed. Edmund Leites (Cambridge: Cambridge University Press, 1988), 214–34.
301 Calderón, *A María el corazón*, auto sacramental.
302 "o sacrílega altivez" (Pérez de Montalbán, *Teágenes, y Clariquea*, Jornada 2).
303 Calderón, *El amor, honor y poder*, Jornada 2.
304 Calderón, *Judás Macabeo*, Jornada 3.
305 Calderón, *El Rey Don Pedro en Madrid, e infanzón de Illescas*, Jornada 2. Most scholars depart from the Teatro Español del Siglo de Oro database in attributing this play instead to Lope de Vega. On Peter I of Castile (Pedro el Cruel) and his representation in the theatre, see the section titled "An Exorcism of Cruelty or a Bejeweling of Blood?" in Forcione, *Majesty and Humanity*, 101–5.
306 Lope de Vega, *El Amor enamorado*, Jornada 1.
307 Calderón, *El valle de la zarzuela*, auto sacramental.
308 Tirso de Molina, *Tanto es lo demás como lo de menos*, Acto 1.
309 For a study which chooses to link Blasphemy instead to Anger, see Maureen Flynn, "Blasphemy and the Play of Anger in Sixteenth-Century Spain," *Past and Present* 149 (1995): 29–56. However, in this article she does make the connection also with arrogance (55).
310 Calderón, *La exaltación de la Cruz*, Jornada 2.
311 Pérez de Montalbán, *El valiente Nazareno*, Jornada 3.
312 Pérez de Montalbán, *Lo que son juicios del cielo*, Jornada 3.
313 Lope de Vega, *La hermosa Ester*, Acto 3.
314 Pérez de Montalbán, *El mariscal de Virón*, Jornada 1.
315 Maureen Flynn confirms that this explicit connection was being made: "the Christian church took seriously the facile use of 'blasphemies' … and tried strenuously to prevent people from violating the third commandment" (Flynn, "Blasphemy and the Play of Anger," 29). This Third Commandment is numbered Two in the enumeration we are using (see figure 1).

316 Tirso de Molina, *Marta la piadosa*, Acto 3; Tirso de Molina, *Santo, y sastre*, Acto 2.

317 Tirso de Molina, *Marta la piadosa*, Acto 3; Tirso de Molina, *Tanto es lo demás como lo de menos*, Acto 3.

318 Lope de Rueda (1510–65), *Medora*, Scena 2. I have not corrected his *algarabía* or mangled speech since in this case the Spanish is not merely antiquated but instead distorted/mispronounced deliberately as a reflection of his low level of education.

319 Maureen Flynn, "Taming Anger's Daughters: New Treatment for Emotional Problems in Renaissance Spain," *Renaissance Quarterly* 51 (1998): 864–86, at 870n23. Flynn cites *Las Siete Partidas del Rey Don Alfonso el Sabio*, Partida vii, Título 28, Ley 4, iii. She confirms that a further infraction was to be punished by the tongue being cut out altogether (Flynn, "Blasphemy and the Play of Anger," 30n4).

320 Tirso de Molina, *Segunda parte de Santa Juana*, Acto 1.

321 Octavio Paz, "Hijos de la Malinche," chapter 4 of *El laberinto de la soledad* (Mexico City: Fondo de Cultura Económica, 1992), 27–36, at 32. Paz waxes eloquent on the unique linguistic and cultural power of swear words: "El poder mágico de la palabra se intensifica por su carácter prohibido. Nadie la dice en público. Solamente un exceso de cólera, una emoción o el entusiasmo delirante, justifican su expresión franca. Es una voz que sólo se oye entre hombres, o en las grandes fiestas. Al gritarla, rompemos un velo de pudor, de silencio o de hipocresía. Nos manifestamos tales como somos de verdad. Las malas palabras hierven en nuestro interior, como hierven nuestros sentimientos. Cuando salen, lo hacen brusca, brutalmente, en forma de alarido, de reto, de ofensa. Son proyectiles o cuchillos. Desgarran" (32).

322 For a magnificent historicization of Spaniards' use of swear words and other insults, see Taylor, *Honor and Violence*, 62–3.

323 Raymond Williams, "Dominant, Residual, and Emergent," in *Marxism in Literature* (Oxford: Oxford University Press, 1977), 121–7, at 122.

2. Greed Breaks the Bag

1 The quotation continues grimly, "porque estaba el oro en él, la codicia hizo tiranos, mató padres, mató hermanos, y propios hijos mató" (Lope de Vega, *El piadoso veneciano*, Acto 2).

2 Lope de Vega, *La prisión sin culpa*, Acto 3.

3 Raymond Williams, "Dominant, Residual, and Emergent," in *Marxism in Literature* (Oxford: Oxford University Press, 1977), 121–7, at 123.

4 "hidrópica sed en sus telas, y diamantes ... codicioso ... de hacienda" (Calderón, *Mañanas de abril, y mayo*, Jornada 3). In the *autos sacramentales*, the allegorical personification of Avarice is invariably seen holding jewels or gold chains: "toma, Avaricia, tus Joyas" (Calderón, *El año santo en Madrid*, auto sacramental) and "la Avaricia [lleva] en una Salva una Cadena de Oro" (Calderón, *El indulto general*, loa for auto sacramental). In a play about a magical finger ring, one character describes

a sparkling diamond stolen by Greed: "Limpio, y claro está el diamante, que le quitó mi codicia" (Lope de Vega, *La sortija del olvido*, Acto 3).

5 Soft cushions: "más contento que en sus sillas de tela el avariento" (Lope de Vega, *Los guanches de Tenerife, y conquista de Canaria*, Acto 3). Rich beds: "Robaron tus ricos lechos, perlas, aljófar, rubíes, colgaduras de oro" (Lope de Vega, *El soldado amante*, Acto 2). King Midas: "¡O hética inagotable de la codicia de Midas, oro gastan tus comidas, tu sed bebe oro" (Tirso de Molina, *La elección por la virtud*, Jornada 2). Counting obsessively: "suele el avariento del cofre cada momento sacar el oro y contarlo" (Lope de Vega, *Los embustes de Zelauro*, Acto 2).

6 A common proverb at this time was "la codicia rompe el saco," or "Greed breaks the bag." This refrain is repeated often throughout the *comedias* as well as other dramatic genres, as in "mire que en tales ganancias la codicia rompe el saco" (Luis Quiñones de Benavente [1593?–1652], *Loa con que empezaron Rueda, y Ascanio*) and "La codicia ha rompido muchos sacos, da siempre mala cuenta de gobiernos" (Lope de Vega, *El valor de las mujeres*, Acto 2). This proverb in fact became the title of a little-known *entremés*, allegedly by Calderón, called *La codicia rompe el saco*, published as a *pliego suelto* in the eighteenth century (Barcelona: Pedro Escuder, 1756). A copy of this short dramatic interlude is preserved at the Biblioteca Nacional in Madrid (call number T/4459) as well as the Bibliothèque Nationale in Paris.

For the desk collapsing, see "escritorio de avariento, que se hunde por su muerte" (Lope de Vega, *El padrino desposado*, Jornada 1). We find frequent references to the miser's desk as the place where he keeps his money at home: "tiene el Avariento en el escritorio el oro" (Lope de Vega, *El Perseo*, Acto 1). The other place where gold was kept was in *arcas*, which were trunks or chests; these were particularly useful for storing gold bars: "guarde el avaro en sus arcas tantas barras como penas" (Tirso de Molina, *Amazonas en las Indias*, Acto 3). These trunks became so heavy with gold that they were impossible to move: "el arca al avariento que no puede moverla del tesoro" (Lope de Vega, *Los prados de León*, Acto 1). The trunks were often buried or otherwise hidden in a cave or some other hiding place by the avaricious hoarder who planned to return for it later: "sacaré toda la plata, y el oro, que en avariento tesoro tanto encerrado oculté" (Calderón, *El gran teatro del mundo*, auto sacramental). We might well ask whether the weight of the gold on it is the only reason the miser's desk sinks into the ground; does the chasm opening beneath it also indicate its owner's proximate journey to hell? That would seem, to this reader, to be the implication.

7 "Fui como rudo villano, que del nido codicioso del ruiseñor amoroso puso en el áspid la mano" (Lope de Vega, *La noche de San Juan*, Acto 1).

8 On Avarice as thirst: "el hinchazón de la Riqueza, y la sed de la Avaricia" (Calderón, *El nuevo hospicio de pobres*, auto sacramental). In another *auto sacramental*, the stage directions read: "ya en el Hidrópico está entendida la Avaricia" (Calderón, *El nuevo hospicio de pobres*, auto sacramental). For the comparison to opium, see "opio vil de la codicia, que bebió en tantas violencias" (Calderón, *No hay instante sin milagro*, auto

sacramental). For arsenic, we find: "[a] sospechar veníamos, que algún traidor tocado del Arsénico de la codicia vil, como vil bárbaro vendió tu sangre" (Lope de Vega, *El soldado amante*, Acto 3).

9 "nacen a la hormiga avara alas para su peligro; pues cuando a Dédalo intenta imitar, de un pajarillo es miserable sustento, sepulcro haciendo su pico" (Tirso de Molina, *El árbol del mejor fruto*, Acto 1).

10 "no todo lo que es brillante riqueza al avaro ofrece, oro la alquimia parece" (Tirso de Molina, *Amazonas en las Indias*, Acto 1). Counterfeit currency was evidently also a problem, as we see in the false gold (along with assorted other fake merchandise) sold by the thief: "sortija sin piedra como escritorio robado, como quien compra al ladrón, el oro falso que vende, como dineros de duende" (Lope de Vega, *El casamiento en la muerte*, Jornada 3).

11 Grave robber: "Si entre tantos desconciertos, tan codiciosa no fueras, ahora no revolvieras las cenizas de los muertos" (Lope de Vega, *El capellán de la Virgen*, Acto 1). Worm: "¡O qué gusano afanado con codicioso ejercicio, parca de su misma vida, labró su muerte hilo!" (Calderón, *La señora, y la criada*, Jornada 1). Entrails: "En sus entrañas admiten el cadáver avariento, que vivo no abrió jamás piadosas puertas al pecho" (Tirso de Molina, *Tanto es lo demás como lo de menos*, Acto 3).

12 As one of Lope de Vega's characters laments, "Ya todo el mundo es engaños, hurtar a vivos y a muertos" (Lope de Vega, *El saber por no saber, y vida de San Julián*, Acto 3). There is a vast bibliography on *desengaño*. For one recent instalment, see Ivan Cañadas, "The Nation in History: Decline, Circularity and *Desengaño* in the Poetry of Fray Luis de León and Francisco de Quevedo," *Ianua: revista philologica romanica* 8 (2008): 203–23.

13 "cuanto he querido intentar codicia y mentira fue, humos fueron de Reinar" (Lope de Vega, *El tirano castigado*, Acto 3).

14 Calderón, *El tesoro escondido*, auto sacramental.

15 Calderón, *El alcalde de sí mismo*, Jornada 2.

16 "la vida se vuelve nauseabunda cuando la fantasía que media nuestro acceso a ella se desintegra" (Slavoj Žižek, "*Azul*, de Krzysztof Kieslowski, o la reconstitución de la fantasía," trans. Román Setton, in *Teoría de la cultura: un mapa de la cuestión*, ed. Gerhart Schröder and Helga Breuninger [Buenos Aires: Fondo de Cultura Económica, 2005], 115–30, at 122).

17 Turning a deaf ear to the poor: "Ventanas que sois oídos de avariento miserable, que no os abrís a los pobres" (Lope de Vega, *El ingrato arrepentido*, Acto 2); "el siempre sordo Afecto de la Avaricia … un Publicano es, que a nadie oye" (Calderón, *El primer refugio del hombre, y probática piscina*, auto sacramental). This kind of greedy person is seen as being liberal, i.e. generous, with himself: "[¿]Ahora sabes, que no deja impío de ser con otros avaro quien es liberal consigo?" (Calderón, *El año santo en Madrid*, auto sacramental). The parable appears in Luke 16:19–31. This whole scene, replete with Abraham, is re-enacted by various characters within the *comedia*

corpus: "le aplaque ninguno, aunque a Lázaro importuno, como otro rico avariento. Fue Rosimundo Abrahán, agua le pedí en su seno, pero …" (Lope de Vega, *El amigo por fuerza*, Acto 2). The rich man and Lazarus appear in at least some iteration in the following plays: Calderón, *El gran teatro del mundo*, auto sacramental; Lope de Vega, *La piedad ejecutada*, Acto 1 (in a passage of dialogue spoken by Ana); and Calderón, *La primer flor de el Carmelo*, auto sacramental. In this last work, the rustic Nabal experiences a metamorphosis, within the play's logic, into the rich man of the parable spoken by Jesus. This transformation is accomplished by Avarice possessing Nabal's chest in what almost sounds like the language of demonic possession: "he querido, que tú, Avaricia, poseas de Nabal el pecho" (Calderón, *La primer flor de el Carmelo*, auto sacramental). This plan fails, however, when Abigail generously disburses Nabal's treasures; at this point, Avarice says: "No me nombres, que ya no soy Avaricia, mirando cuán liberal Abigail desperdicia los Tesoros de Nabal" (Calderón, *La primer flor de el Carmelo*, auto sacramental). The Spanish stage was not the only one where this parable flourished during the Renaissance and Reformation period; for similar scenes penned by German playwrights, see Stephen L. Wailes, *The Rich Man and Lazarus on the Reformation Stage: A Contribution to the Social History of German Drama* (Selinsgrove: Susquehanna University Press, 1997).

This is just one of many instances in which a passage of particular interest from the Bible is reinscribed over and over again, almost obsessively, within the *comedias*. References likewise abound to Jesus's statement that it is more difficult for a rich man to enter heaven than for a camel to pass through the eye of a needle. By extension, "el dinero es aguijón" (Tirso de Molina, *La villana de la Sagra*, Jornada 1).

18 "avariento ese hidrópico cruel, de humanas vidas sediento" (Calderón, *Auristela, y Lisidante*, Jornada 1); "¡Quién la fiera hidropesía de su avara sed templara!" (Calderón, *El primer refugio del hombre, y probática piscina*, auto sacramental).

19 In one of Calderón's *loas* for his auto sacramental *El indulto general*, the allegorical figure of Avarice says: "Para él Avaricia desangre sus venas" (Calderón, *El indulto general*, loa for auto sacramental). Greed's connection to blood is further strengthened by passages which speak of Avarice burning and reigning in the blood: "¡O la codicia vil, que más ardiente reina en la sangre!" (Alarcón, *El semejante a sí mismo*, Acto 1).

20 This kind of miser is "un Avariento rico, pobre con mucho dinero" (Alarcón, *Los pechos privilegiados*, Acto 3). Similarly, another character declares, "Es oro de un avariento, que no se aprovecha de él" (Lope de Vega, *El piadoso veneciano*, Acto 3).

21 "el que siendo rico, por no gastar de avariento, no come … faltando va cada día el sustento" (Moreto, *El secreto entre dos amigos*, Jornada 3).

22 Thus we hear about "el ansia de mi codicia" (Zamora, *Por oír misa, y dar cebada, nunca se perdió jornada*, Acto 1). In contrast, the poor man is said to sleep well at night: "dichoso el pobre que descansa, libre de la solicitud del avariento" (Lope de Vega, *El mejor maestro, el tiempo*, Acto 2).

23 "De dormir se levanta, se levanta sediento el mísero avariento, a quien, ni el hielo, ni el calor espanta" (Lope de Vega, *El cardenal de Belén*, Acto 1); "¡Qué descanso habrá que tenga, quien temeroso imagina, ni quien codicioso piensa!" (Calderón, *En esta vida todo es verdad, y todo mentira*, Acto 1).

24 AFECTO 2: Que me ahogas, suelta, suelta.
DEMONIO: ¿A qué Avaricia, y Envidia no ahoga su misma riqueza?
(Calderón, *El indulto general*, loa for auto sacramental)

25 "Murió de una apoplexia Nineucio, el Rico avariento, blasón, que torpe ha ganado" (Tirso de Molina, *Tanto es lo demás como lo de menos*, Acto 3); "al que muere avaro y rico, compara un sabio al lechón" (Tirso de Molina, *Tanto es lo demás como lo de menos*, Acto 3).

26 "Tú que a la codicia abriste la más anchurosa puerta" (Calderón, *Los tres mayores prodigios*, Jornada 1).

27 "codicia; ordinaria enfermedad, que se pega por contagio" (Matos Fragoso, *El hijo de la piedra*, Jornada 3).

28 Lope de Vega, *El sembrar en buena tierra*, Acto 2; Moreto, *La fortuna merecida*, Jornada 1.

29 "esta Gente es miserable, y avarienta por extremo, mayormente las Mujeres" (Calderón, *La serpiente de metal*, auto sacramental).

30 One of Tirso's characters lists the luxury items by which ladies are often tempted: "de nácar, carey, marfil, con que el interés adula la codicia de las damas" (Tirso de Molina, *La villana de Vallecas*, Acto 2).

31 "En este traje verás a la codicia vestida, y siempre mujer la vida porque siempre pide más" (Lope de Vega, *Virtud, pobreza y mujer*, Acto 2); "ay mujer, que por sacar dineros de un avariento, irá al infierno" (Lope de Vega, *La boda entre dos maridos*, Acto 1).

32 Tirso de Molina, *Don Gil de las calzas verdes*, Acto 1; "amor, y juego son vicios de la edad primera, y la avaricia, y codicia de la que ya canas peina" (Lope de Vega, *Los hidalgos del aldea*, Acto 2).

33 "Dios os guarde tantos años como un avariento rico a un hijo galán, y franco" (Lope de Vega, *La mayor virtud de un rey*, Jornada 3).

34 Lope de Vega, *El Amor enamorado*, Preliminares de obra.

35 Lope de Vega, *La niña de plata*, Acto 1. The trope of the greedy old man goes back at least as far as Aristotle's *Rhetoric*, a classical text which was well known in the Renaissance. See Aristotle, *Rhetoric*, trans. W. Rhys Roberts (New York: Modern Library, 1954), book II, chapter 13, 124. On Golden Age Spanish reception of this text, see Luisa López Grigera, *Anotaciones de Quevedo a la* Retórica *de Aristóteles* (Salamanca: Cervantes, 1998).

36 Father: "mi viejo avariento padre" (Lope de Vega, *La ingratitud vengada*, Acto 1). Father-in-law: "algún avariento suegro" (Lope de Vega, *El Argel fingido y renegado de amor*, Acto 2). Uncle: "[T]engo un tío viejo y avaro, y no lo consentirá, que es mal acondicionado" (Tirso de Molina, *El mayor desengaño*, Acto 1).

37 Moreto, *La misma conciencia acusa*, Jornada 1.

38 "su hacienda cuadre a su avaricia maldita" (Tirso de Molina, *Don Gil de las calzas verdes*, Acto 2), versus "un hombre, a quien dio grande cantidad de hacienda codicia, y contratación" (Calderón, *A secreto agravio, secreta venganza*, Acto 1). The *hacienda* would later give its name to the large, sprawling ranch house emblematic of wealthy landowners on the "New" World colonial frontier.

39 "alguno intenta hacer prueba, guiado de la codicia, para heredarme la hacienda" (Moreto, *El parecido*, Jornada 2).

40 As Cruickshank explains in his recent biography of Calderón regarding laws of primogeniture in Spain, "it was the practice among *hidalgo* families to pass on the inheritance as intact as possible to the eldest son (under the system called *mayorazgo*)" (Don W. Cruickshank, *Don Pedro Calderón* [Cambridge: Cambridge University Press, 2009], 18). Cruickshank in turn cites Ana Guerrero Mayllo, *Familia y vida cotidiana de una élite de poder: los regidores madrileños en tiempos de Felipe II* (Mexico City and Madrid: Siglo XXI, 1993), 11–14. See also Bartolomé Clavero, "*Favor Maioratus, Usus Hispaniae*: Moralidad de Linaje entre Castilla y Europa," in *Marriage, Property, and Succession*, ed. Lloyd Bonfield (Berlin: Duncker and Humblot, 1992), 215–54.

41 Cervantes, *El gallardo español*, Jornada 3.

42 María de Zayas, *La inocencia castigada*, in *Tres novelas amorosas y tres desengaños amorosos*, ed. Alicia Redondo Goicoechea (Madrid: Castalia, 1989), 275–309.

43 "alguno pueda presumir que he muerto a tu hermano por codicia, y por eso darte quiero su estado" (Lope de Vega, *El Duque de Viseo*, Acto 3).

44 Thomas Middleton, *The Phoenix*, ed. John Bradbury Brooks (New York: Garland, 1980). In Middleton's play, the duke's son Phoenix pretends to travel abroad instead of dying; in actuality, his plans are to travel in disguise within his own kingdom in order to discover treachery and root out vice. Both plays are set in Italy; Middleton's ostensibly occurs in Ferrara, while Tirso's drama transpires in Milan. For performance details of Middleton's play, see Hilaire Kallendorf, *Exorcism and Its Texts: Subjectivity in Early Modern Literature of England and Spain* (University of Toronto Press, 2003), 62.

45 Tirso de Molina, *Del enemigo el primer consejo*, Jornada 1.

46 "En confianza de un tío, o de una tía avarienta, llena de hacienda, y de renta, pasa un sobrino hambre" (Lope de Vega, *El bobo del colegio*, Acto 1).

47 "si obediente te pinto, será hipócrita avariento, para que en su testamento te mejore en tercio" (Tirso de Molina, *Tanto es lo demás como lo de menos*, Acto 1).

48 Ysla Campbell, "Nostalgia y transgresión en tres comedias de Lope de Vega," in *Relaciones literarias entre España y América en los siglos XVI y XVII*, ed. Ysla Campbell (Ciudad Juárez [Mexico]: Universidad Autónoma de Ciudad Juárez, 1992), 65–87, at 67, 70.

49 The context of Weber's phrase is his pronouncement: "The fate of our times is characterized by rationalization and intellectualization and, above all, by the 'disenchantment of the world'" (Max Weber, "Science as a Vocation," in *From Max Weber: Essays*

in Sociology, ed. H.H. Gerth and C.W. Mills [New York: Oxford University Press, 1946], 155). Weber's study in turn inspired a work of this title written by Marcel Gauchet, *The Disenchantment of the World: A Political History of Religion*, trans. Oscar Burge (Princeton: Princeton University Press, 1997).

50 Matos Fragoso, *Los indicios sin culpa*, Jornada 3. The female equivalent would be "la mujer honrada tiene sin libertad el albedrío" (Guillén de Castro, *El Narciso en su opinión*, Jornada 2).

51 Council of Trent, proceedings, 24th session, chapter 9, in *The Canons and Decrees of the Sacred and Oecumenical Council of Trent*, ed. and trans. J. Waterworth (London: Dolman, 1848), 192–232, at 203–4. Regarding this decree, Elena del Río Parra reiterates: "el matrimonio concertado … conlleva el riesgo de convertir a las hijas en mercancía de interés" (Elena del Río Parra, *Cartografías de la conciencia española en la Edad de Oro* [Mexico City: Fondo de Cultura Económica, 2008], 249).

52 Lope de Vega, *De cosario a cosario*, Acto 3.

53 Lope de Vega, *San Isidro labrador de Madrid*, Acto 1.

54 Moreto, *De fuera vendrá*, Jornada 2. For a comparative view of women's control over financial resources in Italy and Portugal during this time period, see Jutta Sperling, "Dowry or Inheritance? Kinship, Property, and Women's Agency in Lisbon, Venice, and Florence (1572)," *Journal of Early Modern History* 11.3 (2007): 197–238. On the remarriage of widows in Golden Age literature, see Monique Joly, "Du remariage des veuves: à propos d'un étrange épisode du 'Guzmán,'" in *Amours légitimes, amours illégitimes en Espagne (XVIe-XVIIe siècles)* (Colloque International, Sorbonne, 3, 4, 5 octobre 1984), ed. Augustin Redondo (Paris: Sorbonne, 1985), 327–40. On widowhood in general in Spain during this time period, see Stephanie Fink de Backer, *Widowhood in Early Modern Spain: Protectors, Proprietors, and Patrons* (Leiden: Brill, 2010).

55 Calderón, *El segundo Scipión*, Jornada 3.

56 For information on costumes as financial assets of theatre companies, see Hilaire Kallendorf, "Dressed to the Sevens, or Sin in Style: Fashion Statements by the Deadly Vices in Spanish Baroque *Autos Sacramentales*," in *The Seven Deadly Sins: From Communities to Individuals*, ed. Richard Newhauser (Leiden: Brill, 2007), 145–82, at 178, especially note 113; and Peter Stallybrass, "Worn Worlds: Clothes and Identity on the Renaissance Stage," in *Subject and Object in Renaissance Culture*, ed. Margreta de Grazia, Maureen Quilligan, and Peter Stallybrass (Cambridge: Cambridge University Press, 1996), 289–320.

57 On courtiers' frequent changes of outfits, see Manuel Comba, "A Note on Fashion and Atmosphere in the Time of Lope de Vega," *Theatre Annual* 19 (1962): 46–51, at 46. On investiture ceremonies see Ann Rosalind Jones and Peter Stallybrass, *Renaissance Clothing and the Materials of Memory* (Cambridge: Cambridge University Press, 2000), 2.

58 Calderón, *El encanto sin encanto*, Jornada 2; Lope de Vega, *El Hamete de Toledo*, Acto 1; Lope de Vega, *La Historia de Tobías*, Acto 2.

59 As the servant Tadeo says to his master, the dandy Don Gutierre in *El Narciso en su opinión*:

mira que a dar te condenas
cada día cien cadenas,
cada hora cien diamantes,
o a ser en Madrid tenido
por avaro … (Guillén de Castro, *El Narciso en su opinión*, Jornada 1)

60 "mi dama le hurtó el vestido a Beatriz" (Calderón, *El escondido, y la tapada*, Jornada 3); "te trujese, señora, los dos trocados vestidos, pagándole a su codicia" (Calderón, *El encanto sin encanto*, Jornada 3).

61 "el faldellín es avaro, que es señal de que está rico" (Solís, *Eurídice, y Orfeo*, Jornada 1).

62 Tirso de Molina, *La celosa de sí misma*, Acto 1; Tirso de Molina, *Don Gil de las calzas verdes*, Acto 3.

63 Lope de Vega, *El amigo hasta la muerte*, Acto 1.

64 Lope de Vega, *El Sol parado*, Acto 1.

65 "padre tan avaro, que mi hija, te dé por la codicia de tu hacienda" (Lope de Vega, *La quinta de Florencia*, Jornada 2).

66 Lope de Vega, *La mal casada*, Acto 3.

67 "don Félix arrogante por codicia del dinero, con demostraciones tales se ha desposado con ella" (Lope de Vega, *La villana de Xetafe*, Acto 3); "El enredo es lindo; si él le prende por ladrón, o por yerno, que es lo mismo" (Calderón, *El astrólogo fingido*, Jornada 3).

68 Lope de Vega, *Los melindres de Belisa*, Acto 1.

69 Moreto, *El valiente justiciero*, Jornada 1. Greed appears onstage with Lust, for example, in Calderón's auto *La serpiente de metal*.

70 Lope de Vega, *La dama boba*, Acto 1.

71 Tirso de Molina, *Palabras y plumas*, Acto 1. In a similar vein, sometimes characters dispute the true motives of potential marriage prospects, as when Leonarda declares, "Floriano me quiere a mí," and her interlocutor Lucrecia retorts, "Codicia el talle y la renta" (Lope de Vega, *El dómine Lucas*, Acto 2).

72 "[T]he Inquisition forced penitents to wear a sanbenito or garment of reconciliation which they were then required to hang in the church with their names attached as lasting signs of their disgrace" (Kallendorf, "Dressed to the Sevens," 179). For a visual representation of the *sambenito*, see Francisco de Goya, *Por haber nacido en otra parte* (*For Being Born Somewhere Else*) (ca 1808–14), brown wash drawing, album C, number 85, Prado Museum, Madrid (figure 6).

73 "que comprar el amor, siendo infinito, es hacer simonía el apetito" (Pérez de Montalbán, *El hijo del Serafín, San Pedro de Alcántara*, Jornada 1). An alternative phrase is *buying pleasure*:

GUTIERRE: ¿Y cómo, gusto comprado,
pensáis que lo puede ser?
TADEO: Es amante mercader. (Guillén de Castro, *El Narciso en su opinión*, Jornada 1)

74 Mary Elizabeth Perry, "Deviant Insiders: Legalized Prostitutes and a Consciousness of Women in Early Modern Seville," *Comparative Studies in Society and History* 27.1 (1985): 138–58, at 139–40. See also Mary Elizabeth Perry, "Prostitutes, Penitents and Brothels," chapter 7 of *Gender and Disorder in Early Modern Seville* (Princeton: Princeton University Press, 1990). As Alain Saint-Saëns comments, there was great cognitive dissonance here between the church's message and the state's permissiveness: "People had great difficulty finding an adequate explanation for the paradox between the daily evidence of brothels and the religious message of sexual abstinence … [T]he state was considered by many in Spain to be a pimp … [E]ven the former Holy Roman Emperor Charles V, retired in the Yuste Monastery, regularly visited the local brothel long before the sexual escapades of the syphilitic '*rey pasmado*' Philip IV" (Alain Saint-Saëns, "'It is not a sin!': Making Love according to the Spaniards in Early Modern Spain," in *Sex and Love in Golden Age Spain*, ed. Alain Saint-Saëns [New Orleans: University Press of the South, 1996], 11–25, at 18, 20).

75 Rafael Carrasco, "Lazarillo on a Street Corner: What the Picaresque Novel Did Not Say about Fallen Boys," in Saint-Saëns, ed., *Sex and Love in Golden Age Spain*, 57–69, at 66.

76 Saint-Saëns, "'It is not a sin!'" Appendix I, p. 26.

77 Rojas Zorrilla, *Los áspides de Cleopatra*, Jornada 1; Lope de Vega, *La cárcel de Sevilla*, Acto 1.

78 Moreto, *Trampa adelante*, Jornada 1.

79 Lope de Vega, *Nadie se conoce*, Jornada 2.

80 Fernando de Rojas, *La Celestina: Tragicomedia de Calisto y Melibea* (1499–1502), ed. Dorothy S. Severin (Madrid: Alianza, 1981). The play ends with Melibea's suicide. On the *Celestina* as tragedy, see Edwin J. Webber, "Tragedy and Comedy in the *Celestina*," *Hispania* 35.3 (1952): 318–20.

81 "Certainly slaving activity rose significantly around the Mediterranean after 1500. What had been primarily a luxury trade that might amount to only a few hundred humans a year rapidly grew to a much broader enterprise – one might almost say a social movement – that snared some thousands of victims annually … Slaves were, for Christians as much as for Muslims, a commodity, and a particularly valuable one at that" (Robert Davis, "The Geography of Slaving in the Early Modern Mediterranean, 1500–1800," *Journal of Medieval and Early Modern Studies* 37.1 [2007]: 57–74, at 60–1).

82 Ruth Pike, *Penal Servitude in Early Modern Spain* (Madison: University of Wisconsin Press, 1983), 8–9. On Italian involvement in the Spanish slave trade, see Helen Nader, "Desperate Men, Questionable Acts: The Moral Dilemma of Italian Merchants in the Spanish Slave Trade," *Sixteenth Century Journal* 33 (2002): 401–22.

83 Davis, "The Geography of Slaving," 62–3.

84 Bernard Vincent, "The Affective Life of Slaves in the Iberian Peninsula during the Sixteenth and Seventeenth Centuries," in Saint-Saëns, ed., *Sex and Love in Golden Age Spain*, 71–8, at 71. Vincent also notes that "slaves figure alongside animals in notarial inventories" (73).

85 Calderón, *La niña de Gómez Arias*, Jornada 3. This same basic plot line had received dramatic elaboration earlier by Luis Vélez de Guevara in a play by the same name (1608–14). A similar example of buying Christians occurs in Moreto's *El esclavo de su hijo*:

MULEY: El día que vino a Argel
este Abdenaga inhumano
compré yo a aqueste Cristiano,
que cautivaron con él. (Moreto, *El esclavo de su hijo*, Jornada 2)

On the selling end of the equation, references also abound: "De ti queremos saber, pues que de Valencia viene, unos esclavos que tiene, ¿si nos los querrá vender?" (Moreto, *El esclavo de su hijo*, Jornada 2).

86 This was as true of slaves who were stolen as it was for those who were bought: "Robé a un Capitán famoso una gallarda Cristiana" (Lope de Vega, *Los esclavos libres*, Acto 2).

87 Lope de Vega, *Los melindres de Belisa*, Acto 2. Similar examples abound regarding the theft of human slaves; for example, "De concierto estan él, y sus locos amigos de robar la esclava" (Lope de Vega, *Los melindres de Belisa*, Acto 3).

88 Lope de Vega, *El casamiento en la muerte*, Jornada 3.

89 Tirso de Molina, *La celosa de sí misma*, Acto 3. The phrase in context, which is still ambiguous, appears as the following:

¿Qué Vellocino, qué gato
de avariento tabernero?
¿Qué talegón de arriero,
ni qué robo de mulato
hay que iguale a nuestra presa? (Tirso de Molina, *La celosa de sí misma*, Acto 3)

90 Much of the African slave trade for the Spanish empire was based in Portugal. On Portuguese trafficking in African slaves, see Kenneth Baxter Wolf, "The 'Moors' of West Africa and the Beginnings of the Portuguese Slave Trade," *Journal of Medieval and Renaissance Studies* 24 (1994): 449–69. On Muslim slaves during the late Middle Ages, see P.S. van Koningsveld, "Muslim Slaves and Captives in Western Europe during the Late Middle Ages," *Islam and Christian-Muslim Relations* 6.1 (1995): 5–23. On the surprising lack of visual representation for this recognized social phenomenon, see Carmen Fracchia, "(Lack of) Visual Representation of Black Slaves in Spanish

Golden Age Painting," *Journal of Iberian and Latin American Studies* 10.1 (2004): 23–34.

91 Exaggerated claims have been made that "by the end of the [fifteenth] century the Spanish were already exporting hundreds of Indians back to Europe" (Saul S. Friedman, "Marranos and New Christians: Jews as Traders in the Hispanic World," chapter 4 of *Jews and the American Slave Trade* [New Brunswick: Transaction, 2000], 49). It is alleged that Christopher Columbus himself attempted to sell 500 "New" World natives as slaves in Spain. While it is true that 500 natives were sent back to Spain in Antonio Torres's four ships in 1495, they were arguably prisoners of war captured during the indigenous people's first revolt against the Europeans in 1494. Regardless, Columbus's correspondence makes it clear that his intention for them once they reached Spain was forced servitude.

92 "Ribera advised Philip III to order the distribution of the children among 'Old Christians, officials, and citizens, obliging the children to serve them until the age of twenty-five or thirty years in exchange for food and clothing.' … Philip III … ordered the retention of morisco 'boys and girls under the age of four,' with the consent of their parents … [M]any noble families flouted the decree and retained morisco children without the parents' consent; these 'kidnappings' accounted for many of the three thousand children who remained in Valencia in 1610" (Benjamin Ehlers, *Between Christians and Moriscos: Juan de Ribera and Religious Reform in Valencia, 1568–1614* [Baltimore: Johns Hopkins University Press, 2006], 146–7; Ehlers cites relevant archival documents).

For an unforgettable depiction of the plight of *desaparecidos* and their families during Argentina's Dirty War in the 1970s, see the Argentinian movie *La historia oficial* (1985), directed by Luis Puenzo. On further parallels of the early modern slave trade with current events, see Karen E. Bravo, "Exploring the Analogy between Modern Trafficking in Humans and the Transatlantic Slave Trade," *Boston University International Law Journal* 25 (2007): 209–95.

93 Cervantes, *Los baños de Argel*, Jornada 3. Once again, this phenomenon is historically documentable. In the case of Portugal, where many Jews went initially after fleeing expulsion from Spain, "[m]any Jewish children were taken forcibly from their families and shipped to the São Thomé islands to be raised as Christians" (Esther Benbassa and Aron Rodrigue, *Sephardi Jewry: A History of the Judeo-Spanish Community, 14th–20th Centuries* [Berkeley: University of California Press, 2000], xxxviii).

94 Cervantes, *Los baños de Argel*, Jornada 2.

95 "los Moros que a robar salieron de unas fragatas" (Lope de Vega, *La firmeza en la desdicha*, Acto 3). Archbishop Juan de Ribera, the chief proponent of the Morisco expulsion, nonetheless advocated the relocation of Morisco children into Christian families: "on 27 August 1609, Ribera assured the king that he could retain those children under the age of ten or eleven, 'even if their parents ask for them: because the

parents are apostates, they should be separated from the children so that these will not fall into the same errors'" (Ehlers, *Between Christians and Moriscos*, 146). Ehlers cites archival documents at the Colegio de Corpus Christi, Archivo del Patriarca (Valencia). See also François Martínez, "Les enfants morisques de l'expulsion (1610–1621)," in *Mélanges Louis Cardaillac*, ed. Abdeljelil Temimi (Zaghouan, Tunisia: Fondation Temimi, 1995), 2:499–539.

96 Lope de Vega, *Los esclavos libres*, Acto 3. A similar scene occurs in Moreto's *El esclavo de su hijo*, but this time the father relates his feelings in more moving detail:

FLORENCIO: No digo aquí el sentimiento
que del triste hijuelo hago,
que ya quedaba oprimido
de las Alárabes manos.
HERMITAÑO: ¿Cautiváronsele entonces?
FLORENCIO: ¡Ay Padre! Estaba cercano
del mar, y así fue el primero
de los Cautivos Cristianos. (Moreto, *El esclavo de su hijo*, Jornada 1)

97 María Antonia Garcés, *Cervantes in Algiers: A Captive's Tale* (Nashville: Vanderbilt University Press, 2005), 20, 37. Garcés cites a contemporaneous account, Antonio de Sosa's *Topografía e historia general de Argel* (1612), ed. Diego de Haedo and Ignacio Bauer y Landauer, 3 vols (Madrid: Sociedad de Bibliófilos Españoles, 1927–9), 1:84. On possible religious motives (such as conversion) for capturing Christians, and the spiritual trials they endured, see George Camamis, "El sentido religioso del cautiverio," in *Estudios sobre el cautiverio en el Siglo de Oro* (Madrid: Gredos, 1977), 109–13. For a more general overview of Muslim/Christian relations as portrayed in the theatre, see *Los imperios orientales en el teatro del Siglo de Oro (Actas de las XVI Jornadas de teatro clásico, Almagro, julio de 1992)*, ed. Felipe B. Pedraza Jiménez and Rafael González Cañal (Ciudad Real: Universidad de Castilla-La Mancha, 1994).

98 "Fuele a pagar mi rescate Arnaldo capitán" (Cueva, *El degollado*, Acto 2).

99 Tirso de Molina, *La lealtad contra la envidia*, Acto 2.

100 Matos Fragoso, *Los indicios sin culpa*, Jornada 3.

101 Ellen G. Friedman, *Spanish Captives in North Africa in the Early Modern Age* (Madison: University of Wisconsin Press, 1983), 105–6.

102 Lope de Vega, *La pobreza estimada*, Jornada 3.

103 For example, Muley says to a Jew:

Vengo, amigo Maniqueo,
con este cosario Moro
a emplear cien doblas de oro

en un ganancioso empleo.
Son esclavos de rescate,
según me han dicho, y querría
usar de esta granjería,
y que entre los dos se trate. (Moreto, *El esclavo de su hijo*, Jornada 2)

104 Lope de Vega, *La pobreza estimada*, Jornada 2. The unfortunate captives who did not have wealthy relatives back in Spain found themselves in a terrible dilemma: "Pero vos no escribiréis a tierra, que no tenéis / parientes que hagan por vos" (Moreto, *El esclavo de su hijo*, Jornada 3).

105 Moreto, *El esclavo de su hijo*, Jornada 1. One curious (and certainly unanticipated) consequence of the Spanish government's hands-off policy when it came to the redemption of Spanish captives from enemy hands was that Spaniards became the most sought-after prisoners on the high seas: "The coastal fortifications, on top of lacking ammunitions and guns, were undermanned and in an advanced state of decay. To complicate matters, finding men who were willing to enlist to coastal defence was difficult because of the risky and demanding nature of the work … [T]he Crown did not establish a formal state mechanism for ransoming the thousands of Spaniards who were taken captive but rather left this to private religious orders … Although various organs of the Spanish government – among them the monarch himself – often donated large sums for the redemption of Spanish captives, no tax was levied. From the perspective of the Spanish state, ransoming was a traditional *charity* and not a legal obligation … Moreover, the Crown turned a blind eye to the enrichment of the redemptionist orders, which actually benefited from corsairing due to their intermediary function. Organized redemption made Spaniards the most sought-after captives in the Mediterranean (due to the frequency of the redemption expeditions and the high prices the captives commanded). Therefore, many critics in early modern Spain saw organized redemptionism as a major incentive for the continuance of corsair captive-taking raids and an intolerable drain of money to Spain's enemies" (Oded Löwenheim, *Predators and Parasites: Persistent Agents of Transnational Harm and Great Power Authority* [Ann Arbor: University of Michigan Press, 2007], 96).

106 Luis Vázquez Fernández, "*La redención de cautivos* de Calderón, alegorizada en la Trinidad y en la Merced," in *Calderón 2000: homenaje a Kurt Reichenberger en su 80 cumpleaños. Actas del Congreso Internacional, IV centenario del nacimiento de Calderón* (Universidad de Navarra, septiembre 2000), ed. Ignacio Arellano Ayuso, 2 vols (Pamplona: Universidad de Navarra, 2002), 2:993–1012, at 993–4.

107 Calderón, *La redención de cautivos*, auto sacramental. Vázquez Fernández confirms, "queda patente la referencia directa al fundador de la Merced" and "Aquí está clara la alusión al fundador de la Orden Trinitaria, Juan de Mata" (Vázquez Fernández, "*La redención de cautivos* de Calderón," 1003 and 1005).

108 Calderón, *La redención de cautivos*, auto sacramental. Vázquez Fernández postulates a further layer of symbolism with the Mercedarian friars exiting the doors of the church on the way to embark on their mission of mercy just as Jesus had gone out from His mother's body: "Es transparente la bisemia: claustros de su Templo = Seno de María / salida de los redentores del claustro de sus conventos e iglesias. Las fechas de 25 de marzo y 25 de diciembre = Encarnación del Redentor y Navidad, fechas precisas que aluden a las salidas de embarcación de los redentores, y su llegada a puerto, generalmente en Argel o Túnez" (Vázquez Fernández, "*La redención de cautivos* de Calderón," 1006).

109 Calderón, *La redención de cautivos*, auto sacramental.

110 Lope de Vega, *Pedro Carbonero*, Acto 1. This description of Pedro's livelihood continues:

Tantos en fin ha robado,
que ya el Rey tiene noticia
de aquesta nueva milicia,
de este fronterizo honrado. (Lope de Vega, *Pedro Carbonero*, Acto 1)

111 For an early modern Spanish treatise on the redemption of captives, see Jerónimo Gracián de la Madre de Dios (1545–1614), *Tratado de la redención de cautivos en que se cuentan las grandes miserias que padecen los cristianos que están en poder de infieles y cuán santa obra sea la de su rescate*, ed. Miguel Ángel de Bunes Ibarra and Beatriz Alonso Acero (Seville: Espuela de Plata, 2006).

112 Lope de Vega, *Los donaires de Matico*, Jornada 3.

113 Garcés, *Cervantes in Algiers*, 1. Three of Cervantes's dramatic works that were influenced by his time spent in captivity were undoubtedly *La gran Sultana*, *El gallardo español*, and *Los baños de Argel*. Another Golden Age work which thematizes this subject matter is *Los cautivos de Argel*, attributed to Lope de Vega.

114 Löwenheim, *Predators and Parasites*, 94. Garcés concurs: "the undeclared war fought by the expelled Hispano-Muslims who settled in the Maghrib, fueled by the conflicts between the two great powers that fought for control of the Mediterranean, led to the capture of thousands of Christian captives, some of whom were ransomed, while others remained in Barbary forever" (Garcés, *Cervantes in Algiers*, 16).

115 On the English pirates who were also targeting Spain during this period, see Barbara Fuchs, "Pirating Spain," chapter 6 of *Mimesis and Empire: The New World, Islam, and European Identities* (Cambridge: Cambridge University Press, 2004), 139–63.

116 "The expulsion of the Moriscos brought about a significant change in the operational patterns of the corsairs. Between 1570 and 1609, an average of 31.9 percent of the Spanish captives in Barbary were taken from Spanish shores; between 1610 and 1620, this percentage jumped to 54.2. On average, in the first half of the seventeenth century 42 percent of Spanish people kidnapped were taken from their

own shores … But on top of the raids on the Mediterranean shores, the first decades of the seventeenth century also witnessed the encroachment of the corsairs into the Atlantic … These facts indicate that the corsairs were a significant threat to the personal security of many Spanish and Habsburg civilians" (Löwenheim, *Predators and Parasites*, 95).

117 "saltaron en esta playa ochenta Moros cosarios" (Moreto, *El esclavo de su hijo*, Jornada 1).

118 Moreto, *El esclavo de su hijo*, Jornada 1.

119 Sosa, *Topografía*, 1:52; cited in Garcés, *Cervantes in Algiers*, 34.

120 Garcés, *Cervantes in Algiers*, 35. On renegades, see Bartolomé and Lucile Benassar, *Los cristianos de Alá: la fascinante aventura de los renegados* (Madrid: Nerea, 1989), and Mercedes García Arenal and Miguel Ángel de Bunes, *Los españoles y el Norte de África: siglos XV–XVIII* (Madrid: Mapfre, 1992). Two important papers on this topic have also been delivered recently: Steven Hutchinson, "Journeys across Culture and Religion: 'Renegades' in the Early Modern Mediterranean," lecture delivered at the Melbern G. Glasscock Humanities Research Center, Texas A&M University, spring 2009; and Dauril Alden, "The Ransoming of White Slaves from the Magreb: The Roles of Missionaries, Merchants, and Renegades, 16th to 18th Centuries," paper presented at the Society for Spanish and Portuguese Historical Studies, 37th annual meeting, University of Kentucky, 6–9 April 2006. On Jewish renegades, see David L. Graizbord, *Souls in Dispute: Converso Identities in Iberia and the Jewish Diaspora, 1580–1700* (Philadelphia: University of Pennsylvania Press, 2003), especially chapter 6, "On the Historical Significance of Renegades' Self Subjugation," pp. 171–8. On more general patterns of deceit and disguise like the survival strategies employed by renegades, see Barbara Fuchs, *Passing for Spain: Cervantes and the Fictions of Identity* (Urbana: University of Illinois Press, 2003), especially "Performing Inclusion," 79–86. On Spanish renegades in the context of England, see Barbara Fuchs, "Faithless Empires: Pirates, Renegadoes, and the English Nation," chapter 5 of *Mimesis and Empire*, 118–38.

121 Garcés, *Cervantes in Algiers*, 36. Garcés quotes from Sosa, *Topografía*, 1:53–4. We see the material benefits for Christians of cooperating with their Muslim captors in Moreto's *El esclavo de su hijo* when Abdenaga offers gold and pearls in exchange for a Christian captive's cooperation:

Que por Alá, en quien adoro,
si cumples mi voluntad,
juro a ley de hidalgo Moro
de ponerte en libertad,
cubierto de perlas, y oro. (Moreto, *El esclavo de su hijo*, Jornada 2)

122 Lope de Vega, *El favor agradecido*, Acto 2.

123 Moreto, *El esclavo de su hijo*, Jornada 2.

124 Lope de Vega, *El Nuevo Mundo, descubierto por Cristóbal Colón*, Acto 1. On the placement of lines criticizing Spain in the mouth of a demon, possibly in order to avoid Inquisitorial censorship, by other playwrights such as Calderón, see chapter 8, note 80 of the present work.

125 Lope de Vega, *El Nuevo Mundo, descubierto por Cristóbal Colón*, Acto 3.

126 Lope de Vega, *Arauco domado por el excelentísimo señor don García Hurtado de Mendoza*, Acto 1.

127 Moreto, *El Cristo de los milagros*, Jornada 3. A *talego* was a bag or sack made of coarse sackcloth.

128 Lope de Vega, *De cosario a cosario*, Acto 1. On the pernicious effects upon Spain of the sudden influx of gold from its "New" World colonies, see Elvira Vilches, *New World Gold: Cultural Anxiety and Monetary Disorder in Early Modern Spain* (Chicago: University of Chicago Press, 2010).

129 This name originated with the establishment of the city by Francisco Pizarro on 6 January, the Feast of the Three Kings, but later acquired connotations of great wealth, such as that brought to the Baby Jesus by the original Wise Men.

130 *Chronicle of Colonial Lima: The Diary of Josephe and Francisco Mugaburu, 1640–1697*, trans. and ed. Robert Ryal Miller (Norman: University of Oklahoma Press, 1975), 13. For literary accounts of Hapsburg Peru, see Peter T. Bradley and David Patrick Cahill, eds, *Hapsburg Peru: Images, Imagination and Memory* (Liverpool: Liverpool University Press, 2000). For a more recent historical view, see M.M. Haitin, "Late Colonial Lima: Economy and Society in an Era of Reform and Revolution" (PhD dissertation, University of California at Berkeley, 1983).

131 Lope de Vega, *Amar, servir, y esperar*, Acto 1. In this case *cebo* refers not to food, but to something which excites or foments passion.

132 Lope de Vega, *El Ruiseñor de Sevilla*, Acto 3.

133 Tirso de Molina, *La lealtad contra la envidia*, Acto 3.

134 Lope de Vega, *El honrado hermano*, Acto 3.

135 Lope de Vega, *La hermosa Alfreda*, Acto 3.

136 Lope de Vega, *El soldado amante*, Acto 3.

137 Craig Kallendorf, "Representing the Other: Ercilla's *La Araucana*, Virgil's *Aeneid*, and the New World Encounter," *Comparative Literature Studies* 40.4 (2003): 394–414.

138 The most famous of these controversies was undoubtedly the debate between Juan Ginés de Sepúlveda and Bartolomé de las Casas on whether "New" World natives had souls. The actual debate took place in Valladolid in 1550. They laid out their positions, respectively, in print in Juan Ginés de Sepúlveda, *Democrates alter de justis belli causis apud Indios* (1547), ed. and trans. Marecelino Menéndez y Pelayo as *Tratado sobre las justas causas de la guerra contra los indios* (Mexico City: Fondo de Cultura Económica, 1996), delineating what he saw as the just causes for making

war against the "Indians"; and Bartolomé de las Casas, *Brevísima Relación de la Destruyción de las Indias* (Seville: Sebastian Trugillo, 1552), which many blame for instituting a Black Legend of Spanish cruelty. For a modern study which contextualizes this debate, see Lewis Hanke, *All Mankind Is One: A Study of the Disputation between Bartolomé de las Casas and Juan Ginés de Sepúlveda in 1550 on the Intellectual and Religious Capacity of the American Indians* (DeKalb: Northern Illinois University Press, 1974).

Another, less well-known, political theorist of this time period was Juan de Solórzano Pereira (1575–1654), author of *De indiarum jure*, who tried to justify the conquest on moral and economic grounds. His treatise was written in part as a reponse to Hugo Grotius's *Mare liberum*.

At least three generations of Spanish jurists who "sought legal validation of Spain's right to the territory, labour, and mineral wealth of America" grounded their arguments in explications of Roman law (Barbara Simerka, *Discourses of Empire: Counter-Epic Literature in Early Modern Spain* [University Park: Pennsylvania State University Press, 2003], 1). Simerka also examines a previously understudied but significant discourse within Spain that undermines its justifications for imperial expansion.

139 On rationalizations used historically for the practices of pillaging and taking spoils, see *Violence in War and Peace*, ed. Nancy Scheper-Hughes and Philippe I. Bourgois (Malden, MA: Wiley-Blackwell, 2004). On efforts to extract reparations from a defeated Germany after the First World War, see Bruce Kent, *The Spoils of War: The Politics, Economics and Diplomacy of Reparations* (Oxford: Clarendon, 1989). On similar efforts to recover spoils after the Second World War, see Elizabeth Simpson, *The Spoils of War: World War II and Its Aftermath. The Loss, Reappearance and Recovery of Cultural Property* (New York: H.N. Abrams / Bard Graduate Center for Studies in the Decorative Arts, 1997).

140 Tirso de Molina, *Escarmientos para el cuerdo*, Acto 1.

141 On medieval approaches to pillaging in England, see Denys Hay, "The Division of the Spoils of War in Fourteenth-Century England," *Transactions of the Royal Historical Society* 4, fifth series (1954): 91–109.

142 Lope de Vega, *La amistad pagada*, Jornada 1. This play is normally referenced by its primary title, *La montañesa.*

143 Lope de Vega, *Los españoles en Flandes*, Acto 1.

144 Lope de Vega, *El galán Castrucho*, Acto 1. As far as religious motivation for theft, this was certainly the case during the Crusades, when all sorts of precious objects were spirited out of Jerusalem, more for their religious significance than for any commercial value: "candeleros, vinajeras, los Cálices, patenas, y hostiarios, y otras cosas robaron más crueles, que de Jerusalén cuenta la historia" (Lope de Vega, *Las pobrezas de Reinaldos*, Acto 3). However, the Crusaders often mixed their motives to cover Greed with a modicum of piety; for example, some of the holy reliquaries were

sold after they were stolen, a nefarious tradition also practised in Europe during the Middle Ages, as in "robé los monasterios, y vendí los relicarios" (Lope de Vega, *Las pobrezas de Reinaldos*, Acto 3). In Lope's *San Isidro labrador de Madrid*, the Spaniards steal plunder from the "Moors" and then place some of it as an offering in front of a statue of the Virgin Mary. Still, the play makes it clear that piety is not their only motivation for taking spoils:

ISIDRO: ¿Habéis muerto muchos Moros?
JUAN: Castigados quedan ya,
sus despojos, y tesoros,
se quedan, Isidro, acá. (Lope de Vega, *San Isidro labrador de Madrid*, Acto 1)

Later in the same play, another character reports that the spoils of war are carried triumphantly in a parade through the streets of Madrid: "por Madrid, con las banderas tendidas, entran de despojos llenos" (Lope de Vega, *San Isidro labrador de Madrid*, Acto 1).

145 "no sólo la codicia de las manos llenaréis; mas veréis tantos despojos, que aun hartéis la codicia de los ojos" (Calderón, *Ni Amor se libra de Amor*, Jornada 3).

146 "saco la fortaleza, y mientras el metal roban, que la codicia persigue" (Tirso de Molina, *La vida de Herodes*, Acto 1).

147 On the development of the "New" World mining industry by the Spanish government, see Earl J. Hamilton, "Importaciones de oro y plata americanos," in *El tesoro americano y la revolución de los precios en España, 1501–1650* (Barcelona: Ariel, 1975), 23–59. The Spanish Baroque poet Francisco de Quevedo also lamented the exploitation of the earth's natural treasure by Spanish Greed in his *silva* "A una mina," which begins with the line "Diste crédito a un pino":

¿Qué te han hecho, mortal, de estas montañas
las escondidas y ásperas entrañas?
¿Qué fatigas la tierra?
Deja en paz los secretos de la sierra
a quien defiende apenas su hondura.
¿No ves que a un mismo tiempo estás abriendo
al metal puerta, a ti la sepultura?
¿Piensas (y es un engaño vergonzoso)
que le hurtas riqueza al indio suelo?
¿Oro llamas al que es dulce desvelo
y peligro precioso,
rubia tierra, pobreza disfrazada
y ponzoña dorada?

(Francisco de Quevedo, "A una mina," no. 136 in *Poesía original completa*, ed. José Manuel Blecua [Barcelona: Planeta, 1996], 103, lines 33–45)

148 Rojas Zorrilla, *Los tres blasones de España*, Jornada 1, emphasis mine.

149 Zamora, *Judás Iscariote*, Jornada 2; Tirso de Molina, *La mujer que manda en casa*, Acto 2.

150 Lope de Vega, *El Ruiseñor de Sevilla*, Acto 1; Lope de Vega, *El Amor enamorado*, Jornada 1. This reference to Potosí reflects the Spaniards' interest in Peruvian silver mines. Also in reference to silver: "registrad en los abismos metales, que con temor de la Española avaricia, huyeron de su ambición: dadlos a cerros la plata" (Tirso de Molina, *La lealtad contra la envidia*, Acto 2). In the second half of the sixteenth century silver became the preferred metal to be mined, with demand for it surpassing even the desire for gold: "Tras el descubrimiento de las riquísimas minas de Potosí, Zacatecas y Guanajuato y la introducción del proceso de amalgama en la minería de la plata, hechos todos ellos ocurridos entre 1545 y 1558, la minería del oro fue eclipsada por la de la plata" (Hamilton, "Importaciones de oro y plata," 55).

151 "dicha es envidiar la ajena. Yo, que de Envidia, y Codicia, poseída en Mar, y Tierra, rompí minas en sus senos" (Calderón, *El indulto general*, loa for auto sacramental). Avarice, of course, is speaking.

152 Calderón, *La estatua de Prometeo*, Jornada 1.

153 For a description of the Guatemala earthquake, see Francisco Vásquez, *Breve relación de los terremotos del año de 1717 y sus ruinas* (1717), chapter 26. A transcription by J.G. Alzate of a later chapter of this treatise which nonetheless references the 1651 earthquake is available through the Asociación para el Fomento de los Estudios Históricos en Centroámerica: http://afehc-historia-centroamericana.org/?action=fi_aff&id=2408. Later earthquakes in Guatemala included the 1717 San Miguel as well as the 1773 Santa Marta earthquake, which was one of the most devastating ever to be suffered by that region. For contemporaneous accounts of these two earthquakes – originally published as *relaciones de sucesos* – see the volume *Terremotos: ruina de San Miguel, 29 de septiembre de 1717; Santa Marta, 29 de julio de 1773* (Guatemala: José de Pineda Ibarra, 1980). This volume includes Tomás de Arana's *Relación de los estragos y ruinas que ha padecido la ciudad de Santiago de Guatemala por los terremotos … en este año de 1717*; Cristóbal de Hincapié Meléndez's *Breve relación del fuego, temblores y ruina de la … ciudad de los Caballeros de Santiago de Guatemala, año de 1717*; and Agustín Gómez Carrillo's *Ruina de Santa Marta (29 de julio de 1773)*.

An eyewitness account of the Lima quake reads thus: "Saturday, the 13th of November of the year 1655, at three in the afternoon there was the greatest earthquake so far felt in the major part of Lima … I saw a large section of the island in the bay [San Lorenzo Island] break loose and fall into the ocean. The dust clouds formed were so thick that the island could not be seen for quite a while. Returning later to the town of Callao, I saw the chapel and dome of the Jesuit church of that port caved in. Many houses also collapsed, whereupon all the inhabitants moved into the plazas and the streets to sleep. It caused great damage to all the houses in Lima … In the space of three days there were more than a hundred tremors" (*Chronicle of Colonial Lima*, 36).

154 In addition to their desire for human captives, pirates were also seeking the wealth of Spanish ships; for example, a Turk in Lope's *El gallardo catalán* admits: "no pudiendo, desde aquí a la fragata hurtar, como yo pretendo, algo de oro, o la plata" (Lope de Vega, *El gallardo catalán*, Jornada 1). In another play by the same author, a pirate "viene rico, y soberbio de robar armadas de Indias" (Lope de Vega, *El favor agradecido*, Acto 3).

155 Another *silva* by Francisco de Quevedo, "Exhortación a una nave nueva al entrar en el agua," which begins with the line "¿Dónde vas, ignorante navecilla ...?", specifically warns of divine punishment for Greed by way of shipwreck:

¿Qué codicia te da reino inconstante,
siendo mejor ser árbol que madero,
y dar sombra en el monte al caminante,
que escarmiento en el agua al marinero?
[...]
¡Qué pesos te previene tan extraños
la codicia del bárbaro avariento!
[...]
No invidies a los peces sus moradas;
mira el seno del mar enriquecido
de tesoros y joyas, heredadas
del codicioso mercader perdido:
[...]
No aguardes que naufragios acrediten,
a costa de tus jarcias, mis razones ...

(Francisco de Quevedo, "Exhortación a una nave nueva al entrar en el agua," in *Poesía original completa*, ed. Blecua, 110–11, lines 13–16, 31–2, 49–52, and 61–2)

156 "dio el mar noticia del peligro a que pone la codicia" (Tirso de Molina, *La santa Juana*, Acto 1).

157 Lope de Vega, *De cosario a cosario*, Acto 1.

158 Cervantes, *La entretenida*, Jornada 2.

159 Alarcón, *Las paredes oyen*, Acto 1.

160 Tirso de Molina, *El amor, y el amistad*, Jornada 1.

161 Tirso de Molina, *El mayor desengaño*, Acto 2.

162 Moreto, *El esclavo de su hijo*, Jornada 2.

163 Tirso de Molina, *Escarmientos para el cuerdo*, Acto 1.

164 "y corales rojos, de jaeces de plata, y filigrana, la codicia que brinda por los ojos, en la riqueza bárbara Africana" (Lope de Vega, *La locura por la honra*, Acto 1); "la codicia viene del oro Antártico y plata" (Lope de Vega, *Arauco domado por el excelentísimo señor don García Hurtado de Mendoza*, Acto 2).

165 Calderón, *La nave del mercader*, auto sacramental.

166 The Merchant in this drama does not intend to keep the profit for himself, but instead to use it to ransom captive Man, his brother. Indeed, in a supreme irony, this Merchant turns out to be a type of Christ, who uses His abundant good credit to pay off Man's heavy debts. The fact that the audience might have expected the Merchant to be unscrupulous only adds to their surprise at the end when His true identity is revealed. This elaborate allegory has the Merchant's ship embark at the port of Ostia (meant to symbolize the Host, or wafer, of the Eucharist) and disembark at Cáliz (representing the Chalice containing the communion wine), as opposed to Cádiz, one of Spain's busiest ports:

La Nave del Mercader,
que de su Trigo cargada,
embarcado en Puerto de Ostia,
en Cáliz se desembarca;
a Primero, y Segundo Adán restaura,
en los dos reparando deuda, y fianza.

(Calderón, *La nave del mercader*, auto sacramental)

The ship's cargo, grain, is supremely suitable for Christ to carry as the Bread of Life. Jesus Himself is also likened to a grain of wheat in John 12:24–5: "I say to you, unless the grain of wheat falling into the ground die, Itself remaineth alone. But if it die it bringeth forth much fruit."

167 On Jewish merchants see, for example, "este codicioso Hebreo" (Moreto, *El esclavo de su hijo*, Jornada 2). This particular Jewish character trades in slaves, not merchandise. On actual Jewish seafaring merchants, see Benjamin Arbel, "Jewish Shipowners in the Early Modern Eastern Mediterranean," in *Trading Nations: Jews and Venetians in the Early Modern Eastern Mediterranean* (Leiden: Brill, 1995), 169–84. Arbel attributes the rise of Jewish shipowning specifically to the influx of Jewish immigrants from Spain and Portugal (184). He also notes incidentally that Barabas of Malta, the rich Jewish shipowner in Christopher Marlowe's (1564–93) *The Jew of Malta*, appears to be the earliest depiction of a Jewish shipowner in modern literature (182). Venetian merchants were also deemed avaricious: "cierto Veneciano, de cuya avarienta mano procurarla no conviene" (Lope de Vega, *El caballero del Milagro*, Acto 2). On moneylenders, see *Coin and Conscience: Popular Views of Money, Credit, and Speculation, Sixteenth through Nineteenth Centuries* (Catalog of an Exhibition of Prints from the Bleichroeder Collection, Kress Library of Business and Economics) (Cambridge: Baker Library / Harvard Business School, 1986). Yaron Brook explains how Genoa was uniquely suited to meet the financial needs of businessmen during the Renaissance: "The Italian city of Genoa … had a relatively relaxed attitude toward usury, and moneylenders created

many ways to circumvent the existing prohibitions. It was clear to the city's leaders that the financial activities of its merchants were crucial to Genoa's prosperity, and the local courts regularly turned a blind eye to the usurious activities of its merchants and bankers. Although the Church often complained about these activities, Genoa's political importance prevented the Church from acting against the city" (Yaron Brook, "The Morality of Moneylending: A Short History," *The Objective Standard: A Journal of Culture and Politics* 2.3 [2007]: 9–45). Lope de Vega shows an awareness of Genoa's reputation as a financial centre in his (meant to be paradoxical) title *El Genovés liberal.*

168 Calderón, *El tesoro escondido*, auto sacramental.

169 Calderón, *El veneno, y la triaca*, loa for auto sacramental.

170 "La Avaricia, con Barba" (Calderón, *El nuevo hospicio de pobres*, auto sacramental, Preliminares de obra). As Cyrus Adler notes, "The modern Oriental cultivates his Beard as the sign and ornament of manhood: he swears by his Beard, touching it. The sentiment seems to have been the same in Biblical times. According to the Egyptian and Assyrian monuments, all western Semites wore a full, round Beard, evidencing great care … To mutilate the Beard of another by cutting or shaving is, consequently, considered a great disgrace … Mourners bring a sacrifice by disfiguring themselves in this way … The shaving prescribed for lepers seems intended to call public attention to this dreaded disease" (Cyrus Adler, W. Max Muller, and Louis Ginzberg, "Beard," in the *Jewish Encyclopedia*, http://www.jewishencyclopedia.com). The following contemporaneous paintings by Rembrandt van Rijn give us some idea of how bearded Jews might have looked in the Spanish Netherlands at this time: *Head of a Jew with Scanty Brown Beard and a Dark Cap* (1645), London, Earl of Ellesmere's collection, Bridgewaterhouse; *Bust of a Bearded Jew* (1646), England, Earl Cowper's collection, Panshanger; *Head of a Young Jew with a Red Beard* (1655), Philadelphia, John G. Johnson's collection; and *Rabbi with Black Beard* (1657), London, National Gallery. See also figure 7 of the present volume, *Bust of a Young Jew* (Kimbell Art Museum, Fort Worth, Texas). Rembrandt was known to have lived near the Jewish quarter in Amsterdam. On later relaxations of this fairly rigid fashion code, see Elliott Horowitz, "The Early Eighteenth Century Confronts the Beard: Kabbalah and Jewish Self-Fashioning," *Jewish History* 8.1–2 (1994): 95–115.

171 On atheists and Jews, see "es Ateista, y ladrón, con su punta de Judío" (Rojas Zorrilla, *Los trabajos de Tobías*, Jornada 2). Jews are associated with theft in the lines "sotil ladrón sois Jodío" (Tirso de Molina, *La gallega Mari Hernández*, Acto 1). I have not corrected the errors in this Spanish because it is important to preserve the flavour of the dialect, particularly the pun on *joder*.

172 See Donatella Calabi, "The 'City of the Jews,'" in *The Jews of Early Modern Venice*, ed. Robert C. Davis and Benjamin Ravid (Baltimore: Johns Hopkins University Press, 2001), 31–52.

173 William Shakespeare, *The Merchant of Venice*, in *The Riverside Shakespeare*, ed. G. Blakemore Evans (Boston: Houghton Mifflin, 1974), 3.1.51–8.

174 See Davis and Ravid, eds, *The Jews of Early Modern Venice*, and Benbassa and Rodrigue, *Sephardi Jewry*, xliv.

175 On bibliographical evidence for a community of Spanish Jews living in Venice, see Hilaire Kallendorf, "*Celestina* in Venice: Piety, Pornography, *Poligrafi*," *Celestinesca* 27 (2003): 75–106. Benjamin Arbel notes that in 1589 the Venetian Senate granted a special charter to Jewish merchants, referring to them explicitly as "Levantini, Spagnoli et altri" (Levantines, Spaniards, and others) (Arbel, "Jewish Shipowners," 178). For the text of the charter Arbel cites B. Ravid, "The First Charter of the Jewish Merchants of Venice, 1589," *Association of Jewish Studies Review* 1 (1976): 187–222.

176 Brian Pullan, "Jewish Banks and Monti di Pietà," in Davis and Ravid, eds, *The Jews of Early Modern Venice*, 53–72, at 54–5.

177 Tirso de Molina, *Todo es dar en una cosa*, Acto 3. On usury viewed as Greed in the Hispanic world, see Bartolomé Clavero, *Usura: del uso económico de la religión en la historia* (Madrid: Tecnos / Fundación Cultural Enrique Luño Peña, 1984). In a memorable phrase from a different essay, Clavero calls usury a crime against time, "un delito contra el tiempo" (Bartolomé Clavero, "Delito y pecado: noción y escala de transgresiones," in *Sexo barroco y otras transgresiones premodernas*, ed. Francisco Tomás y Valiente et al. [Madrid: Alianza Universidad, 1990], 57–89, at 81).

178 Pullan, "Jewish Banks," 54. See also Reinhold C. Mueller and Frederic C. Lane, *The Venetian Money Market: Banks, Panics, and the Public Debt, 1200–1500*, vol. 2 (Baltimore: Johns Hopkins University Press, 1997).

179 "Certainly, Jews were not the only ones to carry out such an occupation at this time, but they so dominated the field in the imagination of Christian observers that from the tenth century on, the historical sources contain phrases which virtually equate Jews with business activity … In the midst of the theoretical justification of commerce as a necessary and useful activity, the distrust of merchants as agents of avarice, inherited from Late Antiquity, could not be wholly suppressed" (Richard Newhauser, *The Early History of Greed: The Sin of Avarice in Early Medieval Thought and Literature* [Cambridge: Cambridge University Press, 2000], 126).

180 Rojas Zorrilla, *El profeta falso Mahoma*, Jornada 3; "la Avaricia, con un Estandarte blanco, y en él las cinco Llagas" (Calderón, *El año santo en Madrid*, auto sacramental).

181 Zamora, *Judás Iscariote*, Jornada 2. The gospel account appears in Matthew 26:15.

182 "(¡ay de mí!) la avaricia, infiel calentura interna del alma" (Zamora, *Judás Iscariote*, Jornada 3).

183 "Quien tener me permitió avaricia que me ciegue" (Zamora, *Judás Iscariote*, Jornada 3); "si vio mi avaricia, y me dió el oro, perderme quiso" (Zamora, *Judás Iscariote*, Jornada 3).

184 "De Herodes cuenta la codicia misma Josefo, y historiador de tanto crédito" (Lope de Vega, *El villano en su rincón*, Acto 1).

185 Guillén de Castro, *El mejor esposo*, Jornada 2.

186 For by-now-classic theoretical approaches to the problem of imaginary geography, see Edward Said, *Orientalism* (New York: Vintage, 1994), and Edward Said, *Culture and Imperialism* (New York: Vintage, 1993). As Said notes in a representative essay, "desde Heródoto existe una geografía imaginaria – que se renueva de manera constante – que traza una línea divisoria entre Europa y Oriente sobre la base de la *diferencia*" (Edward Said, "Cultura, identidad e historia," in *Teoría de la cultura: un mapa de la cuestión*, ed. Gerhart Schröder and Helga Breuninger [Buenos Aires: Fondo de Cultura Económica, 2005], 37–54, at 40). On concrete woodcut depictions of imagined geographies in early printed books (including the assertion that "topographical views of near and distant places became so popular that publishers provided them whether they knew what some of the places looked like or not"), see Charles Talbot, "Topography as Landscape in Early Printed Books," in *The Early Illustrated Book: Essays in Honour of Lessing J. Rosenwald*, ed. Sandra Hindman (Washington, DC: Library of Congress, 1982), 105–16, at 105.

187 Benbassa and Rodrigue, *Sephardi Jewry*, xxxvi–xxxvii.

188 Friedman, *Jews and the American Slave Trade*, 52, 51.

189 Recent bibliography on the Sephardic diaspora includes Francesca Trivellato, *The Familiarity of Strangers: The Sephardic Diaspora, Livorno, and Cross-Cultural Trade in the Early Modern Period* (New Haven: Yale University Press, 2009); Renée Levine Melammed, *A Question of Identity: Iberian Conversos in Historical Perspective* (Oxford: Oxford University Press, 2004); Yedida Kalfon Stillman and Norman A. Stillman, eds, *From Iberia to Diaspora: Studies in Sephardic History and Culture* (Leiden: Brill, 1999); and Paloma Díaz Más, *Sephardim: The Jews from Spain* (Chicago: University of Chicago Press, 1992).

190 Benbassa and Rodrigue, *Sephardi Jewry*, xviii. Benbassa and Rodrigue explain: "The Jews obtained protection and privileges, in return for which the king was assured a steady source of revenue in the form of taxes from them" (Benbassa and Rodrigue, *Sephardi Jewry*, xxvii).

191 Sebastián de Covarrubias Orozco, "Judío," in *Tesoro de la lengua castellana o española* (1611), ed. Felipe C.R. Maldonado, rev. Manuel Camarero (Madrid: Castalia, 1995), 688. For more on the economic and cultural impact upon Spain of the Jews' departure, see Henry Kamen, "La expulsión de los judíos y la decadencia de España," in *Judíos, sefarditas, conversos: la expulsión de 1492 y sus consecuencias (Ponencias del congreso internacional celebrado en Nueva York en noviembre de 1992)*, ed. Ángel Alcalá (Valladolid: Ámbito, 1995), 420–33.

192 "Jews were employed as tax farmers and tax collectors. Abraham Seneor and Isaac Abravanel were particularly important in this regard; in fact, Isaac Abravanel was involved in raising funds for the conquest of Granada" (Benbassa and Rodrigue,

Sephardi Jewry, xxxvi). Don Isaac Abravanel also served as finance minister for King João II of Portugal.

193 However, the argument has also been made that it was actually confiscated Jewish wealth that funded the "New" World enterprise: "Spanish Jews paid for the voyages of Columbus not with the proffer of gemstones to Isabella, but through the confiscation of their wealth, seven million maravedi, five times the amount needed to underwrite exploration of the New World" (Friedman, *Jews and the American Slave Trade*, 62).

194 Friedman, *Jews and the American Slave Trade*, 52.

195 "In 1492 King John II (r. 1481–95) allowed wealthy Jewish families from Spain to purchase the right to reside permanently in Portugal. The same privilege was granted to economically useful craftsmen … The extraordinary efflorescence of trade with which Jews were involved between Italy and the Ottoman Empire, as well as farther afield, had made the Jewish presence lucrative for those rulers who wanted to expand their economic activities in their own realms" (Benbassa and Rodrigue, *Sephardi Jewry*, xxxviii, xliii).

196 An interesting coda to this scenario is the question of where the Spanish Jews (i.e., Sephardim) went and what they did after the expulsion: "[T]he Sephardim of Hamburg were among the founders of the Hamburg Bank in 1619, a major financial institution of northern Europe, maintaining forty-six different accounts there by 1623. The number of Sephardic brokers in the city was, percentagewise, even higher than in Amsterdam. They were also very active in maritime insurance and in the stock exchange. The Teixeiras, the Nunes de Costas, the Abensurs, and the Mussaphias were major figures not only in Hamburg but also in the larger European financial scene. There was even a momentary panic at the European stock exchanges when Duarte de Silva, the head of a very important Hamburg family dealing in securities and brokerage, was arrested by the Inquisition on a visit to Spain as a result of a denunciation" (Benbassa and Rodrigue, *Sephardi Jewry*, 1).

Even Golden Age specialists such as George Mariscal, who wish to distance themselves from pronouncements on Spain's decline, must admit of the "so-called crisis period that began near the end of Philip II's reign (1580s and 1590s) and continued throughout that of Philip III" that "there can be no doubt that a complicated network of economic shifts (high inflation, epidemics, royal bankruptcies, decreased industrial production) and political reversals (the armadas against England, the failed attempt at dynastic marriage with the English in 1623) took place in this period" (George Mariscal, "Symbolic Capital in the *Comedia*," *Renaissance Drama* 21 [1990]: 143–69, at 145).

197 Anne J. Cruz, *Discourses of Poverty: Social Reform and the Picaresque Novel in Early Modern Spain* (Toronto: University of Toronto Press, 1999), 40. See especially chapter 2, "The Poor in Spain: Confinement and Control," 39–74.

198 Now held in the Musées Royaux des Beaux-Arts de Belgique, Brussels.

199 Cruz, *Discourses of Poverty*, 42–3.

200 Calderón, *El nuevo hospicio de pobres*, auto sacramental.

201 Calderón, *El primer refugio del hombre, y probática piscina*, auto sacramental.

202 "Este bolsillo toma, porque la codicia satisfagas en los Puertos, para que nadie te impida" (Moreto, *El caballero del Sacramento*, Jornada 2). Seville was the main port of entry in Spain for wealth arriving from the "New" World colonies to be injected into the Spanish economy: "Es en Sevilla donde se reciben los metales americanos y donde se concentra el comercio y la navegación con el Nuevo Mundo" (Campbell, "Nostalgia y transgresión," 82). The centrality of Seville to the "New" World enterprise is still visible in the presence there of the Archivo General de Indias.

203 "Sale la Avaricia vestida de Villano" (Calderón, *La primer flor de el Carmelo*, auto sacramental).

204 Lope de Vega, *El mejor maestro, el tiempo*, Acto 2.

205 "Allí trae sus macetas codicioso el labrador, de Leganés, o Xetafe, Fuenlabrada, o Alcorcón" (Lope de Vega, *Los ramilletes de Madrid*, Acto 1). The proper names mentioned are small villages in Spain.

206 Such was the case during the Revolt of the Comuneros (1520–1), in which the citizens of Castile participated in an uprising against the Emperor Charles V. They were so successful that at one point they temporarily controlled the cities of Valladolid, Tordesillas, and Toledo.

207 Calderón, *El año santo en Madrid*, auto sacramental. On courtly ambitions of Golden Age playwrights, see Margaret Rich Greer, *The Play of Power: Mythological Court Dramas of Calderón de la Barca* (Princeton: Princeton University Press, 1991), which studies a genre of masque written exclusively for performance at court. As Greer points out, Lope de Vega's relative independence as the first writer to live by the fruits of his pen was the exception, not the rule: "the prevailing pattern was still dependence of artists on the patronage of the wealthy and the powerful" (5). Writers such as Calderón de la Barca and Francisco de Quevedo prided themselves on the "Don" before their names, as indicated by the title of Don Cruickshank's recent biography *Don Pedro Calderón* (Cambridge: Cambridge University Press, 2009). A photograph of Quevedo's autograph signature, signed "Don Francisco de Quevedo," is reproduced in Hilaire Kallendorf and Craig Kallendorf, "Conversations with the Dead: Quevedo and Statius, Annotation and Imitation," *Journal of the Warburg and Courtauld Institutes* 63 (2000): 131–68, along with some of his handwritten annotations to one of the books he owned. He, like Calderón de la Barca, further enjoyed the social status that came with being a Caballero del Orden de Santiago (Knight of the Order of Santiago), as evidenced by the fact that he posed for his portrait wearing the Order's traditional garb. We also see class consciousness revealed in such didactic lines as "No es caballero quien es ladrón" (Lope de Vega, *El alcalde mayor*, Acto 3) or "que mal que asienta en un noble el oficio de ladrón" (Lope de Vega, *El ingrato arrepentido*, Acto 3).

208 Lope de Vega, *La amistad pagada*, Jornada 3.

209 Witness such lines as, "un criado, ladrón de casa" (Calderón, *La señora, y la criada*, Jornada 1); "La codicia del criado me logra el intento mío" (Moreto, *El licenciado Vidriera*, Jornada 3); and "es ladrona una criada" (Calderón, *No hay cosa como callar*, Jornada 3). For some reason, theft by servants was considered preferable to theft by roadside bandits: "mejor en toda ocasión, el doméstico ladrón, que el que por la calle pasa" (Lope de Vega, *El príncipe perfecto, parte primera*, Acto 2). Perhaps at least the victims of petty theft within the walls of their own homes did not have to worry about being physically injured by unknown attackers.

210 The tavern-keeper is called either "avariento tabernero" (Tirso de Molina, *La celosa de sí misma*, Acto 3) or "aquel ladrón tabernero" (Moreto, *El caballero del Sacramento*, Jornada 1).

211 Tirso de Molina, *Antona García*, Acto 3. See Cervantes, *El ingenioso hidalgo don Quijote de la Mancha*, ed. Luis Andrés Murillo, 2 vols (Madrid: Castalia, 1987), part I, chapter 16: "De lo que le sucedió al ingenioso hidalgo en la venta que él imaginaba ser castillo."

212 Now held at the Museum Boijmans van Beuningen, Rotterdam.

213 Tirso de Molina, *La venta*, Acto 1.

214 Lope de Vega, *Bamba*, Jornada 1.

215 Richard Pym, *The Gypsies of Early Modern Spain* (New York: Palgrave Macmillan, 2007), 58–9, 99. Pym cites relevant archival documents.

216 Calderón, *El primer refugio del hombre, y probática piscina*, auto sacramental.

217 Calderón, *No hay instante sin milagro*, auto sacramental.

218 Calderón, *La nave del mercader*, auto sacramental. These lines are spoken by a Demon dressed as a Bandit. The traveller he accosts is Man.

219 "Dos valientes salteadores, por un hurto que habían hecho, riñeron, que cada cual lo quiso llevar" (Alarcón, *Las paredes oyen*, Acto 2).

220 "Habiendo delitos del poco culto primero, del mucho terror después, después del avaro afecto, en los términos de Roma, en Real camino" (Calderón, *A María el corazón*, auto sacramental). On early modern European sites of pilgrimage, see Philippe Boutry and Dominique Julia, eds, *Pèlerins et pèlerinages dans l'Europe moderne (Actes de la table ronde organisée para le Département d'histoire et civilisation de l'Institut universitaire européen de Florence et l'École française de Rome, Rome, 4–5 juin 1993)* (Rome: École Française, 2000). Early modern pilgrims might even venture outside of Europe, as we see in F. Thomas Noonan, *The Road to Jerusalem: Pilgrimage and Travel in the Age of Discovery* (Philadelphia: University of Pennsylvania Press, 2007); this book covers other pilgrimage sites as well.

221 For an example of a reference to pilgrims, see "no nueva es en mi bandida saña de robar los Peregrinos" (Calderón, *A María el corazón*, auto sacramental). A passage relating such pilgrims to the Good Samaritan is the following: "el Errado Peregrino de la Parábola, a quien robaron en un camino" (Calderón, *A tu próximo como a ti*, Acto 1).

222 "podrás fingiendo una pequeña herida, decir que te robaron salteadores, que haberlos en el monte no lo ignores" (Lope de Vega, *El leal criado*, Acto 2). Yet another common motif is for *comedia* characters to assume that anyone wearing a mask must be a roadside robber: "con máscara, y sin blanca, yo imagino, que vienes a robar algún camino" (Rojas Zorrilla, *Obligados, y ofendidos*, Jornada 3). However, an urban thief was also expected to wear a disguise: "o de la Noche valido, o el disfraz, vendría el Ladrón a escalar su Domicilio" (Calderón, *A tu próximo como a ti*, Acto 1). "Moorish" costume was typically associated with theft or banditry: "voy a vestirme de Moro para robar el tesoro, que me puede enriquecer" (Lope de Vega, *El conde Fernán González*, Acto 1).

223 Pym, *Gypsies of Early Modern Spain*, 99–100. Pym cites relevant archival documents.

224 Juan de Quiñones de Benavente, *Discurso contra los gitanos* (Madrid: Juan Gonza, 1631), 1–23.

225 Tirso de Molina, *Santo, y sastre*, Acto 3. This equivalency is repeated in the line, "Yo Gitano, yo ladrón" (Lope de Vega, *El arenal de Sevilla*, Acto 3).

226 Solís, *La gitanilla de Madrid*, Jornada 3. For a study comparing this play to the *novela ejemplar* by Cervantes with a similar title from which the *comedia* was derived, see J. Romera Castillo, "De cómo Cervantes y Antonio de Solís construyeron sus 'Gitanillas' (Notas sobre la intervención de los 'actores')," in *Lenguaje, ideología y organización textual en las novelas ejemplares* (Madrid/Toulouse: Universidad Complutense/Université de Toulouse-Le Mirail, 1983), 145–59. On the drama of Antonio de Solís, see Daniel Ernest Martell, *The Dramas of Don Antonio de Solís y Rivadeneyra* (Philadelphia: International Printing Company, 1902). This play is discussed on pp. 10–14.

227 Solís, *La gitanilla de Madrid*, Jornada 3. A similar scenario unfolds in a play by Cervantes: "Hanle dicho a la muchacha, que un ladrón Gitano hurtóla" and "Una gitana hurtada la trujo" (Cervantes, *Pedro de Urdemalas*, Jornada 3, Jornada 1).

228 Pérez de Montalbán, *A lo hecho no hay remedio, y príncipe de los montes*, Preliminares de obra; Calderón, *Agradecer, y no amar*, Preliminares de obra.

229 Calderón, *A María el corazón*, auto sacramental, Preliminares de obra.

230 Lope de Vega, *El Amor enamorado*, Preliminares de obra, emphasis mine.

231 Tirso de Molina, *La celosa de sí misma*, Acto 1.

232 Tirso de Molina, *El melancólico*, Acto 2; Lope de Vega, *Obras son amores*, Acto 3. Sometimes the phrase appears in the singular: "Ni codiciar bien ajeno" (Calderón, *El año santo de Roma*, auto sacramental).

233 Calderón, *A Dios por razón de Estado*, auto sacramental.

3. Lusty Lads and Luscious Ladies

1 Lope de Vega, *La campana de Aragón*, Acto 3; Raymond Williams, "Dominant, Residual, and Emergent," in *Marxism in Literature* (Oxford: Oxford University Press, 1977), 121–7, at 123–4.

2 Calderón, *El laberinto del mundo*, Acto 1. The reference of course is to Saint John the Evangelist, who wrote the book of Revelation on the Isle of Patmos.

3 The stage directions for a representative *auto sacramental* read, "en el segundo Carro una Torre dorada, y en su Capitel la Lascivia, con una Copa dorada en la Mano" (Calderón, *El año santo de Roma*, auto sacramental).

4 Calderón, *El año santo en Madrid*, auto sacramental.

5 In Calderón's great market of the world, it is no accident that Vice sells beds: "Allí vende el Vicio, Camas" (Calderón, *El gran mercado del mundo*, loa for auto sacramental).

6 Lope de Vega, *Las almenas de Toro*, Acto 3; Tirso de Molina, *Santo, y sastre*, Acto 3.

7 Lope de Vega, *Lo que hay que fiar del mundo*, Acto 2. It is fascinating to juxtapose these lines against contemporaneous admonitions by moralists such as Juan Estebán de la Torre about women's lascivious clothing (Juan Estebán de la Torre, *La pecadora santa: vida de Santa María Magdalena. Historia panegírica, política y moral* [Calatayud: Josef Mola, 1688], 26–7; cited in Stephen H. Haliczer, "Sexuality and Repression in Counter-Reformation Spain," in *Sex and Love in Golden Age Spain*, ed. Alain Saint-Saëns [New Orleans: University Press of the South, 1996], 81–93, at 92n37). As Haliczer explains, "Exposing their breasts in low-cut dresses and wearing their hair in a provocative manner, these women turn the houses of God into 'brothels for the soul'" (92).

8 "la Lascivia ufana en sus rizos vierta" (Calderón, *El indulto general*, loa for auto sacramental).

9 Pérez de Montalbán, *El hijo del Serafín, San Pedro de Alcántara*, Jornada 1.

10 Middlebrook borrows the term *courtierization* from Norbert Elias to describe this "joined crisis in Spanish masculine identity and in poetry" (Leah Middlebrook, *Imperial Lyric: New Poetry and New Subjects in Early Modern Spain* [University Park: Pennsylvania State University Press, 2009], 17 and 10. Middlebrook cites Norbert Elias, *Power and Civility: The Civilizing Process*, trans. Edmund Jephcott, vol. 2 [New York: Pantheon, 1982], 104–16, 258–69). For another female scholar's view of this early modern crisis in masculinity, see Elizabeth Lehfeldt, "Ideal Men: Masculinity and Decline in Seventeenth-Century Spain," *Renaissance Quarterly* 61.2 (2008): 463–94.

11 Lope de Vega, *El esclavo de Roma*, Acto 1.

12 "The Spaniards did not bathe themselves very frequently and 'remained astonished' by the frequency with which the Taínos did so … One reason for their astonishment was that 'the Spanish … had never supported regular bathing, public or otherwise, associating it with Islam and thus regarding it as a mere cover for … sexual promiscuity'" (Hilaire Kallendorf, "A Myth Rejected: The Noble Savage in Dominican Dystopia," *Journal of Latin American Studies* 27 [1995]: 449–70, at 465–6). In this passage I cite David E. Stannard, *American Holocaust: Columbus and the Conquest of the New World* (Oxford: Oxford University Press, 1992), 161.

13 Tirso de Molina, *El Aquiles*, Acto 3.

14 The principal study of feminized male actors and theatrical characters to be published in recent years is Sidney Donnell's *Feminizing the Enemy: Imperial Spain, Transvestite Drama, and the Crisis of Masculinity* (Lewisburg: Bucknell University Press, 2003). On a much more limited scale, Sherry Velasco has published a study on the trope of pregnant men (*Male Delivery: Reproduction, Effeminacy, and Pregnant Men in Early Modern Spain* [Nashville: Vanderbilt University Press, 2006]). To this scholarly trend may be added Julio González-Ruiz, *Amistades peligrosas: el discurso homoerótico en el teatro de Lope de Vega* (New York: Peter Lang, 2009). As a counterpoint to these arguments being made about womanly men, see José Reinaldo Cartagena Calderón, *Masculinidades en obras: el drama de la hombría en la España imperial* (Newark, DE: Juan de la Cuesta, 2008). This work, which sees in Lope de Vega's *comedias* a reconquest of masculinity, provides a more balanced picture of what was admittedly a complex gender landscape.

15 Calderón, *A tu próximo como a ti*, Acto 1.

16 Calderón, *El indulto general*, loa for auto sacramental.

17 Lope de Vega, *Adonis, y Venus*, Acto 1.

18 Rojas Zorrilla, *Los trabajos de Tobías*, Jornada 1.

19 "el lascivo, a que dé en malas hierbas verdores, que hermosos, al parecer, son luego adelfas, y hortigas" (Calderón, *La viña del Señor*, auto sacramental).

20 Calderón, *El nuevo hospicio de pobres*, auto sacramental. In another *auto* by Calderón, Lust appears as a villager: "Sale la Lascivia de Villana, con cántaro" (Calderón, *El primer refugio del hombre, y probática piscina*, auto sacramental).

21 "que a la primera jornada la nave adúltera abordes" (Tirso de Molina, *Escarmientos para el cuerdo*, Acto 3); "Carlos, anegado en las ilícitas ondas de lascivo amor profano" (Zamora, *La poncella de Orleans*, Jornada 3).

22 Calderón, *Amar, y ser amado, y divina Philotea*, auto sacramental.

23 "la amarga adelfa de la Lascivia" (Calderón, *No hay instante sin milagro*, auto sacramental). The bitter smell described is of the oleander tree.

24 Calderón, *La nave del mercader*, auto sacramental; Calderón, *A tu próximo como a ti*, Acto 1.

25 Calderón, *Amar, y ser amado, y divina Philotea*, auto sacramental.

26 Rape was an all-too-common occurrence in Golden Age Spain, as evidenced by lawsuits filed in the Chamber of Vizcaya at the Royal Chancery of Valladolid. For the period from 1500 to 1700, at least 220 cases of *estupro* or rape/seduction appear in these court documents (Renato Barahona, "Courtship, Seduction and Abandonment in Early Modern Spain: The Example of Vizcaya, 1500–1700," in Saint-Saëns, ed., *Sex and Love in Golden Age Spain*, 43–55, at 46). *Estupro* is defined here as "the loss of virginity in unmarried women," which could involve forced sexual intercourse but could also include breach of promise to marry (45n12).

Moving from the archive to the repertoire, a horrific case of rape and abduction occurs in Lope de Vega's *La quinta de Florencia*. In this play, the noble César is in love with the *campesina* Laura, who rejects him. His friends propose that he rape her and then give her money later. He abducts, rapes, and then holds her prisoner. When she is freed and appeals to the Duke, he wants to cut off César's head and those of his friends. But at the suggestion of her father – and with her acquiescence – the Duke forces him to marry her instead, giving her and her father each a large dowry.

Perhaps the most famous instance of sexual violation in the entire *comedia* corpus occurs in Calderón's world literature classic *La vida es sueño*. In this play, Rosaura is seduced by Astolfo, who then abandons her for being beneath his noble rank. When he finds out about this stain on the family's honour, her father Clotaldo delivers a soliloquy (in Jornada 1) in which he debates whether to kill his own daughter. Ultimately he does not do so, but the fact that the possibility is raised as a serious option shows just how far honour was prioritized over paternal affection. For further discussion of this compelling scene, see Hilaire Kallendorf, "'¿Qué he de hacer?': The *Comedia* as Casuistry," *Romanic Review* 95.3 (2004): 327–59, at 340–3.

27 "este amor es sodomía" (Moreto, *El poder de la amistad*, Jornada 1). On early modern sodomy in the Hispanic world, see Federico Garza Carvajal, *Butterflies Will Burn: Prosecuting Sodomites in Early Modern Spain and Mexico* (Austin: University of Texas Press, 2003). A total of 445 cases of sodomy were tried by the Inquisitorial tribunals of Aragon from the years 1570 to 1630 (Haliczer, "Sexuality and Repression," 84). From 1566 to 1620, men executed for sodomy numbered 2 in Barcelona, 17 in Valencia, and 34 in Zaragoza (David Greenberg, *The Construction of Homosexuality* [Chicago: University of Chicago Press, 1988], 311–12). For a detailed book-length study of the Valencian Tribunal, see Rafael Carrasco, *Inquisición y represión sexual en Valencia: historia de los sodomitas (1565–1785)* (Barcelona: Laertes, 1985).

28 "válgame Dios, ¿qué es aquesto? ¿Si es amor éste de incesto? Con varias sospechas lucho" (Cervantes, *La entretenida*, Jornada 1). The most famous incest scene in the *comedia* corpus may well occur in the first act of Calderón's *Los cabellos de Absalón*, in which Amon rapes his half-sister Tamar. A song is performed by musicians at the key moment to mask her cries. On the avoidance of incest in the *comedia*, see Henry W. Sullivan, "Sibling Symmetry and the Incest Taboo in Tirso's *Habladme en entrando*," *Revista canadiense de estudios hispánicos* 10.2 (1986): 261–78.

29 Tirso de Molina, *Santo, y sastre*, Acto 2. Playwrights evidently delighted in repeating this classical commonplace, as in "las dos que amaron el Caballo, y Toro" (Guillén de Castro, *El Narciso en su opinión*, Jornada 3). Returning to the archive, a total of 367 cases of bestiality were tried by the Inquisitorial Tribunals of Aragon from the years 1570 to 1630 (Haliczer, "Sexuality and Repression," 84). Specific literary references to bestiality in the *comedias* include the following exchange, in which Mentira and a Demon try to convince Isidro that his wife has been unfaithful to him – not just with every shepherd in the pasture, but even by making love to a horse:

MENTIRA: Que no fue Tais ramera

más loca, pues no hay pastor,
con quien no trate de amor,
en toda aquella ribera.
ISIDRO: ¡Válgame Dios! …
¡Que mi mujer vive así!
DEMONIO: Yo pienso, que le hallaréis,
en la puerta de la Vega,
haciendo mal a un caballo. (Lope de Vega, *San Isidro labrador de Madrid*, Acto 3)

Alain Saint-Saëns claims to have found archival evidence in Inquisitorial *procesos* indicating that fornication was sometimes advocated by defendants as protection against the worse sin of bestiality: "Fornication was not only good, it was also, according to them, a protection against the temptation of bestiality, frequent without doubt" (Alain Saint-Saëns, "'It is not a sin!': Making Love according to the Spaniards in Early Modern Spain," in Saint-Saëns, ed., *Sex and Love in Golden Age Spain*, 11–25, at 23).

30 Moreto, *El lindo Don Diego*, Jornada 1. Calderón de la Barca's *La crítica del amor* likewise alludes to "el pecado nefando" (Calderón, *La crítica del amor*, Jornada 2), a phrase which could refer to bestiality but could also refer to sodomy. On the "nefarious sin," see Mary Elizabeth Perry, "The 'Nefarious Sin' in Early Modern Seville," *Journal of Homosexuality* 16.1–2 (1988): 67–89.

31 "Incest was defined so stringently that even 'social' or 'legal' relatives such as a godsister, etc. ('tu parienta cercana, tu hermana, tu cuñada, tu sobrina, ó finalmente deuda tuya') … were forbidden to marry 'de dentro el cuarto grado,' or within the fourth degree of kinship. This 'parentesco' or kinship was typically enumerated with three possible types: 'cognación espiritual, legal, y terrenal' … 'Spiritual kinship' was defined as originating with the sacraments: 'La cognación espiritual se contrae por el bautismo, y confirmacion, e impide … el matrimonio'" (Hilaire Kallendorf, *Conscience on Stage: The* Comedia *as Casuistry in Early Modern Spain* [Toronto: University of Toronto Press, 2007], 139–40). Here I cite representative passages from two different early modern confessors' manuals: Bartholomé de Alva, *Confesionario mayor, y menor* (Mexico: Francisco Salbago por Pedro de Quiñones, 1634), fol. 22v; and Felipe de la Cruz, *Norte de confesores y penitentes* (Valladolid: Jeronimo Morillo [for] Juan Piñat, 1629), fol. 102v.

32 Cueva, *El Infamador*, Acto 4.

33 Alarcón, *El Anticristo*, Acto 1.

34 "pues sabed que son hermanos, y volvedles el incesto" (Solís, *El doctor Carlino*, Jornada 3). This should not be confused with an earlier play by Luis de Góngora which bears the same title.

35 Tirso de Molina, *Averígüelo Vargas*, Jornada 3.

36 Calderón, *El purgatorio de San Patricio*, Jornada 1.

37 Alarcón, *El Anticristo*, Acto 1.

38 In 1597 the theatres were closed on the occasion of the death of the Duchess of Savoy. Shortly before his death, Philip II ordered the theatres closed once again; and they were not reopened until his successor Philip III, in 1601, resolved to allow less frequent and more limited theatrical productions after consulting with an advisory council of priests and secular authorities. See Modesto Lafuente, Juan Valera et al., *Historia general de España*, vol. 12 (Barcelona: Montaner y Simón, 1889), 103n1.

39 Calderón, *Agradecer, y no amar*, Preliminares de obra.

40 Calderón, *El Joseph de las mujeres*, Jornada 1.

41 See "Mainstream Dramatists Educated by Jesuits," in Kallendorf, *Conscience on Stage*, 22–7, especially 23. Alan Trueblood describes Lope de Vega's infatuation with Elena Osorio, the daughter of a theatrical producer, in *Experience and Artistic Expression in Lope de Vega: The Making of* "La Dorotea" (Cambridge: Harvard University Press, 1974), 2. Their love affair was immortalized in Lope's closet drama. See Hilaire Kallendorf, "Love Madness and Demonic Possession in Lope de Vega," *Romance Quarterly* 51.3 (2004): 162–82. Scholars agree, however, that Dorotea represents a composite portrait of several women in Lope de Vega's life, including other women with whom he also had affairs. See E.S. Morby and A.S. Trueblood, "*La Dorotea*," in *Historia y crítica de la literatura española*, ed. F. Rico, *Siglos de Oro: Barroco,* ed. B.W. Wardropper (Barcelona: Crítica, 1983), 185–97, at 189.

42 Harvard University Press's *History of Private Life* book series, edited by Philippe Ariès and Georges Duby and published beginning in 1992, attempts to reconstruct just such a history. However, in this period, it is also worth remembering that the boundaries between public and private often became quite blurred. For example, Lope de Vega's trial for libel of Elena Osorio and her family became a very public ordeal: "Lope's trial for libel of certain actors (1587–88), an event which marks the end of his four-year liaison with Elena Osorio, daughter of the theatrical producer who brings the charges after Lope responds with slander to the preferment of a wealthier rival … is traumatic in both psychological and esthetic senses" (Trueblood, *Experience and Artistic Expression*, 2).

43 Calderón, *El Joseph de las mujeres*, Jornada 1; Calderón, *Agradecer, y no amar*, Preliminares de obra.

44 Lope de Vega, *El remedio en la desdicha*, Acto 1.

45 Lope de Vega, *El laberinto de Creta*, Acto 1.

46 For example, "de lascivo Hirco a Behemot" (Calderón, *La serpiente de metal*, auto sacramental). Hirco refers to a mountain goat, thought to be a lascivious animal, and one that appeared frequently in Dionysiac rituals. The Behemoth is a legendary monster of Hebrew mythology, a description of which appears in Job 40. We must remember that Lust in classical myths is also not limited to the gods. Often Lust is exhibited by their human counterparts too, such as "lascivo Endimión" (Lope de Vega, *La serrana de Tormes*, Acto 1), who aroused sexual desire in Selene, the goddess of the moon. The satyr is described as lascivious in Calderón's *Agradecer, y*

no amar (Preliminares de obra), as well as Lope de Vega's *La hermosura aborrecida*, Acto 3.

47 Cueva, *La constancia de Arcelina*, Acto 2. In the same play Cueva refers again to "adúltero Egisto" along with "amante Ifis" (Cueva, *La constancia de Arcelina*, Acto 2).

48 Cervantes, *El laberinto de amor*, Jornada 1. Paris stole Helen away from Menelaus in a love triangle which became a common comparison to *comedia* characters.

49 For a discussion of this and other of Aeneas's impieties, see Craig Kallendorf, *The Other Virgil: Pessimistic Readings of the* Aeneid *in Early Modern Culture* (Oxford: Oxford University Press, 2007), 112–18.

50 "el Romano más culpado, eternamente ha llegado a su lascivo vivir" (Lope de Vega, *La hermosura aborrecida*, Acto 3).

51 Cueva, *La libertad de Roma, por Mucio Cevola*, Acto 2.

52 Lope de Vega, *La amistad pagada*, Jornada 1.

53 Calderón, *El Viático Cordero*, auto sacramental. Genesis 39 tells the story of Potiphar's wife, who attempted to seduce Joseph. When he rejected her advances, he was thrown into prison; but from there he ascended to power as Pharaoh's dream interpreter who went on to save his Hebrew people from death by famine.

54 Tirso de Molina, *La mujer que manda en casa*, Acto 3. Jezabel is also seen killing God's prophets in 3 Kings 18:4 (Douay version; corresponds to 1 Kings in most other versions). She is accused of fornication and sorcery in 4 Kings 9:22 (2 Kings in most other versions).

55 Tirso de Molina, *La venganza de Tamar*, Jornada 2. The biblical story appears in 2 Samuel 13 (2 Kings in the Douay version).

56 Matthew 14:4–11.

57 Matthew 2:13–23.

58 Tirso de Molina, *La vida de Herodes*, Acto 3.

59 Calderón, *El primer refugio del hombre, y probática piscina*, auto sacramental. The biblical account appears in John 4.

60 This is the central thesis of Barbara Fuchs, *Exotic Nation: Maurophilia and the Construction of Early Modern Spain* (Philadelphia: University of Pennsylvania Press, 2009). The Moriscos were definitively expelled from 1609 to 1614. For events leading up to the expulsion see Benjamin Ehlers, *Between Christians and Moriscos: Juan de Ribera and Religious Reform in Valencia, 1568–1614* (Baltimore: Johns Hopkins University Press, 2006).

61 Lope de Vega, *El primer Fajardo*, Acto 2.

62 Lope de Vega, *La doncella Teodor*, Acto 3.

63 Lope de Vega, *El casamiento en la muerte*, Jornada 1. Lope de Vega's most extended treatment of this founding myth of Spain's national history occurs in *El último godo* (alternatively titled *El postrer godo de España*). There are many early modern Spanish ballads dealing with La Cava. Some representative examples are "Amores trata Rodrigo" (1570); "En Ceuta está don Julián" (1550; alternatively titled "Romance de

cómo el conde don Julián, padre de la Cava, vendió a España"); "Las huestes de don Rodrigo" (1547); "Profecía de la pérdida de España" (1573); and "Penitencia del rey don Rodrigo" (1547). These are all available online through the Pan-Hispanic Ballad Project at http://depts.washington.edu/hisprom/. In several traditional accounts, a snake devours the live King Rodrigo's genitals in punishment for his sins. Barbara Fuchs affirms, "traditional accounts emphasize the individual, fatal flaw of King Rodrigo, who single-handedly lost Spain to the Moors through his implacable lust for Florinda" (Barbara Fuchs, *Mimesis and Empire: The New World, Islam, and European Identities* [Cambridge: Cambridge University Press, 2004], 112).

64 Eric J. Griffin, *English Renaissance Drama and the Specter of Spain: Ethnopoetics and Empire* (Philadelphia: University of Pennsylvania Press, 2009), 188–9. See also the comments on Spaniards' preoccupation with virginity in the third chapter (devoted to Lust) of Fernando Díaz-Plaja, *El español y los siete pecados capitales* (Madrid: Alianza, 1980). This classic of impressionistic criticism has been translated by John Inderwick Palmer as *The Spaniard and the Seven Deadly Sins* (New York: Charles Scribner's Sons, 1967).

65 Lope de Vega, *El serafín humano*, Acto 1. For the explicit connection between Helen of Troy and La Cava being made by Lope de Vega, see Patricia E. Grieve, "Spain's Second Helen," in *The Eve of Spain: Myths of Origins in the History of Christian, Muslim, and Jewish Conflict* (Baltimore: Johns Hopkins University Press, 2009), 180–5. Another particularly relevant and suggestive section of Grieve's book in this context is "The Woman's Body and the Fate of the Nation," 125–8.

66 Lope de Vega, *La fe rompida*, Acto 1.

67 Tirso de Molina, *La mujer que manda en casa*, Acto 1. This lascivious king was Achab, son of Amri and consort of Queen Jezabel. According to 3 Kings 16:30–3 (1 Kings in most other versions), Achab did evil in the sight of God: he worshipped Baal and set up an altar and temple to this pagan god in Samaria. Thus he did more to provoke God than any other king of Israel.

68 Tirso de Molina, *La mujer que manda en casa*, Acto 3.

69 Adultery – that is, sex by a married person with someone other than his or her spouse – should not be confused with fornication, defined for this specific time and place by historians of the period as "sex between an unmarried man and an unmarried woman – most often a prostitute" (Georgina Dopico Black, *Perfect Wives, Other Women: Adultery and Inquisition in Early Modern Spain* [Durham: Duke University Press, 2001], 27).

70 On repressive attitudes toward sexuality among early modern Spaniards, including a pedagogy of sexual anxiety which allegedly inculcated prudery, see Haliczer, "Sexuality and Repression," especially 87. He cites, among other contemporaneous sources, Pedro Galindo's *Excelencias de la castidad y virginidad* (Madrid, 1681). As Haliczer explains, confessors were told "to ask married persons about their sexual relations and warn them that it was a mortal sin to have an 'adulterous' marriage in which the

object of sexual relations was sensual pleasure instead of procreation. So-called unnatural sexual positions were also condemned because they were considered less likely to result in insemination" (86). Mary-Elizabeth Perry confirms: "Moralists described in minute detail the correct sexual behavior of married couples" (Mary-Elizabeth Perry, Foreword to Saint-Saëns, ed., *Sex and Love in Golden Age Spain*, 7–8, at 8). For a recent study of one of these moralists, the Andalusian Tomás Sánchez, see F. Alfieri, *Nella camera degli sposi: Tomás Sánchez, il matrimonio, la sessualità (secoli XVI–XVII)* (Bologna: Il Mulino, 2010).

On the origins of a cult of chastity surrounding Isabel the Catholic, see Chiyo Ishikawa, "*La llave de palo*: Isabel la Católica as Patron of Religious Literature and Painting," chapter 6 of *Isabel la Católica, Queen of Castile: Critical Essays*, ed. David A. Boruchoff (New York: Palgrave Macmillan, 2003), 103–54, at 103. As Carmen Martín Gaite describes the "enseñanzas y prédicas de la Sección Femenina" of Franco's dictatorship, which appropriated the figure of Queen Isabel to propagandistic purposes, "La retórica de la postguerra se aplicaba a desprestigiar los conatos de feminismo que tomaron auge en los años de la República y volvía a poner el acento en el heroísmo abnegado de madres y esposas, en la importancia de su silenciosa y oscura labor como pilares del hogar cristiano … [L]a teníamos demasiado conocida, demasiado mentada: era Isabel la Católica. Se nos ponía bajo su advocación, se nos hablaba de su voluntad férrea y de su espíritu de sacrificio" (Carmen Martín Gaite, *El cuarto de atrás* [Barcelona: Destino, 1992], 93, 95).

71 Jayme de Corella, *Práctica de el confessionario* (Madrid: Antonio González de Reyes, 1696), 85, 84. Corella's manual further includes this hypothetical exchange between confessor and female penitent:

> [PENITENTE]: Padre, acúsome, que algunas veces yo ya consentía, en que mi marido, *tempore seminandi extraheret membrum, & extra vas semen flueret*. Y aun muchas veces retiraba yo el cuerpo a ese tiempo por no hacerme preñada.
>
> [CURA]: Pecó Vuestra Merced gravemente, y demás de la malicia de ser *contra naturam* esa efusión del semen, tenía también malicia de adulterio … Y es la razón, porque si el marido, teniendo polución con mujer ajena, hace injusticia a su mujer, porque la priva del semen, *ad quod ius habet: eodem modo eam privat, si copulando cum ea semen perdit.*
>
> (Corella, *Práctica de el confessionario*, 84, emphasis added to differentiate Latin from Spanish)

72 Rojas Zorrilla, *Los trabajos de Tobías.*

73 Lope de Vega, *La Historia de Tobías*, Acto 1 and Acto 3.

74 Lope de Vega, *La Historia de Tobías*, Acto 1, emphasis mine.

75 Currently located in the Museum Bredius, The Hague.

76 Lope de Vega, *Adonis, y Venus*, Acto 3.

77 William Shakespeare, *Hamlet*, in *The Riverside Shakespeare*, ed. G. Blakemore Evans (Boston: Houghton Mifflin, 1974), 3.4.8, 40–51.

78 "[W]hile it is true that 'catholic' means 'universal,' it would be a mistake to believe that the Catholic of Burgos or Valencia reacts the same way to prohibitions or injunctions as the one from Boston or Holland" (Díaz-Plaja, *The Spaniard and the Seven Deadly Sins*, 8).

79 Moreto, *El caballero del Sacramento*, Jornada 2.

80 Lope de Vega, *Ursón y Valentín, hijos del rey de Francia*, Jornada 3. This play is known by the alternative title *El nacimiento de Ursón y Valentín*.

81 Rojas Zorrilla, *Progne y Filomena*, Jornada 3.

82 Lope de Vega, *La inocente Laura*, Acto 3.

83 Lope de Vega, *El perseguido*, Jornada 3.

84 Moreto, *El caballero del Sacramento*, Jornada 2.

85 Rojas Zorrilla, *Los áspides de Cleopatra*, Jornada 1.

86 Lope de Vega, *El amigo hasta la muerte*, Acto 3.

87 Nonetheless, that is exactly what multitudes of early modern men seemed determined to do: "In Spain … in the sixteenth and seventeenth centuries, the body and soul of the married woman became the site of an enormous amount of anxious inquiry, a site subject to the scrutiny of a remarkable array of gazes: inquisitors, theologians, religious reformers, confessors, poets, playwrights, and, not least among them, husbands" (Dopico Black, *Perfect Wives, Other Women*, xiii).

88 Calderón, *Agradecer, y no amar*, Preliminares de obra.

89 Calderón, *A Dios por razón de Estado*, auto sacramental, emphasis mine.

90 Calderón, *El año santo de Roma*, auto sacramental.

91 "Spaniards read the Decalogue as the Seven Sins" (Lu Ann Homza, *Religious Authority in the Spanish Renaissance* [Baltimore: Johns Hopkins University Press, 2000], 166).

92 The perceived change in mores I am signalling here refers to change in general over the course of the early modern period, with the new era defined as the dawn of early modernity. It would be exceedingly difficult to narrow the time period in question to a particular decade or generation of playwrights. Change is messy.

93 Lope de Vega, *La buena guarda*, Acto 2 and Acto 3.

94 Lope de Vega, *La buena guarda*, Acto 3; Lope de Vega, *Los Porceles de Murcia*, Acto 2.

95 "Trial by ordeal was widespread, if not ubiquitous, in olden times … [I]n a feudal Europe ruled by military standards of conduct the ordeal could turn into something much more exceptional, trial by combat. This was inspired by the belief, readily cherished by the stronger or luckier, that the outcome was overruled by Providence" (Victor Gordon Kiernan, *The Duel in European History: Honour and the Reign of Aristocracy* [Oxford: Oxford University Press, 1988], 1). On jousting, see Richard W. Barber and Juliet R.V. Barker, *Tournaments: Jousts, Chivalry and Pageants in the Middle Ages* (New York: Weidenfeld and Nicolson, 1989), especially the section on Spain (91–102). There is unfortunately a lack of good secondary scholarship

synthesizing the common ground shared between these two overlapping traditions. It is clear, however, that in certain contexts they were one and the same: "Joust ... was a combat between two persons, and in this was unlike the tournament; and it differed in the further particular, that, by agreement, it might be a mortal fight, or common duel ... At first the weapons were blunt, and the contests commonly harmless; but sharp weapons were finally introduced, and combats occurred that hardly differed from the modern duel" (Lorenzo Sabine, *Notes on Duels and Duelling* [Boston: Crosby, Nichols, 1855], 21, 16). Kiernan would seem to concur that over time, the two customs became virtually indistinguishable: "Between the ordeal by combat, intended to determine right or wrong, and the joust, or exhibition of courage and prowess, the spirit of the modern duel would waver, but with its leaning more and more towards the latter" (Kiernan, *The Duel*, 1–2). Scott Taylor traces this evolution more explicitly, pinpointing the sixteenth century as the time when these two parallel traditions ceased to be coterminous: "By the sixteenth century the Castilian duel had evolved from its medieval origins as a public judicial instrument controlled by royal law into a private recourse for settling points of honor" (Scott K. Taylor, *Honor and Violence in Golden Age Spain* [New Haven: Yale University Press, 2008], 21). See especially chapter 2, "The Duel and the Rhetoric of Honor," 17–64. On duels fought in Spain over alleged cases of Adultery, see Kiernan, *The Duel*, 73. José Luis Bermejo Cabrero summarizes the usual scenario: "Uno de los casos más destacados es el de la acusación de adulterio cometido por la mujer de un alto dignatario, ya sea condesa, duquesa o incluso reina. El duelo será la forma de dirimir la acusación. Aunque las variantes son numerosas de unos casos a otros, suele salir al combate en defensa del honor de la dama algún miembro de su familia, ya sea uno de los hijos o el propio marido" (José Luis Bermejo Cabrero, "Duelos y desafíos en el derecho y en la literatura," in *Sexo barroco y otras transgresiones premodernas*, ed. Francisco Tomás y Valiente et al. [Madrid: Alianza Universidad, 1990], 109–26, at 124).

96 Lope de Vega, *El testimonio vengado*, Jornada 1. For a good discussion of this play, see Yvonne Yarbro-Bejarano, *Feminism and the Honor Plays of Lope de Vega* (West Lafayette: Purdue University Press, 1994), 231–6.

97 Lope de Vega, *El testimonio vengado*, Jornada 3.

98 Lope de Vega, *El gallardo catalán*, Jornada 3. This play is known by the alternative title *El valeroso catalán*.

99 A new study which focuses on the law in the context of marriage and sexual relations – but without much discussion of sin – is María M. Carrión, *Subject Stages: Marriage, Theatre, and the Law in Early Modern Spain* (Toronto: University of Toronto Press, 2010).

100 As these higher standards became more accepted, old practices such as duelling began to fall by the wayside. The Catholic Church was one of the foremost opponents of the practice of duelling, with the Council of Trent decreeing in 1563 that not

only those who engaged in this practice, but also rulers or authorities who failed to stop it, would be excommunicated (Kiernan, *The Duel*, 92). Theoretically duelling had been prohibited in Spain by a law passed in 1480 (Kiernan, *The Duel*, 72), but this statute seems to have been honoured more in the breach.

101 Lope de Vega, *Los Porceles de Murcia*, Acto 3.

102 Lope de Vega, *El testimonio vengado*, Jornada 1.

103 Lope de Vega, *El cardenal de Belén*, Acto 2.

104 Lope de Vega, *Ursón y Valentín, hijos del rey de Francia*, Jornada 3.

105 Lope de Vega, *Los Porceles de Murcia*, Acto 1.

106 Carrión, *Subject Stages*, 86. She further comments that "honour dramas can be interpreted as vehicles to articulate commentaries about the dramatic quality and great possibility for tragedy that such lack of burden of proof represented" (Carrión, *Subject Stages*, 87).

107 Lope de Vega, *El ejemplo de casadas y prueba de la paciencia*, Acto 1.

108 Lope de Vega, *La resistencia honrada y Condesa Matilde*, Jornada 3.

109 Shakespeare's famous scene unfolds thus:

IAGO: Have you not sometimes seen a handkerchief
  Spotted with strawberries in your wive's hand?
OTHELLO: I gave her such a one; 'twas my first gift.
IAGO: I know not that; but such a handkerchief
  (I am sure it was your wive's) did I to-day
  See Cassio wipe his beard with.
OTHELLO: If it be that –
IAGO: If it be that, or any [that] was hers,
  It speaks against her with the other *proofs*.

(William Shakespeare, *Othello*, in *The Riverside Shakespeare*, 3.3.434–41, emphasis mine)

110 "este anillo, y un papel escrito" (Pérez de Montalbán, *Teágenes, y Clariquea*, Jornada 3). The persuasive power of these tokens is reaffirmed later:

y si una información tan verdadera,
por alivio no basta en mi conflicto,
consultad el Oráculo de Apolo.

(Pérez de Montalbán, *Teágenes, y Clariquea*, Jornada 3)

111 Sebastián de Covarrubias Orozco, "Indicio," *Tesoro de la lengua castellana o española* (Madrid: Luis Sánchez, 1611), ed. Felipe C.R. Maldonado, rev. Manuel Camarero (Madrid: Castalia, 1995), 666. However, in "Justicia penal y teatro barroco," José Luis Bermejo Cabrero makes a potentially crucial distinction between *indicios* and

pruebas: "no bastan los simples indicios para condenar … es preciso aportar pruebas convincentes" (José Luis Bermejo Cabrero, "Justicia penal y teatro barroco," in *Sexo barroco*, ed. Tomás y Valiente et al., 91–108, at 96). Once again, though, a disclaimer becomes necessary, considering the fact that for certain so-called *delitos notorios*, the judge did not wait to collect these proofs: "cuando el delito ofrezca suficiente notoriedad – los denominados delitos notorios … – el juez actuará sumariamente pasando a dictar sentencia sin mayor género de averiguaciones" (Bermejo Cabrero, "Justicia penal y teatro barroco," 96).

112 "esas señales violentas escritas en tu jubón, que son rasgos, que me dicen, si letras formadas, no; Enrique, en aqueste pecho hay oculta una traición" (Matos Fragoso, *Los indicios sin culpa*, Jornada 2).

113 Matos Fragoso, *Los indicios sin culpa*, Jornada 1.

114 Matos Fragoso, *Los indicios sin culpa*, Jornada 3, emphasis mine.

115 Rojas Zorrilla, *El profeta falso Mahoma*, Jornada 2.

116 Lope de Vega, *La resistencia honrada y Condesa Matilde*, Jornada 3.

117 Lope de Vega, *La cortesía de España*, Acto 2.

118 Lope de Vega, *Las ferias de Madrid*, Jornada 3.

119 Diamante, *El nacimiento de Cristo*, Acto 2.

120 Guillén de Castro, *El mejor esposo*, Jornada 2.

121 Lope de Vega, *El cardenal de Belén*, Acto 2.

122 See Karl Menninger, "Sin into Crime," chapter 5 of *Whatever Became of Sin?* (New York: Hawthorn, 1973), 50–73. The nuances of this problematic distinction have been explored by Bartolomé Clavero in "Delito y pecado: noción y escala de transgresiones," in *Sexo barroco*, ed. Tomás y Valiente et al., 57–89, and by Francisco Tomás y Valiente, in "Delincuentes y pecadores," in the same essay collection, 11–31. As Clavero explains, "[t]ienden ciertamente a apreciarse de modo objetivo los delitos y subjetivo los pecados; se definirían unos por resultado, por intención los otros" (Clavero, "Delito y pecado," 61). Here he notes the influence of Saint Augustine on Hispanic legal thought, particularly in a distinction made by a jurist by the name of Lorenzo Hispano: "Apartarse del bien es delito; pecado, incurrir en el mal. El delito puede cometerse inconscientemente; el pecado requiere deliberación" (61). Later in the same essay he writes of a process in the history of ideas which he calls "la criminalización del pecado" (65).

123 Moreto, *La fuerza de la ley*, Jornada 1.

124 On the similar double standard experienced by women in fifteenth-century England, see Ruth Mazo Karras, "Two Models, Two Standards: Moral Teaching and Sexual Mores," in *Bodies and Disciplines: Intersections of Literature and History in Fifteenth-Century England*, ed. Barbara Hanawalt and David Wallace (Minneapolis: University of Minnesota Press, 1996), 123–38.

125 William Shakespeare, *Macbeth*, in *The Riverside Shakespeare*, 2.1.

126 Lope de Vega, *La buena guarda*, Acto 2.

127 Tirso de Molina, *Escarmientos para el cuerdo*, Acto 3.
128 Calderón, *El pastor fido*, auto sacramental.
129 Rojas Zorrilla, *Progne y Filomena*, Jornada 3.
130 Lope de Vega, *El perseguido*, Jornada 3.
131 Lope de Vega, *Las ferias de Madrid*, Jornada 3.
132 Tomás y Valiente, "El crimen y pecado contra natura," in *Sexo barroco*, ed. Tomás y Valiente et al., 33–56, at 44.
133 Lope de Vega, *La venganza venturosa*, Acto 1; Moreto, *El caballero del Sacramento*, Jornada 3.
134 Tirso de Molina, *La república al revés*, Acto 2.
135 Lope de Vega, *Los embustes de Zelauro*, Acto 2.
136 For a study comparing these two plays, see Joseph Gillet, "Cueva's *Comedia del Infamador* and the Don Juan Legend," *Modern Language Notes* 37.4 (1922): 206–12.
137 Cueva, *El Infamador*, Acto 2.
138 Tirso de Molina, *La santa Juana*, Acto 2.
139 See Arthur W.H. Adkins, "'Honour' and 'Punishment' in the Homeric Poems," *Bulletin of the Institute of Classical Studies* 7.1 (2010): 23–32.
140 Lope de Vega, *La buena guarda*, Acto 1.
141 Lope de Vega, *El laberinto de Creta*, Acto 1.
142 Alarcón, *La crueldad por el honor*, Acto 2.
143 Quevedo invokes the phrase *al revés* in three out of his five *Sueños y discursos*: "Al revés lo haces" (*El mundo*, 299); "Todo lo entendéis al revés" (*Infierno*, 219); "Todo lo hacen al revés" (*Muerte*, 352); and "Al fin, es gente hecha al revés" (*Infierno*, 231) (in Francisco de Quevedo, *Sueños y discursos*, ed. James O. Crosby [Madrid: Castalia, 1993]).
144 Tirso de Molina, *La república al revés*, Acto 2.
145 Lope de Vega, *Ursón y Valentín, hijos del rey de Francia*, Jornada 1.
146 Lope de Vega, *La campana de Aragón*, Acto 1.
147 Tirso de Molina, *La prudencia en la mujer*, Jornada 1.
148 See Antonio Rumeu de Armas, *Hernando Colón, historiador del descubrimiento de América* (Madrid: Instituto de Cultura Hispánica, 1973), 5n1 and 82–3. Hernando's mother, Beatriz Enríquez de Arana, was from Córdoba. Rumeu de Armas affirms, "Hernando Colón fue todo lo contrario de un postergado, pese a su nacimiento irregular" (82). The particulars of Hernando's legal right to receive an inheritance involved a large sum authorized expressly by the Admiral himself: "El patrimonio de que disponía el Colón cordobés hay que calificarlo de cuantioso. En la escritura de *mayorazgo* otorgada en 1498, el Almirante hizo reserva expresa en favor de Hernando de una renta de un millón de maravedíes que podría llegar en circunstancias óptimas a dos millones como máximo" (82–3). His legitimate brother Diego found himself obliged to honour his father's wishes in this matter even after the older man's death, although he did manage to get Hernando to

agree to sign away some of his legal rights in exchange for a hefty allowance: "Por escritura otorgada en La Coruña el 12 de mayo de 1520, el segundo almirante se obliga a pagar a Hernando una renta vitalicia de 200.000 maravedíes a cambio de la renuncia a la herencia paterna" (83). This situation was not unusual, as we see in Vicente Graullera's study of women and morality in Valencia: "Las Cortes Generales del Reino de Valencia tenían, entre sus múltiples funciones, la de servir como vía para acceder a la legitimación de hijos nacidos fuera del matrimonio, fruto de relaciones ilícitas" (Vicente Graullera, "Mujer, amor y moralidad en la Valencia de los siglos XVI y XVII," in *Amours légitimes, amours illégitimes en Espagne [XVIe–XVIIe siècles]* [Colloque International, Sorbonne, 3, 4, 5 octobre 1984], ed. Augustin Redondo [Paris: Sorbonne, 1985], 109–20, at 109). However, Graullera notes that this recognition was granted only by royal privilege, which made it out of reach to the lower class.

149 Don Diego apparently makes this offer in order to convince the noble Porcia to marry his illegitimate son: "Un hijo tengo en una Extranjera dama; ¿querrás casarte con él? Que yo te doy la palabra de casarme con su madre" (Matos Fragoso, *Los indicios sin culpa*, Jornada 3).

150 Lope de Vega, *Los Ponces de Barcelona*, Acto 2.

151 Calderón, *El segundo blasón del Austria*, auto sacramental. These lines are spoken by the Demon to Basilisco, a mythical creature bearing the head of a rooster and the tail of a serpent (and thus logically the monstrous product of an adulterous, unnatural union).

152 See John Mortimer, ed., *The Oxford Book of Villains* (Oxford: Oxford University Press, 1992).

153 Calderón, *La serpiente de metal*, auto sacramental.

154 For an example, see *Relación de un monstruoso portento que nació en Ostrauizxa, tierra del Turco, donde se da cuenta de las espantosas señales de este prodigioso monstruo* (Madrid: Julián de Paredes, 1660). This pamphlet is held by the Real Academia de la Historia, Madrid (sig. 9/5746, n. 32). For a facsimile collection of *relaciones de sucesos*, see Henry Ettinghausen, ed., *Noticias del siglo XVII: relaciones españolas de sucesos naturales y sobrenaturales* (Barcelona: Puvill, 1995). Figure 11 of the present volume shows a baby born with thirty-three eyes, from *Admirables prodigios y portentos que se manifestaron en Bayona* (Barcelona: Lorenço Déu, 1613). This pamphlet is held by the Biblioteca Nacional de Lisboa (sig. RES. 254//12 V).

155 See Elena del Río Parra, *Una era de monstruos: representaciones de lo deforme en el Siglo de Oro español* (Madrid/Frankfurt: Iberoamericana/Vervuert, 2003).

156 Rojas Zorrilla, *El profeta falso Mahoma*, Jornada 2.

157 Alarcón, *El Anticristo*, Acto 1 and Acto 2.

158 See Matteo Bandello, *Novelle* (1554), Part I, novella 26: "Il signor Antonio Bologna sposa la duchessa d'Amalfi, e tutti due sono ammazzati," in *Raccolta di novellieri italiani: novelle di Matteo Bandello, volume primo* (Turin: Cugini Pomba, 1853),

285–94; and Andrés Antonio Sánchez de Villamayor, *La mujer fuerte, asombro de los desiertos, penitente y admirable Santa María Egipciaca* ([Málaga]: [Mateo López Hidalgo], 1677). Departing from Bandello, Lope wrote the play *El mayordomo de la duquesa de Amalfi.*

159 Lope de Vega, *Los embustes de Zelauro*, Acto 1.

160 "el amoroso y torpe fuego de esta mujer lasciva, que Idolatra le postra y le cautiva" (Tirso de Molina, *La mujer que manda en casa*, Acto 1).

161 Lope de Vega, *El mayorazgo dudoso*, Jornada 3.

162 Lope de Vega, *La campana de Aragón*, Acto 1.

163 Lope de Vega, *La resistencia honrada y Condesa Matilde*, Jornada 3.

164 See Fernando Plata, "On Love and Occasion: A Reading of the 'Tale of Inappropriate Curiosity,'" in *Cervantes and Don Quixote: Proceedings of the Delhi Conference on Miguel de Cervantes*, ed. Vibha Maurya and Ignacio Arellano (Hyderabad: Emesco, 2008), 195–210. A representative Occasio emblem appears in Johan Amos Comenius's *Orbis sensualium pictus* (Nuremberg: Michael Endter, 1658). A better-known occurrence is Andrea Alciato's Emblema CXII, "In Occasionem," in *Emblematum liber* (Paris: Christian Wechel, 1534), 20.

165 Lope de Vega, *Nadie se conoce*, Acto 1.

166 Lope de Vega, *Los Porceles de Murcia*, Acto 2.

167 "Humanae cur sit speculum comoedia vitae" ("Why comedy is the mirror of human life") (Lope de Vega, *El arte nuevo de hacer comedias en este tiempo* [1609], ed. Juana de José Prades [Madrid: Clásicos Hispánicos, 1971], line 377).

4. Loath to Call It Sloth: The Plus Side of *Pereza*

1 Diamante, loa for *Alfeo, y Aretusa*; Calderón, *El gran príncipe de Fez*, Acto 1.

2 Raymond Williams, "Dominant, Residual, and Emergent," in *Marxism and Literature* (Oxford: Oxford University Press, 1977), 121–7, at 123.

3 In one of Calderón's *autos sacramentales*, the allegorical figure of Ocio says, "A la pereza del Ocio, o qué mal le suena esto" (Calderón, *El lirio y la azucena*, auto sacramental). The two words are used not just in conjunction, but as actual synonyms, in a number of instances; for example, "¿Como tú, entregado al sueño en dulces delicias blandas, perezosamente duermes, y ociosamente descansas?" (Calderón, *El santo rey don Fernando, segunda parte*, auto sacramental). Another word used as a rough synonym for Sloth, but with the connotation of cowardliness, is *poltronería*. The concomitant noun (and adjective) for a slothful, cowardly person is *poltrón* or *poltrona*.

4 Calderón, *El Viático Cordero*, auto sacramental. This string of characterizations of Sloth appears in lines of various dramatic works, as follows:

Foolish: "el tiempo, que el ocio necio pierde" (Tirso de Molina, *El melancólico*, Acto 2).

Vile: "vil Pereza" (Calderón, *No hay instante sin milagro*, auto sacramental).
Infamous: "la pereza infame" (Cervantes, *La casa de los celos y selvas de Ardenia*, Jornada 2).
Barbaric: "nunca ha podido tanto conmigo el bárbaro ocio" (Tirso de Molina, *Amar por razón de estado*, Acto 1).
Enemy: "el ocio es fuerte enemigo" (Moreto, *Nuestra Señora del Aurora*, Jornada 3).
Flees from work: "el ocio (cuando huye del trabajo)" (Tirso de Molina, *Santo, y sastre*, Acto 3).

5 To leave Sloth behind: "que dejes la enojosa Pereza" (Cueva, *La muerte de Virginia, y Appio Claudio*, Acto 1). Sloth as base weakness: "la pereza, [y] la flojedad torpe" (Cueva, *El Infamador*, Acto 4). Sloth as brutish negligence: "la pereza bruta" (Zamora, *Judás Iscariote*, Jornada 3); "Mostróme mi pereza y negligencia" (Lope de Vega, *La Santa Liga*, Acto 1).
6 "dos veces culpa es la pereza" (Zamora, *Amar, es saber vencer, y el arte contra el poder*, Jornada 2). Waste of time: "el tiempo que el ocio gasta" (Diamante, *Ir por el riesgo a la dicha*, Jornada 1). Frivolous distraction: "Todo es antojo del ocio, que el tiempo pierde" (Tirso de Molina, *Antona García*, Acto 3).
7 "me reduzca la pereza con que inútilmente vivo" (Zamora, *Áspides hay Basiliscos*, Jornada 1). Paradoxically, *ocio* itself is described as the most useless Vice in the *comedias*: "el ocio … por ser el inútil vicio que más aborrezco" (Calderón, *El gran príncipe de Fez*, Acto 1). One wonders, according to this utilitarian logic, which Vices might be more useful.
8 Calderón, *El gran príncipe de Fez*, Jornada 2.
9 "Ya veo, que descuidado, mi mal, mi Pereza fue, de un día en otro dilaté" (Calderón, *El nuevo hospicio de pobres*, auto sacramental); "sólo que sea presto te demando, que en esto la pereza será ocasión de gran inconveniente" (Cueva, *El viejo enamorado*, Acto 2).
10 "la pereza, que antes te entregó al engaño" (Diamante, *Más encanto es la hermosura*, Jornada 2).
11 "La perezosa tardanza de las galeras de Nápoles" (Tirso de Molina, *La huerta de Juan Fernández*, Jornada 2); "pereza me detiene" (Lope de Vega, *San Nicolás de Tolentino*, Acto 1). In Lope de Vega's hawkish comedia *Los españoles en Flandes*, Alexandro worries that Sloth might prevent him from reaching the battlefield in time: "Si hoy muestro en mi partida pereza, no alcanzo los Españoles, y entran en Flandes sin mí" (Lope de Vega, *Los españoles en Flandes*, Acto 1). This historical drama is set against the backdrop of the Battle of Gembloux (31 January 1578), in which the Spaniards defeated the Protestant rebels.
12 In a *comedia* which is a later adaptation of the famous novel, the stage character Don Quijote laments that Sloth has prevented him from rescuing a damsel in distress:

"Que llorando una doncella fui perezoso en llegar a socorrerla" (Guillén de Castro, *Don Quijote de la Mancha*, Jornada 1).

13 Calderón, *El año santo en Madrid*, auto sacramental; Calderón, *Dicha, y desdicha del nombre*, Jornada 1.

14 "cansancio, y pereza me combaten a porfía; yo paro en este mesón" (Lope de Vega, *El Hamete de Toledo*, Acto 3).

15 "El buen intento que tuvo le destruyó la Pereza" (Calderón, *El indulto general*, loa for auto sacramental); "Otros la pereza vende a las Almas, que en sus yerros habituadas, desean enmendar su traje feo" (Calderón, *El gran mercado del mundo*, loa for auto sacramental).

16 "la Pereza, de Leproso Llagado" (Calderón, *El nuevo hospicio de pobres*, auto sacramental); "De este contagio impedido, Paralítico, el Leproso, me semeja al Perezoso, en su culpa envejecido" (Calderón, *El nuevo hospicio de pobres*, auto sacramental).

17 "las Hidras del ocio, que malograron torpemente muchos deseos generosos" (Lope de Vega, *Las aventuras de don Juan de Alarcos*, Preliminares de obra).

18 "Aquel familiar veneno, que prestadamente mata, siendo Hijo de la Pereza" (Calderón, *La siembra del señor*, Acto 1). Another word used for poison in the context of Sloth is *beleño*, or henbane, as in "beleño de la Pereza" (Calderón, *No hay instante sin milagro*, auto sacramental).

19 "¿Qué perezoso letargo es el que sobre mí tengo?" (Calderón, *Sueños hay, que verdad son*, auto sacramental). A common synonym for lethargy is *torpeza*, as in "la torpeza del ocio" (Calderón, *Los misterios de la Misa*, auto sacramental). This lethargy affects the lips ("por ser Gula, y Pereza, tiene un letargo en los labios" [Calderón, *La serpiente de metal*, auto sacramental]) and also the legs: "Ya tardo, que perezoso muevo los pasos" (Matos Fragoso, *El marido de su madre*, Jornada 2). A heaviness in the legs induced by Sloth is further evident in the following exchange:

ANTEO: Con qué pereza me muevo.
LISIPO: Con qué pesadez tan grande. (Diamante, *Lides de amor, y desdén*, Acto 1)

20 "en ocio buey" (Lope de Vega, *Las pobrezas de Reinaldos*, Acto 2); "no demos con la pereza más vigor a la fatiga" (Zamora, *Ser fino, y no parecerlo*, Jornada 2).

21 "sueño profundísimo, y pereza" (Cueva, *El Infamador*, Acto 2); "si … la pereza, y negligencia hallaron su centro en mí, dormiré treinta semanas" (Lope de Vega, *San Nicolás de Tolentino*, Acto 1).

22 "torpe pereza del sueño vil" (Guillén de Castro, *El engañarse engañado*, Jornada 1); "en una vil Camilla, en que le echó su pereza, tan miserable declina, que envejecido en su culpa, ni habla, alienta, ni respira" (Calderón, *El primer refugio del hombre, y probática piscina*, auto sacramental).

23 Tirso de Molina, *Los lagos de san Vicente*, Acto 1.

24 Calderón, *Las armas de la hermosura*, Jornada 1. Lethe and oblivion are two entities which "infunden a quien las bebe sueño, pereza, y olvido" (Calderón, *La hija del aire, primera parte*, Acto 1).

25 Calderón, *El año santo de Roma*, auto sacramental.

26 Lope de Vega, *Con su pan se lo coma*, Acto 3.

27 Lope de Vega, *El soldado amante*, Acto 3.

28 Calderón, *El primer refugio del hombre, y probática piscina*, auto sacramental. Vigilance is evidenced by "aquese heroíco mancebo, tan nada entregado al ocio, tan todo dado al desvelo" (Calderón, *El gran príncipe de Fez*, Acto 1). Care appears in the line, "mi cautela de tu pereza el espejo" (Diamante, *Santa Juliana*, Jornada 1).

29 Calderón, *Lo que va del hombre a Dios*, loa for auto sacramental.

30 Calderón, *El cordero de Isaías*, auto sacramental. The notion that God or heaven is offended by Sloth is repeated in the *comedias*: "ya el cielo se ofende de nuestro ocio … nos despierta y reprehende" (Tirso de Molina, *El árbol del mejor fruto*, Acto 1).

31 Lope de Vega, *La vengadora de las mujeres*, Acto 1. The examples placed in the text are representative of general trends in the *comedias*. A more extreme example of misogyny, tending toward downright insult, occurs in such a burlesque work as Cervantes's comic interlude *El juez de los divorcios*: "y si andáis siempre rostrituerta, enojada, celosa, pensativa, manirrota, dormilona, *perezosa*, pendenciera, gruñidora, con otras insolencias de este jaez" (Cervantes, *El juez de los divorcios*, Acto 1, emphasis mine).

32 "noramala [= en hora mala] holgazana, que hile, y que cosa, que no viva ociosa … si quiere no hacer labor" (Quiñones de Benavente, *El Remediador*, Acto 1).

33 "Marido, cuya grande simpleza, en su vida hizo cosa sin pereza" (Calderón, *Las espigas de Ruth*, auto sacramental). In his comic interlude about divorce, Cervantes even has one husband admit that he is lazy: "yo soy el leño, el inhábil, el dejado, y el perezoso" (Cervantes, *El juez de los divorcios*, Acto 1). For an interpretation of Cervantes as a sort of proto-feminist, see Ruth El Saffar, *Beyond Fiction: The Recovery of the Feminine in the Works of Cervantes* (Berkeley: University of California Press, 1983).

34 Lope de Vega, *San Nicolás de Tolentino*, Acto 3; "sin que en mi obligación haya [de]-mora, o pereza a cumplir el voto al punto me parta" (Calderón, *El gran príncipe de Fez*, Acto 1).

35 "Inspection functions ceaselessly. The gaze is alert everywhere … This surveillance is based on a system of permanent registration … [T]he slightest movements are supervised … all events are recorded … power is exercised without division, according to a continuous hierarchical figure, in which each individual is constantly located, examined and distributed … [A]ll this constitutes a compact model of the disciplinary mechanism" (Michel Foucault, "Panopticism," in *Discipline and Punish: The Birth of the Prison*, trans. Alan Sheridan [New York: Vintage, 1995], 195–308, at 195–7).

36 Lope de Vega, *Los melindres de Belisa*, Acto 1.

37 See Max Weber, *The Protestant Ethic and the Spirit of Capitalism*, trans. Talcott Parsons (New York: Dover, 2003).

38 Tirso de Molina, *El amor médico*, Acto 2.

39 Moreto, *La cautela en la amistad*, Jornada 3.

40 "la atención vana de la juventud ociosa" (Moreto, *Santa Rosa del Perú*, Jornada 1); "vencidos los naufragios … de la juventud ociosa" (Tirso de Molina, *Próspera fortuna de don Álvaro de Luna*, Jornada 2).

41 Diamante, *Santa Juliana*, Jornada 1; Moreto, *No puede ser*, Jornada 1.

42 Calderón, *El nuevo hospicio de pobres*, auto sacramental. On students who did not study: "para las letras me faltaba habilidad y me sobraba pereza" (Lope de Vega, *La discreta venganza*, Acto 2). On vacations from school: "Las fiestas que ocioso estaba de mis liciones [= lecciones]" (Lope de Vega, *El cardenal de Belén*, Acto 1).

43 "la Pereza Viejo, con Báculo" (Calderón, *El año santo en Madrid*, auto sacramental); "Esta torpe Anciandad, que perezosa en su Edad, aun hacia el bien no camina" (Calderón, *El nuevo hospicio de pobres*, auto sacramental).

44 "¿Mejor no fuera servir hasta morir, que venir a ser ocioso, y cansado? ¿Y vos viejo?" (Lope de Vega, *La hermosa Ester*, Acto 2).

45 Andrew Solomon, *The Noonday Demon: An Atlas of Depression* (New York: Scribner, 2001), 302. For Sloth's direct connection to depression, see 293.

46 Pérez de Montalbán, *El valiente Nazareno*, Jornada 1; "el pesar es monstruo, que come vidas humanas alimentadas del ocio" (Calderón, *Los cabellos de Absalón*, Jornada 1).

47 Lope de Vega, *Los comendadores de Córdoba*, Jornada 3.

48 Tirso de Molina, *Segunda parte de Santa Juana*, Acto 3.

49 Lope de Vega, *La quinta de Florencia*, Jornada 1.

50 Diamante, *Santa María Magdalena de Pazzi*, Jornada 3.

51 Alarcón, *Todo es ventura*, Acto 3.

52 Moreto's *La fingida Arcadia*, Jornada 2. On melancholy and pastoral in a contemporaneous English context, see Anne-Marie Miller Blaise, "George Herbert's Distemper: An Honest Shepherd's Remedy for Melancholy," *George Herbert Journal* 30.1–2 (2006–7): 59–82.

53 This ambivalence may be found not just in literary portrayals of Sloth, but also in treatises purportedly written to contain this Vice. For example, even Francisco de Luque Fajardo's *Fiel desengaño contra la ociosidad y el juego* (1603) (ed. M. de Riquer [Madrid: Consejo Superior de Investigaciones Científicas, 1955]) found a way to justify *ocio* as long as it was devoted to laudable pursuits; this argument was grounded in the classical concept of *eutrapelia*: "La condena es extendida, pero encontramos una justificación del ocio si se dedica a loables y honestos ejercicios, basado en el conocido concepto de la eutrapelia" (Pedro Ruiz Pérez, "Días lúdicos: juego, ocio y literatura," in *Materia crítica: formas de ocio y de consumo en la cultura áurea*, ed. Enrique García Santo-Tomás [Madrid/Frankfurt: Iberoamericana/Vervuert, 2009], 37–58, at 51).

54 As Pedro Ruiz Pérez points out, the entire genre of pastoral may be read as an extended experiment in literary leisure: "la arcadia pastoril es el escenario de una representación donde los personajes se evaden de su vida cotidiana y entretienen sus ocios" (Ruiz Pérez, "Días lúdicos," 38).

55 Calderón, *Duelos de amor, y lealtad*, Jornada 1.

56 Moreto, *La fingida Arcadia*, Jornada 1.

57 Zamora, *Viento es la dicha de amor*, Acto 1; Calderón, *El nuevo hospicio de pobres*, auto sacramental.

58 Calderón, *El pleito matrimonial*, auto sacramental.

59 Cueva, *La libertad de Roma, por Mucio Cevola*, Acto 3.

60 Diamante, *Alfeo, y Aretusa*, Jornada 2. These lines are pronounced in the house of Desengaño, which is made of mirrors to show those who enter it the true nature of things.

61 Tirso de Molina, *La mujer que manda en casa*, Acto 1.

62 Cueva, *Comedia del príncipe tirano*, Acto 4.

63 Calderón, *Celos aun del aire matan*, Jornada 3. *Ocio* is also spoken of as a recompense for service rendered: "a esos Olmos arredrado, aliento cobre, que algo fatigado, el ocio quiero darle en recompensa" (Calderón, *El orden de Melchisedech*, auto sacramental).

64 Alarcón, *La manganilla de Melilla*, Acto 2. An alternative word used to describe the activity of feet in the context of needing rest is *marchas*, which might appear a curious choice: "*tus fatigadas marchas* puedes aquí descansar, seguro, de que en manjares, lechos, y albergues tendrás las delicias de la vida" (Calderón, *El Viático Cordero*, auto sacramental, emphasis mine). This is obviously a military term, which is actually no surprise considering how many wars Spain fought during this period.

65 Matos Fragoso, *Amor, lealtad, y ventura*, Acto 1.

66 Diamante, *Triunfo de la paz, y el tiempo*, Acto 1, emphasis mine. The candlelight is provided by tapers or *antorchas*: "Así en tranquila paz, en ocio blando, ejércitos de antorchas te coronen" (Pérez de Montalbán, *Cumplir con su obligación*, Jornada 2).

67 Calderón, *La humildad coronada de las plantas*, auto sacramental.

68 Lope de Vega, *La resistencia honrada y Condesa Matilde*, Jornada 3. On the deep sleep of Sloth, we find the lines "reinaba el perezoso sueño, manso, en las libres provincias del descanso" (Diamante, *Santa María del Monte, y convento de San Juan*, Jornada 2); and "la bella dormía en ocio tranquilo" (Solís, *Eurídice, y Orfeo*, Jornada 1). The latter play obviously taps into classical myths which thematize sleep and dreaming. The references to soft beds are found, paradoxically, in the austere Calderón: "se rindió mi pecho al ocio blando del mullido lecho" (Calderón, *Afectos de odio, y amor*, Jornada 2); and "entre Lechos de Pluma mullidos, cuyas Delicias retratan el primero Paraíso" (Calderón, *El año santo de Roma*, auto sacramental). Embroidered sheets appear in Lope de Vega: "si al ocio blando se dieran entre las bordadas camas" (Lope de Vega, *La Santa Liga*, Acto 1).

69 Lope de Vega, *La quinta de Florencia*, Jornada 1; "reposo, y las potencias todas entregado, al descanso, quieto, blando, ocioso, estaba de cuidados apartado" (Cueva, *La muerte de Virginia, y Appio Claudio*, Acto 3).

70 Calderón, *El orden de Melchisedech*, auto sacramental.

71 See Hilaire Kallendorf, "Love Madness and Demonic Possession in Lope de Vega," *Romance Quarterly* 51.3 (2004): 162–82.

72 Lope de Vega, *Las paces de los reyes, y Judía de Toledo*, Acto 1.

73 "bien dicen que se cría en ocio amor, y en dulce fantasía" (Lope de Vega, *La mocedad de Roldán*, Acto 3).

74 Lope de Vega, *El vellocino de oro*, Acto 1.

75 Tirso de Molina, *El melancólico*, Acto 1; Matos Fragoso, *Callar siempre es lo mejor*, Jornada 3.

76 Solís, *El amor al uso*, Jornada 1.

77 Lope de Vega, *El Amor enamorado*, Jornada 1.

78 Moreto, *Santa Rosa del Perú*, Jornada 1.

79 Tirso de Molina, *La huerta de Juan Fernández*, Jornada 2.

80 Lope de Vega, *Hay verdades que en amor*, Acto 3.

81 "Viste un retrato mío, halló la vista ociosa el albedrío: rindióte la pintura, débele mucho el ocio a la hermosura" (Solís, *Las amazonas*, Jornada 1). See Laura R. Bass, *The Drama of the Portrait: Theater and Visual Culture in Early Modern Spain* (University Park: Pennsylvania State University Press, 2008), especially "Introduction: Dramas of the Portrait," 1–11.

82 "que Fabia es hermosa, y que es lástima que esté ociosa, y enamorada, como dice la canción" (Lope de Vega, *La necedad del discreto*, Jornada 2).

83 Calderón, *Amado, y aborrecido*, Jornada 3. A similar example occurs in Agustín Moreto's *La misma conciencia acusa* with the phrase "trocando el ocio por la militar fatiga" (Jornada 1).

84 Zamora, *Áspides hay Basiliscos*, Jornada 2.

85 Calderón, *El lirio y la azucena*, auto sacramental. Likewise, in Guillén de Castro's *El conde de Irlos*, one character says somewhat contemptuously to another, "el ocio, y las paces en tu tierra te entretienen" (Acto 1).

86 Lope de Vega, *La Santa Liga*, Acto 1.

87 "ya olvidados de las bélicas jornadas, los animosos soldados, de las ociosas espadas hacen próvidos arados" (Guillén de Castro, *El mejor esposo*, Jornada 2). The prophecy referenced is Isaiah 2:4, which says of the future Messiah: "And he shall judge the Gentiles and rebuke many people: and they shall turn their swords into ploughshares and their spears into sickles. Nation shall not lift up sword against nation: neither shall they be exercised any more to war."

88 Lope de Vega, *El último godo*, Jornada 2; Lope de Vega, *El postrer godo de España*, Acto 1. The TESO database contains two separate versions of this play: *El último godo* from

a 1647 edition and *El postrer godo de España* from 1617. I have chosen to retain this distinction between the titles due to variations in the text.

89 Guillén de Castro, *El engañarse engañado*, Jornada 1.

90 Tirso de Molina, *El amor médico*, Acto 2.

91 Diamante, *Triunfo de la paz, y el tiempo*, Acto 1.

92 Lope de Vega, *El mayorazgo dudoso*, Jornada 2.

93 Zamora, *El custodio de la Hungría, San Juan Capistrano*, Jornada 3; "Ya le parece mal la vida ociosa, sólo trata de espadas y de lanzas" (Lope de Vega, *La resistencia honrada y Condesa Matilde*, Jornada 2).

94 Lope de Vega, *El bastardo Mudarra*, Acto 2.

95 Lope de Vega, *La noche de San Juan*, Acto 3.

96 Cueva, *La libertad de Roma, por Mucio Cevola*, Acto 4.

97 Lope de Vega, *El rey sin reino*, Acto 2. On the discourse of the Reconquista used to justify "New" World colonization, see Thomas E. Case, "El indio y el moro en las comedias de Lope de Vega," in *Looking at the* Comedia *in the Year of the Quincentennial*, ed. Barbara Mujica and Sharon D. Voros (Lanham, MD: University Press of America, 1993), 13–22. As Case explains, "No olvidemos que en la España de los Reyes Católicos y durante todo el siglo XVI, el llamado descubrimiento de América no era más que una fase de la política de expansión de Castilla que incluía Africa, Alemania, Francia, Italia, y los Países Bajos. El ímpetu de esta expansión se aceleró y se definió con la conquista de Granada en 1492 … La derrota del moro se hizo, por consiguiente, el *sine qua non* de otras conquistas, incluyendo la del Nuevo Mundo" (13).

98 Lope de Vega, *La Santa Liga*, Acto 1.

99 Lope de Vega, *Angélica en el Catay*, Acto 1; Guillén de Castro, *Don Quijote de la Mancha*, Jornada 3.

100 Lope de Vega, *La Santa Liga*, Acto 1; Zamora, *Todo lo vence el Amor*, Jornada 3.

101 Lope de Vega, *Contra valor no hay desdicha*, Acto 1. Conversely, *ocio* can be suspended at will, as in "Ea pues, fuerte Aureliano, deja en suspensión el ocio, logra el laurel que has ceñido" (Calderón, *La gran Cenobia*, Acto 1).

102 Solís, *Las amazonas*, Jornada 3.

103 On Derridian deferral and postponement as applied to *comedia* studies, see Edward H. Friedman, "Deference, *Différance*: The Rhetoric of Deferral," in *The Prince in the Tower: Perceptions of* La vida es sueño, ed. Frederick A. de Armas (Lewisburg: Bucknell University Press, 1993), 41–53.

104 Diamante, *El Hércules de Ocaña*, Jornada 2.

105 Tirso de Molina, *Los lagos de san Vicente*, Acto 1.

106 He says, "Vete, Isidro, a descansar" (Lope de Vega, *San Isidro labrador de Madrid*, Acto 2).

107 On other Golden Age reimaginings of the classical *locus amoenus*, see Alfred Rodríguez and Joel F. Dykstra, "Cervantes's Parodic Rendering of a Traditional Topos:

Locus Amoenus," *Cervantes: Bulletin of the Cervantes Society of America* 17.2 (1997): 115–21.

108 Lope de Vega, *La fortuna merecida,* Acto 1.

109 "en ese monte … en cuya frescura hallé ocio, y descanso" (Calderón, *El Príncipe constante,* Jornada 2).

110 Zamora, *Todo lo vence el Amor,* Jornada 1.

111 Moreto, *El desdén, con el desdén,* Jornada 1.

112 Alarcón, *La prueba de las promesas,* Acto 2.

113 Antonio de Guevara, *Menosprecio de corte y alabanza de aldea* (1539), ed. M. Martínez de Burgos (Madrid: Espasa-Calpe, 1952). Pedro Ruiz Pérez comments on the continuities of this theme running through the pastoral genre: "El discurso pastoril en el XVI español se presenta como una continuación estilizada de los anteriores modelos cortesanos, a través de la incorporación de la filosofía platónica y una forma de menosprecio de corte, que no ha dado aún en gusto por la ciudad" (Ruiz Pérez, "Días lúdicos," 39).

114 As Pedro Ruiz Pérez notes, "Se plasma así en los propios textos la relación de la literatura con el ocio justo en los momentos en que se está convirtiendo, en una parte importante, en negocio y profesionalidad" (Ruiz Pérez, "Días lúdicos," 50).

115 Calderón, *Mujer, llora, y vencerás,* Jornada 3.

116 Calderón, *Apolo, y Climene,* Jornada 3.

117 Calderón, *La devoción de la Misa,* auto sacramental.

118 Tirso de Molina, *El amor médico,* Acto 1.

119 "vanidades, que en humanos libros el ocio escribió" (Calderón, *Los dos amantes del cielo,* Jornada 1).

120 "la quietud reservo, bien es llamar las Musas cuando el ocio se cansa de atender vulgo protervo" (Lope de Vega, *La mayor virtud de un rey,* Preliminares de obra).

121 Pérez de Montalbán, *Cumplir con su obligación,* Preliminares de obra.

122 Alarcón, *La cueva de Salamanca,* Preliminares de obra.

123 Alarcón, *La verdad sospechosa,* Acto 1.

124 Calderón, *Los cabellos de Absalón,* Jornada 2.

125 Lope de Vega, *La mocedad de Roldán,* Acto 3. Pedro Ruiz Pérez comments on the popularity of these courtly leisure activities: "El alejamiento de los escenarios bélicos condujo a su ficcionalización en cañas, torneos y justas" (Ruiz Pérez, "Días lúdicos," 54).

126 Solís, *El alcázar del secreto,* Jornada 3. See Sidney Donnell, *Feminizing the Enemy: Imperial Spain, Transvestite Drama, and the Crisis of Masculinity* (Lewisburg: Bucknell University Press, 2003).

127 Moreto, *Primero es la honra,* Jornada 1.

128 Calderón, *Los cabellos de Absalón,* Jornada 2; Moreto, *Hasta el fin nadie es dichoso,* Jornada 1.

129 "[La] ley jamás prohibió andar a nadie a caballo … Use su poltronería del coche" (Pérez de Montalbán, *Despreciar lo que se quiere*, Jornada 1). On legislation designed to control the use of coaches by noblemen in colonial Mexico and Lima, see Alejandro López Álvarez, "Los vehículos representativos en la configuración de la corte virreinal: México y Lima, 1590–1700," in *Materia crítica: formas de ocio y de consumo en la cultura áurea*, ed. Enrique García Santo-Tomás (Madrid/Frankfurt: Iberoamericana/Vervuert, 2009), 269–92.

130 Don Cruickshank, *Don Pedro Calderón* (Cambridge: Cambridge University Press, 2009), 190.

131 Pérez de Montalbán, *El mariscal de Virón*, Jornada 1.

132 "Poltrón, vil, y afeminado tú verás" (Cueva, *El saco de Roma, y muerte de Borbón*, Acto 3).

133 Rojas Zorrilla, *No hay ser padre siendo Rey*, Jornada 1.

134 Calderón, *El Joseph de las mujeres*, Jornada 1.

135 Lope de Vega, *La bella Aurora*, Acto 2.

136 Tirso de Molina, *No hay peor sordo*, Jornada 3.

137 Tirso de Molina, *La santa Juana*, Acto 1.

138 "mi voz, en quien yo libro de las fatigas del ocio, tal vez el descanso mío" (Moreto, *Lo que puede la aprehensión*, Jornada 1).

139 Lope de Vega, *Las flores de Don Juan, y rico, y pobre trocados*, Acto 2.

140 Tirso de Molina, *Segunda parte de Santa Juana*, Acto 3.

141 Diamante, *Más encanto es la hermosura*, Jornada 2. Gardens are further associated with Sloth in the following lines: "ameno de sus jardines, que hube de hacer del divertimiento pereza" (Calderón, *Fieras afemina amor*, Jornada 1).

142 Leah Middlebrook, *Imperial Lyric: New Poetry and New Subjects in Early Modern Spain* (University Park: Pennsylvania State University Press, 2009), 22.

143 Lope de Vega, *El conde Fernán González*, Acto 1.

144 Diamante, *No aspirar a merecer*, Jornada 1.

145 On this conflict as it was perceived in the classical period, with an interesting foreshadowing of one of the medieval Vices, see Eleanor Winsor Leach, "*Otium* as *Luxuria*: Economy of Status in the Younger Pliny's Letters," *Arethusa* 36.2 (2003): 147–65. On the reception of these classical ideas in Renaissance Spain, in particular in a treatise by Rodrigo Caro bearing the title *Días geniales o lúdicros* (manuscript ca 1626), see Ruiz Pérez, "Días lúdicos," 52–3. Caro's treatise has been published in a modern edition: Rodrigo Caro, *Días geniales o lúdicros*, ed. J.-P. Étienvre (Madrid: Espasa-Calpe, 1978). As Ruiz Pérez explains, "Caro explota el campo semántico que reúne juego, entretenimiento, sueño, ocio y ficción, todos ellos como vías de salida de la realidad del *negotium*, la misma a la que recurren ya de modo amplio en el primer cuarto del XVII quienes quieren sustentarse alimentando el *otium* de los demás, convertidos en compradores y lectores" (53).

146 Lope de Vega, *La resistencia honrada y Condesa Matilde* (1609), Jornada 1, emphasis mine.

147 Zamora, *Judás Iscariote*, Acto 1. "Erasmus was associated with moral virtues or social values held to be admirable; they were tolerance, restraint, moderation" (Bruce Mansfield, *Man on His Own: Interpretations of Erasmus, c. 1750–1920*, 2 vols [Toronto: University of Toronto Press, 1992], 11–12). On the influence of Erasmus's ideas in Spain, see Marcel Bataillon, *Erasme et l'Espagne*, trans. Antonio Alatorre as *Erasmo y España: estudios sobre la historia espiritual del siglo XVI*, 2 vols (Mexico City: Fondo de Cultura Económica, 1950). Alban Forcione explores the impact of Erasmian thought specifically on Golden Age literature: "Erasmus rejected the austere dualisms characteristic of rigid stoicism and ascetic Christianity, which maintained that the affections and instincts were a ruinous part of the human being, ever to be held in check and suppressed through discipline. To be sure, reason is the authentic nature of man, and the passions are never to be glorified as certain naturalistic philosophies had allowed, but they are not to be condemned as totally unnatural. If they are channeled according to the direction of man's true nature, that is, reason, for creative purposes, they are in fact natural and beneficial" (Alban Forcione, *Cervantes and the Humanist Vision: A Study of Four Exemplary Novels* [Princeton: Princeton University Press, 1982], 162).

148 Diamante, *El nacimiento de Cristo*, Acto 2.

149 Moreto, *Lo que puede la aprehensión*, Jornada 1.

150 Solís, *El amor al uso*, Jornada 3.

151 "Llega pícaro poltrón" (Lope de Vega, *El Genovés liberal*, Acto 1).

152 Lope de Vega, *El villano en su rincón*, Acto 2.

153 Lope de Vega, *La hermosa fea*, Acto 1.

154 Lope de Vega, *La bella Aurora*, Acto 2.

155 Lope de Vega, *El bastardo Mudarra*, Acto 3.

156 Diamante, *Cumplirle a Dios la palabra*, Jornada 2.

157 Lope de Vega, *El soldado amante*, Acto 2. Tirso de Molina further associates Sloth with extravagant gift giving: "al ocio, y al regalo den generosos desvelos" (*El mayor desengaño*, Acto 1).

158 Lope de Vega, *Hay verdades que en amor*, Acto 1; "no queda en qué entretener tan largo, y ocioso día, o porque solas estemos, o por no admitir galanes" (Lope de Vega, *Las flores de don Juan, y rico, y pobre trocados*, Acto 2).

159 Alarcón, *La prueba de las promesas*, Acto 2. In "Días lúdicos: juego, ocio y literatura," Pedro Ruiz Pérez addresses this aspect of leisure, i.e. the fact of being waited on and therefore being freed from mundane tasks. He describes "la aparición de un nuevo espacio, que … viene marcado precisamente por ser el de la no ocupación, el de la liberación de las servidumbres de lo cotidiano" (Ruiz Pérez, "Días lúdicos," 54).

160 Diamante, *Amor es sangre, y no puede engañarse*, Jornada 2.

161 Rojas Zorrilla, *Los áspides de Cleopatra*, Jornada 1.

162 Calderón, *El día mayor de los días*, Acto 1.
163 Cueva, *La constancia de Arcelina*, Acto 2.
164 Solís, *El alcázar del secreto*, Jornada 2.
165 Lope de Vega, *El serafín humano*, Acto 2.
166 Isidore in Lope de Vega's *San Isidro labrador de Madrid* recalls the parable in a hypothetical scenario: "Si yo … [f]ui tan malo, y perezoso, que vuestra hacienda no aumento" (Lope de Vega, *San Isidro labrador de Madrid*, Acto 2). On master/servant relationships in the drama, see Hilaire Kallendorf, "Rulers and Subjects, Masters and Servants" in *Conscience on Stage: The* Comedia *as Casuistry in Early Modern Spain* (Toronto: University of Toronto Press, 2007), 113–17.
167 "despertad, que no se da el premio al Perezoso, al Próvido sí" (Calderón, *El primer refugio del hombre, y próbatica piscina*, auto sacramental).
168 Lope de Vega, *Pedro Carbonero*, Acto 1.
169 Middlebrook, *Imperial Lyric*, 146.
170 Lope de Vega, *La ilustre fregona*, Jornada 1. The rural background of these foot soldiers is highlighted explicitly in these plays: "soldado nombres, un villano que ayer tan perezoso los bueyes de su arado iba siguiendo" (Lope de Vega, *Las grandezas de Alejandro*, Acto 1).
171 Quiñones de Benavente, *El mago*, Acto 1.
172 "ríense del perezoso, sepultado en triste olvido" (Lope de Vega, *El rústico del cielo*, Acto 1). On early modern Spaniards' concern over *fama*, or fame, see this book's chapter on Envy.
173 Cervantes, *Los baños de Argel*, Jornada 2.
174 Diamante, *Triunfo de la paz, y el tiempo*, Acto 1.
175 Calderón, *El mayor encanto, amor*, Jornada 3.
176 Calderón, *La serpiente de metal*, auto sacramental.

5. That Gnawing Hunger: The Plus Size of Gluttony

1 Alarcón, *Todo es ventura*, Acto 3; Calderón, *El gran mercado del mundo*, auto sacramental; Lope de Vega, *El postrer godo de España*, Acto 2. Note: *martas* are small carnivorous animals related to the weasel, considered a delicacy in early modern Spain.
2 Calderón, *El jardín de Falerina*, auto sacramental. The *comedias* contain multiple echoes of this forbidden fruit: "no hay cosa más hermosa, ni fruta que a la golosa voluntad así despierta" (Cervantes, *El rufián dichoso*, Jornada 2).
3 Calderón, *El año santo de Roma*, auto sacramental.
4 Calderón, *El primer refugio del hombre, y probática piscina*, auto sacramental.
5 Calderón, *Los encantos de la Culpa*, auto sacramental.
6 Calderón, *La cena de Baltasar*, auto sacramental. This famous meal from the Old Testament (Daniel chapter 5), where God's hand writes on the wall, also provides a standard allusion in other similar works, as when a meal is described as being so

delicious that "la puedan envidiar las Mesas de Baltasar, y los Banquetes de Asuero" (Calderón, *El gran mercado del mundo*, auto sacramental).

7 "de ese Banquete … sus delicias paran en ser sus Viandas tan raras, tan exquisitas" (Calderón, *¿Quién hallará mujer fuerte?* loa for auto sacramental).

8 Calderón, *El diablo mudo*, auto sacramental.

9 Calderón, *El primer refugio del hombre, y probática piscina*, auto sacramental.

10 "en los Jardines, de varias bellezas llenos, donde todo sea Delicias, Bailes, Músicas, y Juegos, a quien seguirán Banquetes tan varios, como opulentos" (Calderón, *La serpiente de metal*, auto sacramental).

11 Calderón, *El nuevo hospicio de pobres*, auto sacramental.

12 "las Delicias, Gula, Envidia, y Ambición hoy mis sentidos posean" (Calderón, *El gran teatro del mundo*, auto sacramental).

13 "en bailes, amores, y banquetes divertida pasa lo más de su vida" (Calderón, *A Dios por razón de Estado*, auto sacramental).

14 "la Gula, y la Lascivia, que el concurso perviertan, la devoción impidan" (Calderón, *A María el corazón*, auto sacramental).

15 Appetite appears in the *autos* as the base child of the bodily or corporeal senses: "el Apetito grosero … hijo de los Sentidos Corporales" (Calderón, *Los encantos de la Culpa*, loa for auto sacramental). In the same play, he enters the stage dressed as a Villano. Appetite clearly encompasses both the realm of sex and the realm of food, as in "aquel Apetito de Lascivias, y Viandas" (Calderón, *La segunda esposa, y triunfar muriendo*, auto sacramental). A related word is *gusto*, used to refer specifically to the sense of taste. Gusto appears as a character in Calderón's auto *El nuevo palacio del retiro*, where he explains his raison d'être: "Yo, que soy el más goloso Sentido, y de más placer; pues sólo trato en comer" (Calderón, *El nuevo palacio del retiro*, auto sacramental). Conversely, the lack of Gusto refers to the inability to enjoy food: "¿Dónde está el Gusto, pues todos los Manjares aborrezco?" (Calderón, *El pleito matrimonial*, auto sacramental). As for the specific relationship of Apetito to Gula, Apetito announces that he is governed by the Affect of Gluttony: "el Afecto de la Gula es el que a mí me gobierna, Vivandero de Campaña" (Calderón, *El indulto general*, loa for auto sacramental). Alternatively, Gluttony appears as an adulterous woman who is the wife of Appetite: "En la Casa de la Gula, una Adúltera perdida … Mujer del Apetito, de sus brazos le desvía" (Calderón, *El primer refugio del hombre, y probática piscina*, auto sacramental). These are clearly related concepts which morph ever so slightly in their relationship to each other from one dramatic work to the next according to each particular author's artistic and theological sensibility. In Golden Age literature, food is frequently associated with sex, as in "Si me prestase la salsa de tu hija hermosa" (Lope de Vega, *El galán Castrucho*, Acto 1). On archival evidence for historical cases linking food with sex, see Scott K. Taylor, *Honor and Violence in Golden Age Spain* (New Haven: Yale University Press, 2008), 219. Taylor affirms, "[t]he exchange and sharing of meals and sex were normally part of the relationship between husbands and

wives" (219). Gluttony is further associated in the *comedias* with women of ill repute, as in "ocuparos en regocijos y fiestas, en banquetes y placeres, en deleites de mujeres honestas, y deshonestas" (Lope de Vega, *Bamba*, Jornada 3).

16 Calderón, *El primer refugio del hombre, y probática piscina*, auto sacramental; "Un glotón, con mano franca, gastaba sólo en comer" (Alarcón, *El semejante a sí mismo*, Acto 3). However, in some iterations Gluttony could mean simply the desire for food, as when a character declares that he is still prone to this Vice, even if he is immune to all the others. He says that Gluttony is "la más natural violencia, pues sin Soberbia, Avaricia, Lascivia, e Ira, me queda el deseo de viandas, y de bebidas diversas, con que me brinda la Gula" (Calderón, *Lo que va del hombre a Dios*, loa for auto sacramental). As Lope de Vega notes ironically in one of his plays, "Nunca ... engendró adulterio la hambre" (Lope de Vega, *El serafín humano*, Acto 1). In this sense Gluttony is perhaps more safe morally than Lust. In the words of Calderón, "el Apetito ... es el vicio que con la vida sólo acaba" (Calderón, *El primer refugio del hombre, y probática piscina*, auto sacramental). Due to the fact that eating is tied to survival, Gluttony is actually the hardest Sin to escape.

17 "este glotón así ejercita la boca que a vómitos se provoca" (Lope de Vega, *Roma abrasada*, Acto 1).

18 "que en banquetes, y en amores, en mujeres, y en manjares, no hay desde estar satisfecho a estar harto dos instantes" (Solís, *El amor al uso*, Jornada 1). *Hartura*, or the condition of being stuffed full of food, is seen to be the next step beyond normal Appetite: "En la casa del placer ha convidado a comer al apetito la hartura" (Tirso de Molina, *Tanto es lo demás como lo de menos*, Acto 1).

19 "la Gula con un Cestillo, o Fuente de Frutas" (Calderón, *El indulto general*, loa for auto sacramental). The cup or *copa* appears in Calderón's *A María el corazón*, auto sacramental.

20 "con más preciosos Vinos, al sabor de otros Manjares en mejor Mesa te brindo" (Calderón, *El año santo en Madrid*, loa for auto sacramental).

21 Drunkenness appears next to Gluttony in phrases such as "la embriaguez del apetito" (Calderón, *El gran príncipe de Fez*, Jornada 2) and "descuidado no vivas entre Baco y entre Venus" (Lope de Vega, *Bamba*, Jornada 3).

22 *Sangría* is specifically referenced as the favourite drink of a glutton: "es goloso, y bebe con Luquete" (Moreto, *Antioco, y Seleuco*, Jornada 1). *Luquete* was a slice of orange with the peel still intact.

23 Calderón, *Dicha, y desdicha del nombre*, Jornada 2; Tirso de Molina, *La venganza de Tamar*, Jornada 3.

24 "goza delicias de caza, y pesca" (Calderón, *Los hijos de la Fortuna Teágenes, y Cariclea*, Jornada 2).

25 Calderón, *El segundo blasón del Austria*, auto sacramental.

26 Rojas Zorrilla, *No hay padre siendo Rey*, Jornada 1; "Delicias de los manjares, viendo festiva a su Reina" (Rojas Zorrilla, *Los Áspides de Cleopatra*, Jornada 2).

27 Lope de Vega, *El hijo de los leones*, Acto 2.

28 Zamora, *Duendes son alcahuetes, alias el foleto, segunda parte*, Jornada 2.

29 Lope de Vega, *Contra valor no hay desdicha*, Acto 2. Note here the wordplay on *plata* (silver) and *platos* (plates or dishes, including different recipes for food).

30 "¡Qué Aparadores tan bellos! ¡Qué Viandas! ¡Qué Bebidas! ¡Qué lucidos Escuderos! ¡Y qué Pajes tan golosos!" (Calderón, *Sueños hay, que verdad son*, auto sacramental); "hoy Cortesano se halla, en sus delicias envuelto" (Calderón, *El año santo en Madrid*, auto sacramental).

31 "resolverme preciso, a seguir hoy Cortesano los rumbos de mi Apetito: Soberbia, Avaricia, Envidia, Pereza, Ira, Gula, Amigos, a vosotros vengo" (Calderón, *El año santo en Madrid*, auto sacramental). Specific courtiers are also described as gluttonous in the *comedias*; for example, one particular countess could not seem to resist stopping at the confectioner's shop: "Señor, advierte una cosa, que esta Condesa es golosa, y esto lo hace por entrar sola en ese confitero" (Moreto, *El lindo Don Diego*, Jornada 3).

32 On anti-clericalism in the picaresque, see David R. Castillo, *(A)wry Views: Anamorphosis, Cervantes, and the Early Picaresque* (West Lafayette: Purdue University Press, 2001), 32.

33 Calderón, *La dama duende*, Jornada 2.

34 Lope de Vega, *El rústico del cielo*, Acto 3.

35 "De mi mesa han de comer sus Sacerdotes manjares dignos de quien sirve altares" (Tirso de Molina, *La mujer que manda en casa*, Acto 1).

36 "y la Gula con otro [Estandarte], y en él pintado un Capelo [cardinal's hat]" (Calderón, *El año santo en Madrid*, auto sacramental).

37 Calderón, *El diablo mudo*, auto sacramental.

38 Calderón, *A María el corazón*, auto sacramental.

39 Calderón, *El diablo mudo*, auto sacramental; "por acudir de Epicuro solamente a la alabanza de sus Manjares" (Calderón, *El nuevo hospicio de pobres*, auto sacramental).

40 Calderón, *El jardín de Falerina*, auto sacramental.

41 "traed, y el Néctar … de Dioses le servid" (Calderón, *El jardín de Falerina*, auto sacramental); "dioses del mundo fueron ambrosia, y nectar. Delicias de los manjares" (Rojas Zorrilla, *Los áspides de Cleopatra*, Jornada 2).

42 "qué golpe de fortuna, ayer dejé el faisán, y otros manjares en suma; hoy una cebolla, y pan" (Lope de Vega, *El último godo*, Jornada 2).

43 "¿pues quién querrá con diferente apetito comer siempre de un manjar?" (Rojas Zorrilla, *Lo que son mujeres*, Jornada 2).

44 The stage directions for one *auto* read, "Sale por debajo del Tablado una Mesa con muchas Viandas" (Calderón, *Los encantos de la Culpa*, auto sacramental). The stark moment of *desengaño* comes when a character announces to the audience, "hoy verás todas aquestas Viandas del Viento desvanecidos, en humo, en polvo, en nada" (Calderón, *Los encantos de la Culpa*, auto sacramental). This last line echoes a famous sonnet

by Góngora, "Mientras por competir con tu cabello" (1582): "en tierra, en humo, en polvo, en sombra, en nada."

45 Tirso de Molina, *El burlador de Sevilla*, Jornada 3.

46 On Jesuit meditation technique in Baroque literature, see Hilaire Kallendorf, "Tears in the Desert: Baroque Adaptations of the Book of Lamentations by John Donne and Francisco de Quevedo," *Journal of Medieval and Early Modern Studies* 39.1 (2009): 31–42.

47 "ninguno interesa más que el Apetito, en que haya Alimentos" (Calderón, *Los alimentos del hombre*, auto sacramental).

48 Calderón, *El diablo mudo*, auto sacramental.

49 "¿cuándo qué apetecer tiene un triste, que no tiene qué poseer?" (Calderón, *Los alimentos del hombre*, auto sacramental).

50 "¿Que me tenga yo mi gula con cuatro dedos de moho? ¿Adónde vive el hartazgo, señores, que no le topo?" (Rojas Zorrilla, *Los tres blasones de España*, Jornada 1).

51 On the Baroque age's obsession with grotesque deformity, see Frances K. Barasch, "Definitions: Renaissance and Baroque, Grotesque Construction and Deconstruction," *Modern Language Studies* 13.2 (1983): 60–7; and James Iffland, *Quevedo and the Grotesque*, 2 vols (London: Tamesis, 1983).

52 "de la gula a la carcoma" (Zamora, *Judás Iscariote*, Jornada 3).

53 Calderón, *La semilla, y la cizaña*, auto sacramental.

54 Tirso de Molina, *Tanto es lo demás como lo de menos*, Acto 1.

55 "[en la] mesa sentado Nineucio abrasándose, y muchos platos, echando de los manjares llamas" (Tirso de Molina, *Tanto es lo demás como lo de menos*, Acto 3).

56 Tirso de Molina, *Tanto es lo demás como lo de menos*, Acto 3. His fate is similar to that of the king in Lope's burlesque comedy *La ventura sin buscarla* who dies from overeating.

57 Calderón, *A tu próximo como a ti*, Acto 1, emphasis mine. The character who experiences these gustatory visions concludes, "Sin duda, que estás, Deseo, en las delicias del Mundo, pues me haces estos acuerdos" (Calderón, *A tu próximo como a ti*, Acto 1).

58 Lope de Vega, *Don Juan de Castro, primera parte*, Acto 2.

59 Tirso de Molina, *La fingida Arcadia*, Jornada 1. A similar reference appears in a *loa* for an *auto* by Calderón: "viandas, y … bebidas diversas, con que me brinda la Gula, desde su abundante Mesa, al aparatoso fausto de gulosas opulencias" (Calderón, *Lo que va del hombre a Dios*, loa for auto sacramental).

60 Calderón, *A María el corazón*, auto sacramental. Note here the wordplay on *rica*, which can mean either *rich* as in "delicious food" or *rich* as in "wealthy."

61 Lope de Vega, *Las flores de Don Juan, y rico, y pobre trocados*, Acto 2.

62 Anonymous, *La vida de Lazarillo de Tormes y de sus fortunas y adversidades*, ed. Julio Cejador y Frauca (Madrid: Espasa-Calpe, 1976), Tratado III, 181.

63 Lope de Vega, *El primer Fajardo*, Acto 1. It is difficult to determine a modern equivalency for this amount because as Scott Taylor explains, a *maravedí* was not an

actual coin but instead a unit of account, basically "a way to fix a price on something" (Taylor, *Honor and Violence*, 43). However, it is possible to tell something about buying power by comparing figures for what a *maravedí* could purchase in a given year or decade. For example, "a poor man was getting by on thirty maravedís a day in the 1620s" (91). So 3,000 *maravedíes* would have been enough to keep a poor man alive for 100 days during that decade.

64 Lope de Vega, *Loa en alabanza de la humildad.*

65 "si el huésped viniera ayer no fuera de casa ayuno. Pero hoy por Dios, que aun apenas tengo pan" (Lope de Vega, *El halcón de Federico*, Acto 3).

66 This is the case with the following exchange among villagers who are celebrating a country wedding:

VILLANOS: Si es que habemos de almorzar,
vamos de aquí, ¿a qué aguardamos?
SILVANO: Padres, no los convidamos,
porque hay poco que tragar. (Moreto, *El esclavo de su hijo*, Jornada 1).

67 Pérez de Montalbán, *El hijo del Serafín, San Pedro de Alcántara*, Jornada 3.

68 However, some cooks were thought to take pleasure merely in cooking – as opposed to tasting – the food. The cook who is of this philosophy is likened to a pimp, who enjoys arranging for couples to meet but does not engage in illicit sexual activity himself: "cocinero, y alcahuete: pues sin probar un bocado de los manjares que ha hecho, suele quedar satisfecho de sólo haberlos guisado" (Calderón, *Peor está que estaba*, Jornada 3).

69 "¿Yo al páramo de las ondas, cuando puedo ir al abrigo de las Ciudades? ¿Yo a ver tribulaciones, peligros, y tormentos, cuando sé que en las delicias del siglo hay músicas, y saraos, banquetes, y regocijos?" (Calderón, *La nave del mercader*, auto sacramental); "divirtamos pesares, pongan aquí la mesa, y los manjares" (Tirso de Molina, *La mujer que manda en casa*, Acto 2).

70 Pérez de Montalbán, *Como amante, y como honrada*, Jornada 1, emphasis mine.

71 Don Cruickshank, *Don Pedro Calderón* (Cambridge: Cambridge University Press, 2009), 10.

72 Margaret Rich Greer, "Constituting Community: A New Historical Perspective on the Autos of Calderón," in *New Historicism and the Comedia: Poetics, Politics and Praxis*, ed. José A. Madrigal (Boulder: Society of Spanish and Spanish-American Studies, 1997), 41–68, at 52–3. She cites a document titled "Chumacero to Felipe IV," 6 Feb. 1647, A.M.E. 42, ff. 7r-7v, as quoted in R.A. Stradling's *Philip IV and the Government of Spain*.

73 Cruickshank detects several allusions to hunger in Calderón's works which might not be immediately obvious, such as in the play *El hombre pobre todo es trazas*, where he finds "jokes about the philosopher Nicomedes (*ni comedes = ni coméis*, nor do you eat)

and the Concilio Niceno (*ni ceno*, nor do I dine) which are also made by the hungry Clarín in *La vida es sueño*" (Cruickshank, *Don Pedro Calderón*, 92).

74 Lope de Vega, *El rústico del cielo*, Acto 1.

75 Tirso de Molina, *La villana de Vallecas*, Acto 2.

76 Lope de Vega, *Los locos por el cielo*, Acto 3.

77 Lope de Vega, *San Nicolás de Tolentino*, Acto 1.

78 Lope de Vega, *El Hamete de Toledo*, Acto 3.

79 Moreto, *El licenciado Vidriera*, Jornada 2.

80 Some stage characters express a wish that Gluttony *were* a problem for them; in that hypothetical case, at least they would be getting enough food to eat: "¡Quién al Apetito viera, que matara la hambre, y fuera la Gula la que matara!" (Calderón, *El primer refugio del hombre, y probática piscina*, auto sacramental).

81 For more specific connections between these two genres, see Edward H. Friedman, "Picaresque Sensibility and the *Comedia*," in *A Companion to Early Modern Hispanic Theater*, ed. Hilaire Kallendorf (Leiden: Brill), forthcoming.

82 As Culpa explains her disguise, which also, incidentally, involved cross-dressing, "Pues yo, si a escucharte llego, que como Apetito vas, ciego por fuerza serás, yo seré Mozo de Ciego" (Calderón, *El gran mercado del mundo*, loa for auto sacramental).

83 "los manjares, que hurtándolos de tu mesa le ministran" (Tirso de Molina, *La mujer que manda en casa*, Acto 2).

84 Moreto, *Santa Rosa del Perú*, Jornada 3.

85 Rojas Zorrilla, *Progne y Filomena*, Jornada 2.

86 Lope de Vega, *Los locos de Valencia*, Acto 3.

87 Moreto, *El mejor amigo, el rey*, Jornada 2.

88 Calderón, *Celos aun del aire matan*, Jornada 2. The dialogue about food continues:

CLARÍN: Ir conmigo no rehúses.
RÚSTICO: No haré, si a comer me llevas.
(Calderón, *Celos aun del aire matan*, Jornada 2)

89 Moreto, *La fuerza del natural*, Jornada 1.

90 Tirso de Molina, *Don Gil de las calzas verdes*, Acto 1.

91 Moreto, *El parecido*, Jornada 1.

92 Gula announces her intention to sell food to foreigners at the inn: "Día es hoy de Forasteros, la ganancia está segura" (Calderón, *El gran mercado del mundo*, auto sacramental).

93 "Salen la Gula, vestida de Ventero, y la Lascivia de Criada" (Calderón, *El gran mercado del mundo*, auto sacramental). In an example of cross-genre continuity, a female innkeeper is also described as gluttonous in a *comedia*: "ella es golosa, chismosa, respondona, y alza el grito, ventanera, y todo" (Moreto, *El lindo Don Diego*, Jornada 1).

94 Lope de Vega, *Los ramilletes de Madrid*, Acto 1.

95 "Gula, y Apetito le sirvan la Mesa" (Calderón, *El indulto general*, loa for auto sacramental).

96 Lope de Vega, *Querer la propia desdicha*, Acto 2.

97 Gluttony is associated with gypsies again through the figurative code of fashion emanating from theatrical costumes: "Salen la Culpa, y Gula de Gitanos" (Calderón, *El gran mercado del mundo*, auto sacramental).

98 Tirso de Molina, *Tanto es lo demás como lo de menos*, Acto 2.

99 Moreto, *Trampa adelante*, Jornada 1. The elderly Florencio in Moreto's *El esclavo de su hijo* languishes as a captive in a "Moorish" jail without food for three days, at the end of which he vilifies his captor:

Sobre el quitarme el sustento
tres días, fiero León,
encarnizado, y hambriento
[¿]pides agua al corazón
que está sin vigor, ni aliento? (Moreto, *El esclavo de su hijo*, Jornada 2)

This man's cruel captor orders that his only food be thoughts, and his only drink be tears: "Hola, estos esclavos lleva a una mazmorra, y en prueba de que los corrige, y doma, éste, pensamientos coma, y de sus lágrimas beba" (Moreto, *El esclavo de su hijo*, Jornada 2).

100 Calderón, *El gran mercado del mundo*, auto sacramental.

101 Calderón, *La nave del mercader*, auto sacramental.

102 Calderón, *El primer refugio del hombre, y probática piscina*, auto sacramental.

103 "que el Apetito, siendo placer, sea pesar" (Calderón, *El pastor fido*, auto sacramental).

104 "en sus Gradas el Apetito, de Villano Ciego" (Calderón, *El nuevo hospicio de pobres*, auto sacramental).

105 Lope de Vega, *Las mujeres sin hombres*, Acto 1.

106 Rojas Zorrilla, *Los áspides de Cleopatra*, Jornada 1; a similar passage is "Mira que la privación levanta todo mortal apetito" (Lope de Vega, *Las mujeres sin hombres*, Acto 1). Alternatively – in both amorous and culinary contexts – deprivation is said to enhance appetite ("siempre la privación fue aumento del apetito" [Tirso de Molina, *Quien calla, otorga*, Acto 2]) or to be the mother of appetite ("toda la privación es del apetito madre" [Tirso de Molina, *La venganza de Tamar*, Jornada 1]).

107 Tirso de Molina, *El castigo del penséque*, Acto 1.

108 Anne J. Cruz, *Discourses of Poverty: Social Reform and the Picaresque Novel in Early Modern Spain* (Toronto: University of Toronto Press, 1999), xi.

109 "Colación, ¿pues es hoy día de ayuno? ¿ Hay tal pedir, pidiera más un pobre?" (Tirso de Molina, *Las viudas*, Acto 1). In a further moral descent, picaresque figures such as Cervantes's Pedro de Urdemalas admit to stealing even from beggars: "a tener hambre

aprendí … Supe hurtar la limosna, y disculparme, y mentir" (Cervantes, *Pedro de Urdemalas*, Jornada 1). Surely this must be some measure of the degree of economic desperation to which Spain had sunk.

110 "advertí, que en el lugar ni una migaja dejaste" (Tirso de Molina, *La villana de Vallecas*, Acto 2).

111 For example, in one scene a supposedly wounded soldier limps onto the stage with a swollen leg:

SOLDADO: Señora pierna ya llega
tarde, porque habrán comido.
Duelos la dé Dios, amen,
si no bastan los que tiene,
porque tan despacio viene,
pues ella come también.
Mal la podré sustentar,
si no me sustenta a mí.
MORATA: ¿Pierna gorda viene aquí?
RUBIO: Pues ¿cuándo suele faltar?
MORATA: Más ducados le ha valido,
que si la tuviera sana;
yo pienso, que toda es lana,
y que aquel bulto es fingido.

(Lope de Vega, *San Isidro labrador de Madrid*, Acto 3)

112 Moreto, *El parecido*, Jornada 3.

113 "But if thy enemy be hungry, give him to eat; if he thirst, give him to drink" (Romans 12:20). This New Testament verse is an echo of Proverbs 25:21. The same assumption extended to such basic needs as minimal clothing: "los vestidos, y manjares comunes los hizo Dios" (Tirso de Molina, *La huerta de Juan Fernández*, Jornada 1).

114 The connection occurs when the glutton receives his comeuppance: "arrepentido lloras aquella Soberbia pasada, aquel Apetito de Lascivias, y Viandas … el Desprecio de los Pobres" (Calderón, *La segunda esposa, y triunfar muriendo*, auto sacramental).

115 See, for example, Pieter Claesz, *Still Life with Peacock Pie, Roasted Fowl, and Fruit* (1627), formerly on the art market in London, figure 18.11 of William B. Jordan, *Juan van der Hamen y León and the Court of Madrid* (New Haven: Yale University Press, 2005), 281 (figure 13).

116 Calderón, *El gran mercado del mundo*, auto sacramental.

117 For actual portraits of persons used as props on the *comedia* stage, see Laura Bass, *The Drama of the Portrait: Theater and Visual Culture in Early Modern Spain* (University Park: Pennsylvania State University Press, 2008). Another *comedia* character

seems to allude to the dead carcasses in the still-life paintings when he remarks gloomily, "En la mesa los manjares me saben a lo que fueron" (Diamante, *El sol de la sierra*, Jornada 2). Even in the realm of food, it would seem, the Baroque age was obsessed with death and decay.

118 Calderón, *La Puente de Mantible*, Jornada 2.

119 Tirso de Molina, *Tanto es lo demás como lo de menos*, Acto 3.

120 For example, "Unas mesas derribadas, sus viandas, y vasos veo … por mísero trofeo de su opulencia" (Calderón, *Los hijos de la Fortuna Teágenes, y Cariclea*, Jornada 2).

121 Calderón, *Lo que va del hombre a Dios*, auto sacramental.

122 On the impact of "New" World exploration on Old World cuisine, see Roger Schlesinger, *In the Wake of Columbus: The Impact of the New World on Europe, 1492–1650* (Wheeling, IL: Harlan Davidson, 1996), especially "American Foods and European Life," 92–103.

123 "el pavo, o faisán que inventó la gula" (Lope de Vega, *El Sol parado*, Acto 1).

124 Tirso de Molina, *Amazonas en las Indias*, Acto 2.

125 For example, "Comíamos a la mesa manjares de gran sazón" (Moreto, *Las travesuras del Cid, burlesca*, Jornada 2). On early modern use of spices to preserve food, along with subsequent misunderstandings of this practice, see John H. Munro, "The Consumption of Spices and Their Costs in Late-Medieval and Early-Modern Europe: Luxuries or Necessities?" Lecture delivered to the Royal Ontario Museum Continuing Education Symposium (University of Toronto): *Silk Roads, China Ships*, on 12 October 1983, http://www.economics.utoronto.ca/munro5/SPICES1.htm.

126 For a historical fiction account of the nagging hunger suffered by the conquistadores, see Uruguayan novelist Napoleón Baccino Ponce de León's *Maluco: la novela de los descubridores* (Barcelona: Seix Barral, 1992). One of the most vivid scenes of the novel is an entire shipload of spices sinking into the bay just off the coast of Spain as the explorers return from an excruciatingly long voyage. The ship's occupants know at that moment that they will not receive even a modest recompense for their labours.

127 Tirso de Molina, *Amazonas en las Indias*, Acto 2. During his stay in the Bahamas, Christopher Columbus reported eating an iguana, saying the meat was white and tasted like chicken (Schlesinger, *In the Wake of Columbus*, 93).

128 Lope de Vega, *Los españoles en Flandes*, Acto 2. A similar example occurs in Juan Bonifacio's Jesuit school drama *Tragicomedia Nabalis*, in which King David's soldiers become so hungry that they eat the soles of their shoes (Juan Bonifacio, *Tragicomedia de Nabal del Carmelo*, in *El Códice de Villagarcía del P. Juan Bonifacio: Teatro clásico del siglo XVI*, ed. Cayo González Gutiérrez [Madrid: Universidad Nacional de Educación a Distancia, 2001], 347–406, at 357).

129 Lope de Vega, *La desdichada Estefanía*, Acto 1. This drama plays out against the backdrop of a battle between the Spaniards and the *almohades* (Muslim holy warriors

who came from Morocco) in Seville. Historically, this battle would have taken place in the twelfth or thirteenth century. Thus in this context returning to Spain means returning to the Christian-controlled part of Spain which is recognizable as such. "Desdichada tierra" refers also to Spain.

130 "¿Por qué vos, hermana hormiga, lisonjera del montón, a la gula dais lición, porque su apetito siga? Siempre del comer amiga" (Tirso de Molina, *Segunda parte de Santa Juana*, Acto 3).

131 A character compares himself to this animal in the phrase, "Cogido me han por la gula, con queso como a ratón" (Lope de Vega, *Los Muertos vivos*, Acto 3).

132 Rueda, *Eufemia*, Scena 3.

133 Rueda, *Timbria*, Acto 1; Guillén de Castro, *El Narciso en su opinión*, Jornada 1.

134 See Francisco Goya, *Saturn Devouring His Son* (1819–23), Museo del Prado, Madrid (figure 14). The *comedias* make reference to Saturn as cannibalistically gluttonous in the phrase "Saturno voraz" (Calderón, *El Joseph de las mujeres*, Jornada 1).

135 Calderón, *El año santo en Madrid*, auto sacramental.

136 "dio de comer tan mal, en Banquete, donde eran Cilicio, Ayuno, y Sayal principios de la Comida" (Calderón, *El pleito matrimonial*, auto sacramental).

137 Calderón, *El año santo en Madrid*, auto sacramental, emphasis mine.

138 Calderón, *El pleito matrimonial*, auto sacramental.

139 Calderón, *El indulto general*, loa for auto sacramental.

140 The Biblical text reads: "And when he had fasted forty days and forty nights, afterwards he was hungry. And the tempter coming said to him: If thou be the Son of God, command that these stones be made bread" (Matthew 4:2–3). In the first *auto*, Naturaleza says of Christ: "Dios es, pues Cuarenta Días resiste Ayuno tan grande" (Calderón, *La cura, y la enfermedad*, Acto 1). In the second *auto*, the devil says to the Prince, who is clearly a figure of Jesus: "toma, y pues ayuno andas el Desierto tantos días, hambre, y cansancio repara" (Calderón, *El valle de la zarzuela*, auto sacramental).

141 Moreto, *Antíoco y Seleuco*, Jornada 1. *Hocico* normally refers to a pig's snout.

142 "publicad general ayuno (como en Israel se acostumbra, cuando se espera algún castigo)" (Tirso de Molina, *La mujer que manda en casa*, Acto 3).

143 From the *autos sacramentales*: "cuarenta de Elías el Celo ayunó, para alcanzar el Viático alimento del subcinericio Pan" (Calderón, *El primer refugio del hombre, y probática piscina*, auto sacramental); "logró en otros cuarenta Moisés de su Ayuno el premio, y Elías de tu fatiga para otros cuarenta" (Calderón, *El santo rey don Fernando, segunda parte*, loa for auto sacramental). From a *comedia*: "hoy comienza como el de Moisés mi ayuno" (Tirso de Molina, *La mujer que manda en casa*, Acto 3).

144 Calderón, *El tesoro escondido*, auto sacramental.

145 "estás flaco, y en ayunas" (Moreto, *El licenciado Vidriera*, Jornada 2).

146 Lope de Vega, *La noche toledana*, Acto 2.

147 Moreto, *El esclavo de su hijo*, Jornada 2.

148 Moreto, *El mejor amigo, el rey*, Jornada 2.

149 "disciplínese ... ayune, y rija su casa" (Tirso de Molina, *Segunda parte de Santa Juana*, Acto 2).

150 Diamante, *Santa María Magdalena de Pazzi*, Jornada 3. Likewise Saint Isidro in Lope's *San Isidro labrador de Madrid* refuses to eat until he has said his morning prayers:

ISIDRO: ¿Lleva pan?
MARÍA: Sí,
toma primero un bocado.
ISIDRO: Hasta que rece, María,
no me he de desayunar. (Lope de Vega, *San Isidro labrador de Madrid*, Acto 2)

151 Cervantes, *El rufián dichoso*, Jornada 2.

152 Tirso de Molina, *Quien no cae no se levanta*, Acto 3.

153 "viéndote rendido a tanto ayuno, lástima he tenido de verte así" (Calderón, *La primer flor de el Carmelo*, auto sacramental).

154 Pérez de Montalbán, *A lo hecho no hay remedio, y príncipe de los montes*, Jornada 1. Later in the same play this character asks rather pitifully what he might do to get a little bread for breakfast without breaking the terms of his fast: "¿Qué haré yo para poder, sin que el ayuno se ofenda, hacer colación un pan, sin las demás menudencias?" (Pérez de Montalbán, *A lo hecho no hay remedio, y príncipe de los montes*, Jornada 1).

155 Calderón, *El gran mercado del mundo*, auto sacramental.

156 Rueda, *Los engañados*, Scena 10.

157 Moreto, *No puede ser*, Jornada 1.

158 Diamante, *El jubileo de Porciúncula*, Jornada 2.

159 Fasting was often undertaken as the result of a command by someone else. There was even a belief that one might choose voluntarily to fast, but could not *obligate* one's self to do so without a command by a superior: "la Cuaresma es precepto, mas ninguna podrá decir que al ayuno está obligada ella misma" (Alarcón, *Los pechos privilegiados*, Acto 2). One *comedia* character rails agains doctors and confessors as two loci of power over other people's bodies, especially in the case of someone who is ill: "señores, pues ¿estar malo es pecar? ¿Sois, mandándole ayunar, Médicos, o Confesores?" (Moreto, *Antíoco y Seleuco*, Jornada 2). Another voices concern that a child's superiors are making him fast too much: "Porque lo veo, y lo siento, a él le hacen ayunar" (Lope de Vega, *El niño inocente de la Guardia*, Acto 2). An example of a medical doctor prescribing fasting as part of a cure occurs in Agustín Moreto's *El licenciado Vidriera*, based on Cervantes's *novela ejemplar* of the same title. In this play, the doctor cures a patient with a special diet, effectively simulating the conditions of Lent: "Embajador de paz, le curó con la dieta: donde aquel ayuno clamó

siete semanas … Pensó usted que era Cuaresma" (Moreto, *El licenciado Vidriera*, Jornada 2). A modern-day equivalent would be the rehabilitation treatments which Hollywood stars use to detoxify their bodies.

160 For example, "hoy aliviados vivan del Ayuno que padecen" (Calderón, *La primer flor de el Carmelo*, auto sacramental). One character complains of migraines induced by fasting on bread and water: "con media azumbre, o con dos, y un zoquete cuando ayuno, luego me da la jaqueca" (Tirso de Molina, *Doña Beatriz de Silva*, Acto 3). Perhaps because of the physical risk involved, monarchs were not expected to fast: "No es obligación de un Rey el ayuno, la abstinencia, la oración, la penitencia, sino el gobierno" (Lope de Vega, *Barlán y Josafa*, Acto 3).

161 This requirement or expectation is voiced explicitly in the *comedias*: "que el que come a su contento, sin trabajar, ni ayunar, no es Fraile sino Seglar retraído en un Convento" (Pérez de Montalbán, *El hijo del Serafín, San Pedro de Alcántara*, Jornada 3).

162 Thus one character announces, "a mí me está mejor que el comer, el ayunar" (Moreto, *Los hermanos encontrados*, Jornada 2).

163 For example, one character explains the decision to fast during Lent: "con mi ayuno esta Cuaresma, yo sin mandarme ayunar, cuando obligación no tuve, no quebré ayuno jamás, y ayunaba a pan, y agua" (Moreto, *No puede ser*, Jornada 1). Another character even chooses to punish the body with perpetual fasting, citing as a reason the life-giving power of penance: "Penitencias nos den vida, perpetuo ayuno le mando a mi cuerpo, sin que guste otro manjar" (Tirso de Molina, *El mayor desengaño*, Acto 3).

164 "mira, primo de mi mujer, no dejes de aconsejarle que si se halla bien con las novenas, que las haga decenas, aunque yo sepa ayunar un día más por su salud" (Rueda, *Paso tercero*, Acto 1). In a somewhat absurd case, a single day's fast (on a Friday) is extended for an entire year, presumably as an excuse not to show proper hospitality to a guest: "en Madrid me recibió un viernes, día de ayuno. ¿Qué ha que dura un año entero? Mire qué extraño rigor" (Tirso de Molina, *El castigo del penséque*, Acto 1). In truly exceptional cases a fast might be extended for as long as three years: "es mucho que una mujer pase tres años de ayuno" (Lope de Vega, *Los amantes sin amor*, Acto 1).

165 On eating too many sweets, there were jokes such as "en los dulces, ya yo he dicho *ite missa est* a dos cajas" (Tirso de Molina, *La celosa de sí misma*, Acto 3). The Latin words *ite missa est* (roughly, "mass is ended") announced the end of the church service, as in "la bendición con el Ite Missa Est da fin a la devoción" (Tirso de Molina, *La villana de Vallecas*, Acto 1). The proverb *por oír misa, y dar cebada, nunca se perdió jornada* appears in the lines "dijo un adagio vulgar, por dar cebada, y oír Misa" (Calderón, *No hay cosa como callar*, Jornada 2). Loosely translated, the phrase means that such seemingly unrequited effort as feeding the livestock or going to mass will not be lost. In a memorable line from the eponymous play by Antonio Zamora,

a servant says in a variation on this theme, "cumpla con la Misa mi amo, y con la cebada yo" (Zamora, *Por oír misa, y dar cebada, nunca se perdió jornada*, Jornada 3). He wants his master to go to mass and leave the eating to him.

166 A feast day is mentioned in the line, "en la Merced, oyendo Misa una Pascua" (Lope de Vega, *Quien ama no haga fieros*, Acto 3). On the infrequency with which communion was received during this time period, see M. Fernández Álvarez, "El *Diario de un estudiante*," in *La sociedad española en el Siglo de Oro*, 2 vols (Madrid: Gredos, 1989), 2:818–46. In Fernández Álvarez's summary of the diary of an Italian student who studied in Spain during the early seventeenth century, Girolamo da Sommaia, the young man "[d]e cuando en cuando cumplía con sus deberes religiosos, confesando y comulgando y yendo a los sermones – en particular en tiempos de Cuaresma" (2:822).

167 A funeral is implied by the "Misa de Requiem" (Zamora, *El custodio de la Hungría, San Juan Capistrano*, Jornada 1). A special feast day was called a *fiesta*, as in "como es hoy fiesta saldrá a Misa" (Cervantes, *La entretenida*, Jornada 3).

168 Matos Fragoso, *El hijo de la piedra*, Acto 1. Typically daily mass was said in the morning ("las mañanas se le pasan en oír Misa" [Cervantes, *El juez de los divorcios*, Acto 1]), for the purpose of starting the day well ("para encaminar el día" [Lope de Vega, *La fortuna merecida*, Acto 1]).

169 "Que tengan Sermón las Fiestas y oigan Misa cada día" (Pérez de Montalbán, *Los templarios*, Jornada 1). We find reference to communion being distributed during the mass: "Dijo allí una santa Misa, dio a todos el sacramento" (Lope de Vega, *Bamba*, Jornada 1).

170 We find allusions to daily mass said for the purpose of alleviating souls' torment in Purgatory:

FRANCO: El alma en pena soy.
DATO: Pues levántele una Misa. (Moreto, *El lego del Carmen*, Jornada 3)

We hear a mass being said to plead for the intercession of Saint Anthony, with the goal or objective of finding a lost object, in the following exchange:

MACARRÓN: Verbum Caro, ay bendito san Antonio, una Misa os doy de hallazgo.
ENRIQUE: ¿Qué has perdido? (Moreto, *El mejor amigo, el rey*, Jornada 3)

A special mass is requested to pray for good health in the line, "Para hacerle decir una misa de salud" (Rueda, *Los engañados*, Scena 10). A mass said for personal safety is described with the words, "[el] cielo guarde su vida, y de hoy en adelante diré Misa cada día por su intención" (Pérez de Montalbán, *El hijo del Serafín, San Pedro de Alcántara*, Jornada 2).

171 "Juntos a la Iglesia, Caballero quiero armaros. Mañana oiremos la Misa; velad las armas, Fajardo" (Lope de Vega, *El primer Fajardo*, Acto 1).

172 The cost of a mass appears to have been one *real*, although this seems to fall on the upper end of the scale for donations:

MARGARITA: Mañana daré un real para una Misa.
LEONELA: ¿Un real? Limosna larga.
(Tirso de Molina, *Quien no cae no se levanta*, Acto 2)

173 Guillén de Castro, *El perfecto caballero*, Acto 1; Calderón, *A María el corazón*, auto sacramental; Calderón, *Los misterios de la Misa*, loa for auto sacramental. A similar message is conveyed by *Lo que puede el oír misa*, by Antonio Mira de Amescua.

174 Calderón, *La devoción de la Misa*, auto sacramental. In a different *auto*, this same playwright explains the etymology further: "Llámase Misa, porque Missa en la Latina lengua quiere decir enviada, si se traduce … del Hijo es una enviada Ofrenda al Padre" (Calderón, *Los misterios de la Misa*, auto sacramental).

175 Calderón, *Agradecer, y no amar*, Preliminares de obra.

176 Calderón, *El segundo blasón del Austria*, auto sacramental.

177 Calderón, *Los misterios de la Misa*, loa for auto sacramental.

178 "saldrás bien de todo, si traes la Misa en el cuerpo" (Zamora, *Por oír misa, y dar cebada, nunca se perdió jornada*, Jornada 2).

179 Zamora, *Por oír misa, y dar cebada, nunca se perdió jornada*, Jornada 3. A concrete example of divine reward for church attendance occurs in Lope's *San Isidro labrador de Madrid* when angels come to plough the fields abandoned by Isidro, a manual labourer, in the fervent intensity of his devotion. His piety centres around daily attendance at mass:

que no amanece el Alba, sin que aguarde,
a la puerta de nuestra Iglesia atento,
a cuando el Sacristán a abrirlas venga,
y que jamás al campo va sin Misa.
(Lope de Vega, *San Isidro labrador de Madrid*, Acto 1)

180 Calderón, *Los misterios de la Misa*, auto sacramental.

181 Tirso de Molina, *El pretendiente al revés*, Acto 3.

182 "Lo que es ayudar a Misa, ni aun sabe decir amén, de las hostias come bien" (Lope de Vega, *El rústico del cielo*, Acto 1).

183 Calderón, *La devoción de la Misa*, auto sacramental.

184 "Alto, dejemos la cama, ¿pensáis que es hoy el Domingo?" (Tirso de Molina, *La peña de Francia*, Acto 3).

185 Tirso de Molina, *La gallega Mari Hernández*, Acto 3.

186 Rojas Zorrilla, *Lo que son mujeres*, Jornada 1.

187 Juan de Zabaleta, *El día de fiesta por la mañana y por la tarde* (1654/1660), ed. C. Cuevas García (Madrid: Castalia, 1983), 162, 387.

188 Francisco de Luque Fajardo, *Fiel desengaño contra la ociosidad y el juego* (1603), ed. M. de Riquer (Madrid: Consejo Superior de Investigaciones Científicas, 1955).

189 Tirso de Molina, *Por el sótano y el torno*, Jornada 2. The first mass, known as the "Misa del gallo" (Lope de Vega, *La viuda valenciana*, Acto 1), was at dawn: "oí a la luz primera, tocar a Misa del Alba" (Calderón, *La devoción de la Misa*, auto sacramental); "una Misa al alba, en que el Sacristán dice cantando el amén" (Tirso de Molina, *La Dama del Olivar*, Acto 1).

190 Calderón, *Guárdate de la agua mansa*, Jornada 2.

191 "en el corto breve espacio de una MISSA" (Calderón, *La devoción de la Misa*, auto sacramental); "a estas horas cantara misa muy presto" (Rojas Zorrilla, *Abrir el ojo*, Jornada 2). The few exceptions to this rule are generally remarked upon for their rarity, as in "oír una misa que decían, que duró hora y media" (Rueda, *Eufemia*, Scena 3).

192 Matos Fragoso, *Los indicios sin culpa*, Jornada 1.

193 Thus one *comedia* character aspires to "Ser tan Rey, que en la Capilla me diga Misa un Bonete" (Calderón, *El escondido, y la tapada*, Jornada 2).

194 "oyendo en su casa Misa, o en la Iglesia alguna vez, si era muy templado" (Guillén de Castro, *La fuerza de la costumbre*, Jornada 1).

195 "la salud no os falta, no oigáis en la cama Misa, que no es cortesía Cristiana" (Lope de Vega, *El príncipe perfecto, parte segunda*, Acto 1).

196 "sale fuera mi señor ... y oye misa de soldado, como otros de cazador" (Rojas Zorrilla, *No hay amigo para amigo*, Jornada 1); "en las naves yo he sabido que dicen la Misa así" (Lope de Vega, *El casamiento en la muerte*, Jornada 3).

197 Alarcón, *El semejante a sí mismo*, Acto 3. This sort of evidence led Américo Castro to conclude that Golden Age churches in fact came to resemble social clubs, or "centros de reunión profanos" (this viewpoint is well summarized by Alfredo Alvar-Ezquerra in "Comer y 'ser' en la corte del Rey Católico," in *Materia crítica: formas de ocio y de consumo en la cultura áurea*, ed. Enrique García Santo-Tomás [Madrid/Frankfurt: Iberoamericana/Vervuert, 2009], 295–320, at 301).

198 Pérez de Montalbán, *Lo que son juicios del cielo*, Jornada 3. Note that two alternatives are presented in explanation: he goes to mass out of custom *or* piety. The desire to see friends is reflected in the lines, "más gusta oír cada día sermón en la Compañía, que Misa en la Soledad. Sola estoy, y no soy santa, perdone" (Tirso de Molina, *Quien no cae no se levanta*, Acto 2).

199 Calderón, *No hay cosa como callar*, Jornada 1.

200 Lope de Vega, *La viuda casada y doncella*, Acto 1.

201 "yo que en la Misa estaba más compuesta, que devota, y más curiosa, que santa" (Guillén de Castro, *La fuerza de la costumbre*, Jornada 1).

202 Lope de Vega, *La hermosa Alfreda*, Acto 1.

203 Guillén de Castro, *El pretender con pobreza*, Jornada 1.

204 Tirso de Molina, *La celosa de sí misma*, Acto 1. A young female character tries to defend to an older, prudish woman the use of church services for amorous trysts: "Tía, amor tratado en Misa será en servicio de Dios" (Lope de Vega, *El acero de Madrid, primera parte*, Acto 3).

205 Lope de Vega, *La bella malmaridada*, Jornada 2.

206 Lope de Vega, *El blasón de los Chaves de Villalba*, Acto 1. This line becomes more scandalous and perhaps more true to life when we consider that "Inquisition records of solicitation cases reveal that the church was a favorite place for priests and their lovers to engage in fondling, masturbation and fornication" (Stephen H. Haliczer, "Sexuality and Repression in Counter-Reformation Spain," in Alain Saint-Saëns, ed., *Sex and Love in Golden Age Spain* [New Orleans: University Press of the South, 1996], 81–93, at 93).

207 Lope de Vega, *El blasón de los Chaves de Villalba*, Acto 2.

208 "mujer es, quien da en cazar, que a Misa va siempre a la Iglesia más lejos" (Alarcón, *La crueldad por el honor*, Acto 1).

209 Tirso de Molina, *Los alcaldes*, Parte 2.

210 Tirso de Molina, *El condenado por desconfiado*, Jornada 1.

211 Tirso de Molina, *Escarmientos para el cuerdo*, Acto 3.

212 "no podré, amigos, comer, santo es mi amor, a él ayuno. Mañana cae su fiesta, guardemos hoy su vigilia" (Lope de Vega, *Las pobrezas de Reinaldos*, Acto 3).

213 "tú eres muy honradita, que afectas mucho el ayuno hipócrita de atenciones, y tomarás dos doblones de mejor gana" (Diamante, *Ir por el riesgo a la dicha*, Jornada 2).

214 Diamante, *El jubileo de Porciúncula*, Jornada 2.

215 Tirso de Molina, *El condenado por desconfiado*, Jornada 2; Calderón, *El gran teatro del mundo*, auto sacramental.

216 "estarán en su oratorio puestas, en disciplina, o en ayuno santo, o en oración, en sólo Dios traspuestas" (Cueva, *La libertad de España por Bernardo del Carpio*, Acto 3).

217 Cervantes, *El rufián dichoso*, Jornada 2, emphasis mine.

218 Rojas Zorrilla, *Santa Isabel reina de Portugal*, Jornada 1; Moreto, *Santa Rosa del Perú*, Jornada 2.

219 "Cilicio traigo en verdad, aunque galana me ves, pues a fe que ha más de un mes que ayuno a la Soledad" (Lope de Vega, *El leal criado*, Acto 1); "mas yo haré hacer oración con disciplina y ayuno por vos" (Lope de Vega, *La buena guarda*, Acto 1).

220 Lope de Vega, *La Historia de Tobías*, Acto 3.

221 "Ayunar a la Cuaresma es precepto" (Alarcón, *Los pechos privilegiados*, Acto 2); "suele obligar las más veces a ayunar esta santa Cuarentena" (Tirso de Molina, *Tanto es lo demás como lo de menos*, Acto 1). The specific prohibition against eating meat is mentioned in Cervantes's *Los baños de Argel*: "viejo ya, vos tenéis ancha la conciencia. ¿Ya coméis carne en los días vedados?" (Cervantes, *Los baños de Argel*, Jornada 2). On efforts to prohibit the legal sale of meat on days of religious abstinence from it, see Alvar-Ezquerra, "Comer y 'ser,'" 300.

222 "¿ayunas mis fiestas en Viernes?" (Tirso de Molina, *La santa Juana*, Acto 1); "[en la] fiesta de mi Anunciación santa cayere, el mismo sea tu ayuno todo el año; mi voluntad lo acepta, la Pastorcilla dijo" (Tirso de Molina, *La santa Juana*, Acto 1).

223 Witness the following exchange:

LUISA: Esta miseria, haz que lo coma, porque no esté en ayunas mi señora.
JUANA: ¿Que tanto ha que no come? (Tirso de Molina, *Las viudas*, Acto 1)

224 Lope de Vega, *La viuda valenciana*, Acto 1.

225 This practice is recommended by Juan Luis Vives in his *Instrucción de la mujer cristiana* (1523): "Before marriage frequent fasts will be beneficial – not those that weaken the body, but that check and control it and extinguish the fires of youth. These are true and holy fasts. Let her nourishment be light, plain, and not highly seasoned" (Juan Luis Vives, *The Education of a Christian Woman: A Sixteenth-Century Manual*, trans. Charles Fantazzi [Chicago: University of Chicago Press, 2000], 87). This commonplace becomes the butt of scabrous jokes in lines such as "está la virtud en ser doncella, casta, y hermosa … No sabes tú las virtudes de una doncella en ayunas" (Lope de Vega, *El bobo del colegio*, Acto 1).

226 Lope de Vega, *Los enemigos en casa*, Acto 2.

227 Lope de Vega, *El saber por no saber, y vida de San Julián*, Acto 2.

228 In the case of a child saint, this extreme amount of fasting was seen as a precursor to great future holiness: "qué extraños principios, tres días en la semana ayunó el niño bendito" (Lope de Vega, *San Nicolás de Tolentino*, Acto 2).

229 "Aunque en la Orden se tenga eterno ayuno, y vigilia; allá se come pescado" (Matos Fragoso, *El hijo de la piedra*, Jornada 2).

230 "Desde que nació, los Viernes ayunó … a quien Dios da los favores que disciernes" (Tirso de Molina, *La santa Juana*, Acto 3).

231 "no da pollo, ni pollera … . Él las más noches condena a ayuno a quien le ha tenido / que parece que ha incurrido en la Bula de la Cena" (Moreto, *La fuerza de la ley*, Jornada 2). The *Él* here refers to Honor, who is pictured by a servant woman as a harsh taskmaster. The *Bula* is meant to be a travesty of a papal bull.

232 Matos Fragoso, *Con amor no hay amistad*, Jornada 3.

233 Lope de Vega, *San Nicolás de Tolentino*, Acto 2.

234 For a detailed description of the Corpus Christi celebrations in fifteenth-century Barcelona, see Kenneth Kreitner, "Music in the Corpus Christi Procession of Fifteenth-Century Barcelona," *Early Music History* 14 (1995): 153–204.

235 The *autos sacramentales* included the symbolic use of food as props, but even a regular *comedia* might lead to a dinner afterward if it was particularly well-received: "after a successful first-night performance, a theatre company might have a celebration. On at least one occasion, there was a dinner party, attended by all the company and by the author, that is, Calderón" (Cruickshank, *Don Pedro Calderón*, 179).

236 Jonathan Gil Harris, "Properties of Skill: Product Placement in Early English Artisanal Drama," in *Staged Properties in Early Modern English Drama*, ed. Jonathan Gil Harris and Natasha Korda (Cambridge: Cambridge University Press, 2006), 35–66, at 43. For a comparison of how this feast day was celebrated in early modern England versus Spain, see Donald T. Dietz, "England's and Spain's Corpus Christi Theaters," in *Parallel Lives: Spanish and English National Drama, 1580–1680*, ed. Louise and Peter Fothergill-Payne (Lewisburg: Bucknell University Press, 1991), 239–51.

237 Cruickshank, *Don Pedro Calderón*, 177 and plate 21.

238 See notes 71 and 72 of the present chapter.

239 Greer, "Constituting Community," 55, 57–8, 56.

240 Calderón, *Llamados, y escogidos*, auto sacramental.

241 Calderón, *El nuevo hospicio de pobres*, auto sacramental.

242 Calderón, *Amar, y ser amado, y divina Philotea*, auto sacramental.

243 Calderón, *Psiquis, y Cupido que escribió para esta villa de Toledo*, auto sacramental.

244 Calderón, *La serpiente de metal*, auto sacramental.

245 Calderón, *El nuevo hospicio de pobres*, auto sacramental.

246 "su sabor suavidades, Sagradas Plumas afirman ser el Manjar de Manjares" (Calderón, *Las espigas de Ruth*, loa for auto sacramental).

247 Calderón, *Psiquis, y Cupido que escribió para esta villa de Madrid*, auto sacramental.

248 The allegorical figure of Pan declares, "se llama mi primer Cuna Belén, que en Hebreo, Casa de Trigo quiere decir" (Calderón, *El verdadero Dios Pan*, auto sacramental). Thanks to my theatre colleague Sarah Misemer for reminding me of this connection.

249 We hear echoes of the Prodigal Son parable in Agustín Moreto's *El parecido*, where the father says: "descanse mi hijo, y las mesas disponed, y buscad manjares ricos, pues mi hacienda es para Lope" (Moreto, *El parecido*, Jornada 1).

250 Calderón, *Llamados, y escogidos*, auto sacramental.

251 Calderón, *El pastor fido*, auto sacramental.

252 In one interesting variation on this theme, a cart bearing a table with the Hebrew synagogue as its centrepiece ("un Carro, en que habrá una Mesa bien adornada de Viandas, y Aparadores, y en ella la Sinagoga. Sube el Hebraísmo") is supplanted by one bearing New Testament imagery (Calderón, *La viña del Señor*, auto sacramental).

253 Calderón, *¿Quién hallará mujer fuerte?*, loa for auto sacramental.

254 Calderón, *La semilla, y la cizaña*, auto sacramental.

255 Calderón, *La viña del Señor*, auto sacramental.

256 Calderón, *La primer flor de el Carmelo*, auto sacramental. In this clearly typological play, the Old Testament figure of Abigail (the virtuous wife of King David) becomes a type of the Virgin Mary. Thus the character David addresses her in words reminiscent of the angel Gabriel's words to Mary during the Annunciation: "Bendita eres

entre las Mujeres, toda Hermosa, y toda Rica de Dones Espirituales" (Calderón, *La primer flor de el Carmelo*, auto sacramental).

257 Quiñones de Benavente, *Loa con que empezó Tomás Fernández en la Corte.*

258 Thus one particularly witty character (who also happens to be a good cook) is urged to keep talking, a clever strategy on the part of the playwright to draw out the script even longer: "prosiga, que es su humor más sazonado, que los manjares que guisa" (Tirso de Molina, *La gallega Mari Hernández*, Acto 3).

259 Calderón, *La vida es sueño*, auto sacramental.

6. Angry Young Murderers

1 Diamante, *Más encanto es la hermosura*, Jornada 1.

2 Lope de Vega, *El mármol de Felisardo*, Acto 3.

3 Moreto, *La misma conciencia acusa*, Jornada 3.

4 Calderón, *La exaltación de la Cruz*, Jornada 1; Calderón, *La lepra de Constantino*, auto sacramental.

5 Calderón, *El año santo de Roma*, auto sacramental; Lope de Vega, *El servir con mala estrella*, Acto 3; Moreto, *El esclavo de su hijo*, Jornada 2.

6 Pérez de Montalbán, *Cumplir con su obligación*, Jornada 1.

7 Cueva, *La libertad de España por Bernardo del Carpio*, Acto 4.

8 The fact of solitude is indicated by the lines, "Vos en voces altas, sola, y colérica, ¿qué es esto señora?" (Calderón, *El Conde Lucanor*, Jornada 2). A similar description appears in Tirso's *La fingida Arcadia*: "voces furiosa da, suspira, y llora" (Tirso de Molina, *La fingida Arcadia*, Jornada 2).

9 Rojas Zorrilla, *El más improprio verdugo por la más justa venganza*, Jornada 2.

10 "colérico y turbado, díjele injurias de amante" (Guillén de Castro, *La verdad averiguada, y engañoso casamiento*, Jornada 1).

11 Lope de Vega, *Válgame Dios, es de veras*, loa.

12 "Y donde dijo Aquiles, borró luego el nombre infame, de coraje ciego: Y dijo así con voz soberbia y brava" (Lope de Vega, *Roma abrasada*, Acto 2).

13 Rojas Zorrilla, *No hay amigo para amigo*, Jornada 1.

14 "la Ira deja mis discursos llenos de más confusión" (Calderón, *La segunda esposa, y triunfar muriendo*, auto sacramental).

15 "Tus raras Proposiciones tan rabiosa ira en mi Pecho han introducido" (Calderón, *La redención de cautivos*, auto sacramental).

16 "siempre el agravio saca palabras que la ira ofrece, y el alma noble aborrece" (Tirso de Molina, *El pretendiente al revés*, Acto 3).

17 Pérez de Montalbán, *La toquera vizcaína*, Jornada 2.

18 "La ira se está vertiendo a los ojos" (Zamora, *Judás Iscariote*, Acto 1).

19 Lope de Vega, *Jorge toledano*, Acto 1.

20 This is the title of chapter 19 of Cliff Richey and Hilaire Richey Kallendorf, *Acing Depression: A Tennis Champion's Toughest Match* (New York: New Chapter Press, 2010).

21 Calderón, *Amado, y aborrecido*, Jornada 2.

22 "Ciego va y turbado, de puro coraje llora" (Lope de Vega, *Lucinda perseguida*, Acto 2).

23 Calderón, *Los cabellos de Absalón*, Jornada 3.

24 "no tiene ojos la ira" (Tirso de Molina, *El castigo del penséque*, Acto 3).

25 "¿El color habéis perdido? ¿La ira os ha demudado, cuando injurias escucháis de Licurgo?" (Alarcón, *El dueño de las estrellas*, Acto 1).

26 Solís, *Las amazonas*, Jornada 1; Lope de Vega, *La mocedad de Roldán*, Acto 3.

27 "bañado en sudor el cuerpo de aquella furiosa acción" (Lope de Vega, *Contra valor no hay desdicha*, Acto 3).

28 "el furor, la ira, la rabia, confunden tanto mis Sentidos, tanto mis Potencias" (Calderón, *La nave del mercader*, auto sacramental); "De qué sirve callar, rabio de celos, afuera, que se acaba la paciencia" (Lope de Vega, *Lucinda perseguida*, Acto 2).

29 Calderón, *Casa con dos puertas mala es de guardar*, Acto 1; "¿En coraje tan profundo, lo arroja así su impaciencia?" (Cueva, *La constancia de Arcelina*, Acto 1).

30 "aun no es posible volverme con ruegos, y persuasiones; colérica e impaciente, yo se le quise quitar" (Calderón, *La vida es sueño [Comedia]*, Jornada 2).

31 Zamora, *El custodio de la Hungría, San Juan Capistrano*, Jornada 2.

32 "se fue tan furiosa, y tan a prisa" (Lope de Vega, *El acero de Madrid, primera parte*, Acto 2); "con desdén huyas colérica" (Lope de Vega, *Angélica en el Catay*, Acto 1).

33 Calderón, *Tambien hay duelo en las damas*, Jornada 2. The implication is that Anger has escaped the *auto sacramental* and reappeared in the disguise of an angry character on the *comedia* stage.

34 For a recent, well-nuanced discussion of slapstick audiovisual language in the *comedias*, including the inventive use of a piece of theatrical machinery known as the *bofetón* (about-face machine), "designed to move objects and actors with the physical action of a slap," see María M. Carrión, *Subject Stages: Marriage, Theatre, and the Law in Early Modern Spain* (Toronto: University of Toronto Press, 2010), 102–7.

35 Rojas Zorrilla, *El más improprio verdugo por la más justa venganza*, Jornada 1. Characters hitting one another: "pegándole muy bien, le dijo con voz furiosa …" (Lope de Vega, *Los Tellos de Meneses*, Acto 3). Characters ripping off clothes and jewellery: "también a mi Beatriz Francesca, a quien con celos, y furiosa rabia quitó la ropa y la cadena" (Lope de Vega, *El caballero del Milagro*, Acto 2).

36 Calderón, *Las tres justicias en una*, Jornada 3. Another character threatens, "mi ardiente fuego … te haga tantos pedazos" (Rojas Zorrilla, *El más improprio verdugo por la más justa venganza*, Jornada 3).

37 Stabbing: "Diome muchas cuchilladas colérico, y pertinaz" (Lope de Vega, *Los amantes sin amor*, Acto 2). Whipping: "su cuerpo hirieron con tal coraje, que inhumanos, y

crueles … azoten, y descansen" (Diamante, *Santa Juliana,* Jornada 3). Beating: "pido consejo a la ira, y levantando la pala le doy lo que parecía" (Lope de Vega, *Guardar, y guardarse,* Acto 1).

38 Guillén de Castro, *Progne, y Filomena,* Acto 2; Lope de Vega, *Las grandezas de Alejandro,* Acto 3.

39 Tirso de Molina, *El árbol del mejor fruto,* Acto 3; Scott K. Taylor, *Honor and Violence in Golden Age Spain* (New Haven: Yale University Press, 2008), 114. A sweeter-smelling variation on this theme was sometimes played with honey. In this instance, the miscreant was covered with honey and birds' feathers, the idea being that the real punishment would be carried out by swarms of flies (Enrique Gacto, "El delito de bigamia y la Inquisición española," in *Sexo barroco y otras transgresiones premodernas,* ed. Francisco Tomás y Valiente et al. [Madrid: Alianza Universidad, 1990], 127–52, at 141).

40 See William T. Riley, Frank A. Treiber, and Gail M. Woods, "Anger and Hostility in Depression," *Journal of Nervous and Mental Disease* 177.11 (1989): 668–74.

41 Lope de Vega, *La ingratitud vengada,* Acto 1; Calderón, *Las órdenes militares,* auto sacramental.

42 "si primero con la ira no me arranco el corazón" (Guillén de Castro, *La humildad soberbia,* Acto 3).

43 Diamante, *El remedio en el peligro,* Acto 1. A bloodbath is reflected in the lines, "Vuelve furiosa, y él queda ensangrentadas las manos" (Calderón, *La cura, y la enfermedad,* auto sacramental).

44 "vencí del mar la ira tirana" (Moreto, *El parecido,* Jornada 2); "a la Fuente … A tu colérica saña, monstruo de vidrio, se entregue mi vida" (Zamora, *Viento es la dicha de amor,* Jornada 2).

45 Lope de Vega, *Los locos por el cielo,* Acto 2.

46 Tirso de Molina, *Los amantes de Teruel,* Jornada 3. An angry storm appears figuratively in the lines, "el estruendo rabioso con que me amaga la tempestad de los celos" (Zamora, *El custodio de la Hungría, San Juan Capistrano,* Jornada 1).

47 Lope de Vega, *La piedad ejecutada,* Acto 2; Cueva, *La libertad de España por Bernardo del Carpio,* Acto 3; Cueva, *Comedia del príncipe tirano,* Acto 1. A similar example would be Don Diego's line, "En coraje estoy ardiendo" (Cueva, *La muerte del Rey don Sancho,* Acto 3).

48 Calderón, *La estatua de Prometeo,* Jornada 2.

49 "la ira es fuego" (Lope de Vega, *El llegar en ocasión,* Acto 1).

50 Calderón, *Apolo, y Climene,* Acto 1.

51 "Pues no te espante el inextinguible ardor de este nativo coraje" (Zamora, *El custodio de la Hungría, San Juan Capistrano,* Jornada 1); "volcán soy, llamas respiro" (Calderón, *La lepra de Constantino,* auto sacramental).

52 "de ira rabio. ¿Yo sin Reinar? Pierdo el juicio, Etna soy, llamas aborto" (Calderón, *La hija del aire,* segunda parte, Acto 1).

53 Guillén de Castro, *El Narciso en su opinión,* Jornada 3; Calderón, *El día mayor de los días,* auto sacramental.

54 "¿Quién eres, fiero homicida? Hidra furiosa, y sangrienta, furia de mano atrevida" (Moreto, *El esclavo de su hijo*, Jornada 2); "de la ira al Basilisco" (Zamora, *Judás Iscariote*, Jornada 3).

55 "la ira de las Langostas (que del Pozo inexorable del Apocalypsis …)" (Calderón, *El día mayor de los días*, auto sacramental). The Scripture reference here is to Apocalypse (Revelation) 9:10, where lobster-like creatures are described as issuing forth from a bottomless pit.

56 Lope de Vega, *La ingratitud vengada*, Acto 3.

57 "una serpiente inflamada del veneno y de la ira" (Lope de Vega, *Sobre una mesa de murtas*, loa).

58 "áspid en el corazón asido, ¿Yo sin mandar? De ira rabio" (Calderón, *La hija del aire, segunda parte*, Acto 1); "yo los siento morderme en el Corazón con más rabioso veneno" (Calderón, *El año santo en Madrid*, auto sacramental).

59 Calderón, *No hay instante sin milagro*, auto sacramental.

60 Calderón, *El primer refugio del hombre, y probática piscina*, auto sacramental; Moreto, *El esclavo de su hijo*, Jornada 1.

61 "espero que como pisado áspid la ponzoña no reviento de la ira en que me abraso" (Calderón, *El gran príncipe de Fez*, Jornada 3).

62 Matos Fragoso, *El yerro de el entendido*, Jornada 2. Hidden venom appears in the lines, "¿Por qué callas? Porque encubres ese rabioso veneno, esa cruel obstinación de tu sangre" (Moreto, *Hacer del contrario amigo*, Jornada 2).

63 Lope de Vega, *Sobre una mesa de murtas*, loa.

64 Rojas Zorrilla, *El más improprio verdugo por la más justa venganza*, Jornada 1.

65 "la mortal cicuta de la Ira" (Calderón, *No hay instante sin milagro*, auto sacramental). On Socrates' death and whether it technically qualifies as a suicide, see R.G. Frey, "Did Socrates Commit Suicide?" *Philosophy* 53.203 (1978): 106–8.

66 Lope de Vega, *El bastardo Mudarra*, Acto 1.

67 "Así, bramo, pateo, rabio, y salto" (Pérez de Montalbán, *El sufrimiento premiado*, Jornada 1); "tan soberbia y furiosa, como víbora pisada" (Lope de Vega, *Los embustes de Fabia*, Jornada 2).

68 Guillén de Castro, *El conde Alarcos*, Jornada 2; Rojas Zorrilla, *El más improprio verdugo por la más justa venganza*, Jornada 1.

69 "la sed rabiosa que tengo de sangre" (Calderón, *El purgatorio de San Patricio*, Jornada 2).

70 "Beberé su aleve sangre, y en su corazón aleve, can rabioso, haré que apaguen mi hidrópica sed las iras" (Diamante, *El negro más prodigioso*, Jornada 2).

71 Frenzied: "estoy muy trocado, bravo frenesí me ha dado, muero, rabio, desvarío, quítateme de delante" (Lope de Vega, *Los amantes sin amor*, Acto 2). Senseless: "No prosigáis, de enojo, y de corrimiento rabio, sin sentido estoy, Roberto, de mi locura, y engaño" (Lope de Vega, *Las aventuras de don Juan de Alarcos*, Jornada 2). Crazed: "Estoy de coraje loco" (Lope de Vega, *El arenal de Sevilla*, Acto 1).

72 Guillén de Castro, *La verdad averiguada, y engañoso casamiento*, Jornada 1.

73 Robert A. Greene, "Instinct of Nature: Natural Law, Synderesis, and the Moral Sense," *Journal of the History of Ideas* 58.2 (1997): 173–98, at 173.

74 "Yo rabio, yo me endemonio, que ya no tengo temor" (Rojas Zorrilla, *Los áspides de Cleopatra*, Jornada 3). See Hilaire Kallendorf, "The Demon as Scapegoat," in *Exorcism and Its Texts: Subjectivity in Early Modern Literature of England and Spain* (Toronto: University of Toronto Press, 2003), 140–8.

75 Cueva, *La constancia de Arcelina*, Acto 2.

76 Calderón, *El Viático Cordero*, auto sacramental. This traditional comparison is repeated in Gérald Messadié, "The Devil in the Early Church," in *A History of the Devil*, trans. Marc Romano (New York: Kodansha, 1996), 255. A similar image appears in the Bible when Satan is compared to a roaring lion who seeks to devour the faithful (1 Peter 5:8).

77 "¿No soy yo (rabio de envidia) Luzbel? Soy quien soberbio, tanta ilustre Herarquía convocó" (Diamante, *El sol de la sierra*, Jornada 2).

78 Jupiter: "temo la ira del gran Jupiter" (Lope de Vega, *El laberinto de Creta*, Acto 1). Jupiter and Saturn: "Jupiter me dio soberbia de bizarros pensamientos, Saturno cólera y rabia, valor, y ánimo" (Calderón, *El purgatorio de San Patricio*, Acto 1). Jove: "la ira de Jove, y su violencia" (Cueva, *La constancia de Arcelina*, Acto 2). Hercules: "es de Hércules la ira" (Calderón, *Fieras afemina amor*, Jornada 2). Diana: "la ira de Diana" (Zamora, *Ser fino, y no parecerlo*, Acto 1). Pallas Athena: "Palas, y Venus era, tomando de una la ira, y de otra la belleza" (Calderón, *Afectos de odio, y amor*, Acto 1). An alternative name for Hercules also appears in the *comedias* in the context of Anger ("la ira del fuerte Alcides" [Alarcón, *Los pechos privilegiados*, Acto 2]).

79 Calderón, *La exaltación de la Cruz*, Jornada 2.

80 Calderón, *La púrpura de la rosa*, zarzuela.

81 Alarcón, *El Anticristo*, Acto 2; Rojas Zorrilla, *El profeta falso Mahoma*, Jornada 1. The Persian king referred to here is Khusrau II the Victorious (590–628). The historical sacking of Jerusalem by the Persians occurred in 614 AD.

82 Tirso de Molina, *Escarmientos para el cuerdo*, Acto 1, Acto 3.

83 Tirso de Molina, *La prudencia en la mujer*, Jornada 1; Calderón, *Dicha, y desdicha del nombre*, Jornada 2.

84 "en mujer la envidia, el amor, la ira, y la venganza, han tenido siempre más fuerte rigor" (Lope de Vega, *El valor de las mujeres*, Acto 1).

85 Lope de Vega, *Lo que ha de ser*, Jornada 2.

86 Lope de Vega, *El testimonio vengado*, Jornada 2.

87 Zamora, *Ser fino, y no parecerlo*, Acto 1.

88 Guillén de Castro, *Progne, y Filomena*, Acto 2. On this key prototype in Golden Age drama, see Melveena McKendrick, *Woman and Society in the Spanish Drama of the Golden Age: A Study of the* Mujer Varonil (Cambridge: Cambridge University Press, 2010).

89 For example, "brioso está Don Diego, lleno de furia, y de coraje horrible, sin descansar, ni recibir sosiego, deseando la lid fiera" (Cueva, *La muerte del Rey don Sancho*, Acto 3).

90 "el perseguido tiene siempre a la garganta la ira del ofensor, cuchillo que le amenaza" (Tirso de Molina, *Quien habló, pagó*, Jornada 2).

91 Rojas Zorrilla, *Los bandos de Verona*, Jornada 3.

92 Zamora, *No hay deuda que no se pague, y convidado de piedra*, Acto 1.

93 Lope de Vega, *Bamba*, Jornada 3. Face to face: "airado, colérico, loco, y ciego, sacando la espada, ya cara a cara" (Zamora, *Duendes son alcahuetes, alias el foleto, segunda parte*, Acto 1). Waving swords in the eyes: "¿de espadas hoy a los ojos me pones? ¿Qué entrada furiosa es ésta?" (Lope de Vega, *Laura perseguida*, Acto 2).

94 "cometieron sacrilegio tan enorme, del plomo de mi pistola los breves volantes Orbes. Con esto pues despechado saqué rabioso el estoque" (Alarcón, *La verdad sospechosa*, Acto 2).

95 Dagger: "furiosa, airada y resuelta, sacándome de la cinta el puñal" (Alarcón, *La manganilla de Melilla*, Acto 1). Knife: "el honor llama a la ira, ella al brazo, él al cuchillo" (Lope de Vega, *El bastardo Mudarra*, Acto 1). Arrows: "dejad las flechas ya, porque es vileza, que la ira consulte a la destreza" (Rojas Zorrilla, *Persiles, y Sigismunda*, Jornada 1); "ya descansando el brazo está de la fuerza, y de la ira con que tantas flechas tira" (Lope de Vega, *El desprecio agradecido*, Jornada 3). Andalusian arrows specifically: "le detiene la ira de mis Flecheros Andaluces" (Zamora, *Cada uno es linaje aparte, y los Mazas de Aragón*, Jornada 2).

96 Matos Fragoso, *El genízaro de Hungría*, Jornada 3.

97 Armed with a sword: "la Ira, con la Espada" (Calderón, *El año santo en Madrid*, auto sacramental). Selling swords: "la Ira, vende sus Espadas" (Calderón, *El gran mercado del mundo*, loa for auto sacramental). Bandit firing pistols: "salen la Culpa, y la Ira de Bandoleros, con Charpas, y Pistolas" (Calderón, *A María el corazón*, auto sacramental). In a different version evoking the classical goddess of war, Ira appears armed and with wings: "Sale del tercer Carro la Ira, armada, y con alas" (Calderón, *La semilla, y la cizaña*, auto sacramental).

98 This Renaissance notion was a resurrection of an idea previously voiced in Aristotle's *Rhetoric*. See Aristotle, *Rhetoric*, trans. W. Rhys Roberts (New York: Modern Library, 1954), Book II, chapter 12, 122.

99 Lope de Vega, *La boda entre dos maridos*, Acto 1.

100 Rojas Zorrilla, *Obligados, y ofendidos*, Jornada 3.

101 "Buena va la vejez con tanta flema, tras la sangre colérica encendida, que corre ardiendo por los verdes años" (Lope de Vega, *El verdadero amante*, Acto 2).

102 "en mis canas el fuego de mi coraje se templa, más que por nieve le postran, por ceniza" (Matos Fragoso, *Con amor no hay amistad*, Jornada 2).

103 Moreto, *Santa Rosa del Perú*, Jornada 3.

104 Lope de Vega, *La gallarda toledana*, Acto 3.

105 Alarcón, *Los pechos privilegiados*, Acto 2.

106 Rojas Zorrilla, *Entre bobos anda el juego*, Jornada 2.

107 Calderón, *Casa con dos puertas mala es de guardar*, Acto 1. Disloyalty is expressed in the lines, "es la deslealtad de Octavio, por cuyo amoroso agravio celosa, rabio, y suspiro" (Lope de Vega, *Laura perseguida*, Acto 1).

108 "a don Feliz mi enemigo escribe, de celos rabio, un puñal es cada letra, y una herida cada rasgo" (Matos Fragoso, *Con amor no hay amistad*, Jornada 3).

109 Calderón, *Amigo amante, y leal*, Jornada 3. On the restraint of Anger in classical antiquity, see William V. Harris, *Restraining Rage: The Ideology of Anger Control in Classical Antiquity* (Cambridge, MA: Harvard University Press, 2004).

110 Lope de Vega, *El ausente en el lugar*, Acto 3. A variation is the maxim, "love is an angry man": "¿cómo le pintan niño al Amor, si es hombre tan colérico?" (Lope de Vega, *El llegar en ocasión*, Acto 2).

111 "Ella del desdén sentida, y de la afrenta rabiosa" (Alarcón, *Examen de maridos*, Acto 2).

112 Cueva, *La muerte del Rey don Sancho*, Acto 1. A breach of decorum is described as "el rencor, y la ira, y cólera que en mí engendra tanto ofendido decoro" (Calderón, *Apolo, y Climene*, Acto 1).

113 Cervantes, *El laberinto de amor*, Jornada 1. The slap in the face appears as "Bofetada en mi rostro, ya el coraje ha llegado a su punto" (Cervantes, *El laberinto de amor*, Jornada 2).

114 Tirso de Molina, *Quien habló, pagó*, Jornada 1.

115 "ofendido da licencia al enojo, y a la ira" (Pérez de Montalbán, *Los templarios*, Jornada 2).

116 "nuevas causas de enojos, dan ocasión a la ira" (Tirso de Molina, *Los lagos de san Vicente*, Acto 2).

117 Cueva, *La libertad de España por Bernardo del Carpio*, Acto 2.

118 Calderón, *Dicha, y desdicha del nombre*, Jornada 1.

119 Guillén de Castro, *Las mocedades del Cid, Comedia primera*, Acto 1. The desire for revenge is also expressed as "vengaré, si no su muerte, a lo menos, mi coraje" (Calderón, *Amar después de la muerte*, Jornada 3).

120 Lope de Vega, *La mayor virtud de un rey*, Jornada 3.

121 As Elena del Río Parra notes in this regard, "algunos dramaturgos, reconociendo el poder de convocatoria de estos temas, hicieron uso de la paradoja para atraer al auditorio … Otros títulos reflejan situaciones imposibles o anómalas … Las situaciones planteadas, aparentemente imposibles y finalmente resueltas mediante argucias legales, son similares a algunas de las expuestas en la literatura casuística" (Elena del Río Parra, *Cartografías de la conciencia española en la Edad de Oro* [Mexico City: Fondo de Cultura Económica, 2008], 149).

122 Extending even further to non-dramatic contexts, and essentially hopping from the repertoire seamlessly into the archive, Bartolomé Clavero makes the startling pronouncement, "[h]emos llegado al homicidio y se confirma la impresión de que así sin calificar, era para la época antes un acto lícito que ilícito" (Bartolomé Clavero, "Delito y pecado: noción y escala de transgresiones," in *Sexo barroco*, ed. Tomás y Valiente et al., 57–89, at 86).

123 Lope de Vega, *El padrino desposado*, Jornada 3.

124 Killing for one's self is expressed in the lines, "rabio, aquí te he de matar" (Lope de Vega, *El serafín humano*, Acto 2). Having someone killed by a third party is spoken as "no sólo con el labio me castigó, furiosa, pero hacía matarme" (Guillén de Castro, *El engañarse engañado*, Jornada 3).

125 Calderón, *Mañana será otro día*, Jornada 2.

126 "habrá muerto a Doña Elvira, por vengar allí la ira de su injuria" (Lope de Vega, *El vaquero de Morana*, Acto 1).

127 Cueva, *El viejo enamorado*, Acto 2.

128 "Ay Cenobia, peno, rabio, mataré al Emperador, y mejor en venganza de tu agravio" (Calderón, *La gran Cenobia*, Jornada 3).

129 Solís, *Las amazonas*, Jornada 1.

130 Diamante, *Santa María Magdalena de Pazzi*, Jornada 2.

131 Zamora, *Viento es la dicha de amor*, Jornada 2.

132 Calderón, *Duelos de amor, y lealtad*, Jornada 3.

133 Calderón, *La inmunidad del sagrado*, loa for auto sacramental. There is also, of course, the exception that proves the rule: "hay quien sin cólera mate" (Pérez de Montalbán, *Lo que son juicios del cielo*, Jornada 1).

134 Cervantes, *El gallardo español*, Jornada 3.

135 Lope de Vega, *La bella Aurora*, Acto 2.

136 Cueva, *La libertad de España por Bernardo del Carpio*, Acto 1.

137 Matthew D. Stroud, *Fatal Union: A Pluralistic Approach to the Spanish Wife-Murder* Comedias (Lewisburg: Bucknell University Press, 1990), 14–15.

138 Daniel L. Heiple, "The Theological Context of Wife Murder in Seventeenth-Century Spain," in *Sex and Love in Golden Age Spain*, ed. Alain Saint-Saëns (New Orleans: University Press of the South, 1996), 105–21.

139 Heiple, "The Theological Context of Wife Murder," 112. On probabilism, see Miguel Álvarez, "El probabilismo y el teatro español del siglo XVII" (PhD dissertation, New York University, 1982); and Julio Caro Baroja, "Probabilidades, laxitudes y corrupciones," in *Las formas complejas de la vida religiosa: Religión, sociedad y carácter en la España de los siglos XVI y XVII* (Madrid: Akal, 1978), 517–50.

140 Jenaro Artiles, "Bibliografía sobre el problema del honor y la honra en el drama español," in *Filología y crítica hispánica: homenaje al Profesor Federico Sánchez Escribano*, ed. Alberto Porqueras-Mayo and Carlos Rojas (Madrid: Alcalá, 1969), 235–41, at 237.

141 For a particularly well-nuanced recent discussion of this play, see María M. Carrión, "Foundational Violence and the Drama of Honour," chapter 4 of *Subject Stages: Marriage, Theatre, and the Law in Early Modern Spain* (Toronto: University of Toronto Press, 2010), 77–98, especially 77–80. A different play by the same title has been attributed to Lope de Vega.

142 Don Cruickshank links these blood stains to the Jewish Passover ritual of painting the lamb's blood on the door posts, thereby making this scene an elaborate, profane parody of the Ten Commandments: "One of the reasons for the association of the Commandments with doorposts lies in the relationship of the Commandments to the Passover and the delivery from Egypt: Israelites were expected to keep the Commandments in gratitude for their delivery, and both the Passover and the Commandments were supposed to be recorded in phylacteries … The symbolism of Gutierre's bloody hand on the door-post is therefore quite complex. It represents a turning away from the Commandments (especially the first two) to worship the false god of honour … and as a parody and profanation of the Passover, a sign of ingratitude for the delivery from Egypt" (D.W. Cruickshank, "'Pongo mi mano en sangre bañada a la puerta': Adultery in *El médico de su honra*," in *Studies in Spanish Literature of the Golden Age Presented to E.M. Wilson*, ed. R.O. Jones [London: Tamesis, 1973], 45–62, at 51).

143 As Georgina Dopico Black affirms in the context of Spain, "[t]here is no question that sixteenth- and seventeenth-century civil law afforded husbands ample freedom in the disposal of adulterous wives" (Georgina Dopico Black, *Perfect Wives, Other Women: Adultery and Inquisition in Early Modern Spain* [Durham: Duke University Press, 2001], 114). Merry Wiesner adds that husbands were further accorded the freedom to kill their wives' lovers: "In Spain, only in the sixteenth century did the state take over from the husband the right to punish his wife for adultery, and husbandly revenge was still allowed as long as he killed both his wife and her lover" (Merry E. Wiesner, *Women and Gender in Early Modern Europe* [Cambridge: Cambridge University Press, 2000], 40). Scott Taylor notes that ecclesiastical and secular authorities disagreed on this point: "Scholars have made much of how Castilian culture sanctioned the right of a cuckold to kill his adulterous wife and her lover … [W]hile jurists affirmed that the law allowed revenge, Christian moralists discouraged it" (Taylor, "Adultery and Violence," in *Honor and Violence,* 197). See also the review of this book by Lu Ann Homza in the *Journal of Modern History* 82 (2010): 488–90.

144 On Anger as an emotion, and the historiographical ramifications of treating it as such, see Barbara Rosenwein, "Worrying about Emotions in History," *American Historical Review* 107.3 (2002): 821–45. On the shift towards seeing Anger as an emotional disorder in Spain during this time period, see Maureen Flynn, "Taming Anger's Daughters: New Treatment for Emotional Problems in Renaissance Spain," *Renaissance Quarterly* 51 (1998): 864–86. Flynn offers a (perhaps anachronistically) zen view of Renaissance anger-management strategies: "Instead of relying exclusively

on ascetic discipline and rational reflection as means to subdue undesirable emotions, post-medieval therapeutics added a number of mood-altering techniques such as music, dance, conversation, baths, and meditation on graphic images. The psychological premise of the new morality of the Renaissance was not flight from the body but respectful acceptance of its passionate interests" (864). However, she grounds her argument at least in part in the thought of Juan Luis Vives, who "criticized both Plato and Aristotle for dealing with the emotions in most of their writings as purely moral phenomena … As acts of the natural faculties of the soul, he suggested, the emotions are more properly considered within the realm of psychology than of ethics" (879). Flynn cites Vives, *Tratado del alma.*

145 Cueva, *La muerte de Ajax Telamón, sobre las armas de Aquiles*, Acto 1.

146 Diamante, *Lides de amor, y desdén*, Acto 2. The gods' Anger is further expressed in the lines, "los dioses supremos me han mandado que castigue con la ira, y el acero" (Rojas Zorrilla, *Los trabajos de Tobías*, Jornada 1).

147 Cueva, *La muerte de Ajax Telamón*, Acto 2.

148 Lope de Vega, *La limpieza no manchada*, Acto 1.

149 Alarcón, *El Anticristo*, Acto 2.

150 "Mientras no cesa de pecar no cesa la ira divina, que nos quiere castigar" (Tirso de Molina, *La mejor espigadera*, Jornada 1).

151 This sermon was preached in July 1741 to the congregation of Enfield, Massachusetts (later Connecticut). Its most famous image is that of a spider dangling over a fire: "The God that holds you over the pit of hell, much as one holds a spider, or some loathsome insect over the fire, abhors you, and is dreadfully provoked: his wrath towards you burns like fire; he looks upon you as worthy of nothing else, but to be cast into the fire; he is of purer eyes than to bear to have you in his sight." The text is available in pamphlet form through Sword of the Lord Publishers (Murfreesboro, TN, 2000) and has been anthologized in many American literature textbooks.

152 Alarcón, *La manganilla de Melilla*, Acto 3; Diamante, *El jubileo de Porciúncula*, Jornada 3.

153 Lope de Vega, *Angélica en el Catay*, Acto 1. The Old Testament reference here is to Judges 16:25–30.

154 For an early modern sermon which specifically makes this claim, see David Crosley, *Samson a Type of Christ: In a Sermon Preached at Mr Pomfret's Meeting-House in Gravel-Lane near Hounds-Ditch, London: at the Morning-Lecture, on July 22, 1691* (London: for William Marshall, 1691).

155 Mark 11:15–17. Echoes of this scene are heard in Moreto's *El esclavo de su hijo* when the saintly Loco commands: "Vayan del Templo los dos, puesto que aquí no hay lugar / de vender, y contratar, porque en esto imito a Dios" (Moreto, *El esclavo de su hijo*, Jornada 2).

156 Pérez de Montalbán, *El valiente más dichoso, don Pedro Guiral*, Jornada 3.

157 Calderón, *La redención de cautivos*, auto sacramental.

158 Humoural psychology was a complex calculus of different permutations and combinations of a set number of factors:

> Human nature is determined by the sanguine, phlegmatic, melancholic and choleric humours, related to the four qualities (wet, dry, cold, and hot), which are in turn related to the four elements (water, earth, air, and fire) and the four constituents of the human body (humours, homogeneous parts, *spiritus*, and innate heat respectively). The humours are normally, but not always, said to combine into eight combinations which produce specific temperaments and distempers … [I]n each individual, humours are dominantly, not absolutely, sanguine, phlegmatic, melancholic, or choleric. They can even be redundant at certain times of the year. (Ian Maclean, *Logic, Signs and Nature in the Renaissance* [Cambridge: Cambridge University Press, 2007], 241)

159 On Renaissance reception of Galenic thought, as well as challenges to it by Paracelsus and his followers, see Allen G. Debus, *Man and Nature in the Renaissance* (Cambridge: Cambridge University Press, 1978), especially 19–26 and 55–63. The most important Galenic text dealing with the humours was a treatise titled *That the Habits of the Soul Follow the Temperament of the Body* (Nancy G. Siraisi, *History, Medicine, and the Traditions of Renaissance Learning* [Ann Arbor: University of Michigan Press, 2007], 99). Debus explains which part of Galen's theories Paracelsus rejected: "For the Paracelsian the humoral theory of Galenic medicine was no longer adequate. The traditional explanation of disease as an internal imbalance of the humors was rejected by Paracelsus. He preferred to emphasize local malfunctions within the body" (27).

160 Rojas Zorrilla, *Peligrar en los remedios*, Jornada 3.

161 Matos Fragoso, *El amor hace valientes*, Jornada 3.

162 "temporal camaleón, que hoy truecas tu color mismo, vistiéndote de la ira en que tu pasión te ciega" (Rojas Zorrilla, *Los trabajos de Tobías*, Jornada 1). I have explored the moral connotations of dressing and undressing in my article on fashion and the Deadly Vices. See Hilaire Kallendorf, "Dressed to the Sevens, or Sin in Style: Fashion Statements by the Deadly Vices in Spanish Baroque *Autos Sacramentales*," in *The Seven Deadly Sins: From Communities to Individuals*, ed. Richard Newhauser (Leiden: Brill, 2007), 145–82.

163 Lope de Vega, *La batalla del honor*, Acto 2.

164 "poderoso afecto es la ira de un pecho humano" (Moreto, *El valiente justiciero*, Jornada 2).

165 Sebastián de Covarrubias Orozco, "Afecto," in *Tesoro de la lengua castellana o española* (1611), ed. Felipe C.R. Maldonado, rev. Manuel Camarero (Madrid: Castalia, 1995), 22.

166 Zamora, *Siempre hay que envidiar, amando*, Jornada 1 and Jornada 2. One complication in interpreting these lines is that *afecto* can be translated alternately as either

affect or affection. Moreover, multiple affects may correspond to a single concept, as we see in the title of Calderón's *Los tres afectos de amor, piedad, desmayo y valor* and also his *Afectos de odio, y amor*.

167 Calderón, *El primer refugio del hombre, y probática piscina*, auto sacramental. For a medical doctor's perspective on this metamorphosis in the history of ideas, see Karl Menninger, "Sin into Symptom," chapter 6 of *Whatever Became of Sin?* (New York: Hawthorn, 1973), 74–93.

168 Solís, *Las amazonas*, Jornada 3. Nancy Siraisi explains the centrality of blood for humoural psychology: "Blood occupied a special place among the humors. The actual fluid found in the veins was considered to be a sanguineous mass consisting of a mixture of the pure humor blood with a lesser proportion of the other three humors: changes in color and partial separation in drawn blood left standing in a container were advanced as evidence of the presence of the biles and phlegm. The other humors were generated as part of the process of the manufacture of blood; and an important function of yellow and black bile – in their 'good' form – was, respectively, to purify and fortify the blood" (Nancy G. Siraisi, *Medieval and Early Renaissance Medicine: An Introduction to Knowledge and Practice* [Chicago: University of Chicago Press, 1990], 105–6). Scott Taylor confirms that contemporaneous moralists likewise considered Anger to have a physiological aspect: "Pedro Ciruelo also linked a desire for vengeance with rage (*ira*), an emotion that had a moral component as one of the seven deadly sins but also had a physiological aspect, since it boils and inflames the blood, disturbing reason in a man so affected" (Taylor, *Honor and Violence*, 107). Taylor cites Pedro Ciruelo, *Arte de bien confesar* (Seville: Domenico de Robertis, 1548), fol. 42r-42v. For more commentary on fire imagery used in Renaissance Spain in the context of Anger, see Flynn, "Taming Anger's Daughters," 873. Flynn cites Aristotle, *On the Soul*, and Plutarch, *On Anger*, which (as she notes) went through at least four different Spanish translations in the sixteenth century (878n49).

169 Diamante, *Ir por el riesgo a la dicha*, Jornada 1.

170 "¡pasa un afecto en la voz desde el desmayo a la ira!" (Diamante, *La reina María Estuarda*, Jornada 2).

171 For example, "la Avaricia, que es el Afecto, que en ti reina" (Calderón, *La serpiente de metal*, auto sacramental).

172 Jodi Campbell, *Monarchy, Political Culture, and Drama in Seventeenth-Century Madrid: Theater of Negotiation* (Aldershot: Ashgate, 2006), 94–5. See also 97. Campbell's discussion of this play emphasizes a rejection of the people's influence, from the king's perspective.

173 Lope de Vega, *Jorge toledano*, Acto 2.

174 Lope de Vega, *El llegar en ocasión*, Acto 2.

175 Zamora, *El hechizado por fuerza*, Jornada 2.

176 Lope de Vega, *Los tres diamantes*, Jornada 2. The dream is described thus: "mira señor que es sueño, es sombra, es viento, y mil fantasmas, y colores hace de la solicitud del pensamiento."

177 Lope de Vega, *Lucinda perseguida*, Acto 1. Reason subject to Anger: "la razón tan sujeta está a la ira" (Lope de Vega, *La batalla del honor*, Acto 2). Reason displaced by Anger: "Con qué furor intrínseco deshace la ira a la razón el santo imperio" (Lope de Vega, *El Amor enamorado*, Preliminares de obra).

178 Zamora, *Mazariegos, y Monsalves*, Jornada 1. The religious argument is made that "Mira que provocas al cielo con la ira" (Lope de Vega, *El galán de la Membrilla*, Acto 3). This soon gives way, however, to appeals to understanding, such as "consultando sin pasión vuestro claro entendimiento, no deis lugar a la ira" (Lope de Vega, *La mayor virtud de un rey*, Jornada 3).

179 Cueva, *La muerte de Ajax Telamón, sobre las armas de Aquiles*, Acto 2.

180 Lope de Vega, *El animal de Hungría*, Acto 3.

181 Diamante, *El jubileo de Porciúncula*, Jornada 1.

182 Lope de Vega, *San Isidro labrador de Madrid*, Acto 2.

183 Zamora, *Cada uno es linaje aparte, y los Mazas de Aragón*, Acto 1.

184 "Eusebio, yo confieso, que has podido templar en mí la ira con que agraviado te miro" (Calderón, *La devoción de la Cruz*, Jornada 3).

185 Calderón, *El galán fantasma*, Jornada 2.

186 Lope de Vega, *El vaquero de Morana*, Acto 1.

187 Lope de Vega, *La esclava de su galán*, Jornada 1.

188 Lope de Vega, *La Historia de Tobías*, Acto 1; Lope de Vega, *La nueva victoria del marqués de Santa Cruz*, Jornada 1.

189 "por mi fe que la ira … buen capirote os ha puesto" (Lope de Vega, *El valor de las mujeres*, Acto 2).

190 "sin ser disculpa la ira" (Zamora, *Siempre hay que envidiar, amando*, Jornada 1).

191 Calderón, *Auristela, y Lisidante*, Jornada 1. A similar example appears in Diamante's *Pasión vencida de afecto*: "mas es a mi subjeción atenta razón de estado, templar la ira" (Jornada 1).

192 Lope de Vega, *El secretario de sí mismo*, Acto 3; Lope de Vega, *La buena guarda*, Acto 3.

193 "se amansa arrepentido quien colérico se atreve" (Guillén de Castro, *El pretender con pobreza*, Jornada 2); "la ira que, pasada, se arrepiente" (Lope de Vega, *Jorge toledano*, Acto 3).

194 Anger turns to Pity: "vuelta en lástima la ira, muestre, intentando enmendarla" (Calderón, *Celos aun del aire matan*, Jornada 3). The first quotation is from Calderón, *En esta vida todo es verdad, y todo mentira*, Jornada 2. In this play a magician uses spells to tame Focas's rage.

195 Lope de Vega, *La villana de Xetafe*, Acto 3.

196 Rojas Zorrilla, *No hay amigo para amigo*, Jornada 2. A similar example would be "hasta que el tiempo, o los casos aplaquen del Rey la ira" (Alarcón, *Los pechos privilegiados*, Acto 3).

197 Zamora, *El lucero de Madrid, y divino Labrador, san Isidro*, Jornada 3.

198 Calderón, *Fieras afemina amor*, Jornada 3.

199 Lope de Vega, *La fuerza lastimosa*, Jornada 3.

200 1 Samuel 16:23 (1 Kings 16:23 in the Douay-Rheims version).

201 Giambattista Guarini noted that "melody purges the feeling the Greeks call enthusiasm; the Sacred Scriptures in dealing with it say that David, with the harmony of his music, drove away the evil spirits from Saul, the first king of the Hebrews" (Giambattista Guarini, *The Compendium of Tragicomic Poetry* [1599] [excerpts], trans. Allan H. Gilbert in *Literary Criticism: Plato to Dryden*, ed. Allan H. Gilbert [Detroit: Wayne State University Press, 1962], 504–33, at 514). Paolo Beni made a similar connection in his *In Aristotelis poeticam commentarii* (Padua, 1613), cited in Baxter Hathaway, *The Age of Criticism: The Late Renaissance in Italy* (Ithaca: Cornell University Press, 1962), 286.

202 Calderón, *La primer flor de el Carmelo*, auto sacramental.

203 Calderón, *El indulto general*, loa for auto sacramental.

204 "Mas, que pretendéis, que arme la ira, que en el pecho duerme" (Zamora, *Ser fino, y no parecerlo*, Jornada 2).

205 "la Ira con otra Fuente, y en ella un Peto" (Calderón, *El indulto general*, loa for auto sacramental).

206 Diamante, *El sol de la sierra*, Jornada 3.

207 Lope de Vega, *Angélica en el Catay*, Acto 2.

208 Quiñones de Benavente, *El murmurador*, entremés. Of this medical practice, Cruickshank explains: "The remedy most commonly prescribed for almost all ailments was bleeding. 'Bad' blood was removed, in quantities of anything up to 20 ounces, usually from a vein in the wrist, although the seventeenth century saw a sterile controversy about the virtues of letting blood from the ankle. The nature of the controversy was the only sterile feature of the treatment, which was likely to introduce infection, wherever it was carried out" (Don W. Cruickshank, "The Birthplace: Madrid in 1600," chapter 1 of *Don Pedro Calderón* [Cambridge: Cambridge University Press, 2009], 1–13, at 11). On the use of leeches for medical bleeding, see Siraisi, *Medieval and Early Renaissance Medicine*, 140.

209 Matos Fragoso, *Con amor no hay amistad*, Jornada 2.

210 Calderón, *Fortunas de Andrómeda, y Perseo [Comedia]*, Jornada 3.

211 See Elena del Río Parra, "*Suspensio animi*, or the Interweaving of Mysticism and Artistic Creation," in *A New Companion to Hispanic Mysticism*, ed. Hilaire Kallendorf (Leiden: Brill, 2010), 391–410.

212 Calderón, *Darlo todo, y no dar nada*, Jornada 3; Calderón, *El maestrazgo del Toyson*, auto sacramental.

213 "la ira le doma" (Cervantes, *Los baños de Argel*, Jornada 1). According to the theology of Saint John of the Cross, the mystical "seeker abandons himself to the shaping of the Holy Spirit" (Jane Ackerman, "John of the Cross, the Difficult Icon," in *A New Companion to Hispanic Mysticism*, ed. Kallendorf, 149–74, at 168).

214 Diamante, *Triunfo de la paz, y el tiempo* (1670), Acto 1; Lope de Vega, *El hombre de bien*, Acto 3. The opposite action is described as giving Anger free rein: "Dando la rienda a la ira … Soltando el freno a la rabia" (Calderón, *El Golfo de las sirenas*, Acto 1).

215 Cervantes, *El laberinto de amor*, Jornada 1.

216 Calderón, *La hija del aire, primera parte*, Jornada 3.

217 "dale excepción a tu enojo, redúcete más benigno" (Rojas Zorrilla, *Los tres blasones de España*, Jornada 2).

218 "Mira, Tucapel, que muchas veces no te da lugar la ira a ver las causas" (Lope de Vega, *Arauco domado por el excelentísimo señor don García Hurtado de Mendoza*, Acto 2).

219 Cueva, *La muerte de Ajax Telamón, sobre las armas de Aquiles*, Acto 1; "reparada de la ira vuestra Alteza, le pueda con más templanza responder" (Diamante, *El cerco de Zamora*, Jornada 1). Examples abound in the *comedias* of counsellor figures offering advice to rulers; for example, Saint Casilda says to the king, "Reprime, señor, la ira, detén la cólera, mira" (Tirso de Molina, *Los lagos de san Vicente*, Acto 2). On counsellor figures offering advice in these dramas, see Hilaire Kallendorf, "Asking for Advice," chapter 3 of *Conscience on Stage: The* Comedia *as Casuistry in Early Modern Spain* (Toronto: University of Toronto Press, 2007).

220 "de vuestros enojos apelaréis al estrago de la ira, es un error tan ciego, tan temerario cuanto incierto" (Diamante, *El jubileo de Porciúncula*, Jornada 2). For the postmodern version vis-à-vis love, see Robert Hemfelt, Frank Minirth, and Paul Meier, *Love Is a Choice: The Definitive Book on Letting Go of Unhealthy Relationships* (Nashville: Thomas Nelson, 2003).

221 As one character reflects retrospectively, "sin mirar mi error solté la ira, que hay ya quien haga aquello que no mira" (Rojas Zorrilla, *No hay ser padre siendo Rey*, Jornada 3).

222 Lope de Vega, *La batalla del honor*, Acto 2. On the alleged lack of interiority of *comedia* characters, we recall the misguided pronouncement by José Antonio Maravall: "[E]l 'soy quien soy' … [n]o se trata de afirmar un ser íntimo, ni una esencia individual, ni un yo interior" (José Antonio Maravall, *Teatro y literatura en la sociedad barroca* [Madrid: Seminarios y Ediciones, 1972], 103).

223 Joseph Gillet, "The Autonomous Character in Spanish and European Literature," *Hispanic Review* 24.3 (1956): 179–90.

224 Guillén de Castro, *Los mal casados de Valencia*, Acto 3; Rojas Zorrilla, *Persiles, y Sigismunda*, Jornada 3.

225 "Así la ira mitigo de tu obstinado desdén" (Rojas Zorrilla, *Lo que son mujeres*, Jornada 3); "¡el Cielo quiera que acierte a ajustar la ira la venganza con la ofensa!" (Rojas Zorrilla, *Nuestra Señora de Atocha*, Jornada 2).

226 Tirso de Molina, *Amar por razón de estado*, Acto 3.

227 Rojas Zorrilla, *Nuestra Señora de Atocha*, Jornada 2.

228 This unconvincing thesis was advanced by Maravall: "El teatro español es, ante todo, un instrumento político y social" (Maravall, *Teatro y literatura*, 31). McKendrick refutes him thus:

> The trouble with the establishment-propaganda theory is that it is extremely difficult to locate either in seventeenth-century Spain or in seventeenth-century Spanish drama a monolithic set of entirely complementary establishment values – within the immovable boundaries of Catholic devotion itself doctrinal differences and ecclesiastical and other rivalries were openly acknowledged. How, therefore, could the theatre implement some comprehensive ideological brief that did not exist?

(Melveena McKendrick, *Playing the King: Lope de Vega and the Limits of Conformity* [London: Tamesis, 2000], 8)

229 For a discussion of mutable identities in the context of Renaissance stage performance, see Hilaire Kallendorf, "Intertextual Madness in Hamlet: The Ghost's Fragmented Performativity," *Renaissance and Reformation / Renaissance et Réforme* 22.4 (1998): 69–87.

7. Disappearing Deadlies: The End of Envy

1 Rojas Zorrilla, *Persiles, y Sigismunda*, Jornada 3; Lope de Vega, *El blasón de los Chaves de Villalba*, Acto 3; Diamante, *El nacimiento de Cristo*, Acto 2.

2 Raymond Williams, "Dominant, Residual, and Emergent," in *Marxism in Literature* (Oxford: Oxford University Press, 1977), 121–7, at 123.

3 "La envidia es la sombra de la fama" (Lope de Vega, *Las cuentas del Gran Capitán*, Acto 1).

4 Snake biting the heart: "¡qué rigurosa, qué fuerte la víbora de la envidia en el corazón me muerde!" (Calderón, *Los cabellos de Absalón*, Jornada 3). Scorpion's tongue: "bien sabes que con lengua de escorpión pintan la envidia" (Lope de Vega, *El perro del hortelano*, Acto 1). Manufacture of venom: "Basilisco aprecias, criando propia ponzoña sólo de la dicha ajena" (Calderón, *El jardín de Falerina*, auto sacramental). This venom induces vomiting: "o envidia, soberbio trueno, vómitos das de veneno" (Tirso de Molina, *Próspera fortuna de don Álvaro de Luna, primera parte*, Jornada 2). The logical consequence of Envy's heart attack occurs when she strides onto the stage, carrying a heart in her hands. This occurs in allegorical fashion in the stage directions for Lope de Vega's *El nacimiento de Cristo*, Acto 1.

5 "Envidia te ha derribado, que es rayo, aborto del trueno" (Tirso de Molina, *Cautela contra cautela*, Jornada 2).

6 "O envidia, que eres polilla de la próspera fortuna" (Tirso de Molina, *Adversa fortuna de don Álvaro de Luna, segunda parte*, Jornada 3).

7 This is said to be particularly true of medical doctors and poets: "en Médicos y en Poetas, la envidia es sarna incurable" (Tirso de Molina, *El amor médico*, Acto 2).

8 "a nadie de vista pierde la envidia, aunque esté en la Luna" (Lope de Vega, *El remedio en la desdicha*, Acto 1).

9 "lo contrario ven sus ciegos ojos, es porque son de envidia los antojos" (Tirso de Molina, *La santa Juana*, Acto 3). This trope of Envy's eyeglasses is repeated more than once: "mas hála puesto a los ojos la envidia vil sus antojos, y así no ve la razón" (Tirso de Molina, *Segunda parte de Santa Juana*, Acto 1). A variation on this theme is Envy placing a bandage over the eyes: "pues la envidia, le ha puesto en los ojos venda" (Lope de Vega, *La burgalesa de Lerma*, Acto 2). In a typically Baroque distortion of this trope, Envy is sometimes portrayed as having only one eye: "La envidia es tuerta, de suerte que a nadie ha mirado bien" (Lope de Vega, *El ejemplo de casadas y prueba de la paciencia*, Acto 3). In yet another variation, Envy is the cloud which obscures clear vision: "Mirad, Señor, que la envidia, vapor infiel, nube densa, para cegar vuestros ojos, ha ido" (Zamora, *La poncella de Orleans*, Jornada 3).

10 "Que también es la envidia mariposa, que se abrasa en la llama luminosa" (Lope de Vega, *El Amor enamorado*, Preliminares de obra).

11 "a Dios, de envidia muero como las moscas a la miel, o al mosto" (Lope de Vega, *El leal criado*, Acto 3).

12 "la fortuna sube a un hombre paso a paso, y la envidia como a vidrio de un golpe le hace pedazos" (Lope de Vega, *Porfiando vence amor*, Jornada 1).

13 "le convierte en espada la envidia, que como a herido toro la fastidia" (Lope de Vega, *Laura perseguida*, Acto 3).

14 Moreto, *El secreto entre dos amigos*, Jornada 3. This trope is repeated in the line, "Hablas con rústica envidia" (Lope de Vega, *El triunfo de la humildad, y soberbia abatida*, Acto 3).

15 Calderón, *El divino Orfeo*, auto sacramental. These *autos* in turn serve as an intertext for certain *comedias* which reference the cultural commonplaces contained therein. A prime example would be Matos Fragoso's comedia *El hijo de la piedra*, which likewise refers to Envy's rustic dress: "la ciega tirana envidia, que también, como es villana, vive de sayal vestida" (Matos Fragoso, *El hijo de la piedra*, Jornada 2).

16 In a play written about the son of the Roman general Scipio Africanus, the character Scipión exclaims: "¡O villana pasión, hija de la envidia!" (Calderón, *El segundo Scipión*, Jornada 1).

17 "El huerto en cuya fuente puso la mano la villana envidia" (Lope de Vega, *Las bizarrías de Belisa*, Preliminares de obra).

18 Calderón, *El monstruo de los jardines*, Jornada 3.

19 Tirso de Molina, *Adversa fortuna de don Álvaro de Luna, segunda parte*, Jornada 2.

20 Pérez de Montalbán, *A lo hecho no hay remedio, y príncipe de los montes*, Jornada 1.

21 Calderón, *Fortunas de Andrómeda, y Perseo*, Jornada 1. In another *auto sacramental* Calderón once again mentions Envy and Greed in direct proximity to each other: "Envidia, y Codicia" (Calderón, *El indulto general*, loa for auto sacramental).

22 Lope de Vega, *Ello dirá*, Acto 2.

23 Calderón, *La serpiente de metal*, auto sacramental, emphasis mine.

24 "En noblezàs suele descubrirse más, que el envidioso del rico, a decir mal se provoca" (Lope de Vega, *El galán de la Membrilla*, Acto 1). Here a concern over money is expressed instead in passive-aggressive behaviour such as speaking ill of someone or ruining that person's reputation.

25 Coveting of virtues: "No quiera Dios que tal sea, ni que murmure envidioso de las virtudes ajenas" (Lope de Vega, *El castigo sin venganza*, Acto 1). Of learning: "¡Año para los cultos! ¡Qué claridad estudiosa! ¡Qué cultura! Dará envidia" (Lope de Vega, *Las bizarrías de Belisa*, Jornada 2). Of refinement or good taste: "Sólo que tenga Envidia de tu buen gusto" (Lope de Vega, *Al pasar del arroyo*, Acto 2). Of pleasure: "lo primero que topa la Envidia es con el Placer de otros" (Calderón, *El divino Orfeo*, auto sacramental). Of good fortune: "no quiere estar envidioso, de las ajenas fortunas" (Lope de Vega, *El villano en su rincón*, Acto 2). Of happiness: "amar la propria dicha es envidiar la ajena" (Calderón, *El indulto general*, loa for auto sacramental). Of joys: "solamente ser podía, Envidia la que llorara las ajenas alegrías" (Diamante, *El nacimiento de Cristo*, Acto 2).

26 "no se vio Mujer, que envidiosa, confiese, que otra es Hermosa" (Calderón, *Primero, y segundo Isaac*, auto sacramental). A similar example is "es tan hermosa, que ha dado envidia en Granada a los ojos que la han visto" (Pérez de Montalbán, *La ganancia por la mano*, Jornada 2). Physical beauty was a quality not limited to females, however; in Lope de Vega's *Adonis, y Venus*, Venus refers to Adonis as "Bellísimo mancebo, envidia de los hombres" (Lope de Vega, *Adonis, y Venus*, Acto 3).

27 "Con sus caras dan envidia a las damas Toledanas" (Lope de Vega, *El capellán de la Virgen*, Acto 3); "de la planta al cuello, Laura envidia tu hermosura" (Lope de Vega, *Los Tellos de Meneses*, Acto 3).

28 "Desnuda el cuerpo hermoso, dando a la Luna envidia" (Lope de Vega, *Arauco domado por el excelentísimo señor don García Hurtado de Mendoza*, Acto 1). The naked indigenous woman described is named Fresia.

29 "al mozo rubio siempre envidia el cano" (Lope de Vega, *Castelvines, y Monteses*, Jornada 3).

30 "envidioso quedo de tu ingenio milagroso, para disputar con ellos" (Lope de Vega, *El capellán de la Virgen*, Acto 1). Similarly the Licenciado Vidriera (in a comedy Agustín Moreto wrote in imitation of Cervantes's *novela ejemplar*) is renowned for his knowledge of law: "su Escuela te llama luz de las leyes, allí das envidia a Reyes" (Moreto, *El licenciado Vidriera*, Jornada 1). The titular character of Lope de Vega's *La boba para los otros, y discreta para sí* is also gifted by heaven with clear understanding: "el entendimiento claro, que me dio el cielo, aumentara la envidia de mis contrarios" (Acto 1).

31 "Él es buen Caballero, y me tiene envidioso de su acero, de su estilo admirado" (Calderón, *La dama duende*, Acto 1); "¡Qué galán! ¡Qué alentado! Envidia tengo al traje de soldado" (Calderón, *El alcalde de Zalamea*, Jornada 1). This type of chivalric Envy also appears in Moreto's *La fortuna merecida*, where a knight reports after a sword fight: "reñí con él, de suerte peleaba, que me dejó envidioso el noble acero; ¡vive Dios, que es valiente Caballero!" (Jornada 2). Fashion Envy is not limited to

men in the *comedias*; we also find characters alerting women to the fact that other females envy their outfits: "aseguro por Dios que te miran más de dos con envidia de las tocas" (Pérez de Montalbán, *Amor, privanza, y castigo*, Acto 3).

32 "la Envidia, enarbolando en el viento de las Militares Cruzes los Estandartes" (Calderón, *El año santo en Madrid*, auto sacramental). Another specific military order mentioned was the Knights of Malta: "hasta volver a Malta, donde a pesar de tanta envidia y persecución recibió el Hábito" (Lope de Vega, *El rey sin reino*, Preliminares de obra).

33 Musical ability: "¿No das al más noble envidia? ¿Tú no tocas diestramente la guitarra?" (Matos Fragoso, *El yerro de el entendido*, Acto 1). Artistic talent: "cuyo rostro, cuyo brío ha trasladado el pincel, con tan valiente destreza que dejó a naturaleza, con envidia, y celos de él" (Tirso de Molina, *Adversa fortuna de don Álvaro de Luna*, Jornada 2). Social fame: "mi hermano, envidioso de la fama de Céspedes, su peligro se labró" (Diamante, *El Hércules de Ocaña*, Jornada 1).

34 Lope de Vega, *El amigo hasta la muerte*, Acto 1. Later in the same play Bernardo brags about what a good friend he is: "Habla, y cánsate envidioso de ver cuán perfecto amigo hasta la muerte me nombro" (Acto 3).

35 On love triangles as a thematic cornerstone of the *comedias*, see Denise M. DiPuccio, *Communicating Myths of the Golden Age* Comedia (Lewisburg: Bucknell University Press, 1998), 182. Some examples of references to love triangles in the context of Envy might be "la envidiosa mujer olvidada" (Rueda, *Camila*, Acto 1) or "envidiosa de la suerte venturosa con que mi amor solicito" (Tirso de Molina, *Quien calla, otorga*, Acto 2).

36 One trickster complains about his so-far unsuccessful attempts to get a married woman to go to bed with him, saying that his sister "ha dormido con ella cuatro noches, con envidia del mundo y de mi alma" (Lope de Vega, *Los embustes de Zelauro*, Acto 2).

37 Lope de Vega, *La hermosa Ester*, Acto 1.

38 "Las galas y el buen marido envidia toda mujer" (Lope de Vega, *El marido más firme*, Acto 2).

39 Tirso de Molina, *El amor, y el amistad*, Jornada 2. Once again, however, this form of Envy is not limited to females; for example, one luckless male lover complains vehemently to his lady, "háte engañado algún contrario mío envidioso de nuestro casamiento" (Lope de Vega, *La pastoral de Jacinto*, Acto 3). A masculine character likewise comments to his potential rival: "Don Pedro, tú te has casado tan bien, que envidioso quedo" (Lope de Vega, *Servir a señor discreto*, Acto 3).

40 Lope de Vega, *La mayor virtud de un rey*, Jornada 3. Jealousy, however, does not appear to equate with Envy for every author. Calderón would appear to contradict Lope directly in the lines, "aunque no me dan celos, me da envidia" (Calderón, *La desdicha de la voz*, Jornada 1). For more on conceptualizing jealousy in the works of Lope, Cervantes, and Góngora, see Steven Wagschal, *The Literature of Jealousy in the Age of Cervantes* (St Louis: University of Missouri Press, 2006).

41 Zamora, *Siempre hay que envidiar, amando*, Jornada 3.
42 "mas si sabes cuán airadamente impía me ha despreciado, ¿por qué hacerme creer imaginas, que ha nacido mi esperanza más que para ser envidia?" (Zamora, *Siempre hay que envidiar, amando*, Jornada 1).
43 "y pues entre envidia, y celos ninguno me culpará, que amando envidie, y amando, me vengue, me he de vengar" (Zamora, *Siempre hay que envidiar, amando*, Jornada 3).
44 "ardiendo en mi noble envidioso frenesí está el alma" (Zamora, *Siempre hay que envidiar, amando*, Jornada 1).
45 Tirso de Molina, *Las viudas*, Acto 1. Male widowers are also mentioned in the context of Envy, albeit less frequently: "quien con la envidia queda, quedará con un viudo" (Pérez de Montalbán, *Amor, privanza, y castigo*, Acto 1).
46 "casándose otra vez con generosa prosapia, dará envidia a la lisonja, y sucesión a su Casa" (Tirso de Molina, *Amazonas en las Indias*, Acto 3).
47 Tirso de Molina, *Segunda parte de Santa Juana*, Acto 1. The biblical story appears in 1 Kings 3:16–28 (3 Kings 3:16–28 in the Douay-Rheims version).
48 "There was not, in fact, a large number of children in the average family, given the interruption of marriage by death and high infant mortality. Thus, in one parish in seventeenth-century Medina del Campo, despite a consistently high birth rate, 40 per cent of the households had no children living with them, and 25 per cent had only one" (James Casey, *Early Modern Spain: A Social History* [London: Routledge, 1999], 214).
49 Lope de Vega, *El bastardo Mudarra*, Acto 1.
50 Matos Fragoso, *El yerro de el entendido*, Acto 1.
51 Tirso de Molina, *La elección por la virtud*, Jornada 2.
52 We hear this from the mouth of a Vicar General: "soy Vicario General de mi Orden, y por ver la envidia, enojo, y pasión que tiene mi religión, y los poderosos de ella" (Tirso de Molina, *La elección por la virtud*, Jornada 3). Of course, Tirso de Molina – as a Mercedarian friar himself – would have been intimately familiar with this sort of religious infighting. Not even the church was immune to the plague of Envy.
53 "la envidia cortesana" (Lope de Vega, *Las cuentas del Gran Capitán*, Acto 1); "envidioso, o cortesano, todo es una cosa misma" (Calderón, *Mejor está que estaba*, Jornada 1); "O envidia, bien te llamaron hija de la Corte" (Lope de Vega, *La mayor virtud de un rey*, Jornada 3).
54 Lope de Vega, *El bastardo Mudarra*, Acto 1.
55 "Al bohordo que tiré la envidia sola llegó" (Lope de Vega, *El bastardo Mudarra*, Acto 1). The *bohordo* was a type of *caña*, or cane, which was thrown a great distance in a jousting match.
56 "Caballos, lanzas, y galas, matan de envidia los hombres" (Lope de Vega, *El caballero de Olmedo*, Acto 2).

57 Calderón, *Para vencer a Amor, querer vencerle*, Jornada 2; "la envidia fiera, basilisco de Palacio" (Calderón, *Las tres justicias en una*, Jornada 2); "la envidia ... allá se cría en las Cortes" (Lope de Vega, *El hijo de los leones*, Acto 1).

58 Calderón, *Saber del mal, y el bien*, Acto 1.

59 "esta acción me celebraban, con envidia los galanes, y con aplauso las damas" (Matos Fragoso, *El traidor contra su sangre*, Acto 1).

60 On the male side, Federico asks: "¿No te da envidia cuán celebrado Carlos vive? ¿Cuán amado de toda la Corte?" (Calderón, *De una causa dos efectos*, Jornada 1). In the feminine version, Clemencia declares, "Envidia tengo, serrana, al donaire que tenéis, tras vos la Corte os traéis" (Tirso de Molina, *El melancólico*, Acto 2).

61 "a quién no podrá la invidiosa murmuración, enemiga de toda virtud ofender" (Cueva, *Comedia del príncipe tirano*, Preliminares de obra). As with the contemporaneous case of professional golfer Tiger Woods, badmouthing is not necessarily limited to targeting the virtuous: "es del envidioso naturaleza, y costumbre decir mal de lo que envidia" (Calderón, *La cura, y la enfermedad*, Acto 1). On the destruction of Woods's reputation by tabloid reporters, see Neal Gabler, "Why We Can't Look Away: Understanding Our Craven Celebrity Culture," *Newsweek*, 21 December 2009, cover story, 62–7.

62 Zamora, *Siempre hay que envidiar, amando*, Jornada 2.

63 Calderón, *El sitio de Breda*, Acto 1.

64 "como en Palacio murmurando de las vidas ajenas con envidia, del favor, de la hacienda, del suceso, del oficio" (Lope de Vega, *Los tres diamantes*, Jornada 3).

65 "la envidia en los Palacios lisonjera, que lealtades destierra poco a poco" (Tirso de Molina, *El amor, y el amistad*, Jornada 3). In this regard, Tirso's play *La lealtad contra la envidia*, which thematizes Loyalty and Envy, ends on a note of wishful thinking: "pues vence la lealtad siempre a la envidia" (Acto 3). Less optimistically, Envy is equated in the *comedias* with self-serving adulation: "ojalá salgamos ya de las manos de la envidia, y ... aduladores" (Acto 3).

66 "¡se disfrazó la envidia, para que en ella tropiece!" (Moreto, *La fortuna merecida*, Jornada 2). Envy is repeatedly associated with deception ("la envidia, y sus engaños") (Tirso de Molina, *La lealtad contra la envidia*, Acto 3).

67 Calderón, *La banda y la flor*, Jornada 1; Pérez de Montalbán, *Cumplir con su obligación*, Preliminares de obra.

68 "de noche habéis de entrar, porque no os pueda encontrar alguna envidiosa espía, pues la emulación no sabe reposar" (Alarcón, *La crueldad por el honor*, Acto 3).

69 Calderón, *El laberinto del mundo*, Acto 1.

70 "Los ojos de la envidia que excedieron los que ahora el pavón tiene en cuidado" (Lope de Vega, *El leal criado*, Acto 1).

71 Calderón, *Los encantos de la Culpa*, auto sacramental.

72 Calderón, *Los encantos de la Culpa*, auto sacramental. Calderón explains to us this allegorical symbolism even further: "La Envidia, que es toda enojos del bien que en

los otros ve, viendo a la Vista, porque la Envidia, al fin, toda es ojos" (Calderón, *Los encantos de la Culpa*, auto sacramental, emphasis mine). Here we find a typically Baroque wordplay on *enojos* (irritations), which when separated into distinct syllables (*en ojos*), could be taken to mean *in the eyes*. This wordplay is repeated in another drama by Calderón, where we find the line: "al oírla mis enojos, se están muriendo mis ojos de envidia de mis oídos" (Calderón, *Gustos, y disgustos son no más que imaginación*, Jornada 3). In certain other dramas, most notably the *autos sacramentales*, Envy is pictured not as an animal, but instead as a sailor posted as the lookout for a ship. Once again, the emphasis here is on eyes and seeing. This occurs, for example, in Calderón's *El laberinto del mundo*, Acto 1, as well as in his *Psiquis, y Cupido*, auto sacramental. In a terrestrial version of the same topos, Man looks out with Envy at others' happiness from a high watchman's tower or lookout post: "¡Con cuánta Envidia, desde más alta eminencia, viendo estoy las dichas de otros!" (Calderón, *Lo que va del hombre a Dios*, loa for auto sacramental, emphasis mine).

73 "ofendida la Marquesa, o envidiosa de que papeles me escriba, hoy ha reñido con ella" (Tirso de Molina, *Quien calla, otorga*, Acto 2).

74 "rompa el desleal el sello, conspire la envidia ingrata: ea lobos ambiciosos, un cordero simple vala" (Tirso de Molina, *La prudencia en la mujer*, Jornada 1).

75 Witness "la rosa no presuma tener la Monarquía, cortarle descortés mano envidiosa" (Lope de Vega, *El Amor enamorado*, Preliminares de obra), but neither were monarchs said to be immune to this Vice; for example, "Anda la Reina envidiosa" (Lope de Vega, *El testimonio vengado*, Jornada 1). Envy could apply particularly to an evil prince, as in Juan de la Cueva's *Comedia del príncipe tirano*: "De fiera envidia movido, su ánimo codicioso, de un furor ciego ambicioso incitado" (Acto 2).

76 Calderón, *La cisma de Inglaterra*, Jornada 1.

77 This is true of the count Fernán González in Lope de Vega's eponymous play about him: "el Conde volverá presto de las Cortes de León, aunque envidiosa pasión tan mal con el Rey le ha puesto" (Lope de Vega, *El conde Fernán González*, Acto 3).

78 The *comedias* affirm that fraternal envy can be the very worst sort: "si hay envidia entre hermanos, es la más cruel envidia" (Calderón, *La crítica del amor*, Jornada 2).

79 The first pair of brothers, the children of Adam and Eve, appear frequently in the *comedias* in the context of Envy: "Di, ¿qué delito mayor que envidia, y odio entre hermanos? Mira en Caín, y en Abel" (Calderón, *El Rey Don Pedro en Madrid, e infanzón de Illescas*, Jornada 3). A more biblically focused play which makes a similar reference is Calderón's *La torre de Babilonia*, where we find the lines: "yo seré, si me vengo, dos veces Caín, pues tengo envidia de dos Abeles" (Calderón, *La torre de Babilonia*, auto sacramental). These specific fraternal pairs are alluded to more generally in the phrases, "No fuera del Texto el mayor hermano la Envidia hace" (Calderón, *A María el corazón*, auto sacramental) and "nació la envidia de dos hermanos" (Tirso de Molina, *Amor y celos hacen discretos*, Jornada 2).

80 In a *comedia* written about this story, Lope de Vega's Joseph exclaims: "me libraste con tus santas manos del envidioso celo de mis fieros y bárbaros hermanos" (Lope de Vega, *Los trabajos de Jacob*, Jornada 1).

81 This biblically based play refers specifically to "la privanza de Joseph" (Lope de Vega, *Los trabajos de Jacob*, Jornada 1).

82 "su Contador mayor le hizo el Rey, como sabes, con envidia de hombres graves" (Lope de Vega, *La fortuna merecida*, Acto 2).

83 As one king says to his subject, "daréte un oficio tan honroso que cause envidia a la nobleza toda" (Lope de Vega, *El hombre por su palabra*, Acto 2).

84 "ya sabéis cómo abrasa esto de envidia los pechos en Palacio los criados, cuando a otros ven" (Lope de Vega, *El más galán portugués, duque de Braganza*, Acto 2).

85 Thus one servant voices concern to a monarch that he will be the target of Envy by the king's chamber man: "Si tú lo mandas, harélo; mas al Camarero así causar envidia recelo: porque siempre al más privado empresa igual ha tocado" (Alarcón, *Todo es ventura*, Acto 2).

86 "poner escalas de envidia al muro de la privanza" (Lope de Vega, *El piadoso veneciano*, Acto 2).

87 "hay ejemplos infinitos, con sangre del dueño escritos, que la envidia de el que manda siempre a sus espaldas anda" (Lope de Vega, *La primera información*, Jornada 3).

88 "Quien dice que es ser privado dicha, miente, de la envidia es un objeto bizarro" (Tirso de Molina, *Adversa fortuna de don Álvaro de Luna, segunda parte*, Jornada 3).

89 "La envidia (que a la privanza como al blanco suyo tira)" (Tirso de Molina, *Privar contra su gusto*, Acto 1). Alternatively, Envy declares herself to follow after *privanza* as closely as a shadow; in one play, Envidia declares: "soy sin razón, sin leyes, sombra de las privanzas de los Reyes" (Lope de Vega, *San Isidro labrador de Madrid*, Acto 1).

90 Tirso de Molina, *Ventura te dé Dios, hijo*, Jornada 3. This hurling of insults at the king's favourite is not without precedent; in one of Lope de Vega's plays, likewise, a disgruntled courtier threatens: "Pagar tenéis ahora, bellaco mayordomo, entrelacayo, la envidia que me dais con la privanza" (Lope de Vega, *El amante agradecido*, Acto 3).

91 "Cuando en un hoyo, que puso la envidia, que salió a veros, tropezando, renovastes llantos" (Tirso de Molina, *La vida de Herodes*, Acto 1).

92 Calderón, *Argenis y Poliarco*, Jornada 2.

93 As Don Álvaro de Luna warns the king in Tirso's second *comedia* about him, "Mirad, señor, que la envidia vive entre tantas mercedes" (Tirso de Molina, *Adversa fortuna de don Álvaro de Luna, segunda parte*, Jornada 2).

94 Tirso de Molina, *La gallega Mari Hernández*, Acto 3.

95 "Yedra es la privanza humana, arrollóla la envidia, y luego faltóle al favor la sombra" (Tirso de Molina, *El mayor desengaño*, Acto 2). From the *privado's* perspective, this certainly would be a rude awakening (the sort of ultimate *desengaño* of the title).

96 As one disillusioned ex-favourite asks, "¿no es disfavor, que a los tiros de la envidia, en la vanguardia me expongáis al enemigo?" (Tirso de Molina, *Privar contra su gusto*, Acto 1). The very title of this work could be taken as a wordplay on *privado* since *privar* could theoretically mean either to deprive or to enjoy the protection of a prince.

97 The *comedias* chronicle such seismic shifts in the political landscape of the court; for example, "envidia, y celos llevo del Conde, envidia de que ahora será del Rey, por fuerza, la privanza" (Lope de Vega, *La batalla del honor*, Acto 2).

98 "desterrado de la Corte por envidia" (Lope de Vega, *Si no vieran las mujeres*, Jornada 1).

99 See chapter 1, note 249 of this book as well as J.H. Elliott, *The Count-Duke of Olivares: The Statesman in an Age of Decline* (New Haven and London: Yale University Press, 1988).

100 This barb is addressed to the courtiers: "¿Los privados culpáis a la envidia luego, capa de vuestros delitos que hacéis?" (Tirso de Molina, *El amor, y el amistad*, Jornada 2).

101 Alarcón, *El tejedor de Segovia*, Acto 1.

102 Most scholars attribute this play not to Tirso de Molina, but instead to Antonio Mira de Amescua. The historical figure of Álvaro de Luna is mentioned in other plays apart from this duo; for example, one of Lope de Vega's characters remarks that "fue envidia la privanza de don Álvaro de Luna" (Lope de Vega, *El piadoso aragonés*, Acto 1).

103 Manuel Delgado, "Antonio Mira de Amescua (1574–1644)," in *Spanish Dramatists of the Golden Age: A Bio-Bibliographical Sourcebook*, ed. Mary Parker (Westport, CT: Greenwood, 1998), 107–23, at 111.

104 Tirso de Molina, *Adversa fortuna de don Álvaro de Luna, segunda parte*, Jornada 3.

105 Calderón, *Saber del mal, y el bien*, Acto 1.

106 Tirso de Molina, *Averígüelo Vargas*, Jornada 3.

107 Lope de Vega, *El capellán de la Virgen*, Acto 1. The act of dedicating books to powerful patrons was one thing poets could do to try to protect their work from the attacks of Envy: "Dedicar los libros: prevenirles defensa contra la ignorancia, o la envidia, en amparo suficiente; procurarles autoridad para el mundo" (Quiñones de Benavente, *Jácara, que se cantó en la compañía de Ortegón*, Preliminares de obra). It is touching here to see how the author refers to his books with the pronoun *les* as if they were human.

108 Lope de Vega, *El guante de doña Blanca*, Acto 3.

109 Lope de Vega, *El hijo de los leones*, Acto 2.

110 Lope de Vega, *El Hamete de Toledo*, Acto 2.

111 Guillén de Castro, *Progne, y Filomena*, Acto 3.

112 Calderón, *El año santo en Madrid*, auto sacramental, emphasis mine.

113 Lope de Vega, *El hombre por su palabra*, Acto 1.

114 “España, no ha de haber provincia extraña a quien la envidia no mueva” (Lope de Vega, *El Nuevo Mundo, descubierto por Cristóbal Colón*, Acto 3). The Spanish Indies are mentioned specifically as an object of Envy for the King of Portugal: “el Rey no sé qué intenta, si ya no es que envidia sienta de las Indias de Colón” (Lope de Vega, *El príncipe perfecto, parte segunda*, Acto 3). Another character comments that this does not make much sense, given Portugal’s own successful maritime ventures: “Como el Rey don Juan había de envidiar los Castellanos, si sus fuertes Lusitanos llegan donde nace el día” (Lope de Vega, *El príncipe perfecto, parte segunda*, Acto 3).

115 Lope de Vega, *El valiente Céspedes*, Acto 3; Lope de Vega, *La batalla del honor*, Acto 3. This is not the only time Lope de Vega associates the French with Envy. In *Los españoles en Flandes* we find the snide remark “envidia ha traído muchos Monsiures” (Acto 3). From the Spanish perspective, all other nations are foreign, as in “lustre de nuestra nación, y envidia de las extranjeras” (Lope de Vega, *La pobreza estimada*, Preliminares de obra).

116 Lope de Vega, *La doncella Teodor*, Acto 1.

117 “Que te aman, sin la envidia, de una suerte Fiel Flandes, docta Italia España fuerte” (Lope de Vega, *Las bizarrías de Belisa*, Preliminares de obra).

118 “Verás un escuadrón, que dar pudiera envidia al mundo, y siendo necesario, le conquistara” (Lope de Vega, *La octava maravilla*, Acto 1). In the same play a foreign soldier declares to a Spanish soldier: “Aumentas, Español, la envidia mía” (Acto 1).

119 “Águilas negras de tus Imperiales armas … el Sol de envidia las siga, que lleguen donde él no alcanza” (Lope de Vega, *Si no vieran las mujeres*, Jornada 3). This somewhat confusing image is clarified by the fact that for part of the year, the sun cannot reach the North and South Poles; but in this imagining, Spain’s power does reach that far: “de suerte a España en término sucinto, que, dando envidia a las demás naciones, penetren los dos Polos sus pendones” (Lope de Vega, *El vellocino de oro*, loa).

120 “Ea valor de España, asombro de la envidia, ésta es, sin ejemplar, única hazaña” (Tirso de Molina, *La lealtad contra la envidia*, Acto 2).

121 “ser pienso envidia, y admiración de antiguos, y de modernos” (Rojas Zorrilla, *Lo que quería ver el marqués de Villena*, Jornada 2).

122 Lope de Vega, *Al pasar del arroyo*, Preliminares de obra.

123 Tirso de Molina, *Adversa fortuna de don Álvaro de Luna, segunda parte*, Jornada 1. The reference to Envy in the context of Hector appears within an epic catalogue of Spanish warriors in a play designed to showcase Spanish skill at arms: “Gabrio Cerbellón, dos Castros, Bernardo, y Pedro, que dieran envidia al Héctor de Troya, si entonces los viera en Grecia” (Lope de Vega, *El asalto de Mastrique, por el Príncipe de Parma*, Acto 3).

124 “envidia a la edad pasada, gloria a la dichosa nuestra” (Lope de Vega, *La mayor victoria de Alemania de don Gonzalo de Córdoba*, Preliminares de obra); “a Castilla blasón, a Burgos gloria, la fama envidia, a nuestros siglos canta” (Tirso de Molina, *Los lagos de san Vicente*, Acto 3).

125 Lope de Vega, *Servir a señor discreto*, Acto 3.
126 "ha dado al mundo envidia tanto imperio portátil" (Lope de Vega, *La mayor victoria de Alemania de don Gonzalo de Córdoba*, Preliminares de obra).
127 "[al] avestruz las avecillas pequeñas le quieren sacar los ojos de envidia" (Rojas Zorrilla, *Los encantos de Medea*, Jornada 1).
128 "Sol avestruz del Cielo, los Signos, y las estrellas de envidia se han conjurado por ser el mejor planeta" (Rojas Zorrilla, *Los encantos de Medea*, Jornada 1).
129 Calderón, *A Dios por razón de Estado*, Preliminares de obra. The context for this torrent of flattery is the *Aprobación* by Francisco García de Palacios for a volume of Calderón's works to be printed. He seems to indicate that Calderón's genius is so great that he has been accepted into the Spanish pantheon of poets even before death.
130 "ingenio que al de Aurelio iguale, puede dar a Platón envidia, y celos" (Lope de Vega, *El divino africano*, Acto 1).
131 Moreto, *No puede ser*, Jornada 1.
132 Pérez de Montalbán, *El mariscal de Virón*, Jornada 3.
133 Matos Fragoso, *El amor hace valientes*, Jornada 2.
134 Matos Fragoso, *El traidor contra su sangre*, Jornada 2.
135 Lope de Vega, *La envidia de la nobleza*, Acto 2.
136 "de ser estimado nace la envidia con el bien nacido" (Lope de Vega, *La fortuna merecida*, Acto 3).
137 Lope de Vega, *La envidia de la nobleza*, Acto 3. The two families mentioned are the Zegríes and the Bencerrajes, illustrious families from the Kingdom of Granada. A similar example from English literature of this time period would be the ongoing feud between the Montagues and the Capulets in Shakespeare's *Romeo and Juliet*.
138 Tirso de Molina, *La villana de la Sagra*, Jornada 1. In this genealogical economy, half-breeds were considered mongrels and therefore unworthy to ascend the throne: "Quien no revienta de envidia, de ver este Transilvano, Medio Español por su madre, subir" (Lope de Vega, *El rey sin reino*, Acto 1).
139 Lope de Vega, *El Amor enamorado,* Preliminares de obra; Matos Fragoso, *Amor, lealtad, y ventura*, Acto 1. A similar reference to sweet homeland occurs in the prologue to Lope de Vega's *Las bizarrías de Belisa*: "esta preeminencia Cándida honró su dulce Patria, cuando acechaba la envidia su inocencia" (Lope de Vega, *Las bizarrías de Belisa*, Preliminares de obra). Another more puzzling reference refers to Envy and unhappiness as daughters of the homeland: "la envidia, y la desdicha hijas de la patria son" (Lope de Vega, *Don Lope de Cardona*, Acto 1).
140 Envy's arrows: "a toda envidiosa flecha, habrá resistencia en mí" (Lope de Vega, *La nueva victoria del marqués de Santa Cruz*, Jornada 1). Envy's bites: "no las morderá el envidioso" (Rojas Zorrilla, *Casarse por vengarse*, Preliminares de obra). Teeth form a common image for Envy in these plays, as in "el diente venenoso de la infernal envidia" (Alarcón, *El tejedor de Segovia*, Acto 3). In a particularly ferocious image, Envy's teeth are said to belong to *jabalíes*, or wild boars, and they are sharp

enough to penetrate one's honour: "en la ciudad jabalíes que penetran honras con dientes de envidia" (Lope de Vega, *La bella Aurora*, Acto 1). The juxtaposition of the phrase "in the city" to this hunting image from the countryside emphasizes the fact that Lope de Vega's character is speaking here of Envy at the royal court. For an earlier instance of hunting imagery, such as following a falcon, being imported to an urban context, see the first Act of Fernando de Rojas, *La Celestina: Tragicomedia de Calisto y Melibea*, ed. Dorothy S. Severin (Madrid: Alianza, 1981), 45–73.

141 "mármoles, y bronces, que nunca podrán desfigurar las dentelladas de la envidia, ni confundir las injurias de los tiempos" (Calderón, *Basta callar*, Preliminares de obra). One example of a grand city is Calahorra: "a quien ni el tiempo, ni la envidia borra, es, amigos, la antigua Calahorra" (Rojas Zorrilla, *Los tres blasones de España*, Jornada 2). Another Spanish city mentioned as worthy of Envy is Toledo (Tirso de Molina, *Doña Beatriz de Silva*, Acto 3). It is interesting to note that Spanish cities, while offering different attractions, do not seem to envy each other: "no envidia Sevilla los jazmines de Valencia" (Lope de Vega, *Lo cierto por lo dudoso*, Acto 1). There appears to be an innate sense that this sort of inter-regional rivalry would ultimately prove self-defeating; after all, "la Fama … no se adquiere con violencia, detracción, y envidia, sino con méritos, obras, y trabajos" (Lope de Vega, *Los locos de Valencia*, Preliminares de obra).

142 She is "tan bella que no halla en qué ponerla la envidia, ni aun una tacha" (Cervantes, *Pedro de Urdemalas*, Jornada 1).

143 "Hizo un sermón tan tierno y amoroso, que hasta la envidia se bañaba en llanto" (Lope de Vega, *Las bizarrías de Belisa*, Preliminares de obra). The specific Spanish preacher eulogized here is Hortensio Félix Paravicino.

144 Calderón, *Judás Macabeo*, Jornada 3.

145 Calderón, *La cisma de Inglaterra*, Jornada 1.

146 "que tenga el vuestro Reinado al más envidioso mudo" (Lope de Vega, *Las famosas asturianas*, Acto 1); "sabio, que así te llaman hoy varias naciones, y la envidia también, mordiendo el labio" (Lope de Vega, *El blasón de los Chaves de Villalba*, Acto 1).

147 Calderón, *Darlo todo, y no dar nada*, Jornada 3.

148 "das a la envidia dos higas en los mostachos" (Lope de Vega, *El valiente Céspedes*, Acto 2). As Scott Taylor explains, any gesture involving the mustache was considered especially provocative:

> Hats, beards, mustaches, faces, swords, daggers, and capes were the most tangible signs of male identity and therefore, as symbols of male reputation, were vulnerable to attack and necessary to defend … Gestures involving capes, hats, collars, swords, beards, mustaches, and fingers to the tongue or mouth – all of these … had a provocative meaning that was clear to all.

(Scott K. Taylor, *Honor and Violence in Golden Age Spain* [New Haven: Yale University Press, 2008], 153,.49)

149 "tu espada fue con trofeos mayores admiración a la envidia, miedo al hado, horror al Orbe" (Calderón, *Judás Macabeo*, Jornada 2). In this particular play, the victorious ancient Hebrews may be viewed as a prototype of early modern Spaniards. This is particularly interesting in light of Spain's vexed relationship to its Jewish inhabitants during the Golden Age. In this retelling of an apocryphal episode from the Book of Maccabees, the Israelites enter a conquered city in triumphal procession: "[en la] ciudad han entrado los invencibles Hebreos, y con gloriosos trofeos envidia a la fama dado" (Jornada 3).

150 Matos Fragoso, *El amor hace valientes*, Jornada 3.

151 Lope de Vega, *Querer la propia desdicha*, Acto 2.

152 "podáis mejor con hechos extraordinarios, vencer la envidia, y olvido" (Tirso de Molina, *El árbol del mejor fruto*, Acto 2).

153 Pérez de Montalbán, *Los templarios*, Jornada 2; "Hombre, ¿no mires que das pesar, y envidia a otros mil?" (Lope de Vega, *Mirad a quién alabáis*, Acto 1).

154 "¿[quién] tan sobresaltado siga al Poderoso, sino el Afecto de la envidia?" (Calderón, *El primer refugio del hombre, y probática piscina*, auto sacramental). Also, though Envy follows the powerful Spaniards, it does not catch up to them: "pues tanto al Sol le levantan sus virtudes, que la envidia, si le sigue, no le alcanza" (Diamante, *Santa Juliana*, Jornada 1).

155 Rojas Zorrilla, *La traición busca el castigo*, Jornada 1.

156 Calderón, *El origen, pérdida y restauración de la Virgen del Sagrario*, Acto 1. This sentiment is echoed by the Virgin Mary's husband Joseph in Diamante's Christmas zarzuela *El nacimiento de Cristo*: "¿Qué Ángel no estará envidioso, si en el Ángel cabe envidia, de mi ventura?" (Diamante, *El nacimiento de Cristo*, Acto 2).

157 Moreto, *Santa Rosa del Perú*, Jornada 2. Saint Casilda, like Santa Rosa, is an object of great Envy by the devil: "el común enemigo, envidioso de que herede Casilda a Dios los milagros" (Tirso de Molina, *Los lagos de san Vicente*, Acto 3). There are also passages declaring Lucifer's primordial Sin to be Envy, as when Culpa says to him: "Texto hay, que fue tu presunción, envidia" (Calderón, *El pintor de su deshonra*, auto sacramental).

158 "la envidia que causaron sus milagros estupendos" (Lope de Vega, *Barlán y Josafa*, Acto 2).

159 Love: "dejo al mismo amor envidioso de mi bien" (Calderón, *Judás Macabeo*, Jornada 3). The Fates: "me defienda de la envidia de los hados" (Solís, *El alcázar del secreto*, Jornada 1). The Furies: "que voy a España advierte, si no lo estorba la envidiosa Parca" (Lope de Vega, *El caballero del Sacramento*, Acto 3).

160 Zamora, *Cada uno es linaje aparte, y los Mazas de Aragón*, Acto 1.

161 Tirso de Molina, *Quien habló, pagó*, Jornada 3.

162 "fiera condición de la fortuna … ella es tan envidiosa" (Calderón, *Amar después de la muerte*, Jornada 2).

163 Pérez de Montalbán, *El valiente Nazareno*, Jornada 2. References to vile or perverse Fortune include "la vil fortuna que envidiosa estaba" (Guillén de Castro, *Dido, y Eneas*, Jornada 1); and "Fortuna a mi suerte esquiva, cielo envidioso y cruel" (Cervantes, *El gallardo español*, Jornada 2).

164 "para ser envidiosa es la fortuna mujer" (Lope de Vega, *La noche de San Juan*, Acto 1). This is not the only misogynistic comment regarding Envy in the *comedias*. In Calderón's *Guárdate de la agua mansa*, we find the apostrophe: "¡O envidia, o envidia, cuánto daño has hecho a las mujeres!" (Calderón, *Guárdate de la agua mansa*, Jornada 2). Similarly, in a different play by the same author we find the offhand comment that "la común opinión llena está de que son mujer, y envidia una cosa misma" (Calderón, *Los hijos de la Fortuna Teágenes, y Cariclea*, Jornada 2). In another instance, Lope's character states flatly that "es condición de la mujer la envidia" (Lope de Vega, *La burgalesa de Lerma*, Acto 2). For relevant iconography, see the catalogue from a special exhibit at the Folger Shakespeare Library: Leslie Thomson, ed., *Fortune: "All Is but Fortune"* (Washington, DC, Seattle, and London: The Folger Shakespeare Library / University of Washington Press, 2000).

165 "que la envidia fiera emborrache a la fortuna" (Lope de Vega, *Las cuentas del Gran Capitán*, Acto 2).

166 Calderón, *El nuevo hospicio de pobres*, auto sacramental.

167 Moreto, *El desdén, con el desdén*, Jornada 1.

168 Pérez de Montalbán, *Teágenes, y Clariquea*, Jornada 2.

169 Alarcón, *Ganar amigos*, Acto 3.

170 Guillén de Castro, *El Narciso en su opinión*, Jornada 1. Don Gutierre's speech continues, "porque siempre un hombre he sido, que a infinitos los he dado, mas nunca los he tenido."

171 "que honras sólo las envidia quien no las sabe adquirir" (Moreto, *Hasta el fin nadie es dichoso*, Jornada 2).

172 Pérez de Montalbán, *La ganancia por la mano*, Jornada 2; Lope de Vega, *El caballero de Olmedo*, Acto 2; Lope de Vega, *La cortesía de España*, Acto 1.

173 "de mí mismo envidioso tendré mi mismo bien por sospechoso" (Calderón, *La dama duende*, Jornada 2).

174 "por Gracia vengo a ser de mi ventura envidioso, de mí mismo estoy celoso" (Lope de Vega, *El caballero del Sacramento*, Acto 1); "Vuestra Alteza de modo me favorece que de mí mismo me admiro, envidioso" (Tirso de Molina, *Averígüelo Vargas*, Jornada 2).

175 Lope de Vega, *El desconfiado*, Acto 1.

176 Calderón, *El faetonte*, Jornada 2.

177 "fue su envidia rayo que volvió de los espejos" (Lope de Vega, *El primer rey de Castilla*, Acto 3).

178 Pérez de Montalbán, *La doncella de labor*, Jornada 2.

179 Cueva, *El viejo enamorado*, Acto 1.
180 Tirso de Molina, *La celosa de sí misma*, Acto 2.
181 See Charles D. Presberg, *Adventures in Paradox: Don Quixote and the Western Tradition* (University Park: Pennsylvania State University Press, 2001), especially "Paradoxy and the Spanish Renaissance," 37–71.
182 Calderón, *Fuego de Dios en el querer bien*, Jornada 1; Calderón, *El purgatorio de San Patricio*, Acto 1.
183 Diamante, *El Hércules de Ocaña*, Jornada 2.
184 Calderón, *Los tres afectos de amor, piedad, desmayo y valor*, Jornada 1; Tirso de Molina, *Amar por arte mayor*, Acto 2. A similar example spoken in the first person would be "teniendo de él la envidia, de mí la lástima tengas" (Calderón, *El jardín de Falerina*, auto sacramental).
185 Calderón, *Los dos amantes del cielo*, Jornada 1.
186 "hermana que estoy para reventar en lágrimas, y no de envidia que a ti te tengo, sino de lástima" (Cervantes, *El vizcaíno fingido*, Acto 1).
187 Guillén de Castro, *Las mocedades del Cid, Comedia segunda*, Acto 3.
188 Calderón, *Casa con dos puertas, mala es de guardar*, Acto 1.
189 Calderón, *Fortunas de Andrómeda, y Perseo*, Jornada 2.
190 On this rhetorical figure see Yeshayahu Shen, "Zeugma: Prototypes, Categories, and Metaphors," *Metaphor and Symbol* 13.1 (1998): 31–47. The Baroque age delighted in this type of "disforme unión," a phrase used in the *comedias* to describe what is happening in the combination of "piedad" with "envidia feroz" (Lope de Vega, *Servir a buenos*, Acto 2).
191 Calderón, *Andrómeda, y Perseo*, auto sacramental. On perspectivism in the Spanish Renaissance, see Mack Smith, "Chivalry Decoded: Dialogistic and Perspectivist Voices in Don Quixote," in *Literary Realism and the Ekphrastic Tradition* (University Park: Pennsylvania State University Press, 2008), 43–76.
192 Rojas Zorrilla, *Los trabajos de Tobías*, Jornada 1.
193 "a los prudentes da compasión, y no envidia" (Alarcón, *Los pechos privilegiados*, Acto 1); "El que envidia daba ayer, mayor lástima os dé hoy; muévaos a piedad" (Calderón, *La hija del aire*, primera parte, Jornada 3).
194 Calderón, *Psiquis, y Cupido*, auto sacramental. In the same play, this concept is reinforced repeatedly: "no envidia será, sino compasión la que os tenga" (Calderón, *Psiquis, y Cupido*, auto sacramental).
195 Tirso de Molina, *Adversa fortuna de don Álvaro de Luna, segunda parte*, Jornada 2.
196 Tirso de Molina, *Cautela contra cautela*, Jornada 1.
197 Tirso de Molina, *Del enemigo el primer consejo*, Jornada 3.
198 Calderón, *La dama duende*, Jornada 2.
199 "hoy da lástima lo que soy, como envidia lo que fui" (Tirso de Molina, *Cautela contra cautela*, Jornada 2).

200 Calderón, *El galán fantasma*, Jornada 2.

201 "la virtud máxima carece de envidia, por opinión de tantos" (Lope de Vega, *El cardenal de Belén*, Preliminares de obra). On Machiavelli's notion of *virtù* as virile political power, see Victoria Kahn, *Machiavellian Rhetoric: From the Counter-Reformation to Milton* (Princeton: Princeton University Press, 1994), 185–208. Kahn explains that the Machiavellian concept of *virtù* is actually more akin to virtuosity than to piety: "*virtù* is in some respects like the sprezzatura of Castiglione's courtier … '[V]irtue' is the rhetorical effect of success" (187).

202 Pérez de Montalbán, *El hijo del Serafín, San Pedro de Alcántara*, Jornada 2.

203 Calderón, *De una causa dos efectos*, Jornada 2. This sentiment is echoed in the simple phrase, "ni me envidian, ni envidio" (Tirso de Molina, *Privar contra su gusto*, Acto 1). On Baroque nihilism, see Alban Forcione, "El desposeimiento del ser en la literatura renacentista: Cervantes, Gracián y los desafíos de Nemo," *Nueva revista de filología hispánica* 34.2 (1985–6): 654–90.

204 Calderón, *Saber del mal, y el bien*, Jornada 3.

205 "Ni el mal siento de la envidia, ni la congoja de celos: mi honor sólo me apasiona" (Rojas Zorrilla, *Progne y Filomena*, Jornada 2).

206 Lope de Vega, *El capellán de la Virgen*, Acto 2.

207 Lope de Vega, *El cardenal de Belén*, Acto 2.

208 "basta haberla leído a los que, como yo, juzgan sin envidia, aunque con mayores letras, y entendimientos" (Lope de Vega, *Los esclavos libres*, Preliminares de obra).

209 Lope de Vega, *Porfiando vence amor*, Preliminares de obra. On self-fashioning and self-cancellation, see Stephen Greenblatt, *Renaissance Self-Fashioning: From More to Shakespeare* (Chicago: University of Chicago Press, 1980), especially the Introduction (1–9) and chapter 1 (11–73).

210 Lope de Vega, *La primera información*, Jornada 3, emphasis mine.

211 Calderón, *La dama duende*, Jornada 2.

212 For example, "Dichoso el que vive aquí sin envidia y ambición" (Lope de Vega, *El Duque de Viseo*, Acto 3). In his *San Isidro labrador de Madrid*, Envy herself speaks the following apostrophe to a lowly villager:

A, villano simple y llano,
los sabios que el mundo precia
te envidian, pues tan en vano,
todos los que tuvo Grecia,
y vio el aplauso Romano
supieron libros, y ciencias. (Lope de Vega, *San Isidro labrador de Madrid*, Acto 2)

213 Lope de Vega, *La carbonera*, Jornada 1 and Jornada 3.

214 "De las vidas de palacio, con envidia me deshago" (Lope de Vega, *Los locos por el cielo*, Acto 3).

215 "mereces tanta lealtad en tan hermoso pecho [que] un Rey te envidia y por tu humilde estado trocara el suyo" (Lope de Vega, *El molino*, Jornada 2).

216 Tirso de Molina, *Todo es dar en una cosa*, Acto 3.

217 Lope de Vega, *El alcalde mayor*, Preliminares de obra. The play and the letter are dedicated to Doctor Cristóbal Núñez, resident in Mexico. In this case it has been useful to compare the text of the letter from the TESO database with the original imprint, which appears in the *Trecena parte de las comedias de Lope de Vega Carpio* (Madrid: Viuda de Alonso Martín, 1620).

218 "el que no ve mejor suerte, ni la envidia, ni la daña" (Moreto, *La fuerza del natural*, Jornada 1).

219 Calderón, *El hombre pobre todo es trazas*, Acto 1.

220 Calderón, *El sitio de Breda*, Acto 1.

221 Admiration: "la admiración a silencios pregona, y la envidia a voces" (Diamante, *La reina María Estuarda*, Jornada 1). Imitation: "sólo ha dejado a la envidia capacidad para desearle imitar" (Calderón, *Amigo amante, y leal*, Preliminares de obra).

222 Tirso de Molina, *Amazonas en las Indias*, Acto 3.

223 Calderón, *A tu próximo como a ti*, Acto 1.

224 Moreto, *El desdén, con el desdén*, Jornada 2, emphasis mine.

225 Calderón, *Guárdate de la agua mansa*, Jornada 1. On Envy as ambition, note the following lines: "Envidia, y Ambición hoy mis sentidos posean" (Calderón, *El gran teatro del mundo*, auto sacramental). For Envy as a positive example, see Guillén de Castro, *El engañarse engañado*, Jornada 3. On Envy as motivation, witness the declaration, "os motivó el aleve atrevimiento de la envidia" (Diamante, *El cerco de Zamora*, Jornada 3).

226 Alarcón, *Ganar amigos*, Acto 3.

227 Thus Mundo says to Envy, "Mira, Envidia, pues eres el Piloto, que hemos errado todos el Camino" (Calderón, *Psiquis, y Cupido que escribió para la ciudad de Toledo*, auto sacramental). These words are spoken on board an allegorical ship with Envy dressed in nautical costume.

228 Tirso de Molina, *La república al revés*, Acto 1; Diamante, *Santa Juliana*, Jornada 2; Pérez de Montalbán, *El divino portugués, San Antonio de Padua*, Jornada 1.

229 Calderón, *Hado, y divisa de Leonido, y de Marfisa*, Jornada 3; Guillén de Castro, *La fuerza de la costumbre*, Jornada 1. This honourable Envy is the sort felt by kings: "el Rey verá, pues en él cabe envidia tan honrada" (Lope de Vega, *Don Juan de Castro, primera parte,* Acto 3).

230 "pues también hay envidia generosa" (Tirso de Molina, *Los lagos de san Vicente*, Acto 1); "Lástima os tuve a los dos, y envidia santa después" (Tirso de Molina, *Santo, y sastre*, Acto 3). This type of generous Envy is thought to be worthy of princes: "fue … ley de una envidia generosa, ver que intentas una cosa digna de un Príncipe" (Lope de Vega, *El amigo hasta la muerte*, Acto 3).

231 "con envidia honrada una bella retirada mis deseos nobles den" (Tirso de Molina, *El amor, y el amistad*, Jornada 1).

232 Lope de Vega, *La octava maravilla*, Acto 1; Zamora, *Siempre hay que envidiar, amando*, Jornada 1.
233 Calderón, *¿Quién hallará mujer fuerte?*, auto sacramental.
234 "esta gente rústica, bárbara, y pobre me trae una noble envidia" (Lope de Vega, *El Amor enamorado*, Jornada 1).
235 "es noble la envidia, y aun la alabanza, que España, que en más acciones se ha mirado victoriosa, no es razón que quite el nombre a Italia de la victoria" (Calderón, *El sitio de Breda*, Jornada 3).
236 Calderón, *Hado, y divisa de Leonido, y de Marfisa*, Jornada 3.
237 Calderón, *El árbol del mejor fruto*, auto sacramental.
238 Diamante, *Lides de amor, y desdén*, Acto 1.
239 Diamante, *Jupiter, y Semele*, Acto 1.
240 "¿La envidia? ¿Pues tan gallarda?" (Lope de Vega, *El vellocino de oro*, loa).
241 "no la pintaron así tantas edades pasadas" (Lope de Vega, *El vellocino de oro*, loa).
242 Lope de Vega, *El vellocino de oro*, loa.
243 Williams, "Dominant, Residual, and Emergent," 121–7, at 124, emphasis mine.
244 Stanley G. Payne, *A History of Spain and Portugal* (Madison: University of Wisconsin Press, 1973), 268.
245 Paul Hiltpold, "Noble Status and Urban Privilege: Burgos, 1572," *The Sixteenth Century Journal* 12.4 (1981): 21–44.
246 Cervantes, *El ingenioso hidalgo don Quijote de la Mancha* (1605 and 1615), ed. Luis Andrés Murillo, 2 vols (Madrid: Castalia, 1987).
247 Edward Baker, "Breaking the Frame: Don Quixote's Entertaining Books," *Cervantes* 16.1 (1996): 12–31, at 16. Baker cites Noël Salomon, *La vida rural castellana en tiempos de Felipe II*, trans. Francesc Espinet Burunat (Barcelona: Planeta, 1973); and Pierre Vilar, "El tiempo de los hidalgos," in *Hidalgos, amotinados y guerrilleros: pueblo y poderes en la historia de España*, trans. Ferrán Gallego (Barcelona: Crítica, 1982), 17–59.
248 Baker, "Breaking the Frame," 16.

8. Parents and Lies: The Decalogue on the Rise

1 Calderón de la Barca, *El gran teatro del mundo*, auto sacramental.
2 Once again, I refer here to gradual, perceptual change rather than any sudden shift between decades or generations of dramatists.
3 In this vein, Maureen Flynn has noticed "a peculiar Spanish preoccupation with lineage and filial piety" (Maureen Flynn, "Blasphemy and the Play of Anger in Sixteenth-Century Spain," *Past and Present* 149 [1995]: 29–56, at 51). This special resonance should not be construed as exclusive, however; indeed, this Commandment became more relevant for several patriarchal European cultures during the Renaissance. For an example, see Robert James Bast, *Honor Your Fathers: Catechisms*

and the Emergence of a Patriarchal Ideology in Germany, 1400–1600 (Leiden: Brill, 1997).

4 Tirso de Molina, *El condenado por desconfiado*, Jornada 2.

5 Lope de Vega, *El castigo sin venganza*, Acto 3.

6 Lope de Vega, *Las famosas asturianas*, Acto 1.

7 Tirso de Molina, *La santa Juana*, Acto 2.

8 Lope de Vega, *El príncipe perfecto, parte primera*, Acto 1.

9 For more on the nature of filial bonds in Spain during the early modern period, see Darci L. Strother, "Parent-Child Relations," chapter 5 in *Family Matters: A Study of On- and Off-Stage Marriage and Family Relations in Seventeenth-Century Spain* (New York: Peter Lang, 1999), 135–78.

10 Guillén de Castro, *El nacimiento de Montesinos*, Acto 3.

11 Lope de Vega, *El desposorio encubierto*, Preliminares de obra. These words were directed to Jacinto de Piña, son of Juan Izquierdo de Piña, who was the Secretario de Provincia. In this case it has been useful to compare the play's dedication in the TESO database to the original imprint, which appears in the *Trecena parte de las comedias de Lope de Vega Carpio* (Madrid: Viuda de Alonso Martín, 1620).

12 Lope de Vega, *La madre de la mejor*, Acto 1.

13 Lope de Vega, *La obediencia laureada, y primer Carlos de Hungría*, Acto 2.

14 Guillén de Castro, *El perfecto caballero*, Acto 1.

15 Matos Fragoso, *El traidor contra su sangre*, Jornada 2, emphasis mine.

16 On Aeneas's filial piety, see Patricia Johnston, "Piety in Vergil and Philodemus," in *Vergil, Philodemus, and the Augustans*, ed. David Armstrong (Austin: University of Texas Press, 2004).

17 Exodus 20:12.

18 Lope de Vega, *El piadoso aragonés*, Acto 1.

19 Guillén de Castro, *Las mocedades del Cid, Comedia segunda*, Acto 1.

20 Guillén de Castro, *La verdad averiguada, y engañoso casamiento*, Jornada 1.

21 Lope de Vega, *La madre de la mejor*, Acto 1.

22 Lope de Vega, *La serrana de Tormes*, Acto 1.

23 Lope de Vega, *El piadoso aragonés*, Acto 3.

24 Lope de Vega, *La Francesilla*, Preliminares de obra. This phrase repeats this trope from another play: "los niños … espejos de los padres suelen ser" (Lope de Vega, *Los Benavides*, Jornada 2).

25 But wherefore do not you a mightier way
Make war upon this bloody tyrant Time?
And fortify yourself in your decay
With means more blessed than my barren rhyme?

(William Shakespeare, Sonnet 16, in *The Riverside Shakespeare*, ed. G. Blakemore Evans [Boston: Houghton Mifflin, 1974])

26 Calderón, *El año santo en Madrid*, auto sacramental.

27 Lope de Vega, *La Francesilla*, Preliminares de obra.
28 Guillén de Castro, *Cuánto se estima el honor*, Jornada 3.
29 Lope de Vega, *El piadoso aragonés*, Acto 3.
30 Lope de Vega, *El caballero de Olmedo*, Acto 1.
31 Calderón, *El año santo de Roma*, auto sacramental.
32 Lope de Vega, *El niño inocente de la Guardia*, Acto 2.
33 Lope de Vega, *Los locos de Valencia*, Acto 1.
34 Tirso de Molina, *Don Gil de las calzas verdes*, Acto 3.
35 Lope de Vega, *El piadoso aragonés*, Acto 3.
36 Alarcón, *El semejante a sí mismo*, Acto 1.
37 Lope de Vega, *El rey sin reino*, Acto 2.
38 Lope de Vega, *El laberinto de Creta*, Acto 1.
39 Lope de Vega, *El piadoso aragonés*, Acto 2.
40 Diamante, *Santa María Magdalena de Pazzi*, Jornada 1; Cervantes, *La entretenida*, Jornada 3.
41 Lope de Vega, *La viuda casada y doncella*, Acto 1.
42 Tirso de Molina, *El mayor desengaño*, Acto 1.
43 Lope de Vega, *El tirano castigado*, Acto 2.
44 Guillén de Castro, *Las mocedades del Cid, Comedia segunda*, Acto 2.
45 Lope de Vega, *Nadie se conoce*, Acto 1.
46 Lope de Vega, *El molino*, Jornada 2.
47 Lope de Vega, *El ausente en el lugar*, Acto 2.
48 Lope de Vega, *La Francesilla*, Acto 1.
49 See J. Bentham, *Plan of the Panopticon* (1843), figure 3 in Michel Foucault, *Discipline and Punish: The Birth of the Prison*, trans. Alan Sheridan (New York: Vintage, 1995).
50 "The scale of surveillance on the part of the Inquisition in Spain (much more vigorous and strict than anywhere else) reflected a desire to control an imagery that was very often hidden from all institutionalized constraints" (Victor Stoichita, *Visionary Experience in the Golden Age of Spanish Art* [London: Reaktion, 1995], 8).
51 Lope de Vega, *El desposorio encubierto*, Acto 3.
52 Cervantes, *El gallardo español*, Jornada 2.
53 On arranged marriages and the impact of "New" World riches on Spain's economy, values, and social structure, see Ysla Campbell, "Nostalgia y transgresión en tres comedias de Lope de Vega," in *Relaciones literarias entre España y América en los siglos XVI y XVII*, ed. Ysla Campbell (Ciudad Juárez [Mexico]: Universidad Autónoma de Ciudad Juárez, 1992), 65–87. Campbell analyses three plays by Lope de Vega which revolve around these themes, among them *La niña de plata*: "En *La niña de plata* el padre de don Juan, quien es Veinticuatro de Sevilla, no aprueba su matrimonio con Dorotea, la niña de plata, por ser ésta pobre … [S]upedita las cualidades femeninas a los bienes … [M]odifica al sujeto insistiendo en su cosificación al intercambiar las gracias por dinero o metales … [E]l juego dilógico con la palabra 'niña' … permite al

lector medir el grado de monetarización de este personaje" (Campbell, "Nostalgia y transgresión," 66, 67).

54 Lope de Vega, *El verdadero amante*, Acto 2.

55 Calderón, *Las tres justicias en una*, Jornada 1.

56 Guillén de Castro, *El mejor esposo*, Jornada 1.

57 On free will in Cervantes, see Luis Rosales, *Cervantes y la libertad*, 2 vols (Madrid: Cultura Hispánica / Instituto de Cooperación Iberoamericana, 1985).

58 Guillén de Castro, *El nacimiento de Montesinos*, Jornada 3.

59 Rojas Zorrilla, *Los trabajos de Tobías*, Jornada 2.

60 Calderón, *La niña de Gómez Arias*, Acto 1.

61 See Julia Kristeva, *Powers of Horror: An Essay on Abjection* (New York: Columbia University Press, 1982).

62 Lope de Vega, *El piadoso aragonés*, Acto 1.

63 On happy endings and multiple weddings in the *comedias*, see Catherine Connor Swietlicki, "Marriage and Subversion in *Comedia* Endings: Problems in Art and Society," in *Gender, Identity and Representation in Spain's Golden Age*, ed. Anita K. Stoll and Dawn L. Smith (Lewisburg: Bucknell University Press, 2000), 23–46; and Teresa Scott Soufas, "'Happy Ending' as Irresolution in Calderón's *No hay cosa como callar*," *Forum for Modern Language Studies* 24.2 (1988): 163–74.

64 For a Lacanian reading of the *comedias*, see Henry W. Sullivan, "Lacan and Calderón: Spanish Classical Drama in the Light of Psychoanalytic Theory," *Gestos* 10 (1990): 39–55; and Henry W. Sullivan, "Law, Desire, and the Double Plot: Towards a Psychoanalytic Poetics of the *Comedia*," in *The Golden Age* Comedia*: Text, Theory, and Performance*, ed. Charles Ganelin and Howard Mancing (West Lafayette, IN: Purdue University Press, 1994), 222–35.

65 Lope de Vega, *Los Ponces de Barcelona*, Preliminares de obra. This passage comes from the Prologue signed by the author.

66 Calderón, *Los cabellos de Absalón*, Jornada 3.

67 "Pero yo, que, aunque parezco padre, soy padrastro de don Quijote" (Cervantes, *El ingenioso hidalgo don Quijote de la Mancha*, ed. Luis Andrés Murillo, 2 vols [Madrid: Castalia, 1987], 1:50).

68 Lope de Vega, *La mal casada*, Acto 2.

69 "Buen porte de mujer … bachillera es, su autor ¿quién fue?" (Guillén de Castro, *El engañarse engañado*, Jornada 2). Bernarda replies that the father's name was Sánchez.

70 Lope de Vega, *Los cautivos de Argel*, Jornada 1.

71 Lope de Vega, *Los enemigos en casa*, Acto 1.

72 See Douglas Brooks, ed., *Printing and Parenting in Early Modern England* (Aldershot, England: Ashgate, 2005).

73 Cervantes, *Don Quijote*, part 1, chapter 47, 1:563.

74 Calderón, *Afectos de odio, y amor*, Jornada 2.

75 Guillén de Castro, *El mejor esposo*, Jornada 1.

76 Lope de Vega, *La madre de la mejor*, Acto 3.

77 Guillén de Castro, *El mejor esposo*, Jornada 1.

78 Calderón, *Las cadenas del demonio*, Jornada 2.

79 Guillén de Castro, *El mejor esposo*, Jornada 3. The biblical account appears in Luke 2:42–52.

80 Caspar Peucer, *Commentarius de praecipuis divinationum generibus* (1553) (Frankfurt: Printed using the type of Andreas Wechel, by Claudius Marnius and the heirs of Ioannes Aubrius, 1607), 23. Thanks to Craig Kallendorf for his assistance with this translation.

81 Calderón, *El purgatorio de San Patricio*, Jornada 2.

82 Calderón, *El pastor fido*, auto sacramental.

83 Lope de Vega, *El piadoso aragonés*, Acto 2.

84 This biblical episode too is remembered in the *comedias*, as when the Virgin Mary recalls the faith of Abraham: "la misma fe que alcanzaba Abrahán, en mí colijo, pues en tu nombre esperaba la descendencia del hijo que a sacrificar llevaba" (Guillén de Castro, *El mejor esposo*, Jornada 1).

85 Guillén de Castro, *El mejor esposo*, Jornada 1. The biblical account appears in Judges 11.

86 Lope de Vega, *El niño inocente de la Guardia*, Acto 2. In Calderón's *Las tres justicias en una*, the younger Don Lope slaps the man he supposes to be his father in the face when the older Don Lope calls him a liar. The scene was so scandalous that, according to a manuscript recollection by Francisco Bances Candamo (1662–1704), Calderón later regretted having penned it, even though it was allegedly based upon a true historical incident which had occurred in Aragon: "Don Pedro Calderón deseó mucho recoger la comedia … que escribió siendo muy mozo, porque un Galán daba una bofetada a su padre, y, con ser caso verdadero en Aragón y averiguar después que era el Padre supuesto y no natural, y con hacerle morir, no obstante, en pena de la irreverencia, con todo eso Don Pedro quería recoger la comedia por el horror que daba el escandaloso caso" (Francisco Bances Candamo, *Theatro de los theatros de los passados y presentes siglos*, "Primera versión" [1689–90], ed. Duncan W. Moir [London: Tamesis, 1970], 35). I have modernized the spelling.

87 Calderón, *El purgatorio de San Patricio*, Jornada 3.

88 Tirso de Molina, *El condenado por desconfiado*, Jornada 3.

89 Guillén de Castro, *El Narciso en su opinión*, Jornada 2.

90 The awaited dispensation is expected to arrive quickly: "Vendrá la dispensación" (Guillén de Castro, *El Narciso en su opinión*, Jornada 3). On papal dispensations for marrying relatives, and the financial transactions involved for obtaining them, see Augustin Redondo, "Les empêchements au mariage et leur transgression dans l'Espagne du XVIe siècle," in *Amours légitimes, amours illégitimes en Espagne (XVIe-XVIIe siècles)* (Colloque International, Sorbonne, 3, 4, 5 octobre 1984), ed. Augustin Redondo (Paris: Sorbonne, 1985), 31–56.

91 Lope de Vega, *El verdadero amante*, Acto 3.

92 Lope de Vega, *El piadoso aragonés*, Acto 1.

93 As one father describes the bond he formed with his infant son,

tuvimos un hijo solo ...
Crióse solo en mi casa,
con amorosos regalos,
siendo luz de aquestos ojos,
que en los suyos se miraron. (Moreto, *El esclavo de su hijo*, Jornada 1)

This play illustrates intergenerational strife particularly well, as a renegade son in the play unwittingly returns to Valencia as a corsair and ends up enslaving his own father.

94 Lope de Vega, *Los Ponces de Barcelona*, Acto 1.

95 Scott Taylor confirms the conflation of this specific Commandment with the more general practice of lying or even gossip: "moralists also attacked gossip and lying, usually under the rubric of not bearing false witness" (Scott K. Taylor, *Honor and Violence in Golden Age Spain* [New Haven: Yale University Press, 2008], 107).

96 Raymond Williams, "Dominant, Residual, and Emergent," in *Marxism in Literature* (Oxford: Oxford University Press, 1977), 121–7, at 124–5.

97 Leah Middlebrook, *Imperial Lyric: New Poetry and New Subjects in Early Modern Spain* (University Park: Pennsylvania State University Press, 2009).

98 This term is borrowed by Middlebrook from Norbert Elias, *Power and Civility: The Civilizing Process*, trans. Edmund Jephcott, vol. 2 (New York: Pantheon, 1982).

99 Tirso de Molina, *La mujer que manda en casa*, Acto 3; Tirso de Molina, *Privar contra su gusto*, Acto 3. Notice in the first quotation the references to Envy and Pride, two of the Seven Deadly Sins, in light of Lu Ann Homza's thesis that in Spain the Ten Commandments were conflated with the Capital Vices (see the Introduction to this volume, note 18).

100 Calderón, *El médico de su honra*, Acto 1.

101 Lope de Vega, *La cortesía de España*, Acto 2. The sale of witnesses is described thus: "siendo así, ¿bueno sería que aquí el interés no venda Testigos falsos?" (Tirso de Molina, *La celosa de sí misma*, Acto 2). Even when there is no actual monetary transaction, false witnesses may be induced to testify against the accused: "Que bien puede ser que este hombre testigos falsos induzca" (Lope de Vega, *La mal casada*, Acto 3).

102 Lope de Vega, *La inocente sangre*, Acto 2.

103 "os han de sacar los dientes" (Calderón, *El médico de su honra*, Acto 1). Scott Taylor affirms that bearing false witness was illegal (Taylor, *Honor and Violence*, 39).

104 Lope de Vega, *Servir a buenos*, Acto 3.

105 Lope de Vega, *La inocente sangre*, Acto 2.

106 Calderón, *El año santo de Roma*, auto sacramental.

107 For example, "¿Al próximo no matar? ¿No hurtar, mentir, ni desear los bienes, ni la mujer?" (Calderón, *El Joseph de las mujeres*, Jornada 2). A similar list appears in Lope de Vega's *El saber por no saber*: "ser ladrón, ser homicida, decir mal, jurar, mentir, y no temer, ni aun a Dios" (Lope de Vega, *El saber por no saber, y vida de San Julián*, Acto 3).

108 "Doroteo te mintió, a pagar de mi dinero" (Lope de Vega, *El blasón de los Chaves de Villalba*, Acto 2); "La mentira que he fingido al viejo, mentira ha sido a pagar de su dinero" (Calderón, *Antes, que todo, es mi dama*, Jornada 1).

109 Guillén de Castro, *El nacimiento de Montesinos*, Acto 1.

110 Thus we find a wily female character who declares, "soy la que por salvarme puedo engañar, y mentir" (Moreto, *La traición vengada*, Jornada 3). Other lines talk about lies being told out of fear that harm will come to their tellers or those whom they love; for example, "el miedo sería quien a mentir le provoca" (Lope de Vega, *El Amor enamorado*, Jornada 1). In fact, fear can become such a powerful motivation that it essentially obliges someone to tell a lie: "el miedo las ha obligado a mentir" (Lope de Vega, *El animal de Hungría*, Acto 1).

111 Thus a comparison is made to the sun by saying, "yo soy los rayos del cielo, que los otros son mentira" (Lope de Vega, *Roma abrasada*, Acto 3).

112 "el viento mintió, con ser todo lisonjas el viento" (Calderón, *Mujer, llora, y vencerás*, Jornada 3).

113 "Cristalina mentira, que verdad dice aparente" (Calderón, *Lo que va del hombre a Dios*, auto sacramental).

114 "desharán aquesta tela, que tantas marañas urden y tanta mentira enreda" (Tirso de Molina, *La villana de Vallecas*, Acto 2).

115 "notables cosas se ven en este mar de mentira" (Lope de Vega, *La burgalesa de Lerma*, Acto 3).

116 "suelen noches mentir lo que desmienten los días" (Lope de Vega, *Nadie se conoce*, Jornada 2).

117 "vuelve un espejo a quien mira su rostro, que una mentira le hace forma verdadera" (Lope de Vega, *La dama boba*, Acto 2).

118 Zamora, *Judás Iscariote*, Jornada 2.

119 "Quien fuera mentira para volar; pues con eso consiguiera huir" (Calderón, *El tesoro escondido*, auto sacramental); "hurtarle al viento los pasos, y a la mentira las alas" (Guillén de Castro, *El curioso impertinente*, Acto 2).

120 Rojas Zorrilla, *No hay amigo para amigo*, Jornada 1. The Platonic notion of the forms implied that all earthly objects, including human bodies, were only mere copies of their ideal prototypes. See Stephen Watt, "Introduction: The Theory of Forms (Books 5–7)," in Plato, *Republic*, ed. Stephen Watt (London: Wordsworth, 1997), xiv–xvi.

121 "ya Isabela se murió, su hermosura fue mentira" (Tirso de Molina, *Amar por arte mayor*, Acto 1).

122 "de la boca el mal olor es natural accidente; el mentir es liviandad" (Alarcón, *Examen de maridos*, Acto 3). A further layer of congruence is added when we consider that lying requires breath. Thus we find one character admonishing another to save his breath since he will need it to tell a good lie: "descansad, que para mentir importa todo el aliento cabal" (Solís, *Amparar al enemigo*, Jornada 2).

123 Pérez de Montalbán, *El valiente más dichoso, don Pedro Guiral*, Jornada 1.

124 Rojas Zorrilla, *Sin honra no hay amistad*, Jornada 2.

125 Diamante, *Amor es sangre, y no puede engañarse*, Jornada 2.

126 Matos Fragoso, *Con amor no hay amistad*, Jornada 3.

127 Tirso de Molina, *Todo es dar en una cosa*, Acto 1; Diamante, *El nacimiento de Cristo*, Acto 2. In the same *zarzuela*, Envidia asks, "¿Cómo pudieron mentir tus ojos?" (Diamante, *El nacimiento de Cristo*, Acto 2).

128 "son lenguas los ojos, que nunca dicen mentira" (Lope de Vega, *La firmeza en la desdicha*, Acto 3).

129 Tirso de Molina, *El melancólico*, Acto 3. The soul's function as keeper of the tongue is reiterated in Pérez de Montalbán's *A lo hecho no hay remedio*: "el alma, aun mentir no me consiente" (Pérez de Montalbán, *A lo hecho no hay remedio, y príncipe de los montes*, Jornada 2).

130 "llorar y no sentir, es por los ojos mentir, que suele ser por la boca" (Lope de Vega, *La bella Aurora*, Acto 1). Other plays reiterate that "lágrimas pueden mentir" (Rojas Zorrilla, *Sin honra no hay amistad*, Jornada 2).

131 Guillén de Castro, *El conde de Irlos*, Acto 2.

132 Tirso de Molina, *Quien habló, pagó*, Jornada 3.

133 Zamora, *La poncella de Orleans*, Jornada 2.

134 Tirso de Molina, *La huerta de Juan Fernández*, Jornada 2. Witness the following exchange about fame:

2. No puede mentir la fama.
3. Si no miente, es un prodigio. (Diamante, *Cumplirle a Dios la palabra*, Jornada 2)

Lope de Vega reiterates, "suele mentir la fama, que suena más" (Lope de Vega, *El soldado amante*, Acto 2).

135 Calderón, *Cada uno para sí*, Jornada 2.

136 "de nuestros males consuelo, de nuestras penas alivio, de nuestras tormentas puerto, mintió el deseo; mas ¿cuándo dijo verdad el deseo?" (Calderón, *El mayor encanto, amor*, Acto 1).

137 "No entiende a tu lengua, sí tu acción, porque aquélla mentir puede, y ésta ha de decir verdad" (Calderón, *La crítica del amor*, Jornada 1).

138 Tirso de Molina, *Santo, y sastre*, Acto 2.

139 Guillén de Castro, *El perfecto caballero*, Acto 1.

140 "aquel que ya expira no es bien que diga mentira" (Lope de Vega, *El ejemplo de casadas y prueba de la paciencia*, Acto 3).

141 "la hidra de tantas cabezas, cuantas el padre de la mentira en cada anhelito inspira" (Calderón, *La aurora en Copacabana*, Jornada 3).

142 "Todo es envidia, y mentira, todo es tratar con engaño" (Lope de Vega, *El ausente en el lugar*, Acto 3); "Confesó, que había mentido, por tener al Cardenal envidia, y odio mortal" (Lope de Vega, *El cardenal de Belén*, Acto 3).

143 Tirso de Molina, *Santo, y sastre*, Acto 2.

144 Pérez de Montalbán, *El divino portugués, San Antonio de Padua*, Jornada 1.

145 Calderón, *El laberinto del mundo*, Acto 1.

146 Matos Fragoso, *La devoción del Ángel de la Guarda*, Jornada 3; "el mentir aborrezco, y a los que mienten también" (Pérez de Montalbán, *Lo que son juicios del cielo*, Jornada 2).

147 Calderón, *El maestro de danzar*, Jornada 3. A similar example is "Presto el mentir se declara, por más que el que miente jura" (Tirso de Molina, *Marta la piadosa*, Acto 2) along with "ni hay mentira que no salga" (Alarcón, *La verdad sospechosa*, Acto 3). This last line is reminiscent of William Shakespeare's "the truth will out" (William Shakespeare, *The Merchant of Venice*, II.ii.80, in *The Riverside Shakespeare*, ed. G. Blakemore Evans [Boston: Houghton Mifflin, 1974]). These lines in turn echo proverbs in use since at least the eleventh century.

148 Calderón, *Las manos blancas no ofenden*, Jornada 2; Alarcón, *La verdad sospechosa*, Acto 2.

149 "es muy propio, de la mentira no tener salida, sin mucho deshonor" (Lope de Vega, *La corona merecida*, Acto 3).

150 "Mira, que pesará la mentira, y vas caminando a pie" (Lope de Vega, *El marido más firme*, Acto 3).

151 Alarcón, *La prueba de las promesas*, Acto 1.

152 Alarcón, *La verdad sospechosa*, Acto 3.

153 See Hilaire Kallendorf, *Conscience on Stage: The* Comedia *as Casuistry in Early Modern Spain* (Toronto: University of Toronto Press, 2007).

154 Pérez de Montalbán, *Los amantes de Teruel*, Jornada 3.

155 On this doctrine, see *A Treatise of Equivocation* (1592–5), ed. David Jardine (London: Longman, 1851). For its impact on early modern English drama, see Frank Huntley, "*Macbeth* and the Background of Jesuitical Equivocation," *PMLA* 79 (1964): 390–400.

156 Calderón, *El segundo Scipión*, Jornada 1.

157 Calderón, *Fuego de Dios en el querer bien*, Jornada 2.

158 Calderón, *Los tres afectos de amor, piedad, desmayo y valor*, Jornada 3.

159 Guillén de Castro, *Cuánto se estima el honor*, Jornada 1.

160 Moreto, *El poder de la amistad*, Jornada 3.

161 "embozar una verdad cuando me importa el hacerlo, no es mentir, pues siempre queda verdad al correrla el velo" (Calderón, *El segundo Scipión*, Jornada 3); "embelesó la verdad, aquada su puridad" (Calderón, *La crítica del amor*, Jornada 2).

162 In this case the truth becomes "tan vestida, y tan dorada, que se convierte en mentira" (Guillén de Castro, *La Justicia en la piedad*, Jornada 1).
163 Diamante, *El cerco de Zamora*, Jornada 2; Diamante, *Cumplirle a Dios la palabra*, Jornada 1.
164 Matos Fragoso, *Con amor no hay amistad*, Jornada 3. On the use of this signature question ("What must I do?") in the *comedias*, see Hilaire Kallendorf, "'¿Qué he de hacer?': The *Comedia* as Casuistry," *Romanic Review* 95.3 (2004): 327–59.
165 Alarcón, *Los empeños de un engaño*, Acto 1; "el mentir para obligar es alta razón de Estado" (Pérez de Montalbán, *El Señor don Juan de Austria*, Jornada 3).
166 Calderón, *Antes, que todo, es mi dama*, Jornada 1.
167 Diamante, *Santa Teresa de Jesús*, Jornada 2.
168 On the Jesuit education of major Spanish playwrights, see the Introduction to Kallendorf, *Conscience on Stage*, 3–37.
169 Calderón, *Mañanas de abril, y mayo*, Jornada 2.
170 Pérez de Montalbán, *Los amantes de Teruel*, Jornada 1.
171 Pérez de Montalbán, *La toquera vizcaína*, Jornada 1.
172 Lope de Vega, *La mocedad de Roldán*, Acto 2.
173 "me dio la lengua de la mujer, si yo la mentira soy" (Calderón, *Las cadenas del demonio*, Jornada 3).
174 "¿qué mujer, señor, no nació dotada en mentira infusa?" (Calderón, *¿Cuál es mayor perfección?*, Jornada 2).
175 Calderón, *La cura, y la enfermedad*, Acto 1.
176 "Que el mentir, y el disculparse tuvo principio en mujeres" (Lope de Vega, *El Perseo*, Acto 1). There does not, however, seem to be universal acceptance of this narrative, for in the *comedias* we find other lines indicating the opposite: "hombre fue en aqueste mundo el primero que mintió" (Rojas Zorrilla, *Sin honra no hay amistad*, Jornada 1). This vituperation of Adam instead of Eve is echoed in Calderón's *El Rey Don Pedro en Madrid*: "pues tiene en el primer hombre el mentir su antigüedad; mentira es su majestad, mentira es su perfección" (Calderón, *El Rey Don Pedro en Madrid, e infanzón de Illescas*, Jornada 1).
177 "Eres la mujer primera que tiene miedo al mentir" (Lope de Vega, *Quien todo lo quiere*, Jornada 2).
178 Lope de Vega, *El saber por no saber, y vida de San Julián*, Acto 2.
179 Lope de Vega, *Obras son amores*, Acto 2.
180 "no hay mujer que no sepa inventar una mentira" (Lope de Vega, *Quien dice que las mujeres*, loa).
181 Tirso de Molina, *Cautela contra cautela*, Jornada 1.
182 Tirso de Molina, *El castigo del penséque*, Acto 3.
183 Guillén de Castro, *Los mal casados de Valencia*, Acto 1.
184 Lope de Vega, *Las mujeres sin hombres*, Acto 3.
185 "no hay verdad en amor, todo es mentira" (Lope de Vega, *El villano en su rincón*, Acto 2).

186 Guillén de Castro, *Los mal casados de Valencia*, Acto 1.

187 Tirso de Molina, *El melancólico*, Acto 3.

188 "mintió, Violante, tu amor, tus celos mintieron" (Calderón, *El astrólogo fingido*, Jornada 3).

189 "Testigos falsos, Blanca, son los celos, enemigos sofísticos de casa" (Tirso de Molina, *Los lagos de san Vicente*, Acto 3).

190 There are, of course, exceptions to this rule, such as the prince who is found to be a congenital liar:

REY: ¿Que esfuerce así el Infante una mentira?
MARFIRA: Siempre las palabras suyas son mentiras.
(Guillén de Castro, *El conde de Irlos*, Acto 3)

191 Calderón, *Fineza contra fineza*, Jornada 2.

192 Calderón, *El médico de su honra*, Acto 1. This trope is repeated often, as in Doña Jacinta's rhetorical question to Ana in Guillén de Castro's *El vicio en los extremos*: "¿Y cabe en mi calidad el mentir?" (Guillén de Castro, *El vicio en los extremos*, Jornada 2).

193 Zamora, *Duendes son alcahuetes, y el espíritu foleto, primera parte*, Jornada 3.

194 Tirso de Molina, *El pretendiente al revés*, Acto 3.

195 Calderón, *El hombre pobre todo es trazas*, Jornada 3; "bien puede de agradecido mentir un hombre de bien" (Pérez de Montalbán, *Lo que son juicios del cielo*, Jornada 2).

196 Guillén de Castro, *Los mal casados de Valencia*, Acto 1.

197 Zamora, *Duendes son alcahuetes, y el espíritu foleto, primera parte*, Acto 1.

198 Solís, *La gitanilla de Madrid*, Jornada 1.

199 "Pasar por donaire puede, cuando no daña, el mentir; mas no se puede sufrir, cuando ese límite excede" (Alarcón, *La verdad sospechosa*, Acto 3).

200 Lope de Vega, *El Duque de Viseo*, Acto 3.

201 Lope de Vega, *Las famosas asturianas*, Acto 3.

202 Moreto, *El lindo Don Diego*, Jornada 3.

203 "Following the Christian-Neoplatonist foundations of early modern Spanish political theory, the monarchy was conceived ideally as a hierarchy of reflections that emanated from God to the king, God's representative on earth, to his ministers" (Laura Bass, *The Drama of the Portrait: Theater and Visual Culture in Early Modern Spain* [University Park: Pennsylvania State University Press, 2008], 89). This conception of the monarch signals a discontinuity with much of Spain's Roman past; for a new look at themes of lying and deceit in ancient Rome, see Andrew J. Turner et al., eds, *Private and Public Lies: The Discourse of Despotism and Deceit in the Graeco-Roman World* (Leiden: Brill, 2010).

204 Rojas Zorrilla, *Los celos de Rodamonte*, Jornada 1.

205 Lope de Vega, *Por la puente Juana*, Acto 2.

206 Calderón, *Mañanas de abril, y mayo*, Jornada 2. See Fernando de Rojas, *La Celestina: Tragicomedia de Calisto y Melibea* (1499–1502), ed. Dorothy S. Severin (Madrid: Alianza, 1981).

207 Calderón, *El faetonte*, Jornada 2.

208 Calderón, *El maestro de danzar*, Jornada 2.

209 One significant exception to this pattern occurred in historical cases of duels where the accusation of lying became part of the rhetoric of honour: "[T]ruth telling and accusations of lying pointed straight to the heart of honour rhetoric … To *desmentir*, or give the lie to one's opponent, was a crucial component of the duel … [A]ccusations of lying lent seriousness to the dispute, elevating it from a relatively unimportant issue into a matter of truthfulness and the reputation of one's opponent … [A]ccording to dueling manuals, giving the lie was one of the most offensive things a Castilian could do to another, and going back on one's word was a terrible disgrace" (Taylor, *Honor and Violence*, 123, 183, 35, 89). This may also be an instance, however (with apologies to New Historicists looking for "fiction in the archives") where literary evidence diverges from historical sources such as criminal cases. The reference here is to Natalie Zemon Davis, *Fiction in the Archives: Pardon Tales and Their Tellers in Sixteenth-Century France* (Stanford: Stanford University Press, 1987). My objection would be not at all to Professor Davis, an exemplary historian whose work I admire, but instead to some of her sloppier imitators.

210 Pérez de Montalbán, *El Señor don Juan de Austria*, Jornada 3.

211 Lope de Vega, *La corona merecida*, Acto 3.

212 Quiñones de Benavente, *El murmurador*, Acto 1.

213 Witness the following humorous exchange:

FLORA: ¿De quién, dime, has aprendido, Friso, a mentir tan sin miedo?
FRISO: De ti. (Calderón, *Ni Amor se libra de Amor*, Acto 1)

214 Calderón, *La banda y la flor*, Jornada 2.

215 "no hay cosa como mentir para ganar opinión" (Diamante, *Amor es sangre, y no puede engañarse*, Jornada 2).

216 Moreto, *Antíoco y Seleuco*, Jornada 1.

217 "qué fácil en creer, el que no sabe mentir" (Alarcón, *La verdad sospechosa*, Acto 2).

218 Calderón, *El astrólogo fingido*, Jornada 2.

219 Lope de Vega, *La ilustre fregona*, Jornada 1.

220 Solís, *Un bobo hace ciento*, Jornada 3.

221 Alarcón, *La verdad sospechosa*, Acto 2.

222 Calderón, *Los Lances de Amor, y Fortuna*, Jornada 3. I have not standardized this Spanish in order to preserve the rhyme and the lower-class dialect.

223 "Yo haciendo donaire digo, el mentir es cosa usada desde el principio del mundo" (Lope de Vega, *Amar sin saber a quién*, Acto 1).

224 "basta ser casamiento, para empezar a mentir, pues el eco ha de decir, tras el casamiento, miento" (Lope de Vega, *Quien ama no haga fieros*, Acto 3).

225 Calderón, *Agradecer, y no amar*, Jornada 2.

226 "¿Faltará a una mujer una mentira que la saque de otra?" (Calderón, *Mañanas de abril, y mayo*, Acto 1).

227 "Verdad no dirá quien está tan hecho a mentir" (Calderón, *Antes, que todo, es mi dama*, Jornada 1). The implication here is that lying almost instantly becomes a habit, once someone has started down its slippery slope. This facet of its depiction is demonstrated in the following abrupt – but humorous – exchange:

ÁNGELA: ¿Cuándo suelo yo mentir?
LUISA: Ahora. (Calderón, *Fuego de Dios en el querer bien*, Jornada 2)

The repeated habit of lying was also thought to result in someone's having (and here it is impossible not to hear racist overtones) a black face, as in "siempre está de parte del mentir tu negra tez" (Calderón, *El laberinto del mundo*, Acto 1).

228 "tal vez dirá una verdad, y después mentira veinte" (Tirso de Molina, *La venganza de Tamar*, Jornada 3).

229 "pues antes de hablar sé ya que vas a mentir, es vana la disculpa" (Calderón, *Cada uno para sí*, Jornada 1).

230 As one character asks rhetorically, to comic effect: "¿A mí me falta hoy una mentira, no sobrándome otra cosa todo el año?" (Calderón, *El astrólogo fingido*, Jornada 2).

231 Solís, *El doctor Carlino*, Jornada 2.

232 "También eso es mentir, que aun desmentir no sabéis, sino mintiendo" (Alarcón, *La verdad sospechosa*, Acto 2).

233 "tu falsa lengua, como falso miente, y mentirá mil veces, y ha mentido" (Cervantes, *La casa de los celos y selvas de Ardenia*, Jornada 3).

234 Lope de Vega, *La fe rompida*, Acto 2.

235 "Cortesanos (que en eso la mentira aduladora satisface obligaciones, y afectando sentimientos disfraza con cumplimientos)" (Tirso de Molina, *La lealtad contra la envidia*, Acto 3).

236 Lope de Vega, *La fe rompida*, Acto 2.

237 Tirso de Molina, *La prudencia en la mujer*, Jornada 3.

238 Lope de Vega, *Los Tellos de Meneses*, Acto 3.

239 Calderón, *El Arca de Dios cautiva*, auto sacramental.

240 "jamás ha faltado la mentira cortesana, de encarecer su fineza" (Matos Fragoso, *La devoción del Ángel de la Guarda*, Acto 1).

241 Lope de Vega, *Santiago el verde*, Acto 3.

242 Lope de Vega, *El ausente en el lugar*, Acto 3.

243 "Si parabién de una mentira se da, como suele suceder en pretendientes de Corte" (Lope de Vega, *Dios hace reyes*, Acto 3).

244 "nuestra fragilidad nos tiene tan engañados, que una mentira aplaudimos, y una verdad ultrajamos" (Diamante, *El jubileo de Porciúncula*, Jornada 2).

245 "llegado a Palacio, ésta es la puerta por donde la mentira tiene entrada" (Lope de Vega, *El testimonio vengado*, Jornada 3); "la mentira insolente siempre reina en la ciudad" (Lope de Vega, *El testimonio vengado*, Jornada 1).

246 Calderón, *Fuego de Dios en el querer bien*, Jornada 1. This adjective is repeated often in the context of lying, as in "¿ha de faltar una compuesta mentira, que ablande toda esa ira?" (Calderón, *No hay cosa como callar*, Jornada 2).

247 Calderón, *Fuego de Dios en el querer bien*, Jornada 2. A polished lie is described thus: "más pulida saca una mentira" (Lope de Vega, *El cuerdo en su casa*, Acto 2). Conversely, we find objections to lies not on ethical grounds but based upon the fact that they are ill formed, such as "En toda mi vida vi mentira más mal trazada" (Calderón, *Mejor está que estaba*, Jornada 3).

248 Calderón, *El mágico prodigioso*, Jornada 1. I reference Book 2 of Aristotle's *Rhetoric*: "The Emotions are all those feelings that so change men as to affect their judgements" (Aristotle, *Rhetoric* 1378a20–1, trans. W. Rhys Roberts [New York: Modern Library, 1954], 91). For a secondary treatment of this aspect of Aristotle's rhetorical thought, see Ellen Quandahl, "A Feeling for Aristotle: Emotion in the Sphere of Ethics," in *A Way to Move: Rhetorics of Emotion and Composition Studies*, ed. Dale Jacobs and Laura R. Micciche (Portsmouth, NH: Boynton/Cook, 2003), 11–22. For a survey of rhetoric's associations with falsehood, see C. Jan Swearingen, *Rhetoric and Irony: Western Literacy and Western Lies* (Oxford: Oxford University Press, 1991).

249 Tirso de Molina, *El amor, y el amistad*, Jornada 3.

250 "elocuente quien hiciere creer a un pobre oyente dos mil mentira[s]" (Solís, *La gitanilla de Madrid*, Jornada 3). On dexterity in lying, witness "mentir con destreza" (Pérez de Montalbán, *Don Florisel de Niquea*, Jornada 1). On lying persuasively, see the lines, "es la mentira elocuente, y persuasivo el engaño" (Tirso de Molina, *El amor, y el amistad*, Jornada 1). Not all liars, however, are this successful; as one unfortunate character is told, "tenéis en el mentir menos dicha que artificio" (Solís, *La gitanilla de Madrid*, Jornada 2).

251 Alarcón, *La crueldad por el honor*, Acto 2. A similar line appears in the same playwright's *Examen de maridos*: "si ella es mentira, lindamente la han trazado" (Alarcón, *Examen de maridos*, Acto 3).

252 "Entre las gracias de Bato, como le cuesta barato, es mentir con linda traza" (Lope de Vega, *El Amor enamorado*, Jornada 1). Another *gracioso*, Pillán, admits to telling lies to avoid provoking his master: "[si] os provoco con las verdades que os digo, de siempre mentir propongo" (Lope de Vega, *Arauco domado por el excelentísimo señor don García Hurtado de Mendoza*, Acto 1).

253 Lope de Vega, *Los locos por el cielo*, Acto 2.

254 "si este villano ahora ingenio también tuviese, y otra mentira fingiese" (Calderón, *Cómo se comunican dos estrellas contrarias*, Jornada 3); "¿tendremos ingenio para hacer otra mentira?" (Calderón, *La dama duende*, Jornada 2); "La traza alaba discreta de esta ingeniosa mentira" (Tirso de Molina, *Esto sí que es negociar*, Jornada 2). On Baroque *ingenio* see Baltasar Gracián, *Agudeza y arte de ingenio* (1648), ed. Evaristo Corréa Calderón, 2 vols (Madrid: Castalia, 1969).

255 Calderón, *La gran Cenobia*, Acto 1; "en las láminas mintieron las pinturas, y matices" (Calderón, *Argenis y Poliarco*, Acto 1).

256 Pérez de Montalbán, *La deshonra honrosa*, Jornada 3. On the artificial as an aesthetic category characteristic of Baroque and Manneristic painting in Spain, see Duncan T. Kinkead, "Francisco de Herrera and the Development of the High Baroque Style in Seville," in *Painting in Spain 1650–1700: A Symposium*, special issue of the *Record of the Art Museum, Princeton University* 41.2 (1982): 12–23, at 20.

257 "ya representan países, ya batallas representan, siendo una noble mentira de la gran naturaleza" (Calderón, *Darlo todo, y no dar nada*, Jornada 2).

258 Tirso de Molina, *Quien calla, otorga*, Acto 1.

259 Calderón, *El verdadero Dios Pan*, loa for auto sacramental. In the *Republic* Plato banned poets from his ideal society because he believed they would corrupt public morality with their lies. See Plato, *Republic* IX and XXV, in *The Republic of Plato*, trans. Francis MacDonald Cornford (Oxford: Oxford University Press, 1945), 85 and 321–33. To situate Plato's position within the broader context of classical cultures, see Christopher Gill and T.P. Wiseman, eds, *Lies and Fiction in the Ancient World* (Exeter: University of Exeter Press, 1993). As part of the *Nachleben* of Plato in Golden Age Spain, witness the following exchange:

COSME: Señor, yo la compuse.
ELVIRA: Es mentira.
FERNANDO: ¿Sois Poeta? (Lope de Vega, *No son todos ruiseñores*, Jornada 3)

260 "Que a quien le di ésa venera yo, por favor, con mi retrato, aunque me mintió su trato, su nombre no me mintió" (Calderón, *No hay cosa como callar*, Jornada 2).

261 Lope de Vega, *No son todos ruiseñores*, Jornada 3. This generalization could apply to literary as well as visual portraits.

262 Bass, *The Drama of the Portrait*, 8, 10.

263 Quiñones de Benavente, *Loa con que empezaron Rueda, y Ascanio*. These double dealings were frequently associated with financial gain, and hence motivated by Greed: "miente el que algún trato doble por interés cometió. Miente el que promete dar, y no da" (Lope de Vega, *Del mal lo menos*, Acto 1).

264 "de mí vive envidioso; y también de quien recelo alguna doble intención" (Matos Fragoso, *La devoción del Ángel de la Guarda*, Acto 1).
265 Tirso de Molina, *La lealtad contra la envidia*, Acto 3.
266 Rojas Zorrilla, *Persiles, y Sigismunda*, Jornada 3; Diamante, *Pasión vencida de afecto*, Jornada 2.
267 "primero prevenir galas con que enamorar, y trazas con que mentir" (Tirso de Molina, *Don Gil de las calzas verdes*, Acto 1).
268 "el alma cubre de afeite y el corazón de mentira" (Lope de Vega, *Ursón y Valentín, hijos del rey de Francia*, Jornada 1).
269 For example, "mentira azul de las gentes, hipócrita de sus galas" (Calderón, *Peor está que estaba*, Jornada 2).
270 "Los adornos más nocivos, siempre de la voluntad son mentira, y la verdad ha de andar en cueros" (Calderón, *Céfalo, y Pocris*, Jornada 3).
271 "la Mentira, en varias formas mudada, en varios trajes vestida" (Calderón, *El gran mercado del mundo*, auto sacramental).
272 "Huye la Verdad, y la Mentira la quita el Capote, y queda como desnuda … Se viste la Mentira la Capa de la Verdad" (Calderón, *Llamados, y escogidos*, auto sacramental). This imagery is not limited to religious or allegorical contexts; in secular drama, likewise, we find characters who comment that "se suele cubrir una mentira con capa de verdad" (Lope de Vega, *Las bizarrías de Belisa*, Jornada 2).
273 Calderón, *Llamados, y escogidos*, auto sacramental.
274 Tirso de Molina, *Quien no cae, no se levanta*, Acto 2.
275 Tirso de Molina, *Marta la piadosa*, Acto 2. Similarly, a different character of Tirso's asks, "¿tengo cara de mentir?" (Tirso de Molina, *La mujer por fuerza*, Jornada 1).
276 "Porque el semblante en un hombre, ni puede mentir, ni sabe" (Calderón, *Mejor está que estaba*, Jornada 2). On this Neoplatonic concept specifically, as well as the more general relationship of physical beauty to moral virtue, see Martin Porter, *Windows of the Soul: The Art of Physiognomy in European Culture, 1470–1760* (Oxford: Oxford University Press, 2005), especially 187. This trope appears explicitly in the *comedias*, as in "Es como espejo la cara adonde el alma se mira la pena, el amor, la ira, en su cristal se declara" (Lope de Vega, *Arcadia*, Acto 1).
277 Tirso de Molina, *Amazonas en las Indias*, Acto 1.
278 "así con fingir saben los hombres mentir" (Calderón, *Saber del mal, y el bien*, Jornada 2).
279 Zamora, *Por oír misa, y dar cebada, nunca se perdió jornada*, Acto 1.
280 Calderón, *El astrólogo fingido*, Jornada 3.
281 "¿Cómo podrá acreditarse tan conocida mentira para que pase adelante?" (Cervantes, *La entretenida*, Jornada 1). However, a well-formed lie is said to be worthy of some credit: "Mentira tan bien formada, algún crédito merece" (Lope de Vega, *La corona merecida*, Acto 2).
282 Rueda, *Los engañados*, Scena 7; Lope de Vega, *Los prados de León*, Acto 2.

283 Calderón, *La crítica del amor*, Jornada 2. Similarly, a lie is said to be supported by accompanying deception: "no oso contradecir tan gran mentira por ver tan apoyado su embeleco" (Tirso de Molina, *Don Gil de las calzas verdes*, Acto 2).

284 Calderón, *Las manos blancas no ofenden*, Jornada 3.

285 Diamante, *El negro más prodigioso*, Jornada 1.

286 "nunca hay buena mentira sin verdades" (Rojas Zorrilla, *Los celos de Rodamonte*, Jornada 3).

287 Moreto, *El mejor amigo, el rey*, Jornada 3.

288 Eyes: "Nombre, y voz ya no me pueden mentir, ni los ojos, que la noche aun la deja percibir" (Calderón, *La fiera, el rayo y la piedra*, Jornada 2). Ears: "¿Pueden mentir los oídos?" (Calderón, *La gran Cenobia*, Acto 1). Witness: "testigo, que por lo menos, no me dejará mentir" (Calderón, *¿Cuál es mayor perfección?*, Jornada 1). A nascent graphocentrism is demonstrated amply in lines such as "Lo del papel es verdad, lo de los ojos mentira" (Lope de Vega, *El mayordomo de la duquesa de Amalfi*, Acto 1).

289 Lope de Vega, *La doncella Teodor*, Acto 2. A similar concern over forgery appears as, "Dicen que tú, que no sé si es mentira, mi letra, contrahaciéndola, engañaste" (Lope de Vega, *Las almenas de Toro*, Acto 3).

290 "os engañé con escribiros que os vi, nunca os vi, mentí" (Lope de Vega, *Amar sin saber a quién*, Jornada 2).

291 "la mentira, que luego se conoce, si se mira, como moneda falsa" (Lope de Vega, *Las cuentas del Gran Capitán*, Acto 1).

292 Tirso de Molina, *Todo es dar en una cosa*, Acto 1.

293 "mas el papel pudo hacer mayor mentira verdad" (Lope de Vega, *El Argel fingido y renegado de amor*, Acto 3).

294 Lope de Vega, *Las cuentas del Gran Capitán*, Acto 1.

295 Lope de Vega, *El Hamete de Toledo*, Acto 1.

296 Héctor Urzáiz Tortajada, "El libro áureo: un tótem cultural frente a los *Índices* de la Inquisición," in *Materia crítica: formas de ocio y de consumo en la cultura áurea*, ed. Enrique García Santo-Tomás (Madrid/Frankfurt: Iberoamericana/Vervuert, 2009), 127–48, at 144.

297 "aun aquello que se ve, cuanto y más lo que se oye, nos suele mentir tal vez" (Calderón, *Mañana será otro día*, Jornada 3).

298 "¿Si es verdad esto que miro? ¿Si es mentira esto que leo?" (Calderón, *Argenis y Poliarco*, Jornada 2).

299 Calderón, *El astrólogo fingido*, Jornada 2.

300 "formar de una mentira una verdad" (Solís, *El amor al uso*, Jornada 3).

301 Calderón, *No hay cosa como callar*, Jornada 1.

302 Calderón, *El astrólogo fingido*, Jornada 2.

303 "que aunque sepa yo de cierto que es mentira, la creeré, engañándome a mí mismo" (Calderón, *Bien vengas mal*, Jornada 1); "Tú mientes; pero no mientes; es verdad, pues ¿por qué no?" (Solís, *Amparar al enemigo*, Jornada 1).

304 Pérez de Montalbán, *Como amante, y como honrada*, Jornada 3.

305 Lope de Vega, *El premio del bien hablar*, Acto 1. On this philosophical problem see J.C. Beall and Michael Glanzberg, "The Liar Paradox," in the *Stanford Encyclopedia of Philosophy*, ed. Edward N. Zalta (Stanford: Stanford University, 2010), http://plato.stanford.edu.

306 Alarcón, *La verdad sospechosa*, Acto 3.

307 Tirso de Molina, *Ventura te dé Dios, hijo*, Jornada 1.

308 Lope de Vega, *Del mal lo menos*, Acto 1, emphasis mine. The two-faced motif is a repeated one: "En mentira dos visos" (Calderón, *Ni Amor se libra de Amor*, Acto 1).

309 Thus the didactic *autos sacramentales* decry the World's abandonment of Truth for Falsehood as a return to Original Sin or that "first cruelty": "¿el Mundo, atento a su primer crueldad, por la Mentira deje la Verdad?" (Calderón, *El laberinto del mundo*, auto sacramental).

310 Calderón, *Cómo se comunican dos estrellas contrarias*, Jornada 3. This epic battle is described thus: "en la Tierra están luchando la Verdad, y la Mentira" (Calderón, *Llamados, y escogidos*, auto sacramental).

311 Calderón, *En esta vida todo es verdad, y todo es mentira*, Jornada 2 and Jornada 3.

312 Zamora, *El custodio de la Hungría, San Juan Capistrano*, Jornada 1.

313 Calderón, *En esta vida todo es verdad, y todo es mentira*, Jornada 3.

314 Calderón, *La vida es sueño*, Jornada 3.

315 Pérez de Montalbán, *La doncella de labor*, Jornada 1. A similar line is found in Tirso's *Marta la piadosa*: "O qué adornada de mentira pasa la quimera de hoy" (Tirso de Molina, *Marta la piadosa*, Acto 3).

316 Quiñones de Benavente, *La verdad*, entremés.

317 "del Laberinto del Mundo, Fedra, y Ariadna sean la Mentira, y la Verdad" (Calderón, *El laberinto del mundo*, auto sacramental).

318 Calderón, *El laberinto del mundo*, auto sacramental.

319 "¿Cuál es una cosi cosa, tan extraña, que no siendo mentira, ni verdad, es verdad, y mentira a un tiempo?" (Calderón, *El santo rey don Fernando, segunda parte*, auto sacramental). Especially in the realm of romantic love, truth is said to be grounded in lies and vice versa: "es amor una verdad que miente, y una mentira que en verdad se funda" (Lope de Vega, *Obras son amores*, Acto 2).

320 Calderón, *El secreto a voces*, Jornada 2.

321 "el labio hasta la oreja, siendo verdad cuando sale, es mentira cuando llega" (Diamante, *La reina María Estuarda*, Jornada 2).

322 Lope de Vega, *La firmeza en la desdicha*, Acto 1. The use of fiction in the context of lies is a frequent association, as in "esto es mentira, ficción y sueño" (Lope de Vega, *Las mudanzas de Fortuna, y sucesos de don Beltrán de Aragón*, Acto 3).

323 *Fiction* is derived from the Latin root *facere*, to shape or make (also the root of the Spanish verb *hacer*).

Conclusion: The Self Discovered by Sin

1 Calderón, *El diablo mudo*, auto sacramental; Calderón, *La devoción de la Cruz*, Jornada 3.

2 Enrique Gacto, "El delito de bigamia y la Inquisición española," in *Sexo barroco y otras transgresiones premodernas*, ed. Francisco Tomás y Valiente et al. (Madrid: Alianza Universidad, 1990), 127–52, at 140.

3 See note 19 in the Introduction to the present volume.

4 On playwrights who were also priests, see Hilaire Kallendorf, "Mainstream Dramatists Educated by Jesuits," in *Conscience on Stage: The* Comedia *as Casuistry in Early Modern Spain* (University of Toronto Press, 2007), 22–7.

5 Lu Ann Homza, *Religious Authority in the Spanish Renaissance* (Baltimore: Johns Hopkins University Press, 2000), 166.

6 See Barbara Fuchs, *Exotic Nation: Maurophilia and the Construction of Early Modern Spain* (Philadelphia: University of Pennsylvania Press, 2009).

7 For a recent critique of Bossy, see Richard Newhauser, "'These Seaven Devils': The Capital Vices on the Way to Modernity," in *Sin in Medieval and Early Modern Culture: The Tradition of the Seven Deadly Sins*, ed. Richard Newhauser and Susan Ridyard (York: York Medieval Press, 2012), 157–88.

8 On reader-response or reception theory, which emphasizes the reader's (sometimes even above the author's) role in the co-creation of the text, see Wolfgang Iser, *The Act of Reading: A Theory of Aesthetic Response* (Baltimore: Johns Hopkins University Press, 1980); and Hans Robert Jauss, *Toward an Aesthetic of Reception*, trans. Timothy Bahti, with an introduction by Paul de Man (Minneapolis: University of Minnesota Press, 1982). One of the academic fields where this theoretical perspective has taken root most firmly is that of post-classical classical studies, otherwise known as the classical tradition. On the *Nachleben* of classical texts, see C. Martindale and R.F. Thomas, *Classics and the Uses of Reception* (Oxford: Blackwell, 2006), as well as Craig Kallendorf, "Philology, the Reader and the *Nachleben* of Classical Texts," *Modern Philology* 92 (1994): 137–56. Reflecting this recent trend in scholarship, there is now a journal called *Classical Receptions* (published by Oxford University Press) devoted entirely to the reception by later generations of texts dating back to classical antiquity.

9 Louis Montrose, "Professing the Renaissance: The Poetics and Politics of Culture," in *The New Historicism*, ed. Aram Veeser (New York: Routledge, 1989), 15–36.

10 See Luisa López Grigera, *La retórica en la España del Siglo de Oro: teoría y práctica* (Salamanca: Universidad de Salamanca, 1995).

11 *La trace* is a concept borrowed from Jacques Derrida. It appears in *Of Grammatology* (1967) and *Positions* (1972). The French word can be translated variously as *footprint, mark, trail,* or *clue*. Ajay Heble relates it to both Ferdinand de Saussure's concept of the sign and Sigmund Freud's theory of memory, but attributes the term primarily to Derridian deconstruction: "it is the name Derrida gives to the absences, the relations

of difference, that are involved in the production of the sign" (Ajay Heble, "Trace," in *Encyclopedia of Contemporary Literary Theory*, ed. Irena R. Makaryk [Toronto: University of Toronto Press, 1997], 646–7, at 647). For further discussion of the Derridian trace in relation to Golden Age drama and issues of conscience, see Kallendorf, *Conscience on Stage*, 39.

12 This dilemma has been perceived to affect the choices of public figures such as Senator Tom Daschle, whose potential conflicts of interest due to private consulting work torpedoed his bid to become U.S. President Obama's first Secretary of Health and Human Services (Sheryl Gay Stolberg and David D. Kirkpatrick, "Daschle Was Torn between Public and Private Ambitions, His Friends Say," *New York Times*, 5 February 2009, A16). Such current events have also led to debates over whether human nature is naturally more individualistic or more socially oriented: "[The] individualist description of human nature seems to be wrong. Over the past 30 years, there has been a tide of research in many fields, all underlining one old truth – that we are intensely social creatures, deeply interconnected with one another and the idea of the lone individual rationally and willfully steering his own life course is often an illusion" (David Brooks, "The Social Animal," op-ed, *New York Times*, 12 September 2008, A23).

13 José Antonio Maravall, *Teatro y literatura en la sociedad barroca* (Madrid: Seminarios y Ediciones, 1972), 31.

14 Once again see Anthony Cascardi's recent critique of Maravall (Anthony Cascardi, "Beyond Castro and Maravall: Interpellation, Mimesis, and the Hegemony of Spanish Culture," in *Ideologies of Hispanism*, ed. Mabel Moraña [Nashville: Vanderbilt University Press, 2005], 138–59), as well as George Mariscal, "History and the Subject of the Spanish Golden Age," *The Seventeenth Century* 4 (1989): 19–32, at 26–7.

15 McKendrick actually goes so far as to see the theatre as, at least potentially, a radical instrument of subversion: "The theatre itself ... in its assumptions and procedures essentially anti-elitist and anti-aristocratic, can be seen as a paradigm for rebellion in the challenge its very existence and identity offered to the literary, aesthetic and moral orthodoxies of the day, and its readiness to ignore many of the legislative efforts made to control its activities indicates that it was by no means reluctant to adopt an oppositional stance" (Melveena McKendrick, *Playing the King: Lope de Vega and the Limits of Conformity* [London: Tamesis, 2000], 11).

16 "The Greek word conventionally rendered by the English 'honour' is *timē*. This is not to say that 'honour' and *timē* are strictly equivalent ... Homer sees honour as inseparable from such outward manifestations of it as honourable cuts of meat, gifts, and possessions ... [T]he use of the word in the *Iliad* shows that in the majority of the contexts in which it appears the appropriate translation of the Greek *timē* would be 'status' and/or 'prestige' rather than the unqualified 'honour'; judging by Aristotle's argument of the superiority of virtue (*aretē*) over honour (*timē*) because the latter 'is thought to depend on those who bestow honour rather than on him who receives it,'

the same was also true of the classical Greek concept of *timē*" (Margalit Finkelberg, "Timē and Aretē in Homer," *Classical Quarterly* 48 [1998]: 15–28, at 16).

17 The classic essay is Leo Spitzer, "Soy quien soy," *Nueva revista de filología hispánica* 1.2 (1947): 113–27. See also Stephen Gilman, "The Death of Lazarillo de Tormes," *PMLA* 81.3 (1966): 149–66. As Gilman notes, in the picaresque classic, "[t]he 'soy quien soy' of the hero-braggarts of the 'comedia' seems to have been combined with the autobiographical complacency of an Alonso de Contreras or a Pedro de Baeza" (149). Thus we see that the phrase is important for all of Golden Age Spanish literature, not just the genre of the *comedias*.

18 Spitzer, "Soy quien soy," 113.

19 Exodus 3:14.

20 See note 5 of the Introduction to the present volume.

21 Cervantes, *El ingenioso hidalgo don Quijote de la Mancha*, ed. Luis Andrés Murillo, 2 vols (Madrid: Castalia, 1987), part I, chapter 35, 1:437–46.

22 Once again I would reference such valuable projects as DICAT, ARTELOPE, Out of the Wings, and Manos Teatrales (described in note 3 of the Foreword to this volume and also cited in the Bibliography).

23 For a creative, retroactive attempt to piece together a theory for what Cervantes so clearly accomplished in practice, see Stephen Gilman, *The Novel according to Cervantes* (Berkeley: University of California Press, 1989).

24 The classic one is Joseph E. Gillet, "The Autonomous Character in Spanish and European Literature," *Hispanic Review* 24.3 (1956): 179–90.

25 For example, John Shotter, "The Social Construction of Subjectivity: Can It Be Theorized?" review of Julian Henriques, Wendy Holloway, Cathy Urwin, Couze Venn, and Valerie Walkerdine, *Changing the Subject: Psychology, Social Regulation and Subjectivity* (London: Routledge, 1998), in *Contemporary Psychology* 44 (1999): 482–3.

26 See Hilaire Kallendorf, "Intertextual Madness in *Hamlet*: The Ghost's Fragmented Performativity," *Renaissance and Reformation / Renaissance et Réforme* 22.4 (1998): 69–87. The metatextual stripper is first referenced in the spoofish title of a fictional academic paper, "Textuality as Striptease." It is explained further in application to the genre of romance: "the idea of romance as narrative striptease, the endless leading on of the reader, a repeated postponement of an ultimate revelation which never comes" (David Lodge, *Small World: An Academic Romance* [New York: Macmillan, 1984], 20, 29).

27 See once again my Introduction to the present volume, note 5.

28 The proposed title for the volume is *Ateísmo, herejía y libertinaje en la España medieval y del Renacimiento* (to be published by Editorial Academia del Hispanismo). The call for contributions, circulated among Siglo de Oro specialists, also appears on the web at http://www.medievalismo.org/pdf/libertinos.pdf (accessed 4 May 2010).

29 I reference Maravall, *Teatro y literatura en la sociedad barroca*, which was first published three years before Franco's death.

Epilogue: To Avoid Reductionism

1 Calderón, *El día mayor de los días,* auto sacramental.

2 The book series, published jointly by Oxford University Press and the New York Public Library in 2003, originated with a series of public lectures delivered at the Library in 2002 and 2003 by seven famous writers, scholars, and critics who were asked to offer a meditation on temptation in relation to one each of the Seven Deadly Sins. The movie *Se7en* was written by Andrew Kevin Walker and directed by David Fincher (New Line Cinema, 1995). In this same vein, see the recent popular book by Aviad Kleinberg, *7 Deadly Sins: A Very Partial List,* trans. Susan Emanuel (Cambridge: Harvard University Press, 2008).

3 See Margaret R. Greer, "Spanish Golden Age Tragedy: From Cervantes to Calderón," in *A Companion to Tragedy,* ed. Rebecca Bushnell (Oxford: Blackwell, 2005). Professor Greer is preparing a monograph on early modern Spanish tragedy.

4 The striking exception to this trend is Melveena McKendrick, *Playing the King: Lope de Vega and the Limits of Conformity* (London: Tamesis, 2000).

5 Elena del Río Parra, *Cartografías de la conciencia española en la Edad de Oro* (Mexico City: Fondo de Cultura Económica, 2008), 149.

6 I refer to *El animal profeta y dichoso parricida San Julián.* There is debate about whether the play was written by Antonio Mira de Amescua or Lope de Vega. The parricide is unintentional (a young man returns home to find his parents in his bed and kills them on the assumption that they are his wife and her lover). The protagonist later goes on to found a hospital and become a saint, after going on a pilgrimage to Rome to ask for absolution from the pope.

7 In this play, incest is avoided when the brother flees, but such dilemmas are not always resolved in this way. On poetic justification for illegitimate loves in Lope's drama, see Pierre Dupont, "La justification poétique des amours illégitimes dans le théâtre de Lope de Vega," in *Amours légitimes, amours illégitimes en Espagne (XVIe–XVIIe siècles)* (Colloque International, Sorbonne, 3, 4, 5 octobre 1984), ed. Augustin Redondo (Paris: Sorbonne, 1985), 341–56.

Bibliography

Primary Dramatic Sources (*Comedias*)

All *comedias* cited are from the Teatro Español del Siglo de Oro database, distributed by ProQuest: http://teso.chadwyck.com. For plot summaries of many of these plays, see David Castillejo, *Guía de ochocientas comedias del Siglo de Oro* (Madrid: Ars Millenii, 2002). For a complete list of plays cited in this book, see the Index of *Comedias* (p. 387).

General Bibliography

Abraham, James T. "The Other Speaks: Tirso de Molina's *Amazonas en las Indias*." In *El arte nuevo de estudiar comedias: Literary Theory and Spanish Golden Age Drama,* ed. Barbara Simerka. Lewisburg: Bucknell University Press, 1996.

Ackerman, Jane. "John of the Cross, the Difficult Icon." In *A New Companion to Hispanic Mysticism*, ed. Hilaire Kallendorf, 149–74. Leiden: Brill, 2010. http://dx.doi .org/10.1163/ej .9789004183506.i-518.39.

Adkins, Arthur W.H. "'Honour' and 'Punishment' in the Homeric Poems." *Bulletin of the Institute of Classical Studies* 7.1 (2010): 23–32. http://dx.doi.org/10.1111/j.2041-5370.1960.tb00632.x.

Adler, Cyrus, W. Max Muller, and Louis Ginzberg. "Beard." *Jewish Encyclopedia*. http://www.jewish-encyclopedia.com.

Admirables prodigios y portentos que se manifestaron en Bayona. Barcelona: Lorenço Déu, 1613.

Agamben, Giorgio. *Il Regno e la Gloria: Per una genealogia teologica dell'economia e del governo* (*Homo sacer*, II, 2). Vicenza: Neri Pozza, 2007.

Alciato, Andrea. *Emblematum liber*. Paris: Christian Wechel, 1534.

Alden, Dauril. "The Ransoming of White Slaves from the Magreb: The Roles of Missionaries, Merchants, and Renegades, 16th to 18th Centuries." Paper presented at the Society for Spanish and Portuguese Historical Studies, 37th annual meeting, University of Kentucky, 6–9 April 2006.

Alfieri, F. *Nella camera degli sposi: Tomás Sánchez, il matrimonio, la sessualità (secoli XVI–XVII)*. Bologna: Il Mulino, 2010.

Althusser, Louis. "Ideología y aparatos ideológicos de estado." In *Ideología: un mapa de la cuestión*, ed. Slavoj Žižek, 115–56. Mexico City: Fondo de Cultura Económica, 2004.

Alva, Bartholomé de. *Confesionario mayor, y menor*. Mexico: Francisco Salbago por Pedro de Quiñones, 1634.

Alvar-Ezquerra, Alfredo. "Comer y 'ser' en la corte del Rey Católico." In *Materia crítica: formas de ocio y de consumo en la cultura áurea*, ed. Enrique García Santo-Tomás, 295–320. Madrid/Frankfurt: Iberoamericana/Vervuert, 2009.

Álvarez, Miguel. "El probabilismo y el teatro español del siglo XVII." PhD dissertation, New York University, 1982.

Álvarez, Tomás. "Santa Teresa de Ávila en el drama de los judeo-conversos castellanos." In *Judíos, sefarditas, conversos: la expulsión de 1492 y sus consecuencias*, ed. Ángel Alcalá, 609–30. Valladolid: Ámbito, 1995.

El animal profeta y dichoso parricida San Julián (1631). Attributed to both Antonio Mira de Amescua and Lope de Vega. In Lope de Vega, *Obras*. Vol. 10, *Comedias de Vidas de Santos*, ed. Marcelino Menéndez Pelayo, 179–224. Biblioteca de Autores Españoles, vol. 178. Madrid: Atlas, 1965.

Antonucci, Fausta. "El indio americano y la conquista de América en las comedias impresas de tema araucano (1616–1665)." In *Relaciones literarias entre España y América en los siglos XVI y XVII*, ed. Ysla Campbell, 21–46. Ciudad Juárez (Mexico): Universidad Autónoma de Ciudad Juárez, 1992.

Arana, Tomás de. "Relación de los estragos y ruinas que ha padecido la ciudad de Santiago de Guatemala por los terremotos ... en este año de 1717." In *Terremotos: ruina de San Miguel, 29 de septiembre de 1717; Santa Marta, 29 de julio de 1773*. Guatemala City: José de Pineda Ibarra, 1980.

Arbel, Benjamin. "Jewish Shipowners in the Early Modern Eastern Mediterranean." In *Trading Nations: Jews and Venetians in the Early Modern Eastern Mediterranean*, 169–84. Leiden: Brill, 1995.

Arellano, Ignacio. *Historia del teatro español del siglo XVII*. 4th ed. Madrid: Cátedra, 2008.

Ariès, Phillippe, and Georges Duby, eds. *History of Private Life*. Book series. Cambridge, MA: Harvard University Press, 1992–present.

Aristotle. *Rhetoric*. Trans. W. Rhys Roberts. New York: Modern Library, 1954.

Armstrong-Roche, Michael. *Cervantes' Epic Novel: Empire, Religion, and the Dream Life of Heroes in* Persiles. Toronto: University of Toronto Press, 2009.

ARTELOPE. Base de Datos y Argumentos del teatro de Lope de Vega (Universitat de València). Digital database. http://artelope.uv.es/.

Artiles, Jenaro. "Bibliografía sobre el problema del honor y la honra en el drama español." In *Filología y crítica hispánica: homenaje al Profesor Federico Sánchez Escribano*, ed. Alberto Porqueras-Mayo and Carlos Rojas, 235–41. Madrid: Alcalá, 1969.

La aventura humana en el Mediterráneo. Virtual exhibit sponsored by Spain's Ministry of Culture. http://www.mcu.es/archivos/CE/ExpoVisitVirtual/mediterraneo/. Consulted 22 June 2010.

Baker, Edward. "Breaking the Frame: Don Quixote's Entertaining Books." *Cervantes* 16.1 (1996): 12–31.

Bances Candamo, Francisco (1662–1704). *Theatro de los theatros de los passados y presentes siglos*, ed. Duncan W. Moir. London: Tamesis, 1970.

Bandello, Matteo. *Novelle* (1554). Part I, novella 26: "Il signor Antonio Bologna sposa la duchessa d'Amalfi, e tutti due sono ammazzati." In *Raccolta di novellieri italiani: novelle di Matteo Bandello*, vol. 1, 285–94. Turin: Cugini Pomba, 1853.

Barahona, Renato. "Courtship, Seduction and Abandonment in Early Modern Spain: The Example of Vizcaya, 1500–1700." In *Sex and Love in Golden Age Spain*, ed. Alain Saint-Saëns, 43–55. New Orleans: University Press of the South, 1996.

Barasch, Frances K. "Definitions: Renaissance and Baroque, Grotesque Construction and Deconstruction." *Modern Language Studies* 13.2 (1983): 60–7. http://dx.doi.org/10.2307/3194488.

Barber, Richard W., and Juliet R.V. Barker. *Tournaments: Jousts, Chivalry and Pageants in the Middle Ages*. New York: Weidenfeld & Nicolson, 1989.

Bass, Laura R. *The Drama of the Portrait: Theater and Visual Culture in Early Modern Spain*. University Park: Pennsylvania State University Press, 2008.

Bast, Robert James. *Honor Your Fathers: Catechisms and the Emergence of a Patriarchal Ideology in Germany, 1400–1600*. Leiden: Brill, 1997.

Bataillon, Marcel. *Erasme et l'Espagne*. Trans. Antonio Alatorre as *Erasmo y España: estudios sobre la historia espiritual del siglo XVI*. 2 vols. Mexico City: Fondo de Cultura Económica, 1950.

Beall, J.C., and Michael Glanzberg. "The Liar Paradox." *Stanford Encyclopedia of Philosophy*. Ed. Edward N. Zalta. Stanford: Stanford University, 2010. http://plato.stanford.edu.

Benassar, Bartolomé, and Lucile Benassar. *Los cristianos de Alá: la fascinante aventura de los renegados*. Madrid: Nerea, 1989.

Benbassa, Esther, and Aron Rodrigue. *Sephardi Jewry: A History of the Judeo-Spanish Community, 14th–20th Centuries*. Berkeley: University of California Press, 2000.

Beni, Paolo. *In Aristotelis poeticam commentarii*. Padua: F. Bolzettam, 1613.

Bentham, J. *Plan of the Panopticon* (1843). Figure 3 in *Discipline and Punish: The Birth of the Prison*, by Michel Foucault. Trans. Alan Sheridan. New York: Vintage, 1995.

Bermejo Cabrero, José Luis. "Duelos y desafíos en el derecho y en la literatura." In *Sexo barroco y otras transgresiones premodernas*, ed. Francisco Tomás y Valiente et al., 109–26. Madrid: Alianza Universidad, 1990.

– "Justicia penal y teatro barroco." In *Sexo barroco y otras transgresiones premodernas*, ed. Francisco Tomás y Valiente et al., 91–108. Madrid: Alianza Universidad, 1990.

Bernardini, Paolo, and Norman Fiering, eds. *The Jews and the Expansion of Europe to the West, 1400–1800*. Providence, RI: John Carter Brown Library, 2004.

Blair, Ann. "Humanist Methods in Natural Philosophy: The Commonplace Book." *Journal of the History of Ideas* 53.4 (1992): 541–51. http://dx.doi.org/10.2307/2709935.

Bloomfield, Morton W. *The Seven Deadly Sins: An Introduction to the History of a Religious Concept, with Special Reference to Medieval English Literature*. East Lansing: Michigan State University Press, 1952; reprint, 1967.

Bonifacio, Juan. *Tragicomedia de Nabal del Carmelo*. In *El Códice de Villagarcía del P. Juan Bonifacio: Teatro clásico del siglo XVI*, ed. Cayo González Gutiérrez, 347–406. Madrid: Universidad Nacional de Educación a Distancia, 2001.

Boroditsky, Leva. "How Language Shapes Thought." *Scientific American* 304.2 (2011): 62–5. http://dx.doi.org/10.1038/scientificamerican0211-62.

Bossy, John. "Moral Arithmetic: Seven Sins into Ten Commandments." In *Conscience and Casuistry in Early Modern Europe*, ed. Edmund Leites, 214–34. Cambridge: Cambridge University Press, 1988. http://dx.doi.org/10.1017/CBO9780511521430.008.

Boutry, Philippe, and Dominique Julia, eds. *Pèlerins et pèlerinages dans l'Europe moderne (Actes de la table ronde organisée para le Département d'histoire et civilisation de l'Institut universitaire européen de Florence et l'École française de Rome, Rome, 4–5 juin 1993)*. Rome: École Française, 2000.

Bradley, Peter T., and David Patrick Cahill, eds. *Habsburg Peru: Images, Imagination and Memory*. Liverpool: Liverpool University Press, 2000.

Bravo, Karen E. "Exploring the Analogy between Modern Trafficking in Humans and the Transatlantic Slave Trade." *Boston University International Law Journal* 25 (2007): 209–95.

Brook, Yaron. "The Morality of Moneylending: A Short History." *The Objective Standard: A Journal of Culture and Politics* 2.3 (2007): 9–45.

Brooks, David. "The Social Animal." Op-ed. *New York Times*. 12 September 2008. A23.

Brooks, Douglas, ed. *Printing and Parenting in Early Modern England*. Aldershot, England: Ashgate, 2005.

Calabi, Donatella. "The 'City of the Jews.'" In *The Jews of Early Modern Venice*, ed. Robert C. Davis and Benjamin Ravid, 31–52. Baltimore: Johns Hopkins University Press, 2001.

Camamis, George. "El sentido religioso del cautiverio." In *Estudios sobre el cautiverio en el Siglo de Oro*, 109–13. Madrid: Gredos, 1977.

Campbell, Jodi. *Monarchy, Political Culture, and Drama in Seventeenth-Century Madrid: Theater of Negotiation*. Aldershot: Ashgate, 2006.

Campbell, Ysla. "Nostalgia y transgresión en tres comedias de Lope de Vega." In *Relaciones literarias entre España y América en los siglos XVI y XVII*, ed. Ysla Campbell, 65–87. Ciudad Juárez (Mexico): Universidad Autónoma de Ciudad Juárez, 1992.

Cañadas, Ivan. "The Nation in History: Decline, Circularity and *Desengaño* in the Poetry of Fray Luis de León and Francisco de Quevedo." *Ianua: revista philologica romanica* 8 (2008): 203–23.

Caro, Rodrigo. *Días geniales o lúdicros (ms. ca. 1626)*. Ed. J.-P. Étienvre. Madrid: Espasa-Calpe, 1978.

Caro Baroja, Julio. "Probabilidades, laxitudes y corrupciones." In *Las formas complejas de la vida religiosa: Religión, sociedad y carácter en la España de los siglos XVI y XVII*, 517–50. Madrid: Akal, 1978.

Carrasco, Rafael. *Inquisición y represión sexual en Valencia: historia de los sodomitas (1565–1785)*. Barcelona: Laertes, 1985.

– "Lazarillo on a Street Corner: What the Picaresque Novel Did Not Say about Fallen Boys." In *Sex and Love in Golden Age Spain*, ed. Alain Saint-Saëns, 57–69. New Orleans: University Press of the South, 1996.

Carrión, María M. *Subject Stages: Marriage, Theatre, and the Law in Early Modern Spain*. Toronto: University of Toronto Press, 2010.

Cartagena Calderón, José Reinaldo. *Masculinidades en obras: el drama de la hombría en la España imperial*. Newark, DE: Juan de la Cuesta, 2008.

Casagrande, Carla, and Silvana Vecchio. "La classificazione dei peccati tra settenario e decalogo (secoli XIII–XV)." *Documenti e studi sulla tradizione filosofica medievale* 5 (1994): 331–95.

Cascardi, Anthony J. "Allegories of Power." In *The Prince in the Tower: Perceptions of* La vida es sueño, ed. Frederick A. de Armas, 15–26. Lewisburg: Bucknell University Press, 1993.

– "Beyond Castro and Maravall: Interpellation, Mimesis, and the Hegemony of Spanish Culture." In *Ideologies of Hispanism*, ed. Mabel Moraña, 138–59. Nashville: Vanderbilt University Press, 2005.

– "The Subject of Control." In *Culture and Control in Counter-Reformation Spain*, ed. Anne J. Cruz and Mary Elizabeth Perry, 231–54. Minneapolis: University of Minnesota Press, 1992.

Case, Thomas E. "El indio y el moro en las comedias de Lope de Vega." In *Looking at the* Comedia *in the Year of the Quincentennial*, ed. Barbara Mujica and Sharon D. Voros, 13–22. Lanham, MD: University Press of America, 1993.

Casey, James. *Early Modern Spain: A Social History*. London: Routledge, 1999.

Castillejo, David. *Guía de ochocientas comedias del Siglo de Oro*. Madrid: Ars Millenii, 2002.

Castillo, David R. *(A)wry Views: Anamorphosis, Cervantes, and the Early Picaresque*. West Lafayette, IN: Purdue University Press, 2001.

The Catechism of the Council of Trent. Trans. John A. McHugh and Charles J. Callan. http://www.catholicprimer.org/trent/catechism_of_trent.pdf.

Certeau, Michel de. *Heterologies: Discourse on the Other*. Trans. Brian Massumi. Minneapolis: University of Minnesota Press, 1986.

Cervantes, Miguel de. In *El ingenioso hidalgo don Quijote de la Mancha* (1605 and 1615). 2 vols. Ed. Luis Andrés Murillo. Madrid: Castalia, 1987.

Chartier, Roger. "El tiempo que sobra: ocio y vida cotidiana en el mundo hispánico." *Historia, antropología y fuentes orales* 31 (2004): 99–112.

Chronicle of Colonial Lima: The Diary of Josephe and Francisco Mugaburu, 1640–1697. Trans. and ed. Robert Ryal Miller. Norman: University of Oklahoma Press, 1975.

Ciruelo, Pedro. *Arte de bien confesar*. Seville: Domenico de Robertis, 1548.

Clavero, Bartolomé. "Delito y pecado: noción y escala de transgresiones." In *Sexo barroco y otras transgresiones premodernas*, ed. Francisco Tomás y Valiente et al., 57–89. Madrid: Alianza Universidad, 1990.

– "*Favor Maioratus, Usus Hispaniae*: Moralidad de Linaje entre Castilla y Europa." In *Marriage, Property, and Succession*, ed. Lloyd Bonfield, 215–54. Berlin: Duncker and Humblot, 1992.

– *Usura: del uso económico de la religión en la historia*. Madrid: Tecnos / Fundación Cultural Enrique Luño Peña, 1984.

Coin and Conscience. Popular Views of Money, Credit, and Speculation, Sixteenth through Nineteenth Centuries. Catalog of an Exhibition of Prints from the Bleichroeder Collection, Kress Library of Business and Economics. Cambridge, MA: Baker Library / Harvard Business School, 1986.

Comba, Manuel. "A Note on Fashion and Atmosphere in the Time of Lope de Vega." *Theatre Annual* 19 (1962): 46–51.

Comenius, Johan Amos. *Orbis sensualium pictus*. Nuremberg: Michael Endter, 1658.

Corella, Jayme de. *Práctica de el confessionario*. Madrid: Antonio González de Reyes, 1696.

Council of Trent, proceedings. 24th session. Chapter 9 of *The Canons and Decrees of the Sacred and Oecumenical Council of Trent*. Trans. and ed. J. Waterworth, 192–232. London: Dolman, 1848.

Covarrubias Orozco, Sebastián de. *Tesoro de la lengua castellana o española* (1611). Ed. Felipe C.R. Maldonado. Rev. Manuel Camarero. Madrid: Castalia, 1995.

Crosley, David. *Samson a Type of Christ: In a Sermon Preached at Mr Pomfret's Meeting-House in Gravel-Lane near Hounds-Ditch, London: at the Morning-Lecture, on July 22, 1691*. London: for William Marshall, 1691.

Cruickshank, Don. *Don Pedro Calderón*. Cambridge: Cambridge University Press, 2009.

– "*El monstruo de los jardines* and the Segismundization of Clarín." In *The Prince in the Tower: Perceptions of* La vida es sueño, ed. Frederick A. de Armas, 65–78. Lewisburg: Bucknell University Press, 1993.

– "'Pongo mi mano en sangre bañada a la puerta': Adultery in *El médico de su honra*." In *Studies in Spanish Literature of the Golden Age Presented to E.M. Wilson*, ed. R.O. Jones, 45–62. London: Tamesis, 1973.

Cruz, Anne J. *Discourses of Poverty: Social Reform and the Picaresque Novel in Early Modern Spain*. Toronto: University of Toronto Press, 1999.

Dacome, Lucia. "Noting the Mind: Commonplace Books and the Pursuit of the Self in Eighteenth-Century Britain." *Journal of the History of Ideas* 65.4 (2004): 603–25. http://dx.doi.org/10.1353/jhi.2005.0013.

Davis, Natalie Zemon. *Fiction in the Archives: Pardon Tales and Their Tellers in Sixteenth-Century France*. Stanford: Stanford University Press, 1987.

Davis, Robert. "The Geography of Slaving in the Early Modern Mediterranean, 1500–1800." *Journal of Medieval and Early Modern Studies* 37.1 (2007): 57–74. http://dx.doi.org/10.1215/10829636-2006-010.

De Backer, Stephanie Fink. *Widowhood in Early Modern Spain: Protectors, Proprietors, and Patrons*. Leiden: Brill, 2010.

Debus, Allen G. *Man and Nature in the Renaissance*. Cambridge: Cambridge University Press, 1978.

Delgado, Manuel. "Antonio Mira de Amescua (1574–1644)." In *Spanish Dramatists of the Golden Age: A Bio-Bibliographical Sourcebook*, ed. Mary Parker, 107–23. Westport: Greenwood, 1998.

Delgado, Sandra. "La función de los pecados capitales en los autos sacramentales de Calderón de la Barca." PhD dissertation, University of Illinois at Urbana-Champaign. 1993.

Del Río Parra, Elena. *Cartografías de la conciencia española en la Edad de Oro*. Mexico City: Fondo de Cultura Económica, 2008.

– *Una era de monstruos: representaciones de lo deforme en el Siglo de Oro español*. Madrid/Frankfurt: Iberoamericana/Vervuert, 2003.

– "*Suspensio animi*, or the Interweaving of Mysticism and Artistic Creation." In *A New Companion to Hispanic Mysticism*, ed. Hilaire Kallendorf, 391–410. Leiden: Brill, 2010. http://dx.doi.org/10.1163/ej.9789004183506.i-518.83.

Derrida, Jacques. *Of Grammatology*. Trans. Gayatri Chakravorty Spivak. Baltimore: Johns Hopkins University Press, 1997.

– *Positions*. Trans. Alan Bass. Chicago: University of Chicago Press, 1981.

Díaz Balsera, Paloma. *Sephardim: The Jews from Spain*. Chicago: University of Chicago Press, 1992.

Díaz Balsera, Viviana. "Auracanian Alterity in Alonso de Ercilla and Lope de Vega." In *Looking at the* Comedia *in the Year of the Quincentennial*, ed. Barbara Mujica and Sharon D. Voros, 23–36. Lanham: University Press of America, 1993.

Díaz-Plaja, Fernando. *El español y los siete pecados capitales*. Madrid: Alianza, 1980. Trans. John Inderwick Palmer as *The Spaniard and the Seven Deadly Sins*. New York: Charles Scribner's Sons, 1967.

Di Camillo, Ottavio. "Interpretations of the Renaissance in Spanish Historical Thought: The Last Thirty Years." *Renaissance Quarterly* 49.2 (1996): 360–83. http://dx.doi.org/10.2307/2863162.

Dietz, Donald T. "England's and Spain's Corpus Christi Theaters." In *Parallel Lives: Spanish and English National Drama, 1580–1680*, ed. Louise and Peter Fothergill-Payne, 239–51. Lewisburg: Bucknell University Press, 1991.

DiPuccio, Denise M. *Communicating Myths of the Golden Age* Comedia. Lewisburg: Bucknell University Press, 1998.

Ditchfield, Simon. "Introduction" to *Christianity and Community in the West: Essays for John Bossy*, xv–xxix. Aldershot: Ashgate, 2001.

Donnell, Sidney. *Feminizing the Enemy: Imperial Spain, Transvestite Drama, and the Crisis of Masculinity*. Lewisburg: Bucknell University Press, 2003.

Dopico Black, Georgina. *Perfect Wives, Other Women: Adultery and Inquisition in Early Modern Spain*. Durham: Duke University Press, 2001.

Dupont, Pierre. "La justification poétique des amours illégitimes dans le théâtre de Lope de Vega." In *Amours légitimes, amours illégitimes en Espagne (XVIe–XVIIe siècles)*. Colloque International, Sorbonne, 3, 4, 5 octobre 1984. Ed. Augustin Redondo, 341–56. Paris: Sorbonne, 1985.

Edwards, Jonathan. *Sinners in the Hands of an Angry God (1741)*. Murfreesboro: Sword of the Lord Publishers, 2000.

Egginton, William. *How the World Became a Stage: Presence, Theatricality, and the Question of Modernity*. Albany: State University of New York Press, 2003.

Egido, Teófanes. *El linaje judeoconverso de Santa Teresa: pleito de hidalguía de los Cepeda*. Madrid: Editorial de Espiritualidad, 1986.

Ehlers, Benjamin. *Between Christians and Moriscos: Juan de Ribera and Religious Reform in Valencia, 1568–1614*. Baltimore: Johns Hopkins University Press, 2006.

Elias, Norbert. *Power and Civility: The Civilizing Process*. Vol. 2. Trans. Edmund Jephcott. New York: Pantheon, 1982.

Elliott, J.H. *The Count-Duke of Olivares: The Statesman in an Age of Decline*. New Haven/London: Yale University Press, 1988.

– *Imperial Spain: 1469–1716*. London: Penguin, 1990.

– *Spain and Its World, 1500–1700*. New Haven: Yale University Press, 1989.

El Saffar, Ruth. *Beyond Fiction: The Recovery of the Feminine in the Works of Cervantes*. Berkeley: University of California Press, 1983.

Ettinghausen, Henry, ed. *Noticias del siglo XVII: relaciones españolas de sucesos naturales y sobrenaturales*. Barcelona: Puvill, 1995.

Evagrius of Pontus. *The Greek Ascetic Corpus*. Trans. Robert E. Sinkewicz. Oxford: Oxford University Press, 2003.

Felipe de la Cruz. *Norte de confesores y penitentes*. Valladolid: Jeronimo Morillo [for] Juan Piñat, 1629.

Fernández Álvarez, M. "El *Diario de un estudiante*." In *La sociedad española en el Siglo de Oro*. Volume 2, 818–46. Madrid: Gredos, 1989.

Ferrer Valls, Teresa. *Diccionario biográfico de actores del teatro clásico (DICAT)*. Kassel: Reichenberger, 2008.

Finkelberg, Margalit. "Timē and Aretē in Homer." *Classical Quarterly* 48.1 (1998): 15–28. http://dx.doi.org/10.1093/cq/48.1.14.

Flynn, Maureen. "Blasphemy and the Play of Anger in Sixteenth-Century Spain." *Past and Present* 149.1 (1995): 29–56. http://dx.doi.org/10.1093/past/149.1.29.

– "Charitable Ritual in Late Medieval and Early Modern Spain." *Sixteenth Century Journal* 16.3 (1985): 335–48. http://dx.doi.org/10.2307/2540221.

– "'Taming Anger's Daughters': New Treatment for Emotional Problems in Renaissance Spain." *Renaissance Quarterly* 51.3 (1998): 864–86. http://dx.doi.org/10.2307/2901748.

Fontanella, Lee. "Imperial Superimpositions: Graphing Empire." Lecture, Texas A&M University, October 2009.

Forcione, Alban. *Cervantes and the Humanist Vision: A Study of Four Exemplary Novels*. Princeton: Princeton University Press, 1982.

– "El desposeimiento del ser en la literatura renacentista: Cervantes, Gracián y los desafíos de Nemo." *Nueva revista de filología hispánica* 34.2 (1985–6): 654–90.

– *Majesty and Humanity: Kings and Their Doubles in the Political Drama of the Spanish Golden Age*. New Haven: Yale University Press, 2009.

Foucault, Michel. *The Birth of Biopolitics: Lectures at the Collège de France, 1978–1979*. Ed. Michel Sennelart. Trans. Graham Burchell. New York: Palgrave Macmillan, 2010.

– "Panopticism." In *Discipline and Punish: The Birth of the Prison*. Trans. Alan Sheridan, 195–308. New York: Vintage, 1995.

Fracchia, Carmen. "(Lack of) Visual Representation of Black Slaves in Spanish Golden Age Painting." *Journal of Iberian and Latin American Studies* 10.1 (2004): 23–34. http://dx.doi.org/10.1080/1470184042000236251.

Frey, R.G. "Did Socrates Commit Suicide?" *Philosophy* 53.203 (1978): 106–8. http://dx.doi.org/10.1017/S0031819100016375.

Friedman, Edward H. "Deference, *Différance*: The Rhetoric of Deferral." In *The Prince in the Tower: Perceptions of* La vida es sueño, ed. Frederick A. de Armas, 41–53. Lewisburg: Bucknell University Press, 1993.

– "Picaresque Sensibility and the *Comedia*." In *A Companion to Early Modern Hispanic Theater*, ed. Hilaire Kallendorf. Leiden: Brill. Forthcoming.

Friedman, Ellen G. *Spanish Captives in North Africa in the Early Modern Age*. Madison: University of Wisconsin Press, 1983.

Friedman, Saul S. "Marranos and New Christians: Jews as Traders in the Hispanic World." In *Jews and the American Slave Trade*. New Brunswick: Transaction, 2000.

Fuchs, Barbara. *Exotic Nation: Maurophilia and the Construction of Early Modern Spain*. Philadelphia: University of Pennsylvania Press, 2009.

– *Mimesis and Empire: The New World, Islam, and European Identities*. Cambridge: Cambridge University Press, 2004.

– *Passing for Spain: Cervantes and the Fictions of Identity*. Urbana: University of Illinois Press, 2003.

Gabler, Neal. "Why We Can't Look Away: Understanding Our Craven Celebrity Culture." *Newsweek*, 21 December 2009, 62–7.

Gacto, Enrique. "El delito de bigamia y la Inquisición española." In *Sexo barroco y otras transgresiones premodernas*, ed. Francisco Tomás y Valiente et al., 127–52. Madrid: Alianza Universidad, 1990.

Garcés, María Antonia. *Cervantes in Algiers: A Captive's Tale*. Nashville: Vanderbilt University Press, 2005.

García Arenal, Mercedes, and Miguel Ángel de Bunes. *Los españoles y el Norte de África: siglos XV-XVIII*. Madrid: Mapfre, 1992.

García Pardo, Manuela. "La redención de cautivos: una muestra de la religiosidad popular medieval en Úbeda." In *V Estudios de Frontera: Funciones de la red castral fronteriza. Homenaje a Don Juan Torres Fontes (Congreso celebrado en Alcalá la Real en noviembre de 2003)*, ed. Francisco Toro Ceballos and José Rodríguez Molina, 275–87. Jaén: Diputación Provincial, 2004.

García Santo-Tomás, Enrique. *Materia crítica: formas de ocio y de consumo en la cultura áurea*. Madrid/Frankfurt: Iberoamericana/Vervuert, 2009.

Garza Carvajal, Federico. *Butterflies Will Burn: Prosecuting Sodomites in Early Modern Spain and Mexico*. Austin: University of Texas Press, 2003.

Gauchet, Marcel. *The Disenchantment of the World: A Political History of Religion*. Trans. Oscar Burge. Princeton: Princeton University Press, 1997.

Gilbert, Françoise. "Sobre 'La torre de Babilonia,' auto sacramental de Calderón de la Barca." *Criticón* 103–4 (2008): 331–41.

Giles, Ryan. *The Laughter of the Saints: Parodies of Holiness in Late Medieval and Renaissance Spain*. Toronto: University of Toronto Press, 2009.

Gill, Christopher, and T.P. Wiseman, eds. *Lies and Fiction in the Ancient World*. Exeter: University of Exeter Press, 1993.

Gillet, Joseph. "The Autonomous Character in Spanish and European Literature." *Hispanic Review* 24.3 (1956): 179–90. http://dx.doi.org/10.2307/470514.

– "Cueva's *Comedia del Infamador* and the Don Juan Legend." *Modern Language Notes* 37.4 (1922): 206–12. http://dx.doi.org/10.2307/2914667.

Gilman, Stephen. "The Death of Lazarillo de Tormes." *PMLA* 81.3 (1966): 149–66. http://dx.doi.org/10.2307/460799.

– *The Novel According to Cervantes*. Berkeley: University of California Press, 1989.

Girard, René. *The Scapegoat*. Trans. Yvonne Freccero. Baltimore: Johns Hopkins University Press, 1986.

Gómez Carrillo, Agustín. "Ruina de Santa Marta (29 de julio de 1773)." In *Terremotos: ruina de San Miguel, 29 de septiembre de 1717; Santa Marta, 29 de julio de 1773*. Guatemala City: José de Pineda Ibarra, 1980.

González-Ruiz, Julio. *Amistades peligrosas: el discurso homoerótico en el teatro de Lope de Vega*. New York: Peter Lang, 2009.

Gonzálvez Ruiz, Ramón. "Dos bulas para la redención de cautivos." Capítulo VII of *Las bulas de la catedral de Toledo y la imprenta incunable*. Special issue of *Toletum: Boletín de la Real Academia de Bellas Artes y Ciencias Históricas de Toledo* 18, 2nd series (1985): 80–100.

Gracián, Baltasar. *Agudeza y arte de ingenio* (1648). 2 vols. Ed. Evaristo Corréa Calderón. Madrid: Castalia, 1969.

Gracián de la Madre de Dios, Jerónimo (1545–1614). *Tratado de la redención de cautivos en que se cuentan las grandes miserias que padecen los cristianos que están en poder de infieles y cuán santa obra sea la de su rescate*, ed. Miguel Ángel de Bunes Ibarra and Beatriz Alonso Acero. Seville: Espuela de Plata, 2006.

Graizbord, David L. *Souls in Dispute: Converso Identities in Iberia and the Jewish Diaspora, 1580–1700*. Philadelphia: University of Pennsylvania Press, 2003.

Graullera, Vicente. "Mujer, amor y moralidad en la Valencia de los siglos XVI y XVII." In *Amours légitimes, amours illégitimes en Espagne (XVIe–XVIIe siècles)*. Colloque International, Sorbonne, 3, 4, 5 octobre 1984. Ed. Augustin Redondo, 109–20. Paris: Sorbonne, 1985.

Gray, Bennison. "The Semiotics of Taxonomy." *Semiotica* 22.1–2 (1998): 127–50.

Greenberg, David. *The Construction of Homosexuality*. Chicago: University of Chicago Press, 1988.

Greenblatt, Stephen. *Renaissance Self-Fashioning: From More to Shakespeare*. Chicago: University of Chicago Press, 1980.

– *Shakespearean Negotiations: The Circulation of Social Energy in Renaissance England*. Berkeley: University of California Press, 1988.

Greene, Robert A. "Instinct of Nature: Natural Law, Synderesis, and the Moral Sense." *Journal of the History of Ideas* 58.2 (1997): 173–98. http://dx.doi.org/10.1353/jhi.1997.0014.

Greer, Margaret Rich. "Constituting Community: A New Historical Perspective on the Autos of Calderón." In *New Historicism and the Comedia: Poetics, Politics and Praxis*, ed. José A. Madrigal, 41–68. Boulder: Society of Spanish and Spanish-American Studies, 1997.

– *The Play of Power: Mythological Court Dramas of Calderón de la Barca*. Princeton: Princeton University Press, 1991.

– "Spanish Golden Age Tragedy: From Cervantes to Calderón." In *A Companion to Tragedy*, ed. Rebecca Bushnell. Oxford: Blackwell, 2005. http://dx.doi.org/10.1002/9780470996393.ch21.

Grieve, Patricia E. *The Eve of Spain: Myths of Origins in the History of Christian, Muslim, and Jewish Conflict*. Baltimore: Johns Hopkins University Press, 2009.

Griffin, Eric J. *English Renaissance Drama and the Specter of Spain: Ethnopoetics and Empire*. Philadelphia: University of Pennsylvania Press, 2009.

Guarini, Giambattista. "*The Compendium of Tragicomic Poetry* (1599). Excerpts." In *Literary Criticism: Plato to Dryden*, trans. and ed. Allan H. Gilbert, 504–33. Detroit: Wayne State University Press, 1962.

Guerrero Mayllo, Ana. *Familia y vida cotidiana de una élite de poder: los regidores madrileños en tiempos de Felipe II*. Mexico City and Madrid: Siglo XXI, 1993.

Guevara, Antonio de. *Menosprecio de corte y alabanza de aldea* (1539). Ed. M. Martínez de Burgos. Madrid: Espasa-Calpe, 1952.

Gutiérrez Nieto, Juan Ignacio. "La discriminación de los conversos y la tibetización de Castilla por Felipe II." *Revista de la Universidad Complutense* 22.87 (1973): 99–129.

– "*Honra* y utilidad social: en torno a los conceptos de *honor y honra*." In *Calderón: Actas del Congreso Internacional sobre Calderón y el teatro español del Siglo de Oro*, ed. Luciano García Lorenzo, 881–95. Madrid: Consejo Superior de Investigaciones Científicas, 1983.

Haitin, M.M. "Late Colonial Lima: Economy and Society in an Era of Reform and Revolution." PhD dissertation, University of California at Berkeley, 1983.

Haliczer, Stephen H. "Sexuality and Repression in Counter-Reformation Spain." In *Sex and Love in Golden Age Spain*, ed. Alain Saint-Saëns, 81–93. New Orleans: University Press of the South, 1996.

Hamilton, Earl J. "Importaciones de oro y plata americanos." In *El tesoro americano y la revolución de los precios en España, 1501–1650*, 23–59. Barcelona: Ariel, 1975.

Hammer, Paul E.J., ed. *Warfare in Early Modern Europe 1450–1660*. Aldershot: Ashgate, 2007.

Hanke, Lewis. *All Mankind Is One: A Study of the Disputation between Bartolomé de las Casas and Juan Ginés de Sepúlveda in 1550 on the Intellectual and Religious Capacity of the American Indians*. DeKalb: Northern Illinois University Press, 1974.

Harris, Jonathan Gil. "Properties of Skill: Product Placement in Early English Artisanal Drama." In *Staged Properties in Early Modern English Drama*, ed. Jonathan Gil Harris and Natasha Korda, 35–66. Cambridge: Cambridge University Press, 2006.

Harris, William V. *Restraining Rage: The Ideology of Anger Control in Classical Antiquity*. Cambridge: Harvard University Press, 2004.

Hathaway, Baxter. *The Age of Criticism: The Late Renaissance in Italy*. Ithaca: Cornell University Press, 1962.

Haverbeck Ojeda, N. Erwin. "La comedia mitológica calderoniana: soberbia y castigo." *Revista de filología española* 56 (1973): 67–93.

Hay, Denys. "The Division of the Spoils of War in Fourteenth-Century England." *Transactions of the Royal Historical Society* 4, 5th series (1954): 91–109.

Heble, Ajay. "Trace." In *Encyclopedia of Contemporary Literary Theory*, ed. Irena R. Makaryk. Toronto: University of Toronto Press, 1997.

Heiple, Daniel L. "The Theological Context of Wife Murder in Seventeenth-Century Spain." In *Sex and Love in Golden Age Spain*, ed. Alain Saint-Saëns, 105–21. New Orleans: University Press of the South, 1996.

Hemfelt, Robert, Frank Minirth, and Paul Meier. *Love Is a Choice: The Definitive Book on Letting Go of Unhealthy Relationships*. Nashville: Thomas Nelson, 2003.

Hiltpold, Paul. "Noble Status and Urban Privilege: Burgos, 1572." *Sixteenth Century Journal* 12.4 (1981): 21–44. http://dx.doi.org/10.2307/2539877.

Hincapié Meléndez, Cristóbal de. "Breve relación del fuego, temblores y ruina de la … ciudad de los Caballeros de Santiago de Guatemala, año de 1717." In *Terremotos: ruina de San Miguel, 29 de septiembre de 1717; Santa Marta, 29 de julio de 1773*. Guatemala City: José de Pineda Ibarra, 1980.

The Holy Bible, Translated from the Latin Vulgate. Edited by Richard Challoner. New York: Douay Bible House, 1941.

Homza, Lu Ann. *Religious Authority in the Spanish Renaissance*. Baltimore: Johns Hopkins University Press, 2000.

– Review of Scott Taylor, *Honor and Violence in Golden Age Spain*. *Journal of Modern History* 82 (2010): 488–90. http://dx.doi.org/10.1086/651648.

Horowitz, Elliott. "The Early Eighteenth Century Confronts the Beard: Kabbalah and Jewish Self-Fashioning." *Jewish History* 8.1–2 (1994): 95–115.

Huntley, Frank. "*Macbeth* and the Background of Jesuitical Equivocation." *PMLA* 79.4 (1964): 390–400. http://dx.doi.org/10.2307/460744.

Hutchinson, Steven. "Journeys across Culture and Religion: 'Renegades' in the Early Modern Mediterranean." Lecture delivered at the Melbern G. Glasscock Humanities Research Center, Texas A&M University. Spring 2009.

Iffland, James. *Quevedo and the Grotesque*. 2 vols. London: Tamesis, 1983.

Iñiguez Almech, Francisco. "La Casa Real de la Panedería." *Revista de la Biblioteca, Archivo y Museo de Madrid* 16.56 (1948): 129–55.

Iser, Wolfgang. *The Act of Reading: A Theory of Aesthetic Response*. Baltimore: Johns Hopkins University Press, 1980.

Ishikawa, Chiyo. "*La llave de palo*: Isabel la Católica as Patron of Religious Literature and Painting." In *Isabel la Católica, Queen of Castile: Critical Essays*, ed. David A. Boruchoff, 103–54. New York: Palgrave Macmillan, 2003.

Jacobs, Dale, and Laura R. Micciche. *A Way to Move: Rhetorics of Emotion and Composition Studies*. Portsmouth, NH: Boynton/Cook, 2003.

Jauss, Hans Robert. *Toward an Aesthetic of Reception*. Trans. Timothy Bahti. Introduction by Paul de Man. Minneapolis: University of Minnesota Press, 1982.

Johnston, Patricia. "Piety in Vergil and Philodemus." In *Vergil, Philodemus, and the Augustans*, ed. David Armstrong. Austin: University of Texas Press, 2004.

Joly, Monique. "Du remariage des veuves: à propos d'un étrange épisode du 'Guzmán.'" In *Amours légitimes, amours illégitimes en Espagne (XVIe–XVIIe siècles)*. Colloque International, Sorbonne, 3, 4, 5 octobre 1984. Ed. Augustin Redondo, 327–40. Paris: Sorbonne, 1985.

Jones, Ann Rosalind, and Peter Stallybrass. *Renaissance Clothing and the Materials of Memory*. Cambridge: Cambridge University Press, 2000.

Jones, C.A. "Honor in Spanish Golden-Age Drama: Its Relation to Real Life and to Morals." *Bulletin of Hispanic Studies* 35.4 (1958): 199–210. http://dx.doi.org/10.1080/1475382582000335199.

Kahn, Victoria. *Machiavellian Rhetoric: From the Counter-Reformation to Milton*. Princeton: Princeton University Press, 1994.

Kallendorf, Craig. "Commentaries, Commonplaces, and Neo-Latin Studies." In *Acta Conventus Neo-Latini Uppsalensis: Proceedings of the Fourteenth International Congress of Neo-Latin Studies*, ed. A. Steiner-Weber et al. Leiden: Brill, 2012. 1:535–46.

– *The Other Virgil: Pessimistic Readings of the* Aeneid *in Early Modern Culture*. Oxford: Oxford University Press, 2007.

– "Philology, the Reader and the *Nachleben* of Classical Texts." *Modern Philology* 92.2 (1994): 137–56. http://dx.doi.org/10.1086/392229.

– "Representing the Other: Ercilla's *La Araucana*, Virgil's *Aeneid*, and the New World Encounter." *Comparative Literature Studies* 40.4 (2003): 394–414. http://dx.doi.org/10.1353/cls.2003.0031.

Kallendorf, Hilaire. "*Celestina* in Venice: Piety, Pornography, *Poligrafi*." *Celestinesca* 27 (2003): 75–106.

– *Conscience on Stage: The* Comedia *as Casuistry in Early Modern Spain*. Toronto: University of Toronto Press, 2007.

– "Dressed to the Sevens, or Sin in Style: Fashion Statements by the Deadly Vices in Spanish Baroque *Autos Sacramentales*." In *The Seven Deadly Sins: From Communities to Individuals*, ed. Richard Newhauser, 145–82. Leiden: Brill, 2007. http://dx.doi.org/10.1163/ej.9789004157859.i-312.31.

– *Exorcism and Its Texts: Subjectivity in Early Modern Literature of England and Spain*. Toronto: University of Toronto Press, 2003.

– "Intertextual Madness in *Hamlet*: The Ghost's Fragmented Performativity." *Renaissance and Reformation / Renaissance et Réforme* 22.4 (1998): 69–87.

– "Love Madness and Demonic Possession in Lope de Vega." *Romance Quarterly* 51.3 (2004): 162–82. http://dx.doi.org/10.3200/RQTR.51.3.162-82.

– "A Myth Rejected: The Noble Savage in Dominican Dystopia." *Journal of Latin American Studies* 27.02 (1995): 449–70. http://dx.doi.org/10.1017/S0022216X00010828.

– "¿Qué he de hacer?": The *Comedia* as Casuistry." *Romanic Review* 95.3 (2004): 327–59.

– Review of Elena del Río Parra, *Cartografías de la conciencia española en la Edad de Oro. Sixteenth Century Journal* 40.2 (2010): 560–2.

– "Tears in the Desert: Baroque Adaptations of the Book of Lamentations by John Donne and Francisco de Quevedo." *Journal of Medieval and Early Modern Studies* 39.1 (2009): 31–42. http://dx.doi.org/10.1215/10829636-2008-012.

– "Why the Inquisition Dismantles the *Cabeza Encantada*." *Anuario Cervantino* 1 (2004): 149–63.

Kallendorf, Hilaire, and Craig Kallendorf. "Conversations with the Dead: Quevedo and Statius, Annotation and Imitation." *Journal of the Warburg and Courtauld Institutes* 63 (2000): 131–68. http://dx.doi.org/10.2307/751524.

Kamen, Henry. "La expulsión de los judíos y la decadencia de España." In *Judíos, sefarditas, conversos: la expulsión de 1492 y sus consecuencias (Ponencias del congreso internacional celebrado en Nueva York en noviembre de 1992)*, ed. Ángel Alcalá, 420–33. Valladolid: Ámbito, 1995.

Kantorowicz, Ernst. *The King's Two Bodies: A Study in Medieval Political Theology*. Princeton: Princeton University Press, 1981.

Kent, Bruce. *The Spoils of War: The Politics, Economics and Diplomacy of Reparations*. Oxford: Clarendon, 1989.

Kiernan, Victor Gordon. *The Duel in European History: Honour and the Reign of Aristocracy*. Oxford: Oxford University Press, 1988.

Kinkead, Duncan T. "Francisco de Herrera and the Development of the High Baroque Style in Seville." In *Painting in Spain 1650–1700: A Symposium*, special issue of the *Record of the Art Museum, Princeton University* 41.2 (1982): 12–23.

Kirschner, Teresa J. "Enmascaramiento y desenmascaramiento del discurso sobre el 'indio' en el teatro del 'Nuevo Mundo' de Lope de Vega." In *Relaciones literarias entre España y América en los siglos XVI y XVII*, ed. Ysla Campbell, 47–64. Ciudad Juárez (Mexico): Universidad Autónoma de Ciudad Juárez, 1992.

Kleinberg, Aviad. *7 Deadly Sins: A Very Partial List*. Trans. Susan Emanuel. Cambridge, MA: Harvard University Press, 2008.

Koningsveld, P.S. van. "Muslim Slaves and Captives in Western Europe during the Late Middle Ages." *Islam and Christian-Muslim Relations* 6.1 (1995): 5–23. http://dx.doi.org/10.1080/09596419508721039.

Kreitner, Kenneth. "Music in the Corpus Christi Procession of Fifteenth-Century Barcelona." *Early Music History* 14 (1995): 153–204. http://dx.doi.org/10.1017/S0261127900001467.

Kristeva, Julia. *Powers of Horror: An Essay on Abjection*. New York: Columbia University Press, 1982.

Kurtz, Barbara. "Illusions of Power: Calderón de la Barca, the Spanish Inquisition, and the Prohibition of *Las órdenes militares* (1662–1671)." *Revista canadiense de estudios hispánicos* 18.2 (1994): 189–217.

Lafuente, Modesto, and Juan Valera, et al. *Historia general de España*. Vol. 12. Barcelona: Montaner y Simón, 1889.

Las Casas, Bartolomé de. *Brevísima Relación de la Destruyción de las Indias*. Seville: Sebastian Trugillo, 1552.

Lauer, A. Robert. "Honor/Honora Revisited." In *A Companion to Early Modern Hispanic Theater*, ed. Hilaire Kallendorf. Leiden: Brill. Forthcoming.

Leach, Eleanor Winsor. "*Otium* as *Luxuria*: Economy of Status in the Younger Pliny's Letters." *Arethusa* 36.2 (2003): 147–65. http://dx.doi.org/10.1353/are.2003.0013.

Lehfeldt, Elizabeth. "Ideal Men: Masculinity and Decline in Seventeenth-Century Spain." *Renaissance Quarterly* 61.2 (2008): 463–94. http://dx.doi.org/10.1353/ren.0.0024.

Leng, Rainer. *Ars Belli: Deutsche taktische und kriegtechnische Bilderhandschriften und Traktate im 15. und 16. Jahrhundert*. 2 vols. Wiesbaden: Ludwig Reichert, 2002.

Lermeño, Guillermo. "Banned and Confiscated Books of the Jesuits." Trans. Christopher Winks. In *Artes de México, Edición Especial: Biblioteca Palafoxiana*, 93–6. Mexico City: Transcontinental, 2003.

Little, Lester K. "Pride Goes before Avarice: Social Change and the Vices in Latin Christendom." *American Historical Review* 76.1 (1971): 16–49. http://dx.doi.org/10.2307/1869775.

Lodge, David. *Small World: An Academic Romance*. New York: Macmillan, 1984.

Lope de Vega. *El arte nuevo de hacer comedias en este tiempo* (1609), ed. Juana de José Prades. Madrid: Clásicos Hispánicos, 1971.

– *La Dorotea*. Ed. Edwin S. Morby. Madrid: Clásicos Castalia, 1987.

López Álvarez, Alejandro. "Los vehículos representativos en la configuración de la corte virreinal: México y Lima, 1590–1700." In *Materia crítica: formas de ocio y de consumo en la cultura áurea*, ed. Enrique García Santo-Tomás, 269–92. Madrid/Frankfurt: Iberoamericana/Vervuert, 2009.

López Grigera, Luisa. *Anotaciones de Quevedo a la* Retórica *de Aristóteles*. Salamanca: Cervantes, 1998.

– *La retórica en la España del Siglo de Oro: teoría y práctica*. Salamanca: Universidad de Salamanca, 1995.

Löwenheim, Oded. *Predators and Parasites: Persistent Agents of Transnational Harm and Great Power Authority*. Ann Arbor: University of Michigan Press, 2007.

León, Luis de. *La perfecta casada*. Salamanca: Juan Fernández, 1595.

Lukacher, Ned. *Daemonic Figures: Shakespeare and the Question of Conscience*. Ithaca: Cornell University Press, 1994.

Luque Fajardo, Francisco de. *Fiel desengaño contra la ociosidad y el juego* (1603), ed. M. de Riquer. Madrid: Consejo Superior de Investigaciones Científicas, 1955.

Maclean, Ian. *Logic, Signs and Nature in the Renaissance*. Cambridge: Cambridge University Press, 2007.

Madrigal, José Antonio, ed. *New Historicism and the Comedia: Poetics, Politics and Praxis*. Boulder: Society of Spanish and Spanish-American Studies, 1995.

Maestro, Jesús, ed. *Ateísmo, herejía y libertinaje en la España medieval y del Renacimiento*. Vigo: Academia del Hispanismo. In progress.

Manos Teatrales: Early modern Spain theater manuscripts. Digital database (Duke University / Margaret Greer). http://manosteatrales.org.

Mansfield, Bruce. *Man on His Own: Interpretations of Erasmus, c. 1750–1920*. 2 vols. Toronto: University of Toronto Press, 1992.

Maravall, José Antonio. *Teatro y literatura en la sociedad barroca*. Madrid: Seminarios y Ediciones, 1972.

Mariscal, George. *Contradictory Subjects: Quevedo, Cervantes, and Seventeenth-Century Spanish Culture*. Ithaca: Cornell University Press, 1991.

– "History and the Subject of the Spanish Golden Age." *Seventeenth Century* 4 (1989): 19–32.

– "Symbolic Capital in the *Comedia*." *Renaissance Drama* 21 (1990): 143–69.

Martell, Daniel Ernest. *The Dramas of Don Antonio de Solís y Rivadeneyra*. Philadelphia: International Printing Company, 1902.

Martindale, C., and R.F. Thomas, eds. *Classics and the Uses of Reception*. Oxford: Blackwell, 2006. http://dx.doi.org/10.1002/9780470774007.

Martínez, François. "Les enfants morisques de l'expulsion (1610–1621)." In *Mélanges Louis Cardaillac*, vol. 2, ed. Abdeljelil Temimi, 499–539. Zaghouan, Tunisia: Fondation Temimi, 1995.

Martín Gaite, Carmen. *El cuarto de atrás*. Barcelona: Destino, 1992.

Martz, Linda. "Implementation of Pure-Blood Statutes in Sixteenth-Century Toledo." In *In Iberia and Beyond: Hispanic Jews Between Cultures (Proceedings of a Symposium to Mark the 500th Anniversary of the Expulsion of Spanish Jewry)*, ed. Bernard Dov Cooperman, 245–72. Newark, DE: University of Delaware Press, 1998.

Mazo Karras, Ruth. "Two Models, Two Standards: Moral Teaching and Sexual Mores." In *Bodies and Disciplines: Intersections of Literature and History in Fifteenth-Century England*, ed. Barbara Hanawalt and David Wallace, 123–38. Minneapolis: University of Minnesota Press, 1996.

McKendrick, Melveena. *Playing the King: Lope de Vega and the Limits of Conformity*. London: Tamesis, 2000.

– *Woman and Society in the Spanish Drama of the Golden Age: A Study of the* Mujer Varonil. Cambridge: Cambridge University Press, 2010.

Melammed, Renée Levine. *A Question of Identity: Iberian Conversos in Historical Perspective*. Oxford: Oxford University Press, 2004.

Menninger, Karl. *Whatever Became of Sin?* New York: Hawthorn, 1973.

Messadié, Gérald. "The Devil in the Early Church." In *A History of the Devil*, trans. Marc Romano, 251–70. New York: Kodansha, 1996.

Middlebrook, Leah. *Imperial Lyric: New Poetry and New Subjects in Early Modern Spain*. University Park: Pennsylvania State University Press, 2009.

Middleton, Thomas. *The Phoenix*. Ed. John Bradbury Brooks. New York: Garland, 1980.

Miller Blaise, Anne-Marie. "George Herbert's Distemper: An Honest Shepherd's Remedy for Melancholy." *George Herbert Journal* 30.1–2 (2006–7): 59–82.

Mintz, Sidney W. *Sweetness and Power: The Place of Sugar in Modern History*. New York: Penguin, 1985.

Montrose, Louis. "Professing the Renaissance: The Poetics and Politics of Culture." In *The New Historicism*, ed. Aram Veeser, 15–36. New York: Routledge, 1989.

Morby, E.S., and A.S. Trueblood. "La Dorotea." In *Historia y crítica de la literatura española,* ed. F. Rico, *Siglos de Oro: Barroco,* ed. B.W. Wardropper, 185–97. Barcelona: Crítica, 1983.

Mortimer, John, ed. *The Oxford Book of Villains*. Oxford: Oxford University Press, 1992.

Moss, Ann. "The *Politica* of Justus Lipsius and the Commonplace-Book." *Journal of the History of Ideas* 59.3 (1998): 421–36. http://dx.doi.org/10.1353/jhi.1998.0025.

Mueller, Reinhold C., and Frederic C. Lane. *The Venetian Money Market: Banks, Panics, and the Public Debt, 1200–1500*. Vol. 2. Baltimore: Johns Hopkins University Press, 1997.

Munro, John H. "The Consumption of Spices and Their Costs in Late-Medieval and Early-Modern Europe: Luxuries or Necessities?" Lecture delivered to the Royal Ontario Museum Continuing Education Symposium (University of Toronto): *Silk Roads, China Ships*. 12 October 1983. http://www.economics.utoronto.ca/munro5/SPICES1.htm.

Murrin, Michael. *History and Warfare in Renaissance Epic*. Chicago: University of Chicago Press, 1994.

Nader, Helen. "Desperate Men, Questionable Acts: The Moral Dilemma of Italian Merchants in the Spanish Slave Trade." *Sixteenth Century Journal* 33.2 (2002): 401–22. http://dx.doi.org/10.2307/4143914.

Nelson, Bradley J. *The Persistence of Presence: Emblem and Ritual in Baroque Spain*. Toronto: University of Toronto Press, 2010.

Newhauser, Richard. *The Early History of Greed: The Sin of Avarice in Early Medieval Thought and Literature*. Cambridge: Cambridge University Press, 2000. http://dx.doi.org/10.1017/CBO9780511485992.

– "'These Seaven Devils': The Capital Vices on the Way to Modernity." In *Sin in Medieval and Early Modern Culture: The Tradition of the Seven Deadly Sins*, ed. Richard Newhauser and Susan Ridyard, 157–88. York: York Medieval Press, 2012.

Nider, Valentina. Introduction to Calderón de la Barca, *La torre de Babilonia*. Ed. Valentina Nider. Pamplona/Kassel: Universidad de Navarra/Reichenberger, 2007.

Noonan, F. Thomas. *The Road to Jerusalem: Pilgrimage and Travel in the Age of Discovery*. Philadelphia: University of Pennsylvania Press, 2007.

Noyes, Dorothy. "La Maja Vestida: Dress as Resistance to Enlightenment in Late 18th-Century Madrid." *Journal of American Folklore* 111.440 (1998): 197–217. http://dx.doi.org/10.2307/541941.

O'Connor, Thomas A. "*La vida es sueño*, Reason and Renunciation, Versus *La estatua de Prometeo*, Love and Fulfillment." In *The Prince in the Tower: Perceptions of* La vida es sueño, ed. Frederick A. de Armas, 97–110. Lewisburg: Bucknell University Press, 1993.

Orlove, B.S. "Meat and Strength: The Moral Economy of a Food Riot." *Cultural Anthropology* 12.2 (1997): 234–68. http://dx.doi.org/10.1525/can.1997.12.2.234.

Orso, Steven N. *Art and Death at the Spanish Habsburg Court: The Royal Exequies for Philip IV*. Columbia: University of Missouri Press, 1989.

Out of the Wings: Spanish and Spanish American Theatres in Translation. "A contextualised resource of Spanish-language plays for English-speaking practitioners and researchers." Oxford University. http://www.outofthewings.org.

Pan-Hispanic Ballad Project. http://depts.washington.edu/hisprom/.

Parker, Alexander A. *The Allegorical Drama of Calderón: An Introduction to the* Autos Sacramentales. Oxford: Oxford University Press, 1968.

Payne, Stanley G. *A History of Spain and Portugal*. Madison: University of Wisconsin Press, 1973.

Paz, Octavio. "Hijos de la Malinche." Chapter 4 of *El laberinto de la soledad*, 27–36. Mexico City: Fondo de Cultura Económica, 1992.

Pedraza Jiménez, Felipe B., and Rafael González Cañal, eds. *Los imperios orientales en el teatro del Siglo de Oro (Actas de las XVI Jornadas de teatro clásico, Almagro, julio de 1992)*. Ciudad Real: Universidad de Castilla-La Mancha, 1994.

Perry, Mary Elizabeth. "Deviant Insiders: Legalized Prostitutes and a Consciousness of Women in Early Modern Seville." *Comparative Studies in Society and History* 27.1 (1985): 138–58. http://dx.doi.org/10.1017/S0010417500013724.

– "The 'Nefarious Sin' in Early Modern Seville." *Journal of Homosexuality* 16.1–2 (1988): 67–89.

– "Prostitutes, Penitents and Brothels." In *Gender and Disorder in Early Modern Seville*. Princeton: Princeton University Press, 1990.

Peucer, Caspar. *Commentarius de praecipuis divinationum generibus* (1553). Frankfurt: Printed using the type of Andreas Wechel, by Claudius Marnius and the heirs of Ioannes Aubrius, 1607.

Phillips, William D. "The Early Transatlantic Slave Trade." In *Slavery from Roman Times to the Early Transatlantic Trade,* 171–94. Minneapolis: University of Minnesota Press, 1985.

Pike, Ruth. *Penal Servitude in Early Modern Spain*. Madison: University of Wisconsin Press, 1983.

Plata, Fernando. "On Love and Occasion: A Reading of the 'Tale of Inappropriate Curiosity.'" In *Cervantes and Don Quixote: Proceedings of the Delhi Conference on Miguel de Cervantes*, ed. Vibha Maurya and Ignacio Arellano, 195–210. Hyderabad: Emesco, 2008.

Plato. *Republic* IX, XXV. In *The Republic of Plato*, trans. Francis MacDonald Cornford. Oxford: Oxford University Press, 1945.

Poesse, Walter. "Utilización de las palabras '*honor*' y '*honra*' en la comedia española." In *Homenaje a don Agapito Rey*, ed. Josep Roca-Pons, Herman B. Wells, and George P. Hammond, 289–303. Bloomington: Indiana University Department of Spanish and Portuguese, 1980.

Ponce de León, Napoleón Baccino. *Maluco: la novela de los descubridores*. Barcelona: Seix Barral, 1992.

Porter, Martin. *Windows of the Soul: The Art of Physiognomy in European Culture, 1470–1760*. Oxford: Oxford University Press, 2005.

Premática y nueva orden: de los vestidos y trajes, así de hombres como de mujeres. Madrid: Pedro Madrigal, 1600. Reprint, *Semanario pintoresco* 19 (1854): 242–3.

Presberg, Charles D. *Adventures in Paradox:* Don Quixote *and the Western Tradition*. University Park: Pennsylvania State University Press, 2001.

Pullan, Brian. "Jewish Banks and Monti di Pietà." In *The Jews of Early Modern Venice*, ed. Robert C. Davis and Benjamin Ravid, 53–72. Baltimore: Johns Hopkins University Press, 2001.

Pym, Richard. *The Gypsies of Early Modern Spain*. New York: Palgrave Macmillan, 2007. http://dx.doi.org/10.1057/9780230625327.

Quandahl, Ellen. "A Feeling for Aristotle: Emotion in the Sphere of Ethics." In *A Way to Move: Rhetorics of Emotion & Composition Studies*, ed. Dale Jacobs and Laura R. Micciche, 11–22. Portsmouth: Boynton/Cook, 2003.

Quevedo, Francisco de. "A una mina." No. 136 in *Poesía original completa*, ed. José Manuel Blecua. Barcelona: Planeta, 1996.

– "Exhortación a una nave nueva al entrar en el agua." In *Poesía original completa*, ed. José Manuel Blecua, 110–11.

– *Sueños y discursos*. Ed. James O. Crosby. Madrid: Castalia, 1993.

Quiñones de Benavente, Juan de. *Discurso contra los gitanos*. Madrid: Juan Gonza, 1631.

Ravid, B. "The First Charter of the Jewish Merchants of Venice, 1589." *Association of Jewish Studies Review* 1 (1976): 187–222.

Redondo, Augustin. "Les empêchements au mariage et leur transgression dans l'Espagne du XVIe siècle." In *Amours légitimes, amours illégitimes en Espagne (XVIe–XVIIe siècles)*. Colloque International, Sorbonne, 3, 4, 5 octobre 1984. Ed. Augustin Redondo, 31–56. Paris: Sorbonne, 1985.

Reichenberger, Arnold G. "The Uniqueness of the Comedia." *Hispanic Review* 27.3 (1959): 303–16. http://dx.doi.org/10.2307/471021.

– "The Uniqueness of the Comedia." *Hispanic Review* 38 (1970): 163–73.

Relación de un monstruoso portento que nació en Ostrauizxa, tierra del Turco, donde se da cuenta de las espantosas señales de este prodigioso monstruo. Madrid: Julián de Paredes, 1660.

Richey, Cliff, and Hilaire Richey Kallendorf. *Acing Depression: A Tennis Champion's Toughest Match*. New York: New Chapter Press, 2010.

Riley, William T., Frank A. Treiber, and Gail M. Woods. "Anger and Hostility in Depression." *Journal of Nervous and Mental Disease* 177.11 (1989): 668–74. http://dx.doi.org/10.1097/00005053-198911000-00002.

Ringrose, David. *Spain, Europe, and the "Spanish Miracle," 1700–1900*. Cambridge: Cambridge University Press, 1996. http://dx.doi.org/10.1080/03612759.1997.9952724.

Roach, Joseph. "Culture and Performance in the Circum-Atlantic World." In *Performativity and Performance*, ed. Andrew Parker and Eve Kosofsky Sedgwick, 45–63. New York: Routledge, 1995.

Rodríguez, Alfred, and Joel F. Dykstra. "Cervantes's Parodic Rendering of a Traditional Topos: *Locus Amoenus*." *Cervantes: Bulletin of the Cervantes Society of America* 17.2 (1997): 115–21.

Rojas, Fernando de. *La Celestina: Tragicomedia de Calisto y Melibea* (1499–1502). Ed. Dorothy S. Severin. Madrid: Alianza, 1981.

Romera Castillo, J. "De cómo Cervantes y Antonio de Solís construyeron sus 'Gitanillas' (Notas sobre la intervención de los 'actores')." In *Lenguaje, ideología y organización textual en las novelas ejemplares*, 145–59. Madrid/Toulouse: Universidad Complutense / Université de Toulouse-Le Mirail, 1983.

Rosales, Luis. *Cervantes y la libertad*. 2 vols. Madrid: Cultura Hispánica / Instituto de Cooperación Iberoamericana, 1985.

Rosenwein, Barbara. "Worrying about Emotions in History." *American Historical Review* 107.3 (2002): 821–45. http://dx.doi.org/10.1086/532498.

Roth, Cecil. *The Spanish Inquisition*. New York: Norton, 1964.

Ruiz Lagos, Manuel. "Interrelación pintura/poesía en el drama alegórico calderoniano: El caso imitativo de la *Iconología* de C. Ripa." *Goya* 161–2 (1981): 282–9.

Ruiz Pérez, Pedro. "Días lúdicos: juego, ocio y literatura." In *Materia crítica: formas de ocio y de consumo en la cultura áurea*, ed. Enrique García Santo-Tomás, 37–58. Madrid/Frankfurt: Iberoamericana/Vervuert, 2009.

Rumeu de Armas, Antonio. *Hernando Colón, historiador del descubrimiento de América*. Madrid: Instituto de Cultura Hispánica, 1973.

Sabine, Lorenzo. *Notes on Duels and Duelling*. Boston: Crosby, Nichols, 1855.

Said, Edward. "Cultura, identidad e historia." In *Teoría de la cultura: un mapa de la cuestión*, ed. Gerhart Schröder and Helga Breuninger, 37–54. Buenos Aires: Fondo de Cultura Económica, 2005.

– *Culture and Imperialism*. New York: Vintage, 1993.

– *Orientalism*. New York: Vintage, 1994.

Saint-Saëns, Alain. "'It is not a sin!': Making Love according to the Spaniards in Early Modern Spain." In *Sex and Love in Golden Age Spain*, ed. Alain Saint-Saëns, 11–25. New Orleans: University Press of the South, 1996.

Saint-Saëns, Alain, ed. *Sex and Love in Golden Age Spain*. New Orleans: University Press of the South, 1996.

Salomon, Noël. *La vida rural castellana en tiempos de Felipe II*. Trans. Francesc Espinet Burunat. Barcelona: Planeta, 1973.

Sánchez-Albornoz, Claudio. "*Sede Regia* y *Solio Real* en el reino astur-leonés." *Asturiensia medievalia* 3 (1979): 61–86.

Sánchez de Villamayor, Andrés Antonio. *La mujer fuerte, asombro de los desiertos, penitente y admirable Santa María Egipciaca*. [Málaga]: [Mateo López Hidalgo], 1677.

Scheper-Hughes, Nancy, and Philippe I. Bourgois, eds. *Violence in War and Peace*. Malden: Wiley-Blackwell, 2004.

Schlesinger, Roger. *In the Wake of Columbus: The Impact of the New World on Europe, 1492–1650*. Wheeling: Harlan Davidson, 1996.

Schorsch, Jonathan. "Jews and Their Slaves: Theory and Reality." In *Jews and Blacks in the Early Modern World*, 50–69. Cambridge: Cambridge University Press, 2004.

Scott, James C. *The Moral Economy of the Peasant: Rebellion and Subsistence in Southeast Asia*. New Haven: Yale University Press, 1976.

Scott Soufas, Teresa. "'Happy Ending' as Irresolution in Calderón's *No hay cosa como callar*." *Forum for Modern Language Studies* 24.2 (1988): 163–74. http://dx.doi.org/10.1093/fmls/24.2.163.

Sempere y Guarinos, J. *Historia del lujo y de las leyes suntuarias en España*. Ed. Juan Rico Giménez. Valencia: Alfons El Magnànim, 2000.

Sepúlveda, Juan Ginés de. *Democrates alter de justis belli causis apud Indios* (1547). Ed. and trans. Marecelino Menéndez y Pelayo as *Tratado sobre las justas causas de la guerra contra los indios*. Mexico City: Fondo de Cultura Económica, 1996.

The Seven Deadly Sins. Book series. New York: Oxford University Press / New York Public Library, 2003.

Shakespeare, William. *Hamlet*. In *The Riverside Shakespeare*, ed. G. Blakemore Evans. Boston: Houghton Mifflin, 1974.

– *Macbeth*. In *The Riverside Shakespeare*, ed. G. Blakemore Evans. Boston: Houghton Mifflin, 1974.

– *The Merchant of Venice*. In *The Riverside Shakespeare*, ed. G. Blakemore Evans. Boston: Houghton Mifflin, 1974.

– *Othello*. In *The Riverside Shakespeare*, ed. G. Blakemore Evans. Boston: Houghton Mifflin, 1974.

– "Sonnet 16." In *The Riverside Shakespeare*, ed. G. Blakemore Evans. Boston: Houghton Mifflin, 1974.

Shannon, R. "The Staging of America in Golden Age Theater." In *Looking at the* Comedia *in the Year of the Quincentennial*, ed. Barbara Mujica and Sharon D. Voros, 53–68. Lanham: University Press of America, 1993.

Shattuck, Roger. *Forbidden Knowledge: From Prometheus to Pornography*. New York: St Martin's, 1996.

Shen, Yeshayahu. "Zeugma: Prototypes, Categories, and Metaphors." *Metaphor and Symbol* 13.1 (1998): 31–47. http://dx.doi.org/10.1207/s15327868ms1301_3.

Shotter, John. "The Social Construction of Subjectivity: Can It Be Theorized?" Review of Julian Henriques, Wendy Holloway, Cathy Urwin, Couze Venn, and Valerie Walkerdine, *Changing the Subject: Psychology, Social Regulation and Subjectivity* (London: Routledge, 1998). In *Contemporary Psychology* 44 (1999): 482–3.

Simerka, Barbara. *Discourses of Empire: Counter-Epic Literature in Early Modern Spain*. University Park: Pennsylvania State University Press, 2003.

Simpson, Elizabeth. *The Spoils of War: World War II and Its Aftermath. The Loss, Reappearance and Recovery of Cultural Property*. New York: H.N. Abrams / Bard Graduate Center for Studies in the Decorative Arts, 1997.

Siraisi, Nancy G. *History, Medicine, and the Traditions of Renaissance Learning*. Ann Arbor: University of Michigan Press, 2007.

– *Medieval and Early Renaissance Medicine: An Introduction to Knowledge and Practice*. Chicago: University of Chicago Press, 1990.

Smith, Mack. "Chivalry Decoded: Dialogistic and Perspectivist Voices in *Don Quixote*." In *Literary Realism and the Ekphrastic Tradition*, 43–76. University Park: Pennsylvania State University Press, 2008.

Solomon, Andrew. *The Noonday Demon: An Atlas of Depression*. New York: Scribner, 2001.

Sosa, Antonio de. *Topografía e historia general de Argel* (1612). Ed. Diego de Haedo and Ignacio Bauer y Landauer. 3 vols. Madrid: Sociedad de Bibliófilos Españoles, 1927–9.

Sperling, Jutta. "Dowry or Inheritance? Kinship, Property, and Women's Agency in Lisbon, Venice, and Florence (1572)." *Journal of Early Modern History* 11.3 (2007): 197–238. http://dx.doi.org/10.1163/157006507781147470.

Spitzer, Leo. "Soy quien soy." *Nueva revista de filología hispánica* 1.2 (1947): 113–27.

Stallybrass, Peter. "Worn Worlds: Clothes and Identity on the Renaissance Stage." In *Subject and Object in Renaissance Culture*, ed. Margreta de Grazia, Maureen Quilligan, and Peter Stallybrass, 289–320. Cambridge: Cambridge University Press, 1996.

Stannard, David E. *American Holocaust: Columbus and the Conquest of the New World*. Oxford: Oxford University Press, 1992.

Steiner, George. *After Babel: Aspects of Language and Translation*. 3rd ed. Oxford: Oxford University Press, 1998.

Stillman, Yedida Kalfon, and Norman A. Stillman, eds. *From Iberia to Diaspora: Studies in Sephardic History and Culture*. Leiden: Brill, 1999.

Stoichita, Victor. *Visionary Experience in the Golden Age of Spanish Art*. London: Reaktion, 1995.

Stolberg, Sheryl Gay, and David D. Kirkpatrick. "Daschle Was Torn between Public and Private Ambitions, His Friends Say." *New York Times*, 5 February 2009, A16.

Strother, Darci L. "Parent-Child Relations." In *Family Matters: A Study of On- and Off-Stage Marriage and Family Relations in Seventeenth-Century Spain*, 135–78. New York: Peter Lang, 1999.

Stroud, Matthew D. *Fatal Union: A Pluralistic Approach to the Spanish Wife-Murder Comedias*. Lewisburg: Bucknell University Press, 1990.

Sullivan, Henry W. "Lacan and Calderón: Spanish Classical Drama in the Light of Psychoanalytic Theory." *Gestos* 10 (1990): 39–55.

– "Law, Desire, and the Double Plot: Towards a Psychoanalytic Poetics of the *Comedia*." In *The Golden Age* Comedia*: Text, Theory, and Performance*, ed. Charles Ganelin and Howard Mancing, 222–35. West Lafayette: Purdue University Press, 1994.

– "Sibling Symmetry and the Incest Taboo in Tirso's *Habladme en entrando*." *Revista canadiense de estudios hispánicos* 10.2 (1986): 261–78.

Surtz, Ronald E. *The Birth of a Theater: Dramatic Convention in the Spanish Theater from Juan del Encina to Lope de Vega*. Madrid: Castalia, 1979.

Swearingen, C. Jan. *Rhetoric and Irony: Western Literacy and Western Lies*. Oxford: Oxford University Press, 1991.

Swietlicki, Catherine Connor. "Marriage and Subversion in *Comedia* Endings: Problems in Art and Society." In *Gender, Identity and Representation in Spain's Golden Age*, ed. Anita K. Stoll and Dawn L. Smith, 23–46. Lewisburg: Bucknell University Press, 2000.

Talbot, Charles. "Topography as Landscape in Early Printed Books." In *The Early Illustrated Book: Essays in Honor of Lessing J. Rosenwald*, ed. Sandra Hindman, 105–16. Washington: Library of Congress, 1982.

Taylor, Diana. *The Archive and the Repertoire: Performing Cultural Memory in the Americas*. Durham: Duke University Press, 2003.

Taylor, Scott K. *Honor and Violence in Golden Age Spain*. New Haven: Yale University Press, 2008.

Thomson, Leslie, ed. *Fortune: "All Is but Fortune."* Washington, Seattle, and London: The Folger Shakespeare Library / University of Washington Press, 2000.

Tillich, Paul. *Morality and Beyond*. New York: Harper and Row, 1963.

Tomás y Valiente, Francisco. "El crimen y pecado contra natura." In *Sexo barroco y otras transgresiones premodernas*, ed. F. Tomás y Valiente et al., 33–56. Madrid: Alianza Universidad, 1990.

– "Delincuentes y pecadores." In *Sexo barroco y otras transgresiones premodernas*, ed. Francisco Tomás y Valiente et al., 11–31. Madrid: Alianza Universidad, 1990.

Toro, Alfonso de. "Die Ehrbegriffe '*Honor/Honra*' im Spanien des 16. und 17. Jahrhunderts." In *Homenaje a Hans Flasche: Festschrift zum 80. Geburtstag am 25. November 1991*, ed. Karl-Hermann Korner, Gunther Zimmermann, and Rafael Melgar Lapesa, 674–95. Stuttgart: Steiner, 1991.

A Treatise of Equivocation (1592–5). Ed. David Jardine. London: Longman, 1851.

Trecena parte de las comedias de Lope de Vega Carpio. Madrid: Viuda de Alonso Martín, 1620.

Trivellato, Francesca. *The Familiarity of Strangers: The Sephardic Diaspora, Livorno, and Cross-Cultural Trade in the Early Modern Period*. New Haven: Yale University Press, 2009.

Trueblood, Alan. *Experience and Artistic Expression in Lope de Vega: The Making of "La Dorotea."* Cambridge, MA: Harvard University Press, 1974.

Turner, Andrew J., et al., eds. *Private and Public Lies: The Discourse of Despotism and Deceit in the Graeco-Roman World*. Leiden: Brill, 2010. http://dx.doi.org/10.1163/ej.9789004187757.i-439.

Urzáiz Tortajada, Hector. "El libro áureo: un tótem cultural frente a los *Índices* de la Inquisición." In *Materia crítica: formas de ocio y de consumo en la cultura áurea*, ed. Enrique García Santo-Tomás, 127–48. Madrid/Frankfurt: Iberoamericana/Vervuert, 2009.

Vásquez, Francisco. *Breve relación de los terremotos del año de 1717 y sus ruinas* (1717). Transcription by J.G. Alzate. Asociación para el Fomento de los Estudios Históricos en Centroámerica. http://afehc-historia-centroamericana.org/?action=fi_aff&id=2408.

Vázquez Fernández, Luis. "Impacto del 'Nuevo Mundo' en la obra de Tirso de Molina." In *Relaciones literarias entre España y América en los siglos XVI y XVII*, ed. Ysla Campbell, 89–124. Ciudad Juárez (Mexico): Universidad Autónoma de Ciudad Juárez, 1992.

– "*La redención de cautivos* de Calderón, alegorizada en la Trinidad y en la Merced." In *Calderón 2000: homenaje a Kurt Reichenberger en su 80 cumpleaños: actas del Congreso Internacional, IV centenario del nacimiento de Calderón* (Universidad de Navarra, septiembre 2000). Ed. Ignacio Arellano Ayuso. 2 vols. Pamplona: Universidad de Navarra, 2002. 2:993–1012.

Vázquez García, Francisco, and Andrés Moreno Mengíbar. *Sexo y razón: una genealogía de la moral sexual en España (siglos XVI–XX)*. Madrid: Akal, 1997.

Velasco, Sherry. *Male Delivery: Reproduction, Effeminacy, and Pregnant Men in Early Modern Spain*. Nashville: Vanderbilt University Press, 2006.

Verdú Maciá, Vicente, et al., eds. *Fiesta, juego y ocio en la historia*. Salamanca: Universidad de Salamanca, 2003.

La vida de Lazarillo de Tormes y de sus fortunas y adversidades. Ed. Julio Cejador y Frauca. Madrid: Espasa-Calpe, 1976.

Vilar, Pierre. "El tiempo de los hidalgos." In *Hidalgos, amotinados y guerrilleros: pueblo y poderes en la historia de España*, trans. Ferrán Gallego, 17–59. Barcelona: Crítica, 1982.

Vilches, Elvira. *New World Gold: Cultural Anxiety and Monetary Disorder in Early Modern Spain*. Chicago: University of Chicago Press, 2010.

Vincent, Bernard. "The Affective Life of Slaves in the Iberian Peninsula during the Sixteenth and Seventeenth Centuries." In *Sex and Love in Golden Age Spain*, ed. Alain Saint-Saëns, 71–8. New Orleans: University Press of the South, 1996.

Vinge, Louise. *The Narcissus Theme in Western European Literature up to the Early 19th Century*. Lund [Sweden]: Gleerups, 1967.

Vives, Juan Luis. *The Education of a Christian Woman: A Sixteenth-Century Manual*, trans. Charles Fantazzi. Chicago: University of Chicago Press, 2000.

Wagschal, Steven. *The Literature of Jealousy in the Age of Cervantes*. Saint Louis: University of Missouri Press, 2006.

Wailes, Stephen L. *The Rich Man and Lazarus on the Reformation Stage: A Contribution to the Social History of German Drama*. Selinsgrove, PA: Susquehanna University Press, 1997.

Walker, Andrew Kevin. *Se7en*. Directed by David Fincher. New Line Cinema, 1995.

Watt, Stephen. "Introduction: The Theory of Forms (Books 5–7)." In Plato, *Republic*, ed. Stephen Watt, xiv–xvi. London: Wordsworth, 1997.

Webber, Edwin J. "Tragedy and Comedy in the *Celestina*." *Hispania* 35.3 (1952): 318–20. http://dx.doi.org/10.2307/335758.

Weber, Max. *The Protestant Ethic and the Spirit of Capitalism*. Trans. Talcott Parsons. New York: Dover, 2003.

– "Science as a Vocation." In *From Max Weber: Essays in Sociology*, ed. H.H. Gerth and C.W. Mills. New York: Oxford University Press, 1946.

Weever, Jacqueline de. *Chaucer Name Dictionary*. New York: Garland, 1996.

Weiger, John G. "El juego de la originalidad: rasgo de la comedia frente a su carácter paradigmático." *Bulletin of the Comediantes* 35 (1983): 197–206.

Weller, Robert P., and Scott E. Guggenheim. "Moral Economy, Capitalism, and State Power in Rural Protest." In *Power and Protest in the Countryside: Studies of Rural Unrest in Asia, Europe, and Latin America*, 3–12. Durham: Duke University Press, 1982.

Wiesner, Merry E. *Women and Gender in Early Modern Europe*. Cambridge: Cambridge University Press, 2000.

Williams, Raymond. "Dominant, Residual, and Emergent." In *Marxism and Literature*, 121–27. Oxford: Oxford University Press, 1977.

Wolf, Kenneth Baxter. "The 'Moors' of West Africa and the Beginnings of the Portuguese Slave Trade." *Journal of Medieval and Renaissance Studies* 24 (1994): 449–69.

Woods, Richard D. *Spanish Grammar and Culture through Proverbs*. Potomac: Scripta Humanistica, 1989.

Yarbro-Bejarano, Yvonne. *Feminism and the Honor Plays of Lope de Vega*. West Lafayette: Purdue University Press, 1994.

Zabaleta, Juan de. In *El día de fiesta por la mañana y por la tarde (1654 / 1660)*. Ed. C. Cuevas García. Madrid: Castalia, 1983.

Zayas, María de. "La inocencia castigada." In *Tres novelas amorosas y tres desengaños amorosos*, ed. Alicia Redondo Goicoechea, 275–309. Madrid: Castalia, 1989.

Žižek, Slavoj. "*Azul*, de Krzysztof Kieslowski, o la reconstitución de la fantasía." Trans. Román Setton. In *Teoría de la cultura: un mapa de la cuestión*, ed. Gerhart Schröder and Helga Breuninger, 115–30. Buenos Aires: Fondo de Cultura Económica, 2005.

Index of *Comedias*

ALARCÓN, JUAN RUIZ DE (1581–1639)
- *El Antichristo*, 92, 271nn33, 37, 281n157, 316n81, 321n149
- *La crueldad por el honor*, 91, 280n142, 309n208, 332n68, 357n251
- *La cueva de Salamanca*, 290n122
- *El dueño de las estrellas*, 313n25
- *Los empeños de un engaño*, 353n165
- *Examen de maridos*, 232n172, 318n111, 351n122, 357n251
- *Ganar amigos*, 340n169, 343n226
- *La industria, y la suerte*, 233n197
- *La manganilla de Melilla*, 287n64, 317n95, 321n152
- *Mudarse por mejorarse*, 223n32, 238n280
- *Las paredes oyen*, 259n159, 266n219
- *Los pechos privilegiados*, 139, 243n20, 304–5n159, 309n221, 318n105, 324n196, 341n193
- *La prueba de las promesas*, 106, 290n112, 292n159, 352n151
- *El semejante a sí mismo*, 243n19, 295n16, 308n197, 346n36
- *El tejedor de Segovia*, 161, 335n101
- *Todo es ventura*, 112, 286n51, 293n1
- *La verdad sospechosa*, 189, 198, 223n32, 290n123, 317n94, 352nn147, 148, 152, 354n199, 355nn217, 221, 356n232, 361n306

CALDERÓN DE LA BARCA, PEDRO (1600–81)
- *A Dios por razón de Estado*, auto sacramental, 267n233, 276n89, 294n13, 337n129
- *A María el corazón*, auto sacramental, 72, 219n2, 230nn126, 141, 239n301, 266nn220, 221, 267n229, 294n14, 295n19, 296n38, 297n60, 307n173, 317n97, 333n79
- *A secreto agravio, secreta venganza*, 230nn121, 134, 231n161, 245n38
- *A tu próximo como a ti*, auto sacramental, 35, 222n27, 235n234, 266n221, 267n222, 269nn15, 24, 297n57, 343n223
- *Afectos de odio, y amor*, 219n4, 287n68, 316n78, 347n74
- *Agradecer, y no amar*, 77, 267n228, 272nn39, 43, 272–3n46, 276n88, 307n175, 356n225
- *El alcalde de sí mismo*, 220n13, 231n161, 242n15
- *El alcalde de Zalamea*, 329–30n31
- *Los alimentos del hombre*, auto sacramental, 115, 297nn47, 49
- *Amado, y aborrecido*, 288n83, 313n21
- *Amar después de la muerte*, 318n119, 339n162
- *Amar, y ser amado, y divina Philotea*, 269nn22, 25, 311n242
- *Amigo amante, y leal*, 222n23, 318n109, 343n221

– *El amor, honor y poder*, 42, 228n101, 238n289, 239n303
– *Andrómeda, y Perseo*, auto sacramental, 341n191
– *Antes, que todo, es mi dama*, 350n108, 353n166, 356n227
– *El año santo de Roma*, auto sacramental, 83, 267n232, 268n3, 276n90, 285n25, 287n68, 293n3, 312n5, 346n31, 350n106
– *El año santo en Madrid*, auto sacramental, 22, 226nn84, 87, 232n181, 233n190, 240–1n4, 242–3n17, 262n180, 265n207, 268n4, 284n13, 286n43, 295n20, 296nn30, 31, 36, 303nn135, 137, 315n58, 317n97, 330n32, 335n112, 345n26
– *Apolo, y Climene*, 223n36, 290n116, 314n50, 318n112
– *El árbol del mejor fruto*, auto sacramental, 344n237
– *El Arca de Dios cautiva*, auto sacramental, 23, 228n98, 356n239
– *Argenis y Poliarco*, 334n92, 358n255, 360n298
– *Las armas de la hermosura*, 285n24
– *El astrólogo fingido*, 198, 220nn16, 17, 223–4n49, 224n61, 247n67, 354n188, 355n218, 356n230, 359n280, 360nn299, 302
– *Auristela, y Lisidante*, 233n196, 243n18, 324n191
– *La aurora en Copacabana*, 352n141
– *La banda y la flor*, 332n67, 355n214
– *Basta callar*, 338n141
– *Bien vengas mal*, 360n303
– *Los cabellos de Absalón*, 270n28, 286n46, 290nn124, 128, 313n23, 327n4, 347n66
– *Cada uno para sí*, 356n229
– *Las cadenas del demonio*, 182, 183, 348n78, 353n173
– *Casa con dos puertas mala es de guardar*, 313n29, 318n107, 341n188
– *El castillo de Lindabridis*, 34, 235n227
– *Céfalo, y Pocris*, 359n270
– *Celos aun del aire matan*, 287n63, 299n88, 324n194
– *La cena de Baltasar*, auto sacramental, 112, 293–4n6
– *La cisma de Inglaterra*, 35, 160, 233n199, 235n232, 333n76, 338n145
– *La codicia rompe el saco*, 241n6
– *Cómo se comunican dos estrellas contrarias*, 224n66, 358n254
– *Con quien vengo, vengo*, 223n44
– *El Conde Lucanor*, 312n8
– *El cordero de Isaías*, auto sacramental, 220n10, 285n30
– *La crítica del amor*, 224n60, 271n30, 333n78, 352n161, 360n283
– *¿Cuál es mayor perfección?*, 353n174, 360n288
– *El cubo de la Almudena*, 117, 130, 131
– *La cura, y la enfermedad*, auto sacramental, 123, 191, 303n140, 314n43, 332n61, 353n175
– *La dama duende*, 296n33, 329–30n31, 340n173, 341n198, 342n211, 358n254
– *Darlo todo, y no dar nada*, 325n212, 338n147, 358n257
– *De una causa dos efectos*, 332n60, 342n203
– *La desdicha de la voz*, 232n173, 330n40
– *La devoción de la Cruz*, 202, 324n184, 362n1
– *La devoción de la Misa*, auto sacramental, 126, 219n4, 290n117, 307nn174, 183, 308nn189, 191
– *El día mayor de los días*, auto sacramental, 233n186, 293n162, 314n53, 315n55, 365n1
– *El diablo mudo*, auto sacramental, 202, 223n43, 294n8, 296nn37, 39, 297n48, 362n1
– *Dicha, y desdicha del nombre*, 224n62, 284n13, 295n23, 316n83, 318n118
– *Los dos amantes del cielo*, 290n119, 341n185
– *El divino Orfeo*, auto sacramental, 328n15, 329n25
– *Duelos de amor, y lealtad*, 141, 287n55, 319n132
– *Eco y Narciso*, 222n25, 225n71
– *En esta vida todo es verdad, y todo mentira*, 199, 224n52, 229n112, 244n23, 324n194, 361nn311, 313
– *El encanto sin encanto*, 231n150, 246n58, 247n60
– *Los encantos de la Culpa*, auto sacramental, 160, 231n149, 293n5, 294–5n15, 296–7n44, 332n71, 332–3n72
– *El escondido, y la tapada*, 230n122, 247n60, 308n193
– *Las espigas de Ruth*, auto sacramental, 131, 285n33, 311n246

– *La estatua de Prometeo*, 258n152, 314n48
– *La exaltación de la Cruz*, 239n310, 312n4, 316n79
– *El faetonte*, 23, 166, 227nn93, 94, 95, 340n176, 355n207
– *La fiera, el rayo y la piedra*, 360n284
– *Fieras afemina amor*, 227n89, 291n141, 316n78, 324n198
– *Fineza contra fineza*, 354n191
– *Fortunas de Andrómeda, y Perseo*, 227n89, 229n114, 325n210, 328n21, 341n189
– *Fuego de Dios en el querer bien*, 341n182, 352n157, 356n227, 357nn246, 247
– *El galán fantasma*, 168, 324n185, 342n200
– *El Golfo de las sirenas*, 221n22, 326n214
– *La gran Cenobia*, 40, 224nn63, 65, 229n117, 233n191, 234n222, 238n287, 289n101, 319n128, 358n255, 360n288
– *El gran mercado del mundo*, auto sacramental, 33, 112, 219n2, 225nn77, 79, 234n214, 268n5, 284n15, 293n1, 293–4n6, 299nn82, 92, 93, 300nn97, 100, 301n116, 317n97, 359n271
– *El gran príncipe de Fez*, 97, 230n140, 282n1, 283nn7, 8, 285nn28, 34, 295n21, 315n61
– *El gran teatro del mundo*, auto sacramental, 174, 241n6, 242–3n17, 294n12, 309n215, 343n225, 344n1
– *Guárdate de la agua mansa*, 308n190, 340n164, 343n225
– *Gustos, y disgustos son no más que imaginación*, 332–3n72
– *Hado, y divisa de Leonido, y de Marfisa*, 343n229, 344n236
– *La hidalga del valle*, auto sacramental, 222n28
– *La hija del aire, primera parte*, 220n12, 285n24, 326n216, 341n193
– *La hija del aire, segunda parte*, 224n61, 314n52, 315n58
– *Los hijos de la Fortuna Teágenes, y Cariclea*, 295n24, 302n120, 340n164
– *El hombre pobre todo es trazas*, 170, 298–9n73, 343n219, 354n195
– *La humildad coronada de las plantas*, auto sacramental, 287n67
– *La inmunidad del sagrado*, auto sacramental, 319n133
– *El indulto general*, auto sacramental, 149, 225n78, 240–1n4, 243n19, 244n24, 258n151, 268n8, 269n16, 284n15, 294–5n15, 295n19, 300n95, 303n139, 325nn203, 205, 328n21, 329n25
– *El jardín de Falerina*, auto sacramental, 223n42, 234n210, 238n279, 293n2, 296nn40, 41, 327n4, 341n184
– *El Joseph de las mujeres*, 221n20, 272nn40, 43, 291n134, 303n134, 350n107
– *Judás Macabeo*, 42, 219n5, 228n97, 239n304, 338n144, 339nn149, 159
– *El laberinto del mundo*, auto sacramental, 200, 268n2, 332n69, 332–3n72, 352n145, 356n227, 361nn309, 318
– *Los Lances de Amor, y Fortuna*, 219n4, 232n166, 355n222
– *La lepra de Constantino*, auto sacramental, 312n4, 314n51
– *El lirio y la azucena*, auto sacramental, 103, 221–2n22, 282n3, 288n85
– *Lo que va del hombre a Dios*, auto sacramental, 285n29, 295n16, 297n59, 302n121, 332–3n72, 350n113
– *Luis Pérez el gallego*, 223n37
– *Llamados, y escogidos*, auto sacramental, 196, 221n22, 311nn240, 250, 359nn272, 273, 361n310
– *El maestrazgo del Toyson*, auto sacramental, 325n212
– *El maestro de danzar*, 352n147, 355n208
– *El mágico prodigioso*, 33, 37, 234n212, 236n247, 357n248
– *Las manos blancas no ofenden*, 352n148, 360n284
– *Mañana será otro día*, 319n125, 360n297
– *Mañanas de abril, y mayo*, 224n64, 240–1n4, 353n169, 355n206, 356n226
– *El mayor encanto, amor*, 231n159, 293n175
– *El médico de su honra*, 143, 186, 191, 349nn100, 103, 354n192
– *Mejor está que estaba*, 331n53, 357n247, 359n276
– *Los misterios de la Misa*, auto sacramental, 126, 223n40, 284n19, 307nn173, 174, 177, 180
– *El monstruo de los jardines*, 223n43, 328n18
– *Mujer, llora, y vencerás*, 220n12, 290n115, 350n112

– *La nave del mercader*, auto sacramental, 64, 260nn165, 166, 266n218, 269n24, 298n69, 300n101, 313n28
– *Ni Amor se libra de Amor*, 257n145, 355n213, 361n308
– *La niña de Gómez Arias*, 54, 180, 249n85, 347n60
– *No hay cosa como callar*, 198, 266n209, 305–6n165, 308n199, 357n246, 358n260, 360n301
– *No hay instante sin milagro*, auto sacramental, 219n4, 221n20, 221–2n22, 241–2n8, 266n217, 269n23, 282–3n4, 284n18, 315nn59, 65
– *El nuevo hospicio de pobres*, auto sacramental, 119, 241–2n8, 261n170, 269n20, 283n9, 284n16, 286nn42, 43, 287n57, 294n11, 296n39, 300n104, 311nn241, 245, 340n166
– *El nuevo palacio del retiro*, auto sacramental, 294–5n15
– *El orden de Melchisedech*, auto sacramental, 223n39, 287n63, 288n70
– *Las órdenes militares*, auto sacramental, 218n31, 314n41
– *El origen, pérdida y restauración de la Virgen del Sagrario*, 339n156
– *Para vencer a Amor, querer vencerle*, 220n15, 224n59, 332n57
– *El pastor fido*, auto sacramental, 280n128, 300n103, 311n251, 348n82
– *Peor está que estaba*, 298n68, 359n269
– *La peste del pan dañado*, 117
– *El pintor de su deshonra*, auto sacramental, 220n7, 221n20, 339n157
– *El pleito matrimonial*, auto sacramental, 224nn51, 57, 228n97, 238n291, 287n58, 294–5n15, 303nn136, 138
– *El postrer duelo de España*, 30, 232nn167, 170
– *La primer flor de el Carmelo*, auto sacramental, 149, 220n7, 228n99, 242–3n17, 265n203, 305n160, 311–12n256, 325n202
– *El primer refugio del hombre, y probática piscina*, auto sacramental, 219n3, 224nn56, 65, 242–3n17, 243n18, 265n201, 269n20, 273n59, 284n22, 285n28, 293nn167, 4, 294n9, 294–5n15, 295n16, 299n80, 300n102, 303n143, 315n60, 323n167, 339n154
– *Primero, y segundo Isaac*, 329n26
– *El Príncipe constante*, 225n69, 230n121, 233–4n204, 239n294, 290n109
– *Psiquis, y Cupido*, 167, 311nn243, 247, 332–3n72, 341n194, 343n227
– *La Puente de Mantible*, 35, 235n237, 302n118
– *El purgatorio de San Patricio*, 40, 220n10, 221n20, 227n90, 234n217, 238n286, 271n36, 315n69, 316n78, 341n182, 348nn81, 87
– *La púrpura de la rosa*, zarzuela, 316n80
– *¿Quién hallará mujer fuerte?*, auto sacramental, 229n119, 294n7, 311n253, 344n233
– *La redención de cautivos*, auto sacramental, 57, 229n112, 252n107, 253nn108, 109, 312n15, 322n157
– *El Rey Don Pedro en Madrid, e infanzón de Illescas*, 236n243, 239n305, 333n79, 353n176
– *Saber del mal, y el bien*, 332n58, 335n105, 342n204, 359n278
– *El santo rey don Fernando, segunda parte*, auto sacramental, 230n132, 282n3, 303n143, 361n319
– *El secreto a voces*, 361n320
– *La segunda esposa, y triunfar muriendo*, auto sacramental, 294–5n15, 301n114, 312n14
– *El segundo blasón del Austria*, auto sacramental, 126, 281n151, 295n25, 307n176
– *El segundo Scipión*, 228n106, 246n55, 328n16, 352nn156, 161
– *La semilla, y la cizaña*, auto sacramental, 117, 130, 230n136, 297n53, 311n254, 317n97
– *La señora, y la criada*, 242n11, 266n209
– *La serpiente de metal*, auto sacramental, 111, 157, 226n85, 244n29, 247n69, 272–3n46, 281n153, 284n19, 293n176, 294n10, 311n244, 323n171, 328n23
– *La sibila del Oriente*, 233n200
– *La siembra del señor*, 284n18
– *El sitio de Breda*, 27, 228n103, 230nn139, 144, 233n187, 332n63, 343n220, 344n235
– *El socorro general*, auto sacramental, 33, 233n203
– *Sueños hay, que verdad son*, auto sacramental, 284n19, 296n30
– *También hay duelo en las damas*, 313n33

– *El tesoro escondido*, auto sacramental, 123, 242n14, 261n168, 303n144, 350n119
– *La torre de Babilonia*, auto sacramental, 35, 43, 235n239, 236n241, 333n79
– *Los tres afectos de amor, piedad, desmayo y valor*, 223–4n49, 322–3n166, 341n184, 352n158
– *Las tres justicias en una*, 313n36, 332n57, 347n55
– *Los tres mayores prodigios*, 221n22, 244n26
– *El valle de la zarzuela*, auto sacramental, 123, 239n307, 303n140
– *El veneno, y la triaca*, auto sacramental, 65, 261n169
– *El verdadero Dios Pan*, auto sacramental, 131, 311n248, 358n259
– *El Viático Cordero*, auto sacramental, 273n53, 282–3n4, 287n64, 316n76
– *La vida es sueño*, 34, 38, 196, 199, 221–2n22, 223n42, 237nn266, 267, 269–70n26, 298–9n73, 312n259, 313n30, 361n314
– *La viña del Señor*, auto sacramental, 75, 269n19, 311nn252, 255

CASTRO, GUILLÉN DE (1569–1630)
– *El conde Alarcos*, 315n68
– *El conde de Irlos*, 288n85, 351n131, 354n190
– *Cuánto se estima el honor*, 177, 346n28, 352n159
– *El curioso impertinente*, 350n119
– *Dido, y Eneas*, 340n163
– *Don Quijote de la Mancha*, 283–4n12, 289n99
– *El engañarse engañado*, 28, 231n147, 237n271, 284n22, 289n89, 319n124, 343n225, 347n69
– *La fuerza de la costumbre*, 225n80, 232n169, 308nn194, 201, 343n229
– *La humildad soberbia*, 314n42
– *La Justicia en la piedad*, 353n162
– *Los mal casados de Valencia*, 326n224, 353n183, 354nn186, 196
– *El mejor esposo*, 67, 181, 182, 184, 263n185, 279n120, 288n87, 347nn56, 75, 348nn77, 79, 84, 85
– *Las mocedades del Cid, Comedia primera*, 31, 232n177, 235n225, 318n119
– *Las mocedades del Cid, Comedia segunda*, 341n187, 345n19, 346n44
– *El nacimiento de Montesinos*, 175, 179, 345n10, 347n58, 350n109
– *El Narciso en su opinión*, 20, 22, 185, 225nn72, 73, 74, 81, 246n50, 247n59, 247–8n73, 270–1n29, 303n133, 314n53, 340n170, 348nn89, 90
– *El perfecto caballero*, 223n45, 307n173, 345n14, 351n139
– *El pretender con pobreza*, 309n203, 324n193
– *Progne, y Filomena*, 314n38, 316n88, 335n111
– *La verdad averiguada, y engañoso casamiento*, 312n10, 316n72, 345n20
– *El vicio en los extremos*, 354n192

CERVANTES, MIGUEL DE (1547–1616)
– *Los baños de Argel*, 250nn93, 94, 253n113, 293n173, 309n221, 325n213
– *La casa de los celos y selvas de Ardenia*, 238n285, 356n233, 282–3n4
– *Don Quijote*, 58, 70, 172, 173, 181, 207, 239n297, 266n211, 344n246, 347nn67, 73, 364nn21, 23
– *La entretenida*, 259n158, 270n28, 306n167, 346n40, 359n281
– *El gallardo español*, 28, 48, 230n145, 245n41, 253n113, 319n134, 340n163, 346n52
– *La gitanilla*, 267n226
– *La gran Sultana*, 253n113
– *El juez de los divorcios*, 285nn31, 33, 306n168
– *El laberinto de amor*, 273n48, 318n113, 326n215
– *El licenciado Vidriera*, 304–5n159, 329n30
– *Pedro de Urdemalas*, 223n37, 267n227, 300–1n109, 338n142
– *El rufián dichoso*, 129, 293n2, 304n151, 309n217
– *El vizcaíno fingido*, 341n186

CUEVA, JUAN DE LA (1550–1609?)
– *Comedia del príncipe tirano*, 37, 236n256, 236–7n257, 287n62, 314n47, 332n61, 333n75
– *La constancia de Arcelina*, 273n47, 293n163, 313n29, 316nn75, 78
– *El degollado*, 251n98
– *El Infamador*, 90–1, 271n32, 280n137, 283n5, 284n21

– *La libertad de España por Bernardo del Carpio*, 134, 230nn122, 125, 232n174, 236n253, 309n216, 312n7, 314n47, 318n117
– *La libertad de Roma, por Mucio Cévola*, 78, 273n51, 287n59, 289n96
– *La muerte de Ajax Telamón*, 144, 147, 321nn145, 147, 324n179, 326n219
– *La muerte de Virginia, y Appio Claudio*, 283n5
– *La muerte del Rey don Sancho*, 314n47, 317n89, 318n112
– *El saco de Roma, y muerte de Borbón*, 230nn123, 142, 233n195, 291n132
– *El viejo enamorado*, 166, 283n9, 341n179

DIAMANTE, JUAN BAUTISTA (1625–87)
– *Alfeo, y Aretusa*, 97, 282n1, 287n60
– *Amor es sangre, y no puede engañarse*, 292n160, 351n125
– *El cerco de Zamora*, 220n16, 326n219, 343n225, 353n163
– *Cumplirle a Dios la palabra*, 292n156, 351n134, 353n163
– *El Hércules de Ocaña*, 229–30n120, 230n143, 289n104, 330n33
– *Ir por el riesgo a la dicha*, 283n6, 323n169
– *El jubileo de Porciúncula*, 220n9, 304n158, 309n214, 321n152, 324n181, 326n220, 357n244
– *Jupiter, y Semele*, 344n239
– *Lides de amor, y desdén*, 284n19, 321n146, 344n238
– *Más encanto es la hermosura*, 283n10, 291n141, 312n1
– *El nacimiento de Cristo*, 88, 109, 155, 279n119, 292n148, 327n1, 329n25, 339n156, 351n127
– *El negro más prodigioso*, 315n70, 360n285
– *No aspirar a merecer*, 291n144
– *Pasión vencida de afecto*, 146, 324n191, 359n266
– *El remedio en el peligro*, 314n43
– *La reina María Estuarda*, 323n170, 343n221, 361n321
– *Santa Juliana*, 285n28, 286n41, 313–14n37, 339n154, 343n228
– *Santa María del Monte, y convento de San Juan*, 287n68
– *Santa María Magdalena de Pazzi*, 100, 124, 286n50, 304n150, 346n40
– *Santa Teresa de Jesús*, 222n28, 353n167
– *El sol de la sierra*, 301–2n117, 316n77, 325n206
– *Triunfo de la paz, y el tiempo*, 103, 287n66, 289n91, 293n174, 326n214

LOPE DE VEGA (1562–1635)
– *El acero de Madrid, primera parte*, 309n204, 313n32
– *Adonis, y Venus*, 81, 222n25, 227n89, 269n17, 275n76, 329n26
– *Al pasar del arroyo*, 232n178, 329n25, 336n122
– *El alcalde mayor*, 36, 236n243, 265n207, 343n217
– *Las almenas de Toro*, 268n6, 360n289
– *El amante agradecido*, 334n90
– *Los amantes sin amor*, 305n164, 313–14n37, 315n71
– *Amar, servir, y esperar*, 255n131
– *Amar sin saber a quién*, 356n223, 360n290
– *El amigo hasta la muerte*, 157, 247n63, 276n86, 330n34, 343n230
– *El amigo por fuerza*, 30, 232n175, 242–3n17
– *La amistad pagada*, 237n270, 256n142, 265n208, 273n52
– *El Amor enamorado*, 102, 224n54, 234n206, 239n306, 244n34, 258n150, 267n230, 288n77, 324n177, 328n10, 333n75, 337n139, 350n110, 357n252
– *Angélica en el Catay*, 27, 230nn128, 139, 289n99, 313n32, 321n153, 325n207
– *El animal de Hungría*, 324n180, 350n110
– *Arauco domado por el excelentísimo señor don García Hurtado de Mendoza*, 25, 61, 229n115, 255n126, 259n164, 326n218, 329n28, 357n252
– *Arcadia*, 359n276
– *El arenal de Sevilla*, 267n225, 315n71
– *El Argel fingido y renegado de amor*, 244n36, 360n293
– *El arte nuevo de hacer comedias en este tiempo*, 10, 94, 218n30, 282n167
– *El asalto de Mastrique, por el Príncipe de Parma*, 63, 228n100, 336n123
– *El ausente en el lugar*, 318n110, 346n47, 352n142, 357n242
– *Las aventuras de don Juan de Alarcos*, 315n71

– *Bamba*, 221–2n22, 266n214, 294–5n15, 295n21, 306n169, 317n93
– *Barlán y Josafa*, 305n160, 339n158
– *El bastardo Mudarra*, 223n47, 289n94, 292n155, 315n66, 317n95, 331nn49, 54, 55
– *La batalla del honor*, 322n163, 324n177, 326n222, 335n97, 336n115
– *La bella Aurora*, 291n135, 292n154, 319n135, 337–8n140
– *La bella malmaridada*, 309n205
– *Los Benavides*, 345n24
– *Las bizarrías de Belisa*, 238n288, 328n17, 329n25, 336n117, 337n139, 338n143
– *El blasón de los Chaves de Villalba*, 155, 229–30n120, 230n142, 309nn206, 207, 327n1, 338n146, 350n108
– *La boba para los otros, y discreta para sí*, 329n30
– *El bobo del colegio*, 231n155, 245n46, 310n225
– *La boda entre dos maridos*, 244n31, 317n99
– *La buena guarda*, 84, 89, 276nn93, 94, 279n126, 280n140, 309n219, 324n192
– *La burgalesa de Lerma*, 328n9, 340n164, 350n115
– *El caballero de Olmedo*, 331n56, 340n172, 346n30
– *El caballero del Milagro*, 230n143, 233n198, 260–1n167, 313n35
– *El caballero del Sacramento*, 339n159, 340n174
– *La campana de Aragón*, 92, 267n1, 280n146, 282n162
– *El capellán de la Virgen*, 242n11, 329nn27, 30, 335n107, 342n206
– *La carbonera*, 169, 236n254, 342n213
– *La cárcel de Sevilla*, 248n77, 352n142
– *El cardenal de Belén*, 244n23, 278n103, 286n42, 342nn201, 207
– *El casamiento en la muerte*, 228n111, 230n122, 231nn146, 157, 242n10, 249n88, 273–4n63, 308n196
– *Castelvines, y Monteses*, 329n29
– *El castigo sin venganza*, 238n285, 329n25, 345n5
– *Los cautivos de Argel*, 253n113, 347n70
– *Los comendadores de Córdoba*, 286n47
– *Con su pan se lo coma*, 285n26
– *El conde Fernan González*, 267n222, 291n143, 333n77
– *Contra valor no hay desdicha*, 104, 236n248, 238nn273, 277, 289n101, 296n29, 313n27
– *La corona merecida*, 220n7, 352n149, 355n211, 359n281
– *La cortesía de España*, 279n117, 340n172, 349n101
– *Las cuentas del Gran Capitán*, 223n38, 235n235, 327n3, 331n53, 340n165, 360nn291, 294
– *El cuerdo en su casa*, 357n247
– *La dama boba*, 247n70, 350n117
– *De cosario a cosario*, 239n293, 246n52, 255n128, 259n157
– *Del mal lo menos*, 28, 231n148, 358n263, 361n308
– *El desconfiado*, 166, 340n175
– *La desdichada Estefanía*, 227–8n96, 302–3n129
– *El desposorio encubierto*, 175, 345n11, 346n51
– *El desprecio agradecido*, 317n95
– *Dios hace reyes*, 36, 236n244, 357n243
– *La discreta venganza*, 234n205, 286n42
– *El divino africano*, 337n130
– *El dómine Lucas*, 247n71
– *Don Juan de Castro, primera parte*, 297n58, 343n29
– *Don Lope de Cardona*, 337n139
– *La Dorotea*, 11, 219n37, 272n41
– *Los donaires de Matico*, 253n112
– *La doncella Teodor*, 224n53, 273n62, 336n116, 360n289
– *El Duque de Viseo*, 245n43, 342n212, 354n200
– *El ejemplo de casadas y prueba de la paciencia*, 86, 278n107, 328n9
– *Ello dirá*, 328n22
– *La envidia de la nobleza*, 164, 230n131, 337nn135, 137
– *Los embustes de Fabia*, 315n67
– *Los embustes de Zelauro*, 241n5, 280n135, 282n159, 330n36
– *Los enemigos en casa*, 181, 310n226, 347n71
– *La esclava de su galán*, 324n187
– *El esclavo de Roma*, 228n109, 268n11

– *Los esclavos libres*, 55, 249n86, 251n96, 342n208
– *Los españoles en Flandes*, 62, 256n143, 283n11, 302n128, 336n115
– *Las famosas asturianas*, 338n146, 345n6, 354n201
– *El favor agradecido*, 223n34, 224n54, 254n122, 259n154
– *La fe rompida*, 32, 80, 86, 233n193, 274n66, 356nn234, 236
– *Las ferias de Madrid*, 279n118, 280n131
– *La Filisarda*, 221n20, 227n89
– *La firmeza en la desdicha*, 221n20, 250n95, 361n322
– *Las flores de don Juan, y rico, y pobre trocados*, 291n139, 292n158, 297n61
– *La fortuna merecida*, 233n194, 290n108, 306n168, 334n82, 337n136
– *La Francesilla*, 177, 345n24, 346nn27, 48
– *Fuente Ovejuna*, 38, 237n262
– *La fuerza lastimosa*, 325n199
– *El galán Castrucho*, 256–7n144, 294–5n15
– *El galán de la Membrilla*, 233n202, 324n178, 329n24
– *La gallarda toledana*, 318n104
– *El gallardo catalán*, 259n154, 277n98
– *El Genovés liberal*, 223n30, 260–1n167, 292n151
– *El gran duque de Moscovia, y emperador perseguido*, 236n251
– *Las grandezas de Alejandro*, 223n33, 239n296, 293n170, 314n38
– *Los guanches de Tenerife, y conquista de Canaria*, 24, 228n107, 241n5
– *El guante de doña Blanca*, 222n24, 335n108
– *Guardar, y guardarse*, 313–14n37
– *El halcón de Federico*, 298n65
– *El Hamete de Toledo*, 246n58, 284n14, 299n78, 335n110, 360n295
– *Hay verdades que en amor*, 288n80, 292n158
– *La hermosa Alfreda*, 255n135, 308n202
– *La hermosa Ester*, 40, 228n97, 239nn292, 313, 286n44, 330n37
– *La hermosa fea*, 292n153
– *La hermosura aborrecida*, 272–3n46, 273n50
– *Los hidalgos del aldea*, 237n269, 244n32
– *El hijo de Reduán*, 238n290
– *El hijo de los leones*, 296n27, 332n57, 335n109
– *La Historia de Tobías*, 81, 246n58, 275nn73, 74, 309n220, 324n188
– *El hombre de bien*, 326n214
– *El hombre por su palabra*, 238n283, 334n83, 335n113
– *El honrado hermano*, 15, 219n1, 228nn109, 110, 255n134
– *La ilustre fregona*, 293n170, 355n219
– *La ingratitud vengada*, 244n36, 314n41, 315n56
– *El ingrato arrepentido*, 242–3n17, 265n207
– *La inocente Laura*, 82, 276n82
– *La inocente sangre*, 349nn102, 105
– *Jorge toledano*, 312n19, 323n173, 324n193
– *El laberinto de Creta*, 77, 178, 224n50, 272n45, 280n141, 316n78, 346n38
– *Laura perseguida*, 317n93, 318n107, 328n13
– *El leal criado*, 267n222, 309n219, 328n11, 332n70
– *La limpieza no manchada*, 321n148
– *Lo cierto por lo dudoso*, 338n141
– *Lo que hay que fiar del mundo*, 268n7
– *Lo que ha de ser*, 316n85
– *Loa en alabanza de la humildad*, 298n64
– *Loa: Después, que el famoso César*, 228n108
– *Los locos de Valencia*, 299n86, 338n141, 346n33
– *Los locos por el cielo*, 299n76, 314n45, 342n214, 358n253
– *La locura por la honra*, 259n164
– *Lucinda perseguida*, 313nn22, 28, 324n177
– *El llegar en ocasión*, 314n49, 318n110, 323n174
– *La madre de la mejor*, 345nn12, 21, 348n76
– *La mal casada*, 247n66, 347n68, 349n101
– *El marido más firme*, 330n38, 352n150
– *El mármol de Felisardo*, 312n2
– *El más galán portugués, duque de Braganza*, 334n84
– *El mayor imposible*, 222n26, 234n207
– *La mayor victoria de Alemania de don Gonzalo de Córdoba*, 228n101, 336n124, 337n126
– *La mayor virtud de un rey*, 231n155, 244n33, 290n120, 318n120, 324n178, 330n40, 331n53
– *El mayorazgo dudoso*, 103, 236n255, 282n161, 289n92
– *El mayordomo de la duquesa de Amalfi*, 281–2n158, 360n288

– *El mejor maestro, el tiempo*, 237n259, 243n22, 265n204
– *Los melindres de Belisa*, 99, 247n68, 249n87, 285n36
– *Mirad a quién alabáis*, 229–30n120
– *La mocedad de Roldán*, 191, 288n73, 290n125, 313n26, 353n172
– *El molino*, 343n215, 346n46
– *La montañesa*, 256n142
– *Las mudanzas de Fortuna, y sucesos de don Beltrán de Aragón*, 234n220, 361n322
– *Los Muertos vivos*, 303n131
– *Las mujeres sin hombres*, 300nn105, 106, 353n184
– *El nacimiento de Cristo*, 327n4
– *Nadie se conoce*, 235n230, 248n79, 282n165, 346n45, 350n116
– *La necedad del discreto*, 288n82
– *La niña de plata*, 47, 244n35, 346–7n53
– *El niño inocente de la Guardia*, 304–5n159, 346n32, 348n86
– *No son todos ruiseñores*, 358nn259, 261
– *La noche de San Juan*, 241n7, 289n95, 340n164
– *La noche toledana*, 303n146
– *La nueva victoria del marqués de Santa Cruz*, 324n188, 337–8n140
– *El Nuevo Mundo, descubierto por Cristóbal Colón*, 61, 230n133, 255nn124, 125, 336n114
– *La obediencia laureada, y primer Carlos de Hungría*, 175, 345n13
– *Obras son amores*, 267n232, 353n179, 361n319
– *La ocasión perdida*, 230n127
– *La octava maravilla*, 336n118, 344n232
– *Las paces de los reyes, y Judía de Toledo*, 288n72
– *El padrino desposado*, 241n6, 319n123
– *La pastoral de Jacinto*, 330n39
– *Pedro Carbonero*, 58, 253n110, 293n168
– *El perro del hortelano*, 232n171, 327n4
– *El perseguido*, 223n46, 276n83, 280n130
– *El Perseo*, 241n6, 353n176
– *El piadoso aragonés*, 34, 176, 178, 180, 231n151, 234n216, 335n102, 345nn18, 23, 346nn35, 29, 39, 347n62, 348n83, 349n92
– *El piadoso veneciano*, 45, 240n1, 243n20, 334n86
– *La piedad ejecutada*, 242–3n17, 314n47
– *Los pleitos de Inglaterra*, 224n63, 228n100
– *La pobreza estimada*, 31, 32, 51, 56, 233n185, 234n211, 251n102, 336n115
– *Las pobrezas de Reinaldos*, 256–7n144, 284n20, 309n212
– *Los Ponces de Barcelona*, 231n162, 281n150, 347n65, 349n94
– *Por la puente Juana*, 354n205
– *Los Porceles de Murcia*, 84, 85, 276n94, 278nn101, 105, 282n166
– *Porfiando vence amor*, 328n12, 342n209
– *Porfiar hasta morir*, 227n90
– *El postrer godo de España (El último godo)*, 103, 112, 233n191, 273–4n63, 288–9n88, 296n42
– *Los prados de León*, 241n6, 359n282
– *El premio de la hermosura*, 224n58
– *El premio del bien hablar*, 198, 361n305
– *El primer Fajardo*, 273n61, 297–8n63, 307n171
– *El primer rey de Castilla*, 340n177
– *La primera información*, 230n124, 334n87, 342n210
– *El primero Benavides*, 210
– *El príncipe perfecto, parte primera*, 266n209, 308n195, 345n8
– *El príncipe perfecto, parte segunda*, 336n114
– *La prisión sin culpa*, 45, 240n2
– *Querer la propia desdicha*, 300n96, 339n151
– *Quien ama no haga fieros*, 306n166
– *Quien dice que las mujeres*, loa, 353n180
– *Quien más no puede*, 231n151
– *Quien no ama*, 356n224
– *Quien todo lo quiere*, 231n160, 353n177
– *La quinta de Florencia*, 247n65, 269–70n26, 286n49, 288n69
– *Los ramilletes de Madrid*, 265n205, 300n94
– *El remedio en la desdicha*, 272n44, 328n8
– *La resistencia honrada y Condesa Matilde*, 278n108, 279n116, 282n163, 287n68, 289n93, 292n146
– *El rey sin reino*, 232n176, 289n97, 330n32, 337n138, 346n37
– *Roma abrasada*, 223n48, 295n17, 312n12, 350n111
– *El rústico del cielo*, 293n172, 296n34, 299n74, 307n182
– *El Ruiseñor de Sevilla*, 255n132, 258n150

- *El saber por no saber, y vida de San Julián*, 242n12, 310n227, 350n107, 353n178
- *El saber puede dañar*, 234n208
- *San Isidro labrador de Madrid*, 49, 104, 227–8n96, 246n53, 256–7n144, 270–1n29, 289n106, 293n166, 301n111, 307n179, 324n180, 334n89, 342n212
- *San Nicolás de Tolentino*, 283n11, 284n21, 285n34, 299n77, 310n228
- *La Santa Liga*, 224n54, 230n123, 231n153, 283n5, 287n68, 288n86, 289nn98, 100
- *Santiago el verde*, 225–6n82, 356n241
- *El secretario de sí mismo*, 324n192
- *El sembrar en buena tierra*, 244n28
- *El serafín humano*, 274n65, 293n165, 295n16, 319n124
- *La serrana de Tormes*, 177, 272–3n46, 345n22
- *Servir a buenos*, 186, 341n190, 349n104
- *Servir a señor discreto*, 330n39, 337n125
- *El servir con mala estrella*, 312n5
- *Si no vieran las mujeres*, 234nn215, 218, 335n98, 336n119
- *Sobre una mesa de murtas*, loa, 213n1, 315nn57, 63
- *El Sol parado*, 230n131, 231n152, 247n64, 302n123
- *El soldado amante*, 109–10, 228n104, 233n189, 241n5, 241–2n8, 255n136, 285n27, 292n157
- *La sortija del olvido*, 240–1n4
- *Los Tellos de Meneses*, 313n35, 329n27, 356n238
- *El testimonio vengado*, 84, 85, 277nn96, 97, 278n102, 316n86, 333n75, 357n245
- *El tirano castigado*, 242n13, 346n43
- *Los trabajos de Jacob*, 334nn80, 81
- *Los tres diamantes*, 323n176, 332n64
- *El triunfo de la humildad, y soberbia abatida*, 41, 223n44, 328n14
- *[El nacimiento de] Ursón y Valentín, hijos del rey de Francia*, 82, 92, 276n80, 278n104, 280n145, 359n268
- *Válgame Dios, es de veras*, loa, 312n11
- *El valiente Céspedes*, 25, 229n113, 336n115, 338n148
- *El valor de las mujeres*, 241n6, 316n84, 324n189
- *El vaquero de Morana*, 319n126, 324n186
- *La varona castellana*, 231n154
- *El vellocino de oro*, loa, 171, 288n74, 336n119, 344nn240, 241, 242
- *La vengadora de las mujeres*, 224n64, 285n31
- *La venganza venturosa*, 280n133
- *La ventura sin buscarla*, 237n260, 297n56
- *El verdadero amante*, 185, 317n101, 347n54, 348n91
- *La vida de San Pedro Nolasco*, 226n86
- *La villana de Xetafe*, 247n67, 324n195
- *El villano en su rincón*, 109, 169, 236n243, 263n184, 292n152, 329n25, 353n185
- *Virtud, pobreza y mujer*, 235n240, 244n31
- *La viuda casada y doncella*, 210, 308n200, 346n41
- *La viuda valenciana*, 129, 308n189, 310n224

MATOS FRAGOSO, JUAN DE (1608?–1689)
- *El amor hace valientes*, 322n161, 337n133, 339n150
- *Amor, lealtad, y ventura*, 228n105, 287n65, 337n139
- *Callar siempre es lo mejor*, 288n75
- *Con amor no hay amistad*, 310n232, 317n102, 318n108, 325n209, 351n126, 353n164
- *La devoción del Ángel de la Guarda*, 238n281, 352n146, 356n240, 359n264
- *El genízaro de Hungría*, 317n96
- *El hijo de la piedra*, 244n27, 306n168, 310n229, 328n15
- *Los indicios sin culpa*, 86, 92, 246n50, 251n100, 279nn112, 113, 114, 281nn114, 149, 308n192
- *El marido de su madre*, 210, 284n19
- *El traidor contra su sangre*, 38, 231n153, 237n261, 332n59, 337n134, 345n15
- *El yerro de el entendido*, 315n62, 330n33, 331n50

MORETO, AGUSTÍN (1618–69)
- *Antíoco y Seleuco*, 303n141, 304–5n159, 355n216
- *La cautela en la amistad*, 286n39
- *El caballero del Sacramento*, 227n91, 265n202, 276nn79, 84, 280n133
- *El Cristo de los milagros*, 61, 255n127
- *De fuera vendrá*, 246n54

– *El desdén, con el desdén*, 106, 290n111, 340n167, 343n224
– *El esclavo de su hijo*, 58, 60, 210, 227–8n96, 236n250, 249n85, 251n96, 251–2n103, 252n105, 254nn117, 118, 121, 255n123, 259n162, 260–1n167, 298n66, 300n99, 303n147, 312n5, 315nn54, 60, 321n155, 349n93
– *La fingida Arcadia*, 100, 286n52, 287n56
– *La fortuna merecida*, 223n41, 244n28, 329–30n31, 332n66
– *La fuerza de la ley*, 83, 89, 279n123, 299n89, 310n231
– *La fuerza del natural*, 343n218
– *Hacer del contrario amigo*, 235n223, 315n62
– *Hasta el fin nadie es dichoso*, 238n278, 290n128, 340n171
– *Los hermanos encontrados*, 305n162
– *El lego del Carmen*, 232n165, 306n170
– *El licenciado Vidriera*, 266n209, 299n79, 303n145, 304–5n159, 329n30
– *El lindo Don Diego*, 20, 271n30, 296n31, 299n93, 354n202
– *Lo que puede la aprehensión*, 291n138, 292n149
– *Los más dichosos hermanos*, 223n35
– *El mejor amigo, el rey*, 299n87, 304n148, 306n170, 360n287
– *La misma conciencia acusa*, 245n37, 288n83, 312n3
– *No puede ser*, 286n41, 304n157, 305n163, 337n131
– *Nuestra Señora del Aurora*, 282–3n4
– *El parecido*, 231n162, 245n39, 299n91, 301n112, 311n249, 314n44
– *El poder de la amistad*, 270n27, 352n160
– *Primero es la honra*, 290n127
– *Santa Rosa del Perú*, 288n78, 299n84, 309n218, 318n103, 339n157
– *El secreto entre dos amigos*, 243n21, 328n14
– *La traición vengada*, 41, 239n298, 350n110
– *Trampa adelante*, 248n78, 300n99
– *Las travesuras del Cid, burlesca*, 302n125
– *El valiente justiciero*, 247n69, 322n164

PÉREZ DE MONTALBÁN, JUAN (1602–38)
– *A lo hecho no hay remedio, y príncipe de los montes*, 267n228, 304n154, 328n20, 351n129
– *Los amantes de Teruel*, 189, 229–30n120, 352n154, 353n170
– *Amor, privanza, y castigo*, 39, 222n23, 238n275, 329–30n31, 331n45
– *Como amante, y como honrada*, 298n70, 361n304
– *Cumplir con su obligación*, 134, 231n163, 287n66, 290n121, 312n6, 332n67
– *La deshonra honrosa*, 358n256
– *Despreciar lo que se quiere*, 291n129
– *El divino portugués, San Antonio de Padua*, 235n228, 343n228, 352n144
– *Don Florisel de Niquea*, 357n250
– *La doncella de labor*, 340n178, 361n315
– *La ganancia por la mano*, 329n26, 340n172
– *El hijo del Serafín, San Pedro de Alcántara*, 247–8n73, 268n9, 298n67, 305n161, 306n170, 342n202
– *Lo que son juicios del cielo*, 214n1, 239n312, 308n198, 319n133, 352n146, 354n195
– *El mariscal de Virón*, 237n268, 238n285, 239n314, 291n131, 337n132
– *El Señor don Juan de Austria*, 353n165, 355n210
– *El sufrimiento premiado*, 221–2n22, 315n67
– *Teágenes, y Clariquea*, 86, 239n302, 278n110, 340n168
– *Los templarios*, 223–4n49, 306n169, 318n115, 339n153
– *La toquera vizcaína*, 312n17, 353n171
– *El valiente más dichoso, don Pedro Guiral*, 321n156, 351n123
– *El valiente Nazareno*, 234n221, 238n284, 239n311, 286n46, 340n163

QUIÑONES DE BENAVENTE, LUIS (1593?–1652)
– *Jácara, que se cantó en la compañía de Ortegón*, 335n107
– *Loa con que empezaron Rueda, y Ascanio*, 241n6, 358n263
– *Loa con que empezó Tomás Fernández en la Corte*, 312n257
– *El mago*, 293n171
– *El murmurador*, entremés,193, 325n208, 355n212
– *El Remediador*, 285n32
– *La verdad*, entremés,199, 361n316

ROJAS ZORRILLA, FRANCISCO DE (1607–48)
– *Abrir el ojo*, 308n191
– *Los áspides de Cleopatra*, 248n77, 276n85, 292n161, 295n26, 296n41, 300n106, 316n74
– *Los bandos de Verona*, 317n91
– *Casarse por vengarse*, 337–8n140
– *Los celos de Rodamonte*, 19, 224–5n67, 354n204, 360n286
– *Los encantos de Medea*, 221n20, 235n224, 337n127
– *Entre bobos anda el juego*, 318n106
– *Lo que quería ver el marqués de Villena*, 336n121
– *Lo que son mujeres*, 235n230, 296n43, 308n186, 326n225
– *El más impropio verdugo por la más justa venganza*, 312n9, 313nn35, 36, 315n68
– *No hay amigo para amigo*, 308n196, 312n13, 324n196, 350n120
– *No hay ser padre siendo Rey*, 291n133, 295n26, 326n221
– *Nuestra Señora de Atocha*, 326nn225, 227
– *Obligados, y ofendidos*, 267n222, 317n100
– *Peligrar en los remedios*, 322n160
– *Persiles, y Sigismunda*, 155, 317n95, 326n224, 327n1, 359n266
– *El profeta falso Mahoma*, 27, 87, 92, 230n137, 262n180, 279n115, 281n156, 316n81
– *Progne y Filomena*, 276n81, 280n129, 299n85, 342n205
– *Santa Isabel reina de Portugal*, 37, 236n245, 309n218
– *Sin honra no hay amistad*, 351nn124, 130, 353n176
– *Los trabajos de Tobías*, 180, 236n252, 261n171, 269n18, 275n72, 321n146, 322n162, 341n192, 347n59
– *La traición busca el castigo*, 339n155
– *Los tres blasones de España*, 258n148, 297n50, 326n217, 338n141

RUEDA, LOPE DE (1510–65)
– *Camila*, 330n35
– *Los engañados*, 304n156, 306n170, 359n282
– *Eufemia*, 303n132, 308n191
– *Medora*, 240n318
– *Paso tercero*, 305n164
– *Timbria*, 303n133

SOLÍS, ANTONIO DE (1610–86)
– *El alcázar del secreto*, 34, 110, 235n226, 290n126, 293n164, 339n159
– *Las amazonas*, 224–5n67, 288n81, 289n102, 313n26, 323n168
– *El amor al uso*, 102, 288n76, 292n150, 295n18, 360n300
– *Amparar al enemigo*, 351n122, 360n303
– *Un bobo hace ciento*, 355n220
– *El doctor Carlino*, 76, 194, 271n34, 356n231
– *Eurídice, y Orfeo*, 247n61, 287n68
– *La gitanilla de Madrid*, 72, 267nn226, 227, 354n198, 357n250

TIRSO DE MOLINA (1584?–1648)
– *Adversa fortuna de don Álvaro de Luna*, 29, 231n156, 234n209, 330n33
– *Adversa fortuna de don Álvaro de Luna, segunda parte*, 161, 327n6, 328n19, 334nn88, 93, 335n104, 336n123, 341n195
– *Los alcaldes*, 309n209
– *Los amantes de Teruel*, 314n46
– *Amar por arte mayor*, 341n184, 350n121
– *Amar por razón de estado*, 233n188, 282–3n4, 326n226
– *Amazonas en las Indias*, 196, 241n6, 242n10, 302nn124, 127, 331n46, 343n222, 359n277
– *El amor médico*, 99, 286n38, 289n90, 290n118, 327n7
– *El amor, y el amistad*, 259n160, 330n39, 332n65, 335n100, 343n231, 357nn249, 250
– *Amor y celos hacen discretos*, 333n79
– *Antona García*, 70, 266n211, 283n6
– *El Aquiles*, 75, 229–30n120, 268n13
– *El árbol del mejor fruto*, 233n196, 242n9, 285n30, 314n39, 339n152
– *Averígüelo Vargas*, 271n35, 335n106, 340n174
– *El burlador de Sevilla*, 91, 115, 297n45
– *El castigo del penséque*, 220n8, 300n107, 305n164, 313n24, 353n182
– *Cautela contra cautela*, 327n5, 341nn196, 199, 353n181

– *La celosa de sí misma*, 166, 235n233, 247n62, 249n89, 266n210, 267n231, 305–6n165, 309n204, 341n180, 349n101
– *El condenado por desconfiado*, 128, 309nn210, 215, 345n4, 348n88
– *La Dama del Olivar*, 32, 233n192, 308n189
– *Del enemigo el primer consejo*, 48, 245n45, 341n197
– *Don Gil de las calzas verdes*, 220n8, 244n32, 245n38, 247n62, 299n90, 346n34, 359n267, 360n283
– *Doña Beatriz de Silva*, 223n37, 232n179, 305n160, 338n141
– *La elección por la virtud*, 241n5, 331nn51, 52
– *Escarmientos para el cuerdo*, 90, 256n140, 259n163, 269n21, 280n127, 309n211, 316n82
– *Esto sí que es negociar*, 358n254
– *La fingida Arcadia*, 297n59, 312n8
– *La gallega Mari Hernández*, 261n171, 307n185, 312n258, 334n94
– *La huerta de Juan Fernández*, 283n11, 288n79, 301n113, 351n134
– *Los lagos de san Vicente*, 104, 284n23, 289n105, 318n116, 326n219, 336n124, 339n157, 343n230, 354n189
– *La lealtad contra la envidia*, 229n116, 230n138, 251n99, 255n133, 258n150, 332n66, 336n120, 356n235, 359n265
– *Marta la piadosa*, 230n129, 240nn316, 317, 320, 352n147, 359n275, 361n315
– *El mayor desengaño*, 64, 220n7, 244n36, 259n161, 292n157, 305n163, 334n95, 346n42
– *La mejor espigadera*, 224n55, 321n150
– *El melancólico*, 234n213, 267n232, 282–3n4, 288n75, 332n60, 351n129, 354n187
– *La mujer que manda en casa*, 20, 80, 222n23, 258n149, 273n54, 274nn67, 68, 282n160, 287n61, 296n35, 298n69, 299n83, 303nn142, 143, 349n99
– *La mujer por fuerza*, 359n275
– *No hay peor sordo*, 291n136
– *Palabras y plumas*, 247n71
– *La peña de Francia*, 307n184
– *Por el sótano y el torno*, 308n189
– *El pretendiente al revés*, 307n181, 312n16, 354n194
– *Privar contra su gusto*, 334n89, 335n96, 342n203, 349n99
– *Próspera fortuna de don Álvaro de Luna, primera parte*, 161, 231n156, 286n40, 327n4
– *La prudencia en la mujer*, 280n147, 316n83, 333n74, 356n237
– *Quien calla, otorga*, 300n106, 330n35, 333n73, 358n258
– *Quien habló, pagó*, 317n90, 318n114, 339n161, 351n132
– *Quien no cae no se levanta*, 304n152, 307n172, 308n198, 359n274
– *La república al revés*, 91, 280nn134, 144, 343n228
– *La santa Juana*, 39, 107, 238n274, 259n156, 280n138, 291n137, 310nn222, 230, 328n9, 345n7
– *Santo, y sastre*, 21, 220–1n18, 225n75, 240n316, 267n225, 268n6, 270–1n29, 282–3n4, 343n230, 351n138, 352n143
– *Segunda parte de Santa Juana*, 286n48, 291n140, 303n130, 304n149, 328n9, 331n47
– *Tanto es lo demás como lo de menos*, 31, 232n180, 239n308, 240n317, 242n11, 244n25, 245n47, 295n18, 297nn54, 55, 56, 300n98, 302n119, 309n221
– *Todo es dar en una cosa*, 262n177, 343n216, 351n127, 360n292
– *La venganza de Tamar*, 273n55, 295n23, 300n106, 356n228
– *La venta*, 70, 266n213
– *Ventura te dé Dios, hijo*, 334n90, 361n307
– *La vida de Herodes*, 67, 79, 257n146, 273n58, 334n91
– *La villana de la Sagra*, 242–3n17, 337n138
– *La villana de Vallecas*, 235n236, 244n30, 299n75, 301n110, 305–6n165
– *Las viudas*, 158, 300–1n109, 310n223, 331n45

ZAMORA, ANTONIO DE (1662?–1728)
– *Amar, es saber vencer, y el arte contra el poder*, 35, 220n14, 235n238, 238n280, 283n6
– *Áspides hay Basiliscos*, 283n7, 288n84
– *Cada uno es linaje aparte, y los Mazas de Aragón*, 165, 223n45, 230n130, 317n95, 324n183, 339n160

– *El custodio de la Hungría, San Juan Capistrano*, 32, 220n14, 221n20, 230n135, 233n201, 289n93, 306n167, 313n31, 314nn46, 51, 361n312
– *Duendes son alcahuetes, alias el foleto, segunda parte*, 296n28, 317n93
– *Duendes son alcahuetes, y el espíritu foleto, primera parte*, 354nn193, 197
– *El hechizado por fuerza*, 323n175
– *Judás Iscariote*, 66, 67, 187, 222n26, 238n276, 258n149, 262nn181, 182, 183, 283n5, 292n147, 297n52, 312n18, 315n54, 350n118
– *El lucero de Madrid, y divino Labrador, san Isidro*, 222n27, 324n197
– *Mazariegos, y Monsalves*, 324n178
– *No hay deuda que no se pague, y convidado de piedra*, 317n92
– *La poncella de Orleans*, 229–30n120, 234n212, 269n21, 328n9, 351n133
– *Por oír misa, y dar cebada, nunca se perdió jornada*, 125, 243n22, 305–6n165, 307nn178, 179, 359n279
– *Ser fino, y no parecerlo*, 284n20, 316nn78, 87, 325n204
– *Siempre hay que envidiar, amando*, 158, 322–3n166, 324n190, 331nn41, 42, 43, 44, 332n62, 344n232
– *Todo lo vence el Amor*, 235n229, 289n100, 290n110
– *Viento es la dicha de amor*, 287n57, 314n44

Index

abandonment, 86, 269–70n26
abbess, 84
abdication, 169
abduction, 269–70n26. *See also* kidnapping
Abel, 160, 333n79
Abensurs, 264n196
Abigail, 311–12n256
abjection, 179, 180
Abraham, 27, 184, 242–3n17, 348n84; bosom of, 46
Abravanel, Isaac, 263–4n192
absolution: by the pope, 365n6; by a priest, 148; from a vow, 124
absolutism, 237nn262, 265
abstinence: from food, 122, 123, 128, 129, 130, 305n160; from meat, 130, 309n221; perpetual, 130; sexual, 248n74
accountant, 160, 334n82
accreditation, 197
accusation, 85, 90, 91, 93, 109, 185, 191, 193, 355n209; internalized, 110; unjust, 94
acedia, 98, 215n15
Achab, 274n67
Achilles, 75, 134, 312n12
Ackerman, Jane, 325n213
actor, 133, 134, 135, 137, 272n42; "feminized," 269n14
Adam, 4, 21, 112, 191, 193, 196, 221n19, 260n166, 333n79, 353n176
Adler, Cyrus, 261n170
administrator, 68
admiration, 170, 336n121, 339n149, 340n174, 343n221
Adonis, 22, 165, 329n26
adoption, 55
adornment, 196, 359n270, 361n315
adulation, 194, 332n65
adult, 16
Adultery, 10, 20, 74, 76, 79, 81, 82, 83, 84, 85, 86, 87, 88, 89, 90, 91, 92, 94, 142, 144, 274n69, 275n71, 295n16, 320n143; duels fought over, 276–7n95; of Jupiter, 77; suspicion of, 143
advice, 51, 57, 71, 125, 140, 143, 250n92, 305n164, 313–14n37, 326n219; conflicting, 103; fatherly, 150; moral, 176
Aegisthus, 78, 273n47
Aeneas, 78, 176, 180, 273n49, 345n16
aesthetics, 63, 199; Baroque, 195, 210, 226n88, 358n256
affair, illicit, 78, 96
affect, 111, 145, 146, 150, 157, 225n78, 242–3n17, 266n220, 294–5n15, 322n164, 322–3n166, 323nn170, 171, 339n154; conquering passion, 146
affectation, 194
affection, 160, 166, 292n147, 322–3n166; paternal, 269–70n26
affront, 139, 140, 318n111
Africa, 26, 27, 29, 35, 216n19, 228n106, 289n97; North, 26, 54, 57, 58; riches of, 64, 259n164; slaves from 55, 164, 249–50n90
Afro-Arabic culture, 203

afterlife, 46
Agamemnon, 144
age, 100, 191; old, 317n101
agency, individual, 5, 8, 204, 207
agony, 115
agriculture, 69, 117, 173
Ahab, 20
Ahasuerus, 293–4n6
air, 221n20, 322n158; rending the, 134
Alarcón, Juan Ruiz de, 32. *For list of works see* Index of *Comedias*
Albania, Albanians, 26, 229–30n120; King of, 146
alcalde, 71; *mayor*, 71
alchemy, 5, 46, 242n10
Alciato, Andrea, 282n164
alcohol, 113
Alcorcón, 265n205
Alexander the Great, 17, 24, 41, 171, 239n296
Alfonso of León, King, 231n154
Alfonso VI, King, 161
algarabía, 240n318
Algiers, 51, 54, 55, 56, 57, 58, 59, 68, 123, 249n85, 253n108
Allah, 26, 254n121
allegiance, 210
allegory, 10, 26, 38, 40, 57, 65, 66, 75, 76, 98, 99, 100, 118, 120, 122, 135, 139, 149, 171, 173, 191, 196, 217n21, 237n265, 240–1n4, 243n19, 260n166, 282n3, 327n4, 332–3n72, 343n227, 359n272
alliance, 179
alliteration, 29
allowance, 280–1n148
almohad, 302–3n129
alms, 129, 307n172; theft of, 300–1n109
almud, 130, 131
Alps, 221–2n22
alquicel, 57
altar, 42, 114, 184, 274n67, 296n35
altar boy, 126
Althusser, Louis, 8
altruism, 177
Amalfi, Duchess of, 93, 281–2n158
Amazon, 19, 224–5n67; queen, 141
amber, 75
ambiguity, 86, 87; historical, 172; moral, 170
ambition, 18, 22, 30, 31, 67, 101, 110, 163, 164, 168, 170, 176, 220n12, 222n23, 223n31, 224n63, 258n150, 294n12, 333nn74, 75, 342n212, 343n225; courtly, 70, 265n207; imperial, 61; of *labrador*, 70
ambrosia, 114, 296n41
amends, 148
America, Americans, 144, 209, 255–6n138, 321n151; "discovery" of, 289n97
Ammonites, 184
ammunition, 252n105
Amon, 78, 270n28
Amri, 274n67
Amsterdam, 261n170, 264n196
amulet, 126
anagram, 236n249
anathema, 49
ancestor, 206
ancients vs moderns, 163, 336n121
Andalusia, 29, 71, 117, 139, 274–5n70
Andrieszen, Hendrik, 38
angel, 20, 36, 61, 105, 165, 177, 183, 307n179, 339n156; fallen, 35; Gabriel, 311–12n256
Anger, 15, 31, 97, 133–52, 155, 215n15, 219n4, 221–2n22, 227n90, 232n181, 238n282, 239n309, 295n16, 296n31, 357n246, 359n276; as emotion, 320–1n144; management, 320–1n144; righteous, 144; romantic, 146
Angry Young Men, 139
anguish, 204
animal, 5, 17, 40, 136, 160, 177, 187, 188, 227n89, 249n84, 303n131, 332–3n72; behaviour like, 137; carnivorous, 293n1; fantastic, 78; kingdom, 222n23; lascivious, 272–3n46; skins of, 21, 196; specimens, 214n6
annotation, 265n207
annoyance, 140
Annunciation, 311–12n256
ant, 45, 121, 242n9, 303n130; anthill, 303n130
Antarctica, 64, 259n164
anthropology, 5, 6
Antichrist, 76, 92, 93; mother of, 93
anti-clericalism, 296n32
antidote, 63, 104, 122
antiquity, 102, 104, 169; late, 262n179

anxiety, 46, 82, 89, 99, 108, 117, 126, 174, 186, 243n22, 276n87, 342n205; cultural, 186; sexual, 274–5n70
Apocalypse, 136, 315n55
Apocrypha, 81, 339n149
Apollo, 77; oracle of, 278n110. *See also* Helios
apology, 170, 300–1n109, 356n229
apoplexy, 46, 244n25
aporia, 203
apostasy, 59, 250–1n95
apostle, 66
apostrophe, 88, 150, 157, 166, 186, 340n164, 342n212
apotheosis, 171
appetite, 101, 102, 112, 113, 115, 117, 119, 120, 121, 123, 124, 247–8n73, 294–5n15, 295nn16, 18, 21, 296nn31, 43, 297nn47, 49, 299nn80, 82, 300nn95, 103, 104, 106, 301n114, 303n130; for wealth, 120; loss of, 129; mother of, 300n106; wife of, 294–5n15
appetizer, 115
applause, 159, 332n59, 342n212, 357n244
apple, 112
aprobación, 33, 77, 126, 337n129
Aquinas, Thomas, St, 142
Arab, 26, 27, 54, 56, 79
Arabic, 26, 52, 79, 130; hands, 251n96; name, 60
Aragon, Aragonese, 29, 68, 70, 92, 165, 270n27, 348n86; Tribunal of, 270–1n29
Arbel, Benjamin, 260–1n167, 262n175
arbitration, 84
arch: of cloister, 89; triumphal, 35
archaic, 207
Archangel: Gabriel, 57; Raphael, 81
architecture, 34, 35, 80
archive, ix–x, xii, 7, 10, 38, 43, 53, 63, 68, 82, 84, 90, 200, 202, 203, 204, 207, 250n92, 250–1n95, 266n215, 267n223, 269–70n26, 270–1n29, 294–5n15, 319n122; fiction in the, 355n209
Archivo General de Indias, 265n202
Arellano, Ignacio, xi
aretē, 91, 205, 363–4n16
Argentina, 250n92
Ariadne, 200, 361n317
aristocracy, 172
aristocrat, 108; status, 172
Aristotle, 10, 171, 177, 194, 214n7, 244n35, 317n98, 320–1n144, 323n168, 357n248, 363–4n16
arithmetic: divine, 85; moral, 8, 85
ark, 35
arm, 18, 225n73, 317n95
Armada, 40, 41, 162, 264n196
armour, 116, 191
arms, 170, 175, 183, 233–4n204, 294–5n15; imperial, 336n119; skill at, 336n123; vigil of, 307n171; vs letters, 106, 108, 163
Armstrong-Roche, Michael, 226n83
army, 62, 63, 110; Aragonese, 70
arrest, 71
arrow, 102, 139, 164, 317n95, 337–8n140
arsenic, 45, 241–2n8
art, 35, 80, 195; connoisseur of, 63; form, 206, 209; market, 301n115; pillaged, 63
ARTELOPE, 213n3, 364n22
artifice, 116, 195, 357n250, 358n256
Artiles, Jenaro, 143
artillery, 121
artist, 122, 265n207; artistic talent, 157, 330n33
ascetic: Christianity, 292n147; discipline, 320–1n144
ashes, 138, 139, 242n11, 317n102
Asia, 26, 229n119
aside, 133
asp, 136, 159, 222nn27, 28, 241n7, 315nn58, 61; of wrath, 136
ass, 156
assault, 71, 163
asset, 164; financial, 246n56; non-material, 157; personal, 68
Assumption, Feast of the, 310n222
Assyria, 261n170
astrology, 5
Asturias, 71; kingdom of, 236n247
asylum, 70
atheism, xi, 3, 65, 208, 261n171
Athena, 137
Atlantic, 253–4n116; Ocean, 64; ports, 54
Atlantis, 22, 227n89
atonement, 184
attorney, 83
auction, 54

audience, 23, 24, 65, 73, 94, 106, 130, 132, 133, 136, 156, 186, 260n166, 296–7n44, 318n121
Augustine, St, 6, 142, 279n122
aunt, 47, 245n46
austerity, 226n83
authority, 182, 277–8n100, 335n107; acts against, 221–2n22; divine, 90; earthly, 187; ecclesiastical, 142, 320n143; figure, 177; of nature, 237n265; own, 142; secular, 90, 122, 142, 196, 272n38, 320n143
authorship, 180, 181, 347n69, 363n8; first, 181
auto de fe, 226n83
auto sacramental, ix–xi, 21, 22, 23, 26, 27, 33, 35, 38, 40, 42, 43, 57, 64, 65, 70, 72, 79, 98, 99, 111, 112–15, 117, 118, 119, 120, 122, 123, 125, 126, 130, 131, 132, 135, 137, 139, 149, 156, 157, 160, 162, 167, 170, 196, 200, 217n21, 219nn2, 3, 4, 220nn7, 10, 221n20, 221–2n22, 222nn27, 28, 223nn39, 40, 42, 43, 224nn51, 56, 57, 225nn77, 78, 79, 226nn84, 85, 87, 228nn97, 98, 99, 229n119, 230nn126, 136, 141, 231n149, 232n181, 233nn186, 190, 203, 234nn210, 214, 235n234, 236n241, 237n266, 238nn279, 291, 239nn301, 307, 240n4, 241n6, 241–2n8, 242n14, 242–3n17, 243nn18, 19, 244nn24, 29, 247n69, 252n107, 253nn108, 109, 258n151, 260nn165, 166, 261nn168, 169, 170, 262n180, 265nn200, 201, 203, 207, 266nn216, 217, 218, 220, 221, 267nn229, 232, 233, 268nn3, 4, 5, 8, 269nn16, 19, 20, 22, 23, 24, 25, 272–3n46, 273nn53, 59, 276nn89, 90, 280n128, 281nn151, 153, 282n3, 282–3n4, 283n9, 284nn13, 15, 16, 18, 19, 22, 285nn25, 29, 33, 286n42, 286n43, 287nn57, 58, 63, 64, 67, 68, 288nn70, 85, 290n117, 293nn167, 176, 1, 2, 3, 4, 5, 293–4n6, 294nn7, 8, 9, 10, 11, 12, 13, 14, 294–5n15, 295nn16, 19, 20, 25, 296nn30, 31, 36, 37, 38, 39, 40, 296–7n44, 297nn47, 48, 49, 53, 59, 60, 298n69, 299nn80, 82, 92, 93, 300nn95, 97, 100, 101, 102, 103, 104, 301nn114, 116, 302n121, 303nn135, 136, 137, 138, 139, 140, 143, 144, 305n160, 307nn173, 174, 176, 177, 180, 183, 308nn189, 191, 309n215, 310n235, 311nn240, 241, 242, 243, 244, 245, 246, 247, 248, 250, 251, 252, 253, 254, 255, 311–12n256, 312nn259, 4, 5, 14, 15, 313nn28, 33, 314nn41, 43, 51, 53, 315nn55, 58, 59, 60, 65, 316n76, 317n97, 319n133, 322n157, 323nn167, 171, 325nn202, 203, 205, 212, 327n4, 328nn15, 21, 23, 329nn25, 26, 330n32, 332n71, 332–3n72, 333n79, 335n112, 339nn154, 157, 340n166, 341nn184, 191, 194, 343nn225, 227, 344nn233, 237, 1, 345n26, 346n31, 348n82, 350nn106, 113, 119, 356n239, 358n259, 359nn271, 272, 273, 361nn309, 310, 317, 318, 319, 362n1, 365n1; lost, 117
autobiography, 11, 25, 364n17
autonomy, 150, 207
Avarice, 8, 15, 31, 44, 45–73, 79, 155, 185, 207, 215n15, 220n6, 238n282, 295n16, 296n31, 323n171. *See also* Greed

Baal, 20, 92, 274n67
Babel, 35, 36
baby, 185, 281n154
Babylon, 39, 43, 235n233
Bacchus, 295n21
bacon, 135
Baeza, Pedro de, 364n17
bag, 241n6, 249n89, 255n127, 265n202
baker, 130
Baker, Edward, 172, 173
balcony, 20
ballad, 80, 273–4n63
Balthasar, 293–4n6
Bances Candamo, Francisco, 348n86
Bandello, Matteo, 93, 281–2n158
bandit, 70, 71, 266nn209, 218, 219, 221, 267n222, 317n97; dress of a, 139, 267n222
banishment, 194
bank, banker, 66, 260–1n167, 264n196
bankruptcy, 116, 264n196
banquet, 112, 113, 114, 116, 121, 122, 132, 293–4n6, 294nn7, 10, 13, 294–5n15, 295n18, 298n69, 303n136
Banquo, 89
baptism, 10, 271n31
Barabas of Malta, 260–1n167
Barahona, Renato, 269–70n26

barbarity, 26, 42, 98, 100, 134, 148, 157, 162, 241–2n8, 259nn155, 164, 282–3n4, 334n80, 344n234
Barbary, 58, 253n114, 253–4n116
Barcelona, 106, 270n27
bargain, 64, 65
bark, 187
Baroque, 8, 9, 17, 19, 20, 22, 29, 34, 38, 46, 63, 76, 79, 91, 113, 115, 128, 157, 166, 168, 194, 195, 199, 210, 217n21, 257n147, 297nn46, 51, 301–2n117, 328n9, 332–3n72, 341n190; aesthetics, 210, 226n88; artifice, 224n55; ingenuity, 358n254; mannerism, 226n88; nihilism, 342n203; painting, 358n256; virtuosity, 226n88
basilisk, 136, 159, 281n151, 315n54, 327n4, 332n57
basket, 113, 295n19
Basque, 216n19
Bass, Laura, 195, 354n203
bastard, 91, 92, 93
bath, 75, 268n12, 320–1n144
Bathsheba, 161
battle, 18, 25, 26, 27, 39, 104, 121, 302–3n129, 317n89, 358n257; epic, 199, 361n310; field, 20, 104, 139, 184, 283n11; front line of, 161; of Gembloux, 283n11; infernal, 137; of Lepanto, 54; literary, 33; naval, 41
beach, 18, 216n19, 254n117
beard, 21, 65, 261n170, 278n109, 338n148; mutilation, 261n170
beast, 67, 136, 156
beata, 149, 182
beating, 71, 135, 185, 313–14n37
beatus ille, 106, 169
beauty, 18, 19, 20, 52, 54, 74, 112, 157, 162, 164, 171, 221n20, 224n57, 288nn81, 82, 294–5n15, 316n78, 329n26, 338n142, 350n121; and virtue, 359n276; daughter of, 224n54; earthly, 187
bed, 45, 74, 88, 98, 99, 102, 241n5, 268n5, 284n22, 287n64, 307n184, 330n36, 365n6; baby's, 311n248; bedroom, 81; bedsheet, 50; deathbed, 189; feather, 287n68; getting out of, 127; hearing mass in, 127, 308n195; marriage, 81; soft, 287n68
beef, 112
beggar, 68, 69, 75, 116, 119, 120, 148; devout, 122; theft from, 300–1n109
behaviour: codes of, 108; lascivious, 142; passive-aggressive, 329n24; womanly, 347n69
Behemoth, 272–3n46
belief, 304–5n159; persecution for, 190; structures of, 173
Benbassa, Esther, 263n190, 263–4n192, 264nn195, 196
benefice: ecclesiastical, 114; sale of, 159
Benjamin, Walter, 237n265
bequest, 48, 125
Berber, 68
Bermejo Cabrero, José Luis, 231n164, 276–7n95, 278–9n111
Bernini, Gian Lorenzo, 210
bestiality, 76, 270–1n29, 271n30
bestiary, 5
Bethlehem, 131, 311n248
betrayal, 84, 140, 170, 279n112
betrothal, 166, 247n67
bias, 84
Bible, 6, 23, 31, 35, 40, 67, 73, 78, 80, 136, 138, 144, 182, 202, 216–17n20, 225n68, 236n241, 242–3n17, 261n170, 273nn55, 59, 303n140, 316n76, 331n47, 333n79, 334n81, 348nn79, 84, 85
bienes ajenos, 73, 157, 160, 169, 267n232, 350n107
bigamy, 202
bile, 323n168
binary, 203
biography, 265n207
bird, 22, 177, 187; large, 163; nest of, 45; plague-stricken, 136; of prey, 46; simple, 70; small, 163, 242n9, 337n127
birth, 16, 38, 55, 92, 159, 174, 182, 191, 310n230, 337n136; childbirth, 159; irregular, 280–1n148; of Jesus Christ, 79, 88; rate, 331n48; sex after, 81
bite, 315n58, 337–8n140, 338n141; Envy's, 164; the lip, 338n146; snake, 136, 156, 222n28, 327n4; the tongue, 164
Bizerta, 55
black: African, 164; Indian, 228n108
Black Legend, 80, 255–6n138
blame, 158, 255–6n138, 331n43, 335n100
blanca, 267n222

Blasphemy, 42, 43, 44, 128, 185, 239nn309, 315
bleeding, 243n19; with leeches, 149. *See also* bloodletting
blessing, 305–6n165
blindfold, 143
blindness, 18, 52, 67, 117, 119, 134, 156, 219n4, 223–4n49, 227n89, 262n183, 299n82, 300n104, 312n12, 313n22, 322n162, 326n220, 328nn9, 15, 333n75; moral, 178
blockade, 164
blood, 15, 17, 18, 24, 46, 87, 92, 135, 145, 149, 163, 219n4, 222n28, 223n37, 229n119, 243n19, 315nn54, 62, 317n101, 323n168, 334n87; bad, 325n208; bloodbath, 314n43; bloodletting, 143, 325n208; bloodline, 91; boiling, 323n168; burning, 146; drinking, 137, 219n4, 315n70; excess of, 147; inflammation of, 139, 146, 323n168; innocent, 67; lamb's, 320n142; libel, 68; lineage, 163; manufacture of, 323n168; noble, 163; purity of, 91, 163, 164, 232n182, 232–3n184; relative, 134, 185; royal, 38; selling, 241–2n8; stain, 143, 320n142; thick, 139; weeping, 168; writing with, 86
bloodthirstiness, 104, 137, 315n69
boar, 17, 40; wild, 222n25, 337–8n140
body, 17, 41, 82, 123, 145, 149, 275n71, 307n178, 313n27, 313–14n37, 322nn158, 159; animal, 187; beautiful, 329n29; binding of, 81; of a boar, 227n89; corporeal, 187; detoxification of, 304–5n159; fat, 124; flight from, 320–1n144; food for the, 131, 132; human, 187, 350n120; naked, 329n28; part, 188; power over, 304–5n159; punishment of, 304–5n159; quartered, 71; rest for the, 101; sale of, 70; and soul, 125, 276n87; thin, 124; woman's, 157, 274n65
bofetón, 313n34
Boleyn, Anne, 32
Bologna, Antonio, 281–2n158
book: dedication, 335n107; foreign, 226n83; history, 198; reading of, 108; seller, 72; writing of, 106
boon, 161, 334n93
booty, 71
boredom, 104, 109, 110
Bosch, Hieronymus, 7, 69, 70, 216n17
bosom, 136
boss, 104
Bossy, John, 6, 7, 42, 94, 202, 203, 215–16n16
botany, 5
Bougie, 55
bounty, 55
boutique, 33
branding, 43, 202
bravery, 106, 108, 228n108, 231n152
bread, 43, 99, 117, 118, 123, 124, 194, 298n65, 303n143, 304nn150, 154, 311n248; Eucharistic, 132; from heaven, 123; House of, 130, 131; of Life, 130, 131, 260n166; loaves of, 130; and onion, 296n42; as prop, 130; riot, 130; rotten, 115; stones into, 123, 303n140; supply, 131; and water, 305nn160, 163
breakfast, 129, 300–1n109, 304nn150, 154; begging for, 120
breast, breasts, 63, 138, 258n151, 259n155, 268n7, 279n112, 312n15, 322n164, 325n204, 334n84; beautiful, 343n215; breastplate, 149, 325n205; wounded, 86
breath, 284n22, 300n99, 312n8; bad, 187, 351n122; catching one's, 287n63; exhalation, 136; saving one's, 351n122
bride, 49, 146
bridge, 35
bridle, 17, 37, 67
British, 139
broker, 264n196
bronze, 338n141
Brook, Yaron, 260–1n167
Brooks, David, 363n12
brothel, 248n74; legal, 53; for the soul, 268n7; travelling, 53
brother, 19, 23, 26, 41, 60, 78, 129, 160, 170, 210, 224n63, 240n1, 245n43, 260n166, 330n33, 333nn78, 79, 334n80, 365n7; legitimate, 280–1n148; love affair with, 76, 78, 271n34; older, 48, 67, 333n79; in religion, 66
brutality, 137
bull, 136, 156, 284n20, 293n170; bullfight, 156, 216n19; sex with, 76, 78, 270–1n29; wounded, 328n13
bullet, 139, 317n94

bureaucrat, 194
Burgos, 71, 172, 276n78, 336n124
burial, 257n147, 293n172; live, 48
burlesque, 30, 234n213, 285n31, 297n56
burning, 115, 134, 136, 138, 146, 156, 158, 171, 297n55, 313n36, 314n61, 317n101, 321n151, 328n10, 331n44, 334n84; alive, 83; blood, 139, 243n19; with Envy, 158; with love, 158; with rage, 133, 314n47; of the soul, 67; at the stake, 52, 90
business, 290n114; activity, 262n179
bust, 164
butterfly, 17, 222n23, 328n10
button, 22, 225n81

cadaver, 242n11
Cádiz, 260n166
Caesar Augustus, 67
Cain, 160, 333n79
Calahorra, 338n141
calculus, 322n158
Calderón, 19, 22, 25, 26, 32, 33, 34, 61, 72, 79, 114, 119, 122, 126, 131, 132, 137, 146, 157, 162, 169, 179, 181, 209, 216–17n20, 225n77, 227n89, 238n282, 255n124; biography, 245n40, 265n207, 310n235. *For list of works see* Index of *Comedias*
Callao (Peru), 258n153
camel, 243n17
cameo, 102, 147, 148
Campbell, Jodi, 146, 323n172
Campbell, Ysla, 265n202, 346–7n53
campesino, 269–70n26
Canary Islands, 24
cancer, 43
candle, 87, 101, 256–7n144, 287n66
cane, 100, 290n125, 331n55
cannibalism, 137; canon, 11, 23, 206; law, 143
cape, 22, 196, 225n78, 335n100, 338n148, 359n272; of Truth, 359n272
Capital Vices, 5, 6, 7, 8, 15, 21, 33, 40, 41, 42, 44, 45, 46, 47, 48, 69, 73, 76, 94, 98, 99, 101, 109, 111, 112, 129, 131, 133, 136, 142, 145, 146, 147, 149, 150, 151, 155, 168, 169, 170, 173, 174, 190, 202, 203, 209, 211, 217n21, 219n4, 238n282, 268n5, 283n7, 291n145, 295n16, 322n162, 349n99. *See also* Seven Deadly Sins
capitalism, 69, 172
captatio benevolentiae, 93
captive, 51, 55, 57, 59, 249n85, 252nn104, 105, 259n154, 300n99; chained, 57; Christian, 58, 251n96, 253n114, 254n121; Man, 260n166; North African, 57; price of, 58; ransom of, 56; redemption, 57, 58, 253n111; sale of, 56, 58; by sin, 57; Spanish, 253–4n116
captivity, 176, 251nn96, 97; in Algiers, 123; by love, 102; quasi-captivity, 179
captor, 254n121, 300n99
capture, 196, 251n97, 253n114
cardinal, 114, 296n36, 352n142
caress, 187
cargo, 260n166
caricature, 106
Caro, Rodrigo, 291n145
carpe diem, 93, 103, 114
carpet, 235n230
Carpio, Bernardo del, 134
carriage, 108, 118
Carrión, María Mercedes, 85, 278n106, 313n34
cart, 132, 268n3, 311n252, 317n97
carta de hidalguía, 233n185
Cartagena Calderón, José Reinaldo, 269n14
Cartama, 27
Carthage, Carthaginians, 24, 228n106
cartography, 5
cartoon, 45
Cascardi, Anthony, 237n265
Case, Thomas E., 289n97
case: criminal, 355n209; extreme, 210; study, 210
Casey, James, 331n48
Casilda, St, 326n219, 339n157
Castile, 29, 71, 162, 239n305, 265n206, 336n124; Council of, 70, 117; expansion of, 289n97; northern, 172
Castilian, 29, 37, 55, 336n114; culture, 320n143; duel, 276–7n95; language, 180
Castillejo, David, xi, 227n92
castle, 34, 266n211
Castro, Américo, 308n197
Castro, Guillén de. *For list of works see* Index of *Comedias*
casuistry, 5, 7, 137, 141, 143, 189, 190, 218n32, 234n213, 318n121
cat, 70, 165, 249n89

Catalan, 29, 216n19
Catalonia, 68, 71
catechism, 6, 187, 215n13; satire of, 118
cátedra, 33
cathedral, 61
Catholics, Catholicism, 6, 23, 26, 27, 35, 43, 71, 82, 84, 112, 125, 126, 159, 189, 202, 276n78; Apocrypha, 81; Church, 277–8n100; devotion, 327n228; faithful, 126; Monarchs, 67, 68, 289n97; ordinary, 129; sacrament, 144; Universal Monarchy, 216–17n20
cattle, 149
La Cava, 80, 273–4n63, 274n65
cavern, 185, 241n6
celebrity, 159
Celestina, 128, 192, 248n80
celibacy, 182
cemetery, 208
censor, 10, 33, 78, 126, 183; censorship, 210, 218n31, 255n124
ceremony, 51, 127, 180, 246n57
Cervantes, Miguel de, 179; jealousy in, 330n40; as proto-feminist, 285n33. *For list of works see* Index of *Comedias*
Céspedes y Meneses, Gonzalo de, 25
Ceuta, 273–4n63
chains, 123, 129; golden, 247n59, 313n35
chair, 50, 102
chalice, 132, 256–7n144, 260n166
Cham, 35
chamber, 160, 334n85
chameleon, 322n162
Chaparro, 70
chapel, 127, 258n153, 308n193, 309n216
chariot, 22, 23, 32
charity, 58, 119, 252n105
Charlemagne, 35
Charles II, King, 226n82
Charles III, King, 216n19
Charles V, Emperor, 34, 69, 169, 226n82, 238n274, 248n74, 265n286
charm, 165
charter, 262n175
chastisement, 188
chastity, 81, 84, 104; assumptions about, 85; cult of, 274–5n70; lack of, 82; vow of, 129
cheese, 115, 303n131
chef, 110, 118
chemistry, 5
chest, 18, 149
chicken, 310n231
child, 52, 62, 79, 80, 117, 118, 119, 159, 169, 178, 179, 180, 184, 214n2, 216–17n20, 236n241, 250n92, 250–1n95, 318n110, 331n48, 333n79; bastard, 91, 92, 280–1n148, 294–5n15; beggar, 120; biological, 180; book as, 181; childhood, 16; Christian, 72; devoured, 122; education of, 215n11; of Envy, 156; face of, 177; godchild, 76; grown, 81; Jesus, 182; Jewish, 55; legitimate, 91; memory of, 209; as mirror of parent, 345n24; Morisco, 55, 250n92, 250–1n95; pious, 176, 184; superiors of, 304–5n159; Turkish, 60; well-behaved, 175
chimera, 115, 199, 361n315
chimney, 48
China, 27
choice, 188
choking, 244n24
Christ, 35, 57, 109, 130, 132, 183, 232–3n184, 260n166, 292n147, 303n140; birth of, 88; flesh of, 132; hungry, 123; as Spouse, 84; type of, 144, 157, 260n166; wounds of, 66, 262n180
Christians, Christianity, 3, 6, 20, 23, 26, 27, 54, 55, 58, 65, 66, 99, 104, 127, 133, 189, 248n81, 249n86, 250n93, 254n121, 302–3n129, 354n203; buying, 249n85; captives, 58, 251n97, 254n121; children, 72; Church, 239n315; courtesy, 308n195; faith, 60, 61; families, 55, 250–1n95; God, 144; humanism, 22, 177; infants, 55; kidnapping of, 59; moralists, 320n143; Old, 69, 250n92; principality, 236n247; prisoners, 56; relations with Muslims, 251n97; renegade, 59; ships, 55; Spain, 56; tradition, 138; valour, 144
Christmas, 58, 125, 253n108, 339n156
chronicle, 80
church, 39, 89, 104, 114, 124, 182, 232–3n184, 247n72, 253n108, 260–1n167, 307n171, 308n194, 331n52; attendance, 125, 127, 128, 307n179; being quiet in, 128; Catholic, 277–8n100; Christian, 239n315; church/state, 150, 159, 208, 209; doctrine, 118; door, 253n108, 307n179; far-away, 128, 309n208; Jesuit, 258n153;

lovers in, 128, 309n204; as meeting place, 308n197, 309n206; message of, 248n74; parish, 52; as pimp, 128; plundered, 55; prayer in, 127; service, 125, 305–6n165; and state, 209, 216–17n20; theft in, 72; tokens exchanged in, 128
Chus, 35, 236n241
Cid, 31, 163
Cinderella, 138, 169
cinema, 24, 139
circumlocution, 190
circumstance, 190
Ciruelo, Pedro, 323n168
citizen, 121, 250n92, 265n206
city, 43, 46, 54, 65, 71, 106, 131, 164, 255n129, 260–1n167, 290n113, 298n69, 337–8n140, 357n245; conquered, 339n149; council, 172; grand, 338n141; Italian, 260–1n167; of Kings, 61; life, 169; planners, 109; sacking of, 62, 63
clandestine, 187
class: oppression, 109; structure, 171
classical: antiquity, 169, 318n109, 362n8; cultures, 358n259; ideas, 291n145, 363–4n16; period, 291n145; post-classical, 362n8; reception, 362n8; text, 244n35; tradition, 144, 362n8
Clavero, Bartolomé, 262n177, 279n122, 319n122
Cleopatra, 78, 113
cleric, 114
clerk, 194
client, 172
cloak, 57, 161
cloister, 89, 180, 253n108
closet drama, 11, 53, 272n41
clothing, 51, 62, 196, 250n92, 301n113, 329–30n31, 359n271; of courtiers, 246n57; lavish, 52, 331n56; pretty, 158, 330n38; ripping off, 135, 313n35; sheep's, 160; stripping off, 71, 207. *See also* dress; fashion; garment
cloud, 131, 147, 221n22, 238n285, 258n153, 328n9
Clytemnestra, 78
coach, 71, 291n129
coast, 55, 58, 252n105, 302n126
coat of arms, 31, 32, 175
coat of many colours, 160
co-dependency, 150
code: of fashion, 300n97; figurative, 300n97; moral, 203; social, 205; switching, 150
cognitive dissonance, 248n74
coin, 297–8n63, 360n291
cold, 136
Colón, Diego, 280–1n148
Colón, Hernando, 92, 280–1n148
colonization, 62
colony, 61, 63, 255n128, 265n202
colour, 323n176; change of, 170, 322n162, 323n168; of the face, 134; losing, 313n25
Columbus, Christopher, 65, 92, 250n91, 264n193, 302n127, 336n114
column, 144
combat, 276–7n95; mortal, 84; mounted, 84; trial by, 276n95
combustion, 166
comedia de santos, 100, 129
comedia suelta, 133
comendador, 209
Comenius, Johan Amos, 282n164
Commandments, Ten, 3, 5, 6, 7, 8, 42, 44, 73, 84, 91, 111, 129, 140, 141, 150, 155, 157, 160, 169, 173, 174–201, 202, 204, 207, 209, 210, 211, 215n11, 320n142, 344n1–361n323; First, 320n142; Second, 43, 239n315, 320n142; Third, 125, 128, 239n315; Fourth, 180; Fifth, 140, 150; Sixth, 83; Seventh, 72, 73; Eighth, 186–201; Ninth, 156, 157; Tenth, 73, 156, 157; emergent, 174. *See also* Decalogue
commerce, 262n179
commodification, 173
commodity, 187, 248n81
commoner, 70, 82
commonplace books, 11, 219n38
communal: sin as, 94, 166; world view, 91, 143
communion, 125, 126, 306nn166, 169
community, 7, 73, 94, 262n175
Company of Jesus, 308n198. *See also* Jesuit
compass, 223n45
compassion, 145, 167, 341nn193, 194
comparative literature, 9
compensation, 176
competition, 170
compliance, 180
complicity, 188
Comuneros' Revolt, 38, 69

conceptista, 33, 200
concepto, 200
condemned, 185
conduct manual, 19
confectioner, 296n31
confession, 84, 126, 141, 143, 162, 306n166, 324n184, 352n142; confessional booth, 141, 204, 207; sacramental, 148
confessor, 5, 33, 81, 124, 143, 203, 234n213, 274–5n70, 275n71, 276n87, 304–5n159
confessors' manual, 4, 7, 142, 203, 204, 271n31, 275n71
confirmation, sacrament of, 271n31
conflagration, 185
congregation, 321n151
conjecture, 86
Connor Swietlicki, Catherine, 347n63
conquest, 24, 25, 27, 61, 162, 227n96, 228nn106, 108, 336n118; of Granada, 263–4n192, 289n97; Muslim, 103; "New" World, 55, 104, 289n97
conquistadores, 24, 25, 46, 61, 162, 302n126
conscience, 4, 7, 137, 176, 189, 214n4, 362–3n11; examination of, 4; guilty, 89; "wide," 309n221
consciousness, 4, 11, 214n4; of class, 265n207; lack of, 279n122; of sin, 89
consecration, 181, 184
consort, 274n67
consumption, 226n82
containment, 182
contamination, 47, 191, 236–7n257, 244n27, 284n16
contentment, 168
contract, 186
Contreras, Alonso de, 364n17
control, 346n50, 363n15
convenience, 179
convent, 57, 84, 116, 180, 253n108, 305n161
conversation, 320–1n144
conversion, 40, 60, 129, 251n97
converso, 31, 69
cook, 110, 112, 116, 118, 298n68, 312n258
copper, 63
copulation, 35, 275n71. *See also* sex
coral, 259n164
cord, 86
Córdoba, 29, 53, 117, 280–1n148
Corella, Jayme de, 275n71
Corpus Christi, feast of, 35, 57, 130, 132, 135, 310n234
corral, 144, 156
corruption, 115
corsair, 26, 59, 60, 61, 252n105, 253–4n116; Muslim, 55, 58, 251–2n103. *See also* piracy
Cortes, 226n82; of León, 333n77
La Coruña, 280–1n148
Cosdroes, 138
cosmetics, 75, 187, 196, 359n268
cost, 307n172
costume, 21, 22, 159, 196, 217n21, 238n282, 300n97; as asset, 246n56; change, 196; "Moorish," 267n222; nautical, 343n227
counsel, counsellor, 148, 150, 326n219
Count-Duke of Olivares, 30, 37, 161, 225–6n82, 236n249
Counter-Reformation, 20, 39, 99, 115, 131, 209, 210, 211, 226n83
counterfeit, 197, 242n10, 360n291
courage, 163, 276–7n95
court, 8, 22, 30, 31, 37, 38, 57, 104, 107, 114, 159, 160, 162, 169, 174, 194, 195, 233n185, 331n53, 332nn57, 60, 335nn97, 98, 337–8n140; atmosphere, 199; cares of the, 105; courtroom, 83, 141; culture, 159, 186; daughter of the, 159; of the devil, 34; documents, 269–70n26; entertainment, 106; of God, 37; local, 260–1n167; in Madrid, 106; performance, 265n207; poet, 162; pretender, 194, 357n243; royal, 102, 186; scorn for the, 290n113; Supreme, 209
courtesy, 159, 308n195; discourtesy, 333n75
courtier, 31, 51, 75, 102, 104, 108, 114, 116, 160, 161, 162, 169, 186, 194, 232n181, 268n10, 296nn30, 31, 334n90, 335n100, 342n201, 356n235; class, 173; clothes of, 246n57; disloyal, 160; effete, 107; female, 194; feminized, 106; Spanish, 108
courting, 192
courtly: ambitions, 265n207; favours, 110; game, 161; intrigue, 169; landscape, 160; leisure, 186, 290n125; lie, 194; lifestyle, 116; love, 102; models, 290n113; office, 159; pastime, 107
courtyard, public, 35
cousin, 305n164
Covarrubias, Sebastián de, 68, 86

coveting, 45, 73, 83, 156, 163, 178, 232n181, 333n75, 350n107; Commandments concerning, 157; of virtues, 329n25; a wife, 156, 350n107
cowardice, 104, 282n3
creed, 114
crime, 71, 83, 87, 89, 94, 97, 109, 141, 150, 178, 196, 220n7, 266n220, 279n122, 333n79, 335n100; excuse for, 142; narrowly defined, 144; notorious, 278–9n111; penalty for, 90; scene, 85
Crime Scene Investigation (*CSI*), 86, 87
criminal, petty, 68, 109
criminal behaviour, 86; criminality, 90, 109, 215n11
criminalization, 141, 279n122
cripple, 69, 120
crop, 117
cross-dressing, 19, 225n67, 299n82. *See also* transvestism
crown, 32, 34, 38, 56, 68, 139, 146, 108, 252n105
crucifix, 89, 90
cruelty, 135, 184, 185, 190, 228n97, 243n18, 256n138, 256–7n144, 300n99, 313–14n37, 333n78, 340n163, 361n309
Cruickshank, Don, 221–2n22, 225–6n82, 232–3n184, 236n249, 245n40, 298–9n73, 310n235, 311n237, 320n142, 325n208
crumb, 301n110
Crusades, 145, 256–7n144
Cruz, Anne J., 69, 119, 120
crying, 161, 178, 188, 312n8, 313n22, 329n25, 334n91, 338n143, 351n130
crystal, 187
cuckold, 320n143
Cueva, Juan de la. *For list of works see* Index of *Comedias*
cuisine, 118, 120
culpability, 84, 184, 190, 299n82, 300n97, 317n97, 339n157
culteranismo, 199
culterano, 33
cup, 74, 113, 268n3, 295n19, 302n120
Cupid, 81, 102
cure, 147, 148, 304–5n159
curiosity, 106, 308n201
curse, 3, 178, 185, 214n2, 216–17n20
cushion, 241n5
custom, 308n198, 332n61
Cuzco, 62
cynicism, 128
Cyprus, 77

Daedalus, 242n9
dagger, 89, 139, 144, 158, 317n95, 318n108, 338n148
dalliance, 86
dance, 101, 294nn10, 13, 298n69, 320–1n144
dandy, 20, 22, 247n59, 292n158, 332n59
danger, 189, 257n147, 259n156, 298n69, 330n33
Daniel, 42, 293n6
Dante Alighieri, 209
Danube, 221n20
darkness, 67
Darwin, Charles, 177
daughter, 37, 52, 57, 78, 80, 90, 91, 146, 169, 178, 179, 180, 185, 246n51, 269–70n26, 272nn41, 42, 294–5n15; of Anger, 141; of beauty, 224n54; of the court, 159, 331n53; of Envy, 328n16; of the homeland, 337n139; honour of, 143; incest with, 77; of men, 236n241; oldest, 146; only, 184; treasonous, 210; unwed, 179
David, King, 50, 148, 149, 161, 302n128, 311–12n256, 325n201; wife of, 311–12n256
Davis, Natalie Zemon, 355n209
Davis, Robert, 53, 66, 248n81
dawn, 129, 307n179, 308n189
day, 303n140, 350n116
De la Cruz, Felipe, 271n31
De la Torre, Juan Estebán, 268n7
death, 20, 46, 58, 87, 92, 99, 100, 109, 114, 125, 127, 133, 134, 140, 143, 179, 184, 185, 231n164, 233n185, 241n6, 242nn11, 12, 260n166, 272n38, 286n44, 301–2n117, 315n71, 318n119, 328n11, 330n34, 331n48, 332–3n72, 337n129, 348n86, 350n121; as Anger's daughter, 141; deathbed, 189; in despair, 83; by famine, 273n53; heroic, 167; just, 83; knell, 151; from overeating, 297n56; point of, 128, 351n140; power of, 142; pretended, 48, 245n44; as punishment, 82, 84, 85, 90;

of royal family, 77; of a social class, 172; of Socrates, 315n65; by starvation, 117; without heirs, 60
debate, 255–6n138
debt, 184, 216–17n20, 260n166; moral, 175
Debus, Allen G., 322n159
Decalogue, 5, 6, 7, 42, 73, 83, 94, 128, 129, 143, 157, 174–201, 202, 203, 209, 276n91. *See also* Commandments, Ten
decay, 98, 115, 297n52, 301–2n117, 345n25
deception, 98, 150, 159, 178, 186, 187, 188, 191, 193, 195, 196, 197, 199, 242n12, 254n120, 257n147, 330n39, 332n66, 350n110, 352n142, 354n203, 357nn244, 250, 360nn283, 289, 290, 303
decision, 305n163
deconstruction, 155, 203, 362–3n11
decorum, 231n159; breach of, 140, 318n112
defamation, 90
deformity, 92, 115, 297n51
deity, 78, 123
Del Río Parra, Elena, works: *Cartografías de conciencia*, 5, 210, 246n51, 318n121; "Suspensio animi," 149
delay, 98
deliberation, 279n122
delicacy, 115, 116, 120, 121, 131, 293n1, 294nn7, 10, 12, 295nn24, 26, 296nn30, 41, 297n57, 298n69, 311n249
delight, 294–5n15
delinquent, 90
delirium, 179, 240n321
democracy, 209
democratic, 47, 237n262
demography, 28, 93
demon, 3, 27, 61, 67, 81, 117, 182, 183, 191, 202, 227n96, 244n24, 266n218, 270–1n29, 281n151, 325n201; demonic possession, 137, 242–3n17, 316n74; demonology, 183; hungry, 118; mouth of, 255n124; noonday, 100; sacrifice to, 78; as scapegoat, 222–3n29
Denia, 56
denunciation, 264n196
depravity, 92
depression, 286n45; agitated, 100; as Anger, 135; catatonic, 100; clinical, 100
deprivation, 300n106, 335n96; of food, 300n106; of sex, 275n71, 300n106
Derrida, Jacques, 10, 104, 362–3n11
desaparecido, 250n92
Descartes, René, 4
descendant, 90
Desdemona, 86
desengaño, 17, 46, 76, 115, 168, 186, 242n12, 296–7n44, 334n95; house of, 287n60
desert, 93, 123, 131, 157, 160, 303n140
deserter, 70, 75
desire, 169, 182, 188, 297n57, 351n136, 352n141; to control, 346n50; for food, 295n16; generous, 284n17; noble, 170, 343n231; revenge, 318n119, 323n168; to see friends, 308n198; sexual, 272–3n46
desk, 45, 241n6, 242n10
despair, 185, 237n262; economic, 300–1n109
dessert, 114
destabilization, 109
detection, 196
determinism, 16
detoxification, 304–5n159
Deuteronomy, 66
devil, 15, 16, 17, 20, 34, 37, 42, 76, 137, 165, 303n140, 339n157
devotion, 113, 127, 294n14, 305–6n165, 307n179, 308n201, 327n328; extraordinary, 129; occasion for, 126; pious, 124, 129; public, 126; religious, 122, 128
dialect, 261n171, 355n222
Diamante, Juan Bautista, 133. *For list of works see* Index of *Comedias*
diamond, 52, 53, 61, 240–1n4, 247n59
Diana, 137, 316n78
diary, 306n166
diaspora, 68, 263n189
Díaz-Plaja, Fernando, 239n299, 276n78
DICAT, 213n3
dictatorship, 55, 210, 274–5n70
didacticism, 144, 176, 185, 188, 189, 265n207, 361n309
Dido, 78
diestro braço, 108, 110
diet, 115, 117, 125, 304–5n159
difference, 263n186, 362–3n11
digital age, 207
digital humanities, 9
digital search tools, 213n3
dignity, 148, 191
dilution, 98

dinner, 112, 131, 129, 310nn231, 235
Dionysus, 272–3n46
director, 206
disarmament, 103
discipline, 99, 129, 178, 210, 285n35, 292n147, 304n149, 309nn216, 219, 320–1n144. *See also* flagellation
disclaimer, 179
discourse, 191, 200
"Discovery," 46, 121, 289n97
discretion, 176, 186
disease, 147, 261n170, 322n159; personal, 99; social, 99; spiritual, 63
"disenchantment of the world," 48, 245–6n49
disfigurement, 164, 261n170
disgrace, 178, 194, 247n72, 261n170, 355n209
disguise, 88, 105, 119, 159, 191, 195, 196, 245n44, 254n120, 267n222, 299n82, 313n33, 332n66, 356n235
dismay, 146
disorder, 320–1n144
dispensation: for lying, 190; for marrying relatives, 348n90; papal, 185
dissent, 210
distress, 283–4n12
diversion, 291n141, 294n13, 298n69
divorce, 88, 285n33
DNA, 87
doctor, 124, 143, 304–5n159, 323n167, 327n7
doctrine, 118, 183, 190, 352n155
dog, 17, 118, 120; bark of, 222n24; honest, 187; rabid, 136, 137, 315n70; stray, 135
dogma, 99, 209, 210
dome, 258n153
domestic crises, 103
domestication, 85, 94, 142
dominant, 97, 155, 156, 171
Dominic, St, 61
Dominican, 61
Don Juan, 91
Don Quijote, 70, 104, 108, 150, 172, 181, 206, 207, 266n211, 283–4n12, 347n67
donation, 125, 252n105
donkey, 98, 115
Donnell, Sidney, 75, 106
door, 46, 70, 244n26, 257n147, 357n245; church, 253n108, 307n179; post, 320n142
Dopico Black, Georgina, 274n69, 276n87, 320n143
double: bind, 88; dealing, 195, 358n263; intention, 195, 359n264
doubling, 195
doubloon, 251–2n103, 309n213
doubt, 200
dove, 182
dowry, 10, 48, 50, 51, 269–70n26; incentive, 49; stolen, 51
Drake, Francis, 41
dream, 38, 287n68, 291n145, 323n176, 361n322; interpretation, 273n53; of food, 116; strange, 147
dress, 47, 50, 52, 98, 118, 225n81, 244n31, 301n113; as a bandit, 139; for church, 128; devilish, 137; dressing, 322n162; immodest, 74; the king, 160; low-cut, 268n7; as a man, 196; "Moorish," 267n222; rustic, 156, 265n203, 328n15; soldier's, 329–30n31; ugly, 284n15; like women, 191. *See also* clothing; fashion; garment
drink, 46, 112, 113, 114, 137, 168, 295nn16, 22, 296n30, 297n59, 298n66, 300n99, 301n113; blood, 137; drinker, 118; gold, 241n5; waters of Lethe, 285n24
drug, 64
drunkenness, 113, 165, 295n21, 340n165. *See also* inebriation
dualism, 292n147
ducat, 54, 177, 301n111
duel, 30, 84, 141, 231n164, 276–7n95, 277–8n100, 355n209; Castilian, 276–7n95; common, 276–7n95; manual on, 355n209; modern, 276–7n95; prohibition of, 277–8n100
dungeon, 56
duplicity, 186
dust, 115, 296–7n44
Dutch, 63, 216n17
duty, 181, 182, 306n166
dynasty, 164

eagle, 17, 222n23, 336n119
ear, 197, 200, 242–3n17, 332–3n72, 360n288, 361n321
earth, 236n241, 296–7n44, 322n158, 354n203, 361n310; earthquake, 63, 258n153; Mother, 63

Easter, 125, 306n166
eating, 112, 113, 114, 116, 118, 124, 125, 130, 168, 243n21; forbidden fruit, 221n19; human lives, 286n46; meat, 125, 129, 309n221; overeating, 113, 123, 297n56; to break a fast, 129; vassals, 122
echo, 159, 356n224
economics, 6, 215n11; developments, 220n6
economy, 47; agricultural, 173; commercial, 220n6; genealogical, 337n138; moral, 5, 29, 39, 48, 52, 73, 140, 141, 143, 164, 178, 187, 188, 192, 197, 200, 203, 214n10; natural, 173; Spanish, 68, 116, 265n202, 346–7n53
ecstasy, 149
Edwards, Jonathan, 144
effeminate, 291n132
egg, 45
Egginton, William, 9, 218n28
egotism, 177
Egypt, 31, 35, 79, 93, 113, 168; associated with Lust, 78; delivery from, 320n142; Egyptians, 78, 138; flight to, 67; monument in, 261n170
Ehlers, Benjamin, 250n92, 250–1n95
eighteenth century, 54, 216n19
eighth century, 80
ejaculation, 81
elders, 177
elements, 16, 322n158
eleventh century, 220n6, 352n147
Elias, Norbert, 268n10
Elijah, 20, 123, 303n143
Elliott, John: *The Count-Duke of Olivares*, 37; *Imperial Spain*, 226n83
emblem, 165, 196, 218n28; books, 90, 238n282, 282n164; emblematic costumes, 217n21
embroidery, 99, 102, 195
emergence, 151, 155, 172, 186, 207
emergent, 97, 155, 156, 171, 174, 186
emotion, 144, 167, 194, 240n321, 320–1n144, 323n168, 357n248; dealing with, 320–1n144; undesirable, 320–1n144. *See also* feelings
emperor, 33, 34, 40, 141, 234n219; Holy Roman, 69
empire, 25, 34, 46, 62, 85, 89, 110, 148, 162, 163, 233n184, 249n90, 255–6n138; architecture of, 34, 35; builder, 162; Egyptian, 138; furniture of, 35; Hapsburg, 102; Holy Roman, 34; Inca, 61; justification for, 62; Ottoman, 264n195; portable, 163, 337n126; Roman, 67, 75, 78; Spanish, 69, 165
employment, 69, 251–2n103
emulation, 170, 332n68
encyclopedia, 5
ending: conventional, 169; happy, 169, 179, 209, 347n63
Endymion, 272–3n46
enemy, 40, 65, 79, 98, 134, 135, 139, 150, 163, 167, 178, 185, 282–3n4, 301n113, 318n108, 335n96, 339n157; of God, 144; hands, 252n105; prince, 146; sophistical, 191, 354n189; of the soul, 76; of Spain, 252n105; torn apart, 135; of virtue, 99, 332n61
England, 48, 130, 181, 254n120, 256n141, 261n170, 264n196, 279n124, 311n236
English, 8, 9, 26, 32, 41, 48, 176, 190, 264n196, 286n52, 363–4n16; drama, 352n155; Englishmen, 229n120; literature, 337n137; pirates, 253n115
Enlightenment, 5
enredo, 48
Enríquez Gómez, Antonio, 235n239
entertainment, 106, 110, 291n145
enthusiasm, 325n201
entrails, 46, 242n11
entrance, 317n93
entrée, 115
entremés, 70, 193, 199, 241n6, 325n208, 361n316. *See also* interlude
entrepreneur, 64
enterprise, 227n96
environmentalist, 63
Envy, 8, 31, 37, 73, 117, 120, 147, 151, 155–73, 186, 189, 195, 224n63, 232n181, 236n252, 244n24, 258n151, 259n155, 293n172, 293–4n6, 294n12, 296n31, 316nn77, 84, 349n99, 352n142, 359n264; colour of, 170; end of, 168; generous, 343n230; honourable, 343nn229, 231; noble, 344nn234, 235; object of, 162; of one's self, 166; vile, 171; virtuous, 168, 169
epic, 62, 80; age of, 75; battle, 199, 361n310; catalogue, 136, 336n123; valour, 171; warrior, 104, 108

Epicurean, 112, 114
Epicurus, 114, 296n39
epideictic, 163
epidemic, 264n196
epithet, 180
equation, 195
equivocation, 189, 190, 352n155
Erasmus of Rotterdam, 108, 292n147
Ercilla, Alonso de, 62
ergot, 117
error, 189, 198, 250–1n95, 284n15, 326nn220, 221
Esau, 160
escapade, 248n74
escape, 71, 295n16
escudo, 49
Espejo Surós, Javier, 208
espionage, 159
estate, 51, 60, 172, 245n43; country, 105, 106; humble, 343n215; inheritance of, 92; as ransom, 56; squandered, 122. *See also* hacienda
Esther, 23
Estobeo, 219n37
estupro, 269–70n26
ethics, 6, 10, 142, 189, 191, 200, 320–1n144, 357n247
Ethiopia, Ethiopian, 23, 79
ethnopoetics, 26
etymology, 177, 189
Eucharist, 131, 132, 260n166; liturgy of the, 125; sacrament of the, 218n28
eulogy, 172, 338n143
Europe, 5, 7, 9, 26, 43, 63, 68, 69, 73, 93, 121, 162, 173, 202, 203, 216n19, 220n6, 226n83, 231n146, 250n91, 256–7n144, 263n186, 266n220, 276–7n95; Europeans, 250n91; northern, 264n196; western, 172
eutrapelia, 286n53
evangelism, 62
Evagrius Ponticus, 215nn14, 15
Eve, 4, 16, 19, 21, 112, 191, 193, 196, 221n19, 333n9, 353n176
Everyman, 169
evidence, 86, 88, 89, 143, 150, 191, 196, 197, 200, 203, 204, 308n197; archival, 90, 294–5n15, 355n209; bibliographical, 262n175; daily, 248n74; legal, 87; literary, 355n209; lying, 197; physical, 85
evil, 93, 274n67, 333n75; amulet against, 126; greater, 90; spirits, 325n201
evolution, 167, 173
exception, 265n207, 326n217
exchange, 250n92, 294–5n15, 346–7n53
excommunication, 5, 277–8n100
excuse, 148, 179, 190, 194, 305n164, 324n190, 353n176
execution, 67, 269–70n26; executioner, 137, 143; by royal mandate, 161
exemplum, 36, 86, 163
exemption, 124, 172
exercise, 99
exhortation, 176
exile, 68, 82, 85, 167, 332n65, 335n98
exodus, 68
Exodus, book of, 3, 6, 214n2, 216–17n20, 345n17, 364n19
exorcism, 3, 149
expectation, 305n161
expediency, 173
expiation, 184, 216–17n20
exploitation, 257n147
exploration, 61, 64, 120, 121, 264n193, 302nn122, 126
export, 250n91
expulsion, 264n196; Decree of, 68; of the Jews, 206, 250n93; Morisco, 250–1n95, 253–4n116, 273n60
eye, 18, 20, 22, 50, 87, 128, 134, 139, 160, 188, 196, 197, 221n22, 223–4n49, 227n89, 233–4n204, 259n164, 281n154, 312n18, 317n93, 329n26, 332n70, 332–3n72, 360n288; blind, 252n105, 260–1n167, 328n9; envious, 158; eyeglasses, 156, 328n9; greedy, 257n145; light of the, 349n93; lying, 351nn127, 130; of a needle, 242–3n17; one, 328n9; plucking out, 163, 337n127; pure, 321n151; ripped out, 83; spying, 160

fable, 173
fabrication, 194
face, 189, 330n33, 338n148, 350n117, 359n276; black, 356n227; of a child, 177; colour of the, 134; double, 199, 361n308; to face, 317n93; liar's, 196, 359n275; pretty, 157, 329n27; red, 148; slap in the, 140, 318n113

failure, 170
fairy tale, 138
faith, 132, 167, 233–4n204, 348n84; Christian, 60, 123; defender of the, 177; faithfulness, 86, 93, 270–1n29
Fajardo, Francisco de Luque, 127
falcon, 337–8n140
fallibility, 183
falsehood, 186–201
fame, 163, 188, 293n172, 327n3, 330n33, 336n124, 338n141, 339n149, 351n134
family, 48, 55, 56, 80, 90, 91, 165, 232n183, 250nn92, 93, 264n196, 269–70n26, 272n42, 337n137; average, 331n48; biologically unrelated, 76; Christian, 55; dishonoured, 94; Holy, 183; Jewish, 264n195; line, 158; Morisco, 55; noble, 164, 250n92; relationship, 160; royal, 77, 91; sex within, 76; tree, 31
famine, 117, 273n53
Fáñez, Álvar, 164
fantasy, 39, 46, 78, 79, 102, 108, 242n16, 288n73; about food, 116; pastoral, 171
farm, 117
fascism, 210
fashion, 21, 51, 193, 322n162; code, 261n170; courtly, 108; Envy, 329–30n31. *See also* clothing; dress; garment
fasting, 112, 114, 116, 117, 118, 119, 121, 122, 123, 124, 125, 128, 129, 130, 298n65, 303nn136, 140, 142, 304nn149, 153, 154, 304–5n159, 305nn160, 161, 162, 309n216; all day, 129; all year, 310n222; as cause of weight loss, 303n145; command to stop, 124; day of, 300–1n109; diurnal, 130; of Elijah, 303n143; eternal, 310n229; excessive, 124, 304–5n159; on Friday, 305n164, 310n230; hypocritical, 309n213; involuntary, 123; joking references to, 129; during Lent, 305n163, 309n221; at night, 310n231; obligatory, 304–5n159; permission to cease, 124; perpetual, 305n163; prolonged, 124; as punishment, 130; routine, 125; in solitude, 309n219; for symbolic number of days or years, 123; for three years, 305n164; voluntary, 304–5n159; in the wilderness, 123; for a year, 129, 305n164
fate, 41, 164, 167, 169, 245–6n49, 297n56, 339n149
Fates, the, 137, 165, 242n11, 339n159
father, 23, 32, 47, 49, 51, 79, 82, 91, 140, 143, 160, 171, 176, 178, 180, 184, 185, 209, 210, 240n1, 244n36, 251n96, 269–70n26, 273–4n63, 311n249, 346–7n53, 347nn67, 69, 348n86, 349n93; cruel, 185; divine, 181; earthly, 183; father-in-law, 47, 51, 56, 244n36; father/state, 178; fatherly advice, 150; as grandfather, 92, 93; honouring, 174–201; human, 181; Inquisitor, 177; killing of, 207; Law of the, 180; of lies, 189, 352n141; murder of, 178; sins of the, 52, 79, 82, 90, 183, 185, 214n2; step-father, 109, 347n67; wishes of, 280–1n148; woman's, 181
fatherland, 178
fatigue, 98, 101, 108, 109, 110, 117, 127, 284nn14, 20, 286n44, 287n63, 288n83, 291n138, 303nn140, 143
fault, 160, 183
favour, 159, 160, 192, 332n64; disfavour, 335n96; of God, 310n230
fear, 100, 164, 165, 169, 189, 244n23, 316n74, 339n149, 350n110, 353n177; of God, 350n107; of lying, 191; without, 355n213
feast, 104, 112, 113; auditory, 132; day, 125, 127, 128, 129, 286n42, 306nn166, 167, 169, 309n212, 310n222, 311n236; earthly, 132; for the eyes, 63; half-eaten, 120; heavenly, 130, 131, 132; intellectual, 132; New Testament, 132; visual, 132
feather, 22, 226n84, 287n68, 314n39
feelings, 94, 188, 251n96, 325n201, 356n235, 357n248. *See also* emotion
feet, 98, 101, 164, 223n45
female: character, 309n204, 330n39, 350n110; concept, 165; general, 33; innkeeper, 299n93; scholar, 268n10
feminism, 274–5n70, 285n33
feminization, 75
Fernández Álvarez, M., 306n166
fetus, 219n5
feud, 67, 337n137
feudalism, 84, 99, 117, 122, 172, 173, 237n262, 276–7n95
fever, 147
Fez, 68
fiancé, 166

fiction, 291n145, 361nn322, 323; historical, 31, 302n126; in the archives, 355n209; triumph of, 200
fidelity, 143, 191
field, 156
fifteenth century, 11, 203, 219n37, 250n91, 279n124, 310n234
finance, 263–4n192
financier, 68
finger, 164; fingernail, 115; God's, 214n2; to the mouth, 338n148; ring, 240–1n4; to the tongue, 338n148
Finkelberg, Margalit, 363–4n16
fire, 16, 76, 81, 90, 110, 115, 133, 136, 139, 219n4, 221n20, 226n83, 313n36, 314n49, 317n102, 321n151, 322n158, 323n168; amorous, 93; of manhood, 139
fish, 65, 112, 113, 130, 163, 259n155, 295n24, 310n229
flag, 114, 256–7n144, 296n36, 336n119; imperial, 163; of military orders, 157, 330n32; white, 66, 262n180
flagellation, 122, 124, 129. *See also* whip
flame, 136, 156, 221n20, 297n55, 314nn51, 52, 328n10. *See also* fire
Flanders, 63, 283n11, 336n117
flattery, 31, 159, 168, 187, 188, 194, 331n46, 332n65, 337n129, 350n112, 356n235
Flemish, 28
flesh, 65, 137
flies, 314n39, 328n11
flight, 40
flint, 139
flood, 35, 117
Florinda, 80, 273–4n63. *See also* La Cava
flour, 121
flourishing, 170
flower, 75, 159, 169
Flynn, Maureen, 239nn309, 315, 240n319, 320–1n144, 323n168, 344–5n3
foil, 195
fondling, 309n206
food, 46, 110, 112, 113, 115, 116, 118, 120, 121, 131, 132, 156, 241n5, 250n92, 255n131, 287n64; abstinence from, 122, 128; associated with sex, 294–5n15; delicate, 114; desire for, 295n16; dignified, 114; expensive, 114; exquisite, 115; extra, 120; fantasy about, 116; foraging for, 121; for horses, 121; Idolatry of, 115; inability to enjoy, 294–5n15; lack of, 119; literary, 132; preservation, 121, 302n125; as prop, 130, 310n235; purchase of, 120; recipe, 296n29; rustic, 117; scattered, 120; shortage, 117; Spain's, 117; spiritual, 123, 132; stolen, 117, 118; symbolic use of, 310n235; well-seasoned, 121
fool, foolishness, 98, 178, 191, 194, 282–3n4; cap of, 148
foot, 137, 329n27; tired, 287n64
foot soldier, 293n170
Forcione, Alban, 38; *Cervantes and the Humanist Vision*, 292n147; *Majesty and Humanity*, 237n258
foreigner, 118, 299n92
forelock, 93
forgery, 197, 360n289
Formalist, 204
fornication, 85, 215n15, 273n54, 274n69, 309n206
fortress, 257n146
fortune, 157, 159, 185, 227n96, 296n42, 327n6, 328n12, 329n25, 339n156, 340n174
Fortune, 164, 165; depicted as female, 165, 339n162, 340n164; drunk, 340n165; vile, 340n163
Foucault, Michel, 69, 179, 214–15n11; *Discipline and Punish*, 99, 178, 285n35
foul play, 48
founding myth, 273–4n63
fountain, 156, 314n44, 328n17
fourteenth century, 68, 219n37, 220n6
fowl, 112, 120
fragmentation, 185, 208
France, 26, 88, 224–5n67, 230n122, 236n253, 238n295, 289n97; King of, 91, 92; Queen of, 82
Franco, Francisco, 81, 210, 274–5n70
free will, 150, 167, 179, 180, 246n50, 347n57; vs determinism, 220–1n18
freedom 246n50, 254n121, 292n159, 320n143
French, 26, 28, 35, 162, 216n19, 230n122, 336n115
frenzy, 137, 171, 315n71, 331n44
Freud, Sigmund, 39, 362–3n11

friar, 99, 114, 305n161; Mercedarian, 253n108, 331n52
Friday, 118, 125; abstinence from meat on, 129, 130; fasting on, 305n164, 310n230; feast days falling on, 129, 310n222
Friedman, Saul S., 250n91, 264n193
friend, 30, 56, 65, 87, 107, 127, 190, 269–70n26, 296n31, 308n198, 330n34; crazy, 249n87; erstwhile, 140; girlfriend, 190; mask of a, 196; pretended, 159
friendship, 10, 157, 159, 168
frigate, 75, 250–1n95, 259n154. *See also* ship
frivolity, 98, 106, 107
frontier: colonial, 245n38; military, 56, 253n110
fruit, 113; basket, 295n19; bearing, 260n166; coconut, 121; forbidden, 221n19, 293n2; of the pen, 265n207; papaya, 121; pineapple, 121
frying-pan, 50
Fuchs, Barbara, 28; *Exotic Nation*, 26, 203, 231n146; *Mimesis and Empire*, 273–4n63
Fuenlabrada, 265n205
fuero: local, 172; *real*, 142
fugitive, 70
fun, 193
fundamentalist, 79
fundraising, 263–4n192
funeral, 125, 306n167
fungus, 117
Furies, 138, 165, 339n159
furnishings, 47, 235n230

Gabriel, Archangel, 57, 311–12n256
Galen, 145, 322n159
Galicia, 29, 231n152
galleon, 64, 283n11. *See also* ship
galleys, 54, 55, 57, 103
gambling, 108
game, 101, 107, 108, 112, 113, 116, 127, 166, 167, 244n32, 291n145, 294n10; courtly, 161; wargame, 104, 147
gang, 70, 71
Garcés, María Antonia, 59, 251n97, 253n114
García de Palacios, Francisco, 337n129
garden, gardener, 108, 110, 113, 169, 291n141, 294n10, 328n17; of Eden, 17, 21, 191
garment, 145; of love, 159; "Moorish," 57; ornate, 51; of reconciliation, 247n72; rending of, 135; of shame, 52, 196. *See also* clothing; dress; fashion
gaze, 157, 166, 177, 185, 276n87, 285n35
gemstone, 264n193
gender, 16, 19, 47, 186; double standard, 89; landscape, 269n14
genealogy, 10, 80, 337n138; of performance, 218n34
generation, 176
generosity, 109, 170, 171, 242–3n17, 244n33, 292n157, 331n46
Genesis, book of, 35, 235n241, 273n53
genitals, 273–4n63
genius, 33, 337n129
Genoa, 65, 260–1n167
genre, 5, 9, 10, 11, 29, 39, 130, 180, 189, 204, 205, 208, 241n6, 299n81, 364n17; *comedia*, 219n39; cross-genre, 299n93; masque, 265n207; new, 106, 207; pastoral, 100, 287n54, 290n113; picaresque, 114, 118; romance, 364n26; subgenre, 142, 150
Gentile, 288n87
geography, 28; imaginary, 67, 263n186; remote, 79
German, 162, 242–3n17
Germany, 84, 256n139, 289n97
gesture, 133; symbolic, 148, 338n148
ghetto, 65
ghost, 115
giant, 22, 23, 35, 50, 236n241
gift, 49, 278n109, 349n93, 363–4n16; giving, 110, 292n157; from heaven, 329n30; spiritual, 311–12n256
Gillet, Joseph, 150
Gilman, Stephen, 205, 364n17
girl, 267n227, 346–7n53; girlfriend, 143, 190; young, 141, 179
glass, 156, 328n12, 350n113
gloating, 164
global warming, 3
Gluttony, 31, 97, 111, 112–32, 155, 215n15, 232n181, 238n283
goat, 51, 137, 272–3n46
God, 3, 7, 16, 17, 20, 21, 36, 39, 42, 81, 83, 84, 88, 90, 99, 112, 114, 115, 120, 121, 123, 129, 131, 160, 169, 175, 176, 178, 182, 184, 189, 203, 233–4n204, 234n219, 285n30, 301n113, 309n216, 321nn151, 155, 329n25, 339n157, 354n203; altar of,

114; Angry, 144; as Author, 181; blessing of, 126; command by, 124; discourtesy to, 126; displeasure of, 136; the Father, 307n174; favours of, 310n230; fear of, 350n107; finger of, 214n2; hand of, 293–4n6; house of, 268n7; Jewish, 206; justice of, 143; Lamb of, 132; law of, 202; marriage to, 181; name of, 42, 43, 83; prayer to, 126; prophets of, 273n54; punishment by, 85; relationship with, 215–16n16; representative of, 192, 354n203; service of, 181, 309n204; sight of, 274n67; Son of, 126, 233n184, 303n140; sons of, 236n241; vice regent of, 237n262; will of, 182; wrath of, 143
gold, 45, 46, 47, 49, 52, 61, 63, 64, 68, 70, 186, 240n1, 241n5, 243n20, 254n121, 255n128, 257n147, 258n150, 259n154, 262n183; from Antarctica, 259n164; bars, 241n6; chain, 52, 240–1n4; counting, 240–1n4; doubloons, 56, 251–2n103; drinking, 241n5; false, 242n10
Golden Age, 8, 9, 11, 21, 23, 24, 31, 35, 58, 62, 68, 80, 86, 87, 102, 103, 104, 108, 109, 131, 134, 135, 137, 140, 141, 143, 145, 146, 149, 150, 155, 163, 169, 176, 179, 181, 182, 186, 189, 190, 196, 198, 200, 204, 205, 206, 207, 208, 209, 210, 216–17n20, 221n21, 234nn213, 219, 264n196, 265n207, 269–70n26, 292n147, 294–5n15, 308n197, 316n88, 339n149, 358n259, 362–3n11, 364nn17, 28
golf, 159, 332n61
Goliath, 23, 24
Góngora, Luis de, 33, 199
González, Estebanillo, 119
González-Ruiz, Julio, 75
Good Samaritan, 71, 266n221
goods: material, 346–7n53; of neighbour, 73, 83; theft of, 109. See also *bienes ajenos*
Gospels, 79, 110, 262n181
gossip, 107, 299n93, 329nn24, 25, 332nn61, 64, 349n95, 350n107
Goth, 24, 80, 103, 228n106
government, 209, 252n105, 257n147
Goya, Francisco de, 122, 247n72
grace, 39; fall from, 40, 161, 162; social, 194
Gracián de la Madre de Dios, Jerónimo, 253n111
gracioso, 115, 118, 186, 194, 357n252
grain, 65, 260n166; measure of, 130; shortage, 117; of wheat, 260n166
grammar, 165
Granada, 29, 117, 329n26; conquest of, 263–4n192, 289n97; Kingdom of, 337n137
grandchild, 80, 214n2
grandfather, 92; as father, 92, 93
grandmother, 93
grands récits, 174
graphocentrism, 360n288
gratitude, 177, 192, 320n142, 354n195; ingratitude, 320n142, 333n74
Graullera, Vicente, 280–1n148
grave robber, 46, 242n11
gravitas, 139
Great Awakening, 144
Greece, 342n212; classical, 78, 79, 336n123
Greed, 6, 9, 45–73, 120, 156, 328n21, 358n263. *See also* Avarice
Greek, 26, 163, 325n201, 363–4n16; Adultery, 80; ancient, 78, 91; culture, 205; mythology, 137; proud, 229n120; religion, 78
Greer, Meg, 117, 130, 213n3, 265n207, 365n3
Gregory the Great, Pope, 215nn14, 15
Grieve, Patricia E., 274n65
Griffin, Eric, 26
grocery list, 204
grotesque, 115, 297n51
Grotius, Hugo, 255–6n138
Guanajuato, 258n150
Guatemala, 63, 258n153
Guarini, Giambattista, 325n201
Guerra y Ribera, Manuel de, 77, 126
guest, 116, 169, 298n65, 305n164; list, 116; wedding, 158
Guevara, Antonio de, 106
Guggenheim, Scott E., 214n10
"guided culture," 210
guild, 130
guilt, 4, 11, 84, 87, 89, 90, 92, 141, 166, 174, 197, 204, 207, 211, 216–17n20; acknowledgment of, 141; guilty pleasure, 101; proof of, 85
guitar, 330n33
gullibility, 193
gun, 252n105. *See also* pistol
gusto, 294–5n15

gypsy, 61, 68, 69, 70, 71, 72, 109, 118, 192, 223n37, 267nn225, 227, 300n97

habit, 98, 127, 193, 356n227
hacienda, 47, 48, 52, 56, 62, 73, 83, 105, 156, 176, 240–1n4, 245nn38, 39, 46, 293n166, 311n249, 332n64. *See also* estate
Hagar, 27
hagiography, 100, 104; drama based upon, 124, 129; medieval, 93
The Hague, 275n75
Hail Mary, 61
hair, 137; blond, 329n29; brush, 50; curled, 75, 268n8; grey, 139, 244n32, 317n102, 329n29; hanging by the, 135; provocative, 268n7; shirt, 303n136, 309n219; stand on end, 89
Haliczer, Stephen H., 268n7, 274–5n70, 309n206
Hall of Mirrors, 207
hallucination, 45
Haman, 23, 228n97
Hamburg, 264n196
Hamilton, Earl J., 258n150
Hammer, Paul E.J., 228n102
hammock, 101
hand, 18, 81, 91, 102, 104, 108, 143, 156, 163, 164, 177, 178, 189, 223n45, 268n3, 278n109, 315n54, 327n4, 328n17, 332n65, 333n75, 334n80; Arabic, 251n96; beautiful, 166; bloody, 314n43, 320n142; enemy, 252n105; executing, 143; generous, 295n16; of God, 293–4n6; greedy, 257n145, 260–1n167; sleight of, 115, 156
handkerchief, 50, 86, 278n109
handwriting, 360n289
hanging, 71, 162, 185; by the hair, 135
happiness, 99, 101, 157, 329n25, 332–3n72, 342n212; unhappiness, 337n139
Hapsburg, 79, 233n184; armies, 119; civilians, 253–4n116; empire, 102; monarchs, 126; Peru, 255n130; princess, 169
harem, 79
harm, 178, 186
harp, 148
harpy, 222n25
hartura, 295n18, 297n50
harvest, 117
hat, 22, 324n189, 338n148; cardinal's, 114, 296n36; doffing of, 89; plumed, 226n84
hatred, 159, 189, 333n79, 352nn142, 146
head, 17, 148; cutting off, 269–70n26; forehead, 22, 82, 163, 202, 238n283; headache, 124, 305n160; hydra's, 98, 189, 352n141; knife hanging over, 90; on a platter, 78; rooster's, 281n151
health, 305n164, 308n195; good, 125; physical, 125; prayer for, 306n170; prejudicial to, 124; spiritual, 125
hearing, 115, 360n297
heart, 18, 76, 84, 123, 128, 146, 147, 156, 166, 188, 300n99, 315nn58, 70, 327n4, 359n268; attack, 327n4; joy to the, 124; and mind, 77; ripped out, 135, 314n42; spur to the, 149; wounded, 136
heat, 244n23, 262n182, 322n158
heaven, 20, 23, 37, 84, 134, 165, 176, 178, 180, 182, 191, 227–8n96, 233n185, 242–3n17, 285n30, 306n170, 324n178, 326n225, 340n163; Bread from, 123; face of, 82; gift from, 329n30; heavenly pursuits, 169; ire of, 144; manna from, 131; offense to, 82; permission of, 87; reward from, 126; sword of, 89; voice from, 81
Heble, Ajay, 362–3n11
Hebrew, 3, 20, 65, 126, 184, 273n53, 311n248; ancient, 339n149; conquerors, 339n149; expulsion of, 68; king, 325n201; mythology, 272–3n46; name, 131; religion, 78; Scriptures, 78; synagogue, 311n252. *See also* Jewish
Hector of Troy, 163, 336n123
hedonism, 75, 101, 104
heel, 222n28
hegemony, 7, 150, 201
Heiple, Daniel, 142
heir, 51, 60, 158, 177
Helen of Troy, 80, 273n48, 274n65
Helios, 23. *See also* Apollo
hell, 47, 137, 189, 227–8n96, 241n6, 244n31; circles of, 209; pit of, 321n151
hemlock, 137, 315n65
henbane, 284n18
Henry VIII, King, 32
Hercules, 137, 316n78
heresy, 145

heretic, 27, 52, 65, 145
heritage, 200
hermeneutics, 144
hermit, 59
hero, 120, 165; braggart, 364n17; heroic death, 167; heroic virtue, 171
Herod, King, 66, 67, 78, 263n184; brother of, 78; father of, 79
Herodias, 78
Herodotus, 263n186
heroism, 274–5n70, 285n28
heterodox, 69
hidalgo, 108, 171, 175, 232n183, 233n185; families, 245n40; "Moorish," 254n121; petty, 172, 173; status, 172
hierarchy, 285n35, 316n77, 354n203
Hiltpold, Paul, 172
hippie, 103
Hirco, 272–3n46
Hispanic, 10, 43; legal thought, 279n122; world, 262n177
Hispanist, 8, 9, 10
historical drama, 62, 161, 283n11
historicity of texts, 204
historiography, 7, 59, 145, 208, 216n19, 320–1n144
history of ideas, 42, 279n122, 323n167
histrionics, 133
hitting, 135, 313n35
hoard, 46, 241n6
Hollywood, 24, 209
Holy Spirit, 149, 325n213
home, 20, 30, 93, 132, 241n6, 266n209, 365n6; country, 169; comfort of, 104; homeland, 60, 337n139; returning, 184; Christian, 274–5n70
Homer, 75, 363–4n16
homicide, 19, 62, 83, 92, 137, 140, 179, 315n54, 350n107
homosexual, 20
Homza, Lu Ann, 7, 83, 202, 203, 276n91, 349n99
honesty, 147, 168, 187, 192
honey, 131, 156, 314n39, 328n11
honour, 10, 29, 30, 42, 49, 72, 80, 88, 90, 91, 94, 104, 108, 111, 121, 140, 141, 142, 148, 160, 163, 165, 168, 170, 175, 178, 179, 189, 192, 193, 205, 233–4n204, 239n299, 269–70n26, 310n231, 334n83, 337–8n140, 340n171, 342n205, 363–4n16; conjugal, 143; dishonour, 143, 352n149; dramas, 278n106; false god of, 320n142; killing, 142; masculine, 134; parents, 83, 174–201; point of, 276–7n95; restoration of, 138; rhetoric of, 355n209; the Sabbath, 211
hope, 158, 169, 331n42; end of, 170; without, 176
Horace, 106, 108, 169, 215n14
horror, 122, 164, 339n149, 348n86
horse, 17, 22, 23, 40, 159, 331n56; food for, 121; horseback riding, 107, 291n129; sex with, 76, 270–1n29
hospitality, 113, 305n164
host, 116; Eucharistic, 132, 256–7n144, 260n166, 307n182
hostage, 55
house, 86, 105, 110, 121, 178, 266n209, 267n222, 298n65, 304n149, 308n194, 331n46, 349n93, 354n189; big, 114; collapsed, 258n153; defamation of, 90; of Desengaño, 287n60; household, 114, 173, 331n48; of Gluttony, 113, 119, 294–5n15; of God, 268n7; of Grain, 311n248; of pleasure, 295n18; private, 102; ranch, 245n38; throwing out of the, 185
hubris, 163
human, 75, 145, 177, 194, 226n83
humiliation, 91
humility, 25, 32, 39, 41, 129, 147, 149, 184
humour, 107, 132, 147, 149, 150, 199, 312n258, 356n227
humours, 100, 145, 146, 322nn158, 159, 323n168
hunger, 113, 115, 118, 119, 120, 121, 122, 123, 124, 245n46; of Christ, 123; pangs, 117; as punishment, 119; for riches, 63;
hunting, 35, 107, 127, 236n241, 295n24, 308n196, 309n208, 337–8n140
husband, 20, 48, 49, 51, 75, 78, 79, 81, 86, 88, 93, 142, 143, 144, 161, 179, 210, 275n71, 276n87, 294–5n15, 320n143, 339n156; absent, 94; aggrieved, 88; first, 158; good, 330n38; lascivious, 81; lazy, 99; mystical, 84; prospective, 81
hydra, 15, 39, 74, 98, 136, 189, 219n3, 284n17, 315n54, 352n141
hyperbole, 65, 110, 135

hypocrisy, 86, 118, 240n321, 245n47, 359n269

Iago, 278n109
Iberian Peninsula, 24, 26, 64, 79, 231n146
Icarus, 22, 23, 60, 227n96
ice, 136, 244n23
iconography, 136, 165, 340n164
identity, 151, 189, 196, 206, 260n166, 363n15; masculine, 268n10, 338n148; mistaken, 195; mutable, 327n229; unitary, 218n28
ideology, 190, 226n83, 327n228
idleness, 103, 104, 110, 172
Idolatry, 20, 42, 43, 44, 66, 114, 115
Ignatius, St, 131
ignominy, 92, 191
ignorance, 100, 117, 126, 189, 335n107
iguana, 121, 302n127
illegitimacy, 91. *See also* bastard
illiteracy, 126
illness, 100, 127, 157, 304–5n159
illusion, 363n12
imitation, 170, 343n221, 355n209
Immaculate Conception, 89; Feast of the, 57–8
immigrant, 260–1n167
immorality, 192
immortality, 115, 177, 234n219
immunity, 192
impediment, 271n31
impunity, 142
in flagrante delicto, 88
in typo, 41
inbreeding, 79
Inca, 61
Incarnation, Feast of the, 253n108
incentive, 195, 252n105
incest, 78, 93, 270n28; avoidance of, 270n28, 365n7; definition of, 271n31; fostering, 185; product of, 92
incorporation, 97, 171, 186
independence, 265n207
indeterminacy, 199
"Indians," 250n91
indicio, 86, 87, 278–9n111
Indies, 61, 120, 259n154, 336n114
indiscretion, 92
individual, 91, 94, 203, 205; agency, 204; individualism, 6, 11, 143, 150, 203, 217n23, 363n12; rights, 143; sin, 166; subject, 207; unified, 218n28
indoctrination, 190
industry, 99; local, 69; mining, 257n147
inebriation, 165. *See also* drunkenness
infamy, 90, 91, 98, 107, 189, 192, 233n185, 282–3n4, 312n12
infant, 119; mortality, 159, 331n48; slaying, 79; snatching, 55; son, 349n93
infidel, 27, 60, 145
infidelity, 85
inflation, 264n196
infraction, 240n319
ingenuity, 157, 163, 190, 195, 199, 329n30, 337n130, 358n254
ingrate, 185, 190
inheritance, 47, 48, 49, 51, 82, 91, 92, 159, 176, 177, 209, 245nn39, 40, 259n155, 280–1n148; of crown, 146; disinheritance, 178, 236n253; human, 216–17n20; of kingdom, 91; paternal, 280–1n148
injunction, 276n78
injury, 120, 266, 312n10, 313n25, 338n141
inn, 70, 112, 266n211, 284n14, 287n64, 299n92; innkeeper, 70, 118, 299n93; of Gluttony, 112–13
innocence, 84, 87, 88, 191, 197, 337n139; loss of, 193; proof of, 85, 86
innuendo, 10
Inquisition, 10, 31, 52, 78, 159, 177, 183, 196, 210, 216–17n20, 218n31, 226n83, 232–3n184, 247n72, 255n124, 264n196, 270n27, 270–1n29, 276n87, 309n206, 346n50, 362n2
insanity, 39
insect, 121, 321n151
insemination, 274–5n70
insolence, 101, 178, 185, 357n245
insomnia, 46
inspection, 285n35
instincts, 292n147
insult, 70, 85, 134, 140, 156, 240n322, 285n31, 334n90
insurance, 264n196
integrity, 91, 205
intellect: ancient, 163; intellectual history, 7, 85, 145, 170; intellectualization, 245n49
intelligence, 33, 157, 195

intention, 144, 250n91, 279n122, 284n15, 299n92, 306n170; double, 195, 359n264
intercession, 306n170
interest, 188, 244n30, 349n101, 358n263; charging of, 66; conflict of, 363n12; eternal, 126; self-interest, 188
interiority, 94, 150; lack of, 326n222
interlude: comic, 70, 199, 285n33; dramatic, 241n6. See also *entremés*
intertext, 177
intoxication, 113
intrigue, 160; courtly, 169
inventory, 249n84
investiture, 51, 246n57
investment, 65
Iphis, 273n47
iron, 63
irreverence, 348n86
irritation, 332–3n72
Isaac, 184
Isabel the Catholic, Queen, 68, 206, 264n193; chastity of, 81, 274–5n70; cult of, 81, 274–5n70. *See also* Catholics: Monarchs
Isabel of Portugal, Queen, 37
Isaiah, 103, 288n87
Ishikawa, Chiyo, 274–5n70
Ishmael, 27
Isidore, St, 104, 105, 304n150
Islam, 26, 27, 59, 268n12; Islamic harem, 79; Islamic invasion, 80; Islamic Spain, 56
Israel, 33, 160, 303n142; ancient, 67; king of, 149, 274n67
Israelite, 23, 24, 138, 157, 320n142, 339n149
Italian, 26, 65, 162, 229n120, 248n82, 260–1n167, 306n166
Italy, 245n44, 246n54, 264n195, 289n97, 336n117, 344n235; southern, 93, 229n120
itch, 156, 327n7

jacket, 279n112
Jacob, 79, 160
jail, 300n99
James, King, 48
Janus, 28, 199, 210
jasmine, 338n141
jealousy, 86, 136, 139, 158, 165, 191, 313n28, 314n46, 318nn107, 108, 330nn33, 40, 331n43, 335n97, 337n130, 340n174, 342n205, 354nn188, 189; of one's self, 166; romantic, 139, 147
Jephte, 184
Jerome, St, 137
Jerusalem, 67, 182, 256–7n144; sacking of, 138, 316n81; seven mountains of, 221–2n22
Jesuit, 7, 190; church, 258n153; education, 353n168; Jesuitical equivocation, 189; meditation techniques, 115, 297n46; school drama, 234n213, 302n128
Jesus, 57, 66, 79, 123, 242–3n17, 253n108; ancestor of, 131; Baby, 67, 79, 131, 255n129; Child, 182; figure of, 303n140; teenage, 182
Jew, 6, 20, 31, 55, 61, 65, 66, 67, 250n93, 251–2n103, 261n171, 262n179, 263n190, 263–4n192, 339n149; Spanish, 264nn193. *See also* Hebrew
jewel, 45, 46, 51, 61, 71, 72, 112, 240–1n4, 259n155; family, 72; jewellery, 313n35
Jewish: anti-Jewish, 68; beard, 65, 261n170; capital, 68; children, 55, 250n93; doctor, 143; expulsion, 206, 263n191; family, 264n195; God, 206; immigrant, 260–1n167; king, 148; lineage, 232n183; merchant, 66, 260–1n167, 262n175; mother, 232–3n184; Passover, 320n142; persecution, 232–3n184; quarter, 261n170, 262n175; renegade, 254n120; villain, 66; wealth, 68, 264n193; woman, 181
Jezabel, Queen, 20, 78, 80, 273n54, 274n67
Joan of Arc, 234n212
Job, book of, 272–3n46
John, gospel of, 260n166, 273n59
John of the Cross, St, 325n213
John the Baptist, 78
John the Evangelist, St, 74, 268n2
John II of Portugal, King, 263–4n192, 264n195
joke, 125, 129, 189, 298–9n73, 305–6n165; practical, 107
Joseph, 67, 88, 109, 160, 182, 183, 273n53, 334nn80, 81, 339n156
Josephus, 67, 263n184
journey, 88

joust, 84, 106, 159, 276–7n95, 290n125, 331n55
Jove, 137, 316n78
joy, 157, 329n25
Juan II of Castile, King, 161
Juana de la Cruz, Mother, 238n274
Juana la Beltraneja, 169
judaizing, 31, 232–3n184
Judas Iscariot, 39, 66, 67, 187
Judea, 79
judge, 87, 89, 278–9n111; Divine, 88, 89; of the Gentiles, 288n87; guilty, 141; temperament of, 141
Judges, book of, 184, 321n153, 348n85
judgment, 357n248
judicial, 276–7n95
Julian, Count, 80, 273–4n63
Julian, St, 129–30
Julius Caesar, 24, 78, 163
Jupiter, 78, 137, 227n89, 316n78; Adultery of, 77; and the crab, 227n90
jurisdiction, 49
jurist, 142, 255–6n138, 279n122, 320n143
justice, 143, 237n262, 275n71
justification, 189, 190, 289n97, 365n7

Kahn, Victoria, 342n201
Kallendorf, Craig, 11, 62; "Conversations with the Dead," 265n207; *The Other Virgil*, 273n49
Kallendorf, Hilaire: *Conscience on Stage*, 4, 7, 137, 214n4, 234n213, 271n31; "Dressed to the Sevens," 247n72; *Exorcism and Its Texts*, 4; "A Myth Rejected," 268n12
Kantorowicz, Ernst, 234n219
Khusrau II, King, 316n81
kick, 137
kidnapping, 55, 56, 59, 250n92, 253–4n116
Kiernan, Victor Gordon, 276–7n95
killing, 140, 141, 144, 159, 163, 227–8n97, 240n1, 245n43, 256–7n144, 269–70n26, 273n54, 284n18, 331n56, 350n107; without Anger, 319n133; of father, 207; honour, 142; hunger, 299n80; with impunity, 142; for one's self, 319n124; of parents, 178; by a third party, 319n124; wife-killing, 144. *See also* homicide; murder
king, 18, 29, 30, 31, 33, 34, 36, 37, 38, 39, 42, 67, 80, 82, 83, 85, 90, 91, 92, 93, 103, 109, 113, 114, 118, 139, 143, 150, 160, 161, 162, 169, 171, 177, 178, 182, 186, 192, 209, 210, 230n121, 237n262, 250–1n95, 253n110, 263n190, 297n56, 305n160, 308n193, 323n172, 324n196, 326n219, 329n30, 333n77, 334nn82, 83, 85, 89, 90, 93, 335n97, 343nn215, 229, 354nn190, 203; of Albania, 146; divine right of, 234n219; favourite of, 160, 161, 167, 197; favours of, 60; Jewish, 148, 149, 274n67, 325n201; lascivious, 274n67; of Persia, 138, 316n81; of Portugal, 336n114; of Sicily, 161; subjects of, 85
kingdom, 39, 43, 71, 146, 160, 177, 178, 245n44; animal, 40, 222n23; of Asturias, 236n247; of Granada, 337n137; inheritance of, 91; neighbouring, 146
Kings, book of, 20, 225n68, 273n54, 274n67, 325n200, 331n47
kinship, 76, 271n31
kitchen, 121
knife, 86, 138, 139, 317n95; at the throat, 317n90; nightmare of, 90; words as, 240n321
knight, 18, 30, 84, 116, 159, 265n207, 329–30n31; dubbing of, 125, 307n171; errant, 108, 206; knightly competitions, 106; of Malta, 330n32; of the Order of Santiago, 107, 265n207
Kristeva, Julia, 180

La Guardia, 68
labour, 54, 99, 255–6n138, 274–5n70, 285n32, 302n126; divine help with, 104; power, 173
labrador, 32, 43, 70, 105, 110, 169, 265n205, 307n179
labyrinth, 361n317
Lacan, Jacques, 180
lacayo, 186
lady, 107, 109, 139, 141, 158, 244n30, 247n60, 329n27, 330n39, 332n59
lady-in-waiting, 32, 194
lamb, 132, 320n142
lance, 104, 289n93, 331n56
land, 176; holdings, 51; land-owning class, 108, 171, 245n38
landlord, 93
landmine, 24
landscape, 47, 173, 335n97

Las Casas, Bartolomé de, 255–6n138
Latin, 11, 33, 98, 126, 140, 177, 236n247, 275n71, 305–6n165, 307n174, 361n323
Latin America, 43, 55
laughter, 107, 128, 147, 148, 293n172
Laura, 162
laurel wreath, 34, 163, 164, 184, 289n101
law, 4, 6, 22, 24, 60, 83, 92, 126, 142, 146, 185, 277n99, 277–8n100, 291n129, 329n30, 334n89; canon, 143; civil, 320n143; code of, 43; enforcement, 142; of the Father, 180; God as founder of, 90; God's, 202; of the land, 142; natural, 137, 175, 176, 181; penalty of, 89; Poor, 69, 119; of primogeniture, 245n40; Roman, 255–6n138; royal, 276–7n95; secular, 143; sumptuary, 22, 225n82, 226n82
lawsuit, 141, 209, 232n183, 269–70n26
lawyer, 134
layman, 305n161
Lazarillo de Tormes, 119
Lazarus, 46, 242–3n17
lead, 98
ledger, 64
leech, 149
leg, 98, 284n19, 301n111
legal: context, 147; discourse, 216–17n20; framework, 141; legalism, 85; sophistry, 318n121; status, 172; thought, 279n122; validation, 255–6n138
Leganés, 265n205
legislation, 227n82, 291n129, 363n15; of intangibles, 144
legitimacy, 237n265; of children, 91, 280–1n148; legal, 92
leisure, 45, 97, 101, 102, 103, 104, 105, 106, 107, 109, 110, 127, 186, 292n159; activities, 290n125; courtly, 290n125; literary, 287n54; as parenthesis of work, 108; as work, 109
Leng, Rainer, 228n102
Lent, 129, 130, 304–5n159, 305–6n165, 306n166; fasting during, 305n163, 309n221
León, 29, 333n77
leopard, 136, 222n23
leper, 98, 261n170, 284n16
lethargy, 98, 284n19
Lethe, 98, 285n24
letrado, 161, 234n213
letter, 160; of credit, 60; dedicatory, 169, 343n217, 345n11; discovery of, 86; incriminating, 161; love, 128, 139, 143; from prison, 56, 57
Levantines, 262n175
Lex Julia, 142
lexicography, 68, 86, 145
liability, 164
liaison, 272n42
libel, 68, 233n185; trial for, 272n42
libido, 39
licence, 124, 179, 195, 318n115; fee, 66; lascivious, 101; from parents, 175; printing, 226n83
lifestyle, 182
light: of the eyes, 349n93; first, 308n189; moonlight, 187; ray of, 166, 340n177; sunlight, 187
lightning, 136, 156, 178, 327n5
Lima, 61, 62, 63; chronicle of, 255n130; colonial, 291n129; earthquake, 258n153
limpieza de sangre, 31, 232n182
lineage, 111, 164, 181, 232–3n184, 344–5n3; appeal to, 206; Jewish, 232n183; monstrous, 92
linguistic confusion, 173, 214n4
linguistic register, 150
linguistic relativity, 220n11
linguistics, 4, 10, 168, 220n11
Linnaeus, Carl, 214n6
lion, 17, 136, 222n25, 300n99, 316n76; den of, 42; Indian, 222n25; mouth of, 131
lips, 43, 98, 188, 190, 319n124, 338n146, 361n321; lethargic, 284n19; painted, 156
Lisbon, 54
Little, Lester K., 220n6
liturgy, 125, 127
livelihood, 253n110
livestock, 51, 305–6n165
loa, 65, 97, 171, 222n27, 225n78, 231n149, 240–1n4, 243n19, 244n24, 258n151, 261n169, 268nn5, 8, 269n16, 282n1, 284n15, 285n29, 294n7, 294–5n15, 295nn16, 19, 20, 297n59, 298n64, 300n95, 303n139, 307nn173, 177, 311nn246, 253, 312n11, 315nn57, 63, 317n97, 319n133, 325nn203, 205, 328n21, 332–3n72, 344nn240, 241, 242, 353n180, 358n259
locus amoenus, 40, 105, 106, 169, 289–90n107

Lodge, David, 207, 364n26
logic: utilitarian, 283n7; Western, 203
logismoi, 215n15
loitering, 109, 119
loneliness, 100
loophole: legal, 172; moral, 142
Lope de Vega, 9, 10, 33, 37, 38, 39, 40, 62, 67, 74, 77, 93, 129, 163, 168, 169, 177, 180, 200, 213n3, 233n185, 236n243, 238n288, 239n305, 265n207, 269n14, 272nn41, 42, 320n141, 330n40, 365nn6, 7; *La Dorotea*, 11, 219n37, 272n41. *For list of works see* Index of *Comedias*
love, 49, 51, 101, 102, 103, 104, 118, 146, 157, 158, 159, 162, 165, 191, 195, 244n32, 295n18, 270–1n29, 273–4n63, 288n73, 294n13, 309n212, 316n84, 318n110, 326n220, 330n35, 331n43, 332n60, 336n117, 339n159, 350n16, 353n185, 354n188, 359n276; accidental, 140; affair, 272n41; buying, 53, 247–8n73; courtly, 102; and eating, 113, 115; falling in, 166, 169, 191, 288n82; illicit, 157; incestuous, 270n28; lascivious, 83; letter, 128, 139, 143; lovemaking, 103, 270–1n29; lovesickness, 99, 129; for parents, 177; paternal, 184; pretended, 177; profane, 269n21; romantic, 157, 158, 191, 269–70n26, 361n319; story, 128; triangle, 157, 273n48, 330n35; true, 169; and war, 191
lover, 51, 86, 102, 103, 141, 143, 158, 160, 191, 223n37, 320n143, 365n6; caught in Adultery, 142; exchange of tokens by, 128; humour of, 146; luckless, 330n39; male, 177, 330n39; merchant, 247–8n73; name of, 158; priest and, 309n206; tryst for, 128; wooing a, 196
Löwenheim, Oded, 58, 252n105, 253–4n116
loyalty, 58, 159, 192, 332n65, 336n117, 343n215; disloyalty, 139, 160, 318n107, 333n74; divided, 108; holy, 124
Lucifer, 15, 19, 20, 27, 137, 189, 220n7, 316n77, 339n157
luck, 17, 157, 164, 170, 223n33, 340n163, 343n218
Lucrecia, 78
Lukacher, Ned, 214n4
Luke, gospel of, 242–3n17, 348n79
Luna, Álvaro de, 161, 162, 334n93, 335n102
lunch, 112, 118, 124, 298n66
Luque Fajardo, Francisco de, 286n53
luquete, 295n22
Lust, 8, 35, 44, 52, 73, 74–96, 97, 113, 114, 141, 155, 157, 177, 207, 232n181, 294n14, 294–5n15, 295n16, 299n93, 301n114
Luther, Martin, 27
luxury, 78, 111, 244n30; trade, 248n81
lying, 8, 120, 140, 160, 186–201, 242n13, 300–1n109, 350n107; courtly, 356n240; noble, 358n257; redefined, 190

Maastricht, 63
Maccabees, book of, 23, 339n149
Macedonia, 239n296
Machiavelli, Niccolò, 168, 342n201
Maclean, Ian, 322n158
madness, 137, 173, 224n54, 238n276, 270–1n29, 314n52, 315n71
Madrid, 7, 23, 53, 57, 69, 71, 102, 106, 117, 130, 131, 132, 163, 166, 194, 206, 241n6, 247n59, 256–7n144, 303n134, 305n164
Maestro, Jesús, 208
magic, 16, 75, 198, 221n21, 240n321, 240–1n4; magical worldview, 219n28; magician, 33, 37, 324n194
magistrate, 49, 51, 109
magnet, 75
maiming, 120
malfunction, 322n159
malice, 188, 275n71
malnutrition, 117
Malta, 260–1n167; Knights of, 330n32
man, 18, 20, 31, 47, 49, 53, 74, 75, 76, 86, 87, 88, 89, 93, 99, 101, 102, 107, 110, 112, 118, 119, 128, 134, 138, 141, 159, 163, 179, 181, 182, 190, 191, 194, 199, 202, 216n16, 240n321, 260n166, 266n218, 270n27, 276n87, 323n168, 328n12, 329–30n31, 331n56, 332–3n72, 339n153, 340n170, 353n176, 357n248, 359n276; angry, 318n110; beautiful, 329n26; business, 260–1n167; caught in Adultery, 82, 83, 88; chamber, 160; craftsman, 264n195; daughter of, 236n241; enlisted, 252n105; great, 171; happy, 170; manhood, 261n170; man-in-waiting, 160; manliness, 106, 107, 108; mighty, 236n241; militant, 138; mortal, 181; old, 47, 99, 100, 139, 244n35, 286n43, 329n29; older, 280–1n148,

348n86, 359n278; poor, 51, 297–8n63, 300–1n109; province of, 178; rich, 242–3n17; Renaissance, 111; self-made, 181; unmarried, 274n69; womanly, 269n14; young, 77, 93, 99, 100, 139, 223n36, 285n28, 329n29, 365n6
mandate, 174
Manichean, 251–2n103
manna, 131
mannerism, 210, 226n88, 358n256
Manos Teatrales, 213n3, 364n22
Mansfield, Bruce, 292n147
manuscript, 11, 198, 348n86
marauding, 71
Maravall, José Antonio, 8, 9, 205, 208, 210, 326n222, 327n228
maravedí, 49, 53, 116, 264n193, 280–1n148, 297–8n63
marble, 164, 244n30, 338n141
Marcos, Pedro, 71
Marcus Aurelius, 67, 163
María Egipciaca, St, 93
Mariadnes, 79
Mariana, Queen, 79
Mariscal, George, 218n28, 264n196
Mark, gospel of, 321n155
Mark Antony, 78
market: art, 301n115; public, 69; slave, 54; of the world, 268n5
marquis, 52
marriage, 21, 39, 48, 51, 52, 53, 57, 62, 88, 92, 138, 143, 158, 166, 182, 185, 210, 215n11, 231n154, 232–3n184, 271n31, 277n99, 281n149, 330n39, 356n224; adulterous, 274–5n70; arranged, 49, 179, 180, 209, 246n51, 346–7n53; bed, 81; of convenience, 179; dynastic, 264n196; forced, 83, 269–70n26; to God, 181; impediment to, 271n31; interruption of, 331n48; Lust within, 81; with mothers, 79; mystical, 183; obligatory, 146, 181; partner, 175; prospects, 247n71; remarriage, 158, 246n54, 331n46; to a relative, 185, 348n90; as requirement to govern, 146; vows, 82
Mars, 24, 77, 83, 138, 163, 165
martas, 293n1
Martín Gaite, Carmen, 274–5n70
martyr, 79, 124
Marxism, 8
Mary Magdalene, 19
masculinity, 107, 268n10, 269n14
mask, 196, 267n222
masochism, 124
mass, 89, 126; attendance at, 126; cost of, 307n172; daily, 125, 306nn168, 169, 170; at dawn, 308n189; distraction during, 128; first, 308n189; heard from bed, 127, 308n195; hearing, 305–6n165; at home, 308n194; hunter's, 308n196; as lovers' tryst, 128; outdoor, 127; requiem, 306n167; for safety, 306n170; sailor's, 308n196; short, 127; soldier's, 308n196; solicitation during, 128; for soul, 125; on Sunday, 127; sung, 308n191
massacre, 140
master, 53, 110, 111, 118, 192, 247n59, 305–6n165, 357n252; blind, 117; greedy, 54; and servant, 293n166
masturbation, 309n206
Mata, Juan de, 57, 252n107
mathematics, 193
Matías, 70
matins, 127
Matos Fragoso, Juan de. *For list of works see* Index of *Comedias*
Matthew, gospel of, 262n181, 273nn56, 57, 303n140
mattress, 50
maurophilia, 203
Maximilian of Austria, 126
mayorazgo, 245n40, 280–1n148
Maza, 165
McKendrick, Melveena: *Playing the King*, 8, 9, 150, 205, 237n262, 327n228, 363n15
meal, 116, 117, 118, 120, 293–4n6, 294–5n15
meat, 132; abstinence from, 130; cut of, 363–4n16; turkey, 120–1
medical procedure, 149, 325n208; medicalization, 147
medicine, 5; doctor of, 86, 323n167, 327n7; Galenic, 145, 322n159; humoural, 147; Renaissance, 99
medieval, 5, 6, 8, 30, 35, 42, 53, 73, 97, 99, 100, 109, 112, 115, 142, 173, 194, 203, 209, 215n14, 218n28, 220n6, 256n141, 291n145; feudalism, 172; hagiography, 93; mentality, 91, 94; origins, 276–7n95; world view, 84, 91

meditation: by candlelight, 101; on duplicity, 186; on friendship, 157; on good government, 236n243; on graphic images, 320–1n144; Jesuit, 115, 131; on lies, 198; ontological, 199; technique, 297n46; on temptation, 365n2; violent, 179
Mediterranean, 53, 54, 58, 248n81, 252n105, 253n114, 253–4n116
melancholy, 100, 102, 286n52, 322n158
Melibea, 248n80
memento mori, 17, 38, 63, 114
memory, 100, 103, 105, 116, 164, 209; books, 11; theory of, 362–3n11
Menelaus, 273n48
menstruation, 81
mentalités, 145, 146
La Merced, church of, 57
Mercedarian, 57, 252n107; friar, 253n108, 331n52. *See also* Redemptionist
mercenary, 59, 62, 63, 93
merchandise, 70, 246n51, 260–1n167; fake, 242n10
merchant, 56, 64, 65, 120, 247–8n73, 259n155, 260n166, 260–1n167; class, 68; distrust of, 262n179; Jewish, 66, 260–1n167, 262n175; seafaring, 260–1n167; ship, 260n166; Venetian, 260–1n167
mercy, 145; begging for, 141; mission of, 253n108
mesón, 118
Messiah, 288n87
mestizo, 25
metaliterary, 106, 132, 197
metamorphosis, 22, 166, 198, 227n89, 242–3n17
metaphor, 10, 23
metonymy, 194
Mexico, 43, 238n274, 291n129
Midas, King, 45, 62, 241n5
Middle Ages, 84, 173
Middlebrook, Leah, 75, 106, 108, 186, 237n263, 268n10
Middleton, Thomas, 48, 245n44
migraine, 305n160
Milan, 48
military, 32, 110; campaign, 294–5n15; dictatorship, 55; fatigue, 288n83; furor, 103; innovation, 228n102; leader, 32; might, 162; orders, 157, 330n32; prowess, 163; standards of conduct, 276–7n95; technology, 161, 228n102; terms, 287n64
mimesis, 218n28
mineral, 63, 255–6n138
mining, 63, 257n147, 258nn150, 151
minister, 177, 354n203
Mintz, Sidney, 6
Mira de Amescua, Antonio, 231n156, 335n102, 365n6; *Lo que puede el oír misa*, 307n173
Mirabellio, Domenico Nani, 219n37
miracle, 67, 90, 131, 165, 339nn157, 158
mirage, 115
mirror, 50, 74, 166, 177, 185, 285n28, 340n177, 345n24, 350n117, 359n276; cure, 148; house made of, 287n60; of life, 94, 218n35, 282n167; lying, 187; of princes, 86; of wives, 86
miscegenation, 25, 80
mischief, 109, 113
miser, 47, 117, 122, 241n6, 243n20
misognyny, 47, 52, 84, 93, 99, 138, 163, 165, 191, 285n31, 340n164
mistress, 192
moan, 117
mob, 70
moderation, 108, 292n147
modernity, 94, 173, 216n19, 276n92
moderns vs ancients, 163
modesty, 82
monarch, 32, 34, 51, 105, 107, 113, 114, 127, 131, 139, 160, 163, 192, 226n82, 237n258, 252n105, 305n160, 333n75, 334n85; Catholic, 67, 68; conception of, 354n203; foreign, 175; Hapsburg, 126; hereditary, 47; portrait of, 195; pro-monarch, 237n262
monarchy, 333n75, 354n203
monastery, 84, 106, 110, 116, 169, 248n74, 256–7n144
money, 15, 45, 46, 47, 49, 51, 52, 54, 56, 57, 60, 72, 116, 157, 173, 176, 177, 179, 186, 187, 241n6, 242n10, 242–3n17, 243n19, 244n31, 247n67, 269–70n26, 329n24, 346–7n53, 349n101, 350n108; borrowed, 64; drain, 252n105; lack of, 119; lending, 64, 65, 66, 144, 260–1n167; management, 110; use of, 220n6
monk, 99, 100, 124, 168, 215n14

monotheism, 6
monster, 100, 161, 281n154, 286n46; glass, 314n44; legendary, 272–3n46; of palaces, 159
monstrosity, 92
Montecillo Miranda, Francisco de la Puente, 70
Montillo, Manuel, 71
mood, 320–1n144
moon, 17, 156, 157, 187, 272–3n46, 328n8, 329n28
"Moor," 26, 27, 54, 55, 56, 60, 79, 80, 161, 162, 231n146, 250–1n95, 254n117, 256–7n144, 273–4n63; defeat of the, 289n97; garment of, 57; harem of, 79; hidalgo, 254n121; Moorish rule, 80; name of, 58–9; sale of, 58; trading of, 58
moralist, x, 19, 93, 99, 127, 142, 190, 268n7, 274–5n70, 320n143, 323n168, 349n95
morality, 191, 280–1n148; new, 320–1n144; play, 115; Renaissance, 320–1n144
Moreto, Agustín, 117. *For list of works see* Index of *Comedias*
Morisco, 54, 55, 58, 69, 70, 79; children, 55, 250n92, 250–1n95; expulsion, 55, 58, 250n95, 253–4n116, 273n60
morning: mass, 306n168; prayers, 304n150
Morocco, 51, 54
Morpheus, 103
mortal: fight, 276–7n95; sin, 5, 274–5n70
mortality, 159, 237n264, 331n48
Moses, 3, 7, 111, 123, 132, 157, 176, 200, 206, 214n2, 303n143
moth, 156, 327n6
mother, 23, 52, 72, 82, 92, 93, 110, 159, 210, 274–5n70, 280–1n148, 281n149, 337n138; of Antichrist, 93; Earth, 63; honouring, 174–201; Jewish, 232–3n184; marriage with, 79; milk of, 119; of Muhammad, 92; sex with, 76; step-mother, 138
motive, 170, 247n71, 251n97, 256–7n144, 343n225, 350n110
mould, 297n50
Mount Etna, 136, 314n52
Mount Oeta, 221–2n22
mountain, 16, 22, 24, 45, 63, 71, 105, 133, 221n20, 221–2n22, 222n25, 227n89, 228n106, 257n147, 258n150, 259n155, 267n222, 290n109; goat, 272–3n46; of Jerusalem, 221–2n22; swallowing, 221–2n22
mourning, 77, 84, 261n170; by widows, 129
mouse, 121, 303n131
mouth, 63, 75, 91, 187, 188, 190, 200, 295n17, 351nn122, 130; of a demon, 255n124; of the lion, 131
mouthful, 298n68, 304n150
mouthpiece, 209, 210
movie, 209
Mudéjar, 80
Mugaburu, Josephe de, 61
Muhammad, 27, 87, 92; mother of, 92
mujer varonil, 19, 20, 138, 141, 224–5n67
mulatto, 55, 249n89
muleteer, 249n89
Murder, 10, 22, 48, 61, 67, 133–52, 178, 179; multiple, 144; of parents, 210; wife-murder, 142, 143, 150
murmuring, 159
Musa, 80
Muses, 106, 290n120
music, 107, 166, 294n10, 298n69, 320–1n144; musical ability, 157, 330n33; therapy, 148, 325n201
musician, 158, 270n28
Muslim, 26, 27, 29, 54, 58, 59, 60, 79, 80, 248n81; captors, 254n121; conquest, 103; Hispano-Muslim, 253n114; holy warrior, 302–3n129; pirates, 55, 59, 72; prison, 60; relations with Christians, 251n97; slaves, 249–50n90
Mussaphias, 264n196
muteness, 338n146
mutilation, 261n170
mystic, 124, 325n213; mysticism, 104, 149, 169, 180, 181, 182, 183
mystique, 166
mythology, 22, 23, 76, 137, 177, 221–2n22, 227n89, 227–8n96, 272–3n46, 287n68; creatures from, 78, 136, 281n151; Hebrew, 272–3n46

Naboth, 20
Nachleben, 203, 358n259
name, 164, 165, 171, 247n72, 312n12, 348n84, 358n260, 360n288; dishonour to, 90; false, 196; lover's, 158
nap, 77
Naples, 35, 175, 229n120, 283n11
Napoleonic Wars, 216n19

Narcissus, 20, 74, 177, 225n71
nature, 16, 17, 19, 32, 40, 136, 187, 188, 195, 200, 303n140, 330n33, 332n61, 358n257; against, 233n185, 275n71; authority of, 237n265; human, 63, 98, 114, 176, 292n147, 322n158, 363n12; proliferating, 75; resources, 61
nausea, 242n16
Navarre, 26
navigation, 265n202
Nebuchadnezzar, 42
neck, 17, 81, 89, 223n37, 329n27; breaking the, 222n28
nectar, 114, 296n41
negligence, 98, 126, 283n5, 284n21
negotium, 108, 291n145
neighbour, 107, 216n16; goods of, 73, 156; harm to, 73; wife of, 156
Neoplatonism, 16, 187, 196, 221n21, 354n203, 359n276
nephew, 245n46
nest, 241n7
Netherlands, 27, 62, 71, 93, 216n17, 261n170, 289n97
New Historicism, 8, 9, 168, 204, 217n26, 355n209
New Testament, 6, 46, 71, 78, 123, 132, 182, 301n113, 311n252
"New" World, 25, 46, 55, 245n38; colonies, 61, 62, 63, 255n128, 265n202, 289n97; conquest, 68, 289n97; encounter, 64; exploration, 120, 121, 264n193, 302n122; mining, 257n147; natives, 75, 250n91, 255–6n138; resources, 62; riches, 65, 346–7n53; territories, 65, 93
Newhauser, Richard, 262n179
niche, 61
niece, 271n31
night, 86, 91, 117, 187, 243n22, 267n222, 303n140, 310n231, 330n36, 332n68, 350n116, 360n288
nightingale, 241n7
nightmare, 89, 90, 185
nihilism, 168, 342n203
Nile, 221n20
Nimrod, 35, 36, 43, 235nn239, 240, 236n241
nineteenth century, 179
Noah, 35, 36
nobility, 104, 148, 175, 176, 192, 233n185, 329n24, 334n83; repositioning of the, 108; status of the, 172
noble, 106; blood, 163; desires, 170; family, 164, 250n92; lie, 195; master, 192; rank, 269–70n26; soul, 312n16; status, 172, 233n185; subjects, 108
nobleman, 47, 48, 53, 75, 105, 108, 109, 110, 116, 122, 130, 150, 157, 161, 162, 169, 172, 175, 191, 192, 206, 231n154, 269–70n26, 291n129, 330n33
noblesse oblige, 148, 164
noblewoman, 83, 110, 192, 281n149
Nolasco, Pedro, 57
nomad, 71
Noreña, 71
nostalgia, 103, 105, 169
novel, 11, 108, 207, 208, 283–4n12, 302n126
novelist, 302n126
novelistic autonomy, 150
novena, 61, 125, 305n164
Noyes, Dorothy, 216n19
nudity, 17, 21, 40; indigenous, 157, 329n28; of truth, 196, 359nn270, 272
nun, 84, 99, 100, 124, 182, 238n274; instruction to, 124
Nunes de Costas, 264n196
nunnery, 182

oath, 85
obedience, 129, 139, 245n47; disobedience, 182; forced, 179; to parents, 174–201
obesity, 115, 124
obfuscation, 193
object, 125, 306n170
obligation, 175, 176, 190, 214n10, 252n105, 280–1n148, 285n34, 309n221, 353n165, 356n235; toward children, 184; to fast, 305nn160, 163; to lie, 350n110; to marry, 146; natural, 174
oblivion, 98, 100, 168, 170, 285n24
obscurity, 199
obstinacy, 150, 315n62, 326n225
Occasio, 93, 282n164
occasion, 318n116
ocean, 18, 40, 43, 45, 61, 64, 221n20, 258n153; Atlantic, 64. *See also* sea
O'Connor, Tom, 216–17n20
Odysseus, 75

offense, 326n225
offering, 307n174
office, 160, 173
Old Testament, 3, 20, 23, 35, 66, 78, 123, 131, 132, 148, 160, 293–4n6, 311–12n256, 321n153
Old World, 120, 302n122
Olympus, 222n22
omission, 98
onion, 115, 296n42
ontology, 199
opera, 118
opinion, 91, 355n215
opium, 45, 241–2n8
oracle, 278n110
Orán, 55, 68
oratory, 164
ordeal, 276–7n95
order, 180; Mercedarian, 252n107; military, 157, 330n32; redemptionist, 252n105; religious, 130, 159, 252n105, 310n229, 331n52; restoration of, 180, 209; Trinitarian, 252n107
ordination, 124
orgy, 20
"Orient," 263n186; Oriental, 261n170
Original Sin, 16, 80, 184, 361n309
ornament, 261n170
orphan, 141, 197
orthodoxy, 363n15
Osorio, Elena, 272nn41, 42
Ossa, 222n22
ostentation, 116
Ostia, 260n166
Ostrauizxa, 281n154
ostrich, 163, 337n127
Othello, 278n109
Other, 26, 69, 145, 203
otium, 108, 291n145
Out of the Wings, 213n3, 364n22
overlord, 62
ox, 50

Padre Nuestro, 123
padrino, 107
pagan, 20, 23, 42, 114, 163, 165; deities, 78; gods, 77, 114, 137, 139, 144, 164, 165, 272–3n46, 274n67, 296n41, 317n97, 321n146; idols, 92; wisdom, 177
pain, 100
painting, 23, 38, 50, 81, 102, 122, 169, 195, 261n170, 288n81, 358n255; lamb's blood, 320n142; still-life, 120, 301–2n117
palace, 20, 34, 39, 102, 169, 194, 332nn64, 65, 334n84, 342n214, 357n245; monster of, 159; servants, 160
palate, 114
Palenzuela, 71
Pallas Athena, 137, 316n78
Panopticon, 179, 285n35
pantheism, 16
pantheon, 137, 337n129
pantry, 156
paper, 197, 360nn288, 293
parable, 31, 46, 71, 110, 242–3n17, 266n221, 293n166, 311n249
Paracelsus, 145, 322n159
parade, 112, 256–7n144
paradise, 40, 79, 287n68; earthly, 16; foretaste of, 130
paradox, 6, 104, 167, 198, 199, 248n74, 318n121; Baroque, 199; Liar, 198
paralysis, 98
paranoia, 92
pardon, 148
parent, 8, 51, 174–201, 250–1n95, 365n6; biological, 180; consent of, 250n92; earthly, 182; godparent, 76; murder of, 210; obedience to, 174–201; overprotective, 179; parental figure, 179; parenting, 180, 181, 184; sins of the, 216–17n20
Paris, 241n6
Paris, city of, 162, 169
Paris, Prince, 28, 80, 273n48
Parker, Alexander, 225n77
Parma, 133
Parnassus, 163
parody, 234n213, 320n142
parricide, 210, 365n6
party, 112, 113, 116, 121, 240n321, 294–5n15; day, 126; dinner, 115, 310n235; planner, 116; riotous, 115
passenger, 75, 112–13
passion, passions, 111, 139, 145, 150, 160, 168, 191, 225n131, 292n147, 322n162, 328n16, 331n52, 333n77, 342n205; affect conquering, 146; amorous, 102; blind, 134;

for Gluttony, 121; jealous, 139; natural, 145; rustic, 156; taming of, 146; without, 324n178
Passover, 132, 320n142
pastime, 116
pastoral: ambience, 158; discourse, 290n113; drama, 158; fantasy, 171; genre, 100, 287n54, 290n113; landscape, 100; *locus amoenus*, 169; world, 101
paternity, 92
patience, 198; impatience, 104, 134, 135, 141, 224–5n67, 313nn28, 29, 30
patient, 304–5n159
Patmos, Isle of, 74, 268n2
patriarch, 160; Joseph, 78
patriarchal culture, 174, 344–5n3
patriarchy, 20, 177, 180, 185, 186
patricide, 178
patrimony, 280–1n148
patriotism, 10, 164, 167, 177
patron, 175, 335n107; patronage, 265n207
Paul, St, 120
pauper, 69
pawnbroker, 66
payment, 121, 251n98, 334n90, 350n108
Payne, Stanley, 172
Paz, Octavio, 43, 240n321
peace, 39, 104, 106, 109, 180, 288n85; peaceful setting, 169; peacetime, 103; proffer of, 148
peacock, 17, 160, 222n26, 332n70
pearl, 61, 62, 64, 65, 241n6, 254n121
peasant, 237n262
pecado nefando, 76, 271n30
pedagogy, 40, 99, 126, 274–5n70
Peláez, Juan, 161
Peláez, Suero, 161
pelican, 121
Pelion, 222n22
pen, 106; fruit of the, 265n207; sacred, 311n246; vs sword, 147
penalty, 90, 123
penance, 4, 5, 93, 114, 129, 305nn160, 163
penis, 275n71
penitence, 273–4n63
penitent, 115, 207, 208, 247n72; female, 275n71; penitential context, 141; penitential practice, 122
Pentateuch, 3
Pérez de Montalbán, Juan, 3, 72. *For list of works see* Index of *Comedias*
performance, 39, 86, 132, 134, 135, 148, 235n240, 245n44, 270n28, 327n229; at court, 265n207; first-night, 310n235
perfume, 75, 112; Gucci, 165
permission, 175, 303n130
permissiveness, 248n74
Perry, Mary Elizabeth, 53, 274–5n70
persecution, 190, 232–3n184, 330n32
Perseus, 22, 227n89
Persia, King of, 138, 316n81
perspectivism, 167, 211, 341n191
Peru: Hapsburg, 255n130; silver mines in, 258n150; Viceroyalty of, 61
perversity, 76
pestilence, 187
Peter, epistles of, 316n76
Peter I the Cruel, King, 42, 239n305
petition, 172
Petrarch, 162
petticoat, 52, 247n61, 310n231
Phaedra, 200, 361n317
Phaethon, 22, 23, 166, 227–8n96
phantasm, 168, 323n176
Pharaoh, 138, 160, 273n53
pheasant, 115, 296n42, 302n123
Philip II, King, 22, 69, 77, 226nn82, 83, 264n196, 272n38
Philip III, King, 22, 226nn82, 83, 250n92, 264n196, 272n38
Philip IV, King, 37, 79, 117, 161, 226n82, 248n74
Philistine, 23, 24, 34, 144
philosophy, 141, 177, 189, 226n88, 298–9n73, 361n305; Epicurean, 114; moral, 62; naturalistic, 292n147; professor of, 77
phlegm, 317n101, 322n158, 323n168
physiology, 323n168
picaresque, 25, 114, 116, 117, 118, 129, 207, 210, 300–1n109, 364n17; anti-clericalism, 296n32; novel, 69, 119
pícaro, 68, 109, 117, 119, 148
piety, 99, 127, 129, 130, 132, 176, 180, 184, 190, 242n11, 256–7n144, 307n179, 308n198, 342n201; alternative expressions of, 128; filial, 176, 177, 344–5n3, 345n16; impiety, 178, 273n49

pig, 46, 50, 244n25
pike, 110, 111, 139
Pike, Ruth, 54
Pilate, Pontius, 70
pilgrim, 71, 112, 113, 123, 266nn220, 221; pilgrimage, 113, 266n220, 365n6
pillaging, 63, 256nn139, 141
pillow, 50, 102
pilot, 170, 343n227
piracy, 10, 26, 27, 64, 259n154; English, 253n115; Muslim, 55, 58, 59, 61, 72; of editions, 72
pimp, 53, 298n68; church as, 128; state as, 248n74. *See also* procurer
pistol, 70, 139, 317n94; firing, 139, 317n97
pit, 334n91; bottomless, 315n55; of hell, 321n151
pity, 148, 166, 167, 169, 173, 304n153, 324n194, 341nn186, 190, 193, 199, 343n230
Pizarro, Francisco, 255n129
Pizarro, Gonzalo, 121
plague, 103, 136, 236n257
planet, 101, 164, 339n149
plant, 5, 75, 214n6
plate, 114, 115, 117, 118, 132, 296n29, 297n55
Plato, 163, 171, 195, 290n113, 320–1n144, 337n130, 350n120, 358n259
platter, 78
plaza, 35; Mayor (Madrid), 130; Mayor (Yepes), 35, 36; sleeping in the, 258n153; of Valladolid, 162
pleasure, 105, 113, 118, 119, 123, 124, 156, 157, 168, 178, 193, 202, 294–5n15, 300n103, 329n25; buying, 247–8n73; displeasure, 179; house of, 295n18; vs procreation, 274–5n70
pliego suelto, 241n6
Pliny, 163
plough, 293n170
plunder, 55, 58, 62, 256–7n144. *See also* bounty; spoils
Plutarch, 323n168
Pluto, 77
poet, 33, 162, 358n259
poetics, 39, 137, 189
poetry, lyric, 11, 75, 106, 108, 195, 207, 226n88, 237n263, 268n10, 327n7
poise, 148
poison, 15, 87, 88, 91, 98, 117, 136, 137, 219n4, 284n18
policy, 289n97
Polish, 28
political, 33; appointment, 159; expediency, 173; instrument, 327n228; landscape, 335n97; power, 342n201; theory, 255–6n138, 354n203
pollution, 275n71
poltergeist, 242n10
poltrón, 282n3, 291n132
Polyphemus, 22, 227n89
Ponce de León, Napoleón Baccino, 302n126
pope, 35, 89, 159, 365n6
port, 69, 76, 253n108, 258n153, 260n166, 265n202; Atlantic, 54; of Ostia, 260n166
portent, 281n154
portrait, 72, 102, 160, 195, 265n207, 288n81, 301–2n117, 358n260; composite, 272n41; literary, 358n261; miniature, 86; of monarch, 195; visual, 358n261
Portugal, 68, 93, 232–3n184, 246n54, 249–50n90, 250n93, 260–1n167, 264n195, 336n114; Queen Isabel of, 37
Portuguese, 26, 29, 138, 230n121, 249–50n90, 336n114
positivism, 5
postmodern, 143, 174, 185, 207, 208; postmodernity, xi, 3, 7, 16, 63, 211, 326n220
Potiphar, wife of, 78, 273n53
Potosí, 63, 258n150
pouting, 135
poverty, 31, 32, 46, 51, 116, 117, 119, 170, 173, 176, 178, 242–3n17, 243nn20, 22, 257n147, 297–8n63, 301n114, 344n234, 346–7n53
power, 185, 186, 336n119, 339n154; consolidation of, 172; effects, 237n265; exercise of, 285n35; loci of, 304–5n159; magical, 240n321; persuasive, 278n110; political, 342n201; purchasing, 297–8n63; relations, 179; superpower, 148; world, 151
pragmatism, 99, 175, 177, 189
prayer, 126, 129, 305n160, 309nn216, 219; in church, 127; for good health, 306n170; intercessory, 129; morning, 304n150
preacher, 33
precept, 126, 304–5n159, 309n221; holy, 175

prefatory, 163
pregnancy, 81, 88, 91, 92; avoidance of, 275n71
prejudice, 70, 138; against women, 190; confessional, 92
preliminares, 38
presence, 218n28
presumption, 199, 223n31, 227n95, 339n157
price, 187, 252n105, 297–8n63; right, 186; rise in, 69
Pride, ix, 8, 15–44, 79, 97, 155, 161, 168, 186, 192, 215n15, 259n154, 295n16, 296n31, 301n114, 316nn77, 78, 327n4, 349n99
priest, 41, 62, 77, 110, 114, 144, 148, 179, 207, 272n38, 296n35, 308n193, 362n4; high, 182; and lover, 309n206
primogeniture, 48, 110, 245n40
prince, 33, 39, 80, 82, 148, 160, 162, 163, 165, 177, 178, 199, 303n140, 333n75, 335n96, 343n230, 354n190; enemy, 146; junior, 146; lost, 206; mirror of, 86
princess, 84, 160, 169, 178
print, 134, 142; culture, 198; printed books, 263n186; printed page, 133
printer, 72
printing, 66, 181, 226n83
prison, 34, 35, 38, 60, 78, 82, 102, 119, 123, 273n53
prisoner, 19, 26, 57, 167, 249n89, 252n105, 269–70n26; Christian, 56; exchange, 56; of war, 54, 250n91; wealthy, 56
privacy, 77
privado, 37, 160, 197, 334nn88, 95, 335nn96, 100. See also *valido*
privanza, 161, 162, 334nn86, 89, 90, 95, 335nn97, 102
privilege, 264n195; royal, 280–1n148; urban, 172
prize, 293n167, 303n143
probabilism, 142, 319n139
probate, 48
procession, 61, 107, 339n149
procrastination, 98
procreation, 177, 181, 274–5n70
procurer, 53. *See also* pimp
producer, 272nn41, 42
productivity, 111
profanation, 320n142
professionalism, 290n114
professor, 77
profit, 65, 127, 193, 251–2n103, 260n166, 299n92
profligacy, 47, 110
progenitor, 185
progeny, 91, 98
progress, 174
prohibition, 176, 186, 201, 240n321, 260–1n167, 276n78, 277–8n100, 291n129, 309n221
projection, 98
promiscuity, 75, 77, 268n12
promise, 198, 358n263; breach of, 269–70n26; Commandment with a, 176; rash, 184; to marry, 269–70n26
proof, 85, 86, 196, 197, 199, 232–3n184, 278n109, 278–9n111; alleged, 86; burden of, 85, 278n106; infallible, 88
prop, 35, 86, 130, 138, 145, 235n240, 301–2n117; food as, 310n235
propaganda, 9, 274–5n70, 327n228
property, 120, 159, 172
prophecy, 20, 23, 38, 42, 288n87
prophet, 78, 87, 103, 273n54
prosecution, 83, 88, 94, 144
prosperity, 116, 260–1n167
prostitute, 70, 77, 85, 270–1n29, 274n69
prostitution, 53
prostration, 39
protection, 335n96, 336n107
Protestant, 69; Protestantism, 226n83; rebels, 283n11; work ethic, 99
protocol, 110
proverb, 4, 10, 99, 117, 241n6, 305–6n165, 352n147
Proverbs, book of, 93, 301n113
Providence, 131, 276–7n95
provocation, 338n148, 350n110, 357n252
prudence, 107, 147, 150, 167, 175, 341n193; imprudence, 223n32, 224–5n67
Prudentius, 215n14
prudery, 274–5n70
Psalm, 138
psyche, 41; Latin American, 43; Mexican, 43; Spanish, 80, 81, 99
psychodrama, 201
psycholinguistics, 15

psychology, 4, 23, 90, 100, 135, 148, 207, 320–1n144; humoural, 146, 322n158, 323n168; pop, 134, 148, 150
public: figures, 363n12; vs private, 272n42; space, 209
publican, 71, 242–3n17
Pullan, Brian, 66
punishment, 34, 40, 43, 82, 85, 99, 121, 123, 133, 135, 139, 143, 149, 178, 185, 187, 240n319, 256–7n144, 273–4n63, 303n142, 305n163, 314n39, 320n143; for Adultery, 83; begging for, 84; corporal, 128, 188; customary, 186; for dishonour, 90; divine, 61, 64, 85, 115, 178, 259n155, 321n150; ecological, 63; eternal, 43, 178; for false testimony, 186; fasting as, 130; hunger as, 119; hypothetical, 83; of an innocent, 88; just, 67; of parents, 185; self-punishment, 124; stoning as, 93; temporal, 178; threat of, 178; by vengeful deity, 123
pupil, 190. *See also* student
purchase, 186, 187; of books, 291n145; of Christians, 249n85; of slaves, 164, 249n86
purgation, 144
Purgatory, 125, 185, 306n170
purity, 164, 232n182, 232–3n184
pyramid, 35
Pyrenees, 216n19

quarantine, 226n83
quartering, 71
queen, 32, 84, 85, 93, 113, 295n26, 333n75; Amazon, 141; chaste, 82; Cleopatra, 78; evil, 113; of France, 82, 92; Isabel of Portugal, 37; Jezabel, 78, 80
Quevedo, Francisco de, 226n88, 236n249, 257n147, 259n155, 265n207, 280n143
Quiñones de Benavente, Juan de, 71
Quiñones de Benavente, Luis. *For list of works see* Index of *Comedias*

rabbi, 182
rabbit, 118
race, 28, 331n46
racism, 356n227
raid, 58, 252n105, 253–4n116
Ramírez, Beltrán, 161
ransacking, 71
ransom, 51, 56, 58, 251n98, 251–2n103, 252n105, 253n114, 260n166
rape, 71, 76, 78, 92, 269–70n26, 270n28
Raphael, Archangel, 81
rapier, 139, 317n94
rational arguments, 135; reflection, 320–1n144
rationality, 147, 148, 189, 200, 363n12
rationalization, 116, 245–6n49, 256n139
rations, 118
Ravid, Benjamin, 66
reactionary, 210
reader-response theory, 362n8
reading: of books, 291n145; list, 206; practice, 11
real, 186, 307n172
realism, 135
reason, 99, 112, 132, 147, 148, 292n147, 324n177, 334n89; disturbed, 323n168; loss of, 134; for lying, 190; of state, 148, 190, 324n191, 353n165
rebel, Protestant, 283n11
rebellion, 70, 178, 363n15
reception, 244n35, 322n159; theory, 203, 362n8
recompense, 287n63, 302n126
reconciliation, 39, 247n72
Reconquest, 24, 26, 27, 79, 104, 145, 289n97
Recopilación de leyes, 142
recourse, 276–7n95
redemption: of captives, 57, 58, 252n105, 253n111; expeditions, 252n105; of humanity, 57; organized, 252n105; treatise on, 253n111
Redemptionist, 56, 57. *See also* Mercedarian; Trinitarian
reform, 276n87
Reformation, 242–3n17
refuge, 70
refugee, 66
registry, 49
regret, 148, 150, 348n86
regulation, 178
rein, 17, 149, 223nn42, 43, 326n214
rejection, 269–70n26
relaciones de sucesos, 92, 258n153, 281n154
reliquary, 256–7n144
relocation, 250–1n95
remedy, 149
remorse, 106, 204

Renaissance, 4, 6, 8, 9, 11, 16, 23, 28, 42, 44, 46, 47, 48, 51, 53, 62, 66, 99, 100, 102, 138, 139, 144, 145, 149, 163, 166, 172, 173, 174, 181, 187, 194, 196, 207, 211, 226n83, 228n102, 242–3n17, 244n35, 260–1n167, 291n145, 317n98, 320–1n144, 322n159, 323n168, 327n229, 341n191, 344–5n3; man, 111; medicine, 99; morality, 320–1n144
renegade, 54, 59, 60, 254n120, 349n93; Jewish, 254n120; ship, 75
rent, 177, 245n46, 247n71, 280–1n148
renunciation, 280–1n148
reparations, 256n139
repentance, 40, 84, 112, 141, 144, 178, 180, 301n114, 324n193
repertoire, ix, x, xii, 10, 46, 53, 54, 56, 63, 69, 71, 82, 84, 90, 91, 93, 193, 203, 204, 206, 207, 269–70n26, 319n122
repression, 77, 274–5n70
republic, 91
Republic, 274–5n70
reputation, 85, 91, 111, 329n24, 332n61, 338n148, 355n209
requirement, 305n161
rescue, 283–4n12
resentment, 172, 233n185
residue, 8, 73, 74, 85, 89, 91, 94, 97, 109, 155, 156, 180, 186
resistance, 182, 186, 208, 337–8n140
resource, 116, 246n54
rest, 97, 101, 102, 104, 105, 106, 243n22, 282n3, 287nn64, 68, 288n69, 290n109, 291n138, 311n249, 313–14n37; god of, 103; without, 317n89
restraint, 149, 292n147
retaliation, 91
Revelation, book of, 268n2, 315n55
revenge, 58, 64, 65, 89, 91, 133, 137, 138, 140, 141, 143, 145, 148, 158, 187, 196, 316n84, 318n119, 320n143, 323n168, 326n225, 331n43; tragedy, 140
revenue, 263n190
revival, 144
revolt, 250n91; of the Comuneros, 265n206
revolution, 38, 202, 237n262; Commercial, 220n6; moral, 203
reward: divine, 307n179; earthly, 175; heavenly, 175, 176
rhetoric, 10, 134, 166, 167, 181, 188, 194, 204, 244n35, 274–5n70, 342n201; of honour, 355n209; of proof, 86; of validation, 197
rhetorical project, 132
rhetorical question, 354n192, 356n230
rhinoceros, 40
Ribera, Juan de, Archbishop, 250n92, 250–1n95
rich man, parable of the, 46
riddle, 199
rights, 214n10; of cuckolds, 320n143; legal, 280–1n148; of nobles, 172; to remain celibate, 182
ring, 86, 240n4, 242n10, 278n110
La Rioja, 70
riot, 117, 130, 178
Ripa, Cesare, 238n282
risk, 246n51, 252n105, 305n160
rite, 114
ritual, 10, 148, 272–3n46, 320n142
rival, 164, 165, 272n42; rivalry, 327n228, 338n141
river, 16, 221n20, 222n22
Roach, Joseph, 218n34
road, 70, 266n221, 343n227; open, 71; roadside, 71, 112, 118, 267n222; royal, 266n220
robber, 109, 266n221, 267n222; bandit, 71; professional, 70; robbery, 250–1n95, 253n110, 256–7n144, 259n154, 267n222. *See also* thief
Rodrigo, King, 80, 273–4n63
Rodrigue, Aron, 263n190, 263–4n192, 264nn195, 196
Rojas, Fernando de, 53, 248n80
Rojas Zorrilla, Francisco de, 81. *For list of works see* Index of *Comedias*
Roman, 24, 25, 62, 75, 104, 163, 215n14, 273n50, 342n212; ancient, 78; Christianized, 78; civilization, 78; dramatist, 77; empire, 67; general, 328n16; heritage, 228n108; late-empire, 78; law, 142, 255–6n138; mythology, 137; past, 354n203; Republic, 78; senate, 24; warlike, 78
romance, 364n26
Romance languages, 4, 214n4
Romans, epistle to the, 301n113
Rome, 32, 62, 71, 78, 79, 168, 266n220, 365n6

romería, 113
rooster, 136, 281n151, 308n189
Rosa, St, 339n157
rose, 75, 82, 333n75
Royal Palace (Madrid), 23
ruby, 241n5
Rueda, Lope de. *For list of works see* Index of *Comedias*
ruffian, 129
Ruiz Lagos, Manuel, 238n282
Ruiz Pérez, Pedro, 286n53, 287n54, 290nn113, 114, 125, 291n145, 292n159
rumour, 104, 107
rural, 214n10, 293n170
rustic, 242–3n17, 344n234
Ruth, 131

Sabbath, 125, 128, 129, 211
Sabine, Lorenzo, 276–7n95
sackcloth, 303n136, 328n15
sacrament, 48, 141, 144, 148, 218n28, 271n31, 306n169
sacrifice: human, 184, 348n84; of the mass, 125; mourning, 261n170; personal, 128; spirit of, 274–5n70
sacrilege, 42, 239n302, 317n94
sacristan, 55, 307n179, 308n189
sadism, 120
sadness, 100, 117, 145, 183, 185, 215n15, 251n96, 293n172
safety, 70, 125, 306n170
Said, Edward, 263n186
sailor, 127, 187, 259n155, 332–3n72
saint, 100, 105, 124, 129, 149, 365n6; holy day of, 125; image of, 61; not a, 308n198; patron, 125, 231n152; saintly characters, 123, 124, 129, 176, 321n155
Saint-Saēns, Alain, 53, 248n74, 270–1n29
Salamanca, 69, 71, 77
sale, 186, 187, 242n10, 256–7n144, 284n15, 321n155; of captives, 58, 249n85; legal, 309n221; of meat, 309n221; of reliquaries, 256–7n144; of slaves, 58, 164; of Spain, 273–4n63; of witnesses, 349n101
Salé (Morocco), 54
salvation, 57, 143
Samaria, 274n67
Samaritan, 79
sambenito, 52, 196, 247n72
Samson, 144
Samuel, book of, 273n55, 325n200
San Lorenzo Island (Peru), 258n153
San Miguel, 258n153
Sancho Panza, 118
sanctity, 165, 171, 190, 308n201
sand, 223n43, 227n89
sangría, 113, 216n19, 295n22
sanitizing, 226n83
Santa Marta, 258n153
Santiago de Compostela, 71; Knight of the Order of, 107
Santiago the Moor-Slayer, 231n152
São Thomé, 250n93
Sapir-Whorf hypothesis, 220n11
Saracen, 58
Satan, 123, 137, 316n76
satire, 10, 207
Saturn, 122, 137, 227n90, 303n134, 316n78
satyr, 78, 272–3n46
sauce, 294–5n15
Saul, King, 148, 149, 325n201
Saussure, Ferdinand de, 362–3n11
Savoy, 238n285
Saxony, Duchy of, 26, 229–30n120
scandal, 114, 180, 309n206, 348n86
scapegoat, 17, 222n29
scatology, 44
scene, end of, 149
scenery, 36, 145
sceptre, 38, 139
scholastic, 5, 157
school, 286n42, 329n30; drama, 234n213, 302n128; natural, 183; schoolmaster, 194;
Schröder, Gerhart, 242n16
science, 5, 33, 87, 89, 214nn6, 7, 227n89, 342n212
Scipio Africanus, 328n16
scorn, 189, 223n46, 301n114, 313n32, 326n225, 331n42
scorpion, 115, 156, 327n4
Scott, James C., 6
scream, 115, 134, 219n4
script, 93, 312n258
Scripture, 6, 23, 78, 184, 315n55, 325n201
sculpture, 195, 210
sea, 40, 57, 61, 120, 136, 187, 221n20, 221–2n22, 227n90, 227–8n96, 238n283, 251n96, 258n151, 259nn155, 156, 314n44,

350n115; diving into, 75; high, 252n105; predation, 58. *See also* ocean
Sección Femenina, 274–5n70
secret, 91, 93, 191, 257n147
secular: drama, 137; law, 143; legal system, 94; life, 99
secularization, 48, 145, 147, 148
securities, 264n196
security, 253–4n116
seduction, 20, 47, 76, 80, 86, 269–70n26, 273n53
seed, 115
Selene, 272–3n46
self, 4, 7, 166, 205, 207; discovered by sin, 206, 207, 208; self-awareness, 150; self-cancellation, 342n209; self-defeating, 338n141; self-fashioning, 168, 180, 342n209; self-interest, 177, 188; self-serving, 332n65; vs society, 205
semantics, 214n4, 291n145
semen, 275n71
Seneor, Abraham, 263n192
senses, 115, 294–5n15, 313n28, 343n225; confused, 135; imagining with, 131; without, 315n71
sensibility, 294–5n15
sentence, 278–9n111
Sephardic, 68, 263n189
Sephardim, 264n196
sepulchre, 98, 242n9
Sepúlveda, Juan Ginés de, 255–6n138
sermon, 125, 128, 144, 306nn166, 169, 308n198, 321nn151, 154, 338n143
serpent, 16, 17, 222nn25, 28, 315n57; bronze, 157; fabulous, 159; tail of a, 136, 281n151
servant, 20, 21, 22, 30, 53, 110, 111, 114, 116, 117, 118, 146, 160, 192, 247n59, 299n82, 305–6n165, 334nn84, 85; domestic, 70; female, 192, 299n93, 310n231; good, 192; lower-class, 192; maidservant, 27; master and, 293n166; thieving, 266n209
servitude, 54, 292n159; forced, 250nn91, 92; penal, 54
Se7en, 209
Seven Deadly Sins, 5, 6, 7, 8, 15, 31, 42, 44, 52, 61, 73, 74, 77, 83, 84, 94, 97, 98, 100, 109, 111, 128, 136, 140, 141, 143, 144, 145, 147, 150, 157, 160, 170, 173, 174, 189, 195, 200, 202, 203, 204, 209, 210, 211, 215nn11, 14, 15, 220n6, 276n91, 323n168, 349n99, 365n2. *See also* Capital Vices
seventeenth century, 9, 41, 53, 54, 58, 63, 117, 142, 195, 203, 206, 253–4n116, 253–4n116, 276n87, 291n145, 306n166, 320n143, 325n208, 327n228, 331n48
Seville, 53, 54, 117, 265n202, 302–3n129, 338n141; Veinticuatro of, 346–7n53
sewing, 99, 285n32
sex, 20, 35, 53, 79, 113, 274n69, 277n99, 294–5n15; with animals, 76, 270–1n29; anxiety about, 79, 274–5n70; attitudes toward, 274–5n70; after childbirth, 81; correct, 274–5n70; desire for, 272–3n46; with family, 76; forced, 269–70n26; goal of, 274–5n70; by the gods, 77; illicit, 298n68; positions, 274–5n70; promiscuous, 268n12; sexual inconstancy, 80
Sexto Tarquinio, 78
shadow, 334n89
Shakespeare, William, 8, 9; corpus, 206
– works: *Hamlet*, 82; *Macbeth*, 89; *The Merchant of Venice*, 9, 65, 352n147; *Othello*, 278n109; *Romeo and Juliet*, 337n137; sonnets, 177, 345n25
shame, 84, 193, 196, 240n321, 257n147
Shattuck, Roger, 221n19
shaving, 261n170
sheep, 160, 333n74
shepherd, 23, 31, 148, 158, 171, 270–1n29; shepherdess, 310n222
ship, 15, 54, 64, 65, 69, 170, 250n91, 259n155, 332–3n72; adulterous, 269n21; allegorical, 343n227; Christian, 55; galley, 57; load, 302n126; mass onboard, 127, 308n196; merchant, 260n166; occupants of, 302n126; owner of, 64, 260–1n167; passengers of, 75; pirate, 61; prow, 219n2; renegade, 75; shipwreck, 64, 76, 100, 259n155, 286n40; Spanish, 259n154
shipping: manifest, 10; Mediterranean, 58; of children, 250n93
shirt, 50, 126
shore, 253–4n116
shoulder, 223n33
shouting, 240n321
shrew, 138

shrine, 71, 113
Shylock, 65
sibling, 48
Sicily, 177; King of, 161
Siete partidas, 43
sight, 115, 160
sign, 86, 87, 88, 279n112, 281n154, 362–3n11; of disgrace, 247n72
signifier, 129
silence, 101, 343n221
silk, 74, 75, 79
silva, 226n88, 257n147, 259n155
Silva, Duarte de, 264n196
silver, 49, 63, 64, 67, 68, 114, 241n6, 259nn154, 164, 296n29; harness, 259n164; mines, 258n150
Simerka, Barbara, 255–6n138
simony, 247–8n73
simulacrum, 195
Siraisi, Nancy, 323n168
Siren, 75, 221n20
sister, 48, 72, 200, 224n63, 330n36, 341n186; god-sister, 271n31; half-sister, 270n28; long-lost, 210; love affair with, 78, 271n31; sister-in-law, 48, 271n31
sixteenth century, 6, 54, 57, 63, 69, 108, 119, 142, 172, 202, 203, 258n150, 276n87, 276–7n95, 320n143, 323n168
skin, 23
skull, 38
sky, 178, 221–2n22, 350n111
skyscraper, 173
slander, 272n42
slap, 313n34; in the face, 140, 185, 318n113, 348n86
slapstick, 135, 313n34
slaughter, 68, 86; of the Innocents, 67
slave, slavery, 53, 54, 55, 56, 57, 59, 60, 210, 248n81, 249n84, 251–2n103, 349n93; African, 55, 249–50n90; female, 54; galley, 54; of Gluttony, 115; indigenous, 55, 250n91; market, 54; Morisco, 55; Muslim, 249–50n90; punishment of, 135; royal, 54; sale of, 58, 249n85; theft of, 249n86; trade, 55, 248nn81, 82, 249–50n90, 250n92; trader, 164, 260–1n167
sleep, 98, 99, 101, 102, 103, 104, 107, 111, 134, 147, 149, 160, 243n22, 244n23, 282n3, 284nn21, 22, 285n24, 287n68, 325n204; lack of, 117; in the street, 258n153; for 30 weeks, 284n21
sleeve, 22
Sloth, 31, 97–111, 127, 155, 211, 232n181, 296n31; saintly, 104; son of, 284n18
smell, 115, 116, 120; of bacon grease, 135; bad, 351n122; bitter, 76, 269n23; of food, 115; sense of, 123; sweet, 75, 76, 314n39
smoke, 115, 242n13, 296–7n44
snake, 115, 156, 273–4n63, 327n4; morphing into, 137; venomous, 45, 136
snow, 317n102
social: class, 109; club, 308n197; instrument, 327n228; reform, 69, 119; science, 10; structure, 346–7n53; values, 292n147
Socrates, 137, 315n65
sodomy, 76, 270n27, 271n30
soldier, 22, 25, 28, 32, 59, 61, 63, 110, 127, 139, 149, 162, 163, 181, 228n97, 288n87, 302n128, 336n118; deeds of, 181; dress of, 157, 329–30n31; foot, 110, 293n170; of fortune, 62; fugitive, 70; mass of, 308n196; mercenary, 63; parents of, 181; Spanish, 104, 121; wounded, 301n111
solicitation, 128, 309n206
soliloquy, 10, 207, 269–70n26
Solís, Antonio de. *For list of works see* Index of *Comedias*
solitary confinement, 129
solitude, 100, 106, 107, 308n198, 309n219, 312n8
Solomon, King, 158
Solórzano Pereira, Juan de, 255–6n138
Sommaia, Girolamo de, 306n166
son, 23, 27, 31, 35, 76, 83, 84, 91, 92, 93, 159, 161, 175, 176, 177, 180, 185, 210, 236n241, 241n1, 244n33, 245n44, 251n96, 274n67, 328n16, 345n11, 348n84; bastard, 92, 281n149; book as, 181; disobedient, 178; eldest, 245n40; favourite, 160; of God, 126, 232–3n184, 303n140, 307n174; infant, 349n93; of one's works, 181; Prodigal, 31, 50, 132, 311n249; renegade, 349n93; sacrifice of, 184; second, 110; of something, 172; son-in-law, 52, 57, 247n67; step-son, 181; of the sun, 227–8n96; teenage, 183; young, 175
song, 107, 113, 146, 158, 270n28, 288n82; during mass, 308nn189, 191; popular, 102

sonnet, 177, 296–7n44
soot, 76
Sophocles, 200
sorcery, 34, 234n212, 273n54
sorrow, 188
Sosa, Antonio de, 59, 251n97
soul, 37, 42, 60, 67, 82, 118, 123, 171, 183, 187, 188, 236n255, 255–6n138, 262n182, 284n15, 330n36, 331n44, 351n129, 359n268; ambition of the, 101; body and, 125, 276n87; brothel for the, 268n7; burning, 158; enemy of the, 76; faculties of the, 320–1n144; food for the, 131, 132; hygiene of, 125; mass for, 125; noble, 312n16; profit for, 127; in Purgatory, 125, 306n170; of wife, 143; window to the, 196, 359n276
"soy quien soy," 205, 206
Spanish exceptionalism, 7, 203, 216n19
spear, 156, 159, 288n87
spectacle, 218n28
speculum vitae, 9, 94, 282n167
spell, 75, 324n194
spending, 295n16
spendthrift, 122
spice, 64, 121, 302nn125, 126; of humour, 312n258
spider, 187, 321n151
spirit, 148
spiritus, 322n158
Spitzer, Leo, 8, 205
spoils, 55, 63, 164, 256n139; justification for, 62; of war, 256–7n144. *See also* bounty; plunder
spouse, 62, 86, 87, 88, 90, 92, 185, 274n69; absent, 94; divine, 84; jealous, 86
spur, 149
spy, 160, 179, 332n68
squadron, 134, 162, 336n118
squire, 114, 192, 296n30
stabbing, 135, 313–14n37
stage, 24, 26, 27, 28, 31, 32, 38, 40, 45, 52, 55, 65, 70, 72, 74, 77, 80, 83, 114, 115, 117, 120, 133, 134, 137, 140, 144, 145, 151, 158, 171, 182, 195, 206, 207, 208, 210, 217n21, 294–5n15, 301n111, 301–2n117, 313n33, 327n4; directions, 22, 132, 225n77, 241–2n8, 268n3, 296–7n44, 327n4; machinery, 20, 313n34; modern, 81; temporary, 130; under the, 296–7n44; world, 40
stagnation, 98
stain: blood, 320n142; of dishonour, 94, 269–70n26; on bloodline, 91, 164
standard: double, 279n124; moral, 189
star, 227n96, 235n240; lesser, 163; North, 125
starvation, 117, 118, 120, 130
state: mechanism, 252n105; as pimp, 248n74
Statius, 226n88
statue, 35, 42; of the Virgin, 61, 256–7n144
statute, 277–8n100
Steen, Jan, 81
stereotype, 47, 118, 138
steward, 334n90
stigma, 52, 84
still life, 301–2n117
stock exchange, 264n196
Stoichita, Victor, 346n50
Stoicism, 292n147
stomach, 68, 70, 114, 122
stone, 131, 210; tablet, 209, 214n2; turned to bread, 123, 303n140
stoning, 93
storm, 40, 314n46
street, 120, 135, 256–7n144; pickpocketing in, 266n209; sleeping in, 258n153
strife, 185, 349n93
stripper, 207, 364n26
Structuralist, 204
student, 71, 100, 118, 143, 286n42, 306n166. *See also* pupil
subaltern, 180
subject, 18, 118, 120, 139, 162, 207; commodification of, 346–7n53; to a man, 146; positions, 218n28
subjection, 18, 108
subjectivity, 5, 9, 11, 94, 204, 207, 208, 218n28
sublimation, 157
subversion, 182, 184, 185, 207, 210, 363n15
succession, 177, 331n46
suffering, 134, 179, 184, 185; from hunger, 117, 122, 123, 124, 305n160
suffocation, 46
suicide, 75; of Melibea, 248n80; of Socrates, 137, 315n65

suit, 51
suitor, 51, 52, 57
Sumejera, 138
summa, 5
sumptuary laws, 22, 225n82, 226n82
sun, 22, 23, 34, 42, 147, 163, 187, 191, 227–8n96, 238n285, 336n119, 339n154, 350n111; son of the, 227–8n96
Sunday, 126, 127, 128, 211, 307n184
supernatural, 81, 137, 149, 187
surplus, 173
surveillance, 99, 179, 285n35, 346n50
survival, 173, 254n120, 295n16
suspense, 141
suspension, 100, 149; mystical, 149; of *ocio*, 289n101; of valour, 104
suspicion, 86, 188, 189, 192, 241–2n8, 270n28, 340n173
sustenance, 243n21, 291n145, 300n99; daily, 115; spiritual, 132
sutler, 294–5n15
swearing, 42, 43, 240nn321, 322, 254n121, 261n170, 350n107, 352n147. *See also* Blasphemy
sweat, 135, 313n27
sweets, 114, 125, 305–6n165
Swiss, 110
sword, 86, 89, 108, 138, 139, 145, 197, 230n121, 231n152, 289n93, 317nn93, 97, 321n146, 328n13, 329–30n31, 338n148, 339n149; apostrophe to, 88; brandishing, 104; double-edged, 162, 184; fight, 157, 329–30n31; laid down, 106; vs pen, 108; into ploughshare, 103, 288n87; sale of, 139, 317n97; sheath for, 63, 104; swordplay, 30
syllabus, 206
syllogism, 167
symptom, 108, 159; physical, 146, 147; psychological, 147
synagogue, 311n252
syncretism, 7
synderesis, 137
Synod, 49
syphilis, 248n74

table, 114, 115, 117, 120, 131, 132, 295n20, 296n35, 296–7n44, 297n55, 298n69, 299n83, 301–2n117, 302n125, 311nn249, 252; of Balthasar, 293–4n6; of Gluttony, 297n59; moneylenders', 144; overturned, 120, 302n120
tableau, 40, 79, 120
tabloid, 92
tail, 160, 281n151
Taíno, 268n12
tainting, 203
Thaïs, 270–1n29
Talbot, Charles, 263n186
talent, 157, 170, 330n33
talents, parable of the, 31, 110
talisman, 198
Tamar, 78, 270n28
Tangier, 55
tapestry, 75, 241n5
Tartar, 19, 224–5n67
taste, 114, 115, 294–5n15, 295n20, 298n68, 301–2n117, 302n127, 311n246; aftertaste, 115; refined, 157, 329n25
tavern, 70, 249n89, 266n210
tax, 66, 68, 252n105, 263n190; collector, 68, 263–4n192; exemption from, 172; farmer, 263–4n192; relief, 172; taxation, 69
taxonomy, 4, 5, 6, 7, 8, 9, 202, 204, 206, 211, 214nn6, 7
Taylor, Diana, ix, 204
Taylor, Scott, 135, 215–16n16, 276–7n95, 294n15, 297–8n63, 320n143, 323n168, 338n148, 349nn95, 103, 355n209
tears, 93, 134, 164, 166, 167, 300n99, 341n186, 351n130
technology, 24, 161, 207
teeth, 116, 187, 337–8n140; gnashing, 185; pulled out, 186, 187, 349n103
Teixeiras, 264n196
temperament, 322n158
temple, 253n108, 274n67, 321n155; cleansing of the, 144; service in the, 181, 182
temptation, 244n30, 303n140, 365n2; technique to resist, 123
temptress, 93
tercio, 110
Terence, 77
Teresa, St, 232n183
termite, 115
terror, 210, 266n220
Tesiphonte, 22
testament, 10, 48, 245n47. *See also* will

testimony, 85; false, 186–201; induced, 349n101
textuality, 204
Thacker, Jonathan, 213n3
thaumaturgy, 198
theatre: closing, 272n38; company, 246n56, 310n235; open-air, 144; outdoor, 135; ticket, 53
Thebes, 146
theft, 51, 52, 55, 63, 65, 67, 70, 71, 73, 109, 189, 240–1n4, 242n12, 256–7n144, 259n154, 261n171, 266n219, 267n222, 299n83, 350n107; of alms, 300–1n109; from beggars, 300–1n109; of children, 72; in church, 72; of a dress, 247n60; of food, 117, 118, 121; of goods, 109; of Helen, 78; petty, 266n209; of slaves, 249nn86, 87; by vagrants, 109
theologian, 142, 209
theology, 16, 91, 131, 132, 180, 183, 196, 204, 276n87, 325n213; doctor of, 77
therapy, 320–1n144
thief, 52, 53, 61, 70, 71, 187, 199, 242n10, 247n67, 261n171, 265n207, 350n107; gypsy, 72, 267nn225, 227; servant as, 266n209; urban, 267n222
third term, 203
thirst, 45, 46, 115, 122, 124, 137, 221–2n22, 240–1n4, 241n5, 241–2n8, 243n18, 244n23, 301n113, 315n70; for blood, 315n69
thirteenth century, 6, 43, 56, 302–3n129
thorn, 124
thought, 300n99, 316n78, 323n176; evil, 215n15
threat, 49, 141, 180, 189, 253–4n116, 317n90, 334n90
Three Kings, Feast of the, 255n129
throat, 317n90
throne, 34, 39, 41, 105, 194, 235n231, 337n138; abdication of, 169; empty, 235n231; royal, 236n247
thunder, 40, 327nn4, 5
thunderstorm, 136
tiger, 40, 136, 160
Tillich, Paul, 4
time: empty, 100; free, 107; tyranny of, 345n25; waste of, 98, 282–3n4, 283n6
timē, 91, 205, 363–4n16
Tirso de Molina, 91, 135, 161, 188, 245n44, 335n102. *For list of works see* Index of *Comedias*
titillation, 210
titles, 210
token, 86, 128, 160, 278n110
Toledo, 69, 106, 119, 265n206, 329n27, 338n141
Tomás y Valiente, Francisco, 90
tomb, 38, 98, 169
tongue, 188, 194, 198, 351nn128, 137; biting, 164; cutting out, 40, 43, 135, 240n319; false, 356n233; idle, 107; keeper of, 351n129; licentious, 140; lying, 188; scorpion's, 156, 327n4; venom of, 136; woman's, 191, 353n173
topography, 263n186
Tordesillas, 265n206
torment, 100, 116, 138, 298n69, 306n170, 351n136
Torres, Antonio, 250n91
touch, 115
tournament, 276–7n95, 290n125
tower, 35, 36, 38, 39, 216–17n20, 235n240, 332–3n72; of Babel, 35, 36; golden, 74, 268n3
trace, 10, 11, 86, 117, 204, 207, 218n32, 232n183, 279n112, 362–3n11
trade: Jewish, 264n195; luxury, 248n81; route, 64; slave, 250n92
trafficking, 54
tragedy, 93, 210, 248n80, 278n106, 365n3; national, 80; revenge, 140
tragicomedia, 53
traitor, 33, 84, 93, 121, 241–2n8
tranquillity, 168, 169, 191, 287n68
transaction: economic, 48; financial, 348n90; sale, 58
transformation, 98, 109, 111, 150, 155, 168, 171, 187, 190; structural, 220n6; theological, 196
transgression, 201
transubstantiation, 132
transvestism, 191, 196
Transylvania, 337n138
Trastámara, Enrique de, 47
tratadista, 69
trauma, 272n42
travel, 245n44; traveller, 115, 266n218

treachery, 48, 61, 245n44
treason, 38, 138, 162, 178, 210
treasure, 46, 54, 62, 129, 241n6, 242–3n17, 256–7n144, 259n155, 267n222; box, 179; hidden, 65; natural, 257n147; promised, 60; stolen, 45; sunken, 64
treasury, 68
tree, 75, 121, 259n155; branch, 226n88; elm, 287n63; hanging from, 135; oleander, 269n23
trembling, 133, 134
Trent, Council of, 49, 277–8n100; Catechism of, 6
trial, 276–7n95; for libel, 272n42; spiritual, 251n97
tribe, 24
tribulation, 298n69
tribunal, 88
trickster, 68, 330n36
Trinitarian: friar, 57; Order, 57, 252n107. *See also* Redemptionist
Trinity, 76, 113
trip, 113
Trojan, 75
trophy, 167, 302n120, 339n149
troubadour, 194
Troy, 78, 79, 80, 138, 176; Hector of, 163; Helen of, 273n48, 274n65
Trueblood, Alan, 272n42
trumpet, 115
trunk, 51
trust, 179, 189
truth, 187, 191, 197, 199, 200, 352n161, 356n227, 357nn244, 252, 359n272, 360nn286, 293, 300, 303, 361nn309, 310, 317, 319, 321; banished, 194; bending the, 189; cape of, 359n272; diluting, 190, 352n161; embellishing, 190, 353n162; germ of, 197; naked, 196, 359nn270, 272; nature of, 198, 199; orphaned, 197; partial, 190; status of, 198; suspect, 189; telling, 189, 191; verification, 188
Tunis, 55, 253n108
Tunisia, 54
Turk, 28, 41, 60, 79, 259n154; land of the, 281n154; by profession, 59
turkey, 120, 302n123
Turkey, 26
twelfth century, 56, 302–3n129
twentieth century, 6, 9
twin, 85
type, 132
typography, 133
tyranny, 37, 38, 39, 52, 62, 138, 146, 179, 180, 236n255, 240n1, 328n15; of Time, 345n25; of Western logic, 203

Ulysses, 227n89
uncle, 47, 93, 129, 244n36, 245n46
United States, 45, 209
university, 33, 226n83
upbringing, 176
uprising, 117, 265n206
urban, 69; area, 70; building, 235n233; centre, 69; context, 337–8n140; culture, 220n6; privilege, 172
Urraca of Castile, 231n154
Uruguay, 302n126
Urzáiz Tortajada, Héctor, 198
usury, 66, 260–1n167, 262n177
uxoricide, 142

vacation, 100, 286n42
vaccine, 126
vagabond, 68, 69
vagrancy, 109
vagrant, 69, 109
vainglory, 215n15, 223–4n49, 229–30n120, 230n121, 233–4n204
Valdivielso, Joseph de, 33
Valencia, 51, 57, 58, 59, 71, 249n85, 250n92, 250–1n95, 270n27, 276n78, 280–1n148, 338n141, 349n93; Cortes of, 280–1n148; Tribunal of, 270n27
Valera, Juan, 272n38
validation, 197
valido, 37, 197. See also *privado*
Valladolid, 69, 71, 162, 232n183, 255–6n138, 265n206; Royal Chancery, 269–70n26
valour, 28, 104, 163, 165, 170, 171, 316n78, 336n120
values, 327n228, 346–7n53
vampire, 15, 46, 137, 219n4
vanity, 20, 38, 231n159, 290n119
vassal, 122
Vázquez Fernández, Luis, 57, 252n107, 253n108
veil, 166, 352n161

vein, 243n19
Velasco, Sherry, 75
Vélez de Guevara, Luis, 249n85
Venetian, 61, 65; merchants, 260–1n167; Senate, 262n175
venial sin, 5, 81
Venice, 65, 66, 67, 159, 262n175
venom, 45, 137, 156, 257n147, 315nn57, 58, 61, 337–8n140; hidden, 315n62; manufacture of, 327n4. *See also* poison
Venus, 77, 83, 295n21, 316n78, 329n26
veracity, 193, 197, 201. *See also* truth
verb, 133, 134
verdict, 89
verification, 197
Versailles, 207
Vicar General, 331n52
viceroyalty, 37; of Peru, 61
victim, 184, 248n81, 266n209; of Anger, 148; intended, 141
victory, 121, 233–4n204, 344n235
vida retirada, 104
vigil, 129, 309n212, 310n229
vigilance, 99, 129, 285n28
villain, 39, 42, 76, 78; bastardy of, 92; Jewish, 66; ultimate, 92
villano, 32, 39, 43, 70, 117, 118, 121, 156, 169, 192, 241n7, 265n203, 269n20, 293n170, 294–5n15, 298n66, 300n104, 328n15, 342n212, 358n254
Vincent, Bernard, 249n84
vine, 75, 334n95
vineyard, 20, 51
violence, 88, 124, 134, 135, 237n262, 241–2n8, 316n78, 338n141; of animals, 136; militant, 138; natural, 295n16
viper, 136, 315n67, 327n4. *See also* snake
Virgil, 11, 176, 180
virgin, 79, 179, 182, 210
Virgin Mary, 17, 131, 132, 181, 182, 183, 184, 256–7n144, 339n156, 348n84; accused of Adultery, 88; body of, 253n108; confession to, 84; flight to Egypt, 67; pregnant, 88; procession honouring, 61; type of the, 311–12n256; womb of, 57
virginity, 269–70n26, 274n64
virtù, 168, 342n201
virtue, 37, 51, 82, 131, 150, 151, 157, 170, 171, 176, 190, 205, 238n276, 292n147, 339n154, 342n201, 363–4n16; beauty and, 359n276; coveting of, 329n25; discourse of, 149; enemy of, 332n61; maximum, 168; test of, 130
virus, 5
Visigoths, 80, 236n247
vision, 131, 297n57, 328n9
visual culture, 195, 237n264
visual representation, 249–50n90
vituperation, 91, 190, 233n185, 353n176
Vives, Juan Luis, 320–1n144
Vizcaya, 269–70n26
vocation, 84
voice, 145, 185, 188, 291n138, 312n12, 323n170, 360n288; affect passing through, 146; from heaven, 81; male, 84; of a nation, 208; raising the, 134; tone of, 140
volcano, 136, 314n51
vomit, 113, 295n17
vortex, 187
vow, 99, 184; breaking a, 130; of chastity, 129; delay in fulfilling, 285n34; to fast, 124; not to lie, 189; ordination, 124; perpetual, 130
voyage, 58, 64, 264n193, 302n126
voyeurism, 135, 157
Vulgate, 176
vulgo, 115, 290n120

wagon, 53, 132
waitress, 118
wall, 48, 75, 161, 266n209, 334n86; bloodstains on, 143; knocked down, 131; of the Supreme Court, 209; writing on the, 293–4n6
war, 24, 28, 32, 40, 61, 62, 92, 93, 103, 104, 228n102, 287n64, 288n87; Dirty, 250n92; European, 93; games, 104, 147, 290n125; on God, 42; goddess of, 317n97; imperial, 110; just cause for, 255–6n138; love and, 191; Napoleonic, 216n19; among neighbours, 62; prisoner of, 250n91; spoils of, 62, 63, 256–7n144; undeclared, 253n114; upon Time, 345n25
warning, 178, 189, 198, 259n155
warrior, 18, 24, 25, 26, 27, 106, 134, 139, 141, 336n123; culture, 75; epic, 104, 108; ethic, 75; ethos, 104; Hebrew, 184; holy, 302–3n129; mentality, 108; Muslim, 302–3n129; non-warrior, 108
warship, 103
waste, 98, 120

water, 20, 115, 118, 124, 186, 223n43, 242–3n17, 259n155, 300n99, 322n158; body of, 221n20; bread and, 305nn160, 163; drinking, 156; imagery, 136; living, 79; used to toast, 121
wealth, 32, 34, 46, 47, 48, 52, 109, 255n129, 259n154, 297n60, 329n24; Appetite for, 120; colonial, 62; confiscation of, 264n193; cultural, 68; foreign, 69; Jewish, 68, 264n193; material, 68; mineral, 255–6n138; "New" World, 265n202; portable, 51, 68; reallocation of, 62; wealthy, 113, 127, 252n104, 264n195, 265n207
weapon, 99, 116, 138, 139, 276–7n95
weasel, 293n1
weather, 127, 308n194
Weber, Max, 48, 99, 245–6n49
wedding, 125, 158, 180, 347n63
wedlock, 92, 280–1n148
weed, 75, 269n19
weeping, 84, 134, 168. *See also* crying
weevil, 156
well, 79, 160
Weller, Robert P., 214n10
West, 6, 42, 145; Western logic, 203
wheat, 131, 132; grain of, 260n166; house of, 311n248
whip, 112, 122, 124, 129; whipping, 129, 135, 313–14n37. *See also* flagellation
wickedness, 115
widow, 51, 52, 129, 158, 210; remarriage of, 246n54; widower, 331n45; widowhood, 246n54; young, 129
Wiesner, Merry E., 320n143
wife, 20, 50, 81, 83, 87, 88, 93, 94, 270–1n29, 270–1n29, 274–5n70, 275n71, 278n109, 294–5n15, 305n164, 365n6; adulterous, 143, 320n143; another man's, 275n71; of Appetite, 294–5n15; brother's, 78; coveting of, 156, 350n107; faithful, 143; first, 90; mirror of, 86; Potiphar's, 78, 273n53; soul of, 143; theft of, 67; virtuous, 311–12n256; wife-murder, 142, 144, 150
wilderness, 123
will, iron, 274–5n70
will, last, 10, 48, 58, 125. *See also* testament
Williams, Raymond, 8, 44, 45, 74, 97, 155, 172, 173, 180, 186
wind, 16, 28, 101, 159, 187, 221n20, 222n22, 235n233, 296–7n44, 323n176, 330n32, 350nn112, 119
wine, 113, 116, 131, 295n20; communion, 260n166; lack of, 121; new, 206, 328n11; vessel for, 256–7n144; wineskin, 206
wings, 22, 45, 60, 242n9, 317n97, 350n119
Wise Men, 67, 255n129
wit, 312n258
witness, 84, 85, 197, 360n288; false, 186–201; sale of, 349n101
wolf, 160, 333n74
woman, 16, 19, 20, 21, 26, 30, 47, 48, 49, 52, 53, 61, 71, 74, 76, 79, 83, 85, 86, 91, 92, 93, 99, 113, 116, 128, 129, 132, 135, 158, 159, 162, 163, 165, 178, 179, 181, 183, 192, 194, 210, 224n53, 225n72, 237n262, 238n285, 244nn29, 31, 246nn50, 54, 268n7, 272n41, 279n124, 280–1n148, 295n18, 305n164, 309n208, 329n26, 329–30n31, 330n38, 340n164, 353nn173, 174, 353nn176, 177, 180, 356n226; adulterous, 82, 132, 294–5n15; against, 190; Amazon, 224–5n67; angry, 135, 136, 137, 138; bearded, 225n72; beautiful, 164, 287n68, 311–12n256; blessed, 311–12n256; body of, 157, 274n65; dishonest, 294–5n15; educated, 347n69; father of, 181; forgotten, 330n35; of the hand, 166; honest, 294–5n15; of ill repute, 294–5n15; indigenous, 157, 329n28; innocent, 88; lascivious, 93; lower-class, 52; lying, 191; married, 276n87, 330n36; naked, 157, 329n28; older, 51, 309n204; perspective of, 84; pious, 129; pregnant, 88; prudish, 309n204; rich, 110; saintly, 222n28; Samaritan, 79; single, 129, 269–70n26, 274n69; strong, 93; tongue of a, 191; vain, 93; voluptuous, 216n19; young, 52, 54
womanizing, 77
womb, 93
wood, 115
Woods, Richard D., 10
wooing, 191, 196
word: giving one's, 281n149; play, 175, 177, 332–3n72, 346–7n53
work, 99, 101, 109, 252n105, 305n161, 338n141; alternated with leisure, 108; avoidance of, 110, 282–3n4; ethic, 99; leisure as, 109; of war, 104

world, 337n126, 342n212; beginning of the, 356n223; history, 163; literature, 269–70n26; upside-down, 91, 199, 280n143; view, 89
World, 76, 112, 343n227, 361n309; labyrinth of the, 361n317
worm, 17, 22, 46, 98, 222n23, 242n11; silkworm, 74
worry, 178
worship, 114, 182, 274n67
wound, 71, 86, 135, 168, 301n111; of Christ, 262n180; pretended, 267n22; words as, 139, 318n108

Xetafe, 265n205

Yahweh, 3, 206, 214n2
yelling, 134, 299n93, 312n8, 343n221
Yepes, 35
youth, 17, 23, 31, 47, 48, 99, 100, 124, 139, 157, 194, 244n32, 317n101; lapses of, 139; lazy, 107
Yuste, 169

Zabaleta, Juan de, 126, 127
Zacatecas, 258n150
Zamora, 69
Zamora, Antonio de, 105. *For list of works see* Index of *Comedias*
Zaragoza, 270n27
zarzuela, 316n80, 339n156
Zayas, María de, 48
zen, 168, 320n144
zeugma, 167
Žižek, Slavoj, 39, 242n16
zoology, 5